Book of Family Prayer.

Bible Lessons with Meditations for each Day,

Arranged after the Church Year.

BY

N. J. LAACHE.

*Blessed is the man whose delight is in
the law of the Lord, and who meditates in
his law day and night.   Psalm 1. 1. 2.*

Translated from the Norwegian by Peer O. Strømme.

DECORAH, IOWA.
LUTHERAN PUBLISHING HOUSE.
1902.

1. First Sunday in Advent. I.

God, be gracious unto us, bless us, and make thy face to shine upon us. Amen.

Gospel Lesson, Matthew 21, 1–9. And when they drew nigh unto Jerusalem, and were come to Bethphage, unto the mount of Olives, then sent Jesus two disciples, saying unto them, Go into the village over against you, and straightway ye shall find an ass tied, and a colt with her: loose them, and bring them unto me. And if any man say ought unto you, ye shall say, The Lord hath need of them; and straightway he will send them. All this was done, that it might be fulfilled which was spoken by the prophet, saying, Tell ye the daughter of Zion, Behold, thy King cometh unto thee, meek, and sitting upon an ass, and a colt the foal of an ass. And the disciples went, and did as Jesus commanded them, and brought the ass, and the colt, and put on them their clothes, and they set him thereon. And a very great multitude spread their garments in the way; others cut down branches from the trees, and strawed them in the way. And the multitudes that went before, and that followed, cried, saying, Hosanna to the son of David! Blessed is he that cometh in the name of the Lord: Hosanna in the highest!

Jesus Christ is the king of the church. He governs it with meekness and justice, and defends it with divine omnipotence. Jesus Christ, God's only begotten Son, who took our sin upon himself, who died for us on the cross, and bought us with his blood; *he* is our *king.* What a wealth of joy and comfort there is in this truth! In the heart of every Christian is the prayer: Lord Jesus, rule thou over us. Thou, and none other, shalt own my heart. Do thou protect us; thou alone *art* our sun and our shield, and we will have none other beside thee. —Than the words which we hear today, "rejoice exceedingly, daughter of Zion; behold, thy King, the Lord Jesus, cometh unto thee," nothing more glorious could be said to us on the first day of the church year; it is the best possible answer to the prayer of the Christian heart.

He is the king of the church. No enemy, then, however strong, shall prevail against it. No matter how threatening the outlook may seem, the church shall obtain the victory and be saved. With eternal fidelity he keeps watch over his bride, who has been bought with a price; and in his omnipotence he is *able* to defend her against the most terrific assaults on the part of all the hosts of hell. Beyond question the church will soon be called on to face great tribulation; all manner of lying attacks by false spirits, and bitter persecution on the part of the world. Let all who belong to the army of the Lord

4

put on the true armor of the Spirit; but let none lose hope! Christ reigns in the very midst of his enemies, and his church is victorious even while the world rejoices over her destruction.

He is the Lord of the church by reason of his rule in the *hearts* of his own; and they, only, whose hearts he governs are of his people. But he is, in very truth, the king of your heart, you poor sinner, who believe in him and put your trust in him alone. Truly, he is the king of your heart; you are his, and he is yours; do not let the devil persuade you to the contrary. Have faith in the kingly name of Jesus, and trust in the power of his love. Give yourself wholly to him; you can do it by the grace which he bestows; and he will direct your mind and your conduct, protect you, and lead you in the path of righteousness. Serve him willingly, obey him alway, praise his name, extend his kingdom. You are blessed, and shall be a blessing. All things in him, by him, and for him!

In this church year you shall again, with all the saints, experience that he is the same faithful and mighty Savior that he always was. He shall keep you in the state of grace, strengthen your faith, increase your charity, purify your soul in tribulations, and give you victory over the flesh, the world, and the devil. Beware of trusting in your own, or of doubting his strength. You are baptized unto Christ, you hear his voice, you eat his body and blood, you live and breathe in his saving grace and love; he knows you, and he has you in his eye and in his hand day and night. He is meek, and bears with our infirmity; just, and does away with our sin.

Praise be to thee, Lord Jesus, who didst make us thy people! Give us grace to believe in thee with our whole heart, to serve thee in all that we do, and thus to work with all our might for the extension of thy kingdom on earth. Let this year be a blessed one for us, and for all who are thine. This is our most earnest prayer; thou wilt hear it, and thus fulfil thy promises. Amen.*

Jesus shall reign where'er the sun Doth his successive journeys run; His kingdom stretch from shore to shore, Till moons shall wax and wane no more.
Let every creature rise and bring Peculiar honors to our King; Angels descend with songs again, And earth repeat the loud Amen.

---

2. First Sunday in Advent. II.

Lord Jesus, give us grace to hear the rousing call of thy word!

Epistle Lesson, Romans 13, 11–14. And that, knowing the time, that now it is high time to awake out of sleep: for now is our salvation nearer than when we believed. The night is far spent, the day is at hand: let us therefore cast off the works of darkness, and let us put on the armor of light. Let us walk

---

* Here the head of the family says a short morning or evening prayer in his own words, and closes with the Lord's Prayer and the Benediction. This is to be done every day. If the stanzas are not sung, they may be read in their proper place before the impromptu petition and the Lord's Prayer.

honestly, as in the day; not in rioting and drunkenness, not in chambering and wantonness, not in strife and envying. But put ye on the Lord Jesus Christ, and make not provision for the flesh, to fulfil the lusts thereof.

It is now high time to awake out of sleep; the Sun of righteousness is risen upon us; Christ is come to us with life out of death. None shall have occasion to say: "I must yet lie, yet sleep; night broods over us, the darkness will not permit me to rise." No; the glorious day of grace is come; the acceptable year of liberty is here. Christ wakes us, and lets the light of his countenance shine into our eyes. Through the words of the gospel he is in our very midst, lying in the manger, hanging on the cross; eternal mercy, justice, and life proceed from him. In our baptism he is present as the very same Savior that is being baptized in the Jordan, fulfils all righteousness, dies for us, rises for us, and lives for us. In the Holy Supper I receive his very self; he, who is the resurrection and the life, abides in me, and I in him. O ye Christians, will ye sleep, and thus turn this glorious day of life into an awful night of death? God forbid! However, there is here yet more which should wake us up. Our salvation is now nearer than when we believed. The hours are flying fast, and soon we shall be at the end. *Now* Christ comes in the means of grace; but *soon* he shall come in the clouds, in the glory of his Father. How will ye then stand before him, ye sleepy Christians? Awake, therefore, and be vigilant hereafter! Let this new church year become a new life. Cast off the works of darkness, and put on the armor of light. *Arm* yourselves, for a fight is to be faced! Enter into the holiness and love of Jesus Christ, into the lustre and purity of his being! Let the heart be wholly and entirely his! No lukewarmness and sloth, no cowardly shrinking from the fight! Self-denial and vigilance while the struggle continues; faithfulness to the end! Eyes fixed on the crown of life, and victory through him who loved us!

Wake us, faithful Lord Jesus. Wake them that are spiritually dead, that they may repent. Lord, wake them, that they may not dream themselves into everlasting death. Wake thy believers, and give us zeal, courage, and hopefulness in the fight. Let our sanctification increase, and our progress be manifest in all things. Give us faithfulness unto the end, and give us the crown of life. Amen.

(To be followed by prayer in one's own words, the Lord's Prayer, and the Benediction. Thus every day, without special directions hereafter in the book.)

Assist my soul, too apt to stray, A stricter watch to keep; And should I e'er forget thy way, Restore thy wandering sheep.
Make me to walk in thy commands; 'Tis a delightful road; Nor let my head, or heart, or hands, Offend against my God.

3. Monday after First Sunday in Advent.

Psalm 24. A Psalm of David. The earth is the Lord's, and the fulness thereof; the world, and they that dwell therein: For he hath founded it upon the seas, and established it upon the floods. Who shall ascend into the hill of the Lord? or who shall stand in his holy place? He that hath clean hands, and a pure heart; who hath not lifted up his soul unto vanity, nor sworn deceitfully. He shall receive the blessing from the Lord, and righteousness from the God of his salvation. This is the generation of them that seek him, that seek thy face, O Jacob. Selah. Lift up your heads, O ye gates; and be ye lift up, ye everlasting doors; and the King of glory shall come in. Who is this King of glory? The Lord strong and mighty, the Lord mighty in battle. Lift up your heads, O ye gates; even lift them up, ye everlasting doors; and the King of glory shall come in. Who is this King of glory? The Lord of hosts, he is the King of glory. Selah.

David wrote this psalm for the occasion when the ark of the covenant was removed up on Zion, whereby the King of glory himself went up thither; for the ark and the mercy seat were the throne of the Lord in Israel.

This king of glory is none other than the Lord Jesus Christ, who comes to us full of grace and truth, and enters into Zion, the Christian church, through his holy gospel. He is Lord of all the world; he has dominion over the mighty billows of the deep, and the hosts of heaven obey his commands. The prince of our salvation is the Lord Zebaoth. The gates of the world open themselves to him, and he marches onward with victory over death and hell.

Who shall ascend into his hill? Who has communion with the Holy One? Answer:—The children of Jacob, the true believers, none others; not such as are Christians in name only, not mere Sunday saints, but only sincere, true, and honest souls. Is it possible that Jesus Christ could be a king for hypocrites and liars, for heartless, cold, unclean men, or for proud, self-satisfied, self-righteous minds? Can such as these be the people of the Holy One? O, that ye would hear! Let none delude himself. But neither let any lose heart who sees his sin with sorrow and pain. The wretched who are willing to be saved receive righteousness from the king of glory himself, and are made pure. He who in sincerity confesses his sin and longs for holiness will in no wise be cast out. It is for such that God has built his Zion, and of such he fashions unto himself his holy and glorious people.

Try me, O God, and examine my heart, and find whether or not I am of the truth. Thou knowest how prone I am to delude myself. Preserve me from this danger, and give me an upright heart. Thou knowest that this is my sincere prayer. Let me in truth be of thy people. Amen.

To him shall endless prayer be made, And endless praises crown his head; His name, like sweet perfume, shall rise With every morning sacrifice.
People and realms of every tongue Dwell on his love with grateful song; And infant voices shall proclaim Their early blessings on his name.

4. Tuesday after First Sunday in Advent.

Open thou mine eyes, that I may behold wondrous things out of thy law. Amen.

Ephesians 1, 17–23. That the God of our Lord Jesus Christ, the Father
of glory, may give unto you the spirit of wisdom and revelation in the knowledge of him: The eyes of your understanding being enlightened; that ye may
know what is the hope of his calling, and what the riches of the glory of his
inheritance in the saints, and what is the exceeding greatness of his power to
usward who believe, according to the working of his mighty power, which he
wrought in Christ, when he raised him from the dead, and set him at his own
right hand in the heavenly places, far above all principality, and power, and
might, and dominion, and every name that is named not only in this world,
but also in that which is to come; and hath put all things under his feet, and
gave him to be the head over all things to the church, which is his body, the
fulness of him that filleth all in all.

Our Lord Jesus is greater and more mighty than all the angelic
hosts, together with all powers above and below. The spiritual and
unseen forces, the hosts of heaven, and the powers of the deep, and
the might of death, mock all the wisdom and power of the world; but
our Lord Jesus is greater. He vanquished and disarmed, yea even
destroyed, *death*, and seated himself at the right hand of God the
Father, a Lord of all things and over all on high and in the deep.
But this his kingly power he uses for our salvation, namely in creating
and preserving faith in our hearts, and making us partakers of his
life. The new birth and the sanctification of a man are effects of this
exceeding great power of God in the resurrection of Christ. May his
Spirit of wisdom reveal this to us, and open our eyes, that we may
know the greatness and the certainty of our salvation. It is the eternal
God with his sovereign power who dwells in the Christian church.
The power which is greater than that of the creation; the power
which vanquished the prince of death; the power of the resurrection
of Jesus Christ,—this power it is which the Spirit of God has given
within you, Christian believer; and thereby he has turned you from
death to life, and preserves you therein. The Spirit and life of Christ
is in you; the church is his body, and he its head. "And he *must*
protect, preserve, advance, bless, and glorify himself in his own. He
continually relives his life, and reveals all the mysteries of his redemption, in his body, the church. He suffers in its persecuted,
troubled, needy and sick members; as the meek, lowly, loving, and
obedient one, he sighs and prays in them; in eternal and divine power
he continually arises from the dead anew in his church. Blessed be
the king, the bridegroom of the church, the prince of life! In him
our salvation is not uncertain; he lives, and we shall live.

Lord Jesus, dost thou know me, also, as one of thine? Is my
faith in thee a true and living faith? With all who are of my household I earnestly ask of thee this grace unspeakable.—Praise be to the
Lord; he has attended to the voice of my supplications. Amen.

The head that once was crowned with thorns Is crowned with glory now;
A royal diadem adorns The mighty Victor's brow.
The highest place that heaven affords Is his by sovereign right: The King
of kings and Lord of lords, And heaven's eternal Light.

8

5. Wednesday after First Sunday in Advent.

Lord, give us thy word in our hearts, for we are thine; and do thou save us. Amen.

Psalm 72, 1–8. A Psalm for Solomon. Give the king thy judgments, O God, and thy righteousness unto the king's son. He shall judge thy people with righteousness, and thy poor with judgment. The mountains shall bring peace to the people, and the little hills, by righteousness. He shall judge the poor of the people, he shall save the children of the needy, and shall break in pieces the oppressor. They shall fear thee as long as the sun and moon endure, throughout all generations. He shall come down like rain upon the mown grass; as showers that water the earth. In his days shall the righteous flourish; and abundance of peace so long as the moon endureth. He shall have dominion also from sea to sea, and from the river unto the ends of the earth.

Solomon is a type of Christ, and his kingdom of peace is a type of the Christian church. In this psalm God's people pray, that the kingdom of Christ may come; and they sing of the splendors of this kingdom, its extension and its eternal duration. *Christ* is the *righteous* king who secures justice to the poor and needy, but breaks in pieces the oppressor. Them that love sin and live in unrighteousness he rejects and condemns, but he saves those that submit themselves to the law of God and seek his help against sin. He will surely save the needy who cry to him, and the poor who have none to help them. Admit that God is true in his judgments; acknowledge the justice of the correction administered by his law; but, at the same time, credit him with speaking truth in his gospel, also, concerning the obedience and atonement of the Son of God *for you;* then are you righteous and enjoy the peace of grace. The Prince of peace acquits you of everything brought to your charge; and you shall live with him, and reign with him. *Faith* is the one thing on which all depends. It is in faith that Christ is known. Exercise yourself in the faith; do not allow yourself to be led astray by your conceited reason, or by your own views and feelings. As God lives, the man who gives hearty assent to his word is just and accepted in his sight. The proud children of the world, who resist the purpose and righteousness of God, hope to destroy the dominion of this king; but his throne stands, and he shall sit thereon until the sun and moon are no more. The kingdoms of gold and silver and copper and iron shall pass away, but the kingdom of peace is without end. Neither shall any be able to prevent its *extension.* Our heavenly Solomon shall have dominion from sea to sea, and from the river unto the ends of the earth. How good and glorious a truth this is! With holy joy and fear we accept it, and see all kings fall down before him and all nations serve him.

Lord Jesus, give us humble and believing hearts, so that in all our trouble and strife on earth we may taste thy precious peace. God, give the king thy judgments and thy righteousness unto the king's son. Save thy people and bless thine inheritance; provide for them, and exalt them for evermore. Amen.

Dear Refuge of my weary soul, On thee, when sorrows rise, On thee, when waves of trouble roll, My fainting hope relies.
To thee I tell each rising grief, For thou alone canst heal; Thy Word can bring a sweet relief For every pain I feel.

---

6. Thursday after First Sunday in Advent.

Keep us, Lord, in thy tabernacle, hide us in thy pavilion. Amen.

Psalm 48. A Song and Psalm for the sons of Korah. Great is the Lord, and greatly to be praised in the city of our God, in the mountain of his holiness. Beautiful for situation, the joy of the whole earth, is mount Zion, on the sides of the north, the city of the great King. God is known in her palaces for a refuge. For, lo, the kings were assembled, they passed by together. They saw it, and so they marvelled; they were troubled, and hasted away. Fear took hold upon them there, and pain, as of a woman in travail. Thou breakest the ships of Tarshish with an east wind. As we have heard, so have we seen in the city of the Lord of hosts, in the city of our God: God will establish it for ever. Selah. We have thought of thy lovingkindness, O God, in the midst of thy temple. According to thy name, O God, so is thy praise unto the ends of earth; thy right hand is full of righteousness. Let mount Zion rejoice, let the daughters of Judah be glad, because of thy judgments. Walk about Zion, and go round about her: tell the towers thereof. Mark ye well her bulwarks, consider her palaces; that ye may tell it to the generation following. For this God is our God for ever and ever; he will be our guide even unto death.

The earthly Jerusalem typifies, as it were, the church of Christ; and this psalm recites the splendor of the church.

The Lord is in his Zion; the great, eternal God is in the midst of his Christian people. He who is the first and the last and the living, who was dead and is alive for evermore, who has the keys of hell and death, he is in the midst of the seven candlesticks, in the midst of the church, with the sevenfold gifts of his Spirit. This is the glory of the church, that the Lord himself is in it, that it is the city of the Lord of hosts. For this reason are all its enemies put to shame, while its children are victorious over death and hell.

We who are baptized and believe in Jesus dwell together on that Mount Zion which is established forever; we abide within the walls of the city of God, where mercy and righteousness reign, where death and the devil are shut out, and with them all evil, so that bliss and life only are found therein. For our communion is with the Father and the Son in the Holy Ghost. We still have, to be sure, much sin and frailty, but we have full forgiveness of sin every day; Satan throws the darts of temptation against us and often wounds us, but we are continually healed by the blood of Jesus, and we walk not after the flesh but after the spirit. Outside of God's' church the devil rules, and all who dwell there are the children of death. Over us in Zion, in the community of true believers, Christ is king, and all his people are the children of life. Our removal from the church on earth to that in heaven shall in no wise harm us. For the same God is our God for evermore, and he will be our safe guide even unto death. This is truth. The word of God teaches it. We *believe* it and train ourselves always in this faith. We do not see it, neither do we feel it in such manner, that we make this feeling our reliance. But the word of God does not lie, in this word we trust. O, that we might have firm faith in the blessed truth of the word! Then shall we more and more know by experience, that all the promises of God are yea and amen in Christ.

We remember thy lovingkindness, O God, in the midst of thy temple, and praise thee that thou so graciously dost save us. Keep us with thee and gather unto thyself the multitudes of thy redeemed from all the ends of the earth. Amen.

Ye nations round the earth, rejoice Before the Lord, your sovereign King; Serve him with cheerful heart and voice, With all your tongues his glory sing.
The Lord is God, 'tis he alone Doth life and breath and being give; We are his work, and not our own, The sheep that on his pastures live.

---

7. Friday after First Sunday in Advent.

Lord, let thy word enter into and quicken our hearts. Amen.

Romans 5, 17–21. For if by one man's offence death reigned by one; much more they which receive abundance of grace, and of the gift of righteousness, shall reign in life by one, Jesus Christ. Therefore, as by the offence of one judgment came upon all men to condemnation; even so by the righteousness of one the free gift came upon all men unto justification of life. For as by one man's disobedience many were made sinners, so by the obedience of one shall many be made righteous. Moreover, the law entered, that the offence might abound. But where sin abounded, grace did much more abound: That as sin hath reigned unto death, even so might grace reign, through righteousness, unto eternal life, by Jesus Christ our Lord.

By the fall of Adam death became of force and should have ruled over us all, even though we had no further transgressed the law of God. The offence of one was the offence of all. But the like rule obtains also in regard to Christ and his righteousness; to accept this righteousness is to come into possession of the sovereign power of life. There one; here one.—The offence of one, the offence of all; the righteousness of one, the righteousness of all. By his obedience alone, not by his and ours; by his life, his victory, his fulfilment of the law, without the aid of any work of ours, are we saved. He alone has bruised the serpent's head; the highpriest alone entered in with the sacrifice for the sins of the world; David alone slew Goliath; there was none with our Lord when he trod the wine-press of wrath. Furthermore, the obedience of one does not save from the one fall, only, in which we fell in Adam; many other offences have been added to the offence of Adam, but no other saving obedience has been superadded to the one. The law works transgressions, and thereby offences have become many. But by the obedience of Christ *alone* atonement has been made for every offence, so that there is no room for any other atoning obedience in addition to this. Sin abounds in the world; hence the terrible rule of death; but in the kingdom of Christ we have the glorious reign of grace through his righteousness. The unbelievers are the slaves of sin, but all the people of Christ are free. They are not as yet sinless; they feel their guilt with pain, and they could not stand before the judgment of God's holy law; but in Christ they are under grace, not under the law. Than these words nothing can be more beautiful: "As sin has reigned unto death, even so shall grace reign through righteousness unto eternal life by Jesus Christ our Lord." Blessed be Christ!

May this gospel be painted before our eyes throughout our whole life and in our last hour. Grant us this, thou Holy Spirit, for Jesus' sake. Amen.

Blest is the man, forever blest, Whose guilt is pardoned by his God, Whose sins with sorrow are confessed, And covered with his Savior's blood.
Blest is the man, to whom the Lord Imputes not his iniquities, He pleads no merit of reward, And not on works, but grace relies.

8. Saturday after First Sunday in Advent.

Lord Jesus, let thy words of peace and grace force their way into our hearts. Amen.

Revelations 1, 4–7. John to the seven churches which are in Asia: Grace be unto you, and peace, from him which is, and which was, and which is to come; and from the seven Spirits which are before his throne; and from Jesus Christ, who is the faithful witness, and the first begotten of the dead, and the prince of the kings of the earth. Unto him that loved us, and washed us from our sins in his own blood, and hath made us kings and priests unto God and his Father; to him be glory and dominion for ever and ever. Amen. Behold he cometh with clouds; and every eye shall see him, and they also which pierced him: and all kindreds of the earth shall wail because of him. Even so. Amen.

Our Lord Jesus himself has redeemed us with his own blood, so that Satan has no right to hold us captive in sin. The kingdom which Christ founded by his death and resurrection is the kingdom of grace and peace; all who belong to it are kings and priests. The grace of the triune God rests upon them and reigns in them, and the Spirit sanctifies them by the blood of Jesus. In baptism right and access to this kingdom were granted us, and we have entered into it by faith. Therefore we dare to say with Saint Paul: "Who shall lay anything to the charge of God's elect? It is God that justifieth; who is he that condemneth? It is Christ that died, yea rather, that is risen again, who is even at the right hand of God, who also maketh intercession for us. Who shall separate us from the love of Christ?" We are, to be sure, weak in ourselves, but we are strong in him by faith; for we believe that we, baptized unto Christ, who died and arose from the dead for us, are dead from sin by his death, and quickened with him by his resurrection; and while we believe this, it is ours in very truth, so that we live and reign with him and have free access to the Father. Sin continues still to oppress us, but we dare to enter the sanctuary through the blood of Christ and come before the very throne of God, and we receive forgiveness and strength to win the victory. Make use of your kingly power, dear Christian, and of your priestly privilege for the good of yourself and the brethren. Come forward into the light always; confess your sin honestly before the Lord, and pray earnestly for mercy; then shall nothing condemn you, nothing rob you of your peace, and no sin rule over you. Even though you may, at times, feel so weak both in faith and life that you seem certain to succumb at last; yet, for the sake of the blood of Jesus, this shall not come to pass.

Let thy Spirit, O God, the spirit of the Lord, the spirit of wisdom and understanding, the spirit of counsel and might, the spirit of knowledge and of the fear of the Lord, keep us vigilant and pure. Amen.

O for a faith that will not shrink, Though pressed by every foe; That will not tremble on the brink Of any earthly woe!

That will not murmur nor complain Beneath the chastening rod; But, in the hour of grief or pain, Will lean upon its God.

---

9. Second Sunday in Advent. I.

Lord, let thy word rouse us and keep us awake. Amen.

Gospel Lesson, Luke 21, 25–36. And there shall be signs in the sun, and in the moon, and in the stars; and upon the earth distress of nations, with perplexity; the sea and the waves roaring; men's hearts failing them for fear, and for looking after those things which are coming on the earth: for the powers of heaven shall be shaken. And then shall they see the Son of man coming in a cloud with power and great glory. And when these things begin to come to pass, then look up, and lift up your heads; for your redemption draweth nigh. And he spake to them a parable; Behold the fig tree, and all the trees; When they now shoot forth, ye see and know of your own selves that summer is now nigh at hand. So likewise ye, when ye see these things come to pass, know ye that the kingdom of God is nigh at hand. Verily I say unto you, This generation shall not pass away till all be fulfilled. Heaven and earth shall pass away: but my words shall not pass away. And take heed to yourselves, lest at any time your hearts be overcharged with surfeiting, and drunkenness, and cares of this life, and so that day come upon you unawares. For as a snare shall it come on all them that dwell on the face of the whole earth. Watch ye therefore, and pray always, that ye may be accounted worthy to escape all these things that shall come to pass, and to stand before the Son of man.

Many forget entirely that a judgment day is coming, and none remembers it with such vividness of thought and feeling as the gravity of the subject demands. Time flies, and every second brings us nearer to the judgment. Beware lest you forget this. Even though the many who are of the earth forget it, do not you forget it, Christian believer! Indeed, in your innermost heart you long for the second coming of the Lord. "It is appointed unto men once to die, but after this the judgment." The children of the world refuse to believe this, but the event will put their wisdom to shame. They dream that there is no day of doom, the while they sail straight toward the judgment seat of the Lord and stand in the midst of death, the entrance gate to the place of judgment. Yes, the Lord has said that he will come again, and he will keep his promise. Heaven and earth shall pass away, but his word shall not pass away. Rejoice, ye Christians, for soon shall the Son of Man be revealed, the Glorious One, who loves you and whom ye love. Begin now to lift up your heads, for your redemption draws nigh. No terrible judge is he who cites you to appear before him; he is the Son of Man with the stripes and scars in his transfigured body. When you see the sign of the cross you shall know him and be of good cheer, while the proud and valiant men of the world shake with fear, and their hearts fail them in despair. Himself has said that whosoever believes in him shall not be judged, but has crossed over from death to life.

Watch, however; watch! It is but a little while. Away with the cares of the world; away with the lusts of the flesh; away with all sleepiness and sloth! Watch, stand steadfast in the Lord, be manly, be strong. Do not let the mists of unbelief confuse you. Do not let the countless lusts of the flesh master you. Stand with loins girt about and with lights burning. Watch, for Jesus' sake; watch! Lord Jesus, do thou help us always to watch and pray. Faithful Savior, preserve my soul and man me with firm resolve to abide in thee, in order that I may be found watching when thou comest, and that with the elect I may be a guest at thy wedding feast. Amen.

That day of wrath, that dreadful day, When heaven and earth shall pass away, What power shall be the sinner's stay? How shall he meet that dreadful day?

When, shriveling like a parched scroll, The flaming heavens together roll, When louder yet, and yet more dread, Resounds the trump that wakes the dead:

Oh! on that day, that wrathful day, When man to judgment wakes from clay, Be thou, O Christ, the sinner's stay, Though heaven and earth shall pass away.

---

10. Second Sunday in Advent. II.

Lord, give us devout hearts. Amen.

Epistle Lesson, Romans 15, 4–9. For whatsoever things were written aforetime were written for our learning, that we through patience and comfort of the scriptures might have hope. Now the God of patience and consolation grant you to be likeminded one toward another, according to Christ Jesus; that ye may with one mind and one mouth glorify God, even the Father of our Lord Jesus Christ. Wherefore receive ye one another, as Christ also received us, to the glory of God. Now I say that Jesus Christ was a minister of the circumcision for the truth of God, to confirm the promises made unto the fathers; and that the Gentiles might glorify God for his mercy; as it is written, For this cause will I confess to thee among the Gentiles, and sing unto thy name.

The human family has been torn asunder, hearts have been divided, and the world is full of strife. From Babel the peoples go their several ways; and since the time of the patriarchs the people of Israel have kept their independent course like a current through the sea, without assimilating with the others. But that which sin separated and which the wisdom of God long kept asunder, his mercy has again united. Jesus is become the Savior of all peoples. He has fulfilled the law, and he became the suffering servant whom the scriptures promise to the Jews as a redeemer. But he died for us gentiles also, so that the prophecies of the prophets concerning salvation by the mercy of God are fulfilled in him. Satan, the spirit of discord, the prince of death, shall rule no more. As yet we see, to be sure, only the beginning of the union of Jews and gentiles in one fold; there is yet much division in the Christian church; we still suffer sorely by reason of the cunning and power of the enemy. O, if Israel would but know its Savior, how much of added life and power would not be given to the Lord's people! How strong would the church be, were there not, alas, so many parties among the believing children of God! It would capture the world and would soon attain to the perfect estate of glory. Nevertheless, we shall surely conquer through patience and comfort of the scriptures. The Lord, who bears Jews and gentiles in one heart and has redeemed both with one blood, will continue to unite the believing Jews and gentiles into one people. Or, shall not the prophecies be fulfilled which, from the beginning to the end of the Bible, promise a blessed unity of all who are saved? If the promise concerning the service to be rendered by the Son of God for both Jew and gentile has been fulfilled, shall not the promise concerning their union as one blessed people be fulfilled also? The word of God must come true. Our own hearts, also, tell us that we have communion with all the saints of all peoples; even now we live the life of love together in spite of all that divides us; we pray together before the throne; we sing the same song of praise; we labor in the same spirit; we are joined together by one life; —all of which points to the same glorious end as do the words of the Lord wherein he promises to gather all his own where there shall be one fold and one shepherd.

Lord Jesus, bless this church year; unite thy believers; give the Jews repentance; gather unto thyself the fulness of the gentiles; let thy love constrain us, that we receive one another, even as thou hast received us to the glory of God. Amen.

Sing praise to God who reigns above, The God of all creation, The God of power, the God of love, The God of our salvation. With healing balm my soul he fills, And every pain and sorrow stills: To God all praise and glory!

The angel host, O King of kings, Thy praise forever telling, In earth and sky all living things Beneath thy shadow dwelling, Adore the wisdom which could span, And power which formed creation's plan: To God all praise and glory!

11. Monday after Second Sunday in Advent.

Lord, stir our hearts to hear thy word. Amen.

Isaiah 13, 9–13. Behold, the day of the Lord cometh, cruel both with wrath and fierce anger, to lay the land desolate; and he shall destroy the sinners thereof out of it. For the stars of heaven, and the constellations thereof, shall not give their light: the sun shall be darkened in his going forth, and the moon shall not cause her light to shine. And I will punish the world for their evil, and the wicked for their iniquity; and I will cause the arrogancy of the proud to cease, and will lay low the haughtiness of the terrible. I will make a man more precious than fine gold; even a man than the golden wedge of Ophir. Therefore I will shake the heavens, and the earth shall remove out of her place, in the wrath of the Lord of hosts, and in the day of his fierce anger.

It is the doom of Babylon which is described by the prophet in these appalling words; but such judgments on particular peoples are earnest of the judgment on the world, and hence this is also a description of the last day.

The day of the Lord will be a glorious one for God's people, but terrible for his enemies. The brave shall then become cowards; Now they hold the head high, but then they shall cringe with fear. You shall find no *man* among them on that day, though you offer gold in exchange for him. The sun disappears, the stars are blotted out; travail lays hold of the hearts of men, so that their faces are now flushed with shame, now blanched with fear. See, how the eyes of the proud are cast down, how they stand confounded, with what despair they gaze at one another! They mocked at pain and boasted of their courage; now they groan like a woman in labor, and call to the mountains, "fall on us," and to the hills, "hide us from the anger of the Lamb."

The unbelievers mock, saying: "What is become of his advent? We have heard of it so long, but it is no nearer than before." Thus spake also the men of the time of Noah, until the flood came and swept them all away. In like manner also the people of Sodom, until fire and brimstone rained from heaven; and the inhabitants of Jerusalem, until the flames rolled and their own blood ran in torrents through their city. You, then, who are the Lord's believers and know that all things shall pass away, what should your attitude be? In holy living and godliness, you should look for and earnestly desire the coming of the day of God, by reason of which the heavens being on fire shall be dissolved and the elements shall melt with fervent heat. Heaven and earth, as they now are, shall dissolve and pass away; but, according to his promise, we look for new heavens and a new earth, wherein dwelleth righteousness. Wherefore, beloved, seeing that ye look for these things, be diligent that ye may be found in peace, without spot, and blameless in his sight; account that the long-suffering of our Lord is salvation; for he wants the number of his saints to be full.

God, give us the spirit of thy fear and keep us awake, so that we may meet thee with joy. Let that day become for us a day of glorious redemption. Amen.

My soul, be on thy guard; Ten thousand foes arise; And hosts of sin are pressing hard To draw thee from the skies.

O watch, and fight, and pray! The battle ne'er give o'er; Renew it boldly every day, And help divine implore.

---

12. Tuesday after Second Sunday in Advent.

Lord Jesus, grant that we may hear thy word and live. Amen.

Matthew 25, 1–13. Then shall the kingdom of heaven be likened unto ten virgins, which took their lamps, and went forth to meet the bridegroom. And five of them were wise, and five were foolish. They that were foolish took their lamps, and took no oil with them: But the wise took oil in their vessels with their lamps. While the bridegroom tarried, they all slumbered and slept. And at midnight there was a cry made, Behold, the bridegroom cometh; go ye out to meet him. Then all those virgins arose, and trimmed their lamps. And the foolish said unto the wise, Give us of your oil; for our lamps are gone out. But the wise answered, saying, Not so; lest there be not enough for us and you: but go ye rather to them that sell, and buy for yourselves. And while they went to buy, the bridegroom came; and they that were ready went in with him to the marriage: and the door was shut. Afterward came also the other virgins, saying, Lord, Lord, open to us. But he answered and said, Verily I say unto you, I know you not. Watch therefore, for ye know neither the day nor the hour wherein the Son of man cometh.

What shall it profit us to be *called* believers, if we be not such in fact? Or what gain is there in our having, at one time, *been* living Christians, if we do not remain steadfast to the end? What good purpose is served by having lamps, if we have no oil in the vessel? External works that give us the appearance of being true believers, so that we may mix with these and regard ourselves and be regarded by others as good Christians;—this sort of godliness which is not in truth the life of the Spirit in the heart, will, alas, prove a sad delusion at the last. By the oil in the vessel is meant the Spirit and life in the heart, the true life of faith and love; out of this proceeds the true light in deeds and conversation. Take heed that your fear of God be not an empty lamp. Do you in fact have the life of grace in your soul? Is it out of this, from within, that your deeds of piety proceed? Do you live in the Lord, and is his love in you? Does your heart beat with such tenderness for him, that you hasten to meet him with longing and joy when the cry is made: "Behold, the bridegroom cometh"? Is this your innermost thought: Lord Jesus, come quickly; thou, thou art he for whom I am looking and longing; my whole heart is thine in life and death; thou art my only own now and for evermore?—Even the wise virgins are affected in some measure by the drowsy breath of the times, and they slumber; but they are known herein, that, when their rest is disturbed, their hearts are with Jesus. He is their life, and his love is in truth the soul in all their deeds.

Lord Jesus, we earnestly beseech thee, that we may be among the wise virgins; suffer us never to fall into that sleep which is spiritual death. Make us whole and true in the faith; let it burn in our heart and be the light of our life until the end. Amen.

Rise, my soul, to watch and pray, From thy sleep awake thee, Lest at last the evil day Suddenly o'ertake thee: For the foe, well we know, Oft his harvest reapeth, While the Christian sleepeth.

13. Wednesday after Second Sunday in Advent.

Lord, teach us thy word, and help us to walk in the light which it gives. Amen.

Matthew 25, 31–46. When the Son of man shall come in his glory, and all the holy angels with him, then shall he sit upon the throne of his glory: And before him shall be gathered all nations; and he shall separate them one from another, as a shepherd divideth his sheep from the goats: And he shall set the sheep on his right hand, but the goats on the left. Then shall the King say unto them on his right hand, Come, ye blessed of my Father, inherit the kingdom prepared for you from the foundation of the world: For I was an hungred, and ye gave me meat: I was thirsty, and ye gave me drink: I was a stranger, and ye took me in: Naked, and ye clothed me: I was sick, and ye visited me: I was in prison, and ye came unto me. Then shall the righteous answer him, saying, Lord, when saw we thee an hungred, and fed thee? or thirsty, and gave thee drink? When saw we thee a stranger, and took thee in? or naked, and clothed thee? Or when saw we thee sick, or in prison, and came unto thee? And the King shall answer and say unto them, Verily I say unto you, Inasmuch as ye have done it unto one of the least of these my brethren, ye have done it unto me. Then shall he say also unto them on the left hand, Depart from me, ye cursed, into everlasting fire, prepared for the devil and his angels: For I was an hungred, and ye gave me no meat: I was thirsty, and ye gave me no drink: I was a stranger, and ye took me not in: naked, and ye clothed me not: sick, and in prison, and ye visited me not. Then shall they also answer him, saying, Lord, when saw we thee an hungred, or a thirst, or a stranger, or naked, or sick, or in prison, and did not minister unto thee? Then shall he answer them, saying, Verily I say unto you, Inasmuch as ye did it not to one of the least of these, ye did it not to me. And these shall go away into everlasting punishment: but the righteous into life eternal.

Christ and his judgment seat separate us into two divisions. That which decides the eternal fate of each individual is the relation in which he has placed himself to Christ in this life. All who with humble hearts and true faith live in him and do good, shall stand acquitted over yonder and enter into the joy of their Lord. But those who have led a worldly life without Christ, whether it be in outward piety or in open wickedness, must depart into everlasting fire. Those who are saved inherit the kingdom prepared for them from the foundation of the world; they *inherit* it as the children of God in Christ; they have not themselves earned it by their works; they pretend to no merit of their own. When have we done any good to thee, our Lord? They served him unceasingly, but their left hand knew not what their right hand did. The fact, that they were able to do good, was pure grace: how, then, can it be their merit? And

2

yet the Lord counts it as such; he remembers their good works and rewards them. It is he who does good in us, yet regards it as though we had done it of ourselves. The saints depend on his grace alone; there is, indeed, nothing else which has saved and does save them. They are imperfect in all their works, and deserve nothing but punishment; but the Lord disregards their imperfection, and he finds in them only glorious deeds. He sees, that what they have done, down to the most insignificant act, has been done for him, and he permits nothing thereof to lose its reward.

On the other hand we hear the blind, selfrighteous spirit ask: When have we seen thee and not served thee? This is an impious question. Woe be to us, if we are so blind that, knowing neither ourselves nor the grace of God, we pride ourselves on having done well before the Lord! Woe be to us, if he alone is not our righteousness and our life, so that we serve *him* by doing good to his needy members on earth. O, that these words might cut through our very marrow and bones: "These shall go away into everlasting punishment, but the righteous into life eternal."

Holy and righteous God, who of thy mercy didst become the Son of Man, in order that we might have in thee a merciful judge; grant that we may live our life here on earth in true faith and charity, and that we may stand with all who are thine at thy right hand on the day of thy glory. Amen.

Great God, what do I see and hear! The end of things created! The Judge of mankind doth appear, On clouds of glory seated; The trumpet sounds; the graves restore The dead which they contained before; Prepare, my soul, to meet him.

The dead in Christ shall first arise, At the last trumpet's sounding, Caught up to meet him in the skies, With joy their Lord surrounding; No gloomy fears their souls dismay; His presence sheds eternal day On those prepared to meet him.

---

14. Thursday after Second Sunday in Advent.

Lord, give us grace to keep thy word in our hearts. Amen.

Revelations 3, 7–13. And to the angel of the church in Philadelphia write; These things saith he that is holy, he that is true, he that hath the key of David, he that openeth, and no man shutteth; and shutteth, and no man openeth; I know thy works: behold, I have set before thee an open door, and no man can shut it: for thou hast a little strength, and hast kept my word, and hast not denied my name. Behold, I will make them of the synagogue of Satan, which say they are Jews, and are not, but do lie; behold, I will make them to come and worship before thy feet, and to know that I have loved thee. Because thou hast kept the word of my patience, I also will keep thee from the hour of temptation, which shall come upon all the world, to try them that dwell upon the earth. Behold, I come quickly: hold that fast which thou hast, that no man take thy crown. Him that overcometh will I make a pillar in the temple of my God; and he shall go no more out: and I will write upon him the name of my God, and the name of the city of my God, which is New

Jerusalem, which cometh down out of heaven from my God: and I will write upon him my new name. He that hath an ear, let him hear what the Spirit saith unto the churches.

It behooves the church of God to be patient and remain steadfast through poverty and tribulation a little while, then shall it receive the crown. The church must keep the word of Christ's patience; that is, it must *practice* patience and conquer by his word. It must submit to contempt, scorn, and oppression on the part of the wise and mighty of the world, it must suffer without complaining, bear anguish and sorrow, and find support in the word which teaches us, that such is to be the portion of God's people here on earth, especially in these latter days. Though we have but little strength, the power of the Word is great; the faithfulness of the Lord will enable us to keep the truth and thereby vanquish all its opponents. "Be not thou ashamed of the testimony of our Lord, nor of me, his prisoner; but be thou partaker of the afflictions of the gospel according to the power of God." Through the trials of the latter days the church shall be made worthy of the crown of victory. The cross is the Christians' coat-of-arms; the effeminate shall not inherit the kingdom of God. Man thy soul with courage, Zion; be undaunted in the strife; be undaunted always, looking forward to the crown of life. Though the enemy be mighty, life is but a fleeting breath; let thy heart be stout, O Zion, and be faithful unto death.

Faithful Lord Jesus, thou knowest that we can do nothing of ourselves; give us grace that we may confess thee and be willing to suffer for thy name's sake. Grant us patience; keep our eyes directed toward the crown, so that we never may grow faint of heart, but thank and bless thee in our tribulations while life endures. Amen.

Who will but let himself be guided Of God alone, in all his ways, Shall strength receive, be well provided, And safely led through evil days; Who trusts in God's unchanging love, Builds on the Rock that naught can move. Think not, when in the stress of trial, That God hath cast thee off unheard, That he whose hopes meet no denial Must surely be of God preferred; God never will forsake in need The heart that trusts in him indeed.

---

15. Friday after Second Sunday in Advent.

Lord, help us in the time of our adversity by the power of thy word. Amen.

2 Thessalonians 1, 3–12. We are bound to thank God always for you, brethren, as it is meet, because that your faith groweth exceedingly, and the charity of every one of you all toward each other aboundeth; so that we ourselves glory in you in the churches of God, for your patience and faith in all your persecutions and tribulations that ye endure; which is a manifest token of the righteous judgment of God, that ye may be counted worthy of the kingdom of God, for which ye also suffer: Seeing it is a righteous thing with God to recompense tribulation to them that trouble you; and to you who are troubled, rest with us; when the Lord Jesus shall be revealed from heaven with his mighty angels, in flaming fire taking vengeance on them that know not

20

God, and that obey not the gospel of our Lord Jesus Christ: Who shall be punished with everlasting destruction from the presence of the Lord, and from the glory of his power; when he shall come to be glorified in his saints, and to be admired in all them that believe (because our testimony among you was believed) in that day. Wherefore also we pray always for you, that our God would count you worthy of this calling, and fulfil all the good pleasure of his goodness, and the work of faith with power; that the name of our Lord Jesus Christ may be glorified in you, and ye in him, according to the grace of our God and the Lord Jesus Christ.

The saints of God are purified through much suffering. The dross of sin in them is purged away by fire, the flesh is mortified, the lusts die, the soul is drawn toward heaven, their love is increased, their patience is trained. Then they learn to thank God for his grace in all things and to sing heavenly songs of praise to him in the midst of the dark prison. Such glory can not be attained without suffering. Accept as the cross of the Lord all trouble that may befall you; then it also is, in truth, the cross of Christ. In other words, suffer as a Christian, bow to the will of God, accept chastisement from the Most High; then shall selfishness, stubbornness, the cares and the lusts, die. Then will God make you worthy of his call, and perfect his image in you. Thus is his name glorified in us, and thus are we glorified in him, even in this world. How full of grace is the path of suffering! Yet we shun it instead of loving it!

Especially, however, do our sufferings prepare us for the blessed estate in the future life, and to meet him when he comes with his mighty angels on that great day. Then it shall be seen, that our tribulations have not harmed us, but that they have, on the contrary, sanctified, purified and transfigured us. When the ungodly are consumed by the advent of Christ, then shall *our* glory shine in full lustre. The angels shall marvel and adore the Lord; new depths of his wisdom are opened to them and to us. We, who had fallen so low and were in such wretched case, are become so unspeakably glorious. Thereby the Lord receives his new name; forever new it is reflected from us; in this wise we have it written in our foreheads. His name Jesus shines with a splendor forever new throughout all eternity. Every knee bows to him, and all the saints praise him with new tongues.

Then is our time of tribulation gone by, and the eternal wedding days are come.

We are willing to suffer, Lord Jesus; but still, do thou help us thereto. Give us grace so to bear our sufferings, that thy name may be honored here and yonder. Amen.

Nearer, my God, to thee, Nearer to thee! E'en though it be a cross That raiseth me: Still all my song shall be, Nearer, my God, to thee, Nearer to thee.

16. Saturday after Second Sunday in Advent.

Lord, wake us and keep us awake by thy Spirit and word. Amen.

Malachi 4, 1–6. For, behold, the day cometh, that shall burn as an oven, and all the proud, yea, and all that do wickedly, shall be stubble: and the day that cometh shall burn them up, saith the Lord of hosts, that it shall leave them neither root nor branch. But unto you that fear my name shall the Sun of righteousness arise with healing in his wings; and ye shall go forth, and grow up as calves of the stall. And ye shall tread down the wicked; for they shall be ashes under the soles of your feet in the day that I shall do this, said the Lord of hosts. Remember ye the law of Moses my servant, which I commanded unto him in Horeb for all Israel, with the statutes and judgments. Behold, I will send you Elijah the prophet before the coming of the great and dreadful day of the Lord: and he shall turn the heart of the fathers to the children, and the heart of the children to their fathers, lest I come and smite the earth with a curse.

Should not the word concerning the day of the Lord wake us, make us humble, yea, even crush us and make us sincerely contrite of heart? When the Lord through Jonah spoke of doom and destruction to the people of Nineveh, it caused them to put on sackcloth and ashes, for they *believed* the word. Whosoever believes the word of God concerning the return of the Lord, bows the head in acknowledgment of sin, and is afeared and seeks grace. The ungodly despise the word; therefore they feel so secure, and haste without fear toward destruction. There is no lack of warning from the merciful God. Even as he sent Elijah to the apostate Israelites and chastised them with the fiery tongue of the prophet and with hunger and the sword; and as he sent the Baptist to the Israelites of a later day and by his powerful exhortation to repentance shook Jerusalem and all Judæa; in like manner he continues to send new witnesses who cry out, calling people to repentance, and start spiritual movements in this place and that; while unbelief is compelled to show its poverty, as was the case with the Baal-cult in the time of Ahab. And during the time yet to come he shall give his witnesses great power before the peoples and the tribes, (Rev. 11). All in vain! The many will continue in fancied security in their sins and will not repent. Therefore the day ōf doom must become a burning oven and burn them up, leaving them neither root nor branch. For they alone who have been born again and are holy can stand before him that cometh.

Christian soul; live in repentance day by day unto the last. Never feel too secure, be not puffed up, but walk in holy fear, and with David become all the time less worthy in your own eyes. You have learned to lay all your sins on Jesus and have found healing under his wings; never desert your first love. By the light of the Spirit you shall see yourself more and more clearly and feel more deeply your need of grace; neither shall there be any want of the trials necessary to your daily revival and your humiliation; you also shall be led with the Lord from the judgment hall along the path of pain to Calvary; still, push your way deeper into the fellowship of his suffering and deeper into the salvation of grace. The way leads to the Ascension hill, and soon you shall with unclouded eye see that sun which gladdens all the saints with eternal gladness, but sends the horrors of death through all who are puffed up.

Lord Jesus, give us god-fearing and humble hearts, and prepare our souls by thy grace, that we may await with joy the coming of thy day and be accepted of thee. Amen.

Lord Jesus Christ, do not delay, O hasten our salvation! We often tremble on our way In fear and tribulation. Then hear us when we cry to thee; Come, mighty Judge, come, make us free From every evil. Amen!

17. Third Sunday in Advent. I.

Lord, give us grace, that we may understand thy word and believe in thee. Amen.

Gospel Lesson. Matthew 11, 2-10. Now when John had heard in the prison the works of Christ, he sent two of his disciples, and said unto him, Art thou he that should come, or do we look for another? Jesus answered and said unto them, Go and shew John again those things which ye do hear and see: The blind receive their sight, and the lame walk, the lepers are cleansed, and the deaf hear, the dead are raised up, and the poor have the gospel preached to them. And blessed is he, whosoever shall not be offended in me. And, as they departed, Jesus began to say unto the multitudes concerning John, What went ye out into the wilderness to see? A reed shaken with the wind? But what went ye out for to see? A man clothed in soft raiment? behold, they that wear soft clothing are in kings' houses. But what went ye out for to see? A prophet? yea, I say unto you, and more than a prophet. For this is he of whom it is written, Behold, I send my messenger before thy face, which shall prepare thy way before thee.

Jesus, the son of God and of Mary, who was born in Bethlehem, is in truth the Christ, and there in no other king and redeemer of our souls. Neither do we want any other; we need none other, for he is that perfect savior who helps us out of every trouble. In him the prophecies of the prophets concerning the Messiah have been fulfilled to the letter. He is become the least, and is the greatest; the poorest, and the richest; the most despised, but the most glorious. He enters into our nature, but transfigures it into godlike glory; he dies, but death has no part in him; he is the living one in all eternity. Here is Abel and his innocent blood, shed by a brother's hand; here are the wisdom, sale, imprisonment, and the royal splendor of Joseph; here are the highpriest, the lamb, and the blood which is carried into the sanctuary; here is Samuel with his triple office; here is David in his humiliation and then in his glory; here is Solomon, the prince of peace, who builds the temple of the Lord, here is the son of the virgin, of whom Isaiah spake, the child which is the eternal wonderful God; here is the suffering and dying, but again living servant of the Lord, written of in the 53rd chapter of that prophet; the hunted hart of the 22nd psalm of David; here are all the Scriptures. The eyes of the blind are opened and the ears of the deaf are unstopped; the lame man leaps as an hart, and the tongue of the dumb sings with joy. The year of jubilee is come, the prisoners of death are set free. John, whom prophecy calls Elijah, goes before and prepares the way; the greatest of all the prophets is the herald of him who became the least of all.

We also *experience* on ourselves that Jesus is the true Savior. He has opened our eyes, so that we see our sin and know his merit, which takes it away. We see the death in ourselves, but know the life which vanquishes death, and feel the victory of love in our hearts. We hear the music of heaven in the gospel, and the spirit within us answers amen. We feel the cleansing grace of the blood of Jesus and the victorious power of his life in our hearts, so that we taste the peace of God, love our enemies, bear our sufferings, and give thanks for the daily cross. Will you say that this is not the work of the true Savior? We, who of ourselves can only be offended because of his suffering, still love this crucified form with love unspeakable, a thousand times more than all else in the world. We are tempted, and we sin; but we fly to him, and we find in his wounds our city of refuge; we are victorious over sin and death; they can not touch us at the horns of the altar.

Blessed be the Lord Jesus, who came to the world and became our Savior; who comes to us and saves us; who shall come and set us free. Dear Lord, man us with firm faith when we fight our last battle with the devil in the agony of death. Amen.

Let the earth now praise the Lord, Who hath truly kept his word, And the sinner's help and friend Now at last to us doth send.

What the fathers most desired, What the prophet's heart inspired, What they longed for many a year, Stands fulfilled in glory here.

---

18. Third Sunday in Advent. II.

Lord, make us thy faithful servants. Amen.

Epistle Lesson, 1 Corinthians, 4, 1–5. Let a man so account of us, as of the ministers of Christ, and stewards of the mysteries of God. Moreover, it is required in stewards, that a man be found faithful. But with me it is a very small thing that I should be judged of you, or of man's judgment; yea, I judge not mine own self. For I know nothing by myself; yet am I not hereby justified: but he that judgeth me is the Lord. Therefore judge nothing before the time, until the Lord come, who both will bring to light the hidden things of darkness, and will make manifest the counsels of the hearts: and then shall every man have praise of God.

John the Baptist was the servant and steward of Christ, and so are also all the legitimate and true preachers of the word of God; they are appointed of the Lord to administer his mysteries of the gospel. All who have been properly called to the office of the ministry are to be accounted servants of Christ, who have received the office from him and administer it in his stead. In themselves the ministers of the Word are only erring men, but their office exalts them, and the

Lord makes them strong in their testimony concerning the truth. A servant of the Lord must go through many a conflict; the flesh is all the time weak and would like to be clothed in soft raiment. If he is a man of talent and has marked success in his work, he is tempted to fall into the sin of pride and vanity; if he is less richly endowed, or if his labor seems to have no visible results, he is prone to lose heart and sink into apathy. The Baptist calls himself the voice of Christ, and Paul says concerning himself: "I am nothing." This is the spirit which is necessary, in order that a man may remain faithful.

Faithfulness is the one important requirement. The judgment of the Lord concerning us is of moment, but the judgment of men is not. The eye of God is true, while the eye of man is often deceived by mere outward appearances. On that day, when every man's work shall be revealed by fire, much of what is regarded as gold will prove to be nothing but guilded hay and stubble. The Lord demands of us faithfulness, not brilliant exploits; diligence in the use of the talent entrusted to us, not splendid proofs of genius or of great talents. How beautiful are not those little flowers in the garden of God, which, instead of boastfully showing forth their loveliness, hide themselves beneath the others, but which can neither escape the eye of Heaven nor keep back their wealth of strong and sweet odors. Many an obscure country pastor and lowly teacher shall shine more brightly over yonder than famous bishops and scholars. Sincere love and genuine faithfulness count for more, than do any and all great talents.

Assist us by your prayers for us, ye believers, and by obedience to the word which we bring you from the Lord; in order that we may give account of our stewardship with joy, and not with grief. And do thou, Lord Jesus, help us by the light and power of thy Holy Spirit; give to us thy love, that we may serve thee with gladness and be in truth faithful stewards of the wonderful riches of thy house. Amen.

O pour thy Spirit from on high! Lord, thine appointed servants bless; Thy promised power to each supply, And clothe thy priests with righteousness. And, when their work is finished here, Let them in hope their charge resign; Before the throne with joy appear, And there with endless glory shine.

19. Monday after Third Sunday in Advent.

Lord, may our soul preserve thy glorious testimony. Amen.

Isaiah 35. The wilderness, and the solitary place, shall be glad for them; and the desert shall rejoice, and blossom as the rose. It shall blossom abundantly, and rejoice even with joy and singing; the glory of Lebanon shall be given unto it, the excellency of Carmel and Sharon; they shall see the glory of the Lord, and the excellency of our God. Strengthen ye the weak hands, and confirm the feeble knees. Say to them that are of a fearful heart, Be strong, fear not; behold, your God will come with vengeance, even God with a recompence; he will come and save you. Then the eyes of the blind shall be opened, and the ears of the deaf shall be unstopped: then shall the lame man leap as an hart, and the tongue of the dumb sing: for in the wilderness shall waters break out, and streams in the desert. And the parched ground shall become a pool, and the thirsty land springs of water: in the habitation ot dragons where each lay, shall be grass, with reeds and rushes. And an highway shall be there, and a way, and it shall be called the way of holiness; the unclean shall not pass over it; but it shall be for those; the wayfaring men, though fools, shall not err therein. No lion shall be there, nor any ravenous beast shall go up thereon, it shall not be found there: but the redeemed shall walk there. And the ransomed of the Lord shall return, and come to Zion with songs, and everlasting joy upon their heads: they shall obtain joy and gladness, and sorrow and sighing shall flee away.

What this beautiful chapter prophesies concerning the glory of the church of Christ and the riches of God's grace to believers *began* to be fulfilled by the outpouring of the Spirit on the day of Pentecost. How many faint hearts have not become courageous, how many thirsty souls have not drunk of the water of life in the Word and the sacraments! How many blind, deaf, lame, and dumb have not been healed by Jesus! How many simple Christians have not heard the warning, "this is the way which thou shalt go," when they were on the point of going astray to the right or to the left; and who shall number the redeemed who have already come home to the eternal dwelling places of joy in Zion? The words of Isaiah do not sound as though spoken concerning things to come, but as though he saw them already fulfilled; and such prophecies add strength to our faith. O, how true and how strong and safe to lean upon is the word of God!

However, these sublime words have not as yet been *completely* fulfilled. Time shall be, when the parched people of God shall blossom, rejoice unspeakably, and possess the glory of the Lord, the excellency of our God without measure and limit;—when the first heaven and earth have passed away and the new Jerusalem comes down from heaven prepared as a bride adorned for her husband. Here our hearts easily grow faint and our hands weak, here there is yet evil every day and hour; but these things shall be done away with forever, when God himself shall wipe away all tears from our eyes, and there shall be no more sin, nor sorrow, nor death. Now we see through a glass, darkly; but then we shall see face to face. We shall hear the heavenly harps, we shall sing a new song, and we shall drink without hindrance of the river of water proceeding out of the throne of God and of the Lamb. We are yet in danger. Brethren, here it is needful always to watch and pray that we fall not into temptation. But then, there is no more danger; everlasting joy shall be upon our heads; yea, we shall obtain joy and gladness, and sorrow and sighing shall flee away from us. These sayings are faithful and true; the Lord hath spoken them.

Thou comest to us in our misery, Lord Jesus, for the purpose of bringing us into glory; blessed be thy name. Do thou lead us through the wilderness; thou art the fount of life and makest the desert become for us a meadow full of springs of water. Anoint our eyes that we may see thee, open our ears that we may hear thy voice, precious

Savior. Do thou speak into our souls: Be strong and fear not. Hold us fast to thee and do not release thy hold on us, thou strong, faithful God. Amen.

Awake, my soul, in joyful lays, And sing thy great Redeemer's praise; He justly claims a song from me, His lovingkindness, oh, how free! He saw me ruined in the fall, Yet loved me notwithstanding all; He saved me from my lost estate, His lovingkindness, oh, how great!

20. Tuesday after Third Sunday in Advent.

Lord, let thy tender mercies come unto us, thy salvation according to thy word. Amen.

Isaiah 61, 1–3. "The Spirit of the Lord God is upon me; because the Lord hath anointed me to preach good tidings unto the meek: he hath sent me to bind up the broken-hearted, to proclaim liberty to the captives, and the opening of the prison to them that are bound; to proclaim the acceptable year of the Lord, and the day of vengeance of our God; to comfort all that mourn; to appoint unto them that mourn in Zion, to give unto them beauty for ashes, the oil of joy for mourning, the garment of praise for the spirit of heaviness; that they might be called trees of righteousness, the planting of the Lord, that he might be glorified.

In the 25th chapter of Leviticus the Lord ordains that every fiftieth year in Israel was to be a year of jubilee. Then all debts were to be cancelled, every man was to have his possessions returned to him, and all bondmen who were of the children of Israel were to become free. In the kingdom of Christ all our sins are forgiven us, so that no one in this kingdom has guilt and doom hanging over his head. No bondmen are there; all are freeborn, born of God. They are no longer in the prison of the fear of death; neither are they the slaves of Satan, compelled to do his will and walk in sin; for by baptism they have entered into the covenant of a good conscience toward God by the resurrection of Jesus Christ. This is the glorious message of the gospel which Christ has brought us, and which he announces to the world through his servants. Hear this, all ye mourners in Zion: in the church of Christ, of which you became a member by your baptism, to which you earnestly desire to belong, and to which you thus do, in fact, belong,—in the church of Christ, in which you live, the Lord has established the law, that sin is forgiven, so that nothing can condemn you. This is the covenant of God with us: I will forgive your iniquity, and I will remember your sin no more (Jer. 31, 34). Jesus has taken your sin upon himself and paid its wages. Will you not give him at least this reward, that you believe his message of pardon, and rejoice? He asks no more; do not, then, let this much be denied him. He came and established this kingdom and instituted this gospel by his blood. He appointed unto them that mourn in Zion, to give them beauty for ashes, the oil of joy for mourning, the garment of praise for the spirit of heaviness. He will ground you in his righteousness, that you may have your root in the perfect obedience of the Son of God and be able to stand against all the storms of Satan. In yourself you are utterly lost, sold under sin and made the prisoner of death; but in Christ you have liberty and life, righteousness and salvation. This is no dream, no idle words, but truth as certain and sure as God himself. All heavens answer: Amen.

Lord Jesus, we can hardly believe thy glad tidings, but do thou help us. It is a good thing for us that thou dost not break the bruised reed and dost not quench the smoking flax. We thank thee for thy great mercy; do thou help us to believe. Give us the light of the Spirit and grace to believe in thee. Amen.

Enter his gates with songs of joy, With praises to his courts repair; And make it your divine employ To pay your thanks and honors there.

The Lord is good, the Lord is kind; Great is his grace, his mercy sure; And all the race of man shall find His truth from age to age endure.

---

21. Wednesday after Third Sunday in Advent.

Lord, establish our ways in thy word. Amen.

2 Timothy 1, 6-12. Wherefore I put thee in remembrance that thou stir up the gift of God, which is in thee by the putting on of my hands. For God hath not given us the spirit of fear; but of power, and of love, and of a sound mind. Be not thou therefore ashamed of the testimony of our Lord, nor of me his prisoner: but be thou partaker of the afflictions of the gospel according to the power of God; who hath saved us, and called us with an holy calling, not according to our works, but according to his own purpose and grace, which was given us in Christ Jesus before the world began; but is now made manifest by the appearing of our Savior Jesus Christ, who hath abolished death, and hath brought life and immortality to light through the gospel: whereunto I am appointed a preacher, and an apostle, and a teacher of the Gentiles. For the which cause I also suffer these things: nevertheless I am not ashamed: for I know whom I have believed, and am persuaded that he is able to keep that which I have committed unto him against that day.

Even as John the Baptist saw the near approach of death, when, from the prison, he sent his disciples to Jesus, so did Paul know that his dissolution was at hand when he wrote this epistle to Timothy; but he meets death with triumphant confidence. Christ has brought us great things, and how happy are we who live in his church! O, that the Spirit might, in this church year, stir up anew the gift of God which is given us! Let our faith become healthy and strong, let our love become ardent, and let us willingly and gladly endure hardship with God's people. Boldly confess your Savior; himself will give you the necessary spirit and grace. Indeed, he has given you them already in your baptism; the spirit of power and love is yours, if you will but make use of it; and if you do this, the fire in your soul will be fanned into flame. The secret is this, that you are not a servant, but a *child* in God's household. Do good without ceasing, the fountain of love and power will not run dry; your heavenly father has riches without limit. Or are not we also saved and called with an holy calling? Did not Christ die, and does he not live for us? Are we not baptized unto him, do we not hear his gospel and partake of his Holy Supper? Shall we save ourselves anew by our own works, though we are saved already by the grace of God in Christ? Let us not by unbelief abolish what God has done, deny what God has said, and despise our heavenly calling. The death in our flesh, which treatens to palsy us, has been vanquished by our baptism unto the death and resurrection of Christ; for we are united with him in his death and in his victory over death; we are members of the Savior who died and is alive for evermore. Therefore the devil has no power over us and must not be permitted to subdue our courage. Hear how Paul speaks: "Christ hath abolished death, *abolished death*, and brought *life* and *immortality* to light through the gospel." But what Paul has that we also have, in the measure which we need in order to conquer the flesh and defy the devil when he tries to make us fearful and faint-hearted. You, also, Christian brother, know whom you have believed, and know that it is safe to build on him. Have you not entrusted yourself to him with your heart, your life, your all? Have you not placed your soul and salvation in his hand? I know that my Redeemer liveth; I know that it was not I, but he, who chose me, saved me, and called me; and that it is not I, but he, who keeps me; and I know of a certainty that not devil nor death owns me, but that he owns me and dwells in me. Verily, he shall hold me fast and keep me in faith and love, through whatever of suffering it may please him to lead me, and though it may cost me all that I hold dear in this world.

Teach us, Lord, to immerse our soul in thy everlasting grace. Give us grace to live the life of love, to confess thee with ardent heart, and to win disciples for thee round about. Above all else, dear Lord God, let our faith be true and living, that it may prove itself in charity and in victory over our natural faint-heartedness and over all the power of sin. Amen.

O that the Lord would guide my ways, To keep his statutes still! O that my God would grant me grace To know and do his will! Order my footsteps by thy Word, And make my heart sincere; Let sin have no dominion, Lord, But keep my conscience clear.

22. Thursday after Third Sunday in Advent.

Lord, lead us into the sanctuary of thy word, and let us abide there alway. Amen.

Isaiah 42, 5–10. Thus saith God the Lord, he that created the heavens, and stretched them out; he that spread forth the earth, and that which cometh out of it; he that giveth breath unto the people upon it, and spirit to them that walk therein; I the Lord have called thee in righteousness, and will hold thine hand, and will keep thee, and give thee for a covenant of the people, for a light of the Gentiles; to open the blind eyes, to bring out the prisoners from the prison, and them that sit in darkness out of the prison house. I am the Lord; that is my name: and my glory will I not give to another, neither my praise to graven images. Behold, the former things are come to pass, and new things do I declare; before they **spring** forth I tell you of them. Sing unto the Lord a new song, and his praise from the end of the earth, ye that go down to the sea, and all that is therein; the isles, and the inhabitants thereof.

Ye who know the Lord and his grace shall bless him and sing praises to his name. We were blind and walked in the darkness of death; our heart served strange gods, loved the creature rather than the creator, was without peace, and yet knew not its own unhappy state. Jesus came, however, and opened our eyes; we, who were blind, now see. He led us out into the clear daylight of grace, set us free from the fetters of idolatry, and taught us to know the only true God. Now we love him, and he gives our heart peace. Our joy is great; things more glorious still await us: "The lines are fallen unto me in pleasant places; yea, I have a goodly heritage." Therefore, sing unto the Lord a new song; that is, give him sincere thanks for a new revelation of his glory, for a new, ever new look into the depths of his grace. For he ever leads us into new regions of his kingdom, into new mansions of his house; more and more we become able to comprehend with all saints what is the breadth, and length, and depth, and height; and to know the love of Christ, which passeth knowledge. At times it may *seem* to us that our knowledge becomes less, instead of more, clear; but every Christian who lives in daily repentance is ever advancing in the wisdom of God, even when he does not, himself, notice it.

Praise God, all his believers; praise him without ceasing; tell his wonders! Satan has no tongue with which to bless and praise God; he wants to tie our tongues also, but his bands are broken asunder, and our tongue loosened. Sing unto the Lord, ye who dwell on the rock of faith; who shall do it, if ye will not? Give God honor with humble heart; sound his praises, that it may be heard over all the earth. Over all the earth, I say. Your song of praise reaches farther, much farther, than the tones of the greatest musical artists. The thanksgiving of God's people is not heard over all the earth only, but it reaches heaven and is precious to the heart of the Lord our God.

Help us to know thee, Lord, and to praise thee with a song ever new, here and for evermore. Give us this grace for Jesus' sake. Amen.

I know that my Redeemer lives; What comfort this sweet sentence gives! He lives, he lives, who once was dead, He lives, my ever-living Head. He lives to bless me with his love, He lives to plead for me above, He lives my hungry soul to feed, He lives to help in time of need.

23. Friday after Third Sunday in Advent.

Lord, keep us alive by thy word. Amen.

Psalm 13. To the chief Musician, a Psalm of David. How long wilt thou forget me, O Lord? for ever? how long wilt thou hide thy face from me? How long shall I take counsel in my soul, having sorrow in my heart daily? how long shall mine enemy be exalted over me? Consider and hear me, O Lord my God; lighten mine eyes, lest I sleep the sleep of death; lest mine enemy say,

I have prevailed against him; and those that trouble me rejoice when I am moved. But I have trusted in thy mercy; my heart shall rejoice in thy salvation. I will sing unto the Lord, because he hath dealt bountifully with me.

When your soul asks, how long, O Lord? and again, how long, how long? when your heart is like a turbulent sea; when all manner of distracting thoughts and devices perplex you; when you search in vain on every hand for an escape out of your difficulties; when you cry and the Lord does not hear, but hides his face, so that it seems to you to be almost certain, that for you the light has been put out forever; —then you become like the other saints in the imitation of the Son of God, and taste something of the Long Friday. But still, the true Christians hope and wait for the Lord's salvation. How many of the groanings which can not be uttered do not then rise up from the depths of the soul: "O my God, hear my cry; let me again see thy face. Remember not my sins, but according to thy mercy remember thou me for thy goodness' sake. I am thy own, bought with a price; thou must not reject me for evermore. Save me, save me, for Jesus' sake!" We feel our sin, and acknowledge that the Lord would be just, if he should condemn us; but how dreadful it would be! And what a sad and bitter thought it is, that the enemies of the church of God will rejoice, while the name of God will be mocked for my sake, if I fall into despair and become the prey of Satan. The cry comes, therefore, from the depths of my being: "Lord, surely thou must not, thou canst not give me up. Mine enemy shall not be exalted over me. Thou art the God of forgiveness; all my great sin is but a spark as compared with the bottomless sea of thy grace, and all my wretchedness is as nothing in comparison with thy power to deliver me."— The day dawns; the night disappears; the morning comes; a new flood of light is shed on the glory of the grace of God; the name of Jesus becomes tenfold more beautiful; and the gospel of life and salvation in the blood of the Lamb has created a sounding-board in the heart which delights God and his angels. My adversary is thy adversary; he shall not triumph; "but I have trusted in thy mercy; my heart shall rejoice in thy salvation. I will sing unto the Lord, because he hath dealt bountifully with me."

Lead thou us, Lord Jesus, into the fellowship of thy sufferings, and clothe us with the power of thy resurrection. Amen.

When sorrows rise, My refuge lies In thy compassion tender; Within thine arm Can naught alarm; Keep me from harm, Be thou my strong defender.

I have thy word, Christ Jesus, Lord, Thou never wilt forsake me; This will I plead In time of need; O, help with speed, When troubles overtake me!

---

24. Saturday after Third Sunday in Advent.

Lord, purify our hearts by thy word and by faith. Amen.

Malachi 3, 1–6. Behold, I will send my messenger, and he shall prepare the way before me: and the Lord, whom ye seek, shall suddenly come to his temple, even the messenger of the covenant, whom ye delight in: behold, he shall come, saith the Lord of hosts. But who may abide the day of his coming? and who shall stand when he appeared? for he is like a refiner's fire, and like fullers' sope: and he shall sit as a refiner and purifier of silver; and he shall purify the sons of Levi, and purge them as gold and silver, that they may offer unto the Lord an offering in righteousness. Then shall the offering of Judah and Jerusalem be pleasant unto the Lord, as in the days of old, and as in former years. And I will come near to you to judgment; and I will be a swift witness against the sorcerers, and against the adulterers, and against false swearers, and against those that oppress the hireling in his wages, the widow, and the fatherless, and that turn aside the stranger from his right, and fear not me, saith the Lord of hosts. For I am the Lord, I change not; therefore ye sons of Jacob are not consumed.

The messenger of the covenant, whose coming was expected by Israel in the Old Testament, is the Lord Jesus Christ; he establishes a covenant between God and us. This is a covenant in holiness and righteousness, a covenant which unites a holy God and a holy people of God. But, alas, like the Jews, we, also, are reluctant to hear this, and many close their ears entirely to this truth. They are willing to be saved by Christ, but not to be cleansed from sin; they are willing to reign with the Lord, but not to suffer with him; not to crucify the flesh and forego the pleasures of sin. They wish to avoid the pain of repentance and sanctification. But the Lord comes to make us holy; he saves from sin and purifies unto himself a peculiar people, zealous of good works. He refines them as silver and purges them as gold. If you are a true Israelite, you shall not escape the fire of Christ's sufferings. Jesus is himself a refining fire, and our purification is from him. His life in abasement was unbroken suffering, for throughout his whole life here below he bare our sins and was the sacrificed lamb under the wrath of God. In obedience to the will of the Father he was always victorious, but the fire in the sacrifice of the altar was never quenched until he was able to cry: "It is finished!" This propitiatory suffering is ended, but the fire of purification burns; the sufferings of Christ continue in his body, which is the church (Colossians 1, 24), until the last Christian is perfected in holiness. This refining fire consists especially of internal tribulations of many kinds: Fear and dread of death; sad and heavy thoughts; the darts and buffetings of the devil; bitter pain by reason of the evil lusts of the flesh; cares and sorrows; remorse and sadness on account of old and new sins, a remorse in which "hope despairs and despair hopes;"—and the only support of the soul is the Spirit which makes "intercession for us with groanings which can not be uttered." Dear Christian friend, do not allow yourself to be led astray by the circumstances, that you may, perchance, never have felt this very strongly. God adjusts the burden according to the ability of each to carry it. Continue to walk in the light and confess the Lord, and in his own good time he will purge you in the furnace of suffering.

The metaphor concerning the purification of gold and silver in fire is appropriately supplemented by the other figure: "He is like fullers' sope." Out of the heart issues the life; a clean heart means clean hands. The offering of *pure hearts and hands* is pleasant unto the Lord.

God grant that the messenger who goes before with his call to repentance may prepare the way for him to many hearts. Blessed are they which enter into the covenant of the people of sorrow with the Man of sorrows; for they shall also partake of the joy of holiness with the perfectly purged congregation, if they remain faithful unto the end.

Lord Jesus, thou knowest that our flesh shrinks from suffering. Teach us to know the blessedness of bearing thy cross. We feel that there is yet so much of uncleanness in us; cleanse us, faithful Savior; refine us, and purify us, and mold us to be like thee. Amen.

My hope, my all, my Savior thou! To thee, O Lord, my soul I bow; I seek the bliss thy wounds impart, I long to find thee in my heart.
Be thou my strength, be thou my way, Protect me through my life's short day; In all my acts let Wisdom guide, And keep me, Savior, near thy side.

25. Fourth Sunday in Advent. I.

Lord Jesus, give us thy Spirit in our hearts, thy truth and thy humility. Amen.

Gospel Lesson, John 1, 19-28. And this is the record of John, when the Jews sent priests and Levites from Jerusalem to ask him, Who art thou? And he confessed, and denied not; but confessed, I am not the Christ. And they asked him, What then? Art thou Elias? And he saith, I am not. Art thou that prophet? And he answered, No. Then said they unto him, Who art thou? that we may give an answer to them that sent us. What sayest thou of thyself? He said, I am the voice of one crying in the wilderness, Make straight the way of the Lord, as said the prophet Esaias. And they which were sent were of the Pharisees. And they asked him, and said unto him, Why baptizest thou then, if thou be not that Christ, nor Elias, neither that prophet? John answered them, saying, I baptize with water: but there standeth one among you, whom ye know not; he it is, who coming after me is preferred before me, whose shoe's latchet I am not worthy to unloose. These things were done in Bethabara beyond Jordan, where John was baptizing.

If we allow John the Baptist to teach us *truth and humility*, he prepares the way for the Savior, and we receive true Christmas joy.

It would not have been at all surprising, if the brilliant troop of priests and Levites, which were sent to John, had turned his head; and there was still more of a snare in their questions, which gave him honor as the Christ and might well have tempted him to represent himself as being the Messiah. But John confesses the truth here, as he did later before Herod, and does not deny his Lord and Savior. "I am not the Christ," says he; "I am his voice," neither more nor less. I myself am nothing, but Christ makes use of me as his voice. Do not ask concerning me, concerning my person, but ask concerning him. Why will ye not know him who stands among you? *He* is the eternal God, who alone gives power to my words and my baptism; I am an humble servant, not worthy to unloose the latchet of his shoe.

Everybody who has some little knowledge of himself, knows how prone a man is to seek honor, and he must extol the humility of John as a miracle of grace.

John is, indeed, truly great in his love of truth and in his lowliness. He, of all who lived before the Pentecost, sees Jesus with the greatest clearness of vision. And it is because of the fact that the glory and grace of Christ shine so brightly in his soul, that he is so humble. Again, because the Spirit of God teaches him to know himself so well and makes him so humble, therefore he sees the Lord so clearly, while the others do not know him.

And you, my reader; who are you? When you are to confess, and deny not, but confess the truth and say who you are; then, what is your name? What are *you*? What *should* you be? You, also, are destined to greatness, but are become of the smallest. It is only by knowing this, that you again achieve greatness and glory. Have you learned to know yourself? And do you know the One, unknown of the world, who stands among us? Has your eye followed the finger of John, as it points to the Lamb of God, which taketh away the sin of the world? O, that we might obey the Spirit of God, which guides us into all truth, and become lowly of heart; then would we also become great before the Lord. In this wise the soul comes to love the unspeakable gift of the eternal Father.

Merciful God, who gavest John such deep knowledge of self, such truth and humility in his heart; we earnestly ask of thee this same grace. Give us this grace and teach us to receive our Savior aright, that we may have true joy and peace in him. Amen.

Give deep humility; the sense Of godly sorrow give; A strong desire, with confidence, To hear thy voice and live; Faith in the only sacrifice That can for sin atone, To cast our hopes, to fix our eyes, On Christ, on Christ alone.

---

26. Fourth Sunday in Advent. II.

Lord, satisfy us early with thy mercy, that we may rejoice and be glad all our days. Amen.

Epistle, Philippians 4, 4-7. Rejoice in the Lord alway: and again I say, Rejoice. Let your moderation be known unto all men. The Lord is at hand. Be careful for nothing; but in every thing by prayer and supplication, with thanksgiving, let your requests be made known unto God. And the peace of God, which passeth all understanding, shall keep your hearts and minds through Christ Jesus.

How can Paul say that the believers *shall rejoice* in the Lord *alway?* He, himself, had "continual sorrow in his heart" and suffered so much from the buffetings of the devil, that he complains: "O wretched man that I am; who shall deliver me from the body of this death?" We have his own answer: "We approve ourselves in much patience, in afflictions, in necessities, in distresses; we are as sorrowful, yet always rejoicing." But how can this be? Yes, "the Lord is at hand." For this reason the overmuch sadness of believers is turned to joy, their sorrows are dissolved in prayer, their fight ends in that peace of God which passes all understanding. The Lord is at hand; at hand in the word, at hand in death, at hand in the judgment. In every respect this concerns you. In whatever sense you may take these words, "The Lord is at hand," they will tend to open your ears to the apostolic admonition that here precedes and follows them. A little while, and you shall never shed another tear, never heave another sigh; you shall enjoy eternal peace. Have you not reason to rejoice?

Be comforted, believing Christian, and be joyful in the midst of your sorrow; joyful today, and joyful tomorrow; joyful in the time of gladness, and joyful in the year of affliction. *You have reason* to rejoice. God loves us and has given us his Son, who is with us alway. In him you are a child of God and heir to salvation. Your present estate is humiliation, but this is the way to glory; you now have many troubles which are hard to bear, but all things shall work together for your good. "Be careful for nothing," for nothing whatever! There is no wrong for which Jesus has no remedy. The harder the struggle, the greater the victory; the fight itself will strengthen your arm. "In *every* thing by prayer and supplication with thanksgiving let your requests be made known unto God." Speak to God about all your concerns; whatever your trouble may be, take it to the Lord in prayer; then it is yours no longer, for the Lord has made it his own. Give him thanks for his goodness in taking your troubles upon himself. Do exactly what Paul here says; it is God himself who speaks through him and offers us this joy. Pray and give thanks; do not fail to let thanksgiving follow prayer. Submit to this commandment of God; grace to do this has already been given you. Do what God commands, then shall his peace be victorious in you. At all times and everywhere take your every need and care to the Lord your God in prayer. Even if he does not at once take away your outward tribulations or the sorrow and suffering of your heart, he still gives victory in your soul, so that you are able to thank God for your afflictions. Therefore: Rejoice in the Lord alway; and again I say, rejoice! Let your moderation be known unto all men! The Lord is at hand!

How excellent is thy lovingkindness, O God; therefore the children of men put their trust under the shadow of thy wings. They shall be abundantly satisfied with the fatness of thy house; and thou shalt make them drink of the river of thy pleasures. For with thee is the fountain of life; in thy light shall we see light. To this end give us thy Holy Spirit for Jesus' sake. Amen.

Jesus! Thou joy of loving hearts! Thou fount of life! Thou light of men! From the best bliss that earth imparts We turn unfilled to thee again. Thy truth unchanged hath ever stood; Thou savest those that on thee call; To them that seek thee, thou art good, To them that find thee, all in all.

27. Monday after Fourth Sunday in Advent.

Lord, open our ears, that we may hear the admonition and comfort of thy word. Amen.

Isaiah 40, 1–5. Comfort ye, comfort ye my people, saith your God. Speak ye comfortably to Jerusalem, and cry unto her, that her warfare is accomplished, that her iniquity is pardoned: for she hath received of the Lord's hand double for her sins. The voice of him that crieth in the wilderness, Prepare ye the way of the Lord, make straight in the desert a highway for our God. Every valley shall be exalted, and every mountain and hill shall be made low: and the crooked shall be made straight, and the rough places plain: and the glory of the Lord shall be revealed, and all flesh shall see it together: for the mouth of the Lord hath spoken it.

Thy God, O Israel, is great in mercy. By your sins you deserve his wrath, and he gives you—his only begotten Son; double grace for all your sins. "Comfort ye, comfort ye my people," saith he; it has received enough of chastisement and buffetings. Speak ye lovingly to Jerusalem; speak words of comfort deep, deep, into their hearts; let them hear, that for their abounding sin my grace is still more abounding, so that, as sin hath reigned unto death, even so shall grace reign through righteousness unto eternal life by Jesus Christ our Lord.

It is only in order that you may accept this glorious grace, that the Lord afflicts you and chastises you in sharp words by the voice crying in the wilderness and calling to repentance. "Every valley shall be exalted;" that is, the heart which is mired in worldliness and soulless degradation, the soul which is abased in ignorance, or is held captive in doubt and fear, shall be lifted up and learn to see and desire that which is true and eternal. "Every mountain shall be made low;" that is, the haughty and those of high degree shall be brought low, the great become small and humble in themselves. The crooked shall be made straight, and the rough places plain; truth and uprightness shall supplant falsehood, hypocrisy and self-righteousness. In other words, "repent ye, for the kingdom of heaven is at hand." Wake up and know your wretchedness, confess your sins with remorse and pain, and humble yourselves before the Lord. He who hears the voice of the first John, the preacher in the wilderness, calling to repentance, shall hear the second John, also, the son of thunder, with his still more mighty preaching of the gospel of grace, in this wise: "The Word was made flesh and dwelt among us, (and we beheld his glory, the glory as of the only begotten of the Father,) full of grace and truth. And of his fulness have all we received, and grace for grace. For the law was given by Moses, but grace and truth came by Jesus Christ." Blessed preaching of repentance, which opens our ears to this gospel of life! Now I can and will keep these words in the depth of my heart: "Thine iniquity is pardoned, and thou hast received of the Lord's hand double for all thy sins."

Give us, O Lord, humble, simple, believing hearts. Give us grace to hear thy word of chastisement and of comfort. May we feel the power of that which thy mouth speaketh. Amen.

Eternal Spirit, by whose breath The soul is raised from sin and death,
Before thy throne we sinners bend; To us thy quickening power extend.
Jehovah! Father, Spirit, Son! Mysterious Godhead! Three in One!
Before thy throne we sinners bend; Grace, pardon, life, to us extend!

28. Tuesday after Fourth Sunday in Advent.

Lord, let thy work wake us and enlighten us, that we may believe on thee in spirit and in truth. Amen.

John 3, 27–36. John answered and said, A man can receive nothing, except it be given him from heaven. Ye yourselves bear me witness, that I said, I am not the Christ, but that I am sent before him. He that hath the bride is the bridegroom: but the friend of the bridegroom, which standeth and heareth him, rejoiceth greatly because of the bridegroom's voice: this my joy therefore is fulfilled. He must increase, but I must decrease. He that cometh from above is above all: he that is of the earth is earthly, and speaketh of the earth: he that cometh from heaven is above all. And what he hath seen and heard, that he testifieth; and no man receiveth his testimony. He that hath received his testimony hath set to his seal that God is true. For he whom God hath sent speaketh the words of God: for God giveth not the Spirit by measure unto him. The Father loveth the Son, and hath given all things into his hand. He that believeth on the Son hath everlasting life: and he that believeth not the Son shall not see life; but the wrath of God abideth on him.

John the Baptist is extremely lovable in his sincerity and humility. Here we again see how he makes himself of no reputation; he desires no honor for himself, and will not draw away the disciples after himself. He confesses that *he* is of the earth, but that Jesus is of heaven; he rejoices because the bridegroom has the bride, and he turns all men away from himself and directs them to Jesus. Truly, the Baptist is a man to be much beloved; but we would be acting quite contrary to his spirit if we were to rest satisfied and stop with *him* and become enamored of *his* beauty. Not John, but Jesus! John can not give us life, but Jesus is come from heaven with life for us children of death. No man would have risen out of sin and death, if God had not shown mercy and let his Son become man. Before we had any knowledge of it, he had resolved to give us his only begotten Son as a savior. Who could have brought him down from heaven, if he had not come of his own accord? Now he is here, thank God, and has won the human race, the daughter of Adam, as his bride. For with his blood he has redeemed us all from the power of the prince of death, the devil; life has overcome death and is now present in the gospel offering itself to each and all. He that believes the gospel has this life in his heart. By this means there is already a new generation of the sons of Adam, a new and true humanity, the Christian church. And, through the means of grace in the church, God is ever adding to the number of them which believe. No man can believe by his own strength, but the Son gives us the Holy Spirit in the word and sacraments of the church, and creates faith in all who do not stubbornly resist him. You can no more believe or receive the Spirit by your own strength, than you could have brought Christ down from heaven. But as the Son came, sent by the Father, even so the Spirit came, sent by the Father and the Son. Therefore none can say: "I would believe, but I can not." Of yourself you can not, but the Holy Ghost calls you by the gospel and enlightens you with his gifts; and by his grace you can believe in Christ with the true and living faith of a contrite heart. Be affrighted, then, at your unbelief, but ask God to give you faith. He that in sincerity and truth prays God to give him grace to believe has already begun to believe, and has received a portion in the kingdom of grace of Jesus Christ. There heavenly gifts are bestowed upon you; righteousness, peace, joy, life and salvation; all in Jesus Christ, who is himself the life of the believing soul, and is infinitely more precious than all other gifts.

O God, we fervently pray thee, give us faith, the true, living faith in our hearts, that we may belong to the church of thy Son and have life in his name. Amen.

Faith is a living power from heaven, That grasps the promise God hath given, A confidence in Christ alone, Whose grace can not be overthrown.
Faith in the conscience worketh peace, And bids the mourner's weeping cease; By faith the children's place we claim, And give all honor to One Name.

---

29. Wednesday after Fourth Sunday in Advent.

Let thy word, O God, lighten our eyes and shine upon our path. Amen.

Daniel 9, 15–19. And now, O Lord our God, that hast brought thy people forth out of the land of Egypt with a mighty hand, and hast gotten thee renown, as at his day; we have sinned, we have done wickedly. O Lord, according to all thy righteousness, I beseech thee, let thine anger and thy fury be turned away from the city Jerusalem, thy holy mountain; because for our sins, and for the iniquities of our fathers, Jerusalem and thy people are become a reproach to all that are about us. Now therefore, O our God, hear the prayer of thy servant, and his supplications, and cause thy face to shine upon thy sanctuary that is desolate, for the Lord's sake. O my God, incline thine ear, and hear; open thine eyes, and behold our desolations, and the city which is called by thy name: for we do not present our supplications before thee for our righteousnesses, but for thy great mercies. O Lord, hear; O Lord, forgive; O Lord, hearken, and do; defer not, for thine own sake, O my God; for thy city and thy people are called by thy name.

There was a deep sense of sin and guilt in the holy man of God, Daniel. With all his heart he recognized that God had done all things well, but that he and his people had done evil. Daniel was a man of great piety, and he had feared God of a pure heart from his childhood, so that the scriptures do not even make mention of any infirmity in him. But he feels himself most intensely as a unit with his people, so that their sins are his and his sins theirs. *We, we have sinned,* says he. In humble contrition he bows to the judgments of the Lord; his whole soul confesses, that they are righteous. This is the true conversion to God; such hearts receive joy in the Lord.

Let us, also, view our lives in the light of God's countenance. *Has he not gotten himself renown over us?* Could he have shown us greater love than this, that he gave his only begotten Son? Did he not adopt us as his children in holy baptism, and has he not since that time with unspeakably great patience sought us and borne with us? Try to place before your eyes in one heap, as it were, all the gifts which you have received from him, all the spiritual and bodily blessings which he has conferred on you, and then consider in what manner you have thanked and rewarded him; and you will be terrified because of your sin, and wonder at his grace and goodness. Every act of his providence in your life was love; even all his righteous judgments were the servants of his mercy; it was his purpose to enable you to recover yourself out of the snare of the devil, and to give you the peace and happiness of a new heart. For this reason he chastised you and let you taste the bitter fruit of your own sins and those of your fathers. But you did not understand it. "The ox knoweth his owner, and the ass his master's crib; but Israel doth not know, my people doth not consider." O, let the truth control your thoughts now! Do not think contrary to the word of God, but let God the Holy Ghost shape your thought after the word. Then will you have the disposition of Daniel; and he that prays as Daniel did is ready to hear the Christmas gospel.

Grant us this grace, merciful God. Let thy Spirit show us our sins and lead us to the fountain of grace. Amen.

Show pity, Lord! O Lord, forgive! Let a repenting rebel live. Are not thy mercies large and free? May not a sinner trust in thee?
Great God, thy nature hath no bound, So let thy pardoning love be found. O wash my soul from every sin, And make my guilty conscience clean!

---

30. Thursday after Fourth Sunday in Advent.

Lord, let our faith have its foundation in thy word. Amen.

Micah 5, 2–5. But thou, Bethlehem Ephratah, though thou be little among the thousands of Judah, yet out of thee shall he come forth unto me that is to be ruler in Israel; whose goings forth have been from of old, from everlasting. Therefore will he give them up, until the time that she which travaileth hath brought forth; then the remnant of his brethren shall return unto the children of Israel. And he shall stand and feed in the strength of the Lord, in the majesty of the name of the Lord his God; and they shall abide; for now shall he be great unto the ends of the earth. And this man shall be the peace, when the Assyrian shall come into our land; and when he shall tread in our palaces, then shall we raise against him seven shepherds, and eight principal men.

He is born in Bethlehem, but is from everlasting. The prophet here teaches, what the church confesses, that Jesus Christ is God and man in one person. Concerning this, the greatest of all wonders in heaven and on earth, the scriptures testify with clearness and emphasis. He who lies in the manger, this poor, little child, is the eternal God, who owns all things and upholds all things by the word of his power. He is wisdom itself, which gives to all angels and men all that they have of thought and understanding; yet he is become a child in swaddling clothes; his mind, like that of all other children, grows and develops from the dormant state to conscious knowledge. He is the Living One for evermore, but dies on the cross and is laid in the grave. In truth, his name is "Wonderful" and transcends all our wisdom. But such a Lord and Savior we were to have according to the gracious will and counsel of God. He was to be a *man*; for man had sinned, and the blood of man must of necessity be sacrificed in death for our atonement. He was to be true God, in order that the redeeming power of his death and blood might be without limit. The shepherd king David came out of Bethlehem; and in Bethlehem is to be born the shepherd of the soul and the true king of Israel, he who is David and Solomon and Melchizedek and Aaron, all in one person. The name Bethlehem means the house of bread. Out of it comes our Joseph with the bread of eternal life, which he gives to his brethren without price,—he who is degraded to the meanest prison, but also exalted to the right hand of the King, and is great unto the ends of the earth. Truly, out of Bethlehem comes the Shepherd who feeds his flock in the strength of the Lord, in the majesty of the name of the Lord his God.

The scriptures call him "everlasting God," "the only begotten Son of the Father," "God over all, blessed for ever," "the true God and eternal life;" they declare that he is eternal and almighty and omniscient and holy; they inform us that all things were made by him and subsist by him. They call him the Lord over all things, to whom we shall pray and in whom we shall believe. Himself says: "I and my Father are one," "to me is given all power in heaven and on earth," "I am that Son of God." He died as the only begotten Son of God; he rose again and reigns as the only begotten Son of God. Verily, the Second Article of our creed is certain and sure; he that does not see this is blinded by sin and falsehood.

Give me, Lord Jesus, a heart that is obedient to the truth, so that I may believe on thee alway and rejoice in thy glory and grace. Amen.

From highest heaven to earth I come To bear good news to every home; Glad tidings of great joy I bring, Whereof I now will say and sing:
To you this night is born a Child Of Mary, chosen virgin mild; This little child of lowly birth Shall be the joy of all the earth.
'Tis Christ, our God and Lord, is born, To comfort those who weep and mourn; He will himself your Savior be, From all your sins will set you free.

31. Friday after Fourth Sunday in Advent.
Lord, let thy word enlighten us and lead us on the right path.

Matthew 1, 20-23. But while he thought on these things, behold, the angel of the Lord appeared unto him in a dream, saying, Joseph, thou son of David, fear not to take unto thee Mary thy wife; for that which is conceived in her is of the Holy Ghost. And she shall bring forth a son, and thou shalt call his name Jesus: for he shall save his people from their sins. Now all this was done, that it might be fulfilled which was spoken of the Lord by the prophet, saying, Behold, a virgin shall be with child, and shall bring forth a son, and they shall call his name Emmanuel; which being interpreted is, God with us.

In holy modesty and sincere humility Mary had hid from Joseph the announcement which had been made to her by the angel. Therefore, when Joseph became aware of her condition, he naturally thought that she had been unfaithful to him. The saints of God have many gloomy thoughts. Now he might, according to the law, have dragged her before a public court of justice and put her to shame. But he could also give her a bill of divorce, as one who no longer found favor in his eyes; then it would appear as if she were innocent and he faithless. And the piety of Joseph is so great, that he is willing to be regarded as the criminal, though he is innocent, rather than bring disgrace on her, whom he must believe to be guilty. But the Lord solves all difficulties for his own. Joseph is informed of the blessed mystery, and he hears from the mouth of the angel that name which is above every name.

Joseph is called "a just man;" that is, a godly, believing, good and pious Israelite; it was necessary and proper that this should be the character of the ·man who was to become the foster-father of Jesus. However, he is only his *foster-father*. Our Bible lesson for today shows us again most plainly that Jesus is the *Son of God:* "That which is conceived in Mary is of the Holy Ghost;" she is espoused to Joseph, but it still a "virgin;" the son whom she shall bring forth is "Emmanuel, which being interpreted is, *God* with us." What beautiful concord is there not among the evangelists on this point, that Jesus Christ is the only begotten Son of God, conceived of the Holy Ghost, born of the Virgin Mary! What an exact agreement between the prophets of the Old and the evangelists of the New Testament on this point! If Jesus is not the only begotten Son of God, true God and true man, then there is not a word of truth in the Bible; for this is the central doctrine in all the scriptures, the one in which everything from Genesis to Revelations has its root. In the Old Testament this heavenly truth becomes more and more clear, while in the New it beams like the resplendent sun that floods everything with light. The creed of the church is most firmly established in God's own word; the deeper I penetrate into the scriptures, the more thoroughly am I convinced of the truth of our creed. I there find myself in a sanctuary in which Jesus Christ, the eternal God and precious Savior, fills everything with his glory and his grace. God help us to be right-minded and just, as Joseph was, and obedient to the truth, however much it may conflict with our own will and our way of thinking. Then shall we experience, with Joseph, that a righteous man is not shamed, but learns to solve the enigmas and is taught the mystery of godliness. For the secret of the Lord is with them that fear him. This is, indeed, Christmas joy.

Lord our God, give us this grace by the Holy Ghost for the sake of Jesus Christ. Amen.

Come, thou Savior of our race, Choicest gift of heavenly grace! O thou
blessed Virgin's Son, Be thy race on earth begun.
Not of mortal blood or birth, He descends from heaven to earth: By the
Holy Ghost conceived, Truly man to be believed.
Wondrous birth! O wondrous Child! Of the Virgin undefiled! Though
by all the world disowned, Still to be in heaven enthroned.

---

32. Christmas Eve.

O dearest Jesus, holy Child, make thee a bed, soft, undefiled, within my heart!

Isaiah 9, 6. 7. For unto us a child is born, unto us a son is given, and
the government shall be upon his shoulder; and his name shall be called
Wonderful, Counsellor, The mighty God, The everlasting Father, The Prince
of Peace. Of the increase of his government and peace there shall be no end,
upon the throne of David, and upon his kingdom, to order it, and to establish
it with judgment and with justice, from henceforth even for ever. The zeal of
the Lord of hosts will perform this.

Now we will rejoice with exceeding great joy before the Lord,
according to the joy in harvest, and as men rejoice when they divide
the spoil. For the Lord has broken the yoke and the rod and the
staff as in the day of Midian. Gideon has thrown down the altars of
the idols, routed the enemy and made us free. This child is our brother,
but also the only begotten Son of God; one of us, but, at the same time,
the everlasting God. The Father has given us his Son; he is ours, he
that is prince and lord over all, over heaven and earth, over law and
sin, over death and devil;—he is born unto us. He is righteous and
fulfils all righteousness for us; he is the Life, and he bruises the head
of the prince of death; he takes our every concern upon himself,—
for this purpose he is given us; alone he treads the winepress of wrath;
he alone slays Goliah, and he destroys Baal and his prophets. God
has not consigned us to our wretchedness, but he has had mercy on
us and has given us his Son for our Savior, Counsellor, Father, Prince
of Peace. We *were* lost; we *were*, but *are* lost no longer; we *are*
saved and blessed. We *were* in prison, but *are* free. We *were* doomed
to death, but now eternal life is ours. He has atoned for everything
and has brought us righteousness, love, peace and salvation. O my
Jesus, how shall I thank thee? My heavenly Father, how shall I thank
thee?—"Unto us a child is born, unto us a son is given." Note well
the expression, that he is *born* unto us and *given* unto us; it is wholly
grace, and none shall be without help by reason of unworthiness. It
is *grace alone*, purely and solely, so that every idea of merit or worthiness is excluded. It has come to pass; he *is* given unto us, unto *us*
who were lost and damned; unto *us* the child is born, unto *us* the
son is given. This is in very truth joy and salvation.

Truly, God has bestowed on us a great gift. God *has done* it and
the devil can not defeat it. He shall not succeed in defeating it; neither
by the apostles of infidelity about us, nor by the suggestions of infidelity in us. We are saved; the devil is powerless to take away the
work which our God has already accomplished. O, how I rejoice in

writing this down before the very eyes of the enemy, to the honor and glory of my God! And you, my brother; rejoice when you read these words of God! Midian is defeated, though he deny it never so vehemently; all heavens and all the heavenly host assert it, and I declare it with a heart full of joy unspeakable.

Now, let Christmas, the children's happy festival, make us child-like; then shall we surely have great joy. If you rightly believed this thing which God has done for you, you would leap up and stand, and walk, and enter into the temple, walking, and leaping, and praising God. For verily, all your misery is turned to happiness; all your distress, to glory; all your sin, to righteousness; and death now is nothing but life. This is most certainly true; but God hides it from your senses, because he wants you to have *faith*. I, also, hide the beautiful Bible which my child received as a baptismal present, until he becomes old enough to use it. I have told him that it lies hid in my locker, and he does not doubt it, though he has never seen the book. Yes, blessed are you, if you *believe*. And now, may you have a most blessed and happy Christmas!

Heavenly Father, who gavest us thy Son; give us the light and grace of thy Holy Spirit, that we may believe; give us grace to believe and to accept the salvation of grace in Christ. Blessed be God the Father, God the Son, and God the Holy Ghost for evermore! Amen.

Thy little ones, dear Lord, are we, And come thy lowly bed to see; Enlighten every soul and mind, That we the way to thee may find.

With songs we hasten thee to greet, And kiss the dust before thy feet. O blessed hour, O sweetest night, That gave thee birth, our Soul's Delight!

O draw us wholly to thee, Lord, Thou dearest friend, to us accord Thy grace; Thy faith to us impart, That we may hold Thee in our heart.

33. Christmas Day. I.

Lord, let thy tidings of joy permeate our heart. Amen.

Gospel Lesson, Luke 2, 1–14. And it came to pass in those days, that there went out a decree from Cæsar Augustus, that all the world should be taxed. (And this taxing was first made when Cyrenius was governor of Syria.) And all went to be taxed, every one into his own city. And Joseph also went up from Galilee, out of the city of Nazareth, into Judæa, unto the city of David, which is called Bethlehem, (because he was of the house and lineage of David,) to be taxed with Mary his espoused wife, being great with child. And so it was, that, while they were there, the days were accomplished that she should be delivered. And she brought forth her firstborn son, and wrapped him in swaddling clothes, and laid him in a manger; because there was no room for them in the inn. And there were in the same country shepherds abiding in the field, keeping watch over their flock by night. And, lo, the angel of the Lord came upon them, and the glory of the Lord shone round about them: and they were sore afraid. And the angel said unto them, Fear not: for, behold, I bring you good tidings of great joy, which shall be to all people. For unto you is born this day, in the city of David, a Savior, which is Christ the Lord And this shall be a sign unto you:

43

Ye shall find the babe wrapped in swaddling clothes, lying in a manger. And suddenly there was with the angel a multitude of the heavenly host, praising God, and saying, Glory to God in the highest, and on earth peace, good will toward men.

The blessed angelic hosts praise God for that which he has done for us mortals. It is *our* joy with which the angels of heaven rejoice, *our* song of praise in which they join, our thank-offering which they bring before the throne. Therefor it is that they have come down to the earth and make *it* their temple. For God has given his Son to *us;* he is become *our* brother, *our* Lord and Savior; he is born on *earth*, he is become a man. That which was ordained in the eternal decree of the Trinity; that for which preparation was made through thousands of years, and which was promised throughout the whole time of the Old Testament, has today come to pass: *The Son of God is born of a woman.* We have allowed ourselves to be deceived, sold ourselves to the devil, and should of right have been eternally lost; but now we are redeemed and shall inherit eternal life. God himself has become our Savior. The earth shall no more be the kingdom of the devil, wherein anger, falsehood, and murder from hell are supreme; but shall be the home of saints, where God is worshiped in spirit and truth, and where love, peace, and God's good will abound. For here is he who releases our conscience from the bondage of fear, opens our eyes to the truth, cleanses our heart, pours into it the love of the Lord, and unites us with the holy and blessed God. When we believe the love wherewith God loves us, it comes into our soul; we love him because he loved us first. In this way he makes for himself a dwelling-place in our heart.

The Son of God becomes a man for *all* men; he is born of a woman in order that he may give his life for *all.* Hear this, all men of whatever sort: The Son of God came for *you*, he wants to save *you.* Turn to him; seek him in the manger of the stable; that is, in the word and sacraments of the church. Seek him earnestly, in order to be saved from sin; then *shall* you find him and he shall save you.—Ye, needy *sinners*, who grieve on account of your sins, earnestly long for grace and follow after purity; fear not, but rejoice with great joy. You are of the people to whom the angel's sermon is directed; the blessed joy that fills the heavenly host is in the strictest sense yours. For all who humble themselves and confess their sins and earnestly desire to be saved, are now saved; all the wretched and poor that hope in the Lord are his people, and they possess this "great joy." None can describe your happiness, and none can rob you of your bliss. *Love*, the eternal and heavenly love, is yours; and as it is given you by him that has power to give it, so it is preserved in you by the same power and faithfulness. You have a glory which is greater than that of all angels. We speak of this in reverential fear; for Michael and Gabriel and the seraphim before the throne are so glorious and exalted, that we sinners can not see them without terror. But God himself, before whom they hide their face, is our brother, and it is their greatest delight to look into the counsel of God for our salvation. These pure, radiant, heavenly spirits, which stand before God, delight in our delight, join in the joy that is given us according to the eternal good pleasure of God; and their blissful duty is to serve herein, to act as messengers between heaven and earth, and with us to praise the Lord. Are our glory and honor not great? They are stupendously great, and fill the heart with a blessed feeling of humility, and of elevation, and of rapture. For God so loved me from eternity and so loves me now and for evermore, that he gives me his only begotten Son; therefore I love him in return and shall love him forever in this heavenly love. God is my God, and my heart is his for evermore. Glory to God in the highest, and on earth peace, good will toward men!

The happy Christmas comes once more. The heavenly guest is at the door, The blessed words the shepherds thrill, The joyous tidings: Peace, Good-will.

O wake our hearts, in gladness sing, And keep your Christmas with your King, Till living song, from loving souls, Like sound of mighty waters rolls.

Come, Jesus, glorious heavenly guest, Keep thine own Christmas in our breast, Then David's harp-strings, hushed so long, Shall swell our jubilee of song.

---

34. Christmas Day. II.

Lord, give us grace to keep thy words in our heart. Amen.

Luke 2, 15-20. And it came to pass, as the angels were gone away from them into heaven, the shepherds said one to another, Let us now go even unto Bethlehem, and see this thing which is come to pass, which the Lord hath made known unto us. And they came with haste, and found Mary, and Joseph, and the babe lying in a manger. And when they had seen it, they made known abroad the saying which was told them concerning this child. And all they that heard it wondered at those things which were told them by the shepherds. But Mary kept all these things, and pondered them in her heart. And the shepherds returned, glorifying and praising God for all the things that they had heard and seen, as it was told unto them.

These shepherds *believed* what they had heard; therefore they went into Bethlehem and found Mary, and Joseph, and the babe. Here the Spirit of God teaches us how we are to receive the Christmas gift and praise God for it. When we hear the gospel we must not wave it aside and forget it; neither shall we say: "No, it is not possible for me to believe this." But we must ponder it, and speak one to another about it; then will the Spirit of God, which is in the word, help us to believe it. And when the life of faith begins to stir in us, we must encourage one another, search the scriptures, and seek communion with other believers who are farther advanced in their faith. For Mary and Joseph have the babe between them. Jesus is in his church on earth, and the saints have him in their midst. They have the word and baptism and the Lord's supper, and through these he is with them. Do you think, that the believers can be gathered together without their having the word of God among them? But as surely as they have the word of God, just as surely do they have Jesus among them.

He is the very one about whom they gather. There, in the means
of grace in the church, you find the Lord. Say not in your heart:
How shall I be able to lift myself up to heaven and reach Jesus? Or:
To what place shall I make a pilgrimage in order to find him? Or:
What works shall I do in order that he may come and reveal himself to me? In truth, he is much nearer to you than you think: he is
in the Word. However, you must not expect to see the Glorious One
with your eyes. But admit, that the truth is the truth; believe the
Word, then shall you experience in conscience and heart, that he, in
very truth, is there. For all things appertaining to the Lord are little
to be regarded by the bodily eye and the natural understanding. What,
indeed, did the shepherds see? They saw that which was told them:
a babe wrapped in swaddling clothes, lying in a manger. But does it
stand to reason, that this babe is the Savior of all people, God's
anointed, and the joy of the angels? The shepherds *believed;* therefore they found that which the Lord had made known to them, and
this was enough for them. They did not doubt, that this babe was
the promised Savior of Jews and gentiles. You, also, find in the church
of God that which himself has said; namely, the tidings concerning
him, going out into all the world; the sacrament of baptism in the
name of the triune God; the sacrament of the altar, under the bread
and wine, which he instituted the same night in which he was betrayed.
You shall not ask to see more than what himself has said. The announcement made to the shepherds was this: "Unto you is born this
day in the city of David a Savior, which is Christ the Lord. And this
shall be a sign unto you; ye shall find the babe wrapped in swaddling
clothes, lying in a manger." They believed the word, found it true,
and praised God. To us the Son of God has said: I died for you, and
rose again, and am with you alway; and this is the sign: The gospel
shall be preached, and the sacraments of baptism and the altar shall be
administered. Do you not find it true? Have faith, then, and make
known to others the presence and love and grace of Jesus; and when
others speak to you of these things, then follow the example of Mary,
who "kept all these things, and pondered them in her heart."—Then,
again; praise God in word and deed. Begin in earnest, dear Christian,
to bless and thank the Lord during this Christmastide, and continue
doing it all your life. Do you not owe God this much? He has given
you his Son; and you do not thank him for it! Away with this baneful
unbelief, with sloth, with the tormenting bondage under the law, and
with the whimpering and whining of the perverted and sick heart!
By the grace of God's Spirit you can believe with that simple and
childlike faith which enables you to bless and praise the Lord in the
midst of the griefs of this life. I know well enough, that you must feel
sin and sorrow, but I also know, that the joy of the Lord shall prevail
over all our sin and sorrow. For God loves you and has made you
his child. Obey his Spirit, and he shall answer in your heart: Saved,
—saved and blest. Glory be to God! Say we with one another: God
be praised for his unspeakable gift!

To David's city let us fly, Where angels sing beneath the sky; Through
plain and village pressing near, And news from God with shepherds hear.

The lowly Savior meekly lies, Laid off the splendor of the skies; No
crown bedecks his forehead fair, No pearl, nor gem, nor silk is there.
O holy Child, Thy manger streams, Till earth and heaven glow with its
beams, Till midnight noon's bright light has won, And Jacob's Star outshines
the sun.

---

35. Second Christmas Day. I.

Lord Jesus, gather us by thy word under the wings of thy grace. Amen.

Gospel Lesson, Matthew 23, 34-39. Wherefore, behold, I send unto you
prophets, and wise men, and scribes: and some of them ye shall kill and crucify;
and some of them shall ye scourge in your synagogues, and persecute them
from city to city: that upon you may come all the righteous blood shed upon
the earth, from the blood of righteous Abel unto the blood of Zacharias son
of Barachias, whom ye slew between the temple and the altar. Verily I say
unto you, All these things shall come upon this generation. O Jerusalem,
Jerusalem, thou that killest the prophets, and stonest them, which are sent unto
thee, how often would I have gathered thy children together, even as a hen
gathereth her chickens under her wings, and ye would not. Behold, your house
is left unto you desolate. For I say unto you, Ye shall not see me henceforth,
till ye shall say, Blessed is he that cometh in the name of the Lord.

We have been most profoundly corrupted by sin. The enmity
toward God, the wickedness from the kingdom of darkness, which came
into the world by the malice of the devil, has a terrible power and may,
on occasion, develop appalling size and strength in the human heart.
And this is especially true of those who have felt the call of God, but
have hardened their heart against it. In these the devil has sevenfold
power. This is true of the individual and of the people. One illustration of this is furnished by the Jews, and another by the apostate
Christians. The Savior stands in the midst of them; but they are en-
raged, and crucify him.—Did not the Lord know this, before he came
to us on earth? Certainly he did; it is even declared in advance by the
prophets. But his love is greater than all the might and power of hell;
he was determined to come and offer his saving grace to *all* men.
After all, Jesus loves more than the devil hates; the malice of Satan
is great, but the love of the Lord is greater. The fire of life in him
burns a thousand times more fiercely than do the fires of hell. Man
is so precious and dear to him, that he wanted to come to the world,
become a man, and die for us, although he knew how many there were
who would disdain his love.—That this divine power of grace does
not conquer *every* human heart, is a dark and deep mystery which we
are unable to fathom; but this mystery, also, shall some day have a
glorious solution. What pity it is that Jerusalem will not let herself
be gathered by the Lord Jesus under the wings of his grace! Jerusalem, Jerusalem; there is, then, no hope for you! He that rejects
the Lord Jesus rejects himself; for there is not salvation in any other.
But all who believe on him shall learn that he is great and rich; they
shall receive of his Spirit and be allowed to taste his love; yes, even in
the communion of his sufferings, they shall have a better happiness

than the highest rapture experienced by any child of this world. "Greater is he that is in you, than he that is in the world." He shall destroy everything in you that has its root in the kingdom of darkness.

Our gospel lesson for today testifies with mighty voice to the power of sin and the devil in the world; but the voice rings still more strong in testifying to the unspeakable love and mercy of God in Christ.

We thank thee, Lord Jesus, that thou didst come to us and save us out of our deep fall, that thou didst enter into our misery and dost draw us after thee through sorrow and death to glory. Eternal thanks and praise for thy loving kindness, which prevails over everything that is evil in us. Enlighten us more and more to believe in thee, to know thy ways, to love and serve thee, in order that we willingly may suffer with thee and never tire in the exercises of charity and in bearing witness concerning thee in the teeth of resistance and hate on the part of all the world. Precious Lord Jesus, who didst mourn because of the blindness and the unhappiness of thy people; may *we* grieve thy Spirit nevermore. Thou seest how sorrowful we also are; but, alas, how much of the sorrow of the world is there not yet in us, and how little of the pangs of thy holy love! Our soul weeps over our wretchedness and cries to thee, merciful Savior; we have thee, we yearn for thee, we rejoice in thee, our joy and salvation; and yet our soul is full of sadness because we can not, as we ought, believe in thee, love thee, embrace the foot of thy throne, and give ourselves entirely as an offering to thee. Alas, what a sad state of affairs obtains in Christendom,· among the people which bear thy name! Lord, have mercy on us, have mercy on thy brethren, have mercy on our people, have mercy on all the world! Amen.

Arise, O Lord of hosts; Be jealous for thy name, And drive from out our coasts The sins that put to shame. O Lord, stretch forth thy mighty hand, And guard and bless our fatherland.

Thy best gifts from on high In rich abundance pour, That we may magnify And praise thee more and more. O Lord, stretch forth thy mighty hand, And guard and bless our fatherland.

---

36. Second Christmas Day. II.

Lord our God, sanctify us while we live, and save us when we die. Amen.

Acts 6, 8-15 and 7, 54-60. And Stephen, full of faith and power, did great wonders and miracles among the people. Then arose certain of the synagogue, which is called he synagogue of the Libertines, and Cyrenians, and Alexandrians, and of them of Cilicia and of Asia, disputing with Stephen. And they were not able to resist the wisdom and the spirit by which he spake. Then they suborned men, which said, We have heard him speak blasphemous words against Moses, and against God. And they stirred up the people, and the elders, and the scribes, and came upon him, and caught him, and brought him to·the council, and set up false witnesses, which said, This man ceaseth not to speak blasphemous words against this holy place, and the law: for we have heard him say, that this Jesus of Nazareth shall destroy this place, and shall change the customs which Moses delivered us. And all that sat in the council, looking steadfastly on him, saw his face as it had been the face of an angel. When they heard these things, they were cut to the heart, and they gnashed on him with their teeth. But he, being full of the Holy Ghost, looked up steadfastly into heaven, and saw the glory of God, and Jesus standing on the right hand of God, and said, Behold, I see the heavens opened, and the Son of man standing on the right hand of God. Then they cried out with a loud voice, and stopped their ears, and ran upon him with one accord, and cast him out of the city, and stoned him: and the witnesses laid down their clothes at a young man's feet, whose name was Saul. And they stoned Stephen, calling upon God, saying, Lord Jesus, receive my spirit! And he kneeled down, and cried with a loud voice, Lord, lay not this sin to their charge. And when he had said this, he fell asleep.

Stephen is a glorious example, showing how happy is he that believes in Jesus. The Son of God came to the world, in order that we may go to heaven. None of us doubts that Stephen is there. Be as firmly persuaded, that *every one* who believes in Jesus shall go to heaven. By the same grace and faithfulness you and I, also, shall be there. "He that believeth and is baptized shall be saved." You shall not have the same high rank in glory which is accorded to Stephen, who was the first martyr after the ascension of the Lord; but you shall receive the rank that becomes you, and shall in no wise feel any envy. And, indeed, to reach even barely beyond the threshold of the heavenly abode of bliss is more than glory. Look forward to it with joy, let your thoughts dwell upon it, and do not, then, shrink from suffering with the Lord a little while. God, who has ordained how large a cup of suffering you are to drink, has also fixed the time and manner of your death, and he alone knows what is yet before you. He alone knows how much of suffering remains, and how your last hour shall be. But let this suffice, that he knows it; and do you give yourself no concern about the matter. If it shall be your lot to be sorely tried, you shall receive the more strength and see more clearly the coming glory; then, of a sudden, "all sin and suffering are past, and you are saved and free at last; your soul is filled with gladness." —God, who does not lie, promised us his Son; and we have received him. The same God has promised us everlasting life; we shall as certainly receive this; indeed, we have it already in the Son. Stephen went to heaven, not because of his ability to work great wonders and miracles, but by faith alone. In bliss he now praises God for all his grace; but his power to work miracles and his courage to bear witness of the truth, even in the face of death, are included in the one great gift, Jesus Christ; and when, in eternity, he thanks God for salvation, he thereby praises the Lord for redemption by the blood of Jesus. Have not you, also, been bought by the blood of the Lamb? Is not, then, the same song of praise on your lips? Yes, Christian believer, you are saved, and soon you shall see Jesus by the side of Stephen before the throne. The same Spirit that was in him is in you also; you, also, love your enemies, pray for them which despitefully use you, and bless them that curse you. Such is the love of

Christ; it is victorious over death and the devil; and in this love we say at last: Lord Jesus, receive my spirit.

Lord, grant that our faith be true and living, in order that we may be rejoicing in hope, patient in tribulation, active in charity. Live thou in us, precious Lord Jesus, and let us die in thee. Amen.

Jesus, Lover of my soul, Let me to thy bosom fly, While the nearer waters roll, While the tempest still is high.

Hide me, O my Savior, hide, Till the storm of life is past; Safe into the haven guide; O receive my soul at last!

---

37. Third Christmas Day.

Lord Jesus, thou eternal Word; speak to us, that we may believe in thee. Amen.

John 1, 1–13. In the beginning was the Word, and the Word was with God, and the Word was God. The same was in the beginning with God. All things were made by him; and without him was not any thing made that was made. In him was life; and the life was the light of men. And the light shineth in darkness; and the darkness comprehended it not. There was a man sent from God, whose name was John. The same came for a witness, to bear witness of the Light, that all men through him might believe. He was not that Light, but was sent to bear witness of that Light. That was the true Light, which lighteth every man that cometh into the world. He was in the world, and the world was made by him, and the world knew him not. He came unto his own, and his own received him not. But as many as received him, to them gave he power to become the sons of God, even to them that believe on his name: which was born, not of the blood, nor of the will of the flesh, nor of the will of man, but of God.

Jesus Christ is the Life and the Light; he is God from the beginning. All others are but witnesses concerning him; while he is the life itself that quickens the dead; and he is the light that shines in all things having true brilliancy. He is before all things, and he needs no creature in order to be blest; he is himself the untold fulness of life that gives life and light to the whole creation. His glory radiates from the stars of heaven, from the flowers of the field, from the human soul with its admirable faculties, from the circle of angels and the sea of glass before the throne. His vital force throbs in the myriads of crawling creatures under our feet, in the countless fowls of the air and fishes of the sea, and in every living thing. But in a special sense and degree he gives his life and light to the human heart. He, himself, comes to them and abides in them. Though not in visible form, he was in the world from the beginning as the Angel of the Lord, the Prince of the hosts of Israel, the Spirit of the prophets, and the Soul of God's people. He came to the world and became a man and revealed himself to his own people, but they would not know him; some few, only, received him with believing hearts. So it is now, also. He stands in our midst, and most of us reject him. But as many as believe, are by him made the children of God, made partakers of the divine nature, filled with light to know the Father and the Son in the unity of the

4

Holy Ghost, filled with the spirit of counsel and might, the spirit of wisdom and understanding, the spirit of knowledge and of the fear of the Lord; he abides in them and they in him. The human heart was made for receiving life and light willingly. It is formed with the faculty of loving; but he is love and the proper object of our love, and his Spirit alone can teach us to love. Out of love for us he became a man; in love for us he lived, and died, and lives for evermore. He revealed this love to us, in order that we might accept it. Indeed, it was not possible for him to reveal himself otherwise than in love; for he is love. God is love; what else, then, can life and light be? Do you, dear reader, believe in the Son of God? Do you believe that Jesus Christ is the true, eternal God? If you do, you have known this love; you have been born of God, and "child of God" is your name. By this name you are known in heaven. As many as received him, to them gave he power to become the sons of God, even to them that *believe* in his name. Note this: To *believe* in his name is the one important thing, on which all depends. As many as believe, have thereby received him, are born again, and are in truth the children of God. This is a work of God; of the grace, the life, the light, which he gives. Let none say: "He would not come to *me!*" He has come to you already; but you would not receive him, because you loved sin. Do accept him; God will work this in you; then you are a child of God, and your heart the dwelling-place of life.

Lord, give us the grace of the Spirit to believe with a true and living faith of the heart. Create this faith in us, and preserve it, and increase it unto the end. Amen.

O Jesus, Lord of heavenly grace, Thou brightness of thy Father's face,
Thou fountain of eternal light, Whose beams disperse the shades of night!
Come, holy Sun of heavenly love, Send down thy radiance from above,
And to our inmost hearts convey The Holy Spirit's cloudless ray.

---

38. December 28.

Lord, let thy grace and truth shine into our soul. Amen.

John 1, 14–18. And the Word was made flesh, and dwelt among us, (and we beheld his glory, the glory as of the only begotten of the Father,) full of grace and truth. John bare witness of him, and cried, saying, This was he of whom I spake, He that cometh after me is preferred before me: for he was before me. And of his fulness have all we received, and grace for grace. For the law was given by Moses, but grace and truth came by Jesus Christ. No man hath seen God at any time; the only begotten Son, which is in the bosom of the Father, he hath declared him.

The Word was made flesh and dwelt among us; that is, the Son of God became man and lived, like one of us, here on earth. His divine nature assumed the human nature and was united with it in one person, without any commixture or transmutation of the natures. It is the Son of God, the true God, that is born of the Virgin Mary. It is the only begotten Son of God that grows to man's estate in Nazareth.

is baptized in the Jordan, goes about teaching and healing, is hated, and suffers, and dies. "God sent forth his Son, made of a woman," says Paul (Galatians 4, 4); and again: "God has purchased a church with his own blood" (Acts 20, 28). And John declares that the blood of Jesus Christ is the blood of the Son of God (1 John 1, 7). Christ is true God and true man in one person. The Son of God reveals himself in the *man* Jesus Christ. On this point John says in our text: "We beheld his glory, the glory as of the only begotten of the Father, full of grace and truth." To this high and holy doctrine we must cling with unswerving fidelity; for it is the rock of our salvation. Thank God, this truth is too firmly grounded ever to be overthrown by the attacks of the devil and of false prophets!

Because of the fact that Jesus is God and man in one person, he owns all the fulness of grace. Consider this: The eternal God has made himself subject to the law and has fulfilled it for us. Consider, that the very God died as a man. What a stupendous consideration this is! What are your sins as compared with the greatness of his merit? What becomes of a spark of fire thrown into the ocean?— Here is a sufficiency of grace for *all;* here all men might receive healing and salvation. Here is forgiveness for all your trespasses, and here is all the life needed by your poor heart, now dead in sin. Come, then, every sinner that is needy and athirst; receive of his fulness grace for grace. But do not ask to *see* these things. *Believe* the testimony of John and the apostles! You believe the words of the law, and it confirms itself in your conscience; you believe Moses, though you have not seen him. Should you not, then, believe the gospel? Should you not believe Jesus, by whom grace and truth came? Note what the text says: "The law was given by Moses, but grace and truth came by Jesus Christ." This by no means implies that the law is not truth. But the gospel, which declares that we lost sinners are saved by the grace of Jesus, is *the* truth that eclipses all other truths. Will you not believe the truth? Blessed are they that have not seen, and yet have believed. The truth, then, confirms itself in your conscience; you have the witness in yourself that God is true; and then you have learned to know God.

Merciful God, give us thy Holy Spirit, which thou hast promised to them that ask thee. Amen.

Faith feels the Spirit's kindly breath In love and hope that conquer death; Faith worketh joyfulness in God, And trust that blesses e'en the rod.
We thank thee then, O God of heaven, That thou to us this faith hast given; Preserve to us thy Spirit's grace Till we shall see thee face to face.

39. December 29.

My God, let thy grace sanctify me wholly and entirely. Amen.

Titus 2, 11–14. For the grace of God that bringeth salvation hath appeared to all men, teaching us, that, denying ungodliness and worldly lusts, we should live soberly, righteously, and godly, in this present world; looking for that blessed hope, and the glorious appearing of the great God and our Savior Jesus Christ; who gave himself for us, that he might redeem us from all iniquity, and purify unto himself a peculiar people, zealous of good works.

This is the grace of God that brings salvation,—*the saving grace,* —that Christ gave himself for us, in order to justify and sanctify and beatify us. This is *grace:* love for them that are unworthy of it; goodness, directly contrary to what we have deserved. O, that we might learn, that our salvation is *wholly of grace;* then we would enter fully into the blessed estate of freedom.—This grace brings salvation, for the Son of God has redeemed us from all unrighteousness, and has taken away our sin. He that is baptized unto him and believes in him, or, in other words, *accepts this grace,* is righteous, holy, and blest. And then the grace that brings salvation reigns in the heart; it constrains us to deny ungodliness and worldly lusts, and causes us to lead a sober, righteous, and godly life. The ungodly turn away from the Lord in carelessness or in slavish fear; worldlyminded men cling to the world and care not for heaven. But he that accepts the grace of God loves God, rejoices in the hope of eternal life, looks forward to the coming again of the Lord; yea, yearns for his glorious appearing, and prepares himself for it in holy living and godliness. The things of this world, its riches and honors and pleasures, are not the desire and aim of the believers; they have something else, something much more grand and beautiful, awaiting them. Concerning this matter the apostle John writes: "Beloved, now are we the sons of God, and it doth not yet appear what we shall be; but we know that, when he shall appear, we shall be like him; for we shall see him as he is."

But if you hope for eternal life, of grace, for Jesus' sake, without denying the worldly lusts, you take his grace in vain; and it is not the Spirit of truth, but the father of lies that is the author of your hope. He deceives so many, because the world *wants* to be deceived. They want to humor the flesh and be on terms of friendship with sin, until they imagine themselves as being at the gate of heaven when they come to die; then they want to bid farewell to sin, in order that they may enter heaven. However, you can not enter life in this wise. The grace and salvation in Christ cleanses the heart and makes us zealous of good works. He that is not zealous against sin, and zealous for his own sanctification, has not accepted the grace of God and has no right to indulge in hope. See to it, that you read what our text says.

Preserve us, O God, from the wickedness of continuing in sin in order that grace may abound. Help us to receive thy grace in true faith, that it may cleanse our heart, make us free and sanctify us, and prepare us for bliss in heaven. Amen.

Anoint me with thy heavenly grace, Adopt me for thine own, That I may see thy glorious face, And worship at thy throne.
Let every thought, and work, and word, To thee be ever given; Then life shall be thy service, Lord, And death the gate of heaven.

40. December 30.

Lord Jesus, Word of life, draw us to thee and to the Father. Amen.

1 John 1, 1–7. That which was from the beginning, which we have heard, which we have seen with our eyes, which we have looked upon, and our hands have handled of the Word of life; (for the life was manifested, and we have seen it, and bear witness, and shew unto you that eternal life, which was with the Father, and was manifested unto us;) that which we have seen and heard declare we unto you, that ye also may have fellowship with us: and truly our fellowship is with the Father, and with his Son Jesus Christ. And these things write we unto you, that your joy may be full. This then is the message which we have heard of him, and declare unto you, that God is light, and in him is no darkness at all. If we say that we have fellowship with him, and walk in darkness, we lie, and do not the truth: But if we walk in the light, as he is in the light, we have fellowship one with another, and the blood of Jesus Christ his Son cleanseth us from all sin.

In this text we again hear John speak of the union of the eternal Word with man in Jesus Christ. He and the other apostles have *seen,* and their hands handled, that which was from the beginning, namely, the Word, the Life, God's only begotten Son, God himself. Clearly, it was the human nature of Jesus which they saw with their eyes and felt with their hands; but still he says, that it was God; hence the two natures are one person in Christ. Furthermore, it is the Word, the Life, the only begotten Son of God, whom we hear in the preaching of the apostles; and he it is with whom we are united when we believe and keep the word in our heart. We have fellowship with the apostles and are one body with them; but our fellowship is in Christ, who is the head of the church. His divine life courses through the whole body; the divine life, the divine love itself, the bond of perfection, unites all the saints in the Lord. By their preaching the apostles take us into their embrace and seat us with themselves at the Lord's supper, and thus they and we have fellowship with the Father and the Son. But God is light; that is, truth and holiness. No one who lives in God can walk in sin and deceit. No one who lives in sin and deceit lives in God. This is not to be understood as meaning, that the children of God here on earth are without sin; but they do not live in sin, do not serve sin. They confess their sin and seek forgiveness, and by grace they advance in holiness, until they shall at last attain to perfect purity. For the blood of Jesus Christ is the blood of the *Son of God;* and how could this blood fail to cleanse from all sin? It gives us full forgiveness every hour, and it sanctifies us wholly. By its means I shall sometime be entirely without sin, and then I shall see him as he is.

Lord Jesus, thou hast given me, also, room in thy heart,—it thrills my whole being to speak of it; thou hast cleansed me, also, with thy blood and quickened me with thy love; thou hast drawn me, also, even me, out of the darkness into the light of life. I kneel before thy throne and bless and praise thy exalted name. Lord, I am wretched and poor, and I am not worthy of the least of all thy mercies. I am still sinful and unclean; cleanse me wholly; wash me with thy blood, that I may become perfectly pure. Then will I praise thee with clean lips out of a blissful heart. Amen.

Thine forever! God of love, Hear us from thy throne above; Thine forever may we be, Here and in eternity.

Thine forever! Lord of life, Shield us through our earthly strife; Thou, the Life, the Truth, the Way, Guide us to the realms of day.

---

41. Sunday after Christmas. I.

Lord, remember us in our youth and in our old age, and give us a blessed end. Amen.

Gospel Lesson, Luke 2, 33–40. And Joseph and his mother marvelled at those things which were spoken of him. And Simeon blessed them, and said unto Mary his mother, Behold, this child is set for the fall and rising again of many in Israel; and for a sign which shall be spoken against; (yea, a sword shall pierce through thy own soul also,) that the thoughts of many hearts may be revealed. And there was one Anna, a prophetess, the daughter of Phanuel, of the tribe of Asar; she was of great age, and had lived with her husband seven years from her virginity; and she was a widow of about fourscore and four years, which departed not from the temple, but served God with fastings and prayers night and day. And she, coming in that instant, gave thanks likewise unto the Lord, and spake of him to all them that looked for redemption in Jerusalem. And when they had performed all things according to the law of the Lord, they returned into Galilee, to their own city Nazareth. And the child grew, and waxed strong in spirit, filled with wisdom; and the grace of God was upon him.

"The righteous shall flourish like the palm tree; he shall grow like a cedar in Lebanon. Those that be planted in the house of the Lord shall flourish in the courts of our God. They shall still bring forth fruit in old age; they shall be fat and flourishing; to shew that the Lord is upright; he is my rock, and there is no unrighteousness in him." These words of the Psalmist we see established in our gospel lesson. "The hoary head is a crown of glory, if it be found in the way of righteousness," says Solomon (Proverbs 16, 31). Old age brings much infirmity and many ills. In the 12th chapter of Eccleciastes this mtater is spoken of metaphorically: "The keepers of the house shall tremble:" that is, the arms and hands; "and the strong men shall bow themselves," that is, the legs; "the grinders cease because they are few," the teeth, namely; "and those that look out of the windows be darkened, and the doors shall be shut in the streets," meaning the eyes and ears. So it is with the several members of the body, and so it is with the mental faculties. Everything is being weakened and blunted, until "the silver cord be loosed, or the golden bowl be broken, or the pitcher be broken at the fountain, or the wheel broken at the cistern;" that is, until the vital force is exhausted, and breathing ceases; and "then shall the dust return to the earth as it was, and the spirit shall return unto God who gave it." But such old people as Simeon and Anna are happy. The life of Jesus in them does not grow old. Let us be like them, whether our life is to be long or short; and may it shape itself like theirs at last. The Spirit has opened the eyes of Simeon, so that he sees the Savior in this child. The name Anna means grace, and Phanuel means the countenance of God. She remains always in the temple serving God; this is the beginning of the bliss in heaven. The same grace may be ours. Jesus is here and wishes to be known and embraced by our hearts in faith. He saves from all sin and gives the soul peace and joy. "He forgiveth all thy iniquities, and healeth all thy diseases. He redeemeth thy life from destruction, and crowneth thee with loving kindness and tender mercies; he satisfieth thy mouth with good things, so that thy youth is renewed like the eagle's." You know where you may find him; he is where he has promised to be. None who earnestly seek him there, shall seek him in vain. In the present degenerate age we still know of old men with the words of Simeon in their heart, "Lord, now lettest thou thy servant depart in peace, according to thy word; for mine eyes have seen thy salvation;" and we likewise know of aged women who, until at the very moment of their death, have the jubilant voice of Anna, the daughter of Phanuel.

Lord, Jesus, we thank thee for the life thou gavest us, which never waxes old and dies. Give to young and old the childlike faith of the venerable Simeon and the pious heart of Anna. Grant us, at the last, that we depart in peace and have a blessed end in thee. Amen.

O draw me, Savior, after thee! So shall I run and never tire. With gracious words still comfort me; Be thou my hope, my sole desire. Free me from every weight: nor fear Nor sin can come, if thou art here.

---

42. Sunday after Christmas. II.

Let thy mercies come also unto me, O Lord, even thy salvation, according to thy word. Amen.

Epistle Lesson, Galatians 4, 1–7. Now I say, That the heir, as long as he is a child, differeth nothing from a servant, though he be lord of all; but is under tutors and governors until the time appointed of the father. Even so we, when we were children, were in bondage under the elements of the world: but when the fulness of the time was come, God sent forth his Son, made of a woman, made under the law, to redeem them that were under the law, that we might receive the adoption of sons. And because ye are sons, God hath sent forth the Spirit of his Son into your hearts, crying, Abba, Father. Wherefore thou art no more a servant, but a son; and if a son, then an heir of God through Christ.

Here we again learn from the Holy Spirit, through Paul, that *the Son of God* is born of a *woman*. Of whom does the Spirit speak but of the babe that was born in Bethlehem, of the man that died on the cross? That which is born of a woman is man. Christ really is very man, and yet the Spirit here says: "*God* sent forth *his Son*, made of a woman." Can this be understood otherwise than as meaning, that

Christ is God and man in one person? The Son of God is the Son of Mary, the Word was made flesh, the only begotten of the Father became man.—He was *made under the law*, and he thereafter, of his own free will, declared himself subject to the law; for this reason he was circumcised, and for this reason he was baptized. He obeyed the law and fulfilled it in all things, its deepest spiritual claim and its every commandment, to the very letter. But though he fulfilled the law, yet he let the punishment for its violation fall upon himself in full measure; he placed himself under the condemnation of the law, and he willingly accepted the sentence: Because thou hast transgressed and hast deserved condemnation and death, thou shalt die the death of the accursed. The Son becomes a servant, the Holy One becomes the sinner, in order that we may become sons and stand acquitted before God. The life and blood of his only begotten Son are sacrificed under the judgment of the law on the accursed tree, that we accursed sinners may be free and have sonship in God.

All this has come to pass, and now the Son of God says: *Believe in me*, and all this is yours. It was not necessary for me to keep the law for my own sake; I am righteous from eternity; I had no sin for which to suffer punishment. I have never transgressed; but all has been done and suffered for you, and you shall believe it; all has been *done*, you shall not do it, but *believe* it. The fulness of time is come; everything which was then to be done has been done; you are redeemed from bondage; if you *believe*, you are a free and blessed child of God. Let the devil, then, no more deceive you with this lying invention of his, that you must satisfy the demands of the law in order to become a child of God. This is nothing less than to deny the perfect work of Christ. Verily, *the law has been fulfilled*, and you are a child of God when you believe this gospel. Now art thou mine, says our Lord Jesus; "thou art mine, and I am thine; and where I am, there shalt thou be; the enemy shall not part us." God help us to understand this! And then, behold, how the Spirit of the Son of God in your heart cries, "Abba, Father!" and bears witness with your spirit, that you are a child of God.

Lord Jesus, blessed God and Savior, give us the simplicity of faith and the liberty of grace; give us the glory and bliss of the adoption of sons. Amen.

Lord Jesus Christ, My Savior blest, My hope and my salvation! I trust in thee, Deliver me From misery; Thy word's my consolation.
Most heartily I trust in thee, Thy mercy fails me never; Dear Lord, abide My helper tried, Thou Crucified, From evil keep me ever.

---

43. New Year's Eve.

Psalm 90. A Prayer of Moses, the man of God. Lord, thou hast been our dwelling place in all generations. Before the mountains were brought forth, or ever thou hadst formed the earth and the world, even from everlasting to everlasting, thou art God. Thou turnest man to destruction; and sayest, Return, ye children of men. For a thousand years in thy sight are but as a yesterday when it is past, and as a watch in the night. Thou carriest them away as with a flood; they are as a sleep: in the morning they are like grass which groweth up. In the morning it flourisheth, and groweth up; in the evening it is cut down, and withereth. For we are consumed by thine anger, and by thy wrath are we troubled. Thou hast set our iniquities before thee, our secret sins in the light of thy countenance. For all our days are passed away in thy wrath; we spend our years as a tale that is told. The days of our years are threescore years and ten; and if by reason of strength they be fourscore years, yet is their strength labor and sorrow: for it is soon cut off, and we fly away. Who knoweth the power of thine anger? even according to thy fear, so is thy wrath. So teach us to number our days, that we may apply our hearts unto wisdom. Return, O Lord, how long? and let it repent thee concerning thy servants. O satisfy us early with thy mercy; that we may rejoice and be glad all our days. Make us glad according to the days wherein thou hast afflicted us, and the years wherein we have seen evil. Let thy work appear unto thy servants, and thy glory unto their children. And let the beauty of the Lord our God be upon us: and establish thou the work of our hands upon us; yea, the work of our hands establish thou it.

It is a sad thought, that the days of our life fly so fast. How soon, alas, do the flowers of our youth wither and die! The serious feature, however, the heaviest and weariest part of the consideration, is this, that *sin* is the cause. It would profit us little, at the close of the year, to indulge in melancholy speculations on the flight of time and the rapid revolution of the years; but it shall profit us much to meditate upon our life and to know our sins. Knowledge of sin is the keynote in this touching prayer of Moses. "For we are consumed by thine anger, and by thy wrath are we troubled. Thou hast set our iniquities before thee, our secret sins in the light of thy countenance. The strength of the days of our years is labor and sorrow." Bow, as did Moses, in deepest humility before the Lord, and pray earnestly for mercy. Make up your account at the close of the year, or year will be added to year with unknown and unforgiven sins, and the amount will be appalling at the last; for sometime the day of reckoning will come.—During this year you have again received a thousand benefits from the Lord; all that he did was done with the kindest purpose. But you, how have you been minded toward him? How have you received his manifold mercies, and what manner of life have you led during these many days of grace? Make a clean breast of it! You have, mayhap, walked without God and served sin? Though you be old, you may, possibly, not as yet have experienced true conversion and given your heart to God? Or do you, perhaps, spend your days in the enjoyment of worldly pleasures or the pursuit of fleeting honors and wealth? However, let me assume, that you are a converted and believing soul;—how much more faithfully and diligently than you have done it, might you not have employed your time! Consider, how much better you might have thanked the Lord, and how much more you might have benefited your fellowmen; how much sin you have committed, and how much good you have *left undone!* Do, then, weigh this with care, and confess it with sorrow; prostrate yourself before the Lord and cry to him for mercy. And, behold, he spreads his hands above you, and forgives you, and blesses you. He takes away your shortcomings in all things, but crowns your work. You carry, then, no debt of sin over from the old into the new year, but only the grace and good will of God in Christ. Blessed be the Lord, who satisfies us early with his mercy; so that we, who have merited everlasting and voiceless sorrow, can sing and be glad all our days. The beauty of our God is upon us, and he shall establish the work of our hands. We close the year as we began it: *In the name of Jesus.*

Accept our poor offering of praise, most high and blessed God. Thanks for everything which we have received or suffered during the year. The Lord gave, and the Lord hath taken away; blessed be the name of the Lord! Amen.

For thy mercy and thy grace, Faithful through another year, Hear our song of thankfulness, Father and Redeemer, hear.
In our weakness and distress, Rock of strength, be thou our stay; In the pathless wilderness, Be our true and living way.

44. New Year's Day. I.

In the name of Jesus. Praise waiteth for thee, O God, in Zion; and unto thee shall the vow be performed. Amen.

Gospel Lesson, Luke 2, 21. And when eight days were accomplished for the circumcision of the child, his name was called Jesus, which was so named of the angel before he was conceived in the womb.

Praise the Lord: the name *Jesus* is written in living characters on the gate through which we enter the new year. The name Jesus relieves us of all our sins in the past, so that we can look back with joy and thanks; and the name Jesus gives us courage to face the future with a heart full of hope.—If we believe, we all the time have trials and tribulations; and still we could not have a happier lot. We lived in the Lord during the year now closed; we enter into the name of Jesus, into his saving love, as we now begin the new year. Could anything better have met us at the dawn of our life than Jesus, the Savior, in our holy baptism? Could anything better meet us on the first morning of the year than the name of Jesus with its fulness of life and peace? Or could we wish for a more beautiful sunset, when our evening comes, than to die in the name of Jesus?

The merciful God has given us his Son for our Savior, and has let him take upon himself the curse of the law and all our sin. From the hour of my baptism I am in him, and out of the kingdom of Satan; in life, and out of death. Everything that Jesus became for all the world, by fulfilling all righteousness, is mine. In his name is included the whole grace of God unto salvation; he is the *Savior*, his name is *Jesus;* that is, he has atoned for sin, destroyed death, and bruised the devil. This he did by his death and resurrection. He has taken me out of the kingdom of Satan and made me his own by means of my baptism; he keeps me every hour, continually renews his grace to me and in me, lives alway at the right hand of the Father, and makes intercession for me, supports my soul by his gospel, and nourishes me with his body and blood. All this I have in the name *Jesus*. Himself, who was dead and yet lives for evermore, my King and my God, my Prince of Life and my Salvation, my Brother and my Bridegroom, is the first to meet me today; which means, that, with the beginning of the year, I come into closer communion with him, and that I shall live all the year in his saving, comforting, and blessed fellowship. Everything we have in Jesus; of him, and through him, and to him, are all things. Every concern of the year shall rest on him, my Savior, and all things shall work together for my salvation. I shall have the name of Jesus with me every day and every hour. In his strength I shall live through the year in holiness and patience, honor him and serve the brethren. O, my heart, you will not believe! Is it, then, not true, is it not right, that the name of Jesus is the entrance gate to the new year? Is it a false signboard? Or do you find yourself unable quite to believe it, because it seems too good to be true? Take a good look at the name Jesus, and what do you see? Do you not see, that the name is surrounded with a halo of grace, grace for needy sinners?

Glory be to thee, great God! I understand but little of the depth of grace in thy name. Give me thy Spirit and let him declare thee in my heart. Amen.

Jesus! Name of wondrous love, Name all other names above! Unto which must every knee Bow in deep humility.
Jesus! Name decreed of old, To the maiden mother told, Kneeling in her lowly cell, By the angel Gabriel.
Jesus! Name of priceless worth To the fallen sons of earth, For the promise that it gave, "Jesus shall his people save."

45. New Year's Day. II.

Thy name, O Jesus, is as ointment poured forth!

Epistle Lesson, Galatians 3, 23-29. But before faith came, we were kept under the law, shut up unto the faith which should afterwards be revealed. Wherefore the law was our schoolmaster to bring us unto Christ, that we might be justified by faith. But after that faith is come, we are no longer under a schoolmaster. For ye are all the children of God by faith in Christ Jesus. For as many of you as have been baptized into Christ, have put on Christ. There is neither Jew nor Greek, there is neither bond nor free, there is neither male or female: for ye are all one in Christ Jesus. And if ye be Christ's, then are ye Abraham's seed, and heirs according to the promise.

"For as many of you as have been baptized into Christ have put on Christ." "These words of Paul," says Luther, "we should keep steadily in view, in order that we may defend the proper meaning and use of our holy baptism against the sect of the Anabaptists, who destroy the majesty and glory of baptism and speak blasphemously of this holy sacrament. Beware of such infernal scoffers; this is my earnest advice; it is much better to hear the grand and comforting words of Saint Paul, who calls baptism 'the washing of regeneration, and renewing of the Holy Ghost' (Titus 3, 5). And here he says, that all who are baptized into Christ have put on Christ. It is as though he had said: You have not received baptism as a mere outward sign from which it may be seen that you are to be counted as Christians,— as the heretics have the habit of speaking in regard to this matter, when they make baptism out to be nothing but a livery, or simply a badge which does no good whatever;—for ye, as many of you as are baptized, he says, have put on Christ. That is, you have been released from the prison of the law, and have been born again in your baptism; you are, therefore, no more under the law, but have put on a new garment, which is the righteousness of Christ."

In very truth, then, the believing Christians are the children and heirs of God, as our epistle lesson says: For ye are all the children of God by faith in Christ Jesus. "And now," says Luther again, "let him that has the gift of finest speech and oratory elaborate in his very best manner on this passage concerning the unspeakable grace and glory which we have in Christ Jesus; and let him discuss this matter at length and as it deserves: this truth, namely, that we poor sinners, who by nature are the children of wrath, reach the high honor of becoming, through faith in Christ, the children and heirs of God, and joint heirs wth Jesus Christ, and lords of heaven and earth;—though, to be sure, no tongue of man or angel can do justice to this glorious truth. I therefore ask each and all to study this matter carefully; it is not in my power to voice it properly, or to understand its full meaning. Here we can only begin to spell our way through it, until we reach the home beyond the sky; then we shall see it, and have everlasting joy in it, and praise God for it, evermore. Grant us this, O God, of thy grace through Jesus Christ our Lord. Amen."

Great God! we sing that mighty hand By which supported still we stand;
The op'ning year thy mercy shows—Let mercy crown it to its close.
By day, by night, at home, abroad, Still we are guarded by our God; By his incessant bounty fed, By his unerring counsel led.

---

46. January 2.

Lord Jesus, lead us into the sanctuaries of thy word. Amen.

Luke 4, 16–21. And he came to Nazareth, where he had been brought up: and, as his custom was, he went into the synagogue on the sabbath day, and stood up for to read. And there was delivered unto him the book of the prophet Esaias. And when he had opened the book, he found the place where it was written, The Spirit of the Lord is upon me, because he hath anointed me to preach the gospel to the poor; he hath sent me to heal the brokenhearted, to preach deliverance to the captives, and recovering of sight to the blind, to set at liberty them that are bruised, to preach the acceptable year of the Lord. And he closed the book, and he gave it again to the minister, and sat down

And the eyes of all them that were in the synagogue were fastened on him. And he began to say unto them, This day is this scripture fulfilled in your ears.

For us this scripture is, in truth, fulfilled. The Lord is here; the year of grace, the blessed time of the New Testament, is come. Hear the gospel, ye needy sinners; believe it, and rejoice. To be sure, you are miserably poor as to righteousness and holiness; but, in spite of this, you are now rich. In the Old Testament year of jubilee the law obtained, that every man was to have his inheritance returned to him. In the kingdom of Christ we receive anew the honor and glory of God together with sonship in him. You are sick; I understand very well how it is with you. But our Savior knows best what aches and pains there are in our sick heart and our depressed spirits; none understands us as well as he; for he was in all points tempted like as we are, yet without sin. We are sick, but he is our physician, who has a remedy for every ill. It is a good thing that we feel our sickness; for only the sick are willing to call the physician. Jesus is the anointed priest and physician of the soul; and do you think, that the Lord God appointed one who was not capable to this office? He is to be relied on as absolutely as is God in heaven; for he is the everlasting God himself. Come to him where he has made an appointment with you, namely in the gospel, that is, in the Word and in the sacraments of baptism and the altar. When he says to you: You, who are baptized into me, have put on my righteousness; you, who eat and drink my body and blood, abide in me and I in you; you are free, and you have power to believe and power to serve me;—then he is near to you, nearer than anything else whatsoever; for what he speaks comes to pass. Therefore, by his grace you actually have power to believe; for he gives sight to the blind. Do you not *see* that you are a lost sinner, hopelessly in debt, and without ability to pay a farthing? Do you not see that you are unclean, diseased, and entirely covered with leprosy, and sold under sin? You have begun to see this. Who was it opened your eyes? Did you do it yourself? Look, then, and you will also see, that he has paid your debt, which has, therefore, been wiped out. Do you not see, that he dies, the righteous for the unrighteous; and do you not see with what unmistakable clearness this is written by God's own finger in the gospel? See, also, that he has taken you into his church, which is his hospital for the healing of the sick. Understand, that you are with Jesus, and that you no longer are in the power of the devil; then your eyes do not deceive you; for this is truth, and the Lord has given you light to see it. But, alas, how perverted is our nature! In selfrighteousness or in a feeling of proud indifference the sinners that dwell in fancied security despise the gospel; while they that have experienced a spiritual awakening want to be assured of the truth by the evidence of their senses before they believe. God gives us true humility, that we may be affrighted at our unbelief, which resists a truth so clear and a grace so ineffable. Here we are; the year of jubilee is begun; Jesus stands among us; the gospel is being preached; the fount of healing is flowing freely; the fetters are broken; the bandage has been taken from our eyes;—and yet we act as if we were blind! We are free, and yet we do not give thanks, but continue to sigh and complain!

Precious Lord Jesus, thy name be praised for evermore! This song of praise shall not die away; but thou wilt perform that which thou hast begun in us, and we will glorify thee forever. Grant this, we pray, of thy great, great mercy. Amen.

O Christ, who diedst and yet dost live, To me impart thy merit; My pardon seal, my sins forgive, And cleanse me by thy Spirit. Beneath thy cross I view the day When heaven and earth shall pass away, And thus prepare to meet thee.

47. January 3.

Create in us clean hearts, O God, and knit us together by thy holy love. Amen.

1 Peter 2, 1–6. Wherefore laying aside all malice, and all guile, and hypocrisies, and envies, and all evil speakings, as newborn babes, desire the sincere milk of the word, that ye may grow thereby: if so be ye have tasted that the Lord is gracious. To whom coming, as unto a living stone, disallowed indeed of men, but chosen of God, and precious, ye also, as lively stones, are built up a spiritual house, an holy priesthood, to offer up spiritual sacrifices, acceptable to God by Jesus Christ. Wherefore also it is contained in the scripture, Behold, I lay in Zion a chief corner stone, elect, precious: and he that believeth on him shall not be confounded.

Peter writes to you who are born again of incorruptible seed by the living word of God. Hear and obey his admonition. What yet remains clinging to you of malice, hypocrisy, and the like, must be laid aside; herein you must employ all diligence and zeal. Else these faults will grow and kill the true life in you. But the strength necessary for your sanctification you receive of our Lord Jesus in and through the word of God. Therefore, as newborn babes hunger after the mother's breast, and very frequently demand nourishment, even so shall you desire the pure word of God. For himself is in this word, and of his love he feeds you with it; and this is the only means by which the new man in you grows, so that you become stronger and more courageous in the fight against the evil one. *Desire* this sincere milk of the word, says the apostle; *desire* it, "if so be ye have tasted that the Lord is gracious." Here we learn that it is *the Lord himself* of whom we partake and whom we taste in the word. Should it not, then, be sweet to the taste, and must it not be strong meat? Let your soul absorb it, and when you read and hear it, then keep it; ponder it, take it into your heart, and make it a part of your life and your conversation; then there shall be no lack of sin or sorrow to make the gospel precious to you and enable you to taste that the Lord is gracious. But do not wait another day, nor even another hour; now, this very moment, the Lord is near. Drink of the fountain, and draw your weapon against all the viper brood of which any symptoms remain in you.

The apostle passes over to another figure of speech, which is taken from several passages of the Old Testament. He lived on the scriptures, he was nourished by the sincere milk of the word. Malice disunites the hearts, destroys the true fellowship, and causes death. The love from the heart of God in Christ is a living cement, which binds together the living stones on the everlasting, living foundation stone, the only begotten Son of God. He is the head stone of the corner, and he is the highpriest; we are the walls of the building, and also the priests of the house. Hypocrites have no business in this house, and the offerings of unclean hearts are not permitted on its altars. Here must be living stones, an holy priesthood, and sacrifices acceptable to God.

Grant us thy grace, O God, through Jesus Christ. May we belong to the communion of the saints; and do thou sanctify us more and more each day, until we shall appear before thee without blemish, perfected in holiness. Amen.

Correct, reprove, and comfort me; As I have need, my Savior be; And if I would from thee depart, Then clasp me, Savior, to thy heart.
In fierce temptation's darkest hour, Save me from sin and Satan's power; Tear every idol from thy throne, And reign, my Savior, reign alone.

48. January 4.

The Lord is my strength and my song; he also is become my salvation. Teach me to believe in thee. Amen.

Isaiah 40, 26–31. Lift up your eyes on high, and behold who hath created these things, that bringeth out their host by number: he calleth them all by names, by the greatness of his might, for that he is strong in power; not one faileth. Why sayest thou, O Jacob, and speakest, O Israel, My way is hid from the Lord and my judgment is passed over from my God? Hast thou not known? hast thou not heard, that the everlasting God, the Lord, the Creator of the ends of the earth, fainteth not, neither is weary? there is no searching of his understanding. He giveth power to the faint; and to them that have no might he increaseth strength. Even the youths shall faint and be weary, and the young men shall utterly fall: but they that wait upon the Lord shall renew their strength; they shall mount up with wings as eagles; they shall run, and not be weary, and they shall walk, and not faint.

This is a glorious text, and strikingly appropriate at the beginning of the year. What is to meet us during the course of this year? We know only that we must through much tribulation enter into the kingdom of God;—"through much tribulation," but "into the kingdom of God." We know that *each* day shall have its evil, but, also, that "*sufficient* to the day is the evil thereof;" hence we need not today bear the ills of yesterday or of tomorrow. Lift up your eyes on high, says the Spirit of God through the prophet. Look upward! We have the habit of opening the eye when we look downward, and of closing it when we look upward. Then we see wretchedness in everything, and do we not see that, *in truth, there is glory shining* over it all. "Who hath created these things?" You know that it was he who is your God, your heavenly Father. Who brings out their host by number, and calls them all by name? Do you think that he will lose any by reason of infirmity or forgetfulness? Does he forget or neglect you? Does he tire of helping and providing for you? Or does his understanding fall short when you are in want of help and guidance? O, we fools; why will we not believe in the Lord, the almighty, everlasting, merciful, faithful God? He has called you by name, and you are his own. How, then, could he forget you? You Christian people, members of his needy, poor, and afflicted church; you are precious to him for Jesus' sake. Do read the above text once more, and keep it in your heart. "Lift up your eyes on high," etc.

Let thy mercies come also unto me, O Lord, even thy salvation, according to thy word. Amen.

Praise to the Lord! O let all that is in me adore him! All that hath life and breath, come now with praises before him! Let the Amen Sound from his people again: Gladly for aye we adore him.

49. Epiphany Eve.

Lord God, let thy tender mercy be known in all the earth, and let it become mighty in our hearts. Amen.

Isaiah 12. And in that day thou shalt say, O Lord, I will praise thee: though thou wast angry with me, thine anger is turned away, and thou comfortedst me. Behold, God is my salvation; I will trust, and not be afraid: for the Lord Jehovah is my strength and my song; he also is become my salvation. Therefore with joy shall ye draw water out of the wells of salvation. And in that day shall ye say, Praise the Lord, call upon his name, declare his doings among the people, make mention that his name is exalted. Sing unto the Lord; for he hath done excellent things: this is known in all the earth. Cry out and shout, thou inhabitant of Zion: for great is the Holy One of Israel in the midst of thee.

You that really live in the church of Christ have infinitely great reason to thank the Lord. You *were* a child of wrath, but are one no more. He surrounds you with nothing but love and grace; goodness and mercy, only, follow you all the days of your life. I am not speaking of what your *feelings* may say, but of what *really is*. God himself, the Eternal and Glorious One, is your strength and your life; God, the very fulness of salvation, is your salvation. Can he be moved? Can the rock of your salvation totter? Can the well of your salvation run dry? You may yet have to bear the brunt of many a fight before you shall have achieved your last victory; but the Lord Jehovah is your strength, and, surely, none shall be able to strike him down. Incessantly you shall receive new grace, and new love and new joy; for in this kingdom all things are new; a new and fresh life pours out from the Father and the Son in the Holy Ghost, flows through the whole church and refreshes and nourishes the hearts. With joy you shall draw water out of the wells of salvation. "Whosoever drinketh of the water of Sychar shall thirst again; but whosoever drinketh of the water that Jesus giveth shall never thirst; but the water shall be in him a well of water springing up into eternal life." "But this living water, what is it but the life in God, which is given us in our baptism? What is this water but the life of Christ, which nourishes us in the body and blood of the sacrament of the altar? What is this water but the life of the Holy Ghost, which is given us in the gospel? Yes, this water it is that wells up out of the heart of God the Father, is a flood of glory in all the angels, is the lifebeat of the elect; and on the bosom of this river all who drink of it are carried forward to the boundless sea of the Divine Being, the universal and eternal mother, whence the rivers come, and whither they return."

Praise the Lord, ye members of his church; declare his doings among the people, make mention that his name is exalted. Let his saving glory shine over all the earth. Is not your Savior set for an ensign to the peoples, that the heathen shall inquire after him? Cry out and shout, inhabitants of Zion; call the heathen by the thousands to come and dwell in the tent of the Lord. Why are you still silent? Is there not room? Is there not abundance of the water of life? Have you been forbidden to invite the peoples, or is your voice too weak, or your strength too little. The Lord, who commands you to make his name known in all the earth, is himself your strength and your song. He has done excellent things for us; let this be declared throughout the whole earth.

Grant thy blessings herein, gracious God; glorify thy name, and give salvation to the heathen for Jesus' sake. Amen.

Put forth thy glorious power, That Gentiles all may see, And earth present her store In converts born to thee: God, our own God, his church will bless, And fill the world with righteousness.

To God the only wise, The one immortal King, Let hallelujahs rise From every living thing: Let all that breathe, on every coast, Praise Father, Son, and Holy Ghost.

---

50. Sunday after New Year. I.

Lord, remember thy congregation which thou hast purchased of old, which thou hast redeemed to be the tribe of thine inheritance. Amen.

Gospel Lesson, Matthew 2, 19–23. But when Herod was dead, behold, an angel of the Lord appeareth in a dream to Joseph in Egypt, saying, Arise, and take the young child and his mother, and go into the land of Israel: for they are dead which sought the young child's life. And he arose, and took the young child and his mother, and came into the land of Israel. But when he heard that Archelaus did reign in Judæa in the room of his father Herod, he was afraid to go thither: notwithstanding, being warned of God in a dream, he turned aside into the parts of Galilee: and he came and dwelt in a city called Nazareth: that it might be fulfilled which was spoken by the prophets, He shall be called a Nazarene.

Our Lord became an exile and was despised here on earth. He was persecuted by that instrument of the devil, Herod, and compelled, shortly after his birth, to depart into Egypt; and on his return he was not permitted to grow up in the city of his father David, but had to become the despised Nazarene. In this connection we note three things: 1) This came to pass, in order that the scripture might be fulfilled. The people of Israel, who are called the firstborn son of God, were strangers in the land of Egypt, and took possession of Canaan; and this was a prophecy concerning Jesus, as the Lord says: "I called my Son out of Egypt." The Glorious One was to grow up in despised Galilee, the land of Zebulon and Naphtali (Isaiah 9, 1–7). The Lord was to be a tender plant, a little root, called Nezer in the Hebrew, despised and rejected (Isaiah 11, 1; 53, 2. 3). Herod and Archelaus were obliged to assist in causing these prophecies to be fulfilled. 2) It was a part of the atonement for our sin that the Son of God became not only a poor, but an exiled and utterly despised man on earth. For not only did Adam deserve to be driven out of paradise on account of sin, but all of us have richly deserved to be driven from our country and from all that we have; yet, by the the the grace of the sojourn of Jesus in a strange land, we now dwell in our own land in peace, and in his church with every blessing, and at home in heaven with eternal bliss. We lost the glory of God, and we had incurred the penalty of everlasting shame. From this Jesus now has delivered us by becoming the despised Nazarene, even to the point of dying the death of a malefactor; and we are now honored with the name of the children of God and the sons of Israel, and we shall inherit the crown of glory in heaven. 3) We here learn that our path to glory with Christ leads through contumely, persecution, and tribulation. Let it be our honor that we become like Jesus; let our comfort be that he has preceded us on this path; and let this be our strength, that in this wise are fulfilled on us, also, the holy scriptures.

Help us, Lord God, our heavenly Father, that, saved by the blood of Jesus, we may reach our home in the eternal fatherland. Amen.

He whom the world could not inclose Doth in Mary's arms repose; He is become an infant small, Who by his might upholdeth all. Hallelujah!

He came to earth despised and poor, Man to pity and restore, And make us rich in heaven above, With angels equal, through his love. Hallelujah!

51. Sunday after New Year. II.

Lord, instruct us; teach us the path of true righteousness. Amen.

Epistle Lesson, Romans 3, 19–22. Now we know, that what things soever the law saith, it saith to them who are under the law; that every mouth may be stopped, and all the world may become guilty before God. Therefore by the deeds of the law there shall no flesh be justified in his sight: for by the law is the knowledge of sin. But now the righteousness of God without the law is manifested, being witnessed by the law and the prophets; even the righteousness of God, which is by faith of Jesus Christ, unto all and upon all them that believe: for there is no difference.

It is your bounden duty to keep the holy law of God; for God created you with ability to do this, and the demands of the law are just. It can not be altered, and there can be no abatement of any part of its claim. But as soon as you make a serious effort to keep the law, you find that you are not competent to do it. Many do not know that they are transgressors of the law, and do not feel that the law condemns them; they have never seriously tried to keep it. When we honestly obey the commandment without any sort of compromise, its demands begin more and more to touch our hidden springs of action and our innermost self; we did not know how thorough and exacting the law was, until we seriously began to obey it. When we have done everything which we thought that it demanded; when we have lived piously, shunned evil, and done good to God and man, the law still demands much more than this; it demands the whole heart full of pure love, and does not tolerate even one selfish or unclean desire in us. It promptly pronounces us guilty, and we must admit that the verdict is just. It stops our mouth and puts us under the judgment of God as criminals deserving of condemnation. No man is justified before God by the deeds of the law; the law works wrath; it shows us our sin, but does not take it away. The law *demands* love, demands it by right and with authority; but it can only *demand*, not *give;* it can give nothing at all. But the gospel can; it shews forth the grace of God in Christ. He has fulfilled the law in our stead; and God has ordained that all who believe this and trust in Christ shall be partakers of the benefit of his fulfilment of the law and of his suffering. The gospel says: All is finished, and all things are given you. Thus faith is born in the poor heart that has been troubled by the law; and we then take refuge in Jesus, are covered by the mantle of his righteousness, and in him we stand justified before God. And behold, when you thus had been loosed from the bands of the law, you became heartily attached to it, and began to love it as a revelation of the will of your heavenly Father, your most precious rule of conduct; and the demands of the law are fulfilled in you, for now you love both God and your neighbor. But your righteousness is not that of the law, but that which is of *faith in Jesus Christ*. It is of the utmost importance that you have this experience.

Enlighten us by thy Holy Spirit, O Lord, that we may understand the office of the law, be moved to sincere knowledge of sin, be driven to seek Christ, and truly be justified by faith. Amen.

All that I was, my sin, my guilt, My death, was all my own; All that I am, I owe to thee, My gracious God, alone.
The evil of my former state Was mine **and** only mine; The good in which I now rejoice Is thine and only thine.

---

52. Epiphany (January 6). I.

O, Praise the Lord, all ye nations, praise him, all ye people! For his merciful kindness is great toward us; and the truth of the Lord endureth for-ever. Praise ye the Lord.

Gospel Lesson, Matthew 2, 1–12. Now when Jesus was born in Bethlehem of Judæa, in the days of Herod the king, behold, there came wise men from the east to Jerusalem, saying, Where is he that is born King of the

Jews? for we have seen his star in the east, and are come to worship him. When Herod the king had heard these things, he was troubled, and all Jerusalem with him. And when he had gathered all the chief priests and scribes of the people together, he demanded of them where Christ should be born. And they said unto him, In Bethlehem of Judæa: for thus it is written by the prophet; And thou Bethlehem, in the land of Juda, art not the least among the princes of Juda: for out of thee shall come a Governor, that shall rule my people Israel. Then Herod, when he had privily called the wise men, inquired of them diligently what time the star appeared. And he sent them to Bethlehem; and said, Go and search diligently for the young child; and when ye have found him, bring me word again, that I may come and worship him also. When they had heard the king, they departed: and, lo, the star, which they saw in the east, went before them, till it came and stood over where the young child was. When they saw the star, they rejoiced with exceeding great joy. And when they were come into the house, they saw the young child with Mary his mother, and fell down, and worshipped him: and when they had opened their treasures, they presented unto him gifts; gold, and frankincense, and myrrh. And being warned of God in a dream that they should not return to Herod, they departed into their own country another way.

The wise men are servants and worshippers of Christ, do his errands, and spread abroad the perfume of his name; while in Herod and the scribes we have his enemies. The true people of Christ's kingdom look upward, and see what others do not see, their hearts belong to the invisible world, and they follow other laws than those followed by the children of unbelief. Jesus Christ is their king, and their effort is in all things to promote his honor. When they understand that it is his will, they leave home and country, and journey to strange peoples. For him they willingly sacrifice gold and treasure and all that they have. Him they worship, and to him they seek to gather souls from far and near. The countenance of God in Christ, the sun over our earth, has burst upon their sight. The things of eternity and heaven have become real and present to their hearts; and hence they no longer live unto themselves, but unto him, who died for us, and gave himself for us. In other words, they *believe* without seeing; they follow the star : that is, the light of God in his works; and they follow the word; that is, the holy scriptures. The wise men followed the star, and it led them to that which was written by the prophet. The prophecy pointed to Bethlehem; they accepted its guidance, and the star again attended them on their way to Christ. —The case of Herod and the scribes is entirely different. They have the word; but they see only its letter, and care nothing for Christ as the king of the souls. The world is their all. They live only for that which is of the earth. The eternal and divine things are nothing to them. Therefore they will not give themselves the trouble of going to Bethlehem. Herod reasons in this wise: "Should it prove that there is some truth in what these men say, I will in good time adopt the measures necessary for my own safety." For this reason he asks the wise men to return to him.—This is the exact position taken by the children of the world among us. They know the word, and most of them do not deny its truth; but Christ, the heavenly and living substance of the word, has no real existence in their *hearts*. Therefore they do not worship him in truth, do not give themselves to him, do not sacrifice their treasures in his honor. Some of them may support the work of mission societies and the charities of the church, but their heart is not in it; and when it comes to a real test, they prefer to deny their Savior.

However, our gospel lesson also teaches that *all* must serve the Lord's cause whether or no, and that he saves his own from the snares of the wicked. The stars of heaven and the highways of earth, astronomy and natural science, the railroads and waterways, the gold and frankincense, Herod and the scribes; all things and all men are made use of by the Lord for the extension of his kingdom. Who was victorious, Herod or Christ? Who accomplished their purpose, the wise men from the east or the scribes of Jerusalem? Thou humble child of Bethlehem, who afterward didst become the despised and crucified Nazarene, and now art the glorified king of heaven; thou sun and magnet of my soul, draw us to thee; make us feel assured of this that thy right hand shall obtain the victory; and show us as much of thy glory as we can bear to see, that we may walk with joy on the paths which thou hast appointed. Draw us, Lord, after thee, make us thy servants, extend thy kingdom, let the forces of the gentiles and the abundance of the sea make haste to come unto thee. Amen.

As with gladness men of old Did the guiding star behold; As with joy they hailed its light, Leading onward, beaming bright: So, most gracious God may we Evermore be led to thee.

As with joyful steps they sped To that lowly manger-bed, There to bend the knee before Him whom heaven and earth adore: So may we with willing feet Ever seek thy mercy-seat.

---

53. Epiphany. II.

Lord, speak; and grant that we give ear to thy voice. Amen.

Isaiah 60, 1–6. Arise, shine; for thy light is come, and the glory of the Lord is risen upon thee. For, behold, the darkness shall cover the earth, and gross darkness the people: but the Lord shall arise upon thee, and his glory shall be seen upon thee. And the Gentiles shall come to thy light, and kings to the brightness of thy rising. Lift up thine eyes round about, and see: all they gather themselves together, they come to thee: thy sons shall come from far, and thy daughters shall be nursed at thy side. Then thou shalt see, and flow together, and thine heart shall fear, and be enlarged; because the abundance of the sea shall be converted unto thee, the forces of the Gentiles shall come unto thee. The multitude of camels shall cover thee, the dromedaries of Midian and Ephah; all they from Sheba shall come: they shall bring gold and incense; and they shall shew forth the praises of the Lord.

Was Isaiah an over-sanguine fanatic, do you think; full of foolish dreams and vain expectations, so that his words are not to be relied on? Not at all. Read his book entire, and you will see that he takes a sober view of the situation, and sees its dark as well as its bright features. He prophesies of punishment as well as of salvation and glory. His speech is not fable; he speaks moved by the Holy Ghost. But this being so, the people of God have great things awaiting them, in spite of the troublous times now at the door. Do let the word of the Lord govern our thought, and decide what we are to expect;—the word of the Lord, and not our own gloomy forebodings. If we have begun to open our eyes, do we not see that the scripture is being fulfilled? Is not the light come, and the glory of the Lord risen upon Israel? And, again: Does not darkness cover the earth, and gross darkness the people? Yes, it is as Isaiah has said. But then the remainder of what he says shall come to pass, also: The gentiles and kings shall come to the light of Israel; the Jews shall return, and the multitude of the gentiles shall be converted and become the Lord's people. In accord herewith is the royal command of Christ: "I have all power in heaven and in earth; go ye therefore, and make all nations my disciples." This does not mean that every individual of the heathen shall be saved; but that the light shall travel around the earth, and all nations be saved, so that there shall be a complete human family, including all races and generations of men, on the new earth. You, also, shall see it, my Christian reader. Your hearts, Christian people, shall beat and tremble in joyous astonishment; shall be enlarged, become spacious as the heavens, and hold an everlasting fulness of love and joy. Make yourselves ready; the light, our Lord Jesus Christ, is come to you, and the glory of the Lord is risen upon you. Lord Jesus, anoint our eyes, that we may walk in thy light; give us grace to believe thy word, to hold thy standard aloft, and to hold fast the confidence and rejoicing of the hope, firm to the end. Amen.

O Christ, our true and only light, Enlighten those who sit in night;
Let those afar now hear thy voice And in thy fold with us rejoice.
Fill with the radiance of thy grace The souls now lost in error's maze,
And all whom in their secret minds Some dark delusion haunts and blinds.

---

54. Monday after Epiphany.

Blessed are the undefiled in the way, who walk in the law of the Lord.

Genesis 17, 1–6. And when Abram was ninety years old and nine, the Lord appeared to Abram, and said unto him, I am the Almighty God: walk before me, and be thou perfect. And I will make my covenant between me and thee, and will multiply thee exceedingly. And Abram fell on his face: and God talked with him, saying, As for me, behold, my covenant is with thee, and thou shalt be a father of many nations. Neither shall thy name any more be called Abram, but thy name shall be Abraham; for a father of many nations have I made thee. And I will make thee exceeding fruitful, and I will make nations of thee, and kings shall come out of thee.

Out of his love God has chosen Abraham, and made a covenant with him in the faith. This is pure grace. He says: "I am thy God, and thou art my servant. I bless thee; do thou with full confidence give thyself to me. I make my face to shine upon thee; do thou walk before me in this light." But this is a covenant with us also, if we believe; for it is an everlasting covenant with all the children of Abraham; that is, all who believe unto the end.

It is a covenant *with each one of us*, a precious and blessed covenant between God and my heart. The *almighty* God has promised to protect me, and has said that I shall walk before his face; and hereby he effects that I do according to his word. He is my commander, and he orders me to be perfect; that is, thoroughly honest of purpose, with no wish to cater to any sin, or to compound with the flesh. He has given me grace to believe; and hence I trust in him, and love him, and find happiness in walking before his face. The covenant is not one in the spirit of bondage, but in the spirit of the adoption of sons, and in a good conscience.

It is a covenant *with all Israel*. God promises his church that it shall be extended to embrace all peoples; which promise is implied in the change of the name Abram to the covenant name *Abraham*. Say to Sarai, who was childless, that she shall become the mother of great multitudes. "Sing, O barren, thou that didst not bear; break forth with singing, and cry aloud, that thou didst not travail with child; for more are the children of the desolate than the children of the married wife, saith the Lord. Enlarge the place of thy tent, and let them stretch forth the curtains of thine habitations; spare not, lengthen thy cords, and strengthen thy stakes; for thou shalt break forth on the right hand and on the left; and thy seed shall inherit the gentiles, and make the desolate places to be inhabited." (Isaiah 54).

Abraham had been kept waiting until he was 99 years old, and Isaac was given him by a miracle; afterwards he sacrificed him, and was again given him by a new miracle. Herein there is a valuable lesson for us; study it, and let it edify you.

Gracious God, give us faith, and increase our faith. Help us to walk before thee. Confirm us in thy covenant, that against hope we may believe in hope and await the fulfilment of thy promise. Amen.

When tempests shake the world around, The rock-built Church secure is found; The gates of hell **may here assail** Whom Christ defends, but not prevail.

To God the Father, God the Son, And God the Spirit, Three in One, Be praise: do thou, whom we adore, Teach us to praise thee evermore.

---

55. Tuesday after Epiphany.

Verily, God is good to Israel, even to such as are pure in heart; Lord, let me be of them.

Isaiah 45, 4–8. For Jacob my servant's sake, and Israel mine **elect,** I have even called thee by thy name: I have surnamed thee, though thou hast not known me. I am the Lord, and there is none else, there is no God beside me: I girded thee, though thou hast not known me: That they may know from the rising of the sun, and from the west, that there is none beside me: I am the Lord, and there is none else. I form the light, and create darkness; I make peace, and create evil. I the Lord do all these things. Drop down, ye heavens, from above, and let the skies pour down righteousness; let the earth open, and let them bring forth salvation, and let righteousness spring up together. I the Lord have created it.

This is spoken to Cyrus, whom the Lord called to lead his people home from Babylon. Everything that happens in the world is done by the Lord for the sake of his people; this he teaches us clearly in our text. All kings and nobles, all men of rank and learning, all the rich and great, have by the Lord been given the positions that they hold, and been equipped with all that they have, in order that they may serve his church. He is the Lord, and there is none else. Cyrus and Nebuchadnezzar do not know it; Julian and Voltaire refuse to believe it; Alexander and Napoleon regard themselves as lords, and imagine that they can do whatever they like. But all of them are compelled to serve the Babe in the manger, the Man on the cross, the Lord at the right hand of God. Cyrus is also, in his way, a prototype of Christ in making arrangements for the return of God's people to Canaan. He is also called the anointed of the Lord, for the reason that God made him a mighty ruler, and called him to this work. The counsel of God for the salvation of the world governs the whole history of the world. Christ is the root on which all rests; therefore historic branches, reminding one of him, have been put forth even in the pagan world.—There are not, as the pagans have supposed, two original forces, light and darkness. There is but one God, and all things that come to pass are under his direction. There is, to be sure, a prince of darkness, also called the god of this world, by whom all sin came; but the evil that he does and the mischief that he causes, reach no farther than the Lord permits, and must in the end serve the cause of God's kingdom. Therefore every Christian shall feel firmly assured that Satan can not touch us without the permission of God, and that he can not, through his instruments, accomplish anything but that which God has ordained, as in the case of the Jews who murdered Christ. This is a most important and comforting truth. Hold it fast, and do not let the evil one delude you into the belief that he can do anything to you without permission of your heavenly Father. If you harbor this belief, it is merely a lie by means of which the tempter wants to lure you away from the rock on which you stand. No; Satan is powerless to harm a hair of your head without the permission of the Lord.—That Cyrus is a prototype of Christ is clearly indicated by the closing words of our text: "Drop down, ye heavens, from above, and let the skies pour down righteousness; let the earth open, and let them bring forth salvation, and let righteousness spring up together; I the Lord have created it." This is the blessing in Christ; it shall fill all the earth.

The name of the Lord be praised! Give us for that purpose a firm and childlike faith. Amen.

All hail the power of Jesus' name! Let angels prostrate fall; Bring
forth the royal diadem, And crown him Lord of all!
Ye seed of Israel's chosen race, Ye ransomed from the fall, Hail him who
saves you by his grace, and crown him Lord of all!

56. Wednesday after Epiphany.

*God hath concluded all in unbelief, that he might have mercy upon all.
Lord, help us to believe thy word.*

Jeremiah 31, 1-4. At the same time, saith the Lord, will I be the God
of all the families of Israel, and they shall be my people. Thus saith the
Lord, The people which were left of the sword found grace in the wilderness;
even Israel, when I went to cause him to rest. The Lord hath appeared of old
unto me, saying, Yea, I have loved thee with an everlasting love; therefore
with lovingkindness have I drawn thee. Again I will build thee, and thou
shalt be built, O virgin of Israel: thou shalt again be adorned with thy tabrets,
and shalt go forth in the dances of them that make merry.

Surely, the people of Israel is not in its entirety cast away; there
are many prophecies which encourage the hope that many Jews shall be
converted. Such conversions are always a cause of great rejoicing to
the church of God. It is to this people that the Lord has said: "I have
loved thee with an everlasting love; therefore with lovingkindness have
I drawn thee." Let us labor zealously for the conversion of pagans and
Jews, and let us earnestly pray: "Thy kingdom come." Then "shall
they come with weeping, and with supplications will he lead them;
he will cause them to walk by the river of waters in a straight way,
wherein they shall not stumble; for he is a father to Israel, and Ephraim
is his firstborn. He will bring them from the north country, and
gather them from the coasts of the earth." Is it possible that the
people of Israel continue to live only that they may be a curse and a
sign of wrath? No, the Lord has loved this people with an everlasting love; his bowels are troubled for Ephraim, and he surely shall
continue to perform his saving work upon him.

However, these words are true of you and me also, who by baptism and faith have been made members of Israel. Let this truth
come home to you today, and do you never forget it. Your God says
to you: "I have loved you with an everlasting love." Could anything
more glorious than this be spoken to you? Your heart must be harder
than stone, if this does not cause it to melt. If you would but hear
and believe these words of the Lord to you, it could not fail that
you would be unspeakably happy in the midst of the troubles and
sorrows of his earthly existence. God holds you in his heart from
everlasting to everlasting. Pause in your reading for some moments,
and let your mind dwell on this: God loves you with an everlasting
love. Verily, this is almost beyond belief; but God is such an one;
his love for us is greater than we can understand.—"Therefore with
lovingkindness have I drawn thee," says he, and brought thee near
to me. This I have, indeed, experienced, and do experience every

hour. I would never have come to thee, my God, hadst thou not
drawn me. This was lovingkindness on thy part; for I had deserved
something entirely different. Now, however, I shall surely be saved.
God is my God; his love and mercy govern me, he forgives me my
sins, he turns my sorrow into joy, gives me rest and happiness, and
places songs of gladness on my lips. His *eternal* love shall obtain
victory, and I am *eternally* saved.

Blessed be the Lord God, the God of Israel, who only doeth
wondrous things. And blessed be his holy name forever; and let the
whole earth be filled with his glory. Amen, and Amen.

Jesus, my truth, my way, My sure unerring light, On thee my feeble
soul I stay, Which thou wilt lead aright.

My wisdom and my guide, My counsellor thou art; O let me never leave
thy side, Nor from thy paths depart.

---

57. Thursday after Epiphany.

*Blessed be the Lord God, the God of Israel; and let the whole earth be
filled with his glory.*

Isaiah 45, 22–25. Look unto me, and be ye saved, all the ends of the
earth; for I am God, and there is none else. I have sworn by myself, the
word is gone out of my mouth in righteousness, and shall not return, That unto
me every knee shall bow, every tongue shall swear. Surely, shall one say,
in the Lord have I righteousness and strength: even to him shall men come:
and all that are incensed against him shall be ashamed. In the Lord shall all
the seed of Israel be justified, and shall glory.

It is the will of God that all people shall come to him and be
saved; and when he wills a thing he wills it earnestly. Our Bible
text for today is another of those faith-creating and faith-strengthen-
ing passages whereof the scriptures have so many, and wherein the
Lord assures us that he will reach the end at which he aims, in spite
of all obstacles. "Look unto me, and be ye saved, all the ends of the
earth," says he; "for I am God, and there is none else." When
the mouth of the Lord has spoken it, shall it not come true? Most
certainly, there are many in all parts of the earth who resist his call;
many who turn away from him, instead of turning to him, and who
are lost, instead of being saved. Whosoever refuses to accept the love
of God and be saved shall, of necessity, perish. But this shall not prevent the Lord from gathering unto himself a congregation of the
saved from all the ends of the earth. There is none other God than
the God of Israel, none other God than this one, whom we see and
know in Jesus Christ. Before him every knee shall bow, and every
tongue shall confess that in him only is there salvation. And as many
as believe in him shall glory in him; for they are justified and quickened in his name, and drawn together into a holy and glorious congregation. In what manner it shall come to pass that every knee of
"things under the earth," that is, of them that are lost, shall bow unto
the Lord Jesus, we do not know exactly; neither do we wish to know.

God preserve us, dear readers, from ever learning it of our own knowledge and experience! But this we do know that all who are saved shall be saved in Jesus; and we do know that all believers, all true children of Israel, shall be saved, and that every nation shall form a separate branch on the olive tree of Israel. When there shall be one fold and one shepherd, all the blessed shall be knit together into a unity in the Lord, and sin shall divide them no more. And yet every person shall preserve his individuality, and every people its identity; the glorified people of God shall consist in a unity of the multitude of nations (Matthew 28, 19; Revelations 21, 24). Note that the Lord says: "I have sworn by myself, the word is gone out of my mouth in righteousness, and shall not return." The object at which our mission work aims is certain and glorious.

Quicken our faith, O God, and make us feel assured that our labor is not in vain in the Lord. Amen.

O Spirit of the living God In all thy plenitude of grace, Where'er the foot of man hath trod, Descend upon our fallen race. Give tongues of fire and hearts of love To preach the reconciling Word; Give power and unction from above, Where'er the joyful sound is heard.

---

58. Friday after Epiphany.

God, teach us to know our nakedness; and do thou clothe us with the garment of righteousness. Amen.

Romans 10, 4–10. For Christ is the end of the law for righteousness to every one that believeth. For Moses describeth the righteousness which is of the law, That the man which doeth those things shall live by them. But the righteousness which is of faith speaketh on this wise, Say not in thine heart, Who shall ascend into heaven? (that is, to bring Christ down from above:) Or, who shall descend into the deep? (that is, to bring up Christ again from the dead.) But what saith it? The word is nigh thee, even in thy mouth, and in thy heart: that is, the word of faith, which we preach; That if thou shalt confess with thy mouth the Lord Jesus, and shalt believe in thine heart that God hath raised him from the dead, thou shalt be saved. For with the heart man believeth unto righteousness; and with the mouth confession is made unto salvation.

We note two things in this text: 1) "Christ is the end of the law for righteousness to every one that believeth;" 2) Christ is in the mouth and the heart of the believers by means of the word. Today we will consider only the first of these points: "Christ is the end of the law for righteousness to every one that believeth." This means: The law is a schoolmaster to bring us to Christ, has him as its goal; and, then again, Christ has fulfilled the law. Whosoever believes in Christ is justified from the curse of the law, and the love of the law is perfected in him. Paul is exceedingly zealous for the justice of God. There can be no abatement of the law's demands; there can be no haggling with the holy and just God. Do all that the law demands, all in its full sense inwardly and outwardly; have

76

love in its true intensity, and let it govern your every thought and word and deed; then shall the law justify you; but if you fall short of this, the law condemns you. Whosoever will recognize this, and earnestly strive to do it, shall feel the severe might of the law; he becomes a sinner, and is chastened to Christ. For Christ alone has fulfilled the law.—But he that in this way comes to Christ and believes on him, is regarded of God as being one with Christ; what Christ has done I have done, what Christ has suffered I have suffered; I have kept the law, because Christ has kept it for me; I have atoned for my transgressions, because Christ has suffered death for me. I have really come to the end of the law, and am rid of it and dead from it by the body of Christ; I no more belong to the law, but to him that died for me, and lives for me. The law is not destroyed, but fulfilled. Now it is being fulfilled in me, also; for now I love God and my neighbor with all my heart; and Christ in me shall perfect this love in my heart, until finally, at death, all my evil flesh and blood, which still is under the scourge of the law, shall be utterly destroyed.

The second lesson that is emphasized by our text, and that is equally as precious as is the first, we will by the grace of God consider tomorrow. Let your thoughts dwell on Christ today; and understand, that he is the end of the law for righteousness to every one that believeth.

O God, give us the open eyes of the Spirit to see the just demands of the law; and give us hearts which feel our sin with sorrow and believe in Jesus Christ, that we may in truth have part in his righteousness. Amen.

Christ, the life of all the living, Christ, the death of death our foe, Who, thyself for us once giving To the darkest depths of woe, Patiently didst yield thy breath But to save my soul from death: Thousand, thousand thanks shall be, Blessed Jesus, unto thee.

59. Saturday after Epiphany.

Lord, lay bare to our soul the glorious mysteries of thy word. Amen.

Romans 10, 4–10. For Christ is the end of the law, etc. (same as for the preceding day).

Yesterday we impressed on one another that portion of this text which teaches that Christ is the end of the law for righteousness to every one that believes. Closely connected with this truth is the one which we will particularly consider today; namely this, that Christ, by means of the word, is in the mouth and the heart of the believers. The righteousness which is of the *law* has *its* scriptural text: "This do, and thou shalt live." The righteousness which is of *faith* has *its* scripture text also: "Say not, who shall ascend into heaven, and bring Christ down? or, descend into the deep, and bring him up? The word is very nigh unto thee, in thy mouth and in thy heart." This passage is taken from Deuteronomy 30, 11–14. Paul here teaches us to find Christ everywhere in the scriptures, even in the passages in which we might least expect to discover him. Truly, this is a wonderful lesson in the proper manner of reading the Old Testament. In the word Christ is nearer to us than tongue can tell. You shall not trouble yourself to ascend and descend, or to go hither and thither, in order to be justified. The law places upon us the burdensome duty of doing the deeds commanded; but here, in the gospel, there is no room for any deeds as a means of obtaining righteousness. Do not attempt the irksome task of bringing Christ up from below, or down from above; be came to us long ago, is risen from the dead, has obtained victory over the kingdom of death, has taken away the curse of the law, has torn down the walls of our prison, and has been glorified, so that his power and his presence have no limit. Such he is in the word, in that word which his church preaches. When you have this word in your mouth and in your heart, then are you righteous; for then Christ, who became man for you, and died and is risen for you, is with you and in you, and every demand of the law has been satisfied. The glorified Savior is in the word; the very Christ, not merely his teaching and spirit and power; himself is in the word, and thereby he is in me, and I in him. I have long enough imagined that I must rise up to heaven on the wings of the spirit and of devotion in order to find him, or bury myself deep in the anguish of hell in order to become worthy of him. My soul flitted hither and thither. I knew the teaching of the gospel concerning justification of grace by faith alone, and my heart hungered after peace with God, but I thought that Christ must reveal himself to me from on high or from the deep; until, at last, the Spirit of God in the word succeeded in teaching me that Christ is there, there in the word. And now I want to say to you, my honest reader: Christ is near to you in the word. Do you not believe the word of God? Do you not credit the testimony of Paul? May the Spirit make this clear to you; else you will grope about in the dark, trying to find him who is with you already, in your mouth and in your heart.—Confess him in word and deed, as far as your knowledge reaches, and call upon his name; then shall affliction, sin. and distress teach you to find him in the word.

Do, dear God, let the scales fall from our eyes. Amen.

Abiding, steadfast, firm, and sure, The teachings of the word endure: Blest he who trusts this steadfast word, His anchor holds in Christ, the Lord.
We have a sure, prophetic word, By inspiration of the Lord; And though assailed on every hand, Jehovah's word shall ever stand.

---

60. First Sunday after Epiphany. I.

Let thy work appear unto thy servants, and thy glory unto their children.

Gospel Lesson, Luke 2, 42-52. And when he was twelve years old, they went up to Jerusalem, after the custom of the feast. And when they had fulfilled the days, as they returned, the child Jesus tarried behind in Jerusalem; and Joseph and his mother knew not of it. But they, supposing him to have been in the company, went a day's journey; and they sought him among their kinsfolk and acquaintance. And when they found him not, they turned back again to Jerusalem, seeking him. And it came to pass, that after three days they found him in the temple, sitting in the midst of the doctors, both hearing them, and asking them questions. And all that heard him were astonished at his understanding and answers. And when they saw him, they were amazed: and his mother said unto him, Son, why hast thou thus dealt with us? behold, thy father and I have sought thee sorrowing. And he said unto them, How is it that ye sought me? wist ye not that I must be about my Father's business? And they understood not the saying which he spake unto them. And he went down with them, and came to Nazareth, and was subject unto them: but his mother kept all these sayings in her heart. And Jesus increased in wisdom and stature, and in favor with God and man.

Jesus grew up in the same way as do other children. But his heart was pure, and his development was undisturbed by sin. "How is it that ye sought me? wist ye not that I must be about my Father's business?" These words,—the first recorded for us from his lips after he was made flesh, and the only ones that we hear of all that he spoke as a child,—are very significant. He was about his heavenly Father's business; always obedient, and doing his will.

Our children are baptized into Jesus, and they, also, shall by him grow up, and increase in wisdom and stature, and in favor with God and man. The good Spirit of God, which is given them in their baptism, shall surely accomplish this in them; but we parents are to be the servants of the Lord in furthering this work of grace. Here four things are especially important. 1) *Be diligent in prayer for your children.* Speak with God about them early and late, from their conception and birth until your death. When they weep, and when they smile; when they are well, and when they are ill; when they sleep, and when they are awake; let your prayers for them ascend with thanksgiving and faith to the Father in heaven; moisten and refresh them with your tears of supplication, and thus place them in the arms of the Savior. Follow them with your intercessions for them to the school, to their confirmation and holy communion, out from the home into the world full of dangers and temptations; let your prayers everywhere encircle them like a chain of mountains. If your child be poor, yet it is rich, if many prayers for it have been lodged with God. This heritage the child could not afford to exchange for all the gold of the multi-millionaire. 2) *Begin early to teach your children the word of God.* Jesus has said: "Baptize them, and teach them to observe all things whatsoever I have commanded you." Tell your children about Jesus; about his birth, childhood, obedience, love, suffering, death, and resurrection; about the glories of heaven, and the happiness of the blest with Abraham, Isaac, and Jacob; about the saints of God, and his pleasure in them; about Adam and paradise, Cain and Abel, Joseph and Daniel. Teach them the Ten Commandments, the Articles of the Creed, the Lord's Prayer and other prayers; do not leave this to the school; let the home be the temple of the Lord, and let this instruction in the word of God be *the mother's* sacred privilege.

Alas, what is to become of the unfortunate children who do not learn the word of God in their homes? 3) *Administer correction to your children* with good judgment and in love. The Spirit of God will strive against the evil which is in them, and which early comes to the surface; but their new life is like a tender plant needing support, and this you must give it by administering timely correction, and thereby helping them to practice selfdenial and obedience. "He that spareth his rod hateth his son; but he that loveth him chasteneth him betimes," says the wise Solomon. For wilfulness, lying, obstinacy, and similar sins you must punish your child, but never in wrath and bitterness; always calm, loving, suffering with the child, and zealous only against its sins. Do not scold or threaten, or exasperate; be firm, and true to your word; never effeminate and cowardly, never capricious and partial. 4) *Set them a good example in holiness.* Take care that you, yourself, walk before God as his child; let your children breathe the atmosphere of true piety in their homes. Keep up your faith and courage by the grace of God, in spite of all your infirmities; live in the covenant of your baptism, and renounce the devil, and all his works, and all his ways. God, who loves both you and your children with everlasting love in Christ, shall certainly strengthen you herein. It is a sorry condition of affairs when children are exhorted to that which is good, and punished for doing wrong, and at the same time see that their parents and teachers themselves live in sin. Woe to him that offends one of these little ones!

Practise these four things. Then if a strong and conscious growth of the new life does not appear in your children in their early age, it shall nevertheless not fail to appear later on. You and your house shall be saved. God himself has said it.

Help us hereto, heavenly Father, for Jesus' sake. Amen.

O blest the parents who give heed Unto their children's foremost need,
And weary not of care or cost: To them and heaven shall none be lost.
Blest such a house, it prospers well, In peace and joy the parents dwell;
And in their children's lot is shown How richly God can bless his own.

---

61. First Sunday after Epiphany. II.

We will hear what the Lord has commanded thee to speak to us.

Epistle Lesson, Romans 12, 1–5. I beseech you therefore, brethren, by the mercies of God, that ye present your bodies a living sacrifice, holy, acceptable unto God, which is your reasonable service. And be not conformed to this world: but be ye transformed by the renewing of your mind, that ye may prove what is that good, and acceptable, and perfect, will of God. For I say, through the grace given unto me, to every man that is among you, not to think of himself more highly than he ought to think; but to think soberly, according as God hath dealt to every man the measure of faith. For as we have many members in one body, and all members have not the same office; so we, being many, are one body in Christ, and every one members one of another.

Christ has, once for all, brought the sin- and guilt-offering for us, when he sacrificed himself. Shall we, then, not make any sacrifices? Yes, certainly, Christ sacrificed himself; we, also, shall give ourselves as an offering. We shall give God our heart, and present our bodies a living sacrifice, holy, acceptable, unto God. There is no more room for any atonement-offering, but we shall gladly bring to the Lord our thank-offering and our meat-offering. The children of the world give their bodies to the service of sin, and make them instruments of the devil. The believers shall use all their members in the service of Christ, and perform all their work on earth for him. We belong to him, and he employs us in the several vocations in which we are called to labor, as father, mother, child, servant, laborer, teacher, magistrate, etc. It is his will that we use all our faculties in deeds of charity, and employ our tongue in praising God, our hands in helping our neighbor, and our means in promoting the happiness of the poor. The world makes progress in that which is evil, and places an ever increasing distance between itself and God. The serpent in the wicked is nourished by their evil deeds, and grows from day to day; but the saints become more good every day; they reach a better understanding of the ways and the will of God, the humility of their heart increases, Christ takes a more pronounced shape in them, and their whole walk becomes more pleasing to God. The lower a level they reach in their humility, the deeper do they also penetrate into the sacrificial fire of Christ, into God's holy love; and the more tenderly are they united as members of one body. They understand that they live for the purpose of serving one another, and being sanctified with one another, until the whole church, the most pure, most glorious, most precious body of the Lord Jesus, becomes perfectly holy and pleasing before God.

Give me a calm, a thankful heart, From every murmur free; The blessings of thy grace impart, And let me live to thee.
Let the sweet hope that thou art mine My path of life attend; Thy presence through my journey shine, And crown my journey's end.

62. Monday after First Sunday after Epiphany.

Lord, thou knowest us; give us grace to hear thy word and keep thy ways. Amen.

Genesis 18, 17-19. And the Lord said, Shall I hide from Abraham that thing which I do; seeing that Abraham shall surely become a great and mighty nation, and all the nations of the earth shall be blessed in him? For I know him, that he will command his children and his household after him, and they shall keep the way of the Lord, to do justice and judgment; that the Lord may bring upon Abraham that which he hath spoken of him.

Of the Virgin Mary we read that she "kept all these things, and pondered them in her heart;" and, again, that she "kept all these sayings in her heart." This is great praise for Mary, and *she* was made the blessed among women. In that she so faithfully kept the word of God in her heart, she received the unspeakable grace and glory of instructing Jesus in the word of God. Abraham was blessed, and was made a blessing, became the progenitor of Christ, and the father of all the faithful, in that he kept the words of God in his heart. To his son Isaac the Lord says: "I will make thy seed to multiply as the stars of heaven, and will give unto thy seed all these countries; and in thy seed shall all the nations of the earth be blessed; because that Abraham obeyed my voice, and kept my charge, my commandments, my statues, and my laws." (Genesis 26, 4. 5). Our Lord Jesus himself was always about his Father's business; he lived and had his strength in the word of God, and was everywhere obedient. The faithful in all ages are like him, and shall *endeavor* to be like him. But to keep the word in the heart is to *think* on it, ponder it, let its truths pass in review and stand still before the mind's eye, seek to find and preserve its heavenly substance; furthermore, to *accept* the word as true, hold it fast, embrace it with the soul's trust, and never relax our hold of it; from which will follow sincere *obedience* to the word, so that this determines our course, and makes our whole life a divine service. Then the word of God becomes too precious to be lost, and it is our constant care that we may walk in the ways of the Lord,—the exact reverse of the course taken by the heathenish and unbelieving world.

The Lord desires to give this same grace to us; for which reason he has given us his word. The worldly-minded despise it, and rob their children and their household of this blessing; as the servants of Satan they even take pains to rob our people of this their true happiness. The Christians must let themselves be fired with zeal for the word of the Lord, and in very truth make their hearts and homes his temples. Are you willing to leave your children behind you in this wicked world without having given them the word of God in their hearts as a shield and weapon against the devil? God forbid! May the Lord declare concerning us: I will surely bless him and his kindred; for I know him, that he commands his children and his household to keep the way of the Lord, hold his word sacred, and gladly hear and learn it.

Thy testimonies have I taken as an heritage for ever; for they are the rejoicing of my heart. I have inclined mine heart to perform thy statutes alway, even unto the end. I hate vain thoughts; but thy law do I love. Thou art my hiding place and my shield; I hope in thy word. Amen.

The word of God's our heritage; God grant we lose it never! May we and ours, from age to age, Exalt and praise it ever; It is our help alway, In life and death our stay; O God, while worlds endure, Preserve thy statutes pure To us and to our children.

---

63. Tuesday after First Sunday after Epiphany.

Lord, let our young people take heed according to thy word, that they cleanse their way.

2 Timothy 3, 14–17. But continue thou in the things which thou hast learned and hast been assured of, knowing of whom thou hast learned them; and that from a child thou hast known the holy scriptures, which are able to make thee wise unto salvation through faith which is in Christ Jesus. All scripture is given by inspiration of God, and is profitable for doctrine, for reproof, for correction, for instruction in righteousness; that the man of God may be perfect, throughly furnished unto all good works.

We do not doubt that the Spirit of God has through the baptism of our children created a new life in them. All life must, however, be nourished, if it is to grow and not die. The word of God is the nourishment of the spiritual life, for the little ones as well as for those of larger growth. Children do not, themselves, know enough to feed their souls with the bread of the word; hence it is the duty of the parents to care for this matter. Eunice had done this with her son Timothy, and thus Paul can write to him: "I greatly desire to see thee, being mindful of thy tears, that I may be filled with joy; when I call to remembrance the unfeigned faith that is in thee, which dwelt first in thy grandmother Lois, and in thy mother Eunice; and I am persuaded that it dwelleth in thee also." This is a grand thing to say to a young man. From a child Timothy had known the holy scriptures, which are able to make one wise unto salvation through faith in Christ Jesus.—It should be thus in the case of our children and young people, also. Let this be a burning question in our mind and soul. Ask the Lord to give you wisdom and grace in this matter, ye Christian fathers and mothers! It is necessary that your own hearts live in the word of God; for only that which comes from the heart makes its way to the heart. You must not trouble your children with the dead letter of the scriptures, but give them the spiritual and sincere milk of the word. Neither must you seek to cast their manner of life in your moulds, nor measure their experience of sin and grace according to your measure, nor overload them with instruction or admonition. The flesh must be brought into subjection, and in this work you must help your children by exercising Christian discipline; but the growth of the new life itself can not be forced by a surfeit of spiritual nourishment. How prone we are, alas, to step aside from the path in one direction or in the other! Many neglect to teach their children the word of God, and this is directly contrary to the Lord's command. They shift their duty over on to the schools, and let the home be a place of heathenism. Others surfeit their children with the word of God at all times and seasons, thereby creating aversion instead of love for the word, and closing the young hearts to the Spirit of God. Again I say: Pray earnestly to God for wisdom to give the children proper instruction, in order that the man of God may be perfect, thoroughly furnished unto all good works. For Jesus' sake, do not neglect this! God will surely give you all the grace necessary to the performance of this duty. Read James 1, 5.

Lord, give to us parents the Spirit of wisdom and understanding and the strength of love, that our children may, by the instruction and discipline of thy word, be regenerated, sanctified, and saved. Amen.

O blessed house, where little children tender Are laid upon thy heart, with hands of prayer, Thou friend of children, who wilt freely render To them more than a mother's loving care; Where round thy feet they gather, to thee clinging, And hear thy loving voice most willingly, And in their songs, thy hearty praises ringing, Rejoice in thee, O blessed Lord, in thee.

64. Wednesday after First Sunday after Epiphany.

Lord our God, from thee have we received our children, and we return them to thee; let them be thine in time and eternity. Amen.

1 Samuel 1, 20. 24–28. Wherefore it came to pass, when the time was come about after Hannah had conceived, that she bare a son, and called his name Samuel, saying, Because I have asked him of the Lord. And when she had weaned him, she took him up with her, with three bullocks, and one ephah of flour, and a bottle of wine, and brought him unto the house of the Lord in Shiloh; and the child was young. And they slew a bullock, and brought the child to Eli. And she said, Oh, my lord, as thy soul liveth, my lord, I am the woman that stood by thee here, praying unto the Lord. For this child I prayed; and the Lord hath given me my petition which I asked of him: Therefore also I have lent him to the Lord; as long as he liveth he shall be lent to the Lord. And he worshipped the Lord there.

Do like Hannah: Grant your children to the Lord as long as they live. He will receive them, and employ them in his service for some good purpose, and he will take them home to heaven. We may certainly hope that the children whom their parents give to the Lord with believing and persistent prayer, shall become blessed and happy men and women. There are countless possibilities before the little child. Many of the grandest men in the world have been nursed in poverty, and the parents never dreamed that the little boy in their humble cottage was destined to become a blessing to thousands. But the men and women who fill our prisons for criminals, and who fill their own hearts with falsehood and the poison of hell; they, also, were at one time little children; Cain and Judas, as well as Noah and Isaac, were the hope of their parents. Still, God creates no one in order to destroy him. There is no inexorable evil fate hanging over any of our children; there is no necessity which compels them to become vessels of wrath. God gives to reprobation only such as give themselves to reprobation and refuse his mercy. It is to such as these that God says: "Even for this same purpose have I raised thee up, that I might show my power in thee." Do you think that any have become the children of perdition whom the parents carried often to the Lord in prayer, and whom they gave into his keeping? Most certainly not. Nevertheless, pray for grace to bring your children as an offering to the Lord, even as Abraham made an offering of

Isaac, and as Hannah made an offering of Samuel. Your own heart, also, must be a part of the offering; "every one shall be salted with fire, and every sacrifice shall be salted with salt." To be sure, we often see that the children of godly men go wrong. The sons of Samuel, Absalon, Ahaz, and others had pious fathers, and still became ill-fated men. But is it certain, after all, that their parents prayed sedulously for them? Have not even the saints shown, in many matters of grave importance, that they were far from being perfect? Can the promises of God fail, do you think? Shall a child of prayer perish? Impossible! Whatever the will of God in regard to the worldly estate of your sons and daughters, whether it is to be high or lowly; they shall become a blessing, if you early and unceasingly give them to the Lord, and pray for them, trusting in God's promises. He gave them to you, and you gave them back to him in their baptism; continue to give them to him in sincere faith and devotion, regard them and treat them as belonging to him. In truth, they are his own. Shall Satan, then, have power over them? Nevermore! Is this not a blessing of blessings? God be praised for his mercy! We and all ours shall be saved. And not this alone, but they shall also serve the Lord here. Help us, O God, to believe, and gladly to give ourselves and our children as offerings to thee, for Jesus' sake. Amen.

Tender Shephard, never leave us From thy fold to go astray; By thy look of love directed, May we walk the narrow way; Thus direct us, and protect us, Lest we fall an easy prey.

---

65. Thursday after First Sunday after Epiphany.

Psalm 119, 9–20. Wherewithal shall a young man cleanse his way? By taking heed thereto according to thy word. With my whole heart have I sought thee: O let me not wander from thy commandments. Thy word have I hid in mine heart, that I might not sin against thee. Blessed art thou, O Lord: teach me thy statutes. With my lips have I declared all the judgments of thy mouth. I have rejoiced in the way of thy testimonies as much as in all riches. I will meditate in thy precepts, and have respect unto thy ways. I will delight myself in thy statutes: I will not forget thy word. Deal bountifully with thy servant, that I may live, and keep thy word. Open thou mine eyes, that I may behold wondrous things out of thy law. I am a stranger in the earth; hide not thy commandments from me. My soul breaketh for the longing that it hath unto thy judgments at all times.

None other has followed the word of God as closely as did our Lord Jesus, and none other has kept his way as clean as he. He loved his Father's ordinances, and delighted himself in them, and kept his word in his heart; and he is lovable in the sight of God, and comely and fair above any other among the children of men. We will earnestly strive to be like him. Dear young people; do you rejoice in the word of God? If you do not, you are on an unclean and slippery path; the trail that you are following does not lead to the home of light and glory. Reverse your steps, and begin to love the word of the Lord. You have a Bible, which you received as a baptismal gift, or at the time of your confirmation; or if not, there surely is a Bible in your home, or you may easily procure one for yourself. Begin to read it daily, first the books of the New Testament in their sequence, then the Pentateuch, the Psalms, and the Prophets; then the New Testament again, and thereafter the whole Bible. Read with careful attention, ask God to enlighten you that you may understand the word, and *obey* it with honest soul. Do not neglect the divine services in the church, and do not let the wicked one come and catch away the word from you,while you hear it, or while you are on your way to your home. I beseech you by the love of God and by your precious covenant of baptism, obey my advice, keep the word of the Lord in your heart. Would you not like to keep your way clean? Would you not like to resemble Jesus? You aspire to life and happiness, and imagine that you will find them in the pleasures of the world. David rejoiced in the testimonies, and delighted himself in the decrees of the Lord; and with the deepest yearning of his soul he prayed that he might behold the wondrous things in the law of the Lord; that he might live and walk according to the word of God. Should not you do likewise? Verily, it is your sworn enemy who shuts your heart to the word of God. You are a child of God from the hour of your baptism; the Father loves you, Jesus loves you, the Holy Ghost loves you, the holy angels, also, love you. Do not pollute your path with ungodliness, but say in earnestness, sincerity, and fear of God: "Lord, thy word have I hid in mine heart, that I might not sin against thee."

Teach me, O Lord, the way of thy statutes; and I shall keep it unto the end. Turn away mine eyes from beholding vanity; and quicken thou me in thy way. Amen.

Savior! like a shepherd lead us; Much we need thy tend'rest care; In thy pleasant pastures feed us, For our use thy folds prepare. Blessed Jesus, blessed Jesus! Thou hast bought us, thine we are.

66. Friday after First Sunday after Epiphany.

Lord Jesus, give us thy love and obedience. Amen.

John 4, 30–34. Then they went out of the city, and came unto him. In the mean while his disciples prayed him, saying, Master, eat. But he said unto them, I have meat to eat that ye know not of. Therefore said the disciples one to another, Hath any man brought him ought to eat? Jesus said unto them, My meat is to do the will of him that sent me, and to finish his work.

"Wist ye not that I must be about my Fathers business?" Thus spoke Jesus in the temple, and thereby wrote, as it were, the superscription over his whole life. The words of the Father were his delight; obedience to the Father was his life. In our scripture text for today he says: "My meat is to do the will of him that sent me, and to finish his work." He is so entirely resigned, and even devoted, to the will of his Father for the salvation of sinners, that his body, also, is refreshed and revived when he fulfils this purpose, and souls hereby are rescued from death. Hungry and thirsty he sits at the well of Sychar; but to save the Samaritans with the word of life is his meat and drink. The work which his Father had given him was to be accomplished through the most bitter suffering and the keenest agony of death; yet his Father's will was his meat. How unspeakably great, how entirely complete is his loving obedience to the Father, and his loving desire to save us! He goes to his death with such willingness, that he says concerning this will of his Father: It is my meat; it refreshes me, and gives me strength.

What a wealth of life there is for us herein! How full and complete is the righteousness in which we stand clothed before the Father; and what a shining example has been given us for our guidance!

Lord Jesus, we thank thee for all that thou hast done; but we feel that our thanks are nothing as compared with thy boundless love. Thou blessed and glorious God; praise be to thee for thy precious name Jesus, and for all the salvation for us which is contained in that name. Give us thy righteousness, and let thy mind be in us. Give us this grace, that thy will may more and more be our meat, our delight, and our strength, so that we willingly, yea gladly, take up the cross and carry it after thee. Amen.

My God, my Father, while I stray Far from my home, on life's rough way, O teach me from my heart to say, Thy will be done!

Though dark my path and sad my lot, Let me be still and murmur not, Or breathe the prayer divinely taught, Thy will be done!

---

67. Saturday after First Sunday after Epiphany.

Teach me, O Lord, the way of thy statutes; and I shall keep it unto the end. Amen.

Ecclesiastes 11, 9. 10; 12, 1. 2. Rejoice, O young man, in thy youth, and let thy heart cheer thee in the days of thy youth, and walk in the ways of thine heart, and in the sight of thine eyes: but know thou, that for all these things God will bring thee into judgment. Therefore remove sorrow from thy heart, and put away evil from thy flesh: for childhood and youth are vanity. Remember now thy Creator in the days of thy youth, while the evil days come not, nor the years draw nigh, when thou shalt say, I have no pleasure in them; while the sun, or the light, or the .moon, or the stars, be not darkened; nor the clouds return after rain.

Young and healthy trees are luxuriant; young and healthy-minded people are happy. It is a disease, and contrary to nature, when young people mope, see everything in dark colors, and feel life a bitter mockery. Can a child, a healthy and unaffected child, go about mourning? Is it not the child's lot and privilege to be happy? Be they poor or rich, the children are merry and cheerful. This is true, also, of the children of larger growth, the young people, as long as they preserve their childlike disposition. We do not wish our young people to be childish, nor given to levity, nor callous to sorrow, nor unmindful of the serious things of life; but we do wish that, while their understanding is being developed, and they feel the burdens trom which not even youth is exempt, they yet may keep intact their childlike disposition, their roseate view, and their cheerful courage. This can not be, however, unless true piety and fear of God govern in the soul from childhood. Otherwise all manner of wickedness holds sway in the heart; and then, farewell to the child's buoyancy of spirit and brightness of eye. When the young man walks before his God, and daily renews the covenant of his baptism, not by a mere perfunctory repetition of the formula of renunciation and the creed, but with sincere prayer and true faith; when he flees youthful lusts, but trains himself in selfdenial and piety, and follows charity, purity, and an unfeigned faith; when the name of Jesus is the sun that lights his way, and the word of God is his load-star which he always consults in order to learn how to act and what to do;—then the glad spirit of childhood can be preserved through the time of youth, be shaped into the firmness of manhood, and give happiness even in the gloomy days of old age. This is what the Preacher means in our scripture text. But, alas, how difficult a matter this is, especially in our times. Children ripen too early, and hence the young people become peevish children. Vexations and wickedness fill their hearts; their minds are full of vanity and bitterness and foolish dreams of ambition, and they are a long way from remembering their Creator. What, then, must their old age become! Lord, have mercy on us. Enlighten old and young with thy Holy Spirit, and give us true fear of God in our hearts.

Father of eternal grace, Glorify thyself in me! Meekly beaming in my face, May the world thine image see.
Happy only in thy love, Poor, unfriended, or unknown, Fix my thoughts on things above; Stay my heart on thee alone.

68. Second Sunday after Epiphany. I.

Lord Jesus, come to us, and abide with us; unite our hearts in thee, and sanctify our homes. Amen.

Gospel Lesson, John 2, 1-11. And the third day there was a marriage in Cana of Galilee; and the mother of Jesus was there: And both Jesus was called, and his disciples, to the marriage. And when they wanted wine, the mother of Jesus saith unto him, They have no wine. Jesus saith unto her, Woman, what have I to do with thee? mine hour is not yet come. His mother saith unto the servants, Whatsoever he saith unto you, do it. And there were set there six waterpots of stone, after the manner of the purifying of the Jews, containing two or three firkins apiece. Jesus saith unto them, Fill the waterpots with water. And they filled them up to the brim. And he saith unto them, Draw out now, and bear unto the governor of the feast. And they bare it. When the ruler of the feast had tasted the water that was made wine, and know not whence it was: (but the servants which drew the water knew;) the governor of the feast called the bridegroom, and saith unto him, Every man at the beginning doth set forth good wine; and when men have well drunk, then that which is worse: but thou hast kept the good wine until now. This beginning of miracles did Jesus in Cana of Galilee, and manifested forth his glory; and his disciples believed on him.

Jesus did his first miracle before the eyes of his disciples on the occasion of a marriage; and it consisted in turning water into wine, and transforming the sadness of the bridal house into gladness. The marriage relation is the root of human society, planted by God at the creation, and holy from the beginning. But it was corrupted by the fall of man, and the devil continues to rage against it; for he knows that when he destroys the marriage institution, he undermines all social order, and makes us like unto Sodom and Gomorrah. This is the purpose of the doctrine of free love, in the preaching of which the evil enemy is now busying himself.—As many as wish to follow the Lord Jesus must heartily hate this invention of the devil, and maintain the sacred integrity of the marriage tie. Why did the Lord choose a wedding for the first manifestation of his glory? Why was his first miracle done to assist this young bridal pair? He is come to drive the devil out of the house, and to create for himself not only individual saints, but a saintly, or holy *people*. He takes the children into his embrace by means of their baptism; educates the young people by the instruction of the word to fear God; is with them in their wedded life, and makes it a holy estate; and sanctifies their children. In this way the Lord prepares unto himself a bride on earth (Ephesians 5). He watches over the wedded pair with especial solicitude. It is he who brings the bride and bridegroom together. It is in accordance with his decree that they find each other, often in a wonderful way, and directly contrary to all human calculation. Most assuredly there will come many trials of various kinds into the married life of all pious people; they will have temptations and troubles of many sorts; but in the Lord's own good time this water will be turned into wine. Very thin wine, and a too scanty supply, and only the waterpots filled to the brim;—this is the condition of affairs where Jesus is one of the wedding guests; but in the end this poor cheer becomes the choicest wine. However, Jesus will himself fix the time; and even his mother must submit to his decision.—Let us, then, have Jesus with us in our wedding and in our everyday life. He transforms the water of our sinful wretchedness into the wine of holiness and glory. By the wondrous power of his Spirit he renews and elevates our family and social life, and makes us a happy people that shall sing his praises and be perfected at last as the blessed bride of the Lamb, the bride who shall drink of the new wine with him in his kingdom.—Lord Jesus, teach us to pray thee to be a guest in our weddings; and do thou come to us, and sanctify our home life. Be our guide and ruler, and help us thou who alone canst help. Amen.

O blest the house, whate'er befall, Where Jesus Christ is all in all; Yea, if he were not dwelling there, How poor and dark and void it were!
O blest that house where faith ye find, And all within have set their mind To trust their God and serve him still, And do, in all, his holy will.

69. Second Sunday after Epiphany. II.

Blessed is the man whose strength is in thee, in whose heart are the high-ways to Zion.

Epistle Lesson, Romans 12, 6–16. Having then gifts differing according to the grace that is given to us, whether prophecy, let us prophesy according to the proportion of faith; or ministry, let us wait· on our ministering; or he that teacheth, on teaching; or he that exhorteth, on exhortation: he that giveth, let him do it with simplicity; he that ruleth, with diligence; he that sheweth mercy, with cheerfulness. Let love be without dissimulation. Abhor that which is evil; cleave to that which is good. Be kindly affectioned one to another with brotherly love; in honor preferring one another; not slothful in business; fervent in spirit; serving the Lord; rejoicing in hope; patient in tribulation; continuing instant in prayer; distributing to the necessity of saints; given to hospitality. Bless them which persecute you: bless, and curse not. Rejoice with them that do rejoice, and weep with them that weep. Be of the same mind one toward another. Mind not high things, but condescend to men of low estate. Be not wise in your own conceits.

What glorious exhortations! May they be followed in our daily life. Let our hearts be full of unfeigned piety; holy abhorrence of that which is evil; genuine delight in that which is good; hearty affection, brotherly love, and true respect for one another; burning zeal in the service of the Lord; joy in hope, patience in tribulation, and perseverance in prayer. Let us distribute to the necessity of the saints, exercise hospitality, bless them which persecute us, rejoice with them that do rejoice, and weep with them that weep, and be joined together in the same mind and judgment. Let these virtues, with humility, modesty, and a holy contempt for the pride and greatness of the world, adorn our walk, fill our houses, and characterize the Christian homes. Jesus is here, and will work this in us, dear friends. Let us have faith in his miraculous power, live in it, and make use of it. Miraculous power is required, no doubt of that; natural piety will fall short. You have yourself and the devil and the whole world against you; you must all the time sail against the stream, and must not give way to self-will, unbelief, sloth, and the wickedness which you see in the world about you. However, the miraculous power of Jesus is here. He says only: "Fill the waterpots with water to the brim, and draw out now, and bear to the governor of the feast;" and there is in his words a power which causes the servants to do as they are ordered, though it seems utterly unreasonable; a power which likewise has the effect that the water which they draw is wine. He works in us that which the apostle says that we must do. Command, Lord, what thou wilt; and do thou also work in us that which thou dost command. This is our sincere prayer. Help us to obey the exhortations of thy apostle. We hunger and thirst after this blessing; let us receive it by the mighty power of thy rich grace. Amen.

O that the Lord would guide my ways, To keep his statutes still! O that my God would grant me grace To know and do his will!
Make me to walk in thy commands; 'Tis a delightful road; Nor let my head. or heart, or hands, Offend against my God.

70. Monday after Second Sunday after Epiphany.

As for me and my house, we will serve the Lord.

Genesis 24, 1–7. And Abraham was old, and well stricken in age: and the Lord had blessed Abraham in all things. And Abraham said unto his eldest servant of his house, that ruled over all that he had, Put, I pray thee, thy hand under my thigh; and I will make thee swear by the Lord, the God of heaven, and the God of the earth, that thou shalt not take a wife unto my son of the daughters of the Canaanites, among who I dwell: But thou shalt go unto my country, and to my kindred, and take a wife unto my son Isaac. And the servant said unto him, Peradventure the woman will not be willing to follow me unto this land: must I needs bring thy son again unto the land from whence thou camest? And Abraham said unto him, Beware thou, that thou bring not my son thither again. The Lord God of heaven, which took me from my father's house and from the land of my kindred, and which spake unto me, and that sware unto me, saying, Unto thy seed will I give this land, he shall send his angel before thee; and thou shalt take a wife unto my son from thence.

It would be well, if many parents were as solicitous for the welfare of their children as Abraham was for the welfare of Isaac, so that they would do everything possible to secure for them a *Christian* and happy marriage. But is this the case among us? Many parents show great zeal in helping their children to marry money; but the question whether the daughter-in-law be a pious or wicked woman is one with which they are not concerned. Even such a man as the pious King Jehoshaphat forms an alliance by marriage with the ungodly Ahab, and takes the wicked daughter of this man as a wife for his son. It often seems that even Christian parents are more interested in marrying their child to one that is rich, than to one that fears God. Parents should not force upon their children a marriage that is distasteful to them; but they should possess the full confidence of their sons and daughters; in order that they may place experience, wisdom, and Christian judgment in the balance, and give the young people valuable assistance in making their choice. Parents should pray for their children, as Eliezer prayed when he went forth to do the bidding of Abraham and find a wife for his son Isaac; and they should do like Rebekah's parents, who said: "Let us call the damsel and enquire of her, if she will go with this man." Then it can not fail that the Lord will send his angel, and bring bride and bridegroom together according to his own good will.—A happy marriage between a believer and an unbeliever is *possible*, and it is also *possible* that the believing husband or wife may be so fortunate as to win the other for the Lord; but there never can be a complete unity of heart between the two while they go their several ways. And "what knewest thou, O wife, whether thou shalt save thy husband? or how knowest thou, O man, whether thou shalt save thy wife?" The scriptures contain no promise that a woman of heathen mind shall be a blessing to the house of an Israelite. The very opposite is true. Christian parents and their sons should remember the daughter of Beeri, and the daughter of Elon, and the daughter of Ahab. They are mentioned in the Bible as a warning to us. (Genesis 26, 34. 35. 2 Chronicles 18, 1; 21, 5. 6). Be assured that God will give to your sons pious wives, and to your daughters god-fearing husbands, if you appeal to him in prayer, and guide them with kindness. "The price of a virtuous woman is far above rubies. Favor is deceitful, and beauty is vain; but a woman that feareth the Lord, she shall be praised."

God, give our young men and women piety and love in their hearts; bless them with good sense, and make them industrious in their vocations. Preserve us from unhappy marriages, and let the bond of perfection unite man and wife in the palaces of the rich and the cottages of the poor. This is our heartfelt prayer. Hear us for Jesus' sake. Amen.

O blessed house, where man and wife, united In thy true love, have both one heart and mind; Where both to thy salvation are invited, And in thy doctrine both contentment find; Where both, to thee in truth for ever cleaving, In joy, in grief, make thee their only stay, And fondly hope in thee to be believing, Both in the good and in the evil day.

---

71. Tuesday after Second Sunday after Epiphany.

Lord, unite our hearts to thee in the fellowship of love. Amen.

Ephesians 5, 22–33. Wives, submit yourselves unto your own husbands, as unto the Lord. For the husband is the head of the wife, even as Christ is the head of the church: and he is the savior of the body. Therefore as the church is subject unto Christ, so let the wives be to their own husbands in every thing. Husbands, love your wives, even as Christ also loved the church, and gave himself for it; that he might sanctify and cleanse it with the washing of water by the word, that he might present it to himself a glorious church, not having spot, or wrinkle, or any such thing; but that it should be holy and without blemish. So ought men to love their wives as their own bodies. He that loveth his wife loveth himself. For no man ever yet hated his own flesh; but nourisheth and cherisheth it, even as the Lord the church: For we are members of his body, of his flesh, and of his bones. For this cause shall a man leave his father and mother, and shall be joined unto his wife, and they two shall be one flesh. This is a great mystery: but I speak concerning Christ and the church. Nevertheless, let every one of you in particular, so love his wife even as himself; and the wife see that she reverence her husband.

Christ loved the church, and gave himself for it. He left everything for the sake of his church, and gave to this his whole heart; he forgot his divine glory, the heavenly hosts, and all creation; and he came to us, became a man, and sacrificed himself in death, in order that he might win his bride. In baptism he sets her apart from the world, makes her pure, and adorns her with the mantle of his holiness, the proper and becoming ornament of the bride who is to stand at his side before the face of God the Father; and in the Holy Supper he nourishes her with his body and blood. She is sprung from him, as Eve from Adam; she is of his flesh and bone, and in the union with him she lives and grows. He thus wins her undivided love; he tolerates no rival in her affections, but must have her whole heart. And thus the church is in an indissoluble, everlasting, holy marriage covenant with the Lord. It is his work, and on his part everything necessary has been done; therefore the apostle speaks of the holiness of the church as already perfect.

Of this mystery the Christian marriage between man and woman is not only a symbol; it has its root in the union of Christ and the church. If this were not true, how could the apostle, as he does in our text, treat these two unions as one? The union of the Lord with sanctified mankind is the deep and eternal social idea in which all true forms of human society have their origin; and of these the marriage institution is in every respect the first.—How much of encouragement and admonition is there not in this conception of the nature of the union between the Christian man and woman! With the self-denying and self-sacrificing love of Christ the husband shall live with his wife, and help her to grow in holiness; with the tenderness and gentleness of Christ he shall carry her in his heart; and there he shall keep her, not with unclean desire or mean jealousy, but with that unselfish love which, for the sake of her own happiness, wishes her heart to be his. And the woman shall trustfully and gladly give herself into her husband's keeping; esteem him highly for Christ's sake, in spite of his human infirmities; be his faithful helpmeet; and "in that which is not corruptible, even the ornament of meek and quiet spirit," let her make of his house a home of peace, the place of all on earth the best, for the husband. It is a great problem, but it will pay well to work it out. Let none lose heart who believes in Christ. You dwell in the same house with him; he is your wedded husband, who nourishes and strengthens you with his life.

Dear Lord Jesus, we thank thee for thy great grace. Give us thy Spirit, that we may believe; and quicken and sanctify us in thee. Amen.

Renew my will from day to day, Blend it with thine, and take away All that now makes it hard to say, Thy will be done!
Then, when on earth I breathe no more The prayer oft mixed with tears before, I'll sing upon a happier shore, Thy will be done!

---

72. Wednesday after Second Sunday after Epiphany.

The God of patience and consolation grant us to be likeminded according to Christ Jesus. Amen.

James I, 2-12. My brethren, count it all joy when ye fall into divers temptations. Knowing this, that the trying of your faith worketh patience. But let patience have her perfect work, that ye may be perfect and entire, wanting nothing. If any of you lack wisdom, let him ask of God, that giveth to all men liberally, and upbraideth not; and it shall be given him. But let him ask in faith, nothing wavering. For he that wavereth is like a wave of the sea, driven with the wind and tossed. For let not that man think that he shall receive anything of the Lord. A double minded man is unstable in all his ways. Let the brother of low degree rejoice in that he is exalted: But the rich, in that he is made low: because as the flower of the grass he shall pass away. For the sun is no sooner risen with a burning heat, but it withereth the grass, and the flower thereof falleth, and the grace of the fashion of it perisheth: so also shall the rich man fade away in his ways.

Afflictions always come to them in whose heart and house Jesus reigns. It is necessary that we be tried in suffering; for by this means, only, can our hearts learn not to put their trust in the things of this world. I have a hundred times read and thought that I must not expect a quiet, easy time on earth; but before I am aware of it, I have again found myself dreaming that when this or that thing is over, or when such or such an object has been reached, then I will have an earthly paradise, and will take my ease and enjoy myself. Yes, precious soul; you certainly shall receive ample riches, complete rest, and unmixed enjoyment; not, however, before you reach heaven. In order that you may attain this end, it is necessary that you suffer here on earth, and learn to rejoice and glory in your tribulations. You could, were you so disposed, cut loose, depart from the Lord, and seek enjoyment in the pleasures of the world. You might, possibly, find some sort of happiness herein for a short time; but then, you do not know what tomorrow may bring forth. For what is your life? It is even a "vapor, that appeareth for a little time, and then vanisheth away." Earthly wealth and splendor wither like the flowers of the grass. Patience is the only road to daily happiness. As a Christian you must needs have trouble and pain, in order that the old Adam may die with his love of fleeting riches and honor, his craving for sensual pleasures, his unclean lusts, and all his variety of idolatrous ways. You must learn to trust in God alone; you will need to believe in him with your whole heart in order to obtain the victory over your terrible enemies, Satan and death. But such a whole heart you neither have nor can receive except through tribulations. For whether we be rich or poor, we are fond of having some of the good things of this world in reserve; whether we be gross sinners or fine and pious folk, we are prone to trust a little in ourselves. Patience, only, produces a perfect work. The Lord gives, and takes away; leads into the fire, and out of it; permits the devil and the flesh and the world to tempt us. The rich must learn to rejoice in that he is made low; and the one of low degree, in that he is exalted. Thus shall the heart belong wholly to the Lord, and he alone shall be the rock of our reliance. He has promised us wisdom; that is, knowledge of his ways and purposes, in order that we may rejoice and thank him for all things; and he has promised to give us at last the crown of life. Blessed is he that has him alone as his God. To this end he helps us by means of our sufferings. Count it, then, all joy when ye fall into divers temptations. The filled waterpots are vessels full of wine.

Dear heavenly Father, give us true wisdom; give us grace to believe in thee with whole hearts; give us patience, that we may honor

94

thee by rendering thanks to thee for our sufferings; and finally, when our trials are done, give us the crown of life. Amen.

What our Father does is well: Blessed truth! his children tell! Though he send, for plenty, want, Though the harvest store be scant, Yet we rest upon his love, Seeking better things above.

73. Thursday after Second Sunday after Epiphany.

The way of the righteous is made plain. Lord, let me be found among them.

John 1, 47-51. Jesus saw Nathanael coming to him, and saith of him, Behold an Israelite indeed, in whom is no guile! Nathanael saith unto him, Whence knowest thou me? Jesus answered and said unto him, Before that Philip called thee, when thou wast under the fig tree, I saw thee. Nathanael answered and saith unto him, Rabbi, thou art the Son of God; thou art the King of Israel. Jesus answered and said unto him, Because I said unto thee, I saw thee under the fig tree, believest thou? thou shalt see greater things than these. And he saith unto him, Verily, verily, I say unto you, Hereafter ye shall see heaven open, and the angels of God ascending and descending upon the Son of man.

Nathanael was not only one of those of whom the Bible says that "blessed are they in whose spirit is no guile;" but there was in him a peculiar simplicity of soul, which the Lord can not give to all, even if they are upright and true Christians, but which is especially precious and pleasing to him. The Nathanael-souls are pearls among God's people. However, uprightness there must be in all disciples of Jesus. Only the pure eye is bright enough to see God. But this really does see him. Sarai's maid called the name of the angel of the Lord that spoke to her: "Thou God seest me; for she said: Have I also here looked after him that seeth me?" (Genesis 16, 13). The eyes of the Lord were upon Nathanael, and his ears had marked his prayers. "Before that Philip called thee, when thou wast under the fig tree, I saw thee." Then Nathanael answered and said to him: "Rabbi, thou art the Son of God; thou art the King of Israel." And he saw heaven open, and the angels of God ascending and descending upon the Son of man. First God comes to us, then we to him. First he sees us, and descends; then we see him, and ascend. "This ascending and descending of the angels," says Luther, "is precisely the mystery, that God and man are in one and the same person. It is the great and unspeakable glory of the human race, which none may utter, that, by this wonderful union, God has united the human nature with himself. Hence we are by faith carried up, and become one flesh with Christ. We ascend to him; but, before we can do this, he descends to us through the word and sacraments, instructing and training us in the knowledge of him." God give us the light of faith, the single eye, which sees things invisible; then shall we see that the hills around us are covered with mighty heroes, more numerous than all our enemies; that the eye of God watches over us night and day, and that soon we shall be in heaven. God give us a simple and childlike heart, and increase our faith. Amen.

Faith is wisdom from on high, Hearing ear and seeing eye; In the soul a higher light Than the ken of mortal sight; Lively trust and hope serene, Evidence of things not seen.
Faith, in childlike trust, is wise: Trusting him who never lies, By whose grace the weak grow strong, Change their sighing into song. Praise be thine, O Lord of might! Faith shall end in glorious sight.

---

74. Friday after Second Sunday after Epiphany.

God, thou hast done all things well; teach us to know thy love. Amen.

Genesis 2, 18. 21–24. And the Lord God said, It is not good that the man should be alone; I will make him an help meet for him. And the Lord God caused a deep sleep to fall upon Adam, and he slept: and he took one of his ribs, and closed up the flesh instead thereof; and the rib, which the Lord God had taken from man, made he a woman, and brought her unto the man. And Adam said, This is now bone of my bones, and flesh of my flesh: she shall be called Woman, because she was taken out of Man. Therefore shall a man leave his father and his mother, and shall cleave unto his wife: and they shall be one flesh.

Here we learn that of his goodness God created man, "male and female created he them," and ordered that they live together in wedlock. Of his goodness toward us he still continues to lead to each man the woman destined for him; and every man shall receive his wife, and every woman shall receive her husband, as a gift from the Lord. The woman is created to be an helpmeet for man, and the man is to provide for her temporal wants. Each is to promote the temporal and eternal happiness of the other. But it is only through love that this object can be attained. Love unites the hearts and wills of the two, and together they become strong to fight the battle of life and bear the day's burden. In love they gladly serve each other, each of them happy in the happiness of the other, and both having their troubles in common. Then wedlock is a glorious estate, full of trials of all kinds, but rich in grace also, and having an ennobling, refining, and sanctifying influence on man and woman alike. "Out of the harmony of their natures will then spring a new common will, of which the quiet home, with its duties, its occupations, and its joys, shall be the evidence. But, alas, how this most beautiful relation is being desecrated on every hand! The man and woman have their separate opinions and are at cross purposes after their marriage as well as before it; sometimes one has the upper hand, and sometimes the other; and in their secret hearts both are speculating on the question whether or not the advantages of married life balance the loss of one's dear personal liberty. At last each becomes the torment of the other, and in the contemplation of the cold necessity which ties them to each other, love's fire is quenched." No; self-love never has founded a happy marriage. How could selfishness unite hearts in the Lord?

But let the husband and wife be united in the love of God in Christ, and they will become a blessing to each other for time and eternity. Even the frailties which both of them still have shall not prevent this consummation. On the contrary, if they have all things in common, they shall be blessed even through their very infirmities. "Whoso findeth a wife findeth a good thing, and obtained a favor of the Lord."

God, give us happy marriages and happy homes in which love is the bond of union; in which love is the fire; in which love is the strength, and the riches, and the life. Amen.

O blessed house, the joys of which thou sharest, And never art forgot in scenes of joy; O blessed house, for whose sad wounds thou carest, Where all the sick thy healing power employ; Until at last the day's work fully ended, All finally in joyful rapture fly To that blest house to which thou hast ascended, Unto the blessed Father's house on high.

---

75. Saturday after Second Sunday after Epiphany.

Psalm 143. A psalm of David. Hear my prayer, O Lord; give ear to my supplications: in thy faithfulness answer me, and in thy righteousness. And enter not into judgment with thy servant: for in thy sight shall no man living be justified. For the enemy hath persecuted my soul; he hath smitten my life down to the ground: he hath made me to dwell in darkness, as those that have been long dead. Therefore is my spirit overwhelmed within me: my heart within me is desolate. I remember the days of old; I meditate on all thy works; I muse on the work of thy hands. I stretch forth my hands unto thee: my soul thirsteth after thee, as a thirsty land. Selah. Hear me speedily, O Lord; my spirit faileth: hide not thy face from me, lest I be like unto them that go down into the pit. Cause me to hear thy lovingkindness in the morning; for in thee do I trust: cause me to know the way wherein I should walk; for I lift up my soul unto thee. Deliver me, O Lord, from mine enemies: I flee unto thee to hide me. Teach me to do thy will; for thou art my God: thy Spirit is good; lead me into the land of uprightness. Quicken me, O Lord, for thy name's sake: for thy righteousness' sake bring my soul out of trouble. And of thy mercy cut off mine enemies, and destroy all them that afflict my soul: for I am thy servant.

"Thou art my God, and I am thy servant." This is the foundation on which the afflicted and lamenting psalmist builds his hope. "I am a sinner, and this is the cause of all my misery; but thou must take pity on me, as thou art wont to take pity on all who are thine. No man is justified in thy sight, yet thou hast ever helped thy servants; this I remember from the experiences in my own life as well as in the lives of others. My enemies treat me with injustice, and they persecute me in order to satisfy their malice. This thou canst not permit, thou my God of righteousness. I have hid myself in thee; save me for thy name's sake." Great humility and a strong, trusting faith meet us out of the depths of his soul.—Dear reader; when you are in distress, cry to the Lord in the same manner, and he shall hear you for the sake of his his truth and his righteousness. In his day of trouble the

Christian says: "Lord Jesus, have mercy on me and help me. Remember that I am thine, thou most gracious God and Savior. I am a wretched, needy sinner, altogether corrupt, incapable of that which is good, deserving of wrath and punishment; and thou couldst with justice cast me out forever. But still thou hast loved me, and bought me with thine own blood, baptized me, called me, and destined me to salvation. I am thine, and all who are mine belong to thee; thou hast taken us into thy house, and thou art our hiding place. But now, O Lord, my soul is like a thirsty land. Do not hide thy face from me; refresh me, and keep me alive for thy name's sake. Thou hast promised to deliver me, if I call upon thee; hear me for thy truth's sake, and do not let go thy hold of me. All is well, if I but have thy grace; thou art also *my* Savior, and I am thy servant."

It is the nature of the children of God, that the more they suffer, the more do they yearn after the Lord. The others are embittered, or they harden their hearts, or they despair. Where there is no humility there is neither any trust in God, nor is there any heartfelt longing after him. But the lowly in spirit, the true believers, thirst after God all the more by reason of their sufferings.

Stretch out your hands to him; tell him that your soul thirsts after him and can not let him go. Cling to his gracious promises. He has never thrust anyone away who has done this. All the promises of God are yea and amen in Christ Jesus.

Lord, give us humility and a childlike trust in thee. Make with the temptation also a way to escape, that we may be able to bear it. Give us victory, to the glory of thy name. Amen.

What our Father does is well: May the thought within us dwell; Though nor milk nor honey flow In our barren Canaan now, God can save us in our need, God can bless us, God can feed.

---

76. Third Sunday after Epiphany. I.

Lord Jesus, let the cleansing and healing power of thy blood come upon us. Amen.

Gospel Lesson, Matthew 8, 1-13. When he was come down from the mountain, great multitudes followed him. And, behold, there came a leper and worshipped him, saying, Lord, if thou wilt, thou canst make me clean. And Jesus put forth his hand, and touched him, saying, I will; be thou clean. And immediately his leprosy was cleansed. And Jesus saith unto him, See thou tell no man; but go thy way, shew thyself to the priest, and offer the gift that Moses commanded, for a testimony unto them. And when Jesus was entered into Capernaum, there came unto him a centurion, beseeching him, and saying, Lord, my servant lieth at home sick of the palsy, grievously tormented. And Jesus saith unto him, I will come and heal him. The centurion answered and said, Lord, I am not worthy that thou shouldest come under my roof: but speak the word only, and my servant shall be healed. For I am a man under authority, having soldiers under me: and I say to this man, Go, and he goeth; and to another, Come, and he cometh; and to my servant, Do this, and he doeth it. When Jesus heard it, he marvelled, and said to them that followed, Verily I say unto you, I have not found so great faith, no, not in Israel. And I say unto you, that many shall come from the east and west, and shall sit down with Abraham, and Isaac, and Jacob, in the kingdom of heaven. But the children of the kingdom shall be cast out into outer darkness: there shall be weeping and gnashing of teeth. And Jesus said unto the centurion, Go thy way; and as thou hast believed, so be it done unto thee. And his servant was healed in the selfsame hour.

Both these men, the leper and the centurion, had *humble* hearts. They judged themselves unworthy of all grace and honor; it never occurred to them that they were destined to become great and win undying fame. Though the hand of God is heavy upon him, the leper does not repine; and he is willing to continue to bear his affliction, if it be the Lord's pleasure. And the centurion;—what a keen sense he has of his own littleness! Yet, moved by his love of the word of God, he had built the synagogue in Capernaum, and had always been diligent in doing good. But this does not make him great in his own eyes. He feels his heathen origin and his sinful condition with deep humility, and he is entirely sincere in declaring himself not worthy that the Lord should come under his roof.

Both these men are also remarkable for their *faith*. The leper does not doubt that the Lord *can* make him clean, if he deems best. No human being can cure a leper; but still, this leper feels certain that Jesus is able to do it. He had heard of his power and grace; and the word had found lodgment in his soul, which by means of his affliction had been opened to receive it; and he now firmly believes that the Lord can heal him. And now, the centurion! How must not the Lord himself marvel at the childlike faith of this man! There is beauty in the speech of the leper: "Lord, if thou wilt, thou canst make me whole." But still more beautiful are the words of the centurion: "Lord, I am not worthy that thou shouldest come under my roof; but speak the word only, and my servant shall be healed." He has unbounded confidence in the word of Jesus. "For I," reasons he, "am but a man, a man of *little worth;* yet even *my word* has power over my servants. What, then, must the power of *thy word* be! If thou but sayest to the disease that it shall be gone, and to health that it shall come, they will at once obey thy command."

Beautiful twins are these: Humility and Faith. Submit willingly, O thou soul, to the Lord's discipline. Know your poverty; in truth, you are both sinful and diseased, and of no account, but deserve to be thrown out and lost. Admit this truth; confess in your innermost heart that the Lord is right; by his grace you can do this. Then you have in his own word the power to believe. Jesus says to your sin, "be thou wiped out, and cast into the depths of the sea;" and he commands death saying, "be thou annihilated." And it is as he commands. In like manner he says to you, "live, and be saved;" and it comes to pass. He is Lord of life and death. Even as your servant obeys your order, so must sin and death give way, and life and salvation come at the Lord's command. Do you not believe this? Is not Jesus able to do this? Surely, you do believe it. Then, though the

Lord may not have occasion to marvel at the greatness of *your* faith, yet he shall not quench the smoking flax. But *you* shall marvel in all eternity at his lovingkindness to the upright of heart, and at the power of his grace over the weak, as well as the strong, in faith.

Dear Lord Jesus, thou who alone givest all good things; give us humility, and give us faith, that we, also, may experience thy power to save, that we may be sanctified in spirit and soul and body, and live with thee for evermore. Amen.

For thou art our salvation, Lord, Our refuge and our great reward; Without thy grace our life must fade, And wither like a flower decayed.

To heal the sick stretch out thine hand, And bid the fallen sinner stand; Once more upon thy people shine, And fill the world with love divine.

---

77. Third Sunday after Epiphany. II.

O that my ways were directed to keep thy statutes, my God!

Epistle Lesson, Romans 12, 17–21. Recompense to no man evil for evil. Provide things honest in the sight of all men. If it be possible, as much as lieth in you, live peaceably with all men. Dearly beloved, avenge not yourselves; but rather give place unto wrath: for it is written, Vengeance is mine; I will repay, saith the Lord. Therefore if thine enemy hunger, feed him; if he thirst, give him drink: for in so doing thou shalt heap coals of fire on his head. Be not overcome of evil, but overcome evil with good.

Christ has saved you, Christian believer, from sin, death, and the devil; has healed and cleansed you; and this should appear in your conduct. By the power of his grace in your heart you shall obtain victory over the evil influences which tempt and entice you from within and without. The strength to do this you have in your God; now make diligent use of it in faith.

If anyone does you wrong, you must by no means repay him in kind. To do evil is the business of the devil and his servants; to you it is given of God to do good toward all men. In the heart of God you have an unfailing well from which to draw. Make generous use of it; enjoy in full measure the goodness of God, and make some return by practicing without stint deeds of kindness to all men. The most covetous miner can not be as diligent in burrowing for gold as you should be in doing good to all men. No sower has a field so fertile and seed so precious; and your diligence should, therefore, more than equal that of the most tirelessly industrious husbandman in the busy springtime of the year. And now, is it to be so in your case? It is a good resolution, and by the grace of God it should be carried into effect unceasingly.—When justice or the true welfare of your neighbor demands it, you must willingly bear his enmity; you are not to live peaceably with any, if this works harm to him or to others, or if it curtails the honor of God. But in matters of merely personal concern it is neither right nor necessary for you to stir up a quarrel. If you really *wish* to live peaceably, you will find it possible to do so. Suffer injustice, and remember that, in the end, you will be the gainer by it. If any man who has wronged you be in trouble, come to his assistance. If your neighbor be angry with you, quench the fire that makes him so unhappy; quench this fire from hell by doing good to him out of a good heart. Shall not your love be stronger than his hate? Shall not your gentleness, which is of God, gain the victory over his anger, which is of the devil? To the heathen way of thinking it is a mean and pitiful thing to bear an insult or injury without seeking revenge. But viewed in the proper light, it is pitiful to be the slave of one's own anger. In Christ we are free and able to forgive our enemy, disarm the wicked, crush anger out of existence, and shame the devil. Let no Christian allow himself to be overcome. Jesus says: "Love your enemies, and bless them that curse you." Thereby he has done with our anger what he did with the leprosy of the leper and with the palsy of the centurion's servant. When he has said it, shall it not come true? Have a care, that you make use of the strength which you have in his word, and you shall not be shamed; that which is evil shall not make you evil, but your love shall make the evil men good.

My God, how sweeter than honey is thy instruction, and how great are thy power and grace! Give me a deep and overpowering knowledge of sin, in order that thou mayest melt my soul in love and make me a victor over all wickedness.

We give thee but thine own, Whate'er the gift may be: All that we have is thine alone, A trust, O Lord, from thee.
May we thy bounties thus As stewards true receive, And gladly, as thou blessest us, To thee our first-fruits give.

---

78. Monday after Third Sunday after Epiphany.

Lord, thy river is full of water; we pray thee, give us to drink.

John 4, 6–14. Now Jacob's well was there. Jesus therefore, being wearied with his journey, sat thus on the well: and it was about the sixth hour. There cometh a woman of Samaria to draw water: Jesus saith unto her, Give me to drink. (For his disciples were gone away unto the city to buy meat.) Then saith the woman of Samaria unto him, How is it that thou, being a Jew, askest drink of me, which am a woman of Samaria? for the Jews have no dealings with the Samaritans. Jesus answered and said unto her, If thou knewest the gift of God, and who it is that saith to thee, Give me to drink; thou wouldest have asked of him, and he would have given thee living water. The woman saith unto him, Sir, thou hast nothing to draw with, and the well is deep: from whence then hast thou that living water? Art thou greater than our father Jacob, which gave us the well, and drank thereof himself, and his children, and his cattle? Jesus answered and said unto her, Whosoever drinketh of this water shall thirst again: But whosoever drinketh of the water that I shall give him shall never thirst; but the water that I shall give him shall be in him a well of water springing up into everlasting life.

Jesus was wearied with his journey. He well understands our weariness. As the omniscient God he knows how we feel, we who are tired in body and soul; but he also knows it as one who was in all points tempted like as we are, yet without sin. The woman of Samaria, also, was weary, weary of her worldly and sinful life; but she did not know herself, and did not quite understand what it was that ailed her sick heart. Many, alas, who call themselves Christians, as well as many downright infidels, walk the treadmill of wordliness and sin, and are at bottom heartily tired of it; but they have put the yoke on, and do not see their way clear to shaking it off; and so they give up trying, and sink to a still lower level. From the depths of the soul a sigh for freedom continues to rise up many a time and oft; but it dies aborning, and nothing comes of it. Here it is the business of the church with its word in the service of the Lord to come to the aid of the soul, offer it deliverance, touch the proper heartstrings, wake the soul out of its torpid state, and bring its yearnings out into the light of day. This is what the Lord does in the case of the woman of Samaria. He forgets his bodily thirst in the stronger desire to awaken in her the soul's thirst after righteousness. Does he not say, with reference to the salvation of the Samaritans, that his meat is to do the will of his Father? He takes the condition of this woman into careful account. This we also should do when we have to deal with the heathen or with heathenish Christians. He asks her to give him to drink; and then he speaks to her these heavenly words concerning the water of life. Words such as these, every syllable of which is a gem of paradise, are not by him regarded as too precious to be spoken to this wretched heathen woman, sullied by foul sins. Then there is awakened in her a sense of the weariness of her soul, weariness with her miserable life in sin, weariness with the emptiness and soullessness of the world; a sense, however, in which there is more of accusation against God and against others than against herself, more of defiance and despondency than of humility and hope. For there is as yet but little depth in her knowledge of sin. Therefore she says to Jesus: "Sir, give me this water, that I thirst not, neither come hither to draw." But the Spirit of God has begun his good work in her, and he shall perform it.

Lord Jesus, speak to our hearts, also, of thy thirst and of thy water of life; and give us grace so to hear that we may thirst; and give us to drink of this water, that it may be in us a well of water springing up into everlasting life. Amen.

See, the streams of living waters Springing from eternal love, Well supply thy sons and daughters, And all fear of want remove. Who can faint while such a river Ever flows their thirst to assuage? Grace which, like the Lord, the giver, Never fails from age to age.

---

79. Tuesday after Third Sunday after Epiphany.

Lord, do not relax thy hold on me; but make me humble and save me. Amen.

John 4, 15-26. The woman saith unto him, Sir, give me this water, that I thirst not, neither come hither to draw. Jesus saith unto her, Go, call thy husband, and come hither. The woman answered and said, I have no husband. Jesus said unto her, Thou hast well said, I have no husband: For thou hast had five husbands; and he whom thou now hast is not thy husband: in that saidst thou truly. The woman saith unto him, Sir, I perceive that thou art a prophet. Our fathers worshipped in this mountain; and ye say, that in Jerusalem is the place where men ought to worship, Jesus saith unto her, Woman, believe me, the hour cometh, when ye shall neither in this mountain, nor yet at Jerusalem, worship the Father. Ye worship ye know not what: we know what we worship: for salvation is of the Jews. But the hour cometh, and now is, when the true worshippers shall worship the Father in spirit and in truth: for the father seeketh such to worship him. God is a Spirit: and they that worship him must worship him in spirit and in truth. The woman saith unto him, I know that Messias cometh, which is called Christ: when he is come, he will tell us all things. Jesus saith unto her, I that speak unto thee am he.

The woman said to Jesus: "Sir, give me this water." This prayer he began to answer by saying to her: "Go, call thy husband." *Knowledge of sin* is what she needs. He has spoken to her of the water of eternal life, and has awakened in her a longing after this water; and he has won her confidence, and thus prepared her to hear the penitential sermon which he now preaches to her. For that heart only which truly knows its sin and humbles itself can accept the grace of God. In a few words Jesus shows this woman what her whole life has been; and the picture is so striking that it terrifies her, and she tries to evade it by asking a question concerning the place where men ought to worship. Peter said on one occasion: "Depart from me; for I am a sinful man, O Lord." And David says, in Psalm 39: "O spare me, that I may recover strength, before I go hence, and be no more." Such feelings as these now filled the heart of this woman. And her situation becomes no better when she asks whether God is to be worshipped on Mount Gerizim or in Jerusalem; for now the Lord speaks to her in such manner that she can not avoid hearing him,and he tells her the truth about her heathen blindness and her soulless worship. She, the obscene Samaritan woman of Sychar, the city of liars, to talk about the worship of God, who is a Spirit, the Spirit of truth and holiness, the God of believing Israel! However, these words of the Lord are also an invitation, and they inspire in the poor woman some hope that she may receive light. She knows,—O blessed knowledge of the Bible!—she knows that Messias is to bring salvation to both Jew and gentile; and now, when the Lord says, *"I that speak unto thee am he,"* she believes on him; and the light of grace from his countenance shines into the night of her sin, with the result that she confesses him, and leads others to believe in him. Certainly, her light is as yet very feeble, but it is true and living; and therefore she becomes a new creature. Did she continue in her former lascivious life, do you think?—Here we learn that the only way to Christ leads through *knowledge of sin.* Furthermore we learn that Jesus is near when man knows his sin and in all sincerity makes the confession: "It is true; all these things have I done." Then is salvation at hand.

Lord, give us in our hearts a true and living knowledge of sin.

Reveal thyself to us as the Savior of lost sinners; and draw many souls
to thee out of the night of sin, that we may walk together in the
light before thee. Amen.

My lips with shame my sins confess Against thy law, against thy grace:
Lord, should thy judgment grow severe, I am condemned, but thou art clear.

Yet save a trembling sinner, Lord, Whose hope, still hovering round
thy word Would light on some sweet promise there, Some sure support against
despair.

80. Wednesday after Third Sunday after Epiphany.

Lord, increase our faith! Lord, make our faith strong. Amen.

Hebrews 11, 8–12. By faith Abraham, when he was called to go out
into a place which he should after receive for an inheritance, obeyed; and
he went out, not knowing whither he went. By faith he sojourned in the land
of promise, as in a strange country, dwelling in tabernacles with Isaac and
Jacob, the heirs with him of the same promise: For he looked for a city which
hath foundations, whose builder and maker is God. Through faith also Sara
herself received strength to conceive seed, and was delivered of a child when
she was past age, because she judged him faithful who had promised. Therefore
sprang there even of one, and him as good as dead, so many as the stars of
the sky in multitude, and as the sand which is by the sea shore innumerable.

The Lord said unto Abram: "Get thee out of thy country, and
from thy kindred, and from thy father's house, unto a land that I will
shew thee; and I will make of thee a great nation, and I will bless thee,
and make thy name great; and thou shalt be a blessing. And I will bless
them that bless thee, and curse him that curseth thee; and in thee shall
all families of the earth be blessed." And Abram departed, as the Lord
had spoken unto him. And he came into Canaan, and passed through
the land (Genesis 12). Abraham had only the word of God by which
to go, and on which to rely. The word led him to go forth. He had
not seen the land, nor did he have any geographical knowledge of it.
The land had no existence to him save by reason of what the Lord
had said; but the word sufficed him. Neither did the land come
into his possession while he lived; he dwelt in it as a stranger, and
even *bought* there a burying place. Yet he firmly believed that his
seed should inherit the country; and so did Isaac and Jacob also,
though not a foot of it became their property while they lived. The
word of God was their only pledge; but to them this was a better .
certificate of ownership than any deed duly witnessed and recorded.
And after the earthly Canaan they desired an heavenly country, and
expected an everlasting, imperishable city. The faith of Abraham
is like that of the centurion in last Sunday's gospel lesson. Even
Sara is praised for her faith, although for a long time it certainly was
no stronger than it should be. She tempted Abraham to take Hagar
to wife; and she laughed at the promise of God concerning Isaac as
at a fairy tale. But herein we may find much of comfort; for we are
more like Sara than like Abraham. She was, after all, honest and
open to conviction; and faith did obtain victory over unbelief in her

heart. I hope that this may be true of you, also. We have the promise of eternal life. Let the heart leave Mesopotamia, and enter Canaan. Tear yourself away from everything on earth. Forsake all that is dear to you, and devote your heart to the life in the Lord, to the eternal treasures of love in Christ, in his church. God himself has told you that you shall inherit everlasting life. He has promised this to you by name, and placed the pledge in your hand, at the time when you were baptized. You are a stranger here on earth; then live as a stranger here, and hold fast the gift of God. Surely, his promise is more to be relied on, than are any and all human bonds and pledges. Of his grace in Christ Jesus it has pleased him to give you life; at the proper time you shall see that it is as he says, and as you, persuaded of his promises, believe. Or how was it? Did not the seed of Abraham inherit the land? Or the children of Abraham in faith, have they not become a great multitude? Lord God, help us to believe, in order that we may not make thee a liar. Thou hast promised us everlasting life as distinctly as thou didst promise the land of Canaan to Abraham. Give us grace to believe, even as thou didst give such grace to Abraham; for Jesus' sake. Amen.

Faith in meekness, as is meet, Sits and learns at Jesus' feet, Nestles closely to the Lord, Happy in the Master's word; Cleaves to it, defends it then: This to faith is Yea, Amen.
Faith is sure, where sight is blind: While lost sense may nowhere find Hope, to stay a sinking soul When the billows o'er it roll, Faith directs its saving quest To the cross, and there finds rest.

81. Thursday after Third Sunday after Epiphany.

Purge me with hyssop, and I shall be clean; wash me, and I shall be whiter than snow.

Leviticus 14, 2–8. This shall be the law of the leper in the day of his cleansing: He shall be brought unto the priest: And the priest shall go forth out of the camp; and the priest shall look, and, behold, if the plague of leprosy be healed in the leper, then shall the priest command to take for him that is to be cleansed two birds alive and clean, and cedar wood, and scarlet, and hyssop: And the priest shall command that one of the birds be killed in an earthen vessel over running water: As for the living bird, he shall take it, and the cedar wood, and the scarlet, and the hyssop, and shall dip them and the living bird in the blood of the bird that was killed over the running water: And he shall sprinkle upon him that is to be cleansed from the leprosy seven times, and shall pronounce him clean, and shall let the living bird loose into the open field. And he that is to be cleansed shall wash his clothes, and shave off all his hair, and wash himself in water, that he may be clean: and after that he shall come into the camp, and shall tarry abroad out of his tent seven days.

The lepers were excluded from communion with the people of Israel, and were regarded exactly as though dead. They were incurable. It was not until the leprosy had covered the whole body, leaving no sound spot to be seen, that the lepers were cleansed and were to be readmitted as members of society and into communion with God.—The two sparrows are to be regarded as one, and represent the leper. The cedar wood signifies incorruption, scarlet is the life-color, and hyssop represents purification; and the sparrow dies in the man's stead. The blood is mixed with fresh water in a vessel, and into this the living bird is dipped, together with the cedar and scarlet and hyssop; the man is then sprinkled, and the sparrow let loose. The leper is then regarded as having died and been brought to life again, and is clean.

Sin has made us unclean; nay, even dead. In our sin and unbelief we are separated from God and his people. Not until we acknowledge ourselves as wholly sinful, with no part untouched by disease, can we be cleansed. Christ died in our stead, and lives again; he has united his atoning life and blood with the water of our baptism, and lives alway to make intercession for us. By being sprinkled herewith we are cleansed of the foulness of sin, admitted into a covenant with God, and are of his people. For he stepped into our place when he became man, and died, and rose again, and went home to God; and we become one with him in baptism. The little children who receive baptism are cleansed of the leprosy of sin, and are quickened; for they do not resist the grace of God. But when one who has been baptized reaches years of discretion, he must make the grace of baptism his own in conscious faith; and this faith can not be born in our heart, unless we recognize the fact that we are altogether sinful and have no righteousness of our own, and unless we have no hope of life and purity save through Jesus. If you are wholly sinful and altogether lost, you will cling to him as your only and perfect Savior; then you are pure in his sight, and you are of his people. Then you shall wash your clothes, and shave off all your hair, and wash yourself in water; that is, you shall put away your sinful life, and prove yourself a new creature in Christ.

Lord, teach us thy way of grace, and lead us in this way. We are covered with leprosy; do thou cleanse us. We are dead; do thou quicken us. We are lost; have mercy on us, and save us. Make us to see our corruption in all its hideousness, and give us healing in thy life and in thy death. Amen.

Nothing in my hand I bring; Simply to thy cross I cling; Naked, come to thee for dress, Helpless, look to thee for grace, Foul, I to the Fountain fly: Wash me, Savior, or I die!

---

82. Friday after Third Sunday after Epiphany.

Blessed are they that dwell in thy house; they will be still praising thee! Amen

Isaiah 25, 6–9. And in this mountain shall the Lord of hosts make unto all people a feast of fat things, a feast of wines on the lees, of fat things full of marrow, of wines on the lees well refined. And he will destroy in this mountain the face of the covering cast over all people, and the vail that is spread over all nations. He will swallow up death in victory; and the Lord God will wipe away tears from off all faces; and the rebuke of his people shall he take away from off all the earth: for the Lord hath spoken it. And it shall be said in that day, Lo, this is our God; we have waited for him, and he will save us: this is the Lord; we have waited for him, we will be glad and rejoice in his salvation.

Could anything more beautiful be said concerning the glory of our Lord Jesus and the salvation of his people than that which the prophet says in this text? "Many shall come from the east and west, and shall sit down with Abraham, and Isaac, and Jacob, in the kingdom of heaven." The feast shall be prepared for *all* people. All nations shall be there. The Lord of hosts, our Jesus, does not do anything on a small scale. What a feast, what a meal it will be! There the wine is without dregs, and the fat things are all marrow; there is nothing but pure, unmixed joy and bliss, nothing but love, nothing but God himself, who at this feast is all things in all. For the covering that still is cast over all people is taken away, and we know God face to face; we see him in Christ as he is. Then death is wholly and utterly destroyed for ever; it is swallowed up in victory, is gone, has disappeared, even as night with its darkness disappears before the sun. And with death there is an end of sorrow, and crying, and sighing, and wailing. Dishonor and ignominy have been buried out of sight for ever.—These things has the Lord promised to his church; the mouth of the Lord has spoken it. We still await the fufilment in its entirety; but in faith and hope we already possess salvation. Thousands upon thousands of the gentiles sit at the table of God in his church on earth; eat his flesh; drink his blood; live of his life; taste his love; and see him with uncovered face, though still as through a glass, darkly. And who shall number the multitude of those already at home in heaven? But these two, the saints on earth and the saved in heaven, are one people, and stand together in one place, around the same Lord; the only difference being that the saved in heaven see that which we as yet only believe. Who, then, can doubt that the Lord shall do that which he has spoken, and that he shall gather us as one people in the consummation of glory?

Praise be to thee, Lord Jesus! Do thou soon gather into thy church of all peoples as many as can be saved, and as shall furnish thy wedding feast with guests, in order that the glory of the perfect church may come quickly. Amen.

There is a home of sweet repose, Where storms assail no more; The stream of endless pleasure flows On that celestial shore.
There purity with love appears, And bliss without alloy; There they that oft had sown in tears Shall reap eternal joy.

---

83. Saturday after Third Sunday after Epiphany.

Lord, convert us; and in thy light let us see light. Amen.

Matthew 4, 12–17. Now when Jesus had heard that John was cast into prison, he departed into Galilee: And leaving Nazareth, he came and dwelt in Capernaum, which is upon the sea coast, in the borders of Zabulon and Nephthalim: That it might be fulfilled which was spoken by Esaias the prophet, saying, The land of Zabulon, and the land of Nephthalim, by the way of the sea, beyond Jordan, Galilee of the Gentiles; the people which sat in darkness saw great light: and to them which sat in the region and shadow of death, light is sprung up. From that time Jesus began to preach, and to say, Repent: for the kingdom of heaven is at hand.

The Galileans were despised by the other Jews; but Jesus makes his home among them, and there reveals his glory with preaching and miracles. For the Galileans were more ready than were the others to receive the grace of God. It is a blessed change when a man comes out of darkness into the light, and when the sun of righteousness, Jesus Christ, rises on them which sat in the night of death. If you are unconverted, dear reader, it is dark in your heart. For sin then reigns in you; and sin is darkness. In our land the light is shining; thank God! The sun of righteousness is risen over our people. The gospel is preached; Jesus is here; out of his name proceed knowledge of God, forgiveness of sin, charity, and peace; and it has a ray for each and all of us, like the sun in the sky. However, its purpose is to shine into our *heart*. What does the light of the sun profit the blind man? He walks in darkness nevertheless. Thus it is in your case also, as long as you continue with unconverted heart in the service of sin. You neither see your unhappy condition, nor do you see the great love and grace of God. Life is here, and you do not know it; the pearl lies before you, and you tread it under foot. The table is laid which satisfies the wants of the soul, and the fountain flows which forever slakes our thirst; you go by, and grope about after the allurements of sensual pleasure, and allow the devil to lead you to the poisoned waters of death. And what a dark brood it is that lives within you! Yet you dream in the sleep of sin. O, that you might give ear to this, which the Spirit of God speaks to you: "Repent; awake thou that sleepest, and arise from the dead, and Christ shall give thee light." Verily, he is here, and preaches to us. This is his voice: "Repent; for the kingdom of heaven is at hand." And by the power which is in the word it is possible for you to repent and believe. For what purpose has he given us the light, do you think, but that we may see? The sun rises over our hills, in order that we may walk by its light. The kingdom of heaven is come to us, in order that we may repent and believe. If we regard not this time of our visitation, the verdict will be: "Thou, Capernaum, wast exalted to heaven, but thou shalt be thrust down to hell."

O, dear, tender God; turn thou us, and we shall be turned; save thou us, and we shall be saved. Show us our sin, and reveal to us thy grace. Take away from us all self-righteousness and every manner of dead faith; give us humility in our heart, and a true, living, saving faith in thee. Amen.

Forever with the Lord! Amen! so let it be! Life from the dead is in that word, And immortality.
Here in the body pent, Absent from him I roam, Yet nightly pitch my moving tent A day's march nearer home.

84. Fourth Sunday after Epiphany. I.

Lord, take us with thee, and let us abide with thee alway. Amen.

Gospel Lesson, Matthew 8, 23–27. And when he was entered into a ship, his disciples followed him. And behold, there arose a great tempest in the sea, insomuch that the ship was covered with the waves: but he was asleep. And his disciples came to him, and awoke him, saying, Lord, save us: we perish. And he saith unto them, Why are ye fearful, O ye of little faith? Then he arose, and rebuked the winds and the sea; and there was a great calm. But the men marvelled, saying, What manner of man is this, that even the winds and the sea obey him!

The disciples around the Lord Jesus are the Christian church. It is exposed to storm and danger. The devil, with all his hosts, rages against it; for Jesus is to destroy the kingdom of the devil. By his means of grace, which the church administers and uses, Jesus rescues the souls from the prince of darkness, and lays waste his kingdom; therefore the evil enemy makes turbid the great sea of humanity, and attempts to bury the church under its waves. How badly have not the people of God many a time seemed likely to fare! They were persecuted with fire and sword, and the mighty men of the world had firmly resolved to eradicate "the sect of the Nazarenes" from the face of the earth. The devil invented false doctrines, with which he made people drunk to such an extent that they thought they were serving God when they shed the blood of his saints. For the church of our own times the outlook seems still more threatening; for mighty intellects are conspiring to dig for it a deep and safe grave beneath the riotous masses. Philosophy, the natural sciences, the art of poetry, the press, all are incessantly fanning the flames of unbelief in the hearts of men; and thus the Christian peoples are, in truth, like a sea that is stirred from the bottom up and runs high in waves of atheism, materialism, liberalism, socialism; and it looks as if the church might no longer be able to weather the storms, but must be filled with unbelief, and go to the bottom. However, this is nothing new. In the very earliest days of the church the devil thought to crush it by assaults on the part of learned men, and by the intermixture of strong delusions with the pure word of God. In reality there is, after all, no danger whatever that *the church* may perish. But there is danger for each individual believer that he may be swept away by the temptation to infidelity. The ship of the church shall always emerge uninjured out of the angry waves, and keep its proper course; for Jesus is on board. Let each of us, however, watch and pray, that he fall not away in time of temptation. Abide with the Lord; *O, abide with him!* Accept the correction which he administers for the weakness of your faith; hear his word wherein he chastens you, and it shall calm your troubled heart; then shall you be strengthened, and your eye shall behold the glory of God. Make diligent use of the means of grace in the church; then shall you remain with the Lord in the ship. Be assured beyond a doubt that the almighty Lord Jesus shall save the humble and faithful, who willingly let themselves be disciplined for their want of faith, and who cling to him in all their distress; while the sleepy and the conceited and the foolhardy shall surely be swept away by the waves.

Faithful Lord Jesus, preserve us in faith unto the end. Let none of us tempt the deep without thee; and when the danger comes, be thou our refuge and deliverance. "When compassed about with dangers sore, When the waves run high and the tempests roar; Do thou, O Lord, our captain be, And give us faith to trust in thee."

I fear no foe, with thee at hand to bless; Ills have no weight, and tears no bitterness; Where is death's sting? where, grave, thy victory? I triumph still, if thou abide with me!

---

85. Fourth Sunday after Epiphany. II.

My God, give me the love of Christ in my heart. Amen.

Epistle Lesson, Romans 13, 8–10. Owe no man any thing, but to love one another: for he that loveth another hath fulfilled the law. For this, thou shalt not commit adultery, thou shalt not kill, thou shalt not steal, thou shalt not bear false witness, thou shalt not covet; and if there be any other commandment, it is briefly comprehended in this saying, namely, thou shalt love thy neighbor as thyself. Love worketh no ill to his neighbor: therefore love is the fulfilling of the law.

When the world hates, we love all the more; and we return love for hatred. And when the world assaults us, and attempts our overthrow, this shall, by the grace of God, have no other effect than to unite us more closely, and to strenghten the fraternal spirit among us. Love one another. This is the law in the kingdom of Christ. It is our bounden duty to love one another; and the Lord has given us grace to do it. It is a blessed debt. We cheerfully pay it; but, at the same time, we do not wish ever to be rid of it. We strive to fulfil this our obligation, and are happy in being able to do that which is our duty; but we also desire to feel more and more deeply what we owe one another.

"Thou shalt love thy neighbor as thyself." What a kingly commandment this is; and how rich and precious life would be, if the commandment were obeyed! And in Christ this is *possible*. When he says to us: "A new commandment I give unto you, that ye love one another;" he gives us at the same time power to do what he commands. If we believe his words, they work in us that which he speaks. It is owing to the weakness of our faith that we neither love as warmly as we ought, nor prove our love in deed and truth. You have love in your heart, my Christian friend; use it in faith. You are in Christ; and the living vine is not wanting in sap or in life. The perverseness of your nature, which caused you to hate the law, has by the death of Christ been conquered for you and in you, with the result that you now love the law; and it is quite certain that in Christ you have power to live the life of love. "For what the law could not do, in that it was weak through the flesh, God sending his own Son in the likeness of

sinful flesh, and for sin, condemned sin in the flesh; that the righteousness of the law might be fulfilled in us, who walk not after the flesh,
but after the Spirit." Go, then, and live your whole life in love; let
all that you do be done in love. O, how happy you are! What a
blessed thing it is to be with Christ in his church when tempests
roar on every hand.

Lord, again we pray thee: Pour out thy love into our hearts by
thy Holy Spirit. "Give me, O Lord, this greatest bliss I know, A heart
that with thy love doth overflow." Amen.

O gentle Dew, from heaven now fall With power upon the hearts of all,
Thy tenderness instilling; That heart to heart more closely bound, Fruitful
in kindly deeds be found, The law of love fulfilling; No wrath, no strife, then
shall grieve thee; We receive thee: Where thou livest Peace and love and joy
thou givest.

---

86. Monday after Fourth Sunday after Epiphany.

*Lord of hosts, blessed is the man that trusteth in thee. Give us grace to
do this. Amen.*

Exodus 15, 1–11. Then sang Moses and the children of Israel this song
unto the Lord, and spake, saying, I will sing unto the Lord, for he hath triumphed gloriously: the horse and his rider hath he thrown into the sea. The
Lord is my strength and song, and he is become my salvation: he is my God,
and I will prepare him an habitation; my father's God, and I will exalt him.
The Lord is a man of war: the Lord is his name. Pharaoh's chariots and his
host hath he cast into the sea: his chosen captains also are drowned in the
Red sea. The depths have covered them: they sank into the bottom as a stone.
Thy right hand, O Lord, is become glorious in power: thy right hand, O Lord,
hath dashed in pieces the enemy. And in the greatness of thine excellency
thou hast overthrown them that rose up against thee: thou sentest forth thy
wrath, which consumed them as stubble. And with the blast of thy nostrils
the waters were gathered together: the floods stood upright as an heap, and
the depths were congealed in the heart of the sea. The enemy said, I will
pursue, I will overtake, I will divide the spoil; my lust shall be satisfied
upon them; I will draw my sword, my hand shall destroy them. Thou didst
blow with thy wind, the sea covered them: they sank as lead in the mighty
waters. Who is like unto thee, O Lord, among the gods? who is like thee,
glorious in holiness, fearful in praises, doing wonders?

Pharaoh and his whole army were buried in the Red Sea, and
Israel was delivered from bondage. The Lord had redeemed them,
and betrothed himself unto his people. Jehovah is faithfulness. As
his name is, so is he in very truth. He had promised the fathers
to be the God of Israel; and how more than grand is his fulfilment of
this promise! How great a God he is, and how mighty to save! What
enemy can make headway against him? But a moment ago the
situation of his people seemed absolutely desperate. The enemy was
behind and on either side of them, and the sea in front of them. Every
way was closed save the one leading upward to God. And, worst
of all, their faith was very far from being as strong as it should have

been. They cried to God; but it was the cry of despair, rather than of faith. However, they had a leader who believed. Moses said: "'Fear ye not, stand still, and see the salvation of the Lord." But his soul, also, was filled with sore distress.—Now the situation is changed, and they sing in a way to shake the gates of hell. The sea, which had treathened to swallow them, becomes the means of their deliverance and the grave of their enemies. On the enemy that wished to crush them the Lord has, by the waters of the sea, made manifest his power and the glory of his name. Their faith is strengthened, their hearts are full of gratitude, and songs of joy are on their lips. They have barely started on their way to Canaan, and the journey through the wilderness is before them; yet they already sing as though they had reached their destination: "Thou in thy mercy hast led forth the people which thou hast redeemed; thou hast guided them in thy strength unto thy holy habitation." Even if they yet must meet their enemies before the land shall have been won, they have no fear; for "fear and dread shall fall upon them; by the greatness of thine arm they shall be as still as a stone; till thy people pass over, O Lord, till the people pass over, which thou hast purchased. Thou shalt bring them in, and plant them in the mountain of thine inheritance, in the place, O Lord, which thou hast made for thee to dwell in, in the sanctuary, O Lord, which thy hands have established. The Lord shall reign for ever and ever." (Verses 16–18).

Every obstacle which threatens to impede the onward march of the Lord's people, the church of God on earth, shall be removed in due time, and they shall find an open way before them; but their enemies shall be overwhelmed. Thus it shall be in the case of the individual Christian also. When you see no way of escape save the one that leads up toward heaven, then it is as it should be. Follow that way; speak to the Lord, as did Moses, whose heart called until God said: "Wherefore criest thou unto me?" Do likewise, and the Lord shall surely save you, even though your faith be weak. You have a better advocate than Moses was. Put your trust in the Lord; this is what he wants to teach you. Then, though it be your lot to go through deep waters, you shall see his all the more glorious salvation. For "all his enemies shall perish; but they that love him shall be as the sun when he goeth forth in his might."

Lord, thou canst help when earthly armor faileth, Lord, thou canst save when deadly sin assaileth, Lord, o'er thy Rock nor death nor hell prevaileth: Grant us thy peace, Lord!

87. Tuesday after Fourth Sunday after Epiphany.

Psalm 46. God is our refuge and strength, a very present help in trouble. Therefore will not we fear, though the earth be removed, and though the mountains be carried into the midst of the sea; though the waters thereof roar and be troubled, though the mountains shake with the swelling thereof. Selah. There is a river, the streams whereof shall make glad the city of God, the holy place of the tabernacles of the Most High. God is in the midst of her; she shall not be moved: God shall help her, and that right early. The heathen raged, the kingdoms were moved: he uttered his voice, the earth melted. The Lord of hosts is with us; the God of Jacob is our refuge. Selah. Come, behold the works of the Lord, what desolations he hath made in the earth. He maketh wars to cease unto the end of the earth; he breaketh the bow, and cutteth the spear in sunder: he burneth the chariot in the fire. Be still, and know that I am God; I will be exalted among the heathen, I will be exalted in the earth. The Lord of hosts is with us; the God of Jacob is our refuge. Selah.

The waters spoken of in this psalm are the peoples of the earth; and the mountains in the midst of the sea are governments and rulers. There have been many great revolutions in the world; kingdoms have been overthrown, and dynasties destroyed; mighty princes have fallen, and the great sea of humanity has been lashed into foam. Storms yet more severe shall come; and the heathen shall rage, kingdoms be moved, and the mountains shake with the swelling thereof. At last all will unite in making war on the city of the Lord; that is, on the people of God, the Christian church on earth. But God is our reliance and strength; we have no reason to feel fear, no matter what terrors seem to threaten us. *God* is in the midst of his city; the great, almighty God is with his people; and in his means of grace, the word and sacraments, he gives them comfort, peace, and joy. The human sea is seething and troubled, and all manner of filth is ever rising to the surface. However, the church of God, which dwells among the peoples, enjoys rest and peace by the rivers of water. Out of the throne of God in the midst of the church issues the river of life spoken of in the 47th chapter of Ezekiel. This is the life of grace and love by the Holy Ghost in the means of grace committed to the care of the church. This river shall never be swallowed, nor turned out of its course, nor lose itself in the waters of the world; but shall keep itself pure and fresh, and shall exert its influence in all the earth.—The prospect that presented itself to Israel at the Red sea was far from bright. They had been made sore afraid by the proud and powerful king who had asked: "Who is the Lord, that I should obey his voice?" But "in the morning watch" God came and delivered them (Exodus, 14, 24). Sennacherib threatened Jerusalem, and said: "What Lord should deliver Jerusalem out of my hand?" But in the morning his soldiers were all dead corpses (Isaiah 36, 20; 37, 36).—The Lord, the God of hosts is with us. Neither could we be saved by any thing or any one less mighty. For our enemies are principalitites and powers and spiritual wickedness in high places. We need the very Lord Zebaoth for our protector. And he is, in truth, our mighty fortress. "Therefore distress can be our guest for a night, only; in the morning the Lord sends another, a permanent guest, namely salvation." That which this grand psalm says concerning God as the help of Israel is valid for all time. "There is but one church of God through all ages." To this you belong, Christian friend; you dwell in the city of God. Let the concerns of this city be your concerns; then shall you behold the salvation of the Lord, and learn the glorious truth that he is God.

A mighty fortress is our God, A trusty shield and weapon; Our help is he in all our need, Our stay, whate'er doth happen. The old maglinant foe Doth seek to work us woe; His craft and power are great, And, armed with cruel hate, On earth is not his equal.

With might of ours naught can be done, Soon were our loss effected; But for us fights the Valiant One, Whom God himself elected. Ask ye who this may be? Christ Jesus, it is he; Lord Zabaoth is his name, From age to age the same,— He holds the field forever.

---

88. Wednesday after Fourth Sunday after Epiphany.

Lord, let our soul wait upon thee. Amen.

Matthew 14, 24–33. But the ship was now in the midst of the sea, tossed with waves: for the wind was contrary. And in the fourth watch of the night Jesus went unto them, walking on the sea. And when the disciples saw him walking on the sea, they were troubled, saying, It is a spirit; and they cried out for fear. But straightway Jesus spake unto them, saying, Be of good cheer; it is I; be not afraid. And Peter answered him and said, Lord, if it be thou, bid me come unto thee on the water. And he said, Come. And when Peter was come down out of the ship, he walked on the water, to go to Jesus. But when he saw the wind boisterous, he was afraid; and beginning to sink, he cried, saying, Lord, save me! And immediately Jesus stretched forth his hand, and caught him, and said unto him, O thou of little faith, wherefore didst thou doubt? And when they were come into the ship, the wind ceased. Then they that were in the ship came and worshipped him, saying, Of a truth thou art the Son of God.

Our Jesus is now up in the mountain praying. He is at the right hand of God, and makes intercession for us with the Father. But he is among us, also, as he has been glorified and is omnipresent. He has said: "Lo, I am with you alway, even unto the end of the world." When we are in trouble he knows all about it. While Israel was being vexed in Egypt, it seemed as if he took no thought of the matter; but at the proper time he says: "I have surely seen the affliction of my people which are in Egypt, and have heard their crying by reason of their taskmasters; for I know their sorrows." For "we have not an high priest which cannot be touched with the feeling of our infirmities; but was in all points tempted like as we are, yet without sin" (Hebrews 4, 15). Still, we are often besieged with care and tossed with waves in the midst of the sea all night until the fourth, that is the last, watch; and when he comes we do not know him, but are frightened by the manner of his coming. This is the case with the church of God, and with the individual believer. It appears to us as if the word and the church of God must go down. Or you, yourself, are enveloped in such darkness and stormy weather that your eyes are dimmed with weeping, and you do not know the Lord, but are troubled and cry out in fear.—This episode with the disciples on the Sea of Gennesaret is very instructive and edifying. It surely seemed to them that he waited too long; but he came at the right time. They were afraid, but he said: *"Be of good cheer; it is I."* Let us hear this. It is our Lord *Jesus* who is in the storm; it is he who walks on the troubled sea, and does not sink. Remember that the sea represents the great ocean of humanity, through which the ship of the church plows its way. If you do not know him; if his ways seem strange to you, then do you note that he says: "It is I."—As the disciples had gone out onto the sea in obedience to the Lord's command, they *could not* sink; but when Peter chose, of his own accord, to walk on the water, his faith fell short; and yet the Lord stretched forth his helping hand, because Peter cried to him. There is no difficulty in understanding what we are to learn from this. But make the application yourself!

Is not our Jesus in truth the Son of God? Is he not the Lord of glory? His wisdom and power are unsearchable, and likewise his lovingkindness. Neither the church nor you shall sink; but your faith shall increase, and you shall worship him, and joyfully confess: Lord Jesus; of a truth, thou art the Son of God.

Give us to this end the light and grace of thy Holy Spirit. Tell us when we are to go out onto the sea together with them that are thine; never, never alone; and give us courage, and save us, when the tempests blow. Increase our faith, reveal thy glory to us and through us. Rule the world, and bless our people. Amen.

Amen, Lord Jesus, grant our prayer! Great Captain, now thine arm make bare; Fight for us once again! So shall thy saints and martyrs raise A mighty chorus to thy praise, World without end. Amen.

---

89. Thursday after Fourth Sunday after Epiphany.

Hebrew 11, 23–27. By faith Moses, when he was born, was hid three months of his parents, because they saw he was a proper child; and they were not afraid of the king's commandment. By faith Moses, when he was come to years, refused to be called the son of Pharaoh's daughter; choosing rather to suffer affliction with the people of God, than to enjoy the pleasures of sin for a season: Esteeming the reproach of Christ greater riches than the treasures in Egypt: for he had respect unto the recompense to the reward. By faith he forsook Egypt, not fearing the wrath of the king: for he endured, as seeing him who is invisible.

To the eye of faith the invisible is as real as is the visible world; and infinitely more great and glorious, true and enduring. To be sure, the believer still lives in the visible world, but he lives yet more in the invisible; his heart belongs to the Lord, whom he does not see. In him he trusts, and him he loves with his whole soul. It is in the word that our faith finds and holds fast the Invisible One. They of old time had the promise of a Savior who should come; in this promise they trusted, and waited, and suffered affliction, and despised all things for his sake. Their faith was a power in them which governed their whole life. Look at Moses. He could have become a great man in Egypt, but he dwelt with One who was greater than Pharaoh; he saw greater splendors than those of Egypt. In exchange for the spiritual riches belonging to the people of God in the promise made to them concerning Christ, he was willing to give all temporal great- ness, endure hardships, and do the will of God only.—Were the men of old disappointed? Were the parents of Moses put to shame in their faith, do you think? Who had found the rock; Moses,who clung to the Invisible One; or the king of Egypt, who trusted in his own earthly power? Never, at any time, has any man believed in the Lord, and been disappointed; none shall ever be put to shame who holds fast the word of the Lord.

Now, this word proclaims to us salvation in Christ from sin and death, and gives us promise of life eternal. By baptism and faith we have already entered the kingdom of God; "we who believe are come to Mount Zion and the city of the living God, to the heavenly Jeru- salem and the many thousands of angels." We are passed from death unto life, and are already with God. But we do not and shall not *see* it as yet; we walk in faith, not seeing, but believing. We are pressed and worried by sin and the devil; the church is in distress, and the children of the world are in places of authority. We feel anguish and pain, have afflictions of body and soul, suffer persecution and reproach; but we obtain the victory by holding to the invisible and present God and Savior. We can not, will not, shall not, fail to cling to his word; for he will hold us to it. Let the heaven and earth, then, pass away; the word remains for ever.

Faithful God, give us grace to believe, in order that neither any affliction nor pleasure may drag us away from thy word. Keep us in and by this word while life endures; keep us in the word and faith until we die. Amen.

In the faith, O make me steadfast; Let not Satan, death or shame, Of my confidence deprive me; Lord, my refuge is thy name. When the flesh inclines to ill, Let thy Word prove stronger still.

90. Friday after Fourth Sunday after Epiphany.

Psalm 2. Why do the heathen rage, and the people imagine a vain thing? The kings of the earth set themselves, and the rulers take counsel together, against the Lord, and against his anointed, saying, Let us break their bands asunder, and cast away their cords from us. He that sitteth in the heavens shall laugh; the Lord shall have them in derision. Then shall he speak unto them in his wrath, and vex them in his sore displeasure. Yet have I set my king upon my holy hill of Zion. I will declare the decree: the Lord hath said unto me, Thou art my Son; this day have I begotten thee. Ask of me, and I shall give thee the heathen for thine inheritance, and the uttermost parts of the earth for thy possession. Thou shalt break them with a rod of iron; thou shalt dash them in pieces like a potter's vessel. Be wise now, therefore, ye kings; be instructed, ye judges of the earth. Serve the Lord with fear, and rejoice with trembling. Kiss the Son, lest he be angry, and ye perish from the way, when his wrath is kindled but a little. Blessed are all they that put their trust in him.

"The world suffers and tolerates every kind of false, ungodly doctrine and all manner of idolatrous ways; but it can not endure the Lord in heaven and his Christ." (Luther). The kings and rulers of the earth who now take counsel together against the Lord's anointed are the scholars, the kings in the world of letters and oratory. In their eyes the Cristian religion is obsolete. Our age has long ago outgrown the faith of our childhood and the God of the Bible; and above the grave in which they have buried creed and dogma the scholars are now singing their song of triumph, as did the rulers among the Jews after the crucifixion of Christ. Too soon! The counsel of these rulers in the world of intellect is mere vanity. "But this," says Luther, "was written for our learning, that we through patience and comfort of the scriptures might have hope. For that which is written of Christ is true of all Christians. Every upright Christian shall have his Herod and Pilate, who rage, speak many vain things, and take counsel together against him. Therefore every Christian must arm himself. If these assaults on him are not made now by men and devils and his own conscience, they will be made when he is in the agony of death. Then it will be highly necessary that he apply to his heart the comfort contained in scripture passages such as this: 'He that sitteth in the heavens shall laugh; the Lord shall have them in derision.' On this hope he must stand fast and let nothing in heaven or hell persuade him to depart from it.—No matter how strong and mighty the enemies may appear to human eyes, their speech is so vain and their counsel so little to be regarded that God does not even deem it worth while to oppose them, as would be necessary in a matter of great and serious importance; but he laughs at them and derides them as persons engaged in a little, contemptible foolishness, not worth his notice. But O, how strong a faith is not required by these words! For who believed, when Christ suffered and the Jews triumphed, that God laughed at them? And when we suffer and are oppressed, do we not find it extremely difficult to believe that God laughs at our enemies, and has them in derision? For we, indeed, seem plainly to see and feel that we are derided and oppressed by God and man." He, however, that sitteth in the heavens speaks judgment to the enemies and salvation to his believers. He "cares for us; and he dwells secure, without all fear. Though we be troubled and tempted, he who keeps watch over us is entirely serene. We are tossed hither and thither; but he is firm and shall never suffer the righteous to be moved. But all this takes place in such a secret and hidden manner that you are unable to understand it; you could not, indeed, unless you were in heaven. On earth you must suffer, and no creature can help you. You must not expect comfort in your trials and tribulations, before you have left all else behind and reached him who dwells in heaven. Then you, also, dwell in heaven; though, as yet, only in hope and faith. We must, therefore, in our every need, temptation, trial, and adversity, fix our heart on him who dwells in heaven; then shall the misfortunes, anguish, and distress which we must bear in this world not only rest lightly on us, but become a source of great joy."

Blessed be thou, Lord, our strong fortress. Give us the grace of the Spirit to believe, and to place our whole cause in thy hands, to serve thee, and to obey thy voice only. Amen.

Lord, keep us steadfast in thy word; Curb pope and Turk and all that horde Who fain would hurl from off thy throne Christ Jesus, thy beloved Son.

Lord Jesus Christ, thy power make known; For thou art Lord of lords alone; Defend thy Christendom, that we May evermore sing praise to thee.

O Holy Ghost, our comfort, thou With unity thy church endow, Support us in our final strife, And lead us out of death to life.

---

91. Saturday after Fourth Sunday after Epiphany.

Psalm 27, 7–14. Hear, O Lord, when I cry with my voice: have mercy also upon me, and answer me. When thou saidst, Seek ye my face; my heart said unto thee, Thy face, Lord, will I seek. Hide not thy face far from me; put not thy servant away in anger: thou hast been my help; leave me not, neither forsake me, O God of my salvation. When my father and my mother forsake me, then the Lord will take me up. Teach me thy way, O Lord, and lead me in a plain path, because of mine enemies. Deliver me not over unto the will of mine enemies: for false witnesses are risen up against me, and such as breathe out cruelty. I had fainted, unless I had believed to see the goodness of the Lord in the land of the living. Wait on the Lord; be of good courage, and he shall strengthen thine heart: wait, I say, on the Lord.

It is a great mercy that the Lord has given us his promises concerning salvation, and has said that we are to hold these up before him when we cry to him in our distress. He wants to be conquered by means of his own word. When Jacob went to Mesopotamia, God gave him this promise: "I will bring thee again into this land, and I will do that which I have spoken to thee of." However, when Jacob returned, God came at night, and wrestled with him, and threatened his life. Then Jacob held up before the Lord his own promise, and gained the victory. "Lord, thou hast said that thou wouldst bring me again to Canaan; if thou dost now take my life, thy promise will not come true. Thou must do that which thou hast said. Do this, Lord, for the sake of thy mercy and truth." He wept and prayed, and conquered; and, instead of losing his life, he received the blessing of the Lord. Thus did Moses and David and all who were governed by the Spirit of God. The heart shall seek the face of the Lord, abide by that which he has spoken and done; for he has said: "Seek my face." He has said: "Call upon me in the day of trouble; I will deliver thee, and thou shalt glorify me." We shall remind him of his promise; then he cannot do otherwise than help us. These are not empty words, but unfailing truth. He is the God of our salvation, the God who has a remedy against every evil, and has pledged himself to save all who seek him. Human help does not avail against the devil and death. The love of father and mother falls short; but his mercy endures for ever. When I stand forsaken, like a poor, friendless orphan child, the Lord will receive me and care for me.

Shall, then, the people of God always be in danger among enemies
and false brethren? Certainly they shall, while they are here on earth.
The tares sown by the enemy do not die out. And in afflictions we
learn obedience. The church of God thrives best under persecution;
the Christians are sanctified in suffering, and are glorified through
tribulations; gold is purified in fire. Be assured, beyond any doubt,
that the way of distress which you travel is good, and leads to the
land of life, if you do but seek the face of the Lord at all times, and
if you always come forward into the light before him with your heart.
—However, our afflictions shall come to an end. If we did not believe
to see the goodness of the Lord in the land of the living, we had de-
spaired. But now we believe in his power and mercy, and seek his
face; and then himself places the unfailing words of hope on our
lips: "Wait on the Lord; be of good courage, and he shall strengthen
thine heart; wait, I say, on the Lord."

Lord Jesus, thou hast said that we shall believe and hope in thee
alone. Give us grace to do this by thy Holy Spirit. We have no faith,
we can not pray; but we come to thee. Do with us as thou hast said:
We will not let thee go, except thou bless us. Let thy word be
preached in the power of the Spirit, and let it accomplish that whereto
thou dost send it. Amen.

If God himself be for me, I may a host defy, For when I pray, before
me My foes confounded fly. If Christ, my head and master, Befriend me
from above, What foe or what disaster Can drive me from his love?

---

92. Fifth Sunday after Epiphany. I.

Lord Jesus, give us grace to hear thy word and examine ourselves. Amen.

Gospel Lesson, Matthew 13, 24–30. Another parable put he forth unto
them, saying, The kingdom of heaven is likened unto a man which sowed good
seed in his field: But while men slept, his enemy came and sowed tares
among the wheat, and went his way. But when the blade was sprung up, and
brought forth fruit, then appeared the tares also. So the servants of the householder came and said unto him, Sir, didst not thou sow good seed in thy field?
from whence then hath it tares? He said unto them, An enemy hath done this.
The servants said unto him, Wilt thou then that we go and gather them
up? But he said, Nay; lest while ye gather up the tares, ye root up also the
wheat with them. Let both grow together until the harvest: and in the time
of harvest I will say to the reapers, Gather ye together first the tares, and bind
them in bundles to burn them: but gather the wheat into my barn.

In the visible church here on earth tares and wheat grow together.
We need never think to present a pure community of saints before the
end of the world. Christ himself says: Let the children of the kingdom
and the children of the devil grow together. Herein there are several
important lessons for us. 1) It is not ours to judge; the Lord knows
his own; *he* and none other holds the fan in his hand. That the
church is to debar from its Holy Communion them that are manifestly

wicked is another matter (1 Corinthians, 5). 2) You shall not take offense, though it come to your notice that there are hypocrites and wicked men in the church. You shall not, on this account, secede; else you assist the enemy in rending asunder the church of God. Conquer such temptations to pride by calling to mind your own littleness; and pay attention to the lesson which the Lord teaches in this text: Where there is wheat there always will be tares; it would not be a true wheat field, if the enemy did not care to sow tares in it. 3) Do not rely on your being a Christian in name, or on your fellowship with the faithful; examine yourself earnestly before God, and bring forth good fruit unto the Lord. 4) For the sake of his pious children God spares the world. The great and haughty men of the world in the Christian lands are indebted to the despised saints of God for his long-suffering patience. The believers carry the world and the world's culture on their shoulders. 5) An eternal separation is coming, and the angels shall make no mistake as to who the saints are. Then the present order of the universe shall of necessity cease to be, and every human society on earth shall be dissolved; for all their roots shall then be torn apart. 6) Then the church of Christ shall be purged of all hypocrites, and shall consist of saints only.—Now, are you prepared for the day of judgment? Have you the earnest of the Spirit that you are of the elect? Do you keep yourself undefiled of the mind and life of the wordly-minded Christians? All who offend and do iniquity shall be cast into the furnace of fire; there shall be wailing and gnashing of teeth. Then shall the righteous shine forth as the sun in the kingdom of their Father. Who hath ears to hear, let him hear!

Lord Jesus, protect us from the evil enemy; preserve us from carnal security, from spiritual pride, from coming with undisciplined and unclean hearts to thy communion table; from sects and schisms, and from judging without charity. Keep us watchful and prepared for the judgment, and let us stand before thee with honor on that day. Amen.

Our Hope and Expectation, O Jesus, now appear; Arise, thou Sun so longed for, O'er this benighted sphere! With hearts and hands uplifted, We plead, O Lord, to see The day of earth's redemption, That brings us unto thee.

---

93. Fifth Sunday after Epiphany. II.

Lord, give us the Spirit of truth, love, peace, and joy. Amen.

Epistle Lesson, Colossians 3, 12-17. Put on therefore, as the elect of God, holy and beloved, bowels of mercies, kindness, humbleness of mind, meekness, longsuffering; forbearing one another, and forgiving one another, if any man have a quarrel against any: even as Christ forgave you, so also do ye. And above all these things put on charity, which is the bond of perfectness. And let the peace of God rule in your hearts, to the which also ye are called in one body; and be ye thankful. Let the word of Christ dwell in you richly in all wisdom; teaching and admonishing one another in psalms and hymns and spiritual songs, singing with grace in your hearts to the Lord. And whatsoever ye do in word or deed, do all in the name of the Lord Jesus, giving thanks to God and the Father by him.

This is a statement of what we should be as good plants in the Lord's field, his church on earth. Such as here described is his wheat. From within, from the holy life of love, the flower and fruit develop; exhale their fragrance, which is pleasing to the Lord; and are sweet to the taste of men. Than an epistle like this there certainly is no better correction for our vain, separatistic ideas. Let us take this lesson to heart, and practice it with sincere obedience; then shall we surely dwell together in brotherly unity, wash one another's feet, bear one another's infirmities, and never repulse one another, saying: "Keep your distance; I am more holy than you." Look at yourself in these words of the apostle as in a glass. Are you really, yourself, a true grain of wheat? If so, this admonition lays hold of your innermost heart, and awakens in you a living desire to be such a one as the apostle here describes. But you also see that you are as yet a long distance in the rear, and that you are far from following all the way to the end the footsteps of Jesus. O, how grand and beautiful Christianity is, when it is genuine. It is the life; and without there is nothing but death.

God, give us thy Holy Ghost, that he may sanctify us and make the church ready as a pure and perfect bride of the Lord. Thou wilt do this for Jesus' sake. Amen.

Give to our God immortal praise! Mercy and truth are all his ways. Wonders of grace to God belong: Repeat his mercies in your song.
Give to the Lord of lords renown; The King of kings with glory crown. His mercies ever shall endure, When lords and kings are known no more.

---

94. Monday after Fifth Sunday after Epiphany.

Search me, O God, and know my heart, and lead me in the way everlasting. Amen.

Matthew 13, 36–43. Then Jesus sent the multitude away, and went into the house: and his disciples came unto him, saying, Declare unto us the parable of the tares of the field. He answered and said unto them, He that soweth the good seed is the Son of man: The field is the world: the good seed are the children of the kingdom; but the tares are the children of the wicked one: The enemy that sowed them is the devil: the harvest is the end of the world; and the reapers are the angels. As therefore the tares are gathered and burned in the fire; so shall it be in the end of this world. The Son of man shall send forth his angels, and they shall gather out of his kingdom all things that offend, and them which do iniquity; and shall cast them into a furnace of fire: there shall be wailing and gnashing of teeth. Then shall the righteous shine forth as the sun in the kingdom of their Father. Who hath ears to hear, let him hear.

Ignatius, a disciple of the apostle John, was about to be thrown to the wild beasts. Shortly before this he writes to a church which he knew and loved: "I am one of God's grains of corn; I am to be ground by the teeth of the beasts, in order that I may be one of Christ's pure loaves." This is one of the few who have encountered death with a faith in which was no admixture of doubt. Who among us is able to boast of the like? And may not God come this very day? Here the rule that the harvest can not come before the summer does not hold good. The Father has reserved to himself alone the right to fix the time and hour. Neither may we say: "The signs which are to precede this harvest have not yet come to pass." We often are so blind that we neither see nor understand the signs of the times. Nor may we say: "The world is not yet ripe for the harvest." Of this none can judge but the Lord of the harvest, who engages and directs the reapers.—Awake, therefore, ere the time comes to separate the grain and the chaff. God will have no noxious weeds. They may take such firm hold that it is beyond the power of man to destroy them; parasitic plants grow so thick that man is helpless to cope with the situation. But the sickle of God can not be broken. He cuts down princes and paupers as it pleases best himself. Before him all men are as the grass of the field. The ungodly shall not stand in the judgment, nor sinners in the congregation of the righteous.—It will avail you nothing to dissemble before God. There is a sort of spurious wheat which in outward appearance is much like the genuine. A human reaper may mistake it for good grain, and gather it into his barn. Such counterfeit wheat is found in the field of God, also. Many have a form of godliness. But it is only a Christian cloak; the heart has not been renewed in humility and devotion to Jesus Christ. It is not possible to deceive God. He sees the heart, the corn, the kernel. These spurious ears of wheat, also, shall his reapers bind together in bundles to burn them. Make haste, therefore; become good wheat by the power of God. Be not ashamed to do penance. Make haste! The older one is, the more difficult it is to be renewed and become a child of God. Act on the supposition that the day of judgment shall come tomorrow. Today, then, you should take thought that you may be saved. Should God in his mercy prolong your life, you never will repent having found shelter under his grace; for they, only, enjoy life who adorn it with faith.

Give us, O God, this grace, that we may be true grains of wheat, and be gathered into thy glory. Amen.

Ne'er think the victory won, Nor lay thine armor down; Thine arduous work will not be done Till thou obtain thy crown. Fight on my soul, till death Shall bring thee to thy God: He'll take thee, at thy parting breath, To his divine abode.

95. Tuesday after Fifth Sunday after Epiphany.

Lord, have mercy on us, and let thy word of reproof be for our salvation.

Revelations 3, 1-6. And unto the angel of the church in Sardis write; These things saith he that hath the seven Spirits of God, and the seven stars; I know thy works, that thou hast a name, that thou livest, and art dead. Be watchful, and strengthen the things which remain, that are ready to die:

for I have not found thy works perfect before God. Remember therefore how thou hast received and heard; and hold fast, and repent. If therefore thou shalt not watch, I will come on thee as a thief, and thou shalt not know what hour I will come upon thee. Thou hast a few names even in Sardis which have not defiled their garments; and they shall walk with me in white: for they are worthy. He that overcometh, the same shall be clothed in white raiment; and I will not blot out his name out of the book of life, but I will confess his name before my Father, and before his angels. He that hath an ear, let him hear what the Spirit saith unto the churches.

This is spoken to us; it fits the condition in our churches. How may not the solemnity of this declaration cause the heart to quake: "Thou hast a name that thou livest, and art dead." Nothing could be more sad. Of all things life is the best, and death the worst. What could, then, be more terrible than to be called living, and yet to be dead? How impressive a statement this is from the mouth of Jesus: "I have not found thy works perfect before God." And, again: "If thou shalt not watch, I will come on thee as a thief." But such is the state of affairs with the greater number among us. They are called Christians, that is, anointed; but the living Spirit of God does not dwell in them. On the contrary, the prince of death rules in their hearts. O, ye few, who have not defiled your garments; watch, and keep yourselves pure. Fight for your lives. The enemy of your souls wants to rob you of life; fight, therefore, as a man struggles against a mortal foe. Truly, every day is in these times a struggle for life itself,—the life everlasting. Strengthen one another; for many are weak, and on the point of dropping off to sleep in death. Keep close together around our Lord Jesus. Love one another, and bear with one another; but reprove one another, also, and understand that this is love. Admonish one another, and stand together confessing the same faith. For God's sake do not let the devil divide the army of the Lord. Brethren, the white garments of victory and our names written in the book of life, these are a prize well worth fighting for.

O God, my heart burns within me from fear of losing the life which thou didst give me. And the brethren, Lord God; let none of them fall back into the sleep of death. Almighty, merciful God, help us. Quicken us, and make us zealous to testify concerning thee, and to praise thy name. Knit us together; unite our hearts in thy love. Amen.

May the grace of Christ our Savior, And the Father's boundless love, With the Holy Spirit's favor, Rest upon us from above.
Thus may we abide in union With each other and the Lord, And possess, in sweet communion. Joys which earth cannot afford.

---

96. Wednesday after Fifth Sunday after Epiphany.

Psalm 12. Help, Lord; for the godly man ceaseth; for the faithful fail from among the children of men. They speak vanity every one with his neighbor: with flattering lips, and with a double heart, do they speak. The Lord shall cut off all flattering lips, and the tongue that speaketh proud things;

who have said, With our tongue will we prevail; our lips are our own: who is lord over us? For the oppression of the poor, for the sighing of the needy, now will I arise, saith the Lord; I will set him in safety from him that puffeth at him. The words of the Lord are pure words; as silver tried in a furnace of earth, purified seven times. Thou shalt keep them, O Lord, thou shalt preserve them from this generation for ever. The wicked walk on every side, when the vilest men are exalted.

There is a holy sorrow for the distress of the church. Have you known this sorrow? Paul testifies, his conscience also bearing him witness in the Holy Ghost, that he has great heaviness and continual sorrow in his heart because of the blindness of his people; and his heart burns in him at every offence which comes to his notice in the church. This is some of the same fire that melted our Lord Jesus, and caused him to shed tears over Jerusalem. Is there but little distress at the present time, since we know so little of this sorrow? By no means. But the love of many has waxed cold; and we say in the words of our text: "Help, Lord; for the godly man ceaseth." Hypocrisy, security, lukewarmness, unbelief; yes, unbelief, unbelief, have gained the ascendency; and even the hearts of the faithful have been contaminated thereby to such a degree that they do not feel the impressiveness of eternity, the weight of God's wrath, the significance of grace, the importance of the Christian life. Therefore we have in our hearts at the present time but little joy in the Lord, and but little sorrow for the misery of the world and the distress of the church.— But we have the word of the Lord among us; the pure word, as silver refined seven times. Hear this, ye wretched ones, who have been maltreated by the spirit of lies; ye needy, who cry to the Lord; hear his unadulterated word. This revives us, humbles us, gathers us; it creates life in the dead bones. Hear, hear; then shall your soul live.

Thou living God, quicken our hearts; give us the love after which we thirst, that we may know its joy and its sorrow, and that we may spend our years in the exercise of this love. Amen.

Lord Jesus Christ, with us abide, For round us falls the even-tide; Nor let thy word, that heavenly light, For us be ever veiled in night.

In these last days of sore distress Grant us, dear Lord, true steadfastness, That pure we keep—till life is spent—Thy holy word and sacrament.

Lord Jesus, help, thy Church uphold, For we are sluggish, thoughtless, cold; Endow thy word with power and grace, And spread its truth in every place.

---

97. Thursday after Fifth Sunday after Epiphany.

O God, may we be vessels of gold and silver in thy house. Amen.

1 Corinthians 5, 9–13. I wrote unto you in an epistle not to company with fornicators: Yet not altogether with the fornicators of this world, or with the covetous, or extortioners, or with idolaters; for then must ye needs go out of the world. But now I have written unto you not to keep company, if any man that is called a brother be a fornicator, or covetous, or an idolater, or a railer, or a drunkard, or an extortioner; with such a one no not to eat.

For what have I to do to judge them **also that** are without? do not ye judge them that are within? But them that **are** without God judgeth. Therefore put away from among yourselves that wicked person.

When in the pursuance of our vocation it becomes necessary for us to associate with ungodly persons, we must not withdraw from them, although we find their company unpleasant; but neither should we unnecessarily run headlong into the company of wolves. Christians have no spiritual fellowship whatever with the ungodly; their hearts do not belong together, and they shall not cultivate the society of one another. If any man be a drunkard or fornicator, covetous or idolator, reviler or extortioner, and the Christians have brotherhood with such a one, the body of Christ is defiled, the holy name of the church is befouled, and the Lord himself is dishonored. It is a leaven that leavens the whole lump, a foul spot that eats as does a canker. We are not to judge; that is: 1) We do not assume to decide how many there be of the members of the church who are true believers; but in charity we think as well as possible of all, though many of them may exhibit various traits which we do not like. 2) We are to hope that the wicked, also, may repent; and we should remember that in the glory of heaven they may, perhaps, stand nearer than we to the throne. We are not to judge; yet it is our duty to pass judgment on those who give offence in the church by reason of their ungodly life. It is our duty to help the erring and wicked to mend their ways; and this is the very reason why it is our duty to discipline them and exclude them from communion with us at the Lord's table. We know that the unrighteous shall not inherit the kingdom of God; and we shall let them know it and feel it, in order that they may repent.—By the help of God we will exercise discipline, both for the purpose of keeping the church pure, and for the purpose of saving the ungodly. Charity demands this. The decay of church discipline, as well as sectarianism and separatism, has its origin in want of true charity. The church, mark you, the church society, the congregation, sins against God and against the souls when it fails to judge them that are within, and to rid itself of the wicked. God give us the Spirit of love, strength and wisdom. Amen.

How helpless guilty nature lies; Unconscious of its load! The heart, unchanged, can never rise To happiness and God.
O change these wretched hearts of ours, And give them life divine! Then shall our passions and our powers, Almighy Lord, be thine.

---

98. Friday after Fifth Sunday after Epiphany.

Let thy truth and love, O God, penetrate our souls. Amen.

Ephesians 4, 11–16. And he gave some, apostles; and some, prophets; and some, evangelists; and some, pastors and teachers; for the perfecting of the saints, for the work of the ministry, for the edifying of the body of Christ: Till we all come in the unity of the faith, and of the knowledge of the Son of God, unto a perfect man, unto the measure of the stature of the fulness of

Christ: That we henceforth be no more children, tossed to and fro, and carried about with every wind of doctrine, by the sleight of men, and cunning craftiness, whereby they lie in wait to deceive; but, speaking the truth in love, may grow up into him in all things, which is the head, even Christ: From whom the whole body fitly joined together, and compacted by that which every joint supplieth, according to the effectual working in the measure of every part, maketh increase of the body unto the edifying of itself in love.

In the midst of all confusion do you follow your course straight onward in humility and love, and hold fast that which you heard from the beginning. When one cries: "Lo, here is Christ," and another cries: "No; but Christ is here," do not go after them, nor follow them. Now, you have, I trust, enough of faith and knowledge of the Son of God to know that in nothing is the devil more active than in founding sects and parties. To rend, to tear asunder, to cut in pieces the body of Christ; surely, this is the devil's own work. Let us henceforth be no more children, tossed to and fro as waves, and carried about with every wind of doctrine, by the sleight of men, and cunning craftiness, whereby they lie in wait to deceive. Let us now walk as sober men, and labor in truth and love for the Lord, in every way serving one another. Do not retreat by the breadth of a hair from that which you know to be true; but love all the children of God, even if they may not be of one mind with you in all things. Seek to acquire clear and fixed convictions, that you may know what the truth is and cling to it with unswerving loyalty; but though you be never so unyielding, do not violate the law of love, and do not lose your spirit of humility. You shall not seek strife; but neither shall you be a coward and desert your post when you are attacked. "Every one with one of his hands wrought in the work, and with the other hand held a weapon." (Nehemiah 4, 17). Go your way onward in goodness and active charity; then shall you promote your own growth and edify others. The necessary strength has been given us. The word and Spirit are present with the grace required for the growth of the body of Christ. Labor hopefully, however dark the outlook; in the end all who speak the truth in love shall become one in faith. It is a grand object for which to strive. God, give us this great grace, that we may at all times speak the truth in love. Give us this grace, for Jesus' sake. Amen.

Ye servants of the Lord, Each in his office wait, Observant of his heavenly word, And watchful at his gate.
Let all our lamps be bright, And trim the golden flame; Gird up your loins, as in his sight, For awful is his name.

99. Saturday after Fifth Sunday after Epiphany.

Psalm 74, 1–9. 12. Maschil of Asaph. O God, why hast thou cast us off for ever? why doth thine anger smoke against the sheep of thy pasture? Remember thy congregation, which thou hast purchased of old; the rod of thine inheritance, which thou hast redeemed; this mount Zion, wherein thou hast dwelt. Lift up thy feet unto the perpetual desolations; even all that the enemy hath done wickedly in the sanctuary. Thine enemies roar in the midst of thy congregations; they set up their ensigns for signs. A man was famous according as he had lifted up axes upon the thick trees. But now they break down the carved work thereof at once with axes and hammers. They have cast fire into thy sanctuary; they have defiled by casting down the dwelling place of thy name to the ground. They said in their hearts, Let us destroy them together: they have burned up all the synagogues of God in the land. We see not our signs: there is no more any prophet: neither is there among us any that knoweth how long. For God is my King of old, working salvation in the midst of the earth.

It always was a cross for the saints of God that there was such a deal of wickedness in the church. They saw the tares among the wheat, and asked: "Wilt thou, then, that we go and gather them up?" But the open infidelity which denies the divinity of Christ has probably at no time been greater and more shameless than it is now. Must it not be said at this time: "Thine enemies roar in the midst of thy congregations?" And must we not now ask: "O God, how long shall the adversary reproach? shall the enemy blaspheme thy name for ever? For men who call themselves Christians, and dwell in the midst of the Christian people, mock and scoff with the most reckless impudence at Christ and his person and office in his word and servants; and they break down the most sacred and precious jewels of the church with axes and hammers. O God, why dost thou not take thy right hand out of thy bosom? Hast thou forgotten thy congregation, which thou hast purchased; the rod of thy inheritance, which thou hast redeemed? Seest thou not, O Lord, what a fire is kindled in our hearts also; in the hearts of thy poor people, who still cling to thee? See, how the enemy does wickedly against us. Wherefore dost thou not 'turn thy hand again upon thy little ones'?"—Nevertheless, the complaint of this psalm, also, ends in hope and promise. "For God is my King of old, working salvation in the midst of the earth. Thou brakest the heads of leviathan in pieces. The day is thine, the night also is thine. Arise, O God, plead thine own cause; remember how the foolish man reproacheth thee daily."—Help us, help us; help us to believe that which thy mouth has spoken. Amen.

O God! how sin's dread works abound! Throughout the earth no rest is found, And wide has falsehood's spirit spread, And error boldly rears its head.
Oh, grant that in thy holy word We here may live and die, dear Lord. And when our journey endeth here, Receive us into glory there.

On the Sixth Sunday after Epiphany, if there be one, the text for the Twenty-seventh Sunday after Trinity may be read.

100. Septuagesima Sunday. I.

Lord Jesus, speak now thy lesson of life to us all.

Gospel Lesson, Matthew 20, 1–16. For the kingdom of heaven is like unto a man that is an householder, which went out early in the morning to hire laborers into his vineyard. And when he had agreed with the laborers for a penny a day, he sent them into his vineyard. And he went out about the third hour, and saw others standing idle in the marketplace, and said unto them, Go ye also into the vineyard, and whatsoever is right, I will give you. And they went their way. Again he went out about the sixth and ninth hour, and did likewise. And about the eleventh hour he went out, and found others standing idle, and saith unto them, Why stand ye here all the day idle? They say unto him, Because no man hath hired us. He saith unto them, Go ye also into the vineyard; and whatsoever is right, that shall ye receive. So when even was come, the lord of the vineyard saith unto his steward, Call the laborers, and give them their hire, beginning from the last unto the first. And when they came that were hired about the eleventh hour, they received every man a penny. But when the first came, they supposed that they should have received more: and they likewise received every man a penny. And when they had received it, they murmured against the goodman of the house, saying, These last have wrought but one hour, and thou hast made them equal unto us, which have borne the burden and heat of the day. But he answered one of them, and said, Friend, I do thee no wrong: didst not thou agree with me for a penny? Take that thine is, and go thy way: I will give unto this last even as unto thee. Is it not lawful for me to do what I will with mine own? Is thine eye evil, because I am good? So the last shall be first, and the first last: for many be called, but few chosen.

The faithful live before God, and do all their work in the Lord. When we do this we labor in his vineyard. Then we in all things seek the honor of the Lord, and strive after promoting the growth of God's kingdom; namely, by increasing in faith, strengthening the brethren, and bringing the unbelieving to repentance. They only who lead this manner of life, and work for the kingdom of God, are laborers in the Lord's vineyard. The others stand idle in the marketplace. Many men and woman strive and exert themselves to the utmost, but only for the things of this life or in selfrighteousness; in spite of all their labor, they stand idle in the marketplace. The Lord goes out to call the laborers into his vineyard. Some hear the call early, in the morning of their life; and so they live in faith from childhood, and practice deeds of love. Others are converted in their youth, others not until later on, and some at about the eleventh hour of their life. It is a great mercy to serve the Lord from the early morning, and to live a life which is rich in true and good works. None is able to do this of himself; the call is of God, and the power to remain faithful is given of God. "What hast thou that thou didst not receive?"—It is not the fault of the Lord that many continue long in sin, and waste their day of grace. They speak a lie when they say that no man has hired them; the Lord wanted to engage them early in the morning, but they would not listen to his call. In spite of this he calls them again when

128

the day is almost done; and if they then accept the call, he gives them a full day's hire.

If you still stand idle in the marketplace; if you do not as yet labor for the Lord of the church; if you still live your life for the world, and not for Jesus, who lived his whole life for us alone, and who labored for us until he did sweat blood and suffer death on the cross;—then listen to his call today, and come now and labor in his vineyard. If you are young, it is not too early; the Lord was from childhood engaged in the work of the Father. If you are old, it is not too late; the time of grace still endures,—but soon it will have expired.

Besides this invitation to come and labor in the vineyard, our gospel text contains the lesson, that we are to recognize the labor itself and the reward as being *pure grace* on the part of God. If you begin to harbor the thought that you have by your work made God your debtor, you are no longer fit for life in his blessed fellowship. For love is then lost; and you again come under the curse of the law. No, my dear friend, all is grace; God bestows a glorious gift on you when he permits you to labor much for him. How many, who were not converted until late in life, do not continue to weep, because they wasted so much of their time in vanity, and served Satan in the fair days of their youth! The glorious privilege of devoting the whole strength of your life to the Lord's service is a more than sufficient reward of your labor. The others, who now receive full grace for all their sin, and full salvation according to the measure of their ability to receive it, you shall regard, not with envy, but rather with sympathy, and above all with thanks to the Lord who is so unspeakably rich in grace. In the kingdom of God his gracious will and his mercy, which govern all things, are supreme; no human merit, no deeds of whatever degree or dignity have any authority.

Lord God, do thou call quickly all who can be called. Preserve all thine from pride, selfrighteousness and envy. Give us humble hearts, full of love unto the end. Amen.

Hark! the voice of Jesus crying, "Who will go and work today? Fields are white, and harvests waiting, Who will bear the sheaves away?" Loud and long the Master calleth, Rich reward he offers thee: Who will answer, gladly saying, "Here am I; send me, send me"?

---

101. Septuagesima Sunday. II.

Lord Jesus, draw us after thee. Amen.

Epistle Lesson, 1 Corinthians 9, 24-10, 5. Know ye not that they which run in a race run all, but one receiveth the prize? So run, that ye may obtain. And every man that striveth for the mastery is temperate in all things. Now they do it to obtain a corruptible crown; but we an incorruptible. I therefore so run, not as uncertainly; so fight I, not as one that beateth the air: but I keep under my body, and bring it into subjection; lest that by any means, when I have preached to others, I myself should be a castaway. Moreover, brethren,

I would not that ye should be ignorant, how that all our fathers were under the cloud, and all passed through the sea; and were all baptized unto Moses in the cloud and in the sea; and did all eat the same spiritual meat; and did all drink the same spiritual drink; for they drank of that spiritual Rock that followed them: and that Rock was Christ.

The gospel lesson for today, on the laborers in the vineyard, contains a solemn warning against falling from *grace;* or in other words, against falling into the sin of self-righteousness. In like manner this *epistle lesson* earnestly exhorts us to keep in the right path. It is a great thing to be converted, to come over from the road leading to hell onto that which leads to heaven; but it is, if possible, even greater yet to remain faithful unto the end and never to quit the road until the goal is reached. A glorious, incorruptible crown beckons us at the end of the course; but they, only, receive it who are faithful unto the end. The apostle likens the Christians to men who run in a race. Even as these put forth all their strength and exert themselves to the utmost in order to win the prize, so shall we exert ourselves in order to win eternal life. In like manner as they looked intently forward and had nor ear nor eye for anything but the goal, so shall we with *steady* longing look upward and use our every faculty and all our time in the endeavor to secure the crown. Our spiritual exercises and all our work on earth shall be done in the Lord and have heaven as their aim. The men who took part in those athletic games mortified their flesh in order to increase their suppleness; and they willingly abstained from sensual pleasures which might unfit them for the contests;—and all this in order to win a wreath that soon withers. Us there awaits an incorruptible crown. Do we abandon all those things which might weaken us for the struggle? Do we freely renounce the lusts of the flesh for Jesus' sake? Many go out of Egypt; but few, alas, are they who enter Canaan. They are baptized into Christ, but will not follow him; they eat and drink his Holy Supper, but their hearts turn back to the fleshpots of Egypt.

Brethren and sisters; remain faithful to the Lord. Let the work of your salvation be your sacred care. Stand steadfast in the *grace* of God; push all the time more deeply into the fellowship of Jesus. Watch and pray, and take heed unto yourselves; bow to the will of God when he disciplines you and humbles your pride, and become ever less in your own eyes; then shall you become all the time more rich in the Lord's work, and receive his glory as your reward.

"When I am faint and on my dangers ponder, Then let me see the crown that beckons yonder, Of which thou gavest me thy promise true; Then shall I gather strength and heart anew."—Give us, O God, to be faithful unto the end, for the sake of Jesus Christ. Amen.

From strength to strength go on, Wrestle, and fight, and pray; Tread all the powers of darkness down, And win the well-fought day.
Still let the Spirit cry, In all his soldiers, "Come," Till Christ the Lord descends from high, And takes the conqueror home.

102. Monday after Septuagesima Sunday.

I will pay my vows unto the Lord now in the presence of all his people.

Luke 17, 7–10. But which of you, having a servant plowing, or feeding cattle, will say unto him by and by, when he is come from the field, Go and sit down to meat? And will not rather say unto him, Make ready wherewith I may sup, and gird thyself, and serve me, till I have eaten and drunken; and afterward thou shalt eat and drink? Doth he thank that servant because he did the things that were commanded him? I trow not. So likewise ye, when ye shall have done all those things which are commanded you, say, We are unprofitable servants: we have done that which was our duty to do.

Servants in that age were serfs, who with their labor were the absolute property of their master. It was as impossible for them to do more than the service which they owed their master, as it is for my hand to do more than its duty to me. All that which he commanded they were in duty bound to do. In like manner we Christians are, after a *blessed* fashion, the serfs of the Lord. This entirely excludes all merit on our part, and destroys our self-righteousness; but it imbues us with the willing and humble spirit of love. It is not possible for us to *earn* any title to salvation and honor before God; 1) because in Christ we are already righteous, and *born* to be heirs of glory; 2) because all that we have belongs to him. He owns us in fee simple; whatever there may be in us of strength to do that which is good, is his; it is he who works in us both to will and to do. Is this not a grand and good thing for us? The relation is not that of bondage in the *distressing* sense of the word; our hearts are bound to him by the delicious bonds of love and liberty; and thus we belong to him heartily and gladly, and are happy in serving him with joy·and delight. If we did our whole duty to the utmost limit, no merit would be ours; still less can we boast of any merit now that we, unfortunately, do not fulfil our duty. No; that which he has done is our merit, our privilege, our hope; more than this we do not need, and more we do not have. We know that it is not the duty of the master to serve the servant; but this is what our Master has done. He came not to be ministered unto, but to minister; this is our merit, our redemption. Therefore we look into the perfect law of liberty, and do not labor for hire; we are more than paid by being permitted to devote ourselves to him, to love him, and to serve him.

Give us this grace, precious Lord Jesus. We heartily desire to promote thy honor. Give us this grace by thy good Holy Spirit. Amen.

Not the labors of my hands Can fulfil thy law's demands. Could my zeal no respite know, Could my tears forever flow, All for sin could not atone: Thou must save, and thou alone.

103. Tuesday after Septuagesima Sunday.

O, that we may hear thy voice, Lord Jesus!

Matthew 10, 37–42. He that loveth father or mother more than me, is not worthy of me: and he that loveth son or daughter more than me, is not worthy of me. He that findeth his life, shall lose it; and he that loseth his life for my sake, shall find it. He that receiveth you, receiveth me; and he that receiveth me, receiveth him that sent me. He that receiveth a prophet in the name of a prophet, shall receive a prophet's reward; and he that receiveth a righteous man in the name of a righteous man, shall receive a righteous man's reward. And whosoever shall give to drink unto one of these little ones a cup of cold water only in the name of a disciple, verily I say unto you, he shall in no wise lose his reward.

Our Jesus is infinitely more excellent than all things and persons in heaven and on earth. If we know him, we love him above all, and gladly follow him through tribulation and suffering. He becomes our delight, our treasure, our joy; he becomes our life. Says Paul: "I live; yet not I, but Christ liveth in me." He who does not in this wise know Jesus is not his disciple. For he will teach you this, if you take lessons of him. Begin to *do* from your heart what he says and as he did; do good to all, especially to his disciples, to the poor, to the forsaken and the little ones. Do it from the heart; do it out of love; persist in it unto the last. Then you shall come to feel deeply your distress and your need of Jesus, the Savior of sinners; and you shall learn to know his unspeakably great goodness and grace. In this way he becomes precious to the soul. He is the sweet fountain of life, the bottomless well of love; he is the sun in our sky, which drives away the night of death. He is the fulness of glory, the God of all spirits; everything beautiful and noble is but his reflection. In him only does our heart find peace, joy, and salvation. He has demolished my death, extinguished my sorrow, plucked me out of hell, and placed me in his heavenly kingdom,—and has done all this out of pure love; that is his nature. He offered up his life for me in death on the cross; thereby am I become a child of God, and shall live with him alway, and inherit all things. All that I am and have is of him; and yet he rewards me for that which I do in his service. I have deserved nothing whatever with my greatest and best deed; yet will he reward me even for the least. I have the blessed honor of giving him meat and drink and clothing and care; namely, in his needy little ones; and yet I am to receive for this an everlasting reward! What say you? is not this love? is not this life? He that spares his own life, and holds it more dear than Jesus, loses his life. He that will not mortify his flesh; he that will not take his cross, which Jesus gives, and follow after him, and live this life in him, is not worthy of him. So himself says; and so say we also, with all our heart.

O, dear Lord Jesus, teach us to know thee in truth, that we may love thee, and follow after thee. Give us a portion in thee; do thou live in us; and thus let us live, and serve one another in thy love. Amen.

The captive to release, The lost to God to bring, To teach the way of life
and peace, It is a Christ-like thing.
And we believe thy word, Though dim our faith may be; Whate'er we do
for thine, O Lord, We do it unto thee.

---

104. Wednesday after Septuagesima Sunday.

Heavenly Wisdom; enter, and abide in us.

1 Corinthians 3, 18–23. Let no man deceive himself. If any man among
you seemeth to be wise in this world, let him become a fool, that he may be
wise. For the wisdom of this world is foolishness with God: for it is written,
He taketh the wise in their own craftiness. And again, the Lord knoweth the
thoughts of the wise, that they are vain. Therefore let no man glory in men:
for all things are your's; whether Paul, or Apollos, or Cephas, or the world,
or life, or death, or things present, or things to come; all are your's; and ye are
Christ's; and Christ is God's.

Persons who are puffed up with conceit have no place in the
church of Christ. He that seems to himself to be wise is far away
from God; he must become a fool, before he can become wise. He
must learn that he knows nothing; in this way, only, can he receive
instruction of the Spirit of God. For the Holy Ghost shows us
clearly that we are fools, darkened and blinded, without true knowledge of God; but he also teaches us to know God. Furthermore, he
leads us into an ever deeper knowledge of self, and keeps our hearts
humble, by the very fact of his revealing to our souls more and more
of the wisdom of God. As a result we see that we know very little;
but, at the same time, we are enabled to surmise and catch a glimpse
of a depth of glorious and blessed things, and to understand that we
live in the very midst of divine excellencies. What reason have we,
then, to be puffed up? Or what have we in which to glory as against
one another? We are not one another's masters, but servants; we
have not been appointed to rule over one another, but are joint partakers of the wisdom of God, that we may serve one another. And
yet all is ours. Each one of us is part owner of the whole. All the
gifts which are given to *you* are *mine* also, and mine are yours. For
we are one body in Christ. Paul's gifts of grace belong to you, and
you belong to the apostolic church. The property of the father is the
common property of all the children.—No, the wisdom of God does
not lead to conceit and envy. Such things as these come of the wisdom
from below. The wisdom which is from above is humble, pure, peaceable, full of mercy and all the fruits of love. O, that no man among
us might deceive himself!

Lord God, our heavenly Father, enlighten us by thy Spirit; teach
us that we of ourselves understand nothing; and teach us to know
thy wisdom from on high, that we therein may serve one another with
humility and faithfulness as good stewards of thy manifold grace
Amen.

Jesus, our Lord, how rich thy grace! Thy bounties, how complete! How
shall we count the matchless sum, How pay the mighty debt?
High on a throne of radiant light Dost thou exalted shine; What can our
poverty bestow, When all the worlds are thine?

---

105. Thursday after Septuagesima Sunday.

1 Corinthians 9, 19–22. For though I be free from all men, yet have I
made myself servant unto all, that I might gain the more. And unto the Jews
I became as a Jew, that I might gain the Jews; to them that are under the
law, as under the law, that I might gain them that are under the law; to
them that are without law, as without law, (being not without law to God, but
under the law to Christ,) that I might gain them that are without law. To the
weak became I as weak, that I might gain the weak: 1 am made all things to
all men, that I might by all means save some.

It was the glorious calling and duty of the apostles to preach the
gospel; and it is the calling and duty of all Christians to win souls
for the Lord. Every Christian should be able to say that which Paul
here says: "For though I be free from all men, yet have I made
myself servant unto all, that I might gain the more." Faith makes
me free from all men; love makes me the servant of all men. Paul
was no longer bound in conscience to observe the Jewish ordinances,
with abstinence from certain kinds of food, with purifications, vows,
and the like. He could, without doing violence to his own conscience,
have eaten the flesh of swine, and blood, and things strangled, and
anything whatever. But he conformed to their customs notwithstanding. For instance, he caused his head to be shorn in Cenchrea,
because he had made a vow; he observed the rite of purification in
Jerusalem (Acts 18, 18; 21, 26); and he declares concerning meats,
that if it makes his brother to offend, he will eat no flesh while the
world stands (1 Cor. 8, 13). When he could, without wounding the
feelings of the Jews, disregard their customs, and in that way the
more readily gain the gentiles, he did this also. He did not lead a
lawless, heathen life; on the contrary, he was bound by the law of
Christ, which is love, and he led a Christian life in spirit and truth.
To the weak he became as weak; he was made all things to all men,
that he might save some. And this life in true liberty and ministering
love was so important to him that without it he could not be a partaker of the gospel. In the following verses he speaks of the struggle
for the prize. This is worthy of particular notice.—Such a life must
we lead, dear Christians; free from all men; lords with Christ over
all rules and ordinances; not to be judged of the weak or the strong,
and yet in love the servants of all; willing to accommodate ourselves
to all in order to gain them. If we know these things, then may
God help us to do them! Then we shall not be all the time asking:
What am I permitted to do; and what must I deny myself? Love will
point out to us the proper course. Let it be the constant aim of our
whole life to win souls for the Lord by ministering, self-sacrificing

love. Do this, for the sake of God and your salvation. As for yourself, you are saved in Christ without any work of your own; now you should strive to do unto others that which he has done unto you. In this way you shall surely be able to decide upon the better course to take in matters relating to the socalled indifferent things, which are neither commanded nor prohibited.

Lord, give us the true spirit of liberty and charity. Give us grace to walk in this spirit at all times and in all places. Alas, we are as yet very far from doing it; help us, O our God, for Jesus' sake. Amen.

Lead on, O Love and Mercy, O Purity and Power! Lead on, till peace eternal Shall close this battle-hour: Till all who prayed and struggled To set their brethren free, In triumph meet to praise thee, Most holy Trinity.

---

106. Friday after Septuagesima Sunday.

God, anoint our eyes with thy Holy Spirit!

Isaiah 53, 10–12. Yet it pleased the Lord to bruise him; he hath put him to grief: when thou shalt make his soul an offering for sin, he shall see his seed, he shall prolong his days, and the pleasure of the Lord shall prosper in his hand. He shall see of the travail of his soul, and shall be satisfied: by his knowledge shall my righteous servant justify many; for he shall bear their iniquities. Therefore will I divide him a portion with the great, and he shall divide the spoil with the strong; because he hath poured out his soul unto death: and he was numbered with the transgressors; and he bare the sin of many, and made intercession for the transgressors.

The love with which God loves us is inconceivably great; so intense and deep that it *pleased* him—actually *pleased* him—to bruise his only begotten Son and put him to grief, when this was necessary, in order that we might be saved. At what a sacrifice have we not been bought! How great was the labor which was done by the Son of God in order to deliver us from the power of death! Yes, he, *he* has labored for us, and done the pleasure of the Lord, and set us free. He has fulfilled all righteousness, he has done every deed of the law, he has borne the whole punishment, he has paid the whole debt, he has suffered all pain, he has endured all trouble, he has tasted all the bitterness of death in our stead, and brought his work to perfect completion; the pleasure of the Lord has succeeded by his hand. Now he lives alway to intercede for us. What, then, is his reward? His reward is to give us a portion with himself in the joys of heaven. His reward is to own our hearts, to have our trust and our love. Is this, then, worth so much to him? Yes, it is; for the reason that he is love, and for the reason that we are they whom it has pleased him to love so well. Truly, I grow dizzy when I attempt to search this matter out; but I am and shall be inexpressibly rich in joy and glory in and through my Lord Jesus. I am *righteous*, I am holy, I am saved and glorified through him. None can bring anything to my charge; none can condemn me. I believe and confess that Jesus is my righteousness before God; I stay by him, my high priest; in him I am wholly righteous, and there is nothing which I must *do* to become righteous. He has taken away my sin, and I am clothed in his righteousness. All who know him are justified by him. I will therefore give myself wholly to thee, my precious Savior. Thou didst pour out thy soul unto death, in order that I might find room in thee instead of making my home with the devil. Take me in, Lord Jesus; I am thine, I love thee, I serve thee, I live unto thee, and I am blessed in giving myself to thee as the spoil of thy work of salvation; thou whose delight it is to own us, and whose meat it is to be loved by us, thou great and eternally blessed God, praised and glorified by all the hosts of heaven! Amen.

Jesus, thy blood and righteousness My beauty are, my glorious dress; 'Midst flaming worlds, in these arrayed, With joy shall I lift up my head. When from the dust of death I rise, To take my mansion in the skies, This even then shall be my plea: "Jesus hath lived and died for me."

---

107. Saturday after Septuagesima Sunday.

Psalm 119, 25–32. My soul cleaveth unto the dust: quicken thou me according to thy word. I have declared my ways, and thou heardest me: teach me thy statutes. Make me to understand the way of thy precepts: so shall I talk of thy wondrous works. My soul melteth for heaviness: strengthen thou me according unto thy word. Remove from me the way of lying; and grant me thy law graciously. I have chosen the way of truth: thy judgments have I laid before me. I have stuck unto thy testimonies: O Lord, put me not to shame. I will run the way of thy commandments, when thou shalt enlarge my heart.

While our souls inhabit this bodily tenement of dust, they are in great danger of clinging to the dust and departing from the everlasting things in the word. We are tempted to labor for the meat which perishes, and to be caught in the toils of the sorrow of the world. This must not be. The believing children of God do not belong to the world, but are strangers in a strange land. Their labor is not in vain; in reality they labor for Christ in all that they do; and their desire shall, therefore, not be after perishable things, but after God. In the minds of the children of the world covetousness or cares are supreme, and cause much anguish and distress, combined with envy and bitterness, anger and malice; thus making of the soul a veritable by-place of hell. When the fire is no longer tempered by the enjoyment of the things of the world, it will burn fiercely in all eternity. The children of God, also, may oft be sad, even on account of worldly matters, such as poverty, disappointment in the children, bodily ailments, or despondency; they may be wearied with the labor of this earthly existence, and yet feel that they cleave unto the dust. I can well understand your state of mind, you tired wanderer, whose soul by reason of its sadness dissolves in sighs and tears. But after all, your heart is nevertheless in heaven; and your treasure and your comfort endure for ever. Never, then, allow yourself to be overcome by the temptation to despondency and weariness; and never let bitterness against God or man bear sway in your mind. Should it please God to let you be heavy-hearted and depressed, or to be weighed down with trouble and care your whole life long, well and good; this may, perhaps, be the only method after which God can deal with you, if you are to become eternally happy. Cleave to the testimonies and promises of the Lord; and do not let unbelief, with its hideous brood of whining, and obstinacy, and despair, and bitterness, and anger, and enmity toward God and all men, get the better of you. Has not the Son of God saved you? Have you not cost him dear, and do you not belong to him? Has he not called you, and have you not received grace to choose the way of truth? Assuredly, he shall set you free from the dust, and satisfy you for ever with the good things of his house.—Teach me, O Lord, and I shall keep thy law; yea, I shall observe it with my whole heart. But alas, for my impure mind; cleanse it, cleanse it in the blood of Jesus. Make me to go in the path of thy commandments; for therein do I delight. Incline my heart to thy testimonies, and not to covetousness. Turn away mine eyes from beholding vanity; and quicken thou me in thy way. Let thy mercies come also unto me, even thy salvation, according to thy word. Amen.

A pilgrim and a stranger, I journey here below: Far distant is my country, The home to which I go.
Here I must toil and travail, Oft weary and opprest, But there my God shall lead me To everlasting rest.

---

108. Sexagesima Sunday. I.

Help us, Lord, to keep thy word in our heart. Amen.

Gospel Lesson, Luke 8, 4–15. And when much people were gathered together, and were come to him out of every city, he spake by a parable: A sower went out to sow his seed; and as he sowed, some fell by the way side; and it was trodden down, and the fowls of the air devoured it. And some fell upon a rock; and as soon as it was sprung up, it withered away, because it lacked moisture. And some fell among thorns; and the thorns sprang up with it, and choked it. And other fell on good ground, and sprang up, and bare fruit an hundredfold. And when he had said these things, he cried, He that hath ears to hear, let him hear. And his disciples asked him, saying, What might this parable be? And he said, Unto you it is given to know the mysteries of the kingdom of God: but to others in parables; that seeing they might not see, and hearing they might not understand. Now the parable is this: The seed is the word of God. Those by the way side are they that hear; then cometh the devil, and taketh away the word out of their hearts, lest they should believe and be saved. They on the rock are they, which, when they hear, receive the word with joy; and these have no root, which for a while believe, and in time of temptation fall away. And that which fell among thorns are they, which, when they have heard, go forth, and are choked with cares and riches and pleasures of this life, and bring no fruit to perfection. But that on the good ground are they, which, in an honest and good heart, having heard the word, keep it, and bring forth fruit with patience.

The word of God must enter our heart, and remain there, and develop its strength, if we are to be the laborers of the Lord, fruitful in good works. The word of God alone is able to bring this about, and shall have the honor. This is one lesson of our gospel text for today. Let none imagine that he can serve the Lord and be a blessing on earth without receiving and keeping the word of God.

Furthermore our gospel lesson teaches us that the human hearts assume different attitudes toward the word. Over some hearts there is a hard crust through which the seed of the word can not penetrate. They hear it, and at once forget it; it makes no impression on them; there is awakened in them no feeling of unrest or need of salvation; either because they are so self-righteous as never to be sensible of their sin and the danger to their souls, or because they are so worldly-minded that no thought of eternity can be born in them. Should there be a crevice in the hard crust; should the dispensations of the Lord and the troubles of life predispose them, in a measure, to follow the call of God; then, alas, the devil comes and takes the seed away. He at once guides their thoughts in another direction, and says: "Make yourself easy; all is well with you." Or he says: "You are a fool to brood on such matters, which are but idle talk on the part of parsons; be comforted, and enjoy life."—Others are easily moved and begin to repent; but their fruits of repentance soon die, when the heat of the day increases. Affliction, which is as necessary to the fruit of the heart as is the sun to the fruit of the earth, kills the seed which has not struck root in knowledge of sin and true penitence. Do, then, pray God to give you a contrite heart.—Others, again, earnestly repent, and sink the word deep into the soul; but they forget to watch. The thorns, whose roots still remain in the heart, put forth many and vigorous shoots, and choke the fruit of the word; with the result that their spiritual life languishes and dies. How many are there not who at one time were Christians of great promise, but who married, and had children, and contracted debts, or acquired wealth, and who thereafter have lead most pitiable Christian lives. The expected fruits of the ripe seed were choked with cares or with riches. These thorns, whose roots were in the heart, must of necessity crop out above the surface; the Lord shaped the conditions of life after this fashion, in order that the thorns might spring up, and be known as such and be weeded out with holy diligence and struggle and prayer.—Finally, there are some; alas, only some, who in an honest and good heart keep the word, and bring forth fruit with patience. They take up the cross of Christ, practice self-denial, and sustain life on the love of God in Christ, who is the substance of the word.

Let the seed today fall on the good ground. Let the word make good ground of your heart now, if it has not done so heretofore; the word has power to accomplish even this. The word is the pick and plough which can break through the crust; it is the rain and sun which

can disintegrate the rock; it is the *fire* which can burn up the roots
of the thorns. The word is almighty, and can effect all things necessary to our salvation. God wants us to become rich in that which
is good; he wants to reap of us a generous harvest. It is and always
shall be our fault, if this purpose is not achieved.

Lord, do not let the devil take away the word out of our heart.
Let it sink deep into our soul, and work penitence, faith, and sanctification, that we may bear thee abundant and good fruit. Give us
this grace, for Jesus' sake. Amen.

Can aught beneath a power divine The stubborn will subdue? 'Tis thine,
O holy Spirit, thine To form the heart anew.

'Tis thine the passions to recall, And upward bid them rise, And make
the scales of error fall From reason's darkened eyes.

109. Sexagesima Sunday. II.

Before I was afflicted I went astray; but now have I kept thy word.

Epistle Lesson, 2 Corinthians 12, 2–9. I knew a man in Christ above
fourteen years ago, (whether in the body, I cannot tell; or whether out of the
body, I cannot tell: God knoweth;) such a one caught up to the third heaven.
And I knew such a man, (whether in the body, or out of the body, I cannot
tell: God knoweth;) How that he was caught up into paradise, and heard
unspeakable words, which it is not lawful for a man to utter. Of such a one
will I glory: yet of myself will I not glory, but in mine infirmities. For
though I would desire to glory, I shall not be a fool; for I will say the truth:
but now I forbear, lest any man should think of me above that which he seeth
me to be, or that he heareth of me. And lest I should be exalted above
measure through the abundance of the revelations, there was given to me a
thorn in the flesh, the messenger of Satan to buffet me, lest I should be
exalted above measure. For this thing I besought the Lord thrice, that it might
depart from me. And he said unto me, My grace is sufficient for thee: for my
strength is made perfect in weakness. Most gladly therefore will I rather glory
in my infirmities, that the power of Christ may rest upon me.

"Saint Paul is eminent above thousands and thousands; eminent
by reason of his work, and sufferings, and revelations. The Lord made
of him a great light which shines far and wide. But the greater
the light, the greater and darker the shadow. As for the holy apostle,
he would, therefore, be especially liable to be assailed by the temptation to exalt himself above measure. But the Lord saw the danger
before it became visible to men, and the means for the protection of his own against this danger he provides with greater care
than can be exercised by the most loving human heart. In the
case of the apostle, therefore, the Lord provided in advance that
which was needful to counterbalance the power of the temptation.
'Lest I should be exalted above measure through the abundance of
the revelations, there was given to me a thorn in the flesh, the messenger of Satan to buffet me, lest I should be exalted above measure.'
This is the apostle's own statement. Though we may not be able to

understand clearly the full meaning of these words, there is no reason why we should take them in any other than the literal sense, or construe them as an exaggerated description of natural sufferings. On one hand was the grace of heaven, and on the other a counter-weight from hell, which no prayer could drive away, but concerning which the apostle was told that it should continue, yet without any danger to the grace that was in him. He was obliged to keep the thorn and the messenger of Satan and—the grace of God, all together.

"Dear brethren; there always is pride in the heart of every man; but there is this essential distinction, that pride rules in one, while it only tempts the other. The man, such as we sometimes meet him, who assumes an air of superior piety, and says of his neighbor that he is not wholly free of the sin of pride, thereby reveals a sad ignorance of his own heart, and of the human heart in general. Who is there that has no pride? Who has been able to rid himself of it on this side of the grave? As certain as it is that we have in us a tendency to pride, a tendency which easily might corrupt all that we do and make us an abominable caricature of that which we should and could be; just so certainly does the Lord in his mercy bring about the conditions necessary for the lowering of our pride and for our growth in true humility. Let none try to cast from him those things which tend to keep him truly humble in spirit. Let us keep them and thank the merciful Giver, whose purpose it is by this means to perfect us in that which is good and preserve us from evil." (Loehe.)

Lord, deal with us according to thy wisdom and mercy. Do not let the devil tempt us; but if we are to be tried, and must needs have a thorn in the flesh, let us keep thy grace and find it sufficient. Let our hearts be truly humble, that we may become more and more like thee, Lord Jesus. Amen.

When trials sore obstruct my way, And ills I cannot flee, Oh, let my strength be as my day! Dear Lord, remember me!
If worn with pain, disease, and grief, This feeble frame shall be, Grant patience, rest, and kind relief: Hear, and remember me!

---

110. Monday after Sexagesima Sunday.

Speak, Lord, thy servant heareth.

Luke 10, 38–42. Now it came to pass, as they went, that he entered into a certain village: and a certain woman, named Martha, received him into her house. And she had a sister called Mary, which also sat at Jesus' feet, and heard his word. But Martha was cumbered about much serving, and came to him and said, Lord, dost thou not care that my sister hath left me to serve alone? bid her therefore that she help me. And Jesus answered and said unto her, Martha, Martha, thou art careful and troubled about many things: but one thing is needful: and Mary hath chosen that good part, which shall not be taken away from her.

The heart of Mary was good ground for the holy seed. She sat at the feet of Jesus, and heard his word. This is as it should be.

The Lord calls it the one thing needful. Let us note it well. The word of God is as necessary to the heart, if we are to bring forth fruits of the spirit unto everlasting life, as the seed is to the soil, if this is to produce a crop of grain. If the word of God does not enter our heart, we can bring forth only the fruits of sin unto death and perdition. For nothing save noxious weeds grow wild in the heart; not charity, but self-love, hate, and anger; no work for God and heaven, but only worldly pursuits and aspirations. It is necessary to hear the word, even as Mary heard it. There are many who hear, and yet do not hear it. One who has no ear for music may hear the notes and chords, and yet not hear them, the music does not reach his soul or stir his heart. In like manner many hear the word of God, and their cold reason understands it; but they do not hear the heavenly music of the word, and are not sensible of its power to lay hold of the heart.—Do *you* hear these notes of love? Do *you* hear the shepherd voice of Jesus in the word? Do you hear the chime of the heavenly bells?—You are careful and troubled about many things; your ear is so full of the noise and roar of the world that it is deaf to the word of God. But remember, dear friend, that all your works, even the best among them, are barren and without root or kernel, if they are not the fruit of that faith which is a result of hearing the word. Begin in earnest, with your whole heart, to *do* that which Jesus says; then shall you taste how sweet his word is, and feel its regenerating power.—Lord, grant us this grace. Help us to love thy statutes, and to find delight and joy in thy word. Amen.

Father of mercies, in thy word What endless glory shines! For ever be thy name adored For these celestial lines.
Here the Redeemer's welcome voice Spreads heavenly peace around; And life and everlasting joys Attend the blissful sound.

III. Tuesday after Sexagesima Sunday.

Psalm 19, 7-12. The law of the Lord is perfect, converting the soul: the testimony of the Lord is sure, making wise the simple: the statutes of the Lord are right, rejoicing the heart: the commandment of the Lord is pure, enlightening the eyes: the fear of the Lord is clean, enduring forever: the judgments of the Lord are true and righteous altogether. More to be desired are they than gold, yea, than much fine gold; sweeter also than honey and the honeycomb. Moreover, by them is thy servant warned: and in keeping of them there is great reward. Who can understand his errors? cleanse thou me from secret faults.

Nothing on earth is as perfect as is the word of God. The holy scriptures are the pure and clear fountain of Israel, out of which flow knowledge of God, faith, and holiness. This word is *true* and *sure*, and we may rely on it without any fear of being deceived. Take any of the Bible ordinances; for instance, that concerning the marriage relation, and compare with it the law laid down by Mahomet or by any other religious teacher, and you can be in no doubt as to which is right. And equally safe and reliable are the scriptural *promises*. What the Lord has promised he fulfils to the letter. No man has at any time had a bank note more safe than that which you have in the promise of God to give you all that you need here, and eternal happiness in the world to come. No word of all that which the mouth of the Lord has spoken has failed to come true; but should its fulfilment be postponed, then do you wait on the Lord; he shall surely come, he shall not fail to appear. This word is *pure* as refined gold, there is no dross in it; therefore it is incorruptible altogether, and not one jot or tittle of it shall pass away. It is fulfilled, and is being fulfilled, and abides for ever. One by one the structures reared by human philosophy totter and fall; time disintegrates their ruins, they crumble into dust and pass away; but the word of God is everlasting. It is the bright sun without any spots, the perfect light without any dark lines; beautiful and grateful to the eye, and glorious to walk in for the upright. Dear reader; keep the word of God, and you shall know its excellency. "In keeping them there is great reward."

However, none of us is as yet perfect herein. The saints who walk in the light of the word see much sin in themselves at all times, and know that they have many *secret* faults, besides, which they do not perceive. Sin does not have dominion over them, but it oppresses and troubles them. Then the word of God is their help; and in their daily repentance they experience its power to admonish, comfort, and strengthen.

Lord, create in us the desire to understand the truth and purity of thy word. Grant that we may love the word and delight in walking in it; that we may regard it as more to be desired than the finest gold, and as sweeter than honey and the honeycomb. Lord God, thou dost speak to me most beauteous words; let now, I pray thee, the words of my mouth and the meditations of my heart be acceptable in thy sight, my strength and my Redeemer. Amen.

How precious is the Book divine, By inspiration given! Bright as a lamp its doctrines shine, To guide our souls to heaven.
It sweetly cheers our drooping hearts In this dark vale of tears: Life, light, and joy, it still imparts, And quells our rising fears.

---

112. Wednesday after Sexagesima Sunday.

Lord, let thy word of life permeate my whole heart. Amen.

Isaiah 55, 8–13. For my thoughts are not your thoughts, neither are your ways my ways, saith the Lord. For as the heavens are higher than the earth, so are my ways higher than your ways, and my thoughts than your thoughts. For as the rain cometh down, and the snow, from heaven, and returneth not thither, but watereth the earth, and maketh it bring forth and bud, that it may give seed to the sower, and bread to the eater; so shall my word be that goeth forth out of my mouth: it shall not return unto me void; but it shall accomplish that which I please, and it shall prosper in the thing whereto I sent it. For ye shall go out with joy, and be led forth with peace: the mountains and the hills shall break forth before you into singing, and all the trees of the field shall clap their hands. Instead of the thorn shall come up the fir tree, and instead of the brier shall come up the myrtle tree: and it shall be to the Lord for a name, for an everlasting sign that shall not be cut off.

It is not in your power to form a correct idea of the glories which God has reserved for his faithful people. Even though you imagine them as a thousand times more glorious than everything of which you have any knowledge, you still use the things of this world as your measure of comparison; but God's thoughts are of heaven, and are as much higher than your thoughts, as the heavens are higher than the earth. The mercy of God toward us is great beyond conception; his plan for our salvation is a bottomless depth of eternal love and wisdom. Neither have entered into the heart of man the things which God hath prepared for them that love him.—We often, alas, have gloomy thoughts, and it seems to us that our path leads to lower and lower levels. *Our* thoughts are the inconstant thoughts of doubt and despondency, or of levity. But the thoughts of the Lord are thoughts of truth and love, luminous and pure, fixed and immovable; and his ways, in which he conducts us, dear Christian friend, are high, and lead ever upward. Consider this whenever your own thoughts threaten to overwhelm you in the dark hours of your life. *Your* thoughts are wrong; those of the *Lord* are right. Your ways and your plans must go down; those of the Lord shall endure. For he carries out his purpose through a means which can not fail. As his thoughts in heaven are luminous and high, and his counsel fixed; so his *word*, which brings them to us on earth, is living and fruitful, and accomplishes his will. Do not the rain and snow from heaven water our earth and make it fertile? Does this fail? Shall, then, the word that goeth forth out of his mouth fail? Can you doubt that this word is able to transform the earth, create and maintain faith in our hearts, extend and preserve the kingdom of God, release the souls, and lead them at last, through all temptations, to glory? Have you not already begun to feel the power of the heavenly thoughts in the word? What was it which awakened you out of your sleep in sin, and kindled in you faith, the new life, and prayer? What was it which sustained you, and gave you such consolation in the face of all your sin and distress, that you had cause to wonder at the fact of your not having long since dropped back into your former state of unbelief? What is it which ever anew brings spring and summer into your spiritual life, causing the field to become green, blossom, and bring forth fruit? What is it which sustains your hope, and causes you to expect everlasting life and everlasting victory for the church of God? It is the word which does all this; the word of God. Do not hereafter allow any lying thoughts to find room in you. The Lord has thought glorious thoughts, and has spoken glorious promises concerning us. Let all things fall; let the world, with all that it contains, perish. It has pleased our God to ordain that happiness and peace and songs of joy shall at last fill all the earth. Nature shall be renewed, and the name Jesus with the sign of the cross shall illumine all things and make all full of eternal bliss. The word of God shall accomplish this glorious result.

O, our God, may our faith and our hope be firmly established in thy word. Thou knowest what worthless thoughts we think; help us to conquer all our own thoughts by means of thy thoughts, thy thoughts of love and mercy, which we find in thy word. Amen.

How blest are they who hear God's word, And keep and heed what they have heard. They wisdom daily gather; E'er brighter shines their light each day, And while they tread life's weary way, They have the oil of gladness To soothe all pain and sadness.

---

113. Thursday after Sexagesima Sunday

Lord, plant thy seed of life in our hearts. Amen.

1 Peter 1, 22–25. Seeing ye have purified your souls in obeying the truth through the Spirit unto unfeigned love of the brethren, see that ye love one another with a pure heart fervently: being born again, not of corruptible seed, but of incorruptible, by the word of God, which liveth and abideth for ever. For all flesh is as grass, and all the glory of man as the flower of grass. The grass withereth, and the flower thereof falleth away: But the word of the Lord endureth for ever. And this is the word which by the gospel is preached unto you.

You who have been born again, and have been made partakers of the divine nature, have become what you are by the word of God. For the word is the vehicle in which the incorruptible seed and everlasting life enter our hearts. On this point Luther says: "The word is a divine and everlasting force." The sound or voice soon dies away, to be sure, but the kernel remains, namely, the truth itself which is contained in the voice. When I place a cup to the lips I drink the wine, but I do not attempt to swallow the cup also. Thus with the word which the voice brings to us; it enters the heart, and is and remains living, while the sound remains outside and dies away. Therefore the word is a divine force; nay, it is the very God. For thus he says to Moses: "I will be in thy mouth" (Exodus 4, 12); and in Psalm 81, 10, he says: "Open thy mouth wide, and I will fill it," I will be there and speak. Hence the seed is our Lord God himself.

This is the word which by the gospel is preached unto you. It is not necessary for you to open your eyes wide and ask where you are to find the word; it is nearer to you than you are aware; it is the word which we preach. It does not take long to speak it and hear it; but when it enters the heart it can not die or pass away, and neither will it let you die; while you cling to this word it will sustain you. When I hear that Jesus Christ died, that my sin is taken away, and that heaven is given unto me, I hear the gospel. It is not in the power of any man to overthrow this truth. Hell is powerless against it; and even if I were already in the jaws of the devil, but could lay hold of the word, I must perforce be delivered and be where the word is. Therefore he says with truth: You shall expect no other word than that which we preach. For the reason that the seed of God, which is love, has by means of the word found lodgment in you and lives in you, therefore shall you purify yourselves in obeying the truth, unto chaste and fervent love of the brethren; therein shall it be known in the world that you have not heard the word in vain, but that you are, in truth, born of God.

We thank thee, dear and gracious God, for thy most excellent gift of the word. Let it accomplish its purpose in us all; let us feel its quickening power, and let us prove it in holy love of the brethren. Amen.

O may these heavenly pages be My ever dear delight; And still new beauties may I see, And still increasing light.
Divine instructor, gracious Lord, Be thou forever near; Teach me to love thy sacred word, And view my Savior there.

---

114. Friday after Sexagesima Sunday.

Lord Holy Ghost, enlighten us with thy gifts. Amen.

Isaiah 53, 1–5. Who hath believed our report? and to whom is the arm of the Lord revealed? For he shall grow up before him as a tender plant, and as a root out of a dry ground: he hath no form nor comeliness; and when we shall see him, there is no beauty that we should desire him. He is despised and rejected of men; a man of sorrows, and acquainted with grief: and we hid as it were our faces from him; he was despised, and we esteemed him not. Surely he hath borne our griefs, and carried our sorrows: yet we did esteem him stricken, smitten of God, and afflicted. But he was wounded for our transgressions, he was bruised for our iniquities: the chastisement of our peace was upon him; and with his stripes we are healed.

That which God has done for us is so wonderful that none can believe it by his own reason or strength; faith itself, wherever it is kindled in the heart, is a divine miracle wrought by the word. For Christ's outward appearance and his church with its means of grace attract little attention, and do not please the eye. In his birth Jesus is poor and lowly, and has in nothing the appearance of a king who is to rule over all the earth; and it does not seem possible that he can be the only begotten Son of God. During life he was despised and reviled, smitten and afflicted; nay, covered with ignominy and stricken with grief to such a degree that the haughty loathe him, and those of sympathetic nature can not bear to see him. Thus God deals with his own Son for our sake. We have deserved it, but he suffers it. Our idea always had been that only he who deserves punishment is smitten of God; but the Son is innocent, and yet is stricken. What a miracle of divine mercy! And of divine justice! He, he was wounded for our transgressions, he was bruised for our iniquities; the griefs which he has borne, and the sorrows which he has carried, were ours to bear and carry; the chastisement was upon him, and with his stripes we are healed. Thus speaks the gospel. You and I, who have deserved everlasting shame and suffering, shall for his sake receive everlasting honor and bliss; for the shame and suffering have already been undergone; God has done it, and it is not in the power of the devil to do away with this fact. God has decreed that my disgrace is to be the disgrace of the Son, and his honor mine; my sins and their punishment his, and his righteousness mine. This is God's righteous decree. But who could believe it? Our reason can not grasp it. Since God has done this thing, it must of necessity be right and proper; but to our darkened understanding it is nevertheless an impossibility. *Faith alone* is able to grasp it. But to our faith it approves itself as the highest love and eternal justice; as the brightest, greatest, most beautiful, most glorious truth that has been, or can be, revealed to us. The angels also are of this mind, and their desire is to look into this mystery.

We thank thee for the eternal, incontrovertible decree of mercy; we thank thee for the word in which thou dost make thy purpose known to us; and we thank thee for the faith which thou hast kindled in our soul. Preserve and increase it, and give us grace to penetrate ever more deeply into the truth, and to stand immovable on the rock of thy righteousness, that our cure may be perfect, and that we may stand before thee at last without spot or blemish. Amen.

He who bore all pain and loss Comfortless upon the cross, Lives in glory now on high, Pleads for us and hears our cry. Hallelujah!
He who slumbered in the grave, Is exalted now to save; Now through Christendom it rings That the Lamb is King of kings. Hallelujah!

115. Saturday after Sexagesima Sunday.

Psalm 119, 64-72. The earth, O Lord, is full of thy mercy: teach me thy statutes. Thou hast dealt well with thy servant, O Lord, according unto thy word. Teach me good judgment and knowledge: for I have believed thy commandments. Before I was afflicted I went astray; but now have I kept thy word. Thou art good, and doest good: teach me thy statutes. The proud have forged a lie against me: but I will keep thy precepts with my whole heart. Their heart is as fat as grease: but I delight in thy law. It is good for me that I have been afflicted; that I might learn thy statutes. The law of thy mouth is better unto me than thousands of gold and silver.

Pride darkens the eye, that it sees not the glory of God; but the humble soul is open to receive the light from heaven. It is good for us that the Lord afflicts us with troubles of many kinds, and shows us that we understand nothing and can do nothing without his Spirit. The earth is full of his mercy, full of the miracles of his grace. However, we are blind to these things, unless our eyes are anointed by the Spirit; and this is done by means of the word. His works in nature are wonderful, and they are mercy altogether. Could we but see the beauty, the grandeur, the mercy in these works! We walk all the time in an edifice erected by the greatest of masters; in a cathedral of surpassing grandeur, where the achitecture is perfection, and where we find on every hand rows of stately columns with graceful capitals and arches to delight the eye; but do we see it? Walk through the Cologne cathedral at the darkest hour of a dark night, and how much do you see of its splendors? The word of God is the sun; the works of the Lord must be seen in the light of the gospel; and only the lowly of heart walk in the light.—The mercy of God, however, shines with greatest splendor in his *spiritual* temple, the Christian church. In this temple the manifold wisdom of God is revealed in a manner to command the admiration of principalities and powers in heaven. By means of his word God creates the new man, and unites the saints; teaches them his heavenly statutes, and sanctifies their every faculty, so that they adapt themselves to one another, and serve one another. He turns the heart, humbles it, and melts it in tribulations; he stamps his image on it by means of the word; and he allows the peculiar character of each to develop, but in such a manner that each may fit in with the others and fill his special place in the church. If the members and joints of our body must be said to fit one another with admirable ingenuity and beauty, what say you of the members of the holy church, the bride of Christ? We walk in the midst of such miracles, and the light of the word shines upon them before our eyes; but do we see something of the Lord's resplendent mercy? If we do not, the fault lies in the arrogance of our mind.

Lord, thou hast begun to open my eyes; teach me, I humbly pray thee, to walk in thy paths, that thou mayest show me thy wonders. Teach me to fear thee and keep thy word, that thy glory may be revealed to me, and that I may behold the wondrous things in thy law. Amen.

Thy word is everlasting truth: How pure is **every page**! That holy book **shall** guide our youth, And well support our age.

---

116. Quinquagesima Sunday. I.

Lord, send us thy Holy Spirit. Amen.

Gospel Lesson, Matthew 3, 13–17. Then cometh Jesus from Galilee to Jordan, unto John, to be baptized of him. But John forbad him, saying, I have need to be baptized of thee, and comest thou to me? And Jesus answering said unto him, Suffer it to be so now: for thus it becometh us to fulfil all righteousness. Then he suffered him. And Jesus, when he was baptized, went up straightway out of the water: and, lo, the heavens were opened unto him, and he saw the Spirit of God descending like a dove, and lighting upon him: And, lo, a voice from heaven, saying, This is my beloved Son, in whom I am well pleased.

1) By his baptism Jesus entered into our sin. 2) By his baptism he consecrated the water for our baptism, so that we are baptized into his righteousness.
1) He was consecrated as our high priest, prophet, and king. As our *high priest*: He who knew no sin is made to be sin for us. The Righteous One has taken his place in the midst of sinners; and the scripture says: "Behold the Lamb of God, which taketh away the

sin of the world." He is baptized into our sinful estate, in order that he may make atonement for sin by suffering death. From the time of his baptism he enters on a career of pain.—As our *prophet:* From the time of his baptism he enters on his office as a preacher. From now on he goes about teaching the truth, mighty in deed and word before God and all the people; and in his doctrine he reveals heaven on earth.—As our *king:* The fight against the devil, who attacks him with fury, now begins in earnest, until he, in his resurrection, wins a complete victory over the prince of death. As the one who is anointed to be our high priest, prophet and king, he is here declared to be the beloved Son, in whom the Father is well pleased.

2) By his baptism he consecrated the water as the means of baptism for us. What a glorious and precious water is not baptism now become! In it is the blood of Christ and the life of his resurrection. In my baptism I received that which he became for us in his baptism. a) He was baptized into my sin; I was baptized into his righteousness. Says Paul: "For as many as have been baptized into Christ have put on Christ." As my Savior who was sacrificed in death, and as my advocate who now sits on the throne of heaven and makes intercession for me, he is become mine, and I am become his in holy baptism; I am united with him, even as he died for me and lives for me, so that in him I have died for sin and am dead from sin (Romans 6, 3). b) I have received his Spirit, and have entered into the light; I am numbered among his disciples, and am certain that he shall neither lead me wrong, nor permit me to go wrong. c) I have put on him, the victor over the devil; I have been received into his kingdom; I now fight in his strength, and shall therein win a victory in every battle with the evil one. Christ is *my* high priest, *my* prophet, *my* king. — Now the one thing of supreme importance is to have *faith.* All the promises of God are in Christ yea and amen. Blessed is he that believes, and keeps the blessings conferred on him by his baptism. He is the beloved child of God, and in him the heavenly Father is well pleased.

Lord, give us grace to believe, and to preserve in our faith; to stand fast in the grace of our baptism, and remain in living communion with thee unto the end. Amen.

Now Christ, the very Son of God. On sinners sends another flood; It is the water which the Lord Has comprehended in the word.
That by the water and the word We're born again, we thank thee, Lord!
In life and death thine let us be, And thine in all eternity.

---

117. Quinquagesima Sunday. II.

Help us, Lord, that we may hear thy word today. Amen.

Epistle Lesson, 1 Peter 3, 18–22. For Christ also hath once suffered for sins, the just for the unjust, that he might bring us to God, being put to death in the flesh, but quickened by the Spirit: By which also he went and preached unto the spirits in prison; which sometime were disobedient, when once the longsuffering of God waited in the days of Noah, while the ark was a preparing, wherein few, that is, eight souls, were saved by the water. The like figure whereunto, even baptism, doth also now save us, (not putting away of the filth of the flesh, but the answer of a good conscience toward God,) by the resurrection of Jesus Christ: who is gone into heaven, and is on the right hand of God; angels and authorities and powers being made subject unto him.

"Baptism doth save us." In regard to this matter Luther writes: "Every Christian has, throughout his whole life, enough to learn and practice in connection with his baptism; for it behooves him always to labor toward the end that he may firmly believe that which his baptism promises and brings: victory over death and the devil, forgiveness of sins, the grace of God, the whole Christ, and the Holy Ghost with all his gifts. In short, it is so much, that if we in our weakness were able to grasp the whole truth, we would regard it as beyond belief. Suppose that there were found to be a physician whose skill was such that persons treated by him would escape death, or, if they died, would come to life again and live for ever; would not the world rain money on him, and make it impossible for the poor to approach him? Now, in baptism every person receives such a gift without price; there is brought to his very door a remedy which swallows up death and keeps all men alive. Thus must we regard our baptism and make use of its benefits, in order that we may, when oppressed by sin and our conscience, take heart and say: 'After all, I am baptized; and since I am baptized, I have the promise that I shall be saved body and soul, and have everlasting life.' For this reason baptism has two sides, as it were; water is poured over the body, which is not capable of receiving more than this; and the word of God is pronounced over us, in order that the soul, also, may receive benefit. Now, as water and the word taken together constitute baptism, it follows that both soul and body must be saved; the soul by means of the word, in which it believes; but the body, because it is united with the soul and accepts baptism in so far as this is possible. We have, therefore, nothing more valuable for soul or body; for in baptism we receive full sanctification and salvation; something which can not be brought about by a saintly life or by any work of ours whatever. — Thus we see what a high and excellent thing baptism is, which snatches us out of the jaws of the devil, makes us God's own people, destroys and takes away our sin; and then daily strengthens the new man, and endures until we are removed from this world of sorrow into everlasting glory. Every Christian should, therefore, regard his baptism as a garment for everyday use, in order that he may continue in faith and good works, subdue the former man, and grow in the new. For if we wish to be Christians, we must diligently pursue that which makes Christians of us. But if any fall from grace, let him return. For Christ, our mercy seat, does not forsake us; neither does he prohibit us from coming to him, even though we sin. So we continue in possession of all that with which he has endowed us. We have received forgiveness of sin is baptism; and we continue to receive it every day while we live, or, in other words, while we have our old sinful nature with us."

O glorious and precious estate of grace! Give us, O God, thy Holy Spirit, and give us faith in our heart, for the sake of our Lord Jesus' Christ. Amen.

God of eternal love, Our Father and our friend, We lift our hearts to thee above; Do thou our prayer attend.

Baptized into thy name, We all have Christ put on: O may thy love our hearts inflame, The course of truth to run.

118. Monday after Quinquagesima Sunday.

Thou Lamb of God, which didst take away the sin of the world, have mercy on us.

John 1, 29–34. The next day John seeth Jesus coming unto him, and saith, Behold the Lamb of God, which taketh away the sin of the world. This is he of whom I said, After me cometh a man which is preferred before me: for he was before me. And I knew him not: but that he should be made manifest to Israel, therefore am I come baptizing with water. And John bare record, saying, I saw the Spirit descending from heaven like a dove, and it abode upon him. And I knew him not: but he that sent me to baptize with water, the same said unto me, Upon whom thou shalt see the Spirit descending, and remaining on him, the same is he which baptizeth with the Holy Ghost. And I saw, and bare record that this is the Son of God.

From the time of his baptism our Lord Jesus was known of John as the Lamb of God which taketh away the sin of the world. John could not put the Spirit and life into the baptism with which he baptized, for he was only a man; but Jesus could baptize with the Spirit, for he is the Son of God. When he was baptized baptism was hallowed. The water does not make him holy, but is made holy by him; for he is baptized to suffer the baptism of blood. Then he lets the water and the blood flow together from his riven side; and thus baptism becomes a red "stream colored by the blood of Christ, which cures the disease that we inherited from Adam, and the sin that we have done."

He is called the Lamb of God, because he is God. O, miracle of miracles! God, himself, the Son, co-equal with the Father, is the sacrificial lamb for the sins of the world. He is called the Lamb of God for the further reason that God has selected him and given him to us; we have not made this sacrifice without having first received it of God. He is called a Lamb, because he is to be sacrificed, and because he goes to his death with the patience of a lamb. — *He bears the sin of the world;* it was laid on his shoulders when he was baptized, and after that it was heavy on him, and he felt its weight more and more. The wrath of the righteous God, and his judgment on our unrighteousness, on all our infirmities, all our disease of body and soul; this wrath and judgment, which were not to be satisfied with anything short of death and the torments of damnation, were upon him. He lifts all this and carries it away; takes away the punishment and the power of ungodliness; hence sin shall neither condemn us, nor rule over us. He takes away the sin of the *world;* of Jews and gentiles. from the first soul on earth to the last. How heavy a burden on him, but how great a mercy for us! This concerns us all. Blessed be the Lamb; in the eyes of God my sin is no longer mine. The Lamb has taken away my many and grievous sins, which else would have thrust me down into hell. "Now we know where our sins are laid away," says Luther. "The law places them on our conscience and thrusts them into our bosom; but God takes them from us and places them on the shoulders of the Lamb. I know, says God, that your sins are too heavy for your strength; therefore I take them from you, and lay them on my Lamb. This you shall believe; and when you do believe it, you are rid of your sin. Your sin must be in one of two places; either it is with you, in which case you are lost; or it rests on Christ, in which case you are free and shall be saved. Now choose that which you desire." You are baptized, and have a right and access to this grace; do not by your unbelief put it away. "Neither is there salvation in any other."

Blessed be thou, Lord Jesus, who didst take away the sin of all the world, didst suffer death, and art my advocate before the Father. Help me to believe in thee and to let thee carry away and destroy all my sin, that in distress and death I may have my only comfort in thee, gladly follow after thee, suffer with patience, and find a place at the foot of thy throne in heaven. Amen.

O Jesus Christ, thou Lamb of God, Once slain to take away our load, Now let thy cross, thine agony, Avail to save and solace me; Thy death, to open heaven and there Bid me the joy of angels share.

---

119. Tuesday after Quinquagesima Sunday.

Lord Jesus, make our whole life new through thy love. Amen.

2 Corinthians 5, 14–21. For the love of Christ constraineth us; because we thus judge, that if one died for all, then were all dead: and that he died for all, that they which live should not henceforth live unto themselves, but unto him which died for them, and rose again. Wherefore henceforth know we no man after the flesh: yea, though we have known Christ after the flesh, yet now henceforth know we him no more. Therefore if any man be in Christ, he is a new creature: old things are passed away; behold, all things are become new. And all things are of God, who hath reconciled us to himself by Jesus Christ, and hath given to us the ministry of reconciliation; to wit, that God was in Christ, reconciling the world unto himself, not imputing their trespasses unto them; and hath committed unto us the word of reconciliation. Now then we are ambassadors for Christ, as though God did beseech you by us: we pray you in Christ's stead, be ye reconciled to God. For he hath made him to be sin for us, who knew no sin; that we might be made the righteousness of God in him.

Saint Paul is fairly beside himself by reason of God's infinite love and boundless grace toward us. One died for all, then did all die; such was the will and act of God. Christ, the holy and righteous, was sacrificed for us sinners; and God counts this as though we all had died the death of the Righteous One for our sins. As Christ was made to be sin, and was treated as though he were nothing but sin; as he died our death in full, the death of the accursed world; even so are we righteousness only in him, and there is no more any sin for which to die; for Christ died for all sin of whatever kind or degree. God has reconciled the world unto himself in Christ, not imputing their trespasses unto *them*, but imputing them all unto *him*. Here the old things are passed away; the former estate in sin and bondage, and the old mind, troubled with fear and an evil conscience, are at an end. Paul prays and beseeches in Christ's stead that we may believe in Christ and thus enter into this glorious estate of grace. Why will you continue in the service of sin, now that you are free? Why will you continue in fear or in a fiendish obstinacy, now that you are reconciled unto God and have all that which is necessary to a good conscience and a happy, pure and joyful heart? See, says the apostle, I am in all things one of you; and I am dead and risen again with Christ, and live a new life in him; his love throbs in every thought and word and deed; all, all that I do is done in a new spirit quite different from the old. The new spirit manifests itself in me, even to the minutest details in my manner of living. You have what I have; and my heart burns within me as I pray you to accept and make use of this gift of God.— We will follow the light of God's Spirit, dear reader, and hereafter live the life of faith, justified, regenerated, and sanctified in Christ. We poor fools, who have not heretofore understood this! All is finished; we are reconciled unto God by the death of his Son, and shall live by his life. In this love we will now abide, and give ourselves wholly to thee, Lord Jesus. Thou art one with us, and we with thee; let this union continue. Help us to remain in thee, thou who of God art made unto us wisdom, and righteousness, and sanctification, and redemption. Amen.

Come, thou incarnate word, Gird on thy mighty sword, Our prayer attend. Come, and thy people bless, And give thy word success; Spirit of holiness, On us descend.

---

120. Wednesday after Quinquagesima Sunday.

Great is the mercy of the Lord upon us. God, make us to know it. Amen.

Isaiah 53, 6–9. All we, like sheep, have gone astray; we have turned every one to his own way; and the Lord hath laid on him the iniquity of us all. He was oppressed, and he was afflicted; yet he opened not his mouth; he is brought as a lamb to the slaughter, and as a sheep before her shearers is dumb, so he openeth not his mouth. He was taken from prison and from judgment: and who shall declare his generation? for he was cut off out of the land of the living: for the transgression of my people was he stricken. And he made his grave with the wicked, and with the rich in his death; because he had done no violence, neither was any deceit in his mouth.

The human race is like a flock of sheep which are being torn and scattered in all directions by a wolf in the midst of them. In the ears of the proud this statement is offensive. What! are they to be called sheep; sheep gone astray? Nonsense! They are not sheep; they are lions. However, this is the devil's cunning, that they are ignorant of his existence, and do not know their own pitiable condition and need. Pride and blindness are his work. Many are blind to the fact that humanity is torn asunder, and that they turn every one to his own way. And they do not feel that this is a terribly evil power, a foreign force, which is come into the human world. O, that this blindness might pass away, that each of us might see his error! — To let the devil in among us, into our hearts, was a mortal sin on our part; for we had the power to resist him; and in thereafter doing evil, as we all have done, we are guilty of a damnable iniquity. We are wretched, but it is our own fault; and we have done nothing save to stray farther and farther from the right path. — Then God gave us his Son for a Savior; he became the shepherd of the wretched sheep, and took upon himself the punishment for our transgressions. He is assailed by all the hosts of hell, and is the target of all the darts of death. He was called to account for all the sin of the world. He is called to account, and pays the debt; and we are absolved from the liability. See how the Lamb of God was sheared! Look at him as he was scourged; see him on his way to Calvary; see him on the cross. But he goes to his death with perfect patience. He has not gone astray, but was put to grief for our transgressions. As his life is blameless, his suffering is quiet and holy; he lives and dies in perfect obedience unto death, even the death of the cross. Thus he becomes the spiritual father of a regenerated humanity. The branch of the root of David is cut down and re-planted, and we are grafted into him. Christ dies, and lives again; baptized into him we have died and been quickened with him; and thus his Israel is a countless multitude. Atonement has been made for our iniquities, our sins are put away, and eternal righteousness is come. He that believes is a member of the body of Christ, and lives a new and holy life in him.

Lord Jesus, give us the grace of thy Holy Spirit, that we may have sincere faith in thee, experience thy holy life in our heart, and come no more into the power of the devil. When we go astray do thou at once bring us back into the fold, and keep us with thee for evermore. Amen.

We all, like sheep, have gone astray In ruin's fatal road; On him were our transgressions laid; He bore the mighty load.
He died to bear the guilt of men, That sin might be forgiven; He lives to bless them and defend, And plead their cause in heaven.

---

121. Thursday after Quinquagesima Sunday.

Thou Spirit of God, who didst come to us in our baptism, do thou expound the word to us. Amen.

Exodus 1, 22–2, 10. And Pharaoh charged all his people, saying, Every son that is born ye shall cast into the river, and every daughter ye shall save alive. And there went a man of the house of Levi, and took to wife a daughter of Levi. And the woman conceived, and bare a son; and when she saw him that he was a goodly child, she hid him three months. And when she could not longer hide him, she took for him an ark of bulrushes, and daubed it with slime and with pitch, and put the child therein; and she laid it in the flags by the river's brink. And his sister stood afar off, to wit what would be done to him. And the daughter of Pharaoh came down to wash herself at the river; and her maidens walked along by the river's side; and when she saw the ark among the flags, she sent her maid to fetch it. And when she had opened it, she saw the child: and, behold, the babe wept. And she had compassion on him, and said, This is one of the Hebrews' children. Then said his sister to Pharaoh's daughter, Shall I go and call to thee a nurse of the Hebrew woman, that she may nurse the child for thee? And Pharaoh's daughter said to her, Go. And the maid went and called the child's mother. And Pharaoh's daughter said unto her, Take this child away, and nurse it for me, and I will give thee thy wages. And the woman took the child, and nursed it. And the child grew, and she brought him unto Pharaoh's daughter, and he became her son. And she called his name Moses: and she said, Because I drew him out of the water.

This account is, from several points of view, very edifying. We see the faith and courage of the parents of Moses, the wonderful providence of God in saving the life of the child, in caring for his early training in the faith of Israel, and thereafter for his training in the wisdom of Egypt also, in order that he may be properly equipped for the great work of his life. We see how the cruel persecution on the part of the king thus becomes the salvation of God's people; and we are taught the lesson that the Christians' heaviest cross is their best help. The account before us teaches this, and much more in addition. Consider it as a whole and in its details, and it shall strengthen your faith. But our special purpose at this time is to point out how beautiful a prototype of baptism we have in the story here recited. The verdict of death rested on Moses at his birth and while his parents kept him at home. He was a child of wrath and the prey of death. But when his mother brought him home again from the water he was saved; and, furthermore, he was no longer her child merely, but the child of the king's daughter; a royal prince. Pharaoh's daughter had said: "Take this child away, and nurse it for me, and I will give thee thy wages;" and thereafter she regarded him as her own son. If she had not adopted him as her child, the mother would have been robbed of him by the king's executioners.

When you were born you were a child of wrath; for you were shapen in iniquity, and in sin did your mother conceive you. You were in transgressions, and liable to eternal punishment, until you were brought to the washing of water by the word, to the sacred river Jordan which flows through Israel. When your mother took you home from this bath you had become a child of the king, one of the royal children of *heaven*. The church, which is the bride of Christ; nay, Christ himself took you out of the jaws of death, and delivered you from the tyranny of Satan. Your earthly parents were given the care of you; but he it was who said: "Take this child away, and nurse it for me, and I will give you your wages." For in baptism you were rescued from death and adopted as a child of God; and your

name, also, might properly be called Moses, which means *saved*. It
is entirely in order to see, in the ark of Moses on the Nile, a prototype
of baptism; for it is a repetition of Noah's ark, in which Peter finds
a sermon on the saving power of baptism. (1 Peter 3, 20. 21).

Lord God, our heavenly Father, we earnetly beseech thee, give us
grace to believe with childlike simplicity, and to let thy word hold
entire sway over our thoughts. Keep us by this word, and lead us at
last through the waters of death home to thee in heaven. Amen.

Father, Son, and Holy Spirit, I'm baptized in thy dear name; In the seed
thou dost inherit, With the people thou dost claim, I am reckoned, And for
me the Savior came.
Help me in this high endeavor, Father, Son, and Holy Ghost! Bind my
heart to thee forever, Till I join the heavenly host; Living, dying, Let me
make in thee my boast.

122. Friday after Quinquagesima Sunday.

*Lord Jesus, we thank thee for thy life of suffering. Give us grace to follow
after thee. Amen.*

Matthew 16, 21–23. From that time forth began Jesus to shew unto his
disciples, how that he must go unto Jerusalem, and suffer many things of the
elders and chief priests and scribes, and be killed, and be raised again the third
day. Then Peter took him, and began to rebuke him, saying, Be it far from
thee, Lord: this shall not be unto thee. But he turned, and said unto Peter,
Get thee behind me, Satan; thou art an offence unto me; for thou savorest
not the things that be of God, but those that be of men.

The path which Jesus trod was so dangerous and difficult that none
other would have been able to walk it. The devil lay in wait for him
at every turn, and spread his toils before him where it was least to be
expected. When the Savior, in tender and intimate love, prepares the
disciples for his suffering, the devil is at hand, and makes use of Peter's
zeal, which still is altogether too much of the earth, for the purpose
of giving poison to the Lord. He tempts him to step aside from
the path of obedience with its attendant suffering. While we are
here on earth we can hardly have even a suspicion of the great craftiness of the cunning which the deceiver has employed against Jesus.
And how keenly did not the Lord feel all our distress and infirmity!
You need not think that his burden rested lightly on him because he
had such strong shoulders. "He poured out his soul unto death;"
what does this mean? He truly *suffered, suffered unutterable pain*; he
felt our distress, and "*tasted* death for every man." He had the purest
soul and the purest body, the most deep and intense horror of death,
and the keenest sense of its pain. There is none other to whose nature
suffering was as foreign as to his, yet it has not fallen to the lot of any
other to suffer as much as he; none ever hated death as he did, and
yet none has gone to his death with such perfect willingness. Now
the victory is won, the power of the devil is destroyed, and before our
feet is laid the way of the cross, leading straight to the open gate of
heaven. Before *him* everything was closed, everything dark; while

friends and enemies were his tempters. To him the cross was a curse, while death was death and nothing else. To us, on the other hand, the door is opened, the light is burning, and death has been turned into life. However, the path which in self-denial he trod we also must follow. We are baptized into his death, and the old man in us must die, if we are to live. Whosoever will save his life shall lose it; and whosoever will lose his life for his sake shall find it.

Lord Jesus, like Peter we find it very difficult to understand these things. Correct us, but do not reject us. Draw us after thee; help each of us to take up his cross and follow thee, that we may save our souls. Amen.

Here we have a firm foundation, Here the refuge of the lost; Christ's the rock of my salvation: His the name of which we boast.
Lamb of God for sinners wounded! Sacrifice to cancel guilt! None shall ever be confounded Who on thee their hopes have built.

123. Saturday after Quinquagesima Sunday.

Say to us, O Lord, when we are to walk through the darkness of affliction, that thou art with us. Amen.

Jonah 2, 1-9. Then Jonah prayed unto the Lord his God out of the fish's belly, and said, I cried by reason of mine affliction unto the Lord, and he heard me; out of the belly of hell cried I, and thou heardest my voice. For thou hadst cast me into the deep, in the midst of the seas; and the floods compassed me about: all thy billows and thy waves passed over me. Then I said, I am cast out of thy sight; yet I will look again toward thy holy temple. The waters compassed me about, even to the soul: the depths closed me round about, the weeds were wrapped about my head. I went down to the bottoms of the mountains: the earth with her bars was about me for ever: yet hast thou brought up my life from corruption, O Lord my God. When my soul fainted within me I remembered the Lord: and my prayer came in unto thee, into thine holy temple. They that observe lying vanities forsake their own mercy. But I will sacrifice unto thee with the voice of thanksgiving; I will pay that that I have vowed. Salvation is of the Lord.

In the agony of his passion and death Jesus experienced that which Jonah here prays out of the deep. He was in terror, and he cried out of the womb of hell; he was cast into the deep, into the midst of the seas; the floods compassed him about, and all the waves of God's wrath passed over him. He felt himself cast out of the sight of God and entirely forsaken of him; yet he continued to look toward his holy temple, and in faith he held fast the promise of deliverance. The waters compassed him about, even to the soul; the depth closed him round about, the weeds were wrapped about his head. He went down to the bottoms of the mountains; the earth with her bars was about him for ever. He was buried under a load of disgrace and contempt; the accursed thorns which were wrapped about his head held him fast; and all the power of hell barred his way; yea, the mighty bars of God's wrath were drawn before the door, that he might never escape. But his faith saved him; he did not relax his hold on the word, and his prayer forced its way through iron doors and stone walls, and reached the ear of heaven. "Thou hast brought up my life from corruption, O Lord my God."

You, dear Christian, must follow the same course, if you are to reach the gates of thanksgiving and salvation. Nevertheless, there is a great distinction. Jesus had no Savior; he was alone. "He looked, and there was none to help; and he wondered that there was none to uphold." You, however, are not alone; he is with you. If it seem to you that you are alone in the deep, yet is he with you; cry to the Lord. Your weak voice reaches his ear; your poor prayer comes to him in his holy temple; and "he brought up your life from corruption;" you are saved.

Truly, thou knowest best, Lord Jesus, what my soul suffers. I have sinned against the Lord; therefore I will bear his wrath until he shall again lead me out into the light. Meek and patient Savior, give to me thy gentle spirit. God, hear my cry in thy holy temple. Alas, many toils are spread for my feet; many obstacles bar the way before me; I see no escape. Lord, is this the way which thou wilt lead me, through still greater agony and terror? After all, thou art my Savior; thou canst not release thy hold on me, nor can I release mine on thee. Amen.

Yet, gracious God, where shall I flee? Thou art my only trust, And still my soul would cleave to thee, Though prostrate in the dust.
Thy mercy-seat is open still; Here let my soul retreat. With humble hope attend thy will, And wait beneath thy feet.

---

124. First Sunday in Lent. I.

Lord, our God, lead us into the strong fortress of thy word. Amen.

Gospel Lesson, Matthew 4, 1-11. Then was Jesus led up of the Spirit into the wilderness, to be tempted of the devil. And when he had fasted forty days and forty nights, he was afterward an hungred. And when the tempter came to him, he said, If thou be the Son of God, command that these stones be made bread. But he answered and said, It is written, Man shall not live by bread alone, but by every word that proceedeth out of the mouth of God. Then the devil taketh him up into the holy city, and setteth him on a pinnacle of the temple, and saith unto him, If thou be the Son of God, cast thyself down: for it is written, He shall give his angels charge concerning thee: and in their hands they shall bear thee up, lest at any time thou dash thy foot against a stone. Jesus said unto him, It is written again, Thou shalt not tempt the Lord thy God. Again, the devil taketh him up into an exceeding high mountain, and sheweth him all the kingdoms of the world, and the glory of them; and saith unto him, All these things will I give thee, if thou wilt fall down and worship me. Then saith Jesus unto him, Get thee hence, Satan: for it is written, Thou shalt worship the Lord thy God, and him only shalt thou serve. Then the devil leaveth him, and behold, angels came and ministered unto him.

As soon as Jesus was baptized to be our Savior, the devil sought to strike him down. Then begins the struggle on the outcome of which depends the ownership of our souls. The Son of God could not fall; but in the mists of temptation this is hid from his eyes, and he fights and is victorious only by using the scriptures as his weapon.

The Savior *was to be tempted.* It is one of the mysteries of God's power and grace that he really was tempted, and that only by the might of the scripture was he enabled to guard his perfect purity and obedience. Here we hold fast in faith these truths, which our poor reason is unable to reconcile, that the devil is indeed permitted to draw and entice Jesus, while at the same time he is not able to kindle in him a single evil inclination. — The strong cravings of hunger in his pure human nature are made use of by the tempter, who seeks to accomplish his downfall by storming him with thoughts of doubt and defiance of every sort. "Art thou the Son of God? Is this the manner in which a father deals with his son? Is it not written that thou shouldst make the desert to blossom? (Isaiah 35, 1). Shall the Son of God hunger and thirst? (49, 10). Prove to all angels that God is with his only begotten Son, and has given his glory to man." But the Lord is to atone for our sin by suffering the pangs of hunger, and he is victorious by means of the scriptures. — In the second temptation, in which the devil also employs the word of God, — after his own peculiar fashion, of course, — he strives to find a way to the heart of the Lord through his holy desire to glorify the Father. "Reveal thyself to Jerusalem. In thee shall be fulfilled also that word of God which says that the hands of angels shall bear thee up; and then thou shalt at once sit upon the throne of David, and Israel shall praise God." Such thoughts as these laid siege to his soul, and the deceiver employs all his craft and cunning in order to entice him, by means of the scriptures, to desert the scriptures. But the scriptures interpret themselves; and thereby the Lord obtains the victory, and goes forward on the path of humility. — Then the foul fiend seeks to make a snare for the Lord out of his strong and loving desire to rule over all creatures in order to save them. In a moment all the kingdoms of the world and the glory of them are presented to his view, and the tempter says: "The right which I have to these things, since man obeyed me, I give to thee; do thou but kneel once to me, and all is thine." The shameless audacity and cunning of the devil is truly terrible. This bargain which he proposes *seems* to give Jesus everything, but would, in fact, have placed him and everything under the supremacy of the devil. But see, how the arch liar collides with the scriptures at every point, and how he goes down before it every time. "Get thee hence, Satan; for it is written: Thou shalt worship the Lord thy God, and him only shalt thou serve." — Thus Jesus continues steadfast in his obedience, suffering, and fear of God.

Adam was tempted and fell; *abandoned* the *word* of God; believed the liar; and was caught in the toils of unbelief, carnal lust, and pride. In him we all fell and became subjects of the devil. Christ holds on to the word of God; continues in faith, truth, and holiness, and delivers us from the devil. *For* us he fought and won. His victory is your victory, if you believe in him; and he has also won for you the power and grace to do this. Not the devil, but Jesus, is your

master. Yet shall you also be tempted; by this very means you shall
put on the strength of Christ, his faith, his obedience, his self-denial.
Every child of God is led up of the spirit into the wilderness to be
tempted of the devil. Then he assails you with dark doubt concerning God's goodness and fatherly care, and concerning your election
and adoption and estate of grace; and then he sets for your feet the
snares of unrighteousness and sensuality and greed. You are tempted
to follow after fleeting honor, to go ways of your own choosing for
the purpose of advancing God's cause, to buy imaginary spiritual
benefits at the cost of truth; and who shall enumerate all the pitfalls
and all the decoys which the tempter prepares for God's children?
But in all these things his purpose is to lure your heart away from
the word into a feeling of security, or into despondency; into "unbelief
and despair and other vices." In the soul of the Savior there was
nothing to which the tempter could fasten; no unclean desire of any
sort stirred in the Holy One, though his struggle with the tempter
was more violent than any of which we can conceive. In us, on
the other hand, how many things are there not which give the tempter
a vantage ground! And yet, my dear troubled brother, he shall be
put to shame; he is vanquished. You shall be tempted, but you shall
also be victorious. He who conquered *for* you shall also conquer
in you; by means of the scripture you shall escape defeat. You shall
be horribly tempted to desert the word of God; but you shall receive
grace to abide by it, and to remain in faith and patience on the way
of suffering together with our Lord Jesus. Never, while you are on
earth, will the devil desist from tempting you to pride and unbelief,
to disobedience and to that sort of Christianity which consists in the
desire to enjoy the luxury of one's own feelings. Never, while you
are in the flesh, shall you be entirely free of these odious things; but
neither shall the Spirit of God ever cease to teach you humility, obedience in faith, and joy in suffering.

Thanks for thy temptation and thy victory, Lord Jesus. Spare
us, O God, from temptations; for we are very weak. But if we must
be tempted, give us victory; grant that we may overcome, for Jesus'
sake. Amen.

When temptation sorely presses, In the day of Satan's power, In our
times of deep distresses, In each dark and trying hour, By thy mercy, O
deliver us, good Lord!

When the world around is smiling, In the time of wealth and ease, Earthly
joys our hearts beguiling, In the day of health and peace, By thy mercy, O
deliver us, good Lord!

---

125. First Sunday in Lent. II.

*Lord, our God, let the power of thy grace be made manifest in us through
all manner of heavenly virtues. Amen.*

Epistle Lesson, 2 Corinthians 6, 1-10. We then, as workers together with
him, beseech you also that ye receive not the grace of God in vain. (For he
saith, I have heard thee in a time accepted, and in the day of salvation have

I succored thee: behold, now is the accepted time; behold, now is the day of salvation.) Giving no offence in any thing, that the ministry be not blamed: but in all things approving ourselves as the ministers of God, in much patience, in afflictions, in necessities, in distresses, in stripes, in imprisonments, in tumults, in labors, in watchings, in fastings; by pureness, by knowledge, by long-suffering, by kindness, by the Holy Ghost, by love unfeigned, ·by the word of truth, by the power of God, by the armor of righteousness on the right hand and on the left, by honor and dishonor, by evil report and good report: as deceivers, and yet true; as unknown, and yet well known; as dying, and behold, we live: as chastened, and not killed; as sorrowful, yet alway rejoicing; as poor yet making many rich; as having nothing, and yet possessing all things. O ye Corinthians, our mouth is open unto you, our heart is enlarged.

In the lives of the apostles we see clearly reflected the sufferings and the patience of Christ. Afflictions and necessities and distresses and stripes, labors and watchings and fastings, dishonor and evil report, misjudgment, poverty, pain, death,— these were the portion of Jesus; and the same spectacle is presented to us in the lives of his apostles. Are, then, distress and suffering the portion of the saints of God only? No; "Suffering we see, to be sure, everywhere on earth; but the suffering of Jesus is seen nowhere else *in the same degree;* it is only in his servants that we have anything at all like it." Patience, pureness, longsuffering, kindness, unfeigned love, and the like, — these constitute the manner of *Christ's* suffering, his holy style of warfare. In all things the same ministering, self-sacrificing love; in all things the same spirit, and the same object in view; namely, our welfare, our salvation. And the same is true of the apostles in their imitation of his holy example. What a shining example for us to follow; but, alas, how it must also put us to shame! To be sure, we are not called to be apostles, but all Christians are called to be the servants of Christ; and Paul exhorts us in this wise: "Be ye followers of me, even as I also am of Christ." Is it not to be feared, alas, that too many who call themselves Christians have "received the grace of God in vain"? *"Received* the grace of God" — and yet have done it "in vain"! What a remarkable and impressive statement! Does it not mean that too many have, after receiving the grace of God, accepted the offer of the tempter to effect a compromise? Or are we mistaken? Are there perhaps many who with the apostles walk in the footsteps of Christ? Alas, how few are they whom this description fits: "By the word of truth, by the power of God, by the armor of righteousness on the right hand and on the left." But *these* are the weapons with which one must be armed, if he is to stand against the wiles of the devil. It is absolutely *necessary* for us to be thus armed; else we shall succumb, beyond any doubt. And then, what shall the end be? For Jesus' sake, therefore, put on his armor, ye soldiers of the Lord!

Lord God, make us to be true Christians, and let thy strength be perfected in us. Let it be apparent in our whole walk that we are thy disciples; make all the world to know that thou hast a holy people on earth, who are able to labor and suffer and conquer by thy strength.

Teach us also to "drink of the brook in the way, and lift up the head."
Amen.

، Give us faith that keeps the way Till life's last hour is fled, And with a
pure and heavenly ray Lights up a dying bed.

Lord, give us such a faith as this, And then, whate'er may come, We'll
taste, e'en here, the hallowed bliss Of an eternal home.

126. Monday after First Sunday in Lent.

The Lord's truth is a shield and buckler.

Mark 14, 26–31. And when they had sung an hymn, they went out into
the mount of Olives. And Jesus saith unto them, All ye shall be offended
because of me this night: for it is written, I will smite the shepherd, and the
sheep shall be scattered. But after that I am risen, I will go before you into
Galilee. But Peter said unto him, Although all shall be offended, yet will not
I. And Jesus saith unto him, Verily I say unto thee, that this day, even in this
night, before the cock crow twice, thou shalt deny me thrice. But he spake
the more vehemently, If I should die with thee I will not deny thee in any
wise. Likewise also said they all.

Satan desired to sift them as wheat; but the Lord prayed for them,
that their faith might not fail. Himself was strengthened by the
scripture, and thereby he was their strength. The words of the prophet,
"smite the shepherd, and the sheep shall be scattered" (Zach. 13, 7),
are to the Lord as a star shining in the darkness. That which was to
happen was *necessary; he* is taken prisoner, and the disciples are offended; this is the burdensome, but *right* way, which he must go,
in order that the world may be saved. By means of this word of
prophecy the Lord here puts the devil to shame. The enemy desires
to sift Peter and the others, that they may fall and remain down; but
he is only permitted to sift them in such a way that they are purified;
for Jesus does not only die, but rises again, and gathers them again;
and through the comfort of the scriptures Jesus is able to explain
this to them in advance, with the result that they are strengthened
and do not wholly lose their faith under the heavy trial awaiting them.
— How entirely incapable Peter and the others are of defending themselves against Satan! Peter loved the Lord, and knew in his own
heart that he had this love. But he did not know how deceitful his
heart was, nor how dangerous the confidence which he felt in his own
love. Neither did he know how dark were to be the days which the
Lord was approaching, nor the nature of the trials in which he himself was about to be sifted by Satan. He declares: "If I should die
with thee, I will not deny thee in any wise." Peter; how little you
know what the Lord is to suffer! To die with him, to go to *that* death
which he is to taste; this would have been beyond the power of any
man. Not even after the Pentecost would Peter have been able to do
it; how much less, then, the Peter that now was. Was his declaration, then, mere lying and levity? By no means. He meant it in all
seriousness; but for this very reason his example warns us most im-

pressively against all reliance on self, and exhorts us most solemnly to walk in fear and trembling, and to put all our trust in the grace of God alone. None can by his own strength successfully resist any temptation; if the Lord did not sustain us, we would at once fall into the sin of unbelief, and deny our Savior. But his fidelity is unspeakably great. In the midst of his death agony and deepest distress he holds his protecting hand out over his self-willed disciples, and defends them. "Thou (mine enemy) hast thrust sore at me that I might fall; but *the Lord* helped me. *The Lord* is my strength and song, and is become my salvation. The right hand of the Lord is exalted; the right hand of the Lord doeth valiantly." (Psalm 118, 13. 14. 16).

Lord Jesus, let me be found alway among them that are thine; and strengthen me, that nor shame, nor fear, nor unbelief, may hereafter cause me to deny thee. Amen.

Let me, till my latest breath, Christ confess with constant meekness; Let me faithful be till death, Strong in him 'mid all my weakness; Let me live in him, and die Heir of mansions in the sky.

---

127. Tuesday after First Sunday in Lent.

"For their sakes I sanctify myself, that they also might be sanctified through the truth."

John 18, 1. 2. Mark 14, 32–34. When Jesus had spoken these words, he went forth with his disciples over the brook Cedron, where was a garden, into the which he entered, and his disciples. And Judas also, which betrayed him, knew the place: for Jesus ofttimes resorted thither with his disciples. And they came to a place which was named Gethsemane: and he saith to his disciples, Sit ye here, while I shall pray. And he taketh with him Peter and James and John, and began to be sore amazed, and to be very heavy; and saith unto them, My soul is exceeding sorrowful unto death: tarry ye here and watch.

They come to "Gethsemane." The name means *oil-press;* and here is he who "treads the press alone" (Isaiah 63, 3). The disciples are to remain at the entrance to the garden. Only three of them are to go with him farther on into Gethsemane: Peter, who imagines himself more ready than the others to die with him, and the sons of Zebedee, who have said that they can drink of the cup of which he is to drink (Mark 14, 31; 10, 38. 39). But the time arrives when it is the will of the Father that he shall be alone, and be encompassed about by the appalling terrors of death; and then none, not even one, of these three, may or can follow him farther. He is to be without comfort and without help; alone he is to suffer the death agony of all the world, suffer in our stead the damnation which we had deserved; *he*, and he alone, is to taste of death for us all. And *now* the time is come; now Satan is permitted to assail him with all the terrors of hell and all the horrors at the command of the prince of death. Then he begins to be sore amazed, and to be very heavy. The trembling Savior now felt as shall the wicked, when, having left all hope behind, they quake at the final judgment and in unutterable anguish hang on the lips of the Judge, which open to pronounce the inevitable curse on them. Not until that day of wrath without a morrow shall it be revealed to us what Jesus suffered in Gethsemane. Struggling with the terror of hell and death, his racked soul writhes in voiceless agony, and sustains itself by means of those Psalms of which the echo is heard in the moan: "My soul is exceeding sorrowful unto death." (Psalm 22, 15; 40, 12). — It is *my* death and *yours* which he feels; it is the sin of the world which weighs him down. The only begotten Son of God, the Holy and Righteous One, lies here prostrate in the dust, weeping and moaning, and finding no comfort. In most agonizing terror, in utterly unspeakable agony of death, he writhes on the ground like a worm. "He is bruised for *our* iniquities." The Father surrenders his Son to condemnation in our stead, and permits the prince of darkness to deal with him according to his pleasure and our deserts. It is the death of fallen, ungodly, lost and condemned humanity, the death of all *sinners*, which is suffered by the Lamb without blemish. O, how his heart is compassed about with sorrow, how his soul is stricken with dread, as he is to descend into the most agonizing pangs of everlasting perdition! Lord Jesus, what shall I say? I have no words, I have not a heart worthy of thee; but thou hast bought even me with thy precious blood, and I will bless thee for evermore. Amen.

When no eye its pity gave us, When there was no arm to save us, Christ his love and power displayed; By his stripes he wrought our healing, By his death, our life revealing, He for us the ransom paid.

Jesus, may thy love constrain us, That from sin we may refrain us, In thy griefs may deeply grieve; Thee our best affections giving, To thy glory ever living, May we in thy glory live.

128. Wednesday after First Sunday in Lent.

Wake us, Lord Jesus; wake us, and keep us awake with thee. Amen.

Matthew 26, 39–46. And he went a little farther, and fell on his face, and prayed, saying, O my Father, if it be possible, let this cup pass from me! nevertheless, not as I will, but as thou wilt. And he cometh unto the disciples, and findeth them asleep, and saith unto Peter, What! could ye not watch with me one hour. Watch and pray, that ye enter not into temptation; the spirit indeed is willing, but the flesh is weak. He went away again the second time, and prayed, saying, O my Father, if this cup may not pass away from me, except I drink it, thy will be done. And he came and found them asleep again: for their eyes were heavy. And he left them, and went away again, and prayed the third time, saying the same words. Then cometh he to his disciples, and saith unto them, Sleep on now, and take your rest; behold, the hour is at hand, and the Son of man is betrayed into the hands of sinners. Rise, let us be going: behold, he is at hand that doth betray me.

When the old Testament high priest was to carry the blood of atonement into the holy of holies he enveloped himself in frankincense, burning with fire from the altar in the sanctuary. Christ, our high priest, does the like in Gethsemane. — Man has a dread of death; and here Jesus is confronted by death with all its terrors of whatever kind, death and condemnation in the stead of us all. His pure nature *must* of necessity shrink from the pains of death and hell; and this he expresses in the prayer: *"O my Father, if it be possible,* let this cup pass from me." The baptism with which he is to be baptized is so terrible that, in his dread of it, even he, the only Chosen One, our Immanuel, sweats drops of blood. O sin and hell, how dreadful are you! The Lord spoke to the Father exactly what he felt. His terrible dread of death was a necessary part of his atoning passion. This he must suffer; and hence he *can not* pray otherwise than he does: "If it be possible that the world can be saved by other means, let it be done; take this cup from me. If thou, Father, canst forgive me the iniquity of the world, which now is *my* iniquity, without my dying for it, let it be done." But even here, in the greatest possible temptation, his human will bows down before the will of the Father in the deepest, fullest obedience. How perfect a high priest we have; but O how terrible a battle he wages for us! "He offered up prayers and supplications with strong crying and tears unto him that was able to save him from death, and was heard in that he feared." (Hebrews 5, 7). Was, then, the cup taken from him? No; it is necessary that the demands of justice be satisfied; but we see from the words of the Holy Spirit in the epistle to the Hebrews, as we hear it in the Lord's own words also, that what he pleads for first and last is the will of the Father. It becomes clear to him what this will is. He emerges out of the terrible struggle, out of the sweating of blood and the baptism of agony, out of the mists of death; and then he sees clearly that it is the Father who has poured out the cup for him; the angel is able to show him this truth, and then the victory is won. With the fearlessness of the strong lion the timid Lamb now goes to his death willingly and with perfect patience. — But what shall I say? How unutterably great is the love with which he loves us! How infinitely high is the price for which he bought us! Can you hear that which transpires in Gethsemane, and yet despise his grace? Satan has bewitched the world, alas; but I adore thee, Lord Jesus, and thank thee for thy agony, for thy bloody sweat, for thy victory over the devil, here and everywhere. I thank thee for thy burning offering of prayer; and I will fight with patience, suffer without complaint, and renounce all my own will for thy sake. Grant me grace to do this; O give me this *grace*, Lord Jesus. Amen.

What thou, my Lord, hast suffered Was all for sinners' gain; Mine, mine was the transgression, But thine the deadly pain; Lo, here I fall, my Savior! 'Tis I deserve thy place; Look on me with thy favor, Vouchsafe to me thy grace.

129. Thursday after First Sunday in Lent.

Keep our eyes awake, O God. Amen.

Matthew 26, 45-48. Then cometh he to his disciples, and saith unto them, Sleep on now, and take your rest; behold, the hour is at hand, and the Son of man is betrayed into the hands of sinners. Rise, let us be going: behold, he is at hand that doth betray me. And while he yet spake, lo, Judas, one of the twelve, came, and with him a great multitude, with swords and staves, from the chief priests and elders of the people. Now he that betrayed him gave them a sign, saying, Whomsoever I shall kiss, that same is he: hold him fast.

The disciples were unable to keep awake. A peculiar drowsiness was upon them. What; is even *Peter* unable to watch? Can he not watch one hour with the Lord? Alas! *Peter*, who wanted to give his life for him, can not forego one hour's sleep for him. — Do ye still sleep? saith the Lord; the hour is at hand when the shepherd shall be smitten and the sheep scattered, now that the time when you are to be sifted breaks in upon you. Yes, they did not let *him* wake them; they fell asleep at the very time when he, in his burning love and care for them, struggled vehemently and suffered the agony of death for their sake. Let another, then, rouse them from their sleep. — When we also, who now believe in the Lord Jesus, are so heavy with sleep that his love and suffering and the faithful work of his Spirit in our heart can not keep us awake, he finds it necessary to let the tempter come upon us, with the result that we either wake up and repent, or remain thrown down like bits of the wreck after a storm. — Judas was awake while the others slept. How powerful a sermon is preached by this fact! See, there he comes. He should have been a leader in the army of light, and now he leads the mob of Satan, which is advancing for the purpose of seizing Christ. And this man was one of Jesus' disciples! What an opportunity for the devil to taunt the Lord; to wound and maltreat him, who loved so ardently and was so full of zeal for the good, the true, and the honor of God! And yet he does not denounce his flock. Even Judas would have found mercy had he repented and turned from his wickedness. And it is by reason of the Lord's long-suffering patience and fidelity that he has saved all the disciples, excepting only that son of perdition, and has rescued thousands and millions from the clutches of the sneering enemy, in spite of the fact that all of us are so wretchedly sleepy. This is the kind of Savior of whom we were in need, one who would suffer all this, and endure us, and pray for us, when we are offended because of him. Such a Savior we needed, and such a Savior we have. Praise be to God!

By thy grace, Lord Jesus, and by the power of thy Spirit, which since the day of Pentecost reigns in thy church, will we watch and obtain victory over the devil; by thy grace, by that alone. — Thou shalt keep us in thine eye and hand, and never relax thy hold on us; this we believe and know, and it is our strength and our joy. Amen.

Watch! 'tis your Lord's command; And while we speak he's near; Mark the first signal of his hand, And ready all appear.
Oh, happy servant he, In such a posture found! He shall his Lord with rapture see, And be with honor crowned.

130. Friday after First Sunday in Lent.

Reveal to us, Lord Jesus, thy love and thy power. Amen.

John 18, 4–9. Jesus therefore, knowing all things that should come upon him, went forth, and said unto them, Whom seek ye? They answered him, Jesus of Nazareth. Jesus saith unto them, I am he. And Judas also, which betrayed him, stood with them. As soon then as he had said unto them, I am he, they went backward, and fell to the ground. Then asked he them again, Whom seek ye? And they said, Jesus of Nazareth. Jesus answered, I have told you that I am he: if therefore ye seek me, let these go their way: that the saying might be fulfilled which he spake, Of them which thou gavest me have I lost none.

The Lord had said: "No man taketh my life from me, but I lay it down of myself." (John 10, 18). He went to his death of *his own free will;* else he could not have been led to it by any power in the world. The only force that urged him onward was the will of the Father, the eternal counsel of love concerning our salvation by means of his death; his infinite mercy only, with which he embraces us, is the power that led the Lamb of God to the slaughter. Had he gone to his passion reluctantly, with repugnance and aversion, to which the devil in Gethsemane persistently tempted him with the most dreadful craftiness, he would not have been able to take away our load of guilt.

The Lord's simple statement, "I am he," causes the armed band to fall to the ground. He thereby demonstrates to us that of his own free will he allows himself to be bound. Thereby he also preaches a penitential sermon to Judas and the others; for Jesus can not do otherwise than practice his office of love for the benefit of all who come near to him. And are they still determined to lay hands on him to bind him? It was to be expected that his majesty would smite their hearts and cause them to turn back, as did those other servants who had been sent to seize him. (John 7, 46). But no; the hour of darkness is come, and Satan is now to be permitted to make use of these men for the purpose of putting the Son of God in chains. Unhappy the mothers who gave you birth! — And now the Lord uses all his might solely for the salvation of his disciples. "If therefore ye seek me, let these go their way." In these words he gives them a letter of safe conduct which the enemies are compelled to respect. What would have become of the poor disciples, if they also had been seized at this time and led to their death? How strong a Lord is Jesus, and how true! He lays down his life of himself, in order that we may live; and he cares for us everywhere, in the most hopeless circumstances, that he may lose none of them which the Father gave him. Keep this in your heart, and call it to mind when you are being tempted. His power and love and fidelity are with you to save you. Have faith in him.

We heartily thank thee, precious Lord Jesus, that thou dost shelter us under thy wings, save us by thy death, and defend us with thy almighty word. Give us the light and the gifts of thy Holy Spirit, that we may believe in thee, follow thee, and suffer and die with thee. Amen.

Rejected and despised of men, Behold a man of woe! And grief his
close companion still Through all his life below!
Yet all the griefs he felt were ours, Ours were the woes he bore; Pangs,
not his own, his spotless soul With bitter anguish tore.

---

131. Saturday after First Sunday in Lent.

Most patient Lamb of God, give us to be of like mind with thee. Amen.

Matthew 26, 49–54. And forthwith he came to Jesus, and said, Hail,
Master; and kissed him. And Jesus said unto him, Friend, wherefore art thou
come? Then came they and laid hands on Jesus, and took him. And, behold,
one of them which were with Jesus, stretched out his hand, and drew his sword,
and struck a servant of the high priest's, and smote off his ear. Then said
Jesus unto him, Put up again thy sword into his place: for all they that take
the sword, shall perish with the sword. Thinkest thou that I cannot now pray
to my Father, and he shall presently give me more than twelve legions of
angels? But how then shall the scriptures be fulfilled, that thus it must be?

Let us bear in mind that Jesus was *betrayed with a kiss;* the expression and sign of love, of near relationship, of mutual attachment.
There was this degree of intimacy between him and the betrayer. "It
was thou, a man mine equal, my guide, and mine acquaintance. We
took sweet counsel together, and walked unto the house of God in
company." (Psalm 55, 13, 14). The devil has entered into Judas, and
he kisses Jesus. The Lord accepts the kiss; and by what means
could he have suffered himself to be abased lower than this! Could
he in any possible way have shown greater meekness and patience?
And, what is more, immediately after receiving the kiss he speaks
words of mercy to Judas: "Friend, wherefore art thou come? Judas,
betrayest thou the Son of Man with a kiss?" What he says to Judas
is neither hypocrisy nor bitterness; he still wishes to save that unhappy man. Jesus is betrayed with a kiss by one of the members of
his own household, as it were; and on the part of the betrayer this
certainly was an act worthy of the devil. But the spirit in which the
Lord accepts this treatment is truly divine. He receives the kiss with
such perfect meekness and love that the devil does not succeed in
pouring even one drop of the poison of anger and deceit into the pure
soul of the Savior. The Son of Man thus atones for the sins of
duplicity and sham piety; and there is herein much comfort and grace
for us. That which Christ does on this occasion is done by way of
atonement for all the falsehood and anger which have found lodgment in our poor hearts, and of which there is such an abundance
in our sinful lives. Hereafter the devil shall not be able to bring
anything to my charge on account of my hypocritical heart, nor on
account of the deceit which did, and to my sorrow still does, stain
my life. Neither shall it now be necessary for any whom the devil
has led astray into the sins of lying and faithlessness and deceit to
continue with these sins weighing on his conscience, if he will but
confess them. But, on the other hand, neither shall any among us

continue to stain our conduct with these things; for Christ has delivered us from the ways of the devil. Come out into the light with everything. Spread out before the Lord your soul and your life, and all that propensity to deceit which you find in your heart; — and "the blood of Jesus Christ his Son cleanseth us from all sin.' The devil with his greatest masterpiece of cunning is put to shame. Glory be to God!

We thank thee, Lord Jesus, for that thou didst accept the kiss of Judas. Thereby thou hast given me unspeakably great and sweet comfort. I lie prostrate at thy feet, and will for ever lie at the foot of thy throne and thank thee for all the bitterness which thou didst taste for me and take from me. Faithful Savior, give me the light and grace of thy Holy Spirit, that I may believe in thee. Amen.

Hail, thou once despised Jesus! Hail, thou Galilean King! Thou didst suffer to release us, Thou didst free salvation bring. Hail, thou agonizing Savior, Bearer of our sin and shame! By thy merit we find favor; Life is given through thy name.

---

132. Second Sunday in Lent. I.

Humble us, O Lord, that we depart not from thy word. Amen.

Gospel Lesson, Matthew 15, 21-28. Then Jesus went thence, and departed into the coasts of Tyre and Sidon. And, behold, a woman of Canaan came out of the same coasts, and cried unto him, saying, Have mercy upon me, O Lord, thou son of David! my daughter is grievously vexed with a devil. But he answered her not a word. And his disciples came, and besought him, saying, Send her away; for she crieth after us. But he answered and said, I am not sent but unto the lost sheep of the house of Israel. Then came she, and worshipped him, saying, Lord, help me! But he answered and said, It is not meet to take the children's bread, and to cast it to the dogs. And she said, Truth, Lord: yet the dogs eat of the crumbs which fall from their master's table. Then Jesus answered and said unto her, O woman, great is thy faith: be it unto thee even as thou wilt. And her daughter was made whole from that very hour.

They were hard struggles which our Lord Jesus had when he bare, and was to pay the wages of, our sin, when he was to destroy death and the power of the devil, and restore to us everlasting life. No other battle can be compared with his. But all who are to receive and keep the precious gift, deliverance from death and the devil, shall of necessity have their battles to fight also, and if our faith is to shine more brightly to the glory of God, and our souls are to reach greater depths in his grace, we must expect to be the more sorely tried.

Why does the Lord deal so strangely with the woman of Canaan? Why does he say not a word in answer to her most earnest appeal? And when he at last does speak, why do his words sound so much like a stern rebuff? Our text answers these questions, and does it in a way to fire our hearts, if we read the answer aright. But we also have an account in the Old Testament which answers these questions. Joseph made himself strange and stern and hard to his brethren, although he loved them so well that he was obliged to go into his chamber and weep. He wanted them to remember their sin, repent of it, and receive mercy. When the Lord sees that it is necessary to humble us, and that the trial is not greater than we can bear, he hides his loving heart, and shows us nothing but his wrath. It was necessary that this woman be *brought so low*, be made to feel that she was of the heathen, be taught to liken herself to the dogs; her faith was to be strained so hard, put to so severe a test, in order that she might receive the rights of citizenship in Israel. A surgeon who performs a dangerous operation on his own dearest child rejoices when it is done and all is well. So does the Lord in the case before us; his words express his great joy at the rescue of the woman. When he says, "O woman, great is thy faith," we are again reminded of his prototype Joseph, who, when his brethren had stood the test, wept for joy and cried, "I am Joseph; doth my father yet live?"

Precious Savior, it cost thee immeasurable labor to redeem us; and what a weary task thou hast also in creating faith in us and inducing us to accept thy salvation!— And you, dear soul, be persistent in your prayers, even though he seem not to answer. He has answered already. (Isaiah 65, 24). When care oppresses, when the heart is swept by fierce storms, when the soul is in pain, when there is darkness on every hand, when the Lord seems in anger to have put aside his tender mercies; then it is as it should be. You have sinned and been faithless; but do not leave off crying to him. Follow after him, prostrate yourself before him, prefer your prayer again and again. This is his will; this is what he teaches you in the text now before us. — It is entirely necessary that you should be humbled; faith strikes root and grows in humble hearts only. By degrees, as you receive grace to humble yourself, you also receive grace to believe; and it is unto you according to your faith, as the Lord has said, to his honor and to your salvation.

Lord, we understand that it is well that thou dost humble us; but thou knowest how weak we are in the time of trial. Do not deliver us over to our unbelief and impatience; but purge us, and strengthen our faith, to the praise of thy glorious name. Amen.

When in the hour of utmost need We know not where to look for aid; When days and nights of anxious thought Nor help nor counsel yet have brought:
Then this our comfort is alone, That we may meet before thy throne, And cry, O faithful God, to thee For rescue from our misery.

---

133. Second Sunday in Lent. II.

Lord Jesus, cleanse us from the defilement of the unclean spirit, and sanctify us; thou alone canst do it. Amen.

Epistle Lesson, 1 Thessalonians 4, 1-7. Furthermore then we beseech you, brethren, and exhort you by the Lord Jesus, that as ye have received of us how ye ought to walk and to please God, so ye would abound more and more. For ye know what commandments we gave you by the Lord Jesus. For this is the will of God, even your sanctification, that ye should abstain from fornication: that every one of you should know how to possess his vessel in sanctification and honor; not in the lust of concupiscence, even as the Gentiles which know not God: that no man go beyond and defraud his brother in any matter; because that the Lord is the avenger of all such, as we also have forewarned you and testified. For God hath not called us unto uncleanness, but unto holiness.

The will of God is your sanctification. It could not be otherwise; for God is holy. Still it profits us to hear and consider that in laboring and striving after holiness we have the will of God with us. Then we may know that victory is assured, even though the path be difficult, and though we seem to be losing ground. Labor jealously for your purification; strive after it with zeal and earnestness. The apostle beseeches and exhorts us by the Lord Jesus that we would do this. He *beseeches* us; shall we not hear him? He *exhorts* us; shall we despise his exhortation? He beseeches and exhorts by *the Lord Jesus*, in the service and spirit and power of Jesus, by his love, for his blessed name's sake, for the sake of his atoning obedience and death. Shall we not obey him? You made rapid advance in holiness during the earliest period of your Christian life. You displayed great zeal in the work of purging out all sin and of pleasing God. You improved immensely in a short time; your growth was rapid. Shall the blossom not put forth a bud, or shall the bud die without ripening into fruit? You have been taught how we ought to walk. Does not your heart burn within you when the apostle here speaks of *pleasing God* and of *abounding therein more and more?* "To please God," to walk according to the good pleasures of Jesus; — these are things to touch the innermost chords of the Christian heart. "Not in the lust of concupiscence," God forbid! The holy bride of Christ to defile herself with the uncleanness of the gentiles! The very suggestion of such a thing gives us a shock. — Out, then, with the unclean desires; purge the heart of them. Immerse your soulds in the holiness of Jesus, and in his purity, that you "hate even the garment spotted by the flesh." — It is much to be regretted, if you do not *believe* that he will give you strength to do this; for then the devil has unmanned you. As God is holy, he has in Christ given you grace to become holy; and when you neglect it you grieve the Spirit of God. We also beseech and exhort by the Lord Jesus: Be in earnest in the matter of mortifying the lusts of the flesh. You are not called unto uncleanness, as unfortunately seems to the opinion of many nominal Christians; but you are *called unto holiness.* Mark this: *God has called you unto holiness.* Now strive after it with the zeal and perseverance of faith. The commandment of God, and his promise to you in Jesus Christ are true and faithful.

Most holy Lord Jesus, give to us thy pure mind. Help us to mortify the unclean lusts of the flesh and to walk in holiness, that by the Holy Spirit we may please thee and the Father. Lord grant us this great mercy, that we increase in holiness from day to day. Amen.

Oh, for a closer walk with God, A calm and heavenly frame, A light to shine upon the road That leads me to the Lamb.
The dearest idol I have known, Whate'er that idol be, Help me to tear it from thy throne, And worship only thee.

---

134. Monday after Second Sunday in Lent.

Lord Jesus, do make us to see thy fettered hands, which set us free. Amen.

Matthew 26, 50–56. And Jesus said unto him, Friend, wherefore art thou come? Then came they and laid hands on Jesus, and took him. And, behold, one of them which were with Jesus, stretched out his hand, and drew his sword, and struck a servant of the high priest's, and smote off his ear. Then said Jesus unto him, Put up again thy sword into his place: for all they that take the sword, shall perish with the sword. Thinkest thou that I cannot now pray to my Father, and he shall presently give me more than twelve legions of angels? But how then shall the scriptures be fulfilled, that thus it must be? In that same hour said Jesus to the multitudes, Are ye come out as against a thief, with swords and staves for to take me? I sat daily with you teaching in the temple, and ye laid no hold on me. But all this was done, that the scriptures of the prophets might be fulfilled. Then all the disciples forsook him, and fled.

He is ready and willing to suffer death for us. His love is the tie that binds him. Had it not been so, no man would ever have been able to restrain the Lord's hands. But as he suffers for *us*, we may also say that our sins, our perverse will, our disobedience, our unbridled license, and all that irresponsible and spurious liberty which fills the world, have bound these holy hands, which were lifted only to bless, heal, and save. We *all* have our share of the blame; let us confess this, and his bonds shall make us free indeed.

Peter drew his sword to protect him; but what was this save a new attempt on the part of the devil to strike from the Savior's hand the cup which the Father had given him to drink? Secular power for the church is Satan's own invention. Not the sword, but the word, is the weapon of the church; it is not in ruling, but in suffering, that it has the strength which gives assurance of victory; that which makes its fields fruitful is not the blood of its enemies, but the blood of its martyrs. The Lord would have been in no want of champions, had he wished to employ force against his enemies and yours. In place of twelve such men as Peter he could have had more than twelve legions of angels for his protection. But, in that case, how should the scriptures have been fulfilled? Could he have suffered the penalty for our sins and wiped our guilt away? At this time the Lord was to suffer, not govern; or rather, he was to suffer in order that he might govern. In this manner we also shall through suffering fulfil the counsel of God, and the scriptures, and obtain victory over our enemies. When the power of darkness is allowed to rage against us we shall be victorious through him who healed the ear of Malchus, return good for evil, and prove to our adversaries that God in us is stronger than is the devil in them. And when they speak evil we shall either be patient and say nothing, or we shall correct them in a loving desire to save them, as did the Lord when he said: "Why laid ye not hold on me when I sat daily with you in the temple?" He has done this for us, in our stead; learn this truth well, and he shall certainly accomplish it in you also. Why are you not more in evidence, you believers, who should be everywhere engaged in proving that the Spirit and power of the Savior dwell in you? Why do they seem to be so few who walk in his steps; the steps of the patient Savior, who out of his love was willing to suffer, and who unto death had compassion on all his enemies and was their benefactor? — Not as one rendered powerless; not as one vanquished, but as one completely victorious over the devil, the Lord surrenders his own body to these servants of the devil, and allows himself to be led away.

My soul worships thee, Lord Jesus. Thy love has unchained my fetters and thereupon bound me to thee. Willingly and obediently will I follow thee in thy footsteps of suffering; for thou art my delight and my strength. Lord, thou knowest thy servant; be gracious unto me, and help me. Amen.

Thou art my head, my Lord divine: I am thy member, wholly thine;
And in thy Spirit's strength would still Serve thee according to thy will.
Thus will I sing thy praises here, With joyful spirit year by year: And they shall sound before thy throne, Where time nor number more is known.

135. Tuesday after Second Sunday in Lent.

Lord Jesus, draw our eye and heart to thee.

John 18, 12–14. 19, 24. Then the band and the captain and officers of the Jews took Jesus, and bound him, and led him away to Annas first; for he was father in law to Caiaphas, which was the high priest that same year. Now Caiaphas was he, which gave counsel to the Jews, that it was expedient that one man should die for the people. The high priest then asked Jesus of his disciples, and of his doctrine. Jesus answered him, I spake openly to the world; I ever taught in the synagogue, and in the temple, whither the Jews always resort; and in secret have I said nothing. Why askest thou me? ask them which heard me, what I have said unto them: behold, they know what I said. And when he had thus spoken, one of the officers which stood by struck Jesus with the palm of his hand, saying, Answerest thou the high priest so? Jesus answered him, If I have spoken evil, bear witness of the evil: but if well, why smitest thou me? Now Annas had sent him bound unto Caiaphas the high priest.

He who shall judge all men with righteousness is brought before the tribunal of most foul injustice, which, even before the trial, has decided that he shall die. However, the truth of the matter is that the sentence of death unjustly pronounced by the high council of Israel has already been pronounced on the Son of Man in the highest and most righteous council of Israel, for the reason that the Righteous One was made to be sin for us. The truth of the words, "ye thought evil against me, but God meant it unto good," is in nothing established more clearly than in the passion of Christ. In him the wily craftiness and deceit of Satan are defeated; and to such good purpose, that all the evil which befalls the people of God shall be turned to their good. God makes blessings out of the evil counsel of men against the church of God and against its individual members. The thoughts of men are thought by God also, with the most important distinction, however, that men mean it unto evil, while he means it unto good. Nay, what is more; in his love he has long since decreed that all things shall work together for the good of his children. All this abundance of grace and wisdom and love is poured out over us for the sake of *him* who was on trial and was judged by hypocrites and unrighteous men. He has bought the justice of Heaven over to the side of us sinners, and has put us in possession of this mercy by making us members of his body.

In the Lord's reply to the high priest his majesty and his mercy shine as resplendent as does his purity, and fairly blaze before the eyes of the council and the others present. We hear him make still another attempt to turn their hearts to truth and repentance. Who knows but there may have been some Nicodemus among them? But even if they are villains, every one of them, his mercy toward sinners is so great that he must needs throw out the life line to them. His reward is a slap in the face. Satan continued to exercise all his cunning against the Lord, but Jesus is and remains meek; smitten on the right cheek he turns to them the other also. The Son of God, who shall sit on the throne of glory, loves the soul of this wretched slave of sin who tries to curry favor with his betters by striking the Lord in the face. Jesus speaks words of correction to him, in order that he may be brought to know his sin and be saved, if that be possible. In this way he atones for the sin of masters and servants such as these; and at the same time he sanctifies the blows dealt to his people by the slaves of unbelief; and he gives us power to suffer patiently, and to love them that smite us.

Let none of us, dear readers, be found among the unjust judges or the ungodly servants. But do we love our enemies with the love of Jesus, and do we draw them with us to heaven? God, give us grace to do this, for Jesus' sake. Amen.

Humble, holy, all resigned To thy will—thy will be done! Give me, Lord, the perfect mind Of thy well-beloved Son.
Counting gain and glory loss, May I tread the path he trod, Die with Jesus on the cross, Rise with him to thee, my God!

136. Wednesday after Second Sunday in Lent.

God, preserve me; for I am of thy people.

Mark 14, 66–72. And as Peter was beneath in the palace, there cometh one of the maids of the high priest: and when she saw Peter warming himself, she looked upon him, and said, And thou also wast with Jesus of Nazareth.

But he denied, saying, I know not, neither understand I what thou sayest. And he went out into the porch; and the the cock crew. And a maid saw him again, and began to say to them that stood by, This is one of them. And he denied it again. And a little after, they that stood by said again to Peter, Surely thou art one of them; for thou art a Galilean, and thy speech agree thereto. But he began to curse and swear, saying, I know not this man of whom ye speak. And the second time the cock crew. And Peter called to mind the word that Jesus said unto him, Before the cock crow twice, thou shalt deny me thrice. And when he thought thereon, he wept.

The Lord had said to the disciples that he alone, and none with him, should meet death. He had prayed for them, and had assured their safety from the enemy by his command: "Let these go their way." But Peter is not satisfied to abide by the word of the Lord; he insists on following out his own declaration, "I am ready to die with thee;" and thus he puts himself in the way of temptation. He thus lacks the rest and strength in the words of the Lord which are a protection against death and danger; and then devils and men attack the defenceless man with fury, and maltreat him in a dreadful way. John they leave in peace.

The weakest Christian is strong and defeats the devil, when he but holds fast the word of God and remains in the Lord's ways, in humility, the fear of God, and denial of self; but the strongest is as the lightest feather against the devil, when he follows his own devices, departs from the word, imagines himself to be strong, and throws himself in the way of temptation. Defer to the word of God, my Christian friend. This word declares that you walk in the midst of a thousand dangers, that of yourself you are wretchedly weak, that all your strength is nothing but vanity; but it also declares that the Lord is near you, and that none shall pluck you out of his hand. Abide herein, and walk your way with fear and with confidence; then you walk in the Spirit and are borne on the hands of angels. But if you put your faith in your own understanding, if you rely on yourself, or entrust yourself to the wisdom and strength of men, you shall without fail have the bitter experience that "the flesh is weak." Peter was truly a man of courage and heroism, and none was more honestly loyal than he to the Lord. But it requires strength greater than this to stand against "principalities and powers and spiritual wickedness in high places." What, then, shall be the fate of the Christians of our age, so many of whom have been lulled to sleep by the world, and pillow their heads in fancied security on their own imagined piety?

There is a solemn, we may say a terrible, warning in the fall of Peter; but, on the other hand, the grace of the Lord toward the fallen Peter has unspeakable beauty and comfort. Do you know, dear friend, how the cockcrow stirs, and how the look of Jesus melts the heart? I wonder whether you ever have felt yourself weaken in the courtyard of Caiaphas, or in Antioch? (Galatians 2, 11–14). If you have such an experience hereafter, listen and see, and he shall fill your ear with his voice, and your eyes with his person, that you may tast.

the tears of bitter repentance, but also experience the power of his blood and tears to heal the soul.

Lord God, teach us to walk with wise care, that we never in carnal security plunge into temptations. When we are to be sifted by Satan, then let thy intercession and thy strength save us, that we may overcome, and obtain victory. Thou knowest that we are foolish and weak, and that hence we can do nothing without thee. Faithful God, do not let us be made ashamed; do not let the devil triumph, and thy name be mocked. Save us in the time of temptation, keep us from falling, and lift us up, that we may praise and bless thee for ever-more. Amen.

Arise, my soul, arise, Shake off thy guilty fears; The bleeding Sacrifice In my behalf appears; Before the throne my surety stands, My name is written on his hands.

He ever lives above For me to intercede; His all-redeeming love, His precious blood to plead; His blood atoned for all our race, And sprinkles now the throne of grace.

137. Thursday after Second Sunday in Lent.

"I have preached righteousness in the great congregation." Lord, open our ears, that we may hear it.

Matthew 26, 59-68. Now the chief priests, and elders and all the council sought false witness against Jesus, to put him to death; but found none: yea, though many false witnesses came, yet found they none. At the last came two false witnesses, and said, This fellow said, I am able to destroy the temple of God, and to build it in three days. And the high priest arose, and said unto him, Answerest thou nothing? What is it which these witness against thee? But Jesus held his peace. And the high priest answered and said unto him, I adjure thee by the living God, that thou tell us whether thou be the Christ, the Son of God. Jesus saith unto him, Thou hast said: nevertheless I say unto you, Hereafter shall ye see the Son of man sitting on the right hand of power, and coming in the clouds of heaven. Then the high priest rent his clothes, saying, He hath spoken blasphemy; what further need have we of witnesses? behold, now ye have heard his blasphemy. What think ye? They answered and said, He is guilty of death. Then did they spit in his face, and buffeted him: and others smote him with the palms of their hands, saying, Prophesy unto us, thou Christ, Who is he that smote thee?

The Lord holds his peace when the false witnesses testify against him; and by his silence he atones for all the falsehood in the world. The Lamb of God suffers, and opens not his mouth. Neither was it necessary that he say anything in self-defense; for the harder they strive to make him appear guilty, the more clearly is his innocence brought to light. He is, and continues to be one in whom there is no fault. But it has been determined in advance that he shall die; and now the question which troubles his judges is, how they may find something for which to condemn him. They must and shall destroy the temple, the temple of his body, and, at the same time, the temple of Jerusalem, the place of offering; for the old system of sacrifices ceased with the death of the true sacrificial Lamb. They must carry out the decree of God and place Jesus in the sepulchre, in order that he may rise again and build a living temple on the eternal rock of his divinity and his victory. Therefore the high priest himself must carry out the divine plan, and gives the order that Jesus shall testify and swear by the living God whether he be the Christ, the Son of God. And now Jesus speaks, and testifies and swears that he is the Son of God. He knows what they intend the question to mean, namely, whether he be true God, one with the Father, and that it is their purpose to construe an affirmative answer as being blasphemy; and in this sense he makes reply. Note this: Jesus declares before the magistrates of his people, and calls upon God to witness his declaration, that he is the Christ, the only begotten of the Father, and equal God with him. If he be a true teacher, he can not lie, least of all at such a time as this; and we therefore know of a final certainty that he is the Son of God. It is for this very declaration that he is condemned to die; he seals it with his blood. So sure a foundation does the church have for its creed, "I believe in Jesus Christ, God's only Son, our true God, begotten of the Father from eternity;" and so hollow is the foundation on which *they* stand, who regard Christ as being merely a wise and good man. The whole council hears distinctly what the Lord says. He repeats it, that all the world may hear it; and he is condemned because he is the Son of God and the Son of Man. "He is guilty of death." This is the verdict of the jury of God on earth; for it is so ordained in heaven. The only begotten Son of God, in his holy human nature, is made to be sin, in order that the blood of *God* may wash away the sin of all the world.

Be of good cheer, ye Christians; no infidel, who denies Christ; no, not any number of infidels shall be able to overthrow the testimony of the Lord himself which resounds through the creed of the church in support of the truth that he is God from everlasting. The Son of Man sits on the right hand of power, and reigns in the midst of his enemies.

We praise thee, Lord Jesus, and see thy glory, and await the time when we shall see thee come again in the clouds with thy mighty angels, that all the world may see that thou art God. Hold us fast to thee; and give us courage to confess thee in the face of scorn and derision on the part of the worldly wise, and gladly to suffer for thy name's sake. Amen.

Soldiers of Christ, arise, And put your armor on; Strong in the strength which God supplies, Through his eternal Son;
Strong in the Lord of Hosts, And in his mighty power; Who in the strength of Jesus trusts Is more than conqueror.

---

138. Friday after Second Sunday in Lent.

Lord Jesus, give us earnestness and vigilance. Amen.

Matthew 27, 3-10. Then Judas, which had betrayed him, when he saw that he was condemned, repented himself, and brought again the thirty pieces of silver to the chief priests and elders, saying, I have sinned, in that I have betrayed the innocent blood. And they said, What is that to us? see thou to that. And he cast down the pieces of silver in the temple, and departed, and went and hanged himself. And the chief priests took the silver pieces, and said, It is not lawful for to put them into the treasury, because it is the price of blood. And they took counsel, and bought with them the potter's field, to bury strangers in. Wherefore that field was called, The field of blood, unto this day. Then was fulfilled that which was spoken by Jeremy the prophet, saying, And they took the thirty pieces of silver, the price of him that was valued, whom they of the children of Israel did value; and he gave them for the potter's field, as the Lord appointed me.

Judas had, surely, been in a fair way to become a chosen instrument for the Lord, and to shine in eternal glory among the hosts of the blest. He had been joined with the other disciples in preaching, healing, driving out devils, and glorifying the name of the Lord. But now we find him in the darkness of despair. Shortly afterwards he has a noose about his own neck, and goes to his own place as a son of perdition. This is most horrible. May it rouse us and fill our soul with earnestness. It was with this purpose in view that the Spirit of God caused the account to be written.

Every disciple of Jesus has his infirmities, his weak side; and this is especially true of the most highly gifted among them. The devil knows this, and lies in wait at the door; but God gives man the opportunity to obtain victory over himself, and to put the devil to shame. The great weakness of Judas, as of so many others, was covetousness. The Lord had entrusted to him the purse, the management of the common treasury; in the first place, because Judas had a special talent in that line, and was not of the kind who neither will nor can keep within their means; and in the next place, because all the disciples must be put to the proof, in order that they may be educated to gain the mastery over sin. Now if your special weakness, dear reader, is peevishness, for instance, or a domineering disposition, or vanity, or covetousness, God shapes your life in such a way that you have occasion to make use of the assistance of his grace against that particular temptation; and he gives you the necessary strength, that you may put off the old man day by day. Either he leads you among wicked men who stir up that which is evil in you, or among good men who make you to be ashamed. He gives you power and honor, and allows Satan to tempt you through these things, as in the case of Saul and David and Solomon; and the Spirit of God to humble you, as in the case of Jacob and David and Mary; or he sends you poverty and trouble, teaching you self-denial, humility, and trust in God alone, and giving you a distaste for the world, but longing after heaven. It shall not fail that the Holy Spirit will lead you wherever you go; that he will admonish, correct, comfort, and raise you up, thus enabling you to put on the new man, which is created after God. But do not grieve the Spirit, and do not forget that a little offence may easily bring on a greater, and then one yet greater. If you humor your evil desire, it gains strength; give the devil an inch, and he takes an ell. Bear in mind that with the growth of sin conscience is blunted, blindness increases, and the fear of God passes away. This was the case with Judas. He now hated the Lord and wished to be rid of him; at the same time he hoped to cheat the council out of the thirty pieces of silver. With devilish cunning he says: "Seize him and hold him fast." However, the devil himself is more cunning still, and Judas falls into the pit himself had opened. Alas, many have started on the way to heaven, and have then again followed their sinful lusts, and have gone down to perdition. — Nevertheless, you must know that there is no necessity which compels any man to follow in the footsteps of Judas. The Lord can and will keep us.

Faithful God, we heartily beseech thee to grant us this grace. Save us from the way of perdition, for Jesus' sake. Amen.

O God of Bethel, by whose hand Thy people still are fed; Who through this weary pilgrimage Hast all our fathers led:
Our vows, our prayers, we now present Before thy throne of grace: God of our fathers, be the God Of their succeeding race.

---

139. Saturday after Second Sunday in Lent.

From the rising of the sun to the going down thereof let the name of the Lord be blessed.

John 18, 28–32. Then led they Jesus from Caiaphas unto the hall of judgment: and it was early; and they themselves went not into the judgment hall, lest they should be defiled; but that they might eat the passover. Pilate then went out unto them, and said, What accusation bring ye against this man? They answered and said unto him, If he were not a malefactor, we would not have delivered him up unto thee. Then said Pilate unto them, Take ye him, and judge him according to your law. The Jews therefore said unto him, It is not lawful for us to put any man to death: that the saying of Jesus might be fulfilled, which he spake, signifying what death he should die.

Jesus was not to die for the Jews only, but for us also; therefore he is brought to trial and condemned not only by the council of the Jews, but also by the gentile court of justice. And he was not to be put to death by the mode of execution practiced by the Jews, namely that of stoning to death; but he was to be crucified, as himself had said, and as was indicated by the brazen serpent in the wilderness; not a bone of the Lamb of the passover was to be broken. Thus we behold the righteous judge of the quick and the dead, the King of Zion, about to receive his sentence from the unrighteous Roman governor, Pontius Pilate, whose actions were dictated by fear of man and by cowardice. Jesus has watched through the whole night before Good Friday, partly in Gethsemane, partly in the palaces of Annas and

178

Caiaphas during the trials, partly among the ribald servants who derided and maltreated him. Now, early in the morning, he has allowed himself to be led bound to Pilate, and the lords of the council have followed him for the purpose of asking the governor to confirm their sentence of death on him. They represent to Pilate that he may set his mind at rest; for they, who constitute the high council of the righteous Israel, are not in the habit of rendering unjust verdicts. "If he were not a malefactor, we would not have delivered him up unto thee." In their eyes Jesus is one of the scum, a monster of depravity, a leper, a wretch, whom it is a duty to cast out and throw into the fire, in order that he may not defile the entire holy people of Israel. God the Father suffers them to deal in this way with his only Son, who is the glory of all the heavens, and whom the princes of the angelic host worship with eternal reverence. This is the position of the Son of God on earth; but even under these circumstances the wings of his mercy are extended over his accusers and protect them from the tunderbolts of God's wrath. "If he were not a malefactor, we would not have delivered him up unto thee." "Let the question be put to all those whom he has delivered from unclean spirits, to all the palsied whom he has healed, all the lepers whom he has cleansed, all the deaf to whom he has given hearing, all the dumb to whom he has restored speech, all the blind whose eyes he has opened, all the dead whom he has raised again, and — what is still more — to all the fools whom he has made wise unto salvation; and let them answer and say whether or not Jesus is a malefactor." — But who, then, may the malefactors be? Where are they to be found? You have in mind Caiaphas and Pilate; but there are others, and they are nearer to us. You know who they are, I think.

Here you may see yourself as in a glass. In very truth Jesus stands in your place. He is brought forward clothed in your foul rags; it is the sentence on you which is pronounced on him. Nevertheless, even in his degradation you shall see ever more and more of the ineffable and immeasurable love of God to man, and you shall learn how great a salvation awaits all who believe in him.

Lord Jesus, we thank thee and will thank thee for evermore for thy deep abasement and thy unutterable suffering in our stead. Give us the light of thy Holy Spirit, that we more and more may be able to comprehend with all saints what is the breadth, and length, and depth, and the height; and to know the love of Christ, which passeth knowledge. Amen.

Though num'rous hosts of mighty foes, Though earth and hell my way oppose, He safely leads my soul along, His lovingkindness, oh, how strong!
When trouble, like a gloomy cloud, Has gathered thick and thundered loud, He near my soul has always stood, His lovingkindness, oh, how good!

140. Third Sunday in Lent. I.

Lord Jesus, overthrow the power of the devil, and destroy his kingdom. Amen.

Gospel Lesson, Luke 11, 14–28. And he was casting out a devil, and it was dumb. And it came to pass, when the devil was gone out, the dumb spake; and the people wondered. But some of them said, He casteth out devils through Beelzebub the chief of the devils. And others tempting him, sought of him a sign from heaven. But he, knowing their thoughts, said unto them, Every kingdom divided against itself is brought to desolation; and a house divided against a house falleth. If Satan also be divided against himself, how shall his kingdom stand? because ye say that I cast out devils through Beelzebub. And if I by Beelzebub cast out devils, by whom do your sons cast them out? therefore shall they be your judges. But if I with the finger of God cast out devils, no doubt the kingdom of God is come upon you. When a strong man armed keepeth his palace, his goods are in peace: but when a stronger than he shall come upon him, and overcome him, he taketh from him all his armor wherein he trusted, and divideth his spoils. He that is not with me is against me: and he that gathereth not with me scattereth. When the unclean spirit is gone out of a man, he walketh through dry places, seeking rest; and finding none, he saith, I will return unto my house, whence I came out. And when he cometh, he findeth it swept and garnished. Then goeth he and taketh to him seven other spirits more wicked than himself; and they enter in, and dwell there: and the last state of that man is worse than the first. And it came to pass, as he spake these things, a certain woman of the company lifted up her voice, and said unto him, Blessed is the womb that bare thee, and the paps which thou hast sucked. But he said, Yea, rather blessed are they that hear the word of God, and keep it.

Jesus distinctly teaches that the devil has a kingdom, in which are all unbelieving men and all wicked angels. The devil reigns over them, and uses them in his service to make war on Christ and his people. Those things enumerated by Paul in the epistle lesson for today, such as fornication, uncleanness, covetousness, filthiness, foolish talking, and the like, bear witness to the fact that there is a devil; the men who do these things are the servants of the devil. They will not come to Christ, that they may be delivered from the works and ways of the devil; and so they remain the slaves of the wicked one. But as a rule, they are far from being aware of their condition. Did the Pharisees suppose that they were the devil's helpers, do you think? Against their own better knowledge they accused Christ of casting out devils through Beelzebub; and yet they did not doubt that they themselves were the righteous children of Abraham. It is one of the devil's most artful pieces of cunning to hoodwink men and make them blind. Herein he has his greatest strength; and he employs these crafty tactics everywhere. In our times he has induced many to believe that he does not even exist. They are slaves in the most unhappy service of sin; they live in pride, selfishness, and all manner of wickedness; they carry the mark of the devil on their foreheads; and yet they laugh at you who believe that there is a devil.

What better method could he adopt for holding his people fast, and for promoting his designs?

None save *Jesus* is able to deliver us out of the devil's kingdom. He is the stronger who comes upon the strong; and his weapon is *the word of God.* This lays bare the lies of Satan, reveals his wicked purpose, shows his abominable filthiness and infernal tyranny, and teaches us to know how unhappy is the condition of man in the devil's service. By his word the Lord cast the devil out of them that were possessed bodily; and by his word he casts him out of the hearts of men. When his word, which is spirit and life, abides in you, the spirit of lies and of death can find no room in you. When the word which the mouth of the Lord has spoken governs your heart and your tongue, then you serve Christ and renounce the devil. But this is the word of the Lord, that God loves you, a lost and condemned sinner; that Christ died for you, and made the devil powerless; that you are baptized into his victory and his righteousness, and belong to him; and that the devil, therefore, has no authority over you. Blessed are you, if you hear and keep this word. *Then you in very truth have* that which the word says; and the word shall keep you from again falling into the power of the enemy.

How earnestly should we not have at heart to serve the Lord when we hear from his own lips: "He that is not with me is *against* me; and he that gathereth not with me scattereth." There is a most intimate connection between these and the harrowing words which follow close after, concerning the return of the unclean spirit to hearts whence he had been cast out. Let each ask himself: Am I with Christ? Do I gather with him? If not, I am with the devil; in which case I do damage to the cause of Christ, and destroy my own soul and other souls, which Christ bought with his blood. Do not rest before you have the testimony of the Spirit, that Jesus has set you free from the power of the devil.

Lord God, teach us to know to whom we belong, and whom we serve. Be gracious unto us, and let us serve thee. Be merciful, and never permit the devil to hold sway in us. God, preserve all who are thine from the wiles of the wicked enemy. Amen.

Jesus, Lord of life and glory, Bend from heaven thy gracious ear, While our waiting souls adore thee, Friend of helpless sinners, hear! By thy mercy, O deliver us, good Lord!

From the depth of nature's blindness, From the hardening power of sin, From all malice and unkindness, From the pride that lurks within, By thy mercy, O deliver us, good Lord!

141. Third Sunday in Lent. II.

Create in me a clean heart, O God; and renew a right spirit within me.

Epistle Lesson, Ephesians 5, 1–9. Be ye therefore followers of God, as dear children; and walk in love, as Christ also hath loved us, and hath given himself for us, an offering and a sacrifice to God for a sweet smelling savor. But fornication, and all uncleanness, or covetousness, let it not be once named among you, as becoming saints; neither filthiness, nor foolish talking, nor jesting, which are not convenient; but rather giving of thanks. For this we know, that no whoremonger, nor unclean person, nor covetous man, who is an idolater, hath any inheritance in the kingdom of Christ and of God. Let no man deceive you with vain words: for because of these things cometh the wrath of God upon the children of disobedience. Be not ye therefore partakers with them. For ye were sometimes darkness, but now are ye light in the Lord: walk as children of light; (for the fruit of the Spirit is in all goodness and righteousness and truth).

The ungodly find their pleasure in sensuality, carnal lusts, and all manner of uncleanness. No matter how fine an appearance they make, their heart is a foul pit out of which issue filthiness and foolish talking and unseemly jesting. With their foul tongue they pollute their own body and fill the mind of others with their venom. It is incredible what atrocious language is indulged in everywhere, on the highway, in the field, across the table. And it is also incredible what a deal of poison there may be in seemingly pretty words which come out of a corrupt heart. — You, however, who believe in Christ, have received a new heart, and this shall be manifest in your whole life and conversation. Hear the admonition of the holy apostle, and walk in the footsteps of Christ! Follow after holiness; do not tolerate wicked, unclean desires in your soul. You are the dwellingplace of God, the workshop of the Holy Ghost; and he shall sanctify you in spirit and soul and body. Look at Jesus; you should be like him, and to this end he will give you his Spirit and grace. A pure heart is a delight to God and his angels, and as a fragrant field to all the saints. The speech then becomes clean and edifying; and it gives grace to them that hear it. Out of the unclean heart proceed evil thoughts and wicked words; but from the pure heart gush forth holy words which put the devil to flight. *Strive* after this with all possible diligence! Consider how dangerous it is to neglect your sanctification and to allow your tongue unbridled license. If the unclean spirit is gone out, he lies in wait for the purpose of coming in again. If you do not watch, and do not cleanse yourself every day in the blood of Jesus, the devil will accomplish his purpose; and then your last state will be worse than the first. Let it be the burning desire of your heart that you may be sanctified; never allow your zeal in this cause to become cool. Do not at any time let the devil seduce you to make use of foul language, or to indulge in levity of behavior. Watch, watch! for Jesus' sake, be on your guard; especially at the time when you are happy and seem to be on the best of terms with God and your brethren in the faith, or when good fortune and the riches of this world become yours. Put no trust in yourself; do not imagine that the enemy is far away; do not forget that you carry your flesh and blood about with you all the time; pray God day and night to give you a pure, sanctified mind.

Hold us fast to thee, and draw us after thee, Lord Jesus. Give us grace to walk in love, as dear children, of a sanctified heart. Keep us from all uncleanness in thought and word, in life and deed.

Help us to live as Christians should, and to let all the world see that there is a holy people on earth. Lord Jesus, have mercy on us; for we are called by thy name. Amen.

Jesus, still lead on, Till our rest be won! And although the way be cheerless, We will follow, calm and fearless; Guide us by thy hand To our fatherland.

If the way be drear, If the foe be near, Let not doubt and fears o'ertake us; Let not faith and hope forsake us; For through many a foe To our home we go.

142. Monday after Third Sunday in Lent.

Lord Jesus, grant that we may hear thy voice. Amen.

John 18, 33—38. Then Pilate entered into the judgment hall again, and called Jesus, and said unto him, Art thou the King of the Jews? Jesus answered him, Sayest thou this thing of thyself, or did others tell it thee of me? Pilate answered, Am I a Jew? Thine own nation and the chief priests have delivered thee unto me: what hast thou done? Jesus answered, My kingdom is not of this world: if my kingdom were of this world, then would my servants fight, that I should not be delivered to the Jews: but now is my kingdom not from hence. Pilate therefore said unto him, Art thou a king then? Jesus answered, Thou sayest that I am a king. To this end was I born, and for this cause came I into the world, that I should bear witness unto the truth. Every one that is of the truth heareth my voice. Pilate saith unto him, What is truth? and when he had said this, he went out again unto the Jews, and saith unto them, I find in him no fault at all.

Jesus is not the king of the Jews in the sense in which Pilate puts the question to him. Had he made use of his omnipotence in order to wield the sceptre of an earthly king, he would not now have been standing before the governor, accused and derided by the chief rulers of his people. The Jews would, in that case, have done homage to him; for then he would have been such a Messiah as they desired. — We, also, have much of this same spirit. It is easy enough to complain of the blending together of the church and the temporal power as being a church-state or a state-church; but it is more difficult to renounce one's own appetite for rule, and to *live* in the truth that the kingdom of Christ is not of this world. We wish to begin reigning with Christ here on earth. To be trodden under foot; to be despised and slandered, and endure it in silence; to walk with him the way that leads through suffering and death; this we find difficult; difficult to understand, and difficult to practice. Our king shall help us.

As he confessed before the council that he is the Son of God, so he confesses before Pilate that he is *king*. He knows very well what will be the result of this declaration; that he will be mocked with dreadful blasphemy, that he will be outraged, and crowned with thorns; but he goes straight onward against all the daggers of death, and steps not aside by the breadth of a hair from his kingly course. He also knows that the heart of Pilate is as a lump of fat; yet with tireless patience he continues to pour the water of his grace upon it, to exercise his royal right to extend mercy, and to preach his truth unto salvation. At the very time when he is being condemned and suffers death for the whole world, he labors with the individual unhappy soul which is before him. — Pilate asks of him what he has done. Yes; what is the kingly office of Jesus? If Pilate had been *in earnest* when he inquired after the truth, he would himself have been made able to give the answer which you and I have learned from blessed experience: Jesus has vanquished the devil and destroyed death; he has founded a kingdom of salvation, in which he gives to the souls righteousness, peace and joy through his Holy Spirit; he has brought me out of the darkness, regenerated me, given me power to trample sin under foot, given me an heritage in heaven; he comforts and heals me every day, and gives me patience, and sustains me, and never for a moment loses me out of his keeping. Pilate might have answered further: Christ defends his church, leads his people, guides them through the wilderness; and soon he shall give them for their tribulations everlasting glory. His kingdom endures for ever, and his throne does not totter; it is built on the eternal rock of truth. "Every one that is of the truth heareth his voice." It was merely a piece of impertinent pretense on the part of Pilate when he asked: "What is truth?" and therefore he remained a stranger to the kingly office of Christ. Hear it ye, then, who thirst after light and salvation; let it be heard round about in all the earth: Here is truth and victory and eternal life, here and in none other place; nowhere out of the kingdom of Christ is anything but darkness and death. Whom will ye follow and obey, Jesus or Pilate? What shall rule over you, truth or falsehood? Do not wait; make your choice now. For the sake of your soul's salvation, take up the cross, and give your heart to Jesus.

Precious Savior, speak thy word of truth to us, and draw our hearts to thee in true repentance and living faith. Thine will we be; and thee will we serve. Give us this salvation, and accept our poor thanks for thy ineffable grace. Amen.

Jesus, thy boundless love to me No thought can reach, no tongue declare; Unite my thankful heart to thee, And reign without a rival there. Thine wholly, thine alone I am; Be thou alone my constant flame.

---

143. Tuesday after Third Sunday in Lent.

Lord, let me not enter into the path of the wicked. Amen.

Luke 23, 4-12. Then said Pilate to the chief priests and to the people, I find no fault in this man. And they were the more fierce, saying, He stirreth up the people, teaching, throughout all Jewry, beginning from Galilee to this place. When Pilate heard of Galilee, he asked whether the man were a Galilæan. And as soon as he knew that he belonged unto Herod's jurisdiction, he sent him to Herod, who himself also was at Jerusalem at that time. And when Herod saw Jesus, he was exceeding glad: for he was desirous to see

184

him of a long season, because he had heard many things of him; and he hoped to have seen some miracles done by him. Then he questioned with him in many words; but he answered him nothing. And the chief priests and scribes stood and vehemently accused him. And Herod with his men of war set him at nought, and mocked him, and arrayed him in a gorgeous robe, and sent him again to Pilate. And the same day Pilate and Herod were made friends together: for before they were at enmity between themselves.

Pilate had, no doubt, been greatly impressed by the purity and majesty of Jesus, and quaked at the thought of passing sentence on him. He had the greatest reluctance to having any hand in the matter. But the decisive moment is come, and Jesus must be the means of either bringing him down or raising him up. — Jesus has met you and me also. What is he to become to us? None can evade him. Every one must either be offended in him, and deny him; or believe in him, and serve him. "To Pilate there was a certain attraction in the majesty of Jesus, and in his words of truth; but Pilate loved his own advantage and his honor among men so well that, in the face of his better knowledge and conscience, and directly contrary to the admonitions of Christ and his Spirit, he pronounced the sentence of death on the Son of Man. It is a triumph for the innocence of Jesus that Pilate is hard put to it before he is able to prevail upon himself to condemn him. — When I speak of this there is in me a feeling of distress and sadness to think that this man, for whose soul the Lord labored so earnestly, under the crowns of thorns and the purple robe, while being scourged and mocked; — that this man did not allow himself to be vanquished, and that he did not, to the glory of God's everlasting grace, become the second murderer to be saved by the Lord at the time of the crucifixion. For even if Pilate had acted as a just judge, the rage of hell and the eternal decree of the Father would still have brought Jesus to his death." (Loehe). The Lord places a thousand obstacles in the way of men who are determined to go to hell; but Pilate, and many others, alas, with him, fight their way through the difficulties, and imagine that it is wise to sell their conscience and their soul's eternal happiness for fleeting pleasure and empty honor.

The pleasure-hunting Herod Antipas tries to jest with the Lord, and wants him to perform some trickery for his amusement. This also the Lord tolerates, and holds his peace; and thereby he atones for the world's wantonness, but gives his Christians grace to renounce carnal pleasures, and teaches us in what light we are to view the vanities of the world. Those who wish to be called Christians, and who yet take part in the world's unseemly amusements, should look at Jesus as he stands before Herod and his courtiers.

Thou holy Savior, we heartily thank thee for thy walk between Herod and Pilate, and for thy meekness and patience in suffering all these things. We wonder, we fear, and we worship before thy throne, thou glorious Son of God. Have mercy on us, and help us to believe in thee, to renounce the pleasures of the world, and to rejoice in thy salvation. Amen.

God of grace, whose word is sure, Thou who keepest truth forever,
That my trust may rest secure On this ground that wavers never: Let thy
truth be dear to me, That my soul may faithful be.
To the banner of the cross I fidelity have plighted; It will be my endless
loss If this solemn vow be slighted; Therefore Jesus, none but he, Shall my
constant watchword be.

---

144. Wednesday after Third Sunday in Lent.

Mercy and righteousness kiss each other.

Luke 23, 17-24. (For of necessity he must release one unto them at the
feast.) And they cried out all at once, saying, Away with this man, and release
unto us Barabbas: (who for a certain sedition made in the city, and for murder,
was cast into prison.) Pilate therefore, willing to release Jesus, spake again
to them. But they cried, saying, Crucify him, crucify him. And he said unto
them the third time, Why, what evil hath he done? I have found no cause of
death in him: I will therefore chastise him, and let him go. And they were
instant with loud voices, requiring that he might be crucified. And the voices
of them and of the chief priests prevailed. And Pilate gave sentence that it
should be as they required.

Barabbas, *or* Jesus; one to die, and one to live. Either Barabbas
is to die, and Jesus be released; or Jesus must die, in which case Barabbas is free. The death of one buys life for the other. So Pilate has
decided. But his power as a judge is from above; and the decision
of this unrighteous man agrees with that of the righteous God in the
eternal counsel of his will. Barabbas, *or* Jesus! But Barabbas, the
man guilty of sedition and murder, is Adam and all his generation,
who have rebelled against God and brought death into all the world.
The choice, then, lies between these two: sinful humanity and the
righteous Jesus, God's apostate family, and the only begotten and
well beloved Son of the Father. *Justice* demands the death of the
transgressors; but *mercy* toward us has decided on the other course.
"For God so loved the world, that he gave his only begotten Son, that
whosoever believeth in him should not perish, but have everlasting
life." Barabbas means me. My heart is by nature disobedient and
proud, rebellious and prone to anger; and in the sight of God this is
murder. In all sincerity I must confess that, guided by my evil nature
alone, without the grace of God, I would have fallen into the sin of
David; I am guilty, and deserve to die. However, — O, the ineffable
love of God! — I am now entirely safe from his wrath and from the
terror of death. Even as Barabbas obtained full release by the death
of Jesus, so have I, also, by the same means been ransomed and
absolved from the curse of the law, the guilt of sin, and the power of
death. There is herein so much of assurance and comfort, that I no
longer have the least reason to doubt that I shall be saved from
perdition. My death has been suffered already; and even the *justice*
of God demands my acquittal. It is Barabbas *or* Christ; *not both*.
Nevertheless, we must not for a moment forget that the death of
Jesus in our stead has delivered us from the power of the murderer;

and hence we must not serve sin, thereby crucifying the Son of God anew and turning him into derision. Barabbas must not commit new murders and acts of sedition!

O God, how shall we thank thee for thy scheme of love in regard to us poor lost creatures! Blessed be thy name for evermore! In this world and in the next we will lie at thy feet with holy fear and rejoicing, and will worship, thank, and praise thee. Here and in all eternity we will give ourselves as an offering to thee, with soul and body, and live for thee only. Give us this grace; we must come to thee for all that we need. Grant our prayer, we ask it in the name of Jesus. Amen.

Come to Calvary's holy mountain, Sinners ruined by the fall; Here a pure and healing fountain Flows to you, to me, to all, In a full perpetual tide, Opened when our Savior died.

Come in poverty and meanness, Come, defiled without, within; From infection and uncleanness, From the leprosy of sin, Wash your robes and make them white: Ye shall walk with God in light.

---

145. Thursday after Third Sunday in Lent.

Clothe us, Lord, in thy righteousness and purity. Amen.

Matthew 27, 23-25. And the governor said, Why, what evil hath he done? But they cried out the more, saying, Let him be crucified. When Pilate saw that he could prevail nothing, but that rather a tumult was made, he took water, and washed his hands before the multitude, saying, I am innocent of the blood of this just person: see ye to it. Then answered all the people, and said, His blood be on us, and on our children.

"Let him be crucified." This was the cry in answer to the question of the governor demanding to know what evil Jesus had done. He has done no evil; but "let him be crucified." This was the sole argument; and it became the sentence. Before God, who has made the Sinless One to be sin for us, the judgment was as just, as it was outrageously unjust on the part of the mob and its leaders and on the part of Pilate. It was necessary that he be without sin, in order that he might atone for our sin; and as *one without sin* he was to be condemned to death, that we might believe in him. At the very time of his death his innocence was fairly to dazzle the eyes of angels and devils and men in order that we, who are guilty, may have courage in the midst of death, that the evil spirits may get themselves behind us, and that the angels may serve us. The testimony to his innocence is, therefore, unanimous. Caiaphas and the council can lay nothing to his charge save that he is the Son of God. Pilate declares again and again: "I find no fault in this man." The wife of Pilate calls Jesus a just man; and the mob have no argument against him save the cry: "Crucify him!"

Pilate washes his hands. We, however, will confess: I am guilty of the blood of this just man. Then shall this blood cleanse our heart. It is a terrible thing to see Pilate in the act of washing his hands, while at the same time he confesses that he is shedding innocent blood: but it is more terrible still to hear the people of Israel cry: "His blood be on us, and on our children." Let all unjust judges and false witnesses take warning, and ponder the fate of Pilate and the Jews. Yet the people seemed to have no doubt as to the guilt of Jesus. The deceitfulness of the human heart is something terrible; and popular opinion may be a dreadful thing. Thus the devil deceives us when we seek our glory in that which is of the earth. These persons who now ask that his blood may be on them, are the ones who but five days ago hailed him with loud Hosannas. For such as these the Lord is willing to lay down his life! I know not what cries out most loudly, the injustice of Pilate, or the rage of the priests, or the shouts of the rabble, or the love of Christ. Yes, after all, I do know; and so do you who read this.

Thy righteousness and love, my Jesus, are high as the heavens and deep as the pit, and have power to do away with all our sins. Help us by thy Holy Spirit to know this, to believe it, to give thee thanks, and to live of thy grace. Amen.

Still let thy love point out my way; What wondrous things thy love hath wrought! Direct my word, inspire my thought; And if I fall, soon may I hear Thy voice, and know that love is near.

146. Friday after Third Sunday in Lent.

Lord, let it become clear to us how much thou didst suffer, and for what reason. Amen.

John 19, 1. Then Pilate therefore took Jesus, and scourged him.

Four soldiers bound Jesus to a stake, and scourged his back with whips of leather having barbs of iron fastened to the thongs. "I gave my back to the smiters" (Isaiah 50, 6). "Lashes are for the back of the fool. How comes it, then, that they are laid on thy back, thou eternal Wisdom? The disobedient servant shall be beaten with many stripes. How, then, hast thou, the righteous servant of God, deserved them? Thou art wounded for my transgressions, and bruised for my iniquities; thou wast scourged for me, that I might not be scourged in the wrath to come." — When God disciplines us severely, let us pause and look with care at the scourging of his only begotten Son. Jesus, who has taken upon himself our load of guilt, is the object of God's wrath. The stripes which he receives are dealt him in *wrath;* he is *punished* for sin. The fire of God's righteous anger is in every stroke of the lash and in every wound, and burns into his soul. But as *he* has suffered the punishment, it follows that when his believers are now scourged, it is not by way of *punishment.* It is not the sword of judgment, but the rod of the merciful heavenly Father, that smites you, dear Christian. Yet you are to have this honor, that your suffering is of the kind which Christ suffered; and the discipline which you undergo has this blessing, that it gives you a part in his glory. Our God scourgeth every son whom he receiveth. — In the stripes which Jesus receives at the hands of unrighteous men you may see what you have merited; in this manner you should of right have been lashed by the scorpions of hell for your evil lusts. If you acknowledge this, and understand the significance of the scourging administered to the Lord, the holy Lamb of God will heal the wounds which Satan may have given your conscience, give you strength to suffer patiently when the world does you injustice, deliver you from the power of the sinful lusts which still stir in your flesh, and clothe you in his holiness. When by faith we are united with Christ his pure life is ours, and his holy suffering is ours; not only to forgive our sins but also to make our hearts pure, and our lives holy. Our lusts are *punished* in Christ, and *mortified* in him; and thus we are now able to present our bodies as instruments of righteousness. — Never forget the scourging of Christ, ye his disciples!

Lord Jesus, we heartily beseech thee, clothe us in the strength of thy victory, and take us into the fellowship of thy suffering. Give us thy holiness and thy patience in our life full of affliction and distress, when we are to be scourged by Satan and the world; and grant us at last to become partakers of thy glory. Amen.

In suffering, be thy love my peace; In weakness, be thy love my power; And when the storms of life shall cease, Jesus, in that dark final hour Of death, be thou my guide and friend, That I may love thee without end.

---

147. Saturday after Third Sunday in Lent.

"I hid not my face from shame and spitting."

Matthew 27, 27-30. Then the soldiers of the governor took Jesus into the common hall, and gathered unto him the whole band of soldiers. And they stripped him, and put on him a scarlet robe. And when they had platted a crown of thorns, they put it upon his head, and a reed in his right hand: and they bowed the knee before him, and mocked him, saying, Hail, King of the Jews! And they spit upon him, and took the reed, and smote him on the head.

The whole band gathered around Jesus; the Holy One is in the midst of the ungodly, the Lamb among wolves, in order that I may for ever have communion with all the saints. His body is stripped naked, that he may give me the garment of righteousness, and adorn me with heavenly beauty. He allows himself to be decked out as a king, thus giving the rabble something at which to jeer, and causing him sharp pain; they put on him a scarlet robe, which adheres to his wounds and is soaked with his blood; and they crown him with thorns, the curse of the earth, which sink into his flesh, — this is his royal crown! — and they put a reed into his hand as a sceptre; and then he is in derision hailed as the king of the Jews. My God, why is this necessary? He suffers this because I, who should have had dominion over all creatures, had become the slave of my own lusts, and had turned God's blessing on the earth into a curse. This he suffers in order to save me from the dominion of the devil, and give to me the crown of life. — They spat on him, they spat the Son of God in the face; and this the Father saw and tolerated! They took the reed, his royal sceptre, and beat him on the head with it; and yet God did not strike them dead. He, whose is the kingdom, and the power for ever, allows himself to be thus abased, and ill-used, and mocked, in order that he may hold his royal sceptre in grace and mercy over us wretched sinners and give us eternal salvation. Blessed be the Lord Jesus; the shame has been taken away, and the glory remains to us!

If you, dear friend, who by the grace of Jesus have a heart filled with yearning after communion with God's people, must yet a little while dwell among the wicked, remember the Lord as he was in the common hall, endure evil without being angered, and rejoice in the thought that soon you shall be at home, in the house of the Father, in the company of none but saints. When the world seeks to strip you naked and expose to view your infirmities, then think of Jesus in the common hall of judgment; wrap yourself in his righteousness, and adorn your life with his heavenly virtues. And when the thorns of care threaten to prick you, or when it is your lot to suffer poverty, loss, or want, for the sake of your faith; or when you are beaten, or spat on, or you name is dragged in the mire; then remember Jesus in the hall of judgment, and esteem it an honor of which you are not worthy, to be like him. You deserve nothing but punishment; and yet you shall, for the sake of the crown of thorns which Christ wore, receive full reward for your labor, and receive the crown of glory that fadeth not away.

Lord Jesus, we thank thee; we thank and praise thee for all things! Praise be to thee for thy humiliation and suffering! Praise be to thee for thy glory and salvation! Help us to believe in thee, and to praise thee for evermore. Amen.

Father of heaven, whose love profound A ransom for our souls has found, Before thy throne we sinners bend; To us thy pardoning love extend. Almighty Son! Incarnate Word! Our prophet, priest, redeemer, Lord! Before thy throne we sinners bend; To us thy saving grace extend.

---

148. Fourth Sunday in Lent. I.

Lord, give us this bread of life. Amen.

Gospel Lesson, John 6, 1–15. After these things Jesus went over the sea of Galilee, which is the sea of Tiberias. And a great multitude followed him, because they saw his miracles which he did on them that were diseased. And Jesus went up into a mountain, and there he sat with his disciples. And the passover, a feast of the Jews, was nigh. When Jesus then lifted up his eyes, and saw a great company come unto him, he saith unto Philip, Whence shall we buy bread, that these may eat? And this he said to prove him: for he knew himself what he would do. Philip answered him, Two hundred pennyworth of bread is not sufficient for them, that every one of them may take a little. One of his disciples, Andrew, Simon Peter's brother, saith unto him, There is a lad here, which hath five barley loaves, and two small fishes: but what are they among so many? And Jesus said, Make the men sit down. Now there was much grass in the

place. So the men sat down, in number about five thousand. And Jesus took
the loaves; and when he had given thanks, he distributed to the disciples, and
the disciples to them that were set down; and likewise of the fishes as much as
they would. When they were filled, he said unto his disciples, Gather up
the fragments that remain, that nothing be lost. Therefore they gathered them
together, and filled twelve baskets with the fragments of the five barley loaves,
which remained over and above unto them that had eaten. Then those men,
when they had seen the miracle that Jesus did, said, This is of a truth that
prophet that should come into the world. When Jesus therefore perceived that
they would come and take him by force, to make him a king, he departed again
into a mountain himself alone.

The spiritual life requires nourishment, as much as does the life
of the body, for its sustenance and growth. If you have the life in
God, you *must* nourish it with the bread of life, or it will wither and
die. In the case of many Christians the spiritual life droops and
languishes; their eyes are dull, their hands palsied, and their knees
weak. The reason of this is that they do not nourish themselves
sufficiently with the bread from heaven. — What bread is this? *Jesus*
says: *"I am the bread of life."* With his love, grace, Spirit, and life,
he is to be found in his holy gospel; when you make honest use of
this gospel you partake of him. — In what manner is this brought
about? You must be diligent in your calling as a Christian, zealous
in every good work, serve the Lord of a pure heart, become rich in
loving service for others, make the most of your talents, — then you
will feel that there is in you much sin, much weakness, selfishness,
self-righteousness, pride, sloth, cowardice, unbelief, and lukewarmness.
Then you want Jesus more and more; for you need strength and
spirit and courage and understanding, and you need forgiveness of
sins, forgiveness for all that you do, and for all that you omit to do;
and thus is created in you hunger after the bread of life. — Make
diligent use, then, of the word, by yourself alone, and together with
others; renew your baptismal covenant every day, and partake often
of the Lord's Supper. Rise early to gather manna, and you shall find;
the wilderness and the desert places shall blossom, and the rock give
forth water in abundance; you shall eat and live; you shall of a certainty grow in the strength of the Lord. The faith, charity, patience,
hope, peace, joy, in your heart shall increase; Christ shall become
strong in you, while sin and the flesh shall die and be destroyed.

Do you today hunger after the bread of life? Does your heart
pray for life and a willing spirit, for faith and love, for peace and
forgiveness? That which the Lord's servants have to offer you seems,
on the surface, to be of little account, but in truth it contains life and
strength. Eat and drink without price; you are heartily welcome to
it. You shall receive all that you need; and there shall be more than
a sufficiency for all. — On the other hand, if you do not hunger after
him who is that bread of life, you are, without any doubt, spiritually
dead. God help you to wake up before it shall be too late.

Lord Jesus, quicken the dead, and strengthen the quick. Be
thou our life; and, above all things, let us live in thee. Amen.

Thou our only hope and guide, Never leave us, nor forsake; In thy light may we abide Till the endless morning break; Moving on to Zion's hill, Onward, upward, homeward still.

Lead us all our days and years In thy straight and narrow way; Lead us through the vale of tears To the land of perfect day, Where thy people, fully blest, Near thy throne forever rest.

---

149. Fourth Sunday in Lent. II.

"Where the Spirit of the Lord is, there is liberty." God grant that it *may be ours. Amen.*

Epistle Lesson, Galatians 4, 21–31. Tell me, ye that desire to be under the law, do ye not hear the law? For it is written, that Abraham had two sons; the one by a bondmaid, the other by a freewoman. But he who was of the bondwoman was born after the flesh; but he of the freewoman was by promise. Which things are an allegory: for these are the two covenants; the one from the mount Sinai, which gendereth to bondage, which is Agar. For this Agar is mount Sinai in Arabia, and answereth to Jerusalem which now is, and is in bondage with her children. But Jerusalem which is above is free, which is the mother of us all. For it is written, Rejoice, thou barren that bearest not; break forth and cry, thou that travailest not; for the desolate hath many more children than she which hath an husband. Now we, brethren, as Isaac was, are the children of promise. But as then he that was born after the flesh, persecuted him that was born after the Spirit, even so it is now. Nevertheless what saith the scripture? Cast out the bondwoman and her son: for the son of the bondwoman shall not be heir with the son of the freewoman. So then, brethren, we are not children of the bondwoman, but of the free.

The self-righteous are bondmen in the Lord's house; they labor for hire, and they are in fear of punishment. They are born of the flesh, and they look to the law. The believers, on the other hand, are children of the household, born of God, children of grace, born by a miracle of God; their life has its origin in a miracle wrought by the Holy Ghost, directly contrary to nature and reason. They look to the grace and truth in Christ, and expect an inheritance, not of works, but of grace. Paul finds these two classes of people represented in Agar with her son Ishmael on the one hand, and Sara, the mother of Isaac, on the other. Agar was a bondwoman, and was not of Abraham's kindred. Sara was a free woman, and the rightful wife of Abraham. Agar gave birth in accordance with the natural order of things; Sara, by a miracle in accordance with God's promise. Agar and Ishmael mocked Sara and Isaac, but were at last obliged to submit to being cast out; Sara was the mistress, and Isaac the heir. — As it was then, so it is now. We who read this, are we of the lineage of Sara, or are we, mayhap, the children of Agar? We all belong to the church organization; but have we also been born in the Jerusalem which comes down from heaven? Are we God's children, or are we, perhaps, bondmen of the household? Are we under the law, or under grace? Do we live the life of true liberty and holy love? Do we have the Spirit of the adoption of sons, which cries, Abba, Father? Is our citizenship in heaven? Do we seek those things which are from above; or do we, peradventure, seek those which are of the earth? Mark well what the scripture says: "Cast out the bondwoman; for the son of the bondwoman shall not be heir with the son of the free-woman." Let this be of greater concern to your heart than all things else, that you be a child of the freewoman, born after the Spirit from on high, and heir to everlasting life. It is a terrible thing to be one of those against whom is directed this curse: "Cast him out; for he shall in no wise be heir with the children of the household." O, how important it is to be liberated from the law, and to be in the true and blessed estate of grace!

God of mercy, above all things we pray that thou mayest know us as thy children of grace. Lead us out of bondage, and to the blessed liberty of the true disciples of Jesus. Unite us with him in faith, that through him we may be dead from the law, but may live in him, who is risen from the dead. Amen.

The darkness of my former state, The bondage, all was mine; The light of life, in which I walk, The liberty, is thine.
Thy grace first made me feel my sin, It taught me to believe; Then, in believing, peace I found, And now I live, I live.

•

---

150. Monday after Fourth Sunday in Lent.

Lord, Lord, wake us, and show us thy crown of thorns. Amen.

John 19, 4–7. Pilate therefore went forth again, and saith unto them, Behold, I bring him forth to you, that ye may know that I find no fault in him. Then came Jesus forth, wearing the crown of thorns, and the purple robe. And Pilate saith unto them, Behold the man! When the chief priests therefore and officers saw him, they cried out, saying, Crucify him, crucify him. Pilate saith unto them, Take ye him, and crucify him: for I find no fault in him. The Jews answered him, We have a law, and by our law he ought to die, because he made himself the Son of God.

"Behold the man!" Thus speaks Pilate, and presents *the Son of God* as the most wretched, abject, and miserable of men, in order that they may be compelled either to despise him or to take compassion on him. "And he himself, the Holy One whom I worship, whose feet I would embrace and kiss at this moment; I, a miserable sinner, worthy of being accursed; — he stands before us covered with blood, with tear-stained face, weighed down by ignominy, a mockery to all men, a spectacle before which the angels hide their face; a king more abased than would seem possible; and yet there is none to have compassion on him." (Loehe). "Behold the man!" Look at him, all who bear the shape of man; and see what man is become. This is the condition to which Adam and his children have come down. They were to have had dominion over the world, and to have enjoyed every blessing; but they have placed the accursed thorns about their own head. They were created unto glory; but they have lost their honor before God, and have been swallowed up in disgrace. They should have been

kindly affectioned to one another, and should have been the express image of love; but what their hearts now are you may see in the crown of prickly thorns, and the condition of their souls you may see in the face on which they spat, and in the bloody body which they had scourged. Fallen man is, therefore, the slave of Satan; and unless he has been born again he must be cast into everlasting fire. Then all devils shall mock him, saying: Behold man, who was created in the image of God to be the king of creation and the judge of every spirit! What is become of his heavenly crown? Then man shall feel the curse of God as thorns in all his members, and be covered with unending shame.

All this misery, however, Jesus has taken upon himself, that we may be saved from it by faith in him. Behold *the man*, as he receives the deserved punishment in full and with no abatement; with not a drop of sympathy to sweeten the bitterness of the cup. Behold it, heaven and earth and hell, and say whether or not man has atoned, in perfect willingness and in perfect and uncomplaining patience, for the crime of attempting to grasp the kingly crown of God himself. And look at him, ye timid sinners, when you are in terror by reason of the persistent stubbornness of your hearts; look to him, and man yourselves to meet your accuser without fear; behold him, and receive grace to be humble of your innermost heart!

Give us to this end thy Holy Spirit, Lord Jesus; and reign over us from thy throne of glory. Here is my sinful, needy, wicked heart; take it, and reign in it, and exercise dominion over all that I am and all that I have. O, that I might be obedient to thee, and that I might rejoice in walking the way of suffering after thee! Dear Lord Jesus, grant me this grace, I pray thee with all my heart. Amen.

I will leave my Jesus never! On the cross for me he died; Love shall draw me to him ever, At his feet I will abide. Of my life the light forever, I will leave my Jesus never!
In his name I stand acquitted While upon the earth I stay: What I have to him committed He will keep until that day. Be his service my endeavor; I will leave my Jesus never.

151. Tuesday after Fourth Sunday in Lent.

Lord, draw us after thee, and let thy righteousness and truth keep us. Amen.

John 19, 12–16. And from thenceforth Pilate sought to release him: but the Jews cried out, saying, If thou let this man go, thou art not Cæsar's friend: whosoever maketh himself a king, speaketh against Cæsar. When Pilate therefore heard that saying, he brought Jesus forth, and sat down in judgment seat, in a place that is called the Pavement, but in the Hebrew, Gabbatha. And it was the preparation of the passover, and about the sixth hour: and he saith unto the Jews, Behold your King! But they cried out, Away with him, away with him, crucify him! Pilate saith unto them, Shall I crucify your King? The chief priests answered, We have no king but Cæsar. Then delivered he him therefore unto them to be crucified. And they took Jesus, and led him away.

At last Pilate sold his soul for the friendship of Cæsar. Up to this time he had been swaying to and fro, sometimes inclined towards the Lord, and then again yielding to the power of hell. Now he pauses, almost in despair, at the fingerpost which points straight down into the bottomless pit. His fear of the charges which may be brought against him by the furious Jews, and of Cæsar's displeasure on account of the numerous crimes which he has committed, and of which Satan now reminds him, conquers every sentiment of justice and truth in his soul. — Pilate is to teach us that he who fears man rather than the Lord has made a most unhappy choice. What did it profit the wretched man to humor the Jews? His conscience, already weighed down by many sins, now gave him ten times more torture; and the favor of Cæsar is of short duration. Pilate was before long brought before the cruel Emperor Caligula, and was by him exiled to Gaul, where he soon went the way of Judas. That was a terrible bargain which Pilate made when, like Esau, he sold his birthright; and it should serve as a warning to all lukewarm and timid Christians. "The friendship of the world is enmity with God; whosoever therefore will be a friend of the world is the enemy of God." (James 4, 4). O, that all who wish to please both God and the world might understand betimes whither their way leads! Let them bear in mind that they are the brothers of Pilate! They are more fearful of affronting their worldly friends than of casting Jesus off by offending him. They are ashamed of his contumely, and turn aside to escape his cross. They are willing enough to be of his people; but will not confess his name, and will not follow in the footsteps of his sufferings. To them honor and power and reputation among men are more to be desired than are salvation in the Lord and fidelity toward the truth. Yes, many there are who sell their conscience for one gratification of a sensual desire, or for one little wretched and transient gain.

Ye Christians who love the Lord and hold your souls dear; beware of the favor of men, and do not turn aside by the breadth of a hair from the path of a clear conscience. The temptation to seek honors and to fear men will lie in wait for you everywhere; but by the Spirit of *him* who witnessed the good confession before Pontius Pilate, you shall at all times be able to be on your watch, and to tread the temptation under foot.

Give us this grace, merciful and faithful God, for Jesus' sake. Amen.

Watch against the world, that frowns Darkly to dismay thee; Watch when she thy wishes crowns, Smiling to betray thee; Watch and see thou art free From false friends, that charm thee, While they seek to harm thee.

Watch against thyself, my soul, See thou do not stifle Grace that should thy thoughts control, Nor with mercy trifle; Pride and sin lurk within All thy hopes to scatter; List not when they flatter.

152. Wednesday after Fourth Sunday in Lent.

Lord Jesus, draw us after thee. Amen.

Matthew 27, 31. 32. Luke 23, 27–31. And after that they had mocked him, they took the robe off from him, and put his own raiment on him, and led him away to crucify him. And as they came out, they found a man of Cyrene, Simon by name: him they compelled to bear his cross. And there followed him a great company of people, and of women, which also bewailed and lamented him. But Jesus turning unto them, said, Daughters of Jerusalem, weep not for me, but weep for yourselves, and for your children. For, behold, the days are coming, in the which they shall say, Blessed are the barren, and the wombs that never bare, and the paps which never gave suck. Then shall they begin to say to the mountains, Fall on us; and to the hills, Cover us. For if they do these things in a green tree, what shall be done in the dry?

He is condemned to die, and is led away together with "two other malefactors." The scripture says *"two other malefactors"*; and thus it calls him, also, a malefactor. In this manner the Son of God is led through the streets of Jerusalem, bearing his cross. A remarkable pageant it was! Legions of angels were willing to relieve him of the cross, but no man would; Jesus himself *will* and *shall* bear it. Isaac carried the wood for the sacrifice; his father Abraham had laid it on him. But here the only begotten of the Father carries more than the tree on which he is to be sacrificed in the fire of God's wrath; his soul also is crushed by the weight of the awful judgment on him. He *knows* whither the way leads; he feels the fire in his conscience; "murder is done in all his bones." — How terrible a thing is sin, and how awful the justice of God! Could not the mere willingness of the Son of God to put himself in the place of sinners and suffer their punishment have been sufficient to appease God's wrath? Could not the Father have pardoned his only Son without demanding any further suffering? No; the punishment *must* be undergone, and even the well beloved Son is torn with the agony of the damned. Death racks and fells him who is without sin or blemish in mind or body; the fire of hell burns in this most sound, green, and vigorous tree. How great a burning shall there not be, then, when the hollow, dry, dismembered branches are piled up high and set on fire!

The episode with Simon of Cyrene shows how Jesus had poured out his soul unto death, how his strength had failed him. (Isaiah 53, 12. Psalm 38, 10). It is not to be supposed that Satan stops him in his work of atonement; nor is it to be inferred that any other can or shall bear the sins of the world for him or with him; neither Simon of Cyrene, who was forced to carry the cross, nor the two thieves, who by their own deeds had deserved everlasting punishment. No: the purpose of the occurrence here related is to make plain to us, how entirely sin consumes man's strength, and how wholly Jesus has relinquished the use of his omnipotence, how completely he has staked everything for us, and how perfectly he has in this wise made atonement for us.

It was necessarry to lay hold on Simon of Cyrene and *force* him to bear the cross after Jesus. This matter is one with which we should be familiar; for we are in similar case. However, though at first we bear the cross with the greatest reluctance, we learn later on to bear it willingly. To the true cross-bearers the cross becomes the lighter, as it grows more heavy; the dearer, as it lasts the longer; until all our need and misery become altogether bliss and everlasting songs of praise.

Lord Jesus, I thank thee that thou didst bear the accursed cross for me, in order that I may bear the cross of sanctification in the fellowship of thy sufferings. Alas, there yet is much in me which rebels against it; have mercy, and teach me to take up my cross willingly and gladly; and draw me after thee. Amen.

The joy of all who dwell above, The joy of all below, To whom he manifests his love, And grants his name to know.
The cross he bore is life and health, Though shame and death to him: His people's hope, his people's wealth, Their everlasting theme.

---

153. Thursday after Fourth Sunday in Lent.

Lord, let there be silence, that we may hear; and dispel the mists that cloud our vision. Amen.

Matthew 27, 33. 34. John 19, 18. Mark 15, 28. And when they were come unto a place called Golgotha, that is to say, a place of a skull, they gave him vinegar to drink, mingled with gall: and when he had tasted thereof, he would not drink. Where they crucified him, and two other with him, on either side one, and Jesus in the midst. And the scripture was fulfilled which saith, And he was numbered with the transgressors.

The Lord did not wish to taste anything which would blunt his senses; it was his will to taste death for us in all its bitterness. And now the hour is come; now the Lamb of the Passover is to be slaughtered; now the Son of Man is to be lifted up; now all the prophecies concerning his passion in atonement for us are about to be fulfilled; now he is to become the accursed for our sake, as it is written: "Cursed is every one that hangeth on a tree." — Blessed Son of God, my Savior, dearest beloved of my soul; I see thee, as thou art being led to the place of execution for criminals, between two other male-factors. Thou, who didst not know sin, hast been made to be sin for me; but thou art the same alway, love and righteousness itself; and thy divine purity sparkles with undiminished lustre in the fiery crucible of God's wrath. I see thee, as thou dost permit them to lay hold on thy sacred body, again strip it of its robes, lay it down, stretch it on the cross, and drive the nails through hands and feet. They were fastened to the cross with nails, these hands which were never raised to heaven except to bless us and intercede for us, and which were never moved on earth except to do good. I see them raise the cross; and thou, my Jesus, the only begotten of the Father, the glory of all the heavens, dost hang on it, a curse for the sake of us accursed sinners.

Dost thou love us so well, **thou everlasting, blessed God**? Dost thou regard us as being worth so much that thou art willing to become a malefactor and die the death on the cross on Golgotha for our sake; for us wretched and wicked men, for me and all other sinners, who in ourselves are but venom and gall, and are among them that crucified thee, and that walked around the cross and mocked thee? Take, then, my soul as thy spoil; take my heart, and fill it with thy love; take my every vital emotion, my every drop of blood, my every heartbeat; take me wholly and entirely, and let me be thine alway, to serve thee for ever, and to live for thee, for thee only! Crucify everything in me which is displeasing to thee, that I do not henceforth live unto myself, but unto thee, who didst love me and give thyself for me! Precious Lord Jesus, I heartily beseech thee, grant me this grace: have mercy on me, even me, miserable sinner that I am, Lord Jesus! Thou didst let thyself be crucified for me; and I am thine, bought with a price. Let me never, never lose thy cross and the nails that pierced thy hands and feet. Amen.

When I survey the wondrous cross On which the Prince of glory died, My richest gain I count but loss, And pour contempt on all my pride.
Forbid it, Lord, that I should boast, Save in the death of Christ, my God; All the vain things that charm me most, I sacrifice them to his blood.

---

154. Friday after Fourth Sunday in Lent.

Lord Jesus, may we hear the voice of thy intercession for us from the cross. Amen.

Mark 15, 25. Luke 23, 34. Isaiah 53, 12. And it was the third hour; and they crucified him. Then said Jesus, Father, forgive them; for they know not what they do. And they parted his raiment, and cast lots. Therefore will I divide him a portion with the great, and he shall divide the spoil with the strong; because he hath poured out his soul unto death: and he was numbered with the transgressors; and he bare the sin of many, and made intercession for the transgressors.

The following thoughts are suggested to me by the intercession of Jesus for his murderers: 1) *There is nothing save love and mercy in his soul;* not a spark of anger, not a drop of bitterness. They inflict on him the most dreadful suffering; but he excuses them and prays for them. He prays for the soldiers, for Pilate, for the priests, and for all who take part in crucifying him. 2) *While praying for others he sheds his blood.* Naked and bloody, in the garb of shame and affliction, the Pure and Holy One hangs on the cross, and prays that for the sake of his suffering the Father will forgive them that inflict these sufferings on him. "Wholly and entirely compassed about by the waves of affliction, he descends into the depths of distress in the souls of his enemies, and seeks to rescue them." In the service of wickedness they stretch out his hands and nail them to the cross; but thus he is enabled to stretch out his hands in prayer for them. His first words on the cross are *the words of the high priest.* 3) *He earns and asks full forgiveness for all;* and thus the pardon has been made out and is ready, if the sinner will but seek it and accept it. Here he does not pray with the condition, "Father, if thou wilt." On the contrary, he asks without any condition, "Father, forgive them." His blood and death is a perfect, entirely valid payment of the whole world's debt. These men certainly should have known what they were doing; they have no excuse. Yet the Lord makes excuses for them, and provides grace for them, if they would accept it. Such is our high priest, Jesus Christ. My heart praises and worships him. He extends the grace of his vicarious atonement to the most hardened sinners; he takes upon himself the guilt of all, and hence there is in him forgiveness for all. Many of the blind instruments of Satan for whom Jesus prays continue in their unbelief, and are lost; but the reason for this is not that there was no forgiveness for them; had they but repented and turned to him, the blood of Jesus would have cleansed them from all their sin. Thousands of Jews and gentiles have experienced the power contained in the intercession of the crucified Savior, and are now returning thanks to him in everlasting bliss.

We, also, took part in nailing the Son of God to the cross; for *our* sins, also, he died. To *us*, as to all others, he extends the grace which is embraced in his prayer as our high priest; and we may have the full assurance that all our sins are atoned for and wiped out by his blood. Come, my soul, into the sanctuary, before the face of God; receive full pardon for everything, out of the fullness of his merit, and receive likewise the ornament of his priestly purity, patience, and mercy, that you, also, may be of those in whom the Father is well pleased, and that you may love and bless your enemies. Help us, O God, and give us thy blessing herein through thy Holy Ghost. Amen.

See, from his head, his hands, his feet, Sorrow and love flow mingled down! Did e'er such love and sorrow meet, Or thorns compose so rich a crown?
Were the whole realm of nature mine, That were a tribute far too small; Love so amazing, o divine, Demands my soul, my life, my all.

---

155. Saturday after Fourth Sunday in Lent.

The kingdom is the Lord's. Thou, thou art the king of Israel!

John 19, 19-22. And Pilate wrote a title, and put it on the cross. And the writing was, Jesus of Nazareth the king of the Jews. This title then read many of the Jews: for the place where Jesus was crucified was nigh to the city: and it was written in Hebrew, and Greek, and Latin. Then said the chief priests of the Jews to Pilate, Write not, The King of the Jews; but that he said, I am King of the Jews. Pilate answered, What I have written I have written.

The governor wished to mock and insult the Jews, who had caused him so much vexation and uneasiness of conscience, and who had in such a scandalous way forced him to become their obedient servant. He had said to them: "Behold your King!" Now he fastened above the head of the Crucified One a writing which said: "Jesus of Nazareth the King of the Jews." We may see and admire God's glorious providence in all things, but it is especially wonderful in every detail of the passion of our Savior. The surliness of Pilate puts on his lips an answer which was to be proclaimed and heard throughout all the world. "What I have written I have written, and it *shall* so remain; it *shall not* be changed. Jesus, the Nazarene, is the King of the Jews, the Messiah. This despised branch out of the root of David, this Jesus, who hangs on the accursed tree, is the King of the house of Jacob, and for this reason he dies; not because he calls himself, but because he is in very truth the King of the Jews." The writing, "Jesus of Nazareth the King of the Jews," placed above the head of the Savior who was crowned with thorns and crucified, is a summary, as it were, of the prophecies concerning the Messiah as the King of Israel who was to be victorious through suffering and death.

The writing is in Hebrew, and Greek, and Latin. The word of the cross is to be preached not only in Hebrew, that is, in the language of the Jews; but also in the several tongues of the gentiles. The furious Jews forced Pilate to crucify the Lord of glory; but no clamor or threats on the part of earth or hell shall be able to tear this truth down from the cross, or prevent its being preached in all tongues. This gospel shines like the sun over all the earth: This man of Nazareth, who hangs on the cross, is *Jesus*, the Son of God, the Savior of the world, the King who was to come to his people; and for this reason he dies. This is the cause of his death. By his death he acquires the kingdom; he thereby renders the prince of death powerless, and thus he makes *the preaching of the cross* his sword of state. — Be a son of Jacob, an Israelite without guile, dear friend; then it is an established fact that Jesus *is your King*, who with his royal grace as your Savior, a power stronger than the omnipotence that sustains the heavens and the earth, stretches out his sceptre over you to govern and protect you, and writes with indelible letters in your soul: I am your King; the kingdom is mine, and you are of my blessed people.

Precious Savior, Lord of glory, let this come to pass. Extend thy royal power over all the earth; gather thy Israel out of all peoples. Amen.

On my heart imprint thine image, Blessed Jesus, King of grace, That life's riches, cares, and pleasures, Have no power thee to efface; This the superscription be: Jesus, crucified for me, Is my life and glory ever; Nothing me from him shall sever.

156. Annunciation Day. I.

"O, my Immanuel, come and be born in my heart."

Gospel Lesson, Luke 1, 26–38. And in the sixth month the angel Gabriel was sent from God, unto a city of Galilee, named Nazareth, to a virgin espoused to a man whose name was Joseph, of the house of David; and the virgin's name was Mary. And the angel came in unto her, and said, Hail, thou that art highly favored, the Lord is with thee: blessed art thou among women. And when she saw him, she was troubled at his saying, and cast in her mind what manner of salutation this should be. And the angel said unto her, Fear not, Mary, for thou hast found favor with God. And, behold, thou shalt conceive in thy womb, and bring forth a son, and shalt call his name Jesus. He shall be great, and shall be called the Son of the Highest: and the Lord God shall give unto him the throne of his father David: And he shall reign over the house of Jacob for ever; and of his kingdom there shall be no end. Then said Mary unto the angel, How shall this be, seeing I know not a man? And the angel answered and said unto her, The Holy Ghost shall come upon thee, and the power of the Highest shall overshadow thee; therefore also that holy thing which shall be born of thee shall be called the Son of God. And, behold, thy cousin Elisabeth, she hath also conceived a son in her old age: and this is the sixth month with her who was called barren. For with God nothing shall be impossible. And Mary said, Behold the handmaid of the Lord; be it unto me according to thy word. And the angel departed from her.

In the midst of the lenten season we shall consider this gospel lesson, and the divinity of Jesus, and his two natures in one person, that we may not forget who it is that suffers, but may ponder it earnestly and worship his love. Then shall we know this love in our heart, and the Lord himself shall assume shape in us, both as the King of the cross and as the King of glory. It is necessary that Jesus be conceived spiritually in our heart; — and it is a blessed thing, also.

The Holy Ghost testifies in the scripture with such clearness and emphasis concerning the mystery of the divinity in Christ, because it is so absolutely necessary that we recognize this truth. The church has understood this, and therefore it repeatedly presents this testimony of the Spirit for our meditation in our church services. — Can any one who with an honest purpose reads the gospel of the conception of Jesus construe it otherwise than as meaning that the son to whom Mary is to give birth is the Son of *God?* Is it not stated with all possible clearness that he had no father after the natural order on earth? Does not the angel say repeatedly that he shall be *called the Son of God?* But in the scriptural use of language to be *called* the Son of God is to *be* the Son of God. This is what Mary understands to be the meaning of the words spoken by the angel. And does not the angel clearly call attention to the prophecies concerning the Messiah, in which his divinity is announced? We call to mind II Samuel 7, wherein the Lord gives David the promise: I will set up thy seed after thee; I will establish the throne of his kingdom for ever; I will be his father, and he shall be my son. We are reminded of Isaiah 9, wherein the same heir to the throne of David is called "Wonderful, Counsellor, The mighty God, The everlasting Father, The Prince of Peace," with a government of peace without end, in which he reigns from henceforth even for ever. How can the Holy Ghost in the scripture, and how can the angels of the Lord speak in this wise, if this son of Mary be not the only begotten Son of God, very and everlasting God with the Father? The whole Bible teaches that he is conceived by the Holy Ghost, and that he is true God and true man in one person. We dare openly and aloud declare them to be fools who deny that Christ is true God; they read the scripture incorrectly, and do not perceive its true meaning, for the reason that they wish to appear wise above that which is written. When man is led by his own conceit he walks in darkness. — Let us rather bow in worship and thank God for his ineffable gift. It is a glorious thing to be fully assured of the divinity of Christ; for then he is unto us a perfect Savior, and his name is great and beautiful above every name. Why should it trouble me that his person is more exalted and wonderful than anything which my poor reason can grasp? On the contrary; the wisdom and power of God must of necessity be far beyond my comprehension; and here is the miracle of all the miracles of God; the highest, and the deepest, and the greatest; a mystery which the angels desire to look into. I therefore willingly and gladly bow to his power to do wonders, and believe that his love is immeasurably greater than all that we can conceive and understand. For with God *nothing* shall be impossible. — What, then, is to prevent us from saying with Mary: "Be it unto me according to thy word"? God says: "I love you with love eternal; I give you my only begotten Son, and in him I give you life everlasting." To this I make answer: "It be unto me according to thy word." Was Mary disappointed when she believed the word of the Lord? Shall we be disappointed, do you think, if we build on his word? No; it has pleased God in his everlasting love to give us his Son for our Savior, and to let him become man, in order that we may be given a part in his glory. Let the sages and champions of infidelity keep their Messiah, whom they regard as a mere man, whose person and doctrines have their day, and then drop for ever out of sight; — such a Savior will not serve our turn; we must have one who is Lord over time and eternity, earth and heaven, life and death, sin and righteousness, men and angels and devils; and such a one we have, blessed be his name! With the whole Christian church we believe in Jesus Christ, God's only Son, true God and true man, who suffered and died, rose again and lives, and sits at the right hand of God.

God Holy Ghost, give us this simple and childlike spirit. Amen.

We believe in Jesus Christ, His own son, our Lord, possessing An equal Godhead, throne, and might, Thro' whom comes the Father's blessing; Conceived of the Holy Spirit, Born of Mary, Virgin-mother, That lost man might life inherit, Made true man, our elder brother, Was crucified for sinful men, And raised by God to life again.

---

157. Annunciation Day. II.

Lord, what is man, that thou art mindful of him? and the son of man, that thou visitest him?

Lesson Isaiah 7, 10–15. Moreover, the Lord spake again unto Ahaz, saying, Ask thee a sign of the Lord thy God: ask it either in the depth, or in the height above. But Ahaz said, I will not ask, neither will I tempt the

Lord. And he said, Hear ye now, O house of David; Is it a small thing for you to weary men, but will ye weary my God also? Therefore the Lord himself shall give you a sign: Behold, a virgin shall conceive, and bear a son, and shall call his name Immanuel. Butter and honey shall he eat, that he may know to refuse the evil, and choose the good.

Our Lord Jesus is the true "Immanuel;" or, in our tongue, "*God with us.*" He is the true, eternal God, the second person of the holy Trinity, begotten of the Father from eternity; but at the same time he is true man, with body and soul, sprung from Adam, like unto us in all things, yet without sin. He is one with the Father in eternal divinity, and one with us in true human nature. His sacred person forms a wonderful connection between God and us. How near to us is God come, now that the one and same Lord Jesus is both God and man! His birth on earth is the birth of *God's* Son by the *woman* Mary; his human sufferings are the sufferings of the Son of God; and the blood of the man Jesus Christ is the blood of the Son of God. How excellent is human nature become by the union of the Son of God with man in one person! A precious stone is not set in lead, but in gold; yet even to the gold the stone adds new lustre and splendor. Much greater glory do we receive by the personal, indissoluble union of God's only Son with man. The angels have transcendent glory; the thrones and principalities in heaven are close to God; but it is with man only that he is united in one person; the Son of God did not become an angel, but he became a man. How great is man by this means become! But we lay our glory at his feet: for not we, but *he* has done it. He has thus decreed; it was his will to love us in this way; of his free love he has chosen us. The *glory* is not ours; yet it is our *glory.* To us it is at once the deepest humiliation and the highest exaltation. This truth, that the Son of God was made man, is worth more than all our other knowledge, and it contains more of strength and joy for the soul than all else in the world that is beautiful and noble. In wonder and worship the apostle Paul exclaims, 1 Timothy 3, 16: "Great is the mystery of godliness: God was manifest in the flesh, justified in the Spirit, seen of angels, preached unto the gentiles, believed on in the world, received up into glory."

Another of the wonders of grace is this, that the mystery is revealed to the simple. It is for all, and is offered to all; but we must become as children, if we are to lay hold on it and keep it. The truth must rouse us out of our foolish dreams of pride, and teach us to know what we are become. Whosoever does not see that he is a lost sinner can not know the excellence of the person of Jesus Christ. For his *person* and his *offices* can not be separated. He is "Immanuel" in his offices as well as in his person. *He,* God and man in one person, is our *Jesus,* who takes away that which separates us from God. *He* is our *Christ,* the High Priest, who leads us into the presence of God; the Prophet, who brings the truth and life of God to our souls; and the King, who destroys our death, establishes the kingdom. and appoints us to live and reign with him for evermore. If the prophecy concerning "Immanuel" gave Ahaz and Judah sufficient assurance of the continued existence of the nation, because the people of which he was to be born could not cease to be; — how much more shall we, Immanuel's very own people, be saved; we who are sprung from him, and born of him, and are the members of his body, flesh of his flesh, and bone of his bones! Be simple in heart, childlike in mind and spirit; so shall you grasp this in faith. — God help us, that in truth we may be of the people of *Immanuel*. Amen.

Glory to God in highest heaven, The Father of eternal love; To his dear Son, for sinners given, Whose watchful grace we daily prove; To God the Holy Ghost on high,—O ever be his comfort nigh, And teach us free from sin and fear, To please him here, And serve him in the sinless sphere.

---

158. Monday after Annunciation Day.

Lord, teach me to know the shame of my nakedness, and put on me the dearly bought robe of righteousness. Amen.

John 19, 23. 24. Then the soldiers, when they had crucified Jesus, took his garments, and made four parts, to every soldier a part; and also his coat: now the coat was without seam, woven from the top throughout. They said therefore among themselves, Let us not rend it, but cast lots for it, whose it shall be: that the scripture might be fulfilled, which saith, They parted my raiment among them, and for my vesture they did cast lots. These things therefore the soldiers did.

They strip the Lord of his garments; the Son of God is to hang naked on the cross, and thus atone for the world's vanity and passion for all sorts of finery, and buy for us the robe of righteousness. — When parting his garments among them, and casting lots for his coat, the soldiers again unwittingly fulfil the decree of God and the words of the prophets. How could David, a thousand years in advance, know this and write it down in the Twenty-second Psalm, as accurately in all its details as though he had been present and seen it? Or were the soldiers acquainted with the scriptures, and did they do this thing with the purpose of fulfilling the prophecy? Not so; but God wants to help us to believe. If we knew and understood the scriptures well, the conviction that they are true would force itself upon us; for the Old Testament contains the New; human wisdom could by no possibility have written these things. None save the Spirit of God knew what would come to pass after thousands of years.

The coat without seam, woven from the top throughout, which could not be taken apart, and which God did not permit the soldiers to rend, reminds us of the seamless wedding garment of righteousness, which Christ gives to his believers, and which he bought for us when he divested himself of his glory and died for us on the cross in nakedness and disgrace. That garment can not be parted. If you have the righteousness of Christ, you have it complete; not a part of it, but the whole garment. In other words, if you truly believe in our Lord Jesus, you are *entirely* justified before God, *all* your sins are forgiven you, he shelters you completely, there is *no* condemnation whatever for you; you may of a certainty be sure of everlasting life. The sin that you have, and the sin that you commit; your former transgressions, and your daily weaknesses; the disobedience of which you are aware, and your secret faults; — for all these Jesus has atoned, and all that he did and suffered has been given to you in your baptism; if you believe, all is yours. That which the law requires you to love and practice, perfect obedience and perfect holiness, has been *done* by him in your stead; and what he has done for you is set down to your credit; in this wise you have put on Christ when you were baptized into him. Blessed are you, if you believe; for in that case you have the wedding garment; the shame of your nakedness is taken away. Christ was lifted up naked onto the cross; you shall be lifted up to the seat of honor clothed with the robe of salvation.

We bless thee, Lord Jesus, for all that thou didst do and suffer for us, though as yet we understand but little thereof. Give us more and more of the light of the Spirit; make clear to our souls the significance of thy holy passion; and help us to believe with single hearts, in order that we may stand before thee clothed in thy righteousness, and praise thee for evermore. Amen.

O Lamb of God most holy! Who on the cross didst languish, E'er patient meek, and lowly, Though mocked amid thine anguish; Our sins thou bearest for us, Else would despair reign o'er us; Have mercy on us, O Jesus!
O Lamb of God most holy! etc. Have mercy on us, O Jesus!
O Lamb of God most holy! etc. Thy peace be with us, O Jesus!

---

159. Tuesday after Annunciation Day.

Thou art worthy, Lord Jesus, to receive glory and honor and power for ever and ever.

Matthew 27, 39–44. And they that passed by reviled him, wagging their heads, and saying, Thou that destroyest the temple, and buildest it in three days, save thyself. If thou be the Son of God, come down from the cross. Likewise also the chief priests mocking him, with the scribes and elders, said, He saved others, himself he cannot save. If he be the King of Israel, let him now come down from the cross, and we will believe him. He trusted in God; let him deliver him now, if he will have him: for he said, I am the Son of God. The thieves also, which were crucified with him, cast the same in his teeth.

"Our fathers trusted in thee; they trusted in thee, and were not confounded. But I am a worm, and no man; a reproach of men, and despised of the people. All that see me laugh me to scorn; they shoot out the lip, they shake the head, saying: He trusted on the Lord that he would deliver him; let him deliver him, seeing he delighted in him." In these words David has, in the Twenty-second Psalm, recorded that which Jesus felt and to which he gave utterance while hanging on the cross. In another of the Psalms he says: "As with a sword in my bones, mine enemies reproach me; while they say daily unto me: Where is thy God?" (Psalm 42, 10). Let none imagine that the Lord shook off the reproach without feeling it. "Reproach hath broken my heart," he declares, "and I am full of heaviness; and I lookèd for some to take pity, but there was none; and for comforters, but I found none. They gave me also gall for my meat; and in my thirst they gave me vinegar to drink." (Psalm 69, 20 and 21). It was a part of his work of atonement to pay for all the reproach and mockery in which men indulge and delight on this poor earth. How many are there not whose pleasure and pride it is to mock and hold others up to derision. Jesus was to be loaded down with this sort of wickedness also. Let the flippant mockers see and hear that which takes place around the cross of the Lord; that should cure them of their abominable passion for scoffing. The weight of his sacred body, weary unto death, and suspended by the nails driven through his hands and feet, gave him unutterable agony; sufferings, such as none of us can imagine, coursed like a consuming fire through all his members, and every nerve was racked with the pains of death. But wounds yet more deep were inflicted on his soul by the reproach with which he was assailed. It must have been hard, beyond our power to conceive, for the Son of God to bear the foul ignominy and insults which were heaped upon him. My Jesus, if thou hadst descended from the cross, they that reviled thee would have seen with terror that thou art the Son of God. But the nails were forged in the scheme of the Eternal, and therefore they riveted thee fast; thou dost love us with the love that is stronger than death and greater than all the agonies of hell.

I would gladly, then, be despised and reviled for thy· sake. I, also, feel how reproach and contumely have a mighty power to tempt one away from the cross; but I shall gain the victory through thee, and keep the flesh in subjection. To be reviled for thy sake shall to me be an honor a thousand times more great than any which the world can give. Grant me the grace that I may never dishonor thee by an ungodly life or by impatience in suffering; but let me suffer as a Christian should, and be reviled for that I have thy Spirit. — Save me from the awful crime of reviling thee in thy saints on earth. Amen.

Stricken, smitten, and afflicted, See him dying on the tree! 'Tis the Christ by man rejected; Yes, my soul, 'tis he! 'tis he!
·Ye who think of sin but lightly, Nor suppose the evil great, Here may view its nature rightly, Here its guilt may estimate.
Mark the sacrifice appointed! See who bears the awful load; 'Tis the word, the Lord's Anointed, Son of man, and Son of God.

---

160. Wednesday after Annunciation Day.

Lord, give us repentance, and give us a portion in thy kingdom. Amen.

Luke 23, 39–43. And one of the malefactors which were hanged railed on him, saying, If thou be Christ, save thyself and us. But the other answering, rebuked him, saying, Dost not thou fear God, seeing thou art in the same condemnation? And we indeed justly; for we receive the due reward of our deeds: but this man hath done nothing amiss. And he said unto Jesus, Lord, remember me when thou comest into thy kingdom. And Jesus said unto him, Verily I say unto thee, Today shalt thou be with me in paradise.

The penitent thief is the only person of whom the scripture relates that he was converted in his last hour. We infer that it is possible to be converted immediately before death; but it is an extremely rare occurrence. The greater number of these conversions are not genuine. We often observe that persons who have seemed to repent when they were sick and in distress, return to their former wickedness as soon as they regain their health. Let none of us reason in this wise: "I shall have time enough in which to sue for mercy before I die; and then I shall be saved." With thoughts such as these in your heart you commit sin, that grace may the more abound; and if you continue thus from day to day, it is but too certain that you will not be able to turn to the Lord in the agony of your dying hour. — This thief on the cross also presents a remarkable example of sincere repentance. He recognizes his guilt, and confesses that he has deserved death. The contrition of his heart is the more conspicuous by reason of the contrast with the impenitence of the other thief. This is the true conversion, that one knows himself as not only sinful, but *guilty*, and of his heart confesses that he deserves the wrath of God and the sentence of death. Thereafter he declares his faith. While the disciples are offended; while the people and their leaders revile; and while the Lord hangs on the cross in deepest disgrace, the glory of the Savior shines so brightly into the soul of the penitent thief that he believes, and confesses, and worships him as the Son of God. "With the heart man believeth unto righteousness; and with the mouth confession is made unto salvation." He that is able thus to pray of a contrite and believing heart shall be saved, as surely as God is just and truthful; they, *and none other;* for the only road to salvation is by way of repentance and faith.

And now, in words of sublime grandeur, Jesus bestows the gift of paradise upon the thief. With the death which even now he suffers he buys redemption and salvation for all sinners; and hanging on the cross, in the midst of his deepest abasement, he gives to the thief the paradise of glory; by his kingly word he snatches this soul out of death, and translates it into his heavenly kingdom. Is he not the Savior and the King, as is written above his head? Does he carry his crown of thorns in vain? Blessed be thou, Lord Jesus, for all things! We bless thee for that thou didst take *the thief* with thee from *the cross* to *paradise!* Condemned to death, as thou wast, thou didst take this malefactor, who also was under sentence of death, out of death, and didst carry him in triumph to heaven. Give us also of thy mercy true penitence and living faith, and take us to thyself in paradise when our time is come. Help us now, today, to seek thee and find thee in the right order of grace. Amen.

Jesus, may our hearts be burning With more fervent love for thee; May our eyes be ever turning To thy cross of agony;
Till in glory, parted never From the blessed Savior's side, Graven in our hearts for ever, Dwell the cross, the Crucified.

161. Thursday after Annunciation Day.

At thy cross, Lord Jesus, is the home of love; draw me thither. **Amen.**

John 19, 25–27. Now there stood by the cross of Jesus his mother, and his mother's sister, Mary the wife of Cleophas, and Mary Magdalene. When Jesus therefore saw his mother, and the disciple standing by whom he loved, he saith unto his mother, Woman, behold thy son! Then saith he to the disciple, Behold thy mother! And from that hour that disciple took her unto his own home.

After his baptism Jesus had addressed his mother as "Woman," but had cared for her as for his mother. This is now to cease; for he is to be "cut off out of the land of the living" (Isaiah 53, 8), and shall not henceforth be known of any after the flesh. But he does not leave his mother alone and helpless. As he had, of his own free will, taken upon himself the condition of a son, and had shown filial love and duty to Mary, so he now places this love and duty on the shoulders of John; for he has authority in this matter, even while hanging on the cross. And he gives to Mary the rights of a mother in the home of John. He is *Lord* of the Fourth Commandment, but had obeyed it. He pays in full for all our transgressions of this commandment; and how sublimely does he not honor it, and teach us the duty of love toward our parents!

It was a splendid gift which John here received. He received as his mother the blessed of God among women; he is to maintain her, care for her, and, as far as possible, heal her sick soul, which had been pierced by the sword of grief. To John, the apostle of *love*, this was a beauteous and precious gift; but there be many who *claim* to love the Lord, and who yet refuse to accept from him such a gift as this. John led Mary away from the cross as his mother — presumably before the last terrible hours of darkness, — and it is said that she lived with him eleven years before going to her long home. — Now your parents and other old and friendless people are the mother of Jesus (Matthew 12, 48 and following verses) whom he gives to you; and he wants to give you filial love to receive and care for these. If you seek your peace in Jesus, and if his cross is your abiding place, then from his cross he points to them that stand about, and that need your help; and he speaks to you, saying: "Behold thy mother!" It is *your crucified Jesus* who commits them to your care; *receive them from him;* then shall they, with the love which follows them as his gift to your *heart*, become to you the most precious treasure which you can have in your earthly home. "Christ is a most generous testator. He bequeathed to us his body to be our food, his blood to be our drink, his soul to be our ransom, his wounds to be our healing, his arms to be our safe refuge, his cross to be our shield, his pierced heart to be our pledge of love, the water out of his side to be our bath, his sweat to be our cure, his crown of thorns to be our ornament, his word to be our guide, his life to be an example for our imitation; and his members, who believe in him, he appointed to receive the love of them that are beloved of him." (Bernhard)

Give to me also, Lord Jesus, grace to receive and care for them
that are thine. Give me the priceless gift of charity in my poor heart,
and let it rule in my house. Amen.

O blessed house, that cheerfully receiveth Thy visits, Jesus Christ, the
soul's true friend; That, far beyond all other guests, believeth It must to thee
its warmest cheer extend; Where every heart to thee is fondly turning, Where
every eye for thee with pleasure speaks, Where all to know thy will are truly
yearning, And every one to do it promptly seeks.

162. Friday after Annunciation Day.

"My God, be not far from me; for trouble is near; for there is none to help."

Matthew 27, 45-49. Now from the sixth hour there was darkness over
all the land unto the ninth hour. And about the ninth hour Jesus cried with
a loud voice, saying, Eli, Eli, lama sabachthani? that is to say, My God, my
God, why hast thou forsaken me? Some of them that stood there, when they
heard that, said, This man calleth for Elias. And straightway one of them ran,
and took a sponge, and filled it with vinegar, and put it on a reed, and gave
him to drink. The rest said, Let be, let us see whether Elias will come to
save him.

To be forsaken of God is to be damned. Was it the *intent* of God,
then, to deal thus with his Son? Did this take place in accordance
with the Father's positive will? How could it be otherwise than in
accordance with the will of him without whom not even a sparrow
falls to the ground? The scripture expressly declares that when the
Son tasted death for us all, this was done according to the gracious
will of God. (Hebrews 2, 9). Or what power other than his love
could have caused the almighty Father to forsake his well beloved
Son? It was done for our sake, in obedience to his own gracious
purpose. The Father forsook the Son in the agony of death, tempted,
reproached and tortured by devils and men. And the Son knew that
he was forsaken, and fully realized the horror of it; the darkness of
eternal death settled down on him, and his soul was racked with all
the terrors of hell. The whole penalty which the world had deserved
is now executed on him; all the misery with which all men had deserved to be punished for ever and ever is poured into one cup, and
he empties it to the dregs, and tastes *all the bitterness of God's fiery
wrath* which it contains. "I know not what transpired in heaven and
in the soul of the Redeemer to produce this sensation of being forsaken of God; but I shudder at the thought, and a dark dread falls
on my soul, as it did on nature in those last hours. Here it becomes
plain to me that there is no flaw in the doctrine of Saint Paul, and of
Luther, in regard to the vicarious atonement of Jesus. He that does
not see this is more blind than was the night which fell on the land
when Jesus died." (Loehe).— The power of sin, the severity of justice,
the agony of the damned, the greatness of mercy, the eternal value
of my soul in the sight of God, — all these are in nothing revealed
more clearly than in the words of the Lord: "My God, my God, why

hast thou forsaken me?" But how can any poor words of mine, wretched sinner that I am, do justice to this subject? I sink down at the foot of thy throne with a profound sense of my unworthiness to be redeemed at so great a cost, and with my heart full of thanksgiving and worship.

Since thou, my Jesus, didst thus cry out, I am able in the midst of death to say with a glad voice: Blessed be thou for the ineffable grace of redemption. Justice is satisfied; condemnation has passed away. Nothing shall separate me from thy love; life everlasting is mine. Together with all the saints I shall be with thee, and praise and thank thee for evermore. Amen.

We held him as condemned of heaven, An outcast from his God; While for our sins he groaned, he bled, Beneath his Father's rod.

His sacred blood hath washed our souls From sin's polluting stain; His stripes have healed us, and his death Revived our souls again.

163. Saturday after Annunciation Day.

Lord Jesus, give us to understand thy suffering of expiation, and to taste thy love. Amen.

John 19, 28. 29. Psalm 22, 14. 15. Psalm 69, 21. After this, Jesus, knowing that all things were now accomplished, that the scripture might be fulfilled, saith, I thirst. Now there was set a vessel full of vinegar: and they filled a spunge with vinegar, and put it upon hyssop, and put it to his mouth. I am poured out like water, and all my bones are out of joint: my heart is like wax; it is melted in the midst of my bowels. My strength is dried up like a potsherd; and my tongue cleaveth to my jaws; and thou hast brought me into the dust of death. They gave me also gall for my meat; and in my thirst they gave me vinegar to drink.

Christ bore all the evils which sin has brought upon us, without asking relief of men. The snares of death compassed him, the floods of ungodly men made him afraid, the sorrows of death overwhelmed him, the waters came in unto his soul, the floods overflowed him; the fierce anger of the Lord, and all horrors, swept over him; the wrath of God burned him like fire. God forsook him; yet did he cling to God. Though filled with the sense of God's wrath, of having been forsaken by the Father, of the agony of death; he still looks to God, and in faith continues on the rock of his promises. That which is written in the Psalms and Prophets is his strength and deliverance. It did not exempt him from death; — for he should and would suffer death with all its pain and its terrors; — but it gave him strength to suffer patiently and without uttering any complaint, and it enabled him to cleave to God even when he felt in the fullest measure that he had been forsaken and was in the midst of the darkness of death. It is above all for his sake, for the support of his faith, that it is written in the Twenty-second Psalm: "My God, my God, why hast thou forsaken me; why art thou so far from helping me, and from the words of my roaring?" If there had been no such scripture passages to serve as his stay, he could not have gone through death in the manner in which he did, nor have become the prince of our faith. But it is written for the sake of our faith also; and therefore he uttered these words on the cross. We are to see that in him the prophecies concerning the sufferings of the Messiah are fulfilled to the letter in every detail; and among these prophecies are Psalm 22, 14 and 15, and 69, 21. For this reason he now *says:* "I thirst." His preceding cry marks the climax of his *soul's* agony; this expresses his most acute *bodily* pain. He has been suspended on the cross for five or six hours; his wounds are on fire, his blood is exhausted, "he is poured out like water, and all his bones are out of joint; his heart is like wax, melted in the midst of his bowels." His strength is dried up, and the weakness of exhaustion comes upon him; but his faith and love gain the victory. Now vinegar with gall is put to his mouth. This is the last cup drained by the Son of God on earth; men have nothing else to give him in his last moments. — I keep silence, my dear reader, and only pray the Holy Spirit to explain this to you. — Precious Savior, blessed be thy name for ever and ever! The rivers of living water in paradise are thine; yet dost thou thirst unto death and drink vinegar as an expiation for my sinful fleshly desires, in order that thou mayest give me the water of grace while I live, the cup of comfort when I die, and the sweet and blessed draught of eternal life in heaven. Again I say with all my heart: Blessed for ever be the precious name of the Savior! Amen.

In the cross of Christ I glory, Towering o'er the wrecks of time, All the light of sacred story Gathers round its head sublime.

When the woes of life o'ertake me, Hopes deceive, and fears annoy, Never shall the cross forsake me: Lo! it glows with peace and joy.

164. Palm Sunday. I.

Let all those that put their trust in thee rejoice; let them ever shout for joy, because thou defendest them; let them also that love thy name be joyful in thee.

Gospel Lesson, Matthew 21, 1-9. See First Sunday in Advent.

The kings of the nations are distinguished by their glory and splendor; Christ, on the other hand, by his lowliness and humility. The princes of this earth purchase victories with the blood of their subjects; Christ did it with his own blood. Other rulers have climbed into high places in order to gain power and dominion for themselves; Christ has descended to the lowest depths, that he might win glory and salvation for us. How? is he, then, not grand and great? Does he not possess dominion and glory? He upholds all things by the word of his power, and all the hosts of heaven do homage to him. It was not by reason of weakness that he became the least of all, but by reason of his omnipotence and infinite love. Still, his lowliness is by no means a pretense, or a mere assumption of humility; he has in very truth made himself of no reputation, — descending to the depths in order to slay our enemy and snatch us out of the jaws of death. His

kingdom is not of this world, the blessings which he bestows on us
are not of earth, but of heaven; not for the body, but for the soul.
Humility, meekness, patience, love, mercy, peace, and eternal salvation
are his gifts to his people.

He makes this entry into Jerusalem as a king at the very time
when he goes there to suffer and die. This was the necessary order
of things. It is by his death on the cross that he is to destroy the
power of the devil and found his own kingdom. He now comes to
Jerusalem, that he may be lifted up and draw all men unto himself.
(John 3, 14; 8, 28; 12, 32). It is done. He was crucified, and he
ascended to the right hand of the Father. He sits on the throne of
God, and has all power in heaven and on earth; and yet, gentle and
meek, he stands in our midst. All that believe in him are saved from
the power of darkness, and dwell within the ramparts of that kingdom
in which lovingkindness and meekness hold sway, where "mercy and
truth are met together, and righteousness and peace have kissed each
other." In *faith* we now enjoy this grace. A blessed thing for us is
his entrance into Jerusalem on Palm Sunday, when he came and was
made a sin offering for us. A blessed thing for us is the power of
his grace to conquer sin and all evil in our poor hearts. The time is
coming when we shall see him; he shall come once more; and this
coming shall be the occasion of such joy to the faithful that their
shouts of gladness shall continue throughout ages everlasting. — And
now, we thank thee for thy royal pageant on Palm Sunday, we do thee
homage as the king of our hearts; we worship thee as our God; and
we humbly ask of thee this great favor, that we may lay ourselves,
with all that we are and all that we have, at thy feet. Take all that
we have, Lord Jesus, and make use of it for the extension of thy kingdom. Lead us along the way of the cross; and in all things make
use of us for the victory of thy truth and grace on earth. Amen.

Paschal Lamb, by God appointed, All our sins on thee were laid; By almighty love anointed, Thou hast full atonement made. All thy people are
forgiven Through the virtue of thy blood: Opened is the gate of heaven,.
Peace is made 'twixt man and God.

---

165. Palm Sunday. II.

*Lord Jesus, teach us to know thee in thy humiliation and in thine exalta-
tion. Amen.*

Epistle Lesson, Philippians 2, 5-11. Let this mind be in you, which was
also in Christ Jesus: Who, being in the form of God, thought it not robbery
to be equal with God; but made himself of no reputation, and took upon him
the form of a servant, and was made in the likeness of men: and being found
in fashion as a man, he humbled himself, and became obedient unto death,
even the death of the cross. Wherefore God also hath highly exalted him,
and given him a name which is above every name: That at the name of Jesus
every knee should bow, of things in heaven, and things in earth, and things
under the earth; and that every tongue should confess that Jesus Christ is
Lord, to the glory of God the Father.

Jesus descends to the lowest depths of humility; for he is to accomplish all that of which the name *Jesus* is earnest. It is his wish to save us from the devil, and free our hearts from sin; deliver us from endless agony, and make us for ever blest; lift us up out of the deepest degradation, and give us eternal glory and honor in heaven. Therefore he renounces the use of his divine glory, and becomes the least and most humble of servants. When the Son of God became man it would naturally be expected that he must, as a matter of course, be a man of godlike grandeur; that his whole human nature must shine with the lustre lent to it by its union with the divine. But this likeness unto God he put away, and of this glory he stripped himself, and lived on earth in the likeness of sinful flesh. Himself without sin or blemish, he bore our whole burden of sin with all its consequences, poverty, hunger, pain, and death. But when he had suffered all this, and had made full payment of our debt, and had bought us with his own life and blood, he was translated to glory; and now "the Son of Man" is highly exalted, and has dominion over all things in heaven and earth; and he shall come again on the last day to judge the quick and the dead. It was a condescension greater than words can express on the part of the Son of God when he took upon him the form of a servant. On the other hand, man is exalted beyond measure by the personal union with the Son of God. Not only does he deliver us from evil, but he endows us with all honor and glory. It cost him dear to prove his title to the name Jesus; but he knew this from everlasting, and was willing to pay the price. To us this name is more precious than tongue can tell. It does not seem possible that I could refrain from doing it reverence; neither shall any deny me this privilege. The hosts of heaven shall worship him in all eternity, and all principalities and powers above and below shall bow down before him. God is our Savior; the name of the Son of God is Jesus; therefore we have great joy. This name, which fills the heavens with rejoicing, is the name of *our* Savior. Him shall we worship in glory without end, and his beauty shall for ever satisfy our soul's desire. We had deserved to be scullions in the devil's kitchen, and our Savior appoints us to places of honor among the angels around his heavenly throne. Should we not, then, be willing, nay even glad, to endure humiliation and suffering for a little while, and thus become like unto our meek and loving Savior? "Let this mind be in you, which was also in Christ Jesus." These are the opening words of our epistle lesson; and with these words we close, saying to one another: "Let this mind be in you, which was also in Christ Jesus."

O Lord Jesus, grant us the gift of thy Holy Spirit, that we may believe in thee; that we may be like thee, and that we may worship thee and confess thy precious name, here on earth in tribulations and in lowliness, and thereafter in the eternal glory and bliss of heaven. Amen.

Worship, honor, power, and blessing, Thou art worthy to receive; Loudest praises, without ceasing, Meet it is for us to give. Help, ye bright angelic spirits, Bring your sweetest, noblest lays, Help to sing our Savior's merits, Help to chant Immanuel's praise.

166. Monday in Holy Week.

Lord, cleanse our hearts, and teach our lips to show forth thy praise. Amen.

Matthew 21, 10–16. And when he was come into Jerusalem, all the city was moved, saying, Who is this? And the multitude said, This is Jesus, the prophet of Nazareth of Galilee. And Jesus went into the temple of God, and cast out all them that sold and bought in the temple, and overthrew the tables of the moneychangers, and the seats of them that sold doves; and said unto them, It is written, My house shall be called the house of prayer; but ye have made it a den of thieves. And the blind and the lame came to him in the temple; and he healed them. And when the chief priests and scribes saw the wonderful things that he did, and the children crying in the temple, and saying, Hosanna to the son of David! they were sore displeased, and said unto him, Hearest thou what these say? And Jesus saith unto them, Yea: have ye never read, Out of the mouth of babes and sucklings thou hast perfected praise?

Though the meekest of all kings, Christ is nevertheless filled with fiery zeal against wickedness, and does not tolerate ungodly men within the borders of his kingdom. The gentleness in which he deals with the afflicted who wish to be cleansed of their sin is no more pronounced than is the sternness with which he drives out of his church all self-confident and impenitent sinners. He does not crush the broken reed; but he brings low the proud and the stiff-necked. He that will not humble himself shall be cast out; for the kingdom of Christ is the home of humility and meekness and love. He heals the blind and the lame, and the Hosanna of babes is sweetest music to him; but he whips the money changers and traders out of his house, and the haughty scribes he rebukes with the two-edged sword of the word. The temple of burnt offerings is destroyed, and in its place is erected a temple of living stones, a temple in which God is worshiped in spirit and in truth. Let it be fully understood that only such as repent and become little children shall enter this temple. Humility and faith secure admission, while the doors are shut against the worldly, the vain, and the self-righteous. In a great house there are, to be sure, not only vessels of gold and silver, but also of wood and clay; but the former are unto honor and the latter unto dishonor. The tares are, indeed, allowed to grow in the field together with the wheat until the harvest; but they do not belong there, and they shall in due season be separated from the wheat with merciless severity. Let each of us examine himself and find whether or not his heart has been made humble and is cleansed in the blood of Jesus, thus enabling us to give the answer of a good conscience toward God, and to worship him in spirit and in truth; for none other shall be able to stand before him on the day of judgment. Jesus gave himself for us, that he might save us from the ways and works of the devil; and he let water and blood flow from his side for the purification of his peculiar people. Shall we not, then, follow holiness, and be zealous of good works? Now then, by the power of the blood of Christ, leave the ways of darkness: be not unequally yoked with unbelief. Purify your soul in the obedience of truth; let your heart be a holy temple, and your whole life a stainless service devoted to him whom "zeal for the house of God hath eaten up!"

Grant us this grace, merciful God, for Jesus' sake. Amen.

Return, O holy Dove! return, Sweet messenger of rest! I hate the sins that made thee mourn, And drove thee from my breast.
So shall my walk be close with God, Calm and serene my frame; So surer light shall mark the road That leads me to the Lamb.

167. Tuesday in Holy Week.

Lord, may we know the power of thy resurrection, and become partakers of thy sufferings! Amen.

John 12, 23-32. And Jesus answered them, saying, The hour is come, that the Son of man should be glorified. Verily, verily, I say unto you, Except a corn of wheat fall into the ground and die, it abideth alone: but if it die, it bringeth forth much fruit. He that loveth his life shall lose it; and he that hateth his life in this world, shall keep it unto life eternal. If any man serve me, let him follow me; and where I am, there shall also my servant be: if any man serve me, him will my Father honor. Now is my soul troubled; and what shall I say? Father, save me from this hour: but for this cause came I unto this hour. Father, glorify thy name. Then came there a voice from heaven, saying, I have both glorified it, and will glorify it again. The people therefore that stood by, and heard it, said that it thundered: others said, An angel spake to him. Jesus answered and said, This voice came not because of me, but for your sakes. Now is the judgment of this world: now shall the prince of this world be cast out. And I, if I be lifted up from the earth, will draw all men unto me.

Jews and Greeks wanted the Savior to make a splendid appearance in the world. And alas for us all, we much resemble them in this particular. It is a part of our corrupt nature to reach out after worldly fame and power and pleasure. Let all who follow Jesus search their hearts, and discover if these are the things which they seek in him. Let every man examine himself. We are ready enough to walk with him to the wedding feast, but prefer not to be with him in danger. We have no objection whatever to being with him in the glory of his kingdom; but we find it hard to learn the lesson that the way to heaven is the way of the cross. To deny self, to be humble always, to hate life and lose it, to suffer death on the cross; this was the life of Christ. This path he trod, and in this path the faithful follow him. In this way only could he become our Savior, and in this way only can you be a partaker of his suffering and his glory. Had he not died the death of the cross, he could not have delivered us from the devil and made atonement for our sin; and had he not been cut off out of the land of the living, he could not draw us unto himself in heaven. Through death and the grave he is gone to the Father, and who shall number the many whom he has saved? (Isaiah 53, 8). The grain of corn now brings forth much fruit; the cross is become a ladder to heaven. It is the *only* ladder which reaches up into the better world; the only way to heaven leads through suffering; there is none other bridge from death to life. This way of the cross to the glories of heaven has been prepared for all men; and whosoever will, let him come. Hanging on the cross, and sitting on the throne of heaven, the will of the Savior is to draw all men unto himself. But he that will not die with him can not live with him. Our own life, or, in other words, our evil nature, all our sinful lusts, which Paul calls "the body of sin" (Romans 6, 6), the combined force of wicked desires, whose root is wilfulness, and whose strength is pride and deceit; — this life of the world in you must die, if you are to live. In the name of God, sacrifice all this! You have been baptized into the death of Christ, and your old man is crucified with him. Let the efficacy of your baptism prove itself. If you believe in the Lord, be assured that you shall not want the grace to mortify the flesh and lead a new life in him. To this end he helps us by means of our many trials and tribulations from without and within, vexations, temptations, sickness, suffering; but the strength itself comes from the death and resurrection of Christ. There are the roots of your new life; and thence it must receive nourishment, if it is to increase. In his word and sacraments he gives to his believers the strength of his life and death; and through these means we of a truth *receive* grace to mortify the flesh, to take up the cross, and to live for heaven. Help us herein, O God, that we also may bring forth much fruit. Amen.

May earthly feelings die, And fruits of faith increase, And Adam's nature prostrate lie Before the Prince of Peace.

Endue us, Lord, with strength To triumph over sin, That we may with thy saints at length Eternal glory win.

---

168. Wednesday in Holy Week.

"*While the king sitteth at his table, my spikenard sendeth forth the smell thereof.*"

Matthew 26, 1–16. And it came to pass, when Jesus had finished all these sayings, he said unto his disciples, Ye know that after two days is the feast of the passover, and the Son of man is betrayed to be crucified. Then assembled together the chief priests, and the scribes, and the elders of the people, unto the palace of the high priest, who was called Caiaphas, and consulted that they might take Jesus by subtilty, and kill him. But they said, Not on the feast day, lest there be an uproar among the people. Now when Jesus was in Bethany, in the house of Simon the leper, there came unto him a woman having an alabaster box of very precious ointment, and poured it on his head, as he sat at meat. But when his disciples saw it, they had indignation, saying, To what purpose is this waste? For this ointment might have been sold for much, and given to the poor. When Jesus understood it, he said unto them, Why trouble ye the woman? for she hath wrought a good work upon me. For ye have the poor always with you; but me ye have not always. For in that she hath poured this ointment on my body, she did it for my burial. Verily I say unto you, Wheresoever this gospel shall be preached in the whole **world,** there shall also this, that this woman hath done, be told for a memorial of her. Then one of the twelve, called Judas Iscariot, went unto the chief priests, and said unto them, What will ye give me, and I will deliver him unto you? And they covenanted with him for thirty pieces of silver. And from that time he sought opportunity to betray him.

The council assembled in the palace of Caiaphas decides that Jesus must die. Not, however, on the feast day; for at that time Jerusalem is crowded with visitors from Galilee and elsewhere, and there might easily be a riot. But in the high council of God it had been decreed from everlasting that his death should occur at this very time, at the feast of the passover, and in the sight of all the people. The Lamb of the passover is to be made an Easter sacrifice in the presence of Jews and Greeks; for it is the office of Jesus to save from death both Jew and gentile. While the chief priests now take counsel together in the palace of Caiaphas, saying, "not on the feast day," Jesus is being anointed in Bethany. Judas strongly disapproves of this waste, and goes out to replenish the purse; and thus it comes about that the catastrophe takes place at the time of the feast. Though Satan lay his plans with all the cunning of which he is master, and though the wicked take counsel together with all possible caution and prudence, yet the Lord "taketh the wise in their own craftiness." Though it is against their will, they all must serve his purposes. How much more, then, must it be true in regard to the faithful, that they are instruments for the working out of his purposes. This woman loved the Lord. She regarded no ointment as too precious to be poured out for him. Her heart was full of the love which is fragrant of heaven. She cared nothing for the money value of her offering; her delight was to be near Jesus, to serve and please him. And thus she did more than she was aware of; she anointed him for his burial. She loved him for that he loved us with the love that caused him to lay down his life for us; and her love was a precious ointment to his heart, and comforted him for his loss of the unhappy Judas. In the most stupendous event that heaven and earth have witnessed, the passion and death of the Son of God, this woman holds a place of such importance that her deed is recounted wherever the gospel is preached. And why? By reason of her love; the love that gladly gives all that it has, and does not think of the cost when buying ointment for Jesus. The council in the palace of Caiaphas and the company in Bethany are curiously correlated; and the one sheds light on the other. The woman pours out on the head of Jesus ointment to the value of three hundred pence; Judas sells him for thirty pieces of silver.

Avarice is always poor, and robs the heart of every noble impulse; love always has abundance, and is able to fill the house with its divine perfume.

Lord Jesus, give us love, the greatest and best of all things in the world. Amen.

Dear Lord, and shall we ever live At this poor, dying rate? Our love so faint, so cold to thee, And thine to us so great?
Come, Holy Spirit, heavenly dove, With all thy quickening powers, Come, shed abroad a Savior's love. And that shall kindle ours.

169. Thursday in Holy Week. I.

Lord, teach us to understand that which thou doest. Amen.

John 13, 1–15. Now before the feast of the passover, when Jesus knew that his hour was come that he should depart out of this world unto the Father, having loved his own which were in the world, he loved them unto the end. And supper being ended, the devil having now put into the heart of Judas Iscariot, Simon's son, to betray him; Jesus knowing that the Father had given all things into his hands, and that he was come from God, and went to God; he riseth from supper, and laid aside his garments; and took a towel, and girded himself. After that he poureth water into a bason, and began to wash the disciples' feet, and to wipe them with the towel wherewith he was girded. Then cometh he to Simon Peter: and Peter saith unto him, Lord, dost thou wash my feet? Jesus answered and said unto him, What I do thou knowest not now; but thou shalt know hereafter. Peter saith unto him, Thou shalt never wash my feet. Jesus answered him, If I wash thee not, thou hast no part with me. Simon Peter saith unto him, Lord, not my feet only, but also my hands and my head. Jesus saith to him, He that is washed needeth not save to wash his feet, but is clean every whit: and ye are clean, but not all. For he knew who should betray him; therefore said he, Ye are not all clean. So after he had washed their feet, and had taken his garments, and was set down again, he said unto them, Know ye what I have done unto you? Ye call me Master and Lord: and ye say well; for so I am. If I then, your Lord and Master, have washed your feet; ye also ought to wash one another's feet. For I have given you an example, that ye should do as I have done to you.

There are no words of ours which can do justice to this grand text, or can bring out its wondrous beauty. Do thou therefore, O Lord, explain it to us. — The sinner who has been justified is pure and spotless in the sight of God, all his guilt is taken away, he is robed in the seamless and undivided garment of Christ; "there is no condemnation to them which are in Christ Jesus." God has justified them; who, then, shall lay anything to their charge? The justified sinner has been born again, and lives in righteousness and purity. He has a new heart, which loves God and does his will. But he also has flesh and blood, and his life is therefore as yet imperfect; there is more or less of dust which clings to his feet. "Ye are clean," said Jesus to his disciples; but see how their pride causes them to sin. Each of them wants to be first. In like manner all believers have many open and secret faults. Therefore we all the time stand in need of forgiveness and renewal. This is what the Lord means by the ceremony of washing the feet. If he did not grant us every day new forgiveness for the sins which still cling to us, we could not continue in fellowship with him. If we say that we have no sin we deceive ourselves, and the truth is not in us. (John 1, 8). If you do not feel the need of daily forgiveness and continued sanctification, you are not a child of God, and can not from your heart pray the Lord's Prayer; for in this prayer we say: "Forgive us our trespasses." You can not receive forgiveness, if you do not ask it; for in that case you are not in the estate of grace, and have no part in Jesus O, how important it is that we

know **our** sin and obtain mercy! It **is the** only way in which we can
continue in grace, increase in holiness, and become every day more
pure in all our conversation. — But he whom the Lord has made clean,
and whose feet are washed by him from day to day, can and shall also
wash the feet of others. That is to say: He must serve the brethren
in devoted love, bear with their faults, hide their infirmities, and help
them to become better. This is what the Lord would have us do. Let
none of his disciples regard himself as too good to bend down and wash
a brother's feet, however unclean they may be; and let none look on
with unconcern when his brother strays into filthy paths and defiles
himself with sin. Do as the Lord did. He was conscious of being
the Almighty God, and yet he washed the feet of his sinful disciples.
The *greatest* man is most humble. None save *Jesus* can make us clean;
yet we also shall wash one another. He that understands this, let him
practice it! He will find herein the true joy of life. — O, that I may
be pure in thy sight, O Lord, and that I may have need only to wash
the feet! Let me not be among those unhappy ones who will not
allow thee to wash them. Sanctify me, O Lord; wash my feet. Let
no filth of sin cling to me; sanctify me *wholly* and *entirely*, in spirit
and soul and body. Give me humility and charity, that I may cheerfully wash the feet of the brethren. Give me to be like-minded unto
thee, that I may do that which thou hast done. Amen.

Loving Jesus, gentle lamb, In thy gracious hands I am: Make me,
Savior, what thou art, Live thyself within my heart.
I shall then show forth thy praise, Serve thee all my happy days: Then
the world shall always see, Christ, the holy child, in me.

---

170. Thursday in Holy Week. II.

Wash us, O Lord, and clothe us, and make us worthy guests at thy table. Amen.

1 Corinthians 11, 23-29. For I have received of the Lord that which also
I delivered unto you, That the Lord Jesus, the same night in which he was
betrayed, took bread: and when he had given thanks, he brake it, and said.
Take, eat; this is my body, which is broken for you: this do in remembrance
of me. After the same manner also he took the cup, when he had supped,
saying, This cup is the new testament in my blood: this do ye, as oft as ye
drink it, in remembrance of me. For as often as ye eat this bread, and drink
this cup, ye do shew the Lord's death till he come. Wherefore, whosoever
shall eat this bread, and drink this cup of the Lord, unworthily, shall be guilty
of the body and blood of the Lord. But let a man examine himself, and so
let him eat of that bread, and drink of that cup. For he that eateth and
drinketh unworthily, eateth and drinketh damnation to himself, not discerning
the Lord's body.

Among the things which the Lord revealed to Paul was instruction
in regard to the Holy Supper. How important a matter is this sacrament, and how full of meaning! It was instituted in the most solemn
night of the Lord's life on earth; and after his ascension to heaven
he gives Paul instruction concerning this sacrament, at the time of

calling him to the office of an apostle To Paul he repeats the exact words which he used when instituting the sacrament. The account which Paul gives after his meeting with the Savior tallies exactly with what the other apostles report in regard to the events of the night in which he was betrayed. Let us understand that the Holy Supper is of more importance in our Christian life than words can express; and let us therefore hold it in highest esteem, and approach it with reverence.

It was on this Thursday evening that he sat with his disciples in a room in Jerusalem. He had already sacrificed himself, and had been anointed as one who had already died for our sins. And now, before finally yielding up his spirit, this night, while eating the passover with his disciples, it is his will to institute this sacrament, which gives us his body and blood to eat and drink, and which carries us back to the time and place of his death of atonement for our sins. In the hour of his death it must be done, that we may not only receive his body and blood, which he sacrificed for us, but may also sit at the altar on which the sacrifice was made, and shew the Lord's death. He took bread, gave thanks, brake it, and said: *Take, eat; this is my body which is broken for you.* After the same manner also he took the cup, when he had supped, saying: *This cup is the new testament in my blood; this ye do, as oft as ye drink it, in remembrance of me.* The *Lamb of the passover* in a striking way *represents* Jesus; but that is all. Here, in this new sacrament, we surely must have something more than a mere sign or symbol; and the Lord declares in express words: *This is my body.* With divine omnipotence he gives the disciples his glorified and heavenly body, even while he still sits among them in the form of a servant; and by his almighty word he commands that the bread and wine of the sacrament shall, for all time, give us his true body and blood. As surely as Jesus is truthful and almighty, the Sacrament of the altar is "the true body and blood of our Lord Jesus Christ, under the bread and wine." But while the bread does not merely *represent* the body of Christ, neither does it *cease* to be bread, and become the body of the Lord instead. No; when you eat the bread of the sacrament, *the Lord gives therein his body.* He makes no mention of the bread, he speaks as you would in administering medicine to the sick. You call it after the healing drug which it contains, and say nothing about the water in which you give it. Because the body and blood of Christ is *united with* bread and wine in the sacrament, Paul says: "The cup of blessing which we bless, is it not the communion of the blood of Christ? The bread which we break, is it not the communion of the body of Christ?" What a precious thing is this sacrament! And it shall remain unchanged and unchangeable to the end of time; and the Christians who partake of it thereby proclaim their faith, that Christ, the Son of God, died, and lives, and shall come again in his glory.

The Christians of our day do not come as often as they should to the Lord's table. The earliest Christians partook of this sacrament much more frequently. Is it not highly necessary in our case also to be strengthened in faith, quickened in love, to be more firmly estab-lished in hope, to come nearer to Jesus, to taste his divine goodness, to have a powerful reminder of his death, to be led deeper into communion with him in his suffering, to be more closely knit together in brotherly love, to be made more zealous in bearing witness concerning our Savior; in short, to become more Christlike? O, how great is our need of all this! Therefore, dear brethren in the Lord; make more diligent use of this sacrament than has heretofore been your practice. There is no other place here below where Christ comes so near to us. In this sacrament he has agreed to meet you; here he gives himself to you; here you are with him in that awful night of his suffering and death; here the fire of love sets your soul aglow; for himself has said: "He that eateth my flesh and drinketh my blood dwelleth in me, and I in him." Blessed supper, in which my Lord Jesus himself is set before me! I will come often to this thrice blessed feast.

Now, since the Holy Supper is the body and blood of the Lord, by virtue of his own word, so that all, believers and unbelievers, who partake of it, eat and drink the body and blood of Jesus; it is of paramount importance that we examine ourselves. The Spirit of God testifies that if you receive this sacrament unworthily, you are guilty of the Lord's body and blood. You outrage the Lord himself, you betray him, you give him the kiss of Judas, you crucify and blaspheme him; you eat and drink damnation to yourself! In God's name, examine yourself! He will give you the necessary light. But if you know yourself as one indeed unworthy, and sincerely desire to be cleansed of sin; and if you believe that the gifts received are the body and blood of Christ, then you are properly prepared to partake of this Supper. Do not neglect it, as do the many who despise the Lord's command: "Do this in remembrance of me."

Help us, O God, to come often and in the right way to thy Supper, there to be strengthened in our faith, to be made sure of thy favor, and to enter into a closer communion with thee and with all the saints. Guard us from the danger of eating and drinking damnation to ourselves. Forgive us the sins which we have committed when partaking of Holy Communion; and, when we come to thy Supper, do thou carry us back over time and space, that we may be with thee and the twelve on that Thursday night in the room in Jerusalem, and there may forget all things else, and taste nothing save thy love. Amen.

Come, ye disconsolate, where'er ye languish, Come to the mercy-seat, fervently kneel; Here bring your wounded hearts, here tell your anguish; Earth has no sorrow that heaven cannot heal.
Here see the bread of life; see waters flowing Forth from the throne of God, pure from above; Come to the feast of love; come ever knowing: Earth has no sorrow but heaven can remove.

---

171. Good Friday. I.

O, thou Lamb of God that didst take away the sins of the world, have mercy on us.

John 19, 30. Luke 23, 46. When Jesus therefore had received the vinegar, he said, It is finished: and he bowed his head, and gave up the ghost. And when Jesus had cried with a loud voice, he said, Father, into thy hands I commend my spirit: and having said thus, he gave up the ghost.

221

Every prophecy in regard to the work and the passion ot the Messiah in his estate of lowliness has now been brought to its conclusion; Jesus has fulfilled everything which the law demands of us. He has made complete satisfaction for us all. *"It is finished."* This truth is the one which I need more than anything else in the world. *"For that he hath done this,"* says the Twenty-second Psalm, therefore the kingdom is the Lord's, and there is salvation for Jew and gentile, for high and low, from the first sinner to the last on earth, for all, from one end of the earth to the other. *All* is finished, for me and for all men. The law condemns me; for I have disobeyed it; but Christ sets me free, for he has kept it in my stead, and has suffered the punishment which I had deserved. He has redeemed me; his is the kingdom, and I belong to him. The work of Christ embraces every work necessary for our justification; all is finished, and there is no room for any work of ours by which we might hope to attain righteousness. *He has done it all;* and in his kingdom, therefore, the questions as to any merit on our part, or as to the power of the law to save or to condemn, have been finally disposed of; for that which he has done is done, and is not *to be done* by any other. Hence he says: "Come; *for all things are now ready."* This will I proclaim aloud; O, that it might resound to the ends of the earth! This will I confess while I live; and when my last hour comes I will bid the world farewell, bow my head in death, and commend my soul to God, trusting in his' declaration: *"It is finished."*

The first words spoken by the Lord on the cross, and the last, were a *prayer to the Father.* What he said, from the first word to the last, we have heard. How much he suffered none can say, nor even faintly surmise. And all was done for our sake. By reason of his having done this for me, and having baptized me into his death, he is with me and in me; and in every affliction and in my dying hour I therefore can say: "Heavenly Father, hear my prayer, and save me." Thus Stephen in the midst of death was able to pray: "Lord Jesus, receive my spirit." And Luther: "Into thy hand I commit my spirit; thou hast redeemed me, O Lord God of truth." (Psalm 31, 5). Whosoever believes in Jesus and lives in him, the Victor over death, shall with him go from earth to paradise. Live and suffer every day trusting in these shouts of victory from the lips of Jesus: "It is finished," "Father, into thy hands I commend my spirit." When you do this you are absolved and dead from the law; and in your dying hour the faithful Holy Spirit shall whisper these words of Jesus into your soul. Then you can not perish; but, as God lives, you shall enter into life everlasting.

"May my soul be calm and fearless As I lie expecting death; May thy love so great and peerless Lauded be with my last breath. When at last I fall asleep, Dearest Jesus, may I keep Firm the faith that life and heaven By thy death to me were given." Amen.

For thy sorrows we adore thee, For the pains that wrought our peace; Gracious Savior! we implore thee, In our souls thy love increase.
Here we feel our sins forgiven, While upon the land we gaze; And our thoughts are all of heaven, And our lips o'erflow with praise.

172. Good Friday. II.

Lord Jesus, may our faith in thy blood be firmly established on the truth of the scriptures. Amen.

John 19, 31-37. The Jews therefore, because it was the preparation, that the bodies should not remain upon the cross on the sabbath day, (for that sabbath day was an high day,) besought Pilate that their legs might be broken, and that they might be taken away. Then came the soldiers, and brake the legs of the first, and of the other which was crucified with him. But when they came to Jesus, and saw that he was dead already, they brake not his legs: but one of the soldiers with a spear pierced his side, and forthwith came thereout blood and water. And he that saw it bare record, and his record is true; and he knoweth that he saith true, that ye might believe. For these things were done, that the scripture should be fulfilled, A bone of him shall not be broken. And again another scripture saith, They shall look on him whom they pierced.

As the Victor over death Jesus commits his spirit to his Father, and his body to the grave. Nevertheless he felt the inevitable agony at the moment of dissolution; for this, also, was a part of the wages of sin. But this was the end of his sufferings; and his head sinks upon his breast; life has departed from the sacred body. The soul has winged its flight to paradise. How did the angelic host receive him? What say Death and Hell now? Do they still refuse to admit defeat? The fight is over whether or no; the victory is the Lord's and — ours for evermore!

Our passover is sacrificed; and now come the soldiers to break the legs of the two thieves. Shall they not break his also? No; the scripture forbids it. (Exodus 12, 46). His body is not to be mutilated; they are not permitted to maim it. Thus they are made to fulfil yet another passage of scripture, Zechariah 12, 10, — all parts of the Bible are linked together in Christ. They pierce his side, and bring the water of life for our souls to flow from his heart. The lamb was to be sacrificed for us; but we may at all times sprinkle its blood on our hearts and be safe from the angel of death. The words of the gospel are: "And forthwith came there out blood and water." In his epistle the same John writes: "This is he that came by water and blood, even Jesus Christ; not by water only, but by water and blood; . . . there are three that bear witness in earth, the spirit, and the water, and the blood; and these three agree in one." (1 John 5). St. Augustine writes: "Even as from the side of the sleeping Adam a rib was taken and made into a woman, to whom Adam said that she was bone of his bone and flesh of his flesh; in like manner did Christ, the heavenly Adam, fall asleep on the cross; and from his side came there out blood and water, the sacraments of the new covenant, by which he builds up his bride, the church; concerning which the apostle says: 'For we are members of his body, of his flesh, and of his bones.'" Jesus Christ died on the cross for our sins; "he died for our sins according to the scriptures." This is certainly true; for God has said it. John did not doubt it; and Paul and all the other apostles were equally confident. But it is quite

as certain, according to the testimony of the apostles and of all the
scriptures, that we, who are baptized into him, have a part in the blood
and water which flowed from his side in the hour of his death. On
so sure a foundation does our faith rest; and there is nothing can shake
our hope of everlasting life through the death of the Son of God. But
whosoever does not believe, and does not surrender his heart to this
truth, makes God a liar in the highest revelation of his love, and
tramples the blood of Jesus under foot. God deliver us from this
danger.

I thank thee, Lord Jesus, for thy death; for the blood and water
from thy side; for thy full and perfect atonement; and for the holy
means of grace, through which thou dost make me a partaker in thy
salvation. Thou knowest that I yearn after thee; thou knowest that
of my heart I ask of thee this favor, that I may have a place among
the needy sinners who stand at the foot of thy cross, and who are
cleansed by thy sacred blood. Thou knowest how precious these fountains of life are to my soul, how happy I am to dwell in thy church on
earth and there enjoy them. But, alas, Lord Jesus, sin and unbelief
still have a strong hold on me. Precious, faithful Savior, increase my
faith; and let me daily die with thee, and live in thee alway. Lord
Jesus, be thou my life. Sanctify me, and wash me, and kindle the fire
of thy love in my poor soul. How blest I would be, if I could of my
whole heart live for thee. Grant me, grant us all this blessing, thou
most loving and precious Savior. Amen.

Sweet the moments, rich in blessing, Which before the cross we spend;
Life, and health, and peace possessing, From the sinner's dying friend.
Truly blessed is this station, Low before his cross to lie, While we see
divine compassion Beaming in his gracious eye,

---

173. Saturday in Holy Week.

Lord Jesus, make it clear to our faith that thou hast made of the grave a
place of pleasant slumber. Amen.

Matthew 27, 57–66. When the even was come, there came a rich man of
Arimathæa, named Joseph, who also himself was Jesus' disciple: he went to
Pilate, and begged the body of Jesus. Then Pilate commanded the body
to be delivered. And when Joseph had taken the body, he wrapped it in a
clean linen cloth, and laid it in his own new tomb, which he had hewn out in
the rock: and he rolled a great stone to the door of the sepulchre, and departed. And there was Mary Magdalene, and the other Mary, sitting over
against the sepulchre. Now the next day, that followed the day of the preparation, the chief priests and Pharisees came together unto Pilate, saying,
Sir, we remember that that deceiver said, while he was yet alive, After three
days I will rise again. Command therefore that the sepulchre be made sure
until the third day, lest his disciples come by night, and steal him away, and
say unto the people, He is risen from the dead; so the last error shall be
worse than the first. Pilate said unto them, Ye have a watch: go your way,
make it as sure as ye can. So they went, and made the sepulchre sure, sealing
the stone, and setting a watch.

None of the disciples of Jesus had the courage or the strength to inter his body. Shall it, then, be thrown into the valley of Hinnom to be eaten by the dogs? The mere question wounds us and seems sacrilegious. Have no fear; for it is written by the prophet Isaiah that his body would be delivered to a rich man, and that a watch of wicked men would be set to guard his sepulchre. (Isaiah 53). The Father in heaven has caused a rich man, a member of the high council, to hew out in the rock a tomb for himself in his garden near Calvary; and now God puts it into this man's mind to ask for the body of Jesus and to give it burial in his own new tomb. But the high priests are to fulfil the prophecy in regard to the watch; and thus they are compelled, against their will and in more ways than one, to make more sure our faith in the resurrection of our Lord. For not only does the setting of the watch at the grave furnish proof of the truth of scripture; but all that transpired, with the flight of the soldiers and their lying account of what had taken place, is most conclusive evidence that the Lord is risen and the sepulchre empty.

"Set a watch, and seal the stone well; — the earth shall tremble, and your seal be broken, and the stone thrown aside. The situation is changed, and the power is yours no longer. All that you could do was to deliver him into the hands of the governor to be crucified. Now that the soul of Jesus has found rest in paradise, and has vanquished death; now that all the saints in heaven are making ready for the joyous Easter jubilee, your power even over the body of Jesus is at an end. You may seal the grave, if you like; him you shall see no more. Go your ways; and fare well, if you can. Soon you shall hear something, and be forced to step aside to make way for the triumphal car of the Crucified One. You have rejected the precious stone; but he is become the chief stone of the corner. He shall crush you, or you shall be broken on him, if you do not soon wake up and repent.

"Gentle Jesus, victorious Hero; thy body lies in the grave from Friday until Sunday! Who can say why thou didst rest so long, or why thou didst not rise again sooner? Who knows what took place in paradise during these three days? Blessed mystery, which thy Spirit shall explain to us in the next world. Certain it is that thou didst not shun or avoid the condition in which the blessed dead now are, and into which we soon shall enter. For thou wast out of the body, as other souls are, and thy body rested as a deserted habitation of God, alone and lifeless in the grave. If thou art become like unto us, we shall become like unto thee; and no fear shall keep us back from the path which thou didst tread; for thou hast sanctified it and robbed it of every danger and terror." (Loehe).

To the unbelievers death is terrible, and the grave full of horrors. They are forced to tell themselves that the dark, cold tomb is the end and all of their course, the comfort and reward for all their labor and their struggles, the unutterably sad and hopeless answer to their longing and groping and questioning. Alas they are forced to go further, and to tell themselves that there is beyond the grave something yet more dark awaiting them because they serve sin. — But rejoice, ye believers! *Your* grave is the grave of *Jesus,* and his grave is yours. For was it not for *our* sin that he died? He died *our* death, and he slept in *our* grave; what is our burial, then, but the laying of our bodies to rest in the grave of Jesus? — God give us faith! The grave still seems so dark to me. I am weary and wish to go to rest; but I would like to have another bed. And yet; where could I hope to find a better bed than the one in which thou didst rest, thou who art the resurrection and the life? Praise be to thee, Lord Jesus, for thy burial; for this and for all other benefits! Amen.

Teach us to know that Jesus died, And rose again, our souls to save; Teach us to take him as our guide, Our help from childhood tc the grave.
Then shall not death with terror come, But welcome as a bidden guest, The herald of a better home, The messenger of peace and rest.

174. Easter Day. I.

The voice of rejoicing and salvation is in the tabernacles of the righteous.

Gospel Lesson, Mark 16, 1–7. And when the sabbath was past, Mary Magdalene, and Mary the mother of James, and Salome, had brought sweet spices, that they might come and anoint him. And very early in the morning, the first day of the week, they came into the sepulchre at the rising of the sun. And they said among themselves, Who shall roll us away the stone from the door of the sepulchre? And when they looked, they saw that the stone was rolled away: for it was very great. And entering into the sepulchre, they saw a young man sitting on the right side, clothed in a long white garment: and they were affrighted. And he saith unto them, Be not affrighted: Ye seek Jesus of Nazareth, which was crucified: he is risen; he is not here: behold the place where they laid him. But go your way, tell his disciples and Peter that he goeth before you into Galilee: there shall ye see him, as he said unto you.

"Who shall roll us away the stone from the door of the sepulchre?" anxiously inquired the women; but "when they looked, they saw that the stone was rolled away; for it was very great." The stone which imprisons us in death and the grave is sin. It is so large and heavy that no man and no angel could have removed it. It would without any question have held us for ever in the cave of death, separated from God, shut out from all life and light. But Jesus has taken away sin, and burst open the grave; then the angel rolls the stone away, that the victory may become known. Go to the grave of Jesus; and behold, the stone is rolled away! He who died for the sins of the world, and who said, "It is finished," *he is risen,* and the truth of his announcement has been established. If he had not in truth fully paid for our sins and fulfilled all things for us, the death to which he delivered himself would have held him bound. Now we know of a certainty that he is risen; and hence it is clear that the cup of death has been drained to the dregs, and that the whole burden of sin has been taken away. The stone is rolled away. Should sin still rest heavy on your conscience, and death still have terrors for you, then bear in

15

mind that you are baptized into him who was dead and is alive, and that hence you are dead with him and risen again with him. Sin has no more any right to cause you death. In Christ death *has* already been suffered; *it is finished.* — Neither shall death be able to make your heart a grave filled with death's ugly brood, a habitation for the evil powers of darkness. You are united with the *living* Christ; you are one with him, over whom death has no authority whatever. Christ is risen; therefore the stone is rolled away. Christ is risen; and thereby sin is vanquished, and death destroyed. To me there is nothing, and can be nothing, more grand than the declaration of Paul (2 Tim. 1, 10), that "Jesus Christ hath abolished death." Death, this terrible reality; death abolished, done away with! Hallelujah! O, that we might make our shout of victory heard in all the earth! Verily, death is abolished, death for us and death in us. We are saved from the greatest of all terrors; for we are members of *his* body, who died and rose again, and are one with him in his death and in his resurrection. To be sure, our faith still is weak; but it is founded on the word of God, and is therefore stronger than all the gates of hell.

The grave of Jesus is the door to all graves in which the bodies of the faithful are laid to rest. The seal is broken, and the stone rolled away; he is the resurrection and the life. "He that believeth in me, though he were dead, yet shall he live; and whosoever liveth and believeth in me shall never die." (John 11, 25. 26). My reader, believest thou this? There is no doubt whatever of its truth; himself, who is the truth, has spoken it, and you may trust in it with absolute safety. Blessed are you, if you believe! Yes, blessed is every one who *in truth believes*, even though his faith be weak and he be obliged to fight continually against unbelief. — How shall I thank thee, Lord Jesus, for thy victory over death and the devil, and for life, everlasting life, which thou hast given me! Grant me grace to live for thee while life endures, to confess thy name by walking in godliness, and to bring forth much fruit for thy kingdom. And let me then for ever lie at the foot of thy throne with praise and thanksgiving. Thou knowest that it is my innermost heart which says: Blessed be thy glorious name evermore! How blest shall I be to praise thee with a new tongue in thy kingdom for ever and ever! Amen.

Christ the Lord is risen today, Sons of men and angels say; Raise your joys and triumphs high, Sing, ye heavens, and earth reply.
Lives again our glorious king; Where, O death, is now thy sting? Dying once, he all doth save; Where thy victory, O grave?

175. Easter Day. II.

Lord Jesus, our living Savior; quicken us, and sanctify us with thee. Amen.

Epistle Lesson, 1 Corinthians 5, 7. 8. Purge out therefore the old leaven, that ye may be a new lump, as ye are unleavened. For even Christ our passover is sacrificed for us: Therefore let us keep the feast, not with old leaven, neither with the leaven of malice and wickedness; but with the unleavened bread of sincerity and truth.

The use of leaven was, under penalty of death, prohibited among the children of Israel during the Easter festival. *They* ate the passover every year; and with the faith of our heart *we* eat the true passover all the time. Christ was sacrificed for us, and they that believe in him live in communion with him alway, and celebrate Easter without ceasing. "Except ye eat the flesh of the Son of Man, and drink his blood, ye have no life in you." (John 6, 63). Reference is here had to the union of the *heart* with Jesus. In this union only is there life. But do you hear what the apostle says in regard to the leaven? Do you remember that the leaven is prohibited, and that it is death itself? "The old leaven" is the nature and life of the natural man. War must be made on *all* the lusts of the flesh, even as the Israelites were to have no leaven in the house at the time of Easter. It means death, if you again conclude peace with any of your carnal lusts. "The leaven of malice and wickedness" means an evil and deceitful mind. Is it possible, do you think, that hate and anger, the spirit of Esau and Saul, can be united with Jesus, who is all love? Or how should malice, deceit, and craftiness be connected in any way with our holy and blameless Lamb of the passover? No, sincerity and truth shall be our bread. You, the Lord's believers, are a new lump, unleavened and pure; and this is what you *should* be. The passover is sacrificed; and thereby you *are become* a new lump, says the apostle. How happy we would be, did we but understand the word of God and believe the truth! As you *are* a new lump you can and shall purge out the old leaven. Your whole life shall be a life in sincerity and truth. It shall be lived in the power of Christ's resurrection and in the fellowship of his suffering. Your whole life shall be on a high plane; you shall not wallow in the mire of sin, but climb the heights, bathe in the sunshine of truth and holiness, and breathe the pure and heavenly spirit of Jesus. In like manner as a leaven leavens the whole lump, so shall the new life, the life of Christ's resurrection, be manifest in all that you do. It is a life of the heart, and must be seen in every act down to the least important, even as the heart-beat sends the blood coursing through the body out into the tips of the fingers.

God help us to be true believers, and to lead a life of true holiness. Amen.

The strife is o'er, the battle done! The victory of life is won; The song of triumph has begun, Hallelujah!
The powers of death have done their worst, But Christ their legions hath dispersed; Let shouts of holy joy outburst, Hallelujah!

176. Easter Monday. I.

Come, Lord Jesus, and speak to our hearts. Amen.

Gospel Lesson, Luke 24, 13–35. And behold, two of them went that same day to a village called Emmaus, which was from Jerusalem about threescore furlongs. And they talked together of all these things which had happened. And it came to pass, that while they communed together and reasoned, Jesus himself drew near, and went with them. But their eyes were holden, that they should not know him. And he said unto them. What manner of communications are these, that ye have one to another, as ye walk, and are sad? And the one of them, whose name was Cleopas, answering said unto him, Art thou only a stranger in Jerusalem, and hast not known the things which are come to pass there in these days? And he said unto them, What things? And they said unto him, Concerning Jesus of Nazareth, which was a prophet mighty in deed and word before God and all the people: And now the chief priests and our rulers delivered him to be condemned to death, and have crucified him. But we trusted that it had been he which should have redeemed Israel: and beside all this, today is the third day since these things were done. Yea, and certain women also of our company made us astonished, which were early at the sepulchre; and when they found not his body, they came, saying, that they had also seen a vision of angels, which said that he was alive. And certain of them which were with us went to the sepulchre, and found it even so as the women had said: but him they saw not. Then he said unto them, O fools, and slow of heart to believe all that the prophets have spoken! Ought not Christ to have suffered these things, and to enter into his glory? And beginning at Moses, and all the prophets, he expounded unto them in all the scriptures the things concerning himself. And they drew nigh unto the village whither they went: and he made as though he would have gone further. But they constrained him, saying, Abide with us: for it is toward evening, and the day is far spent. And he went in to tarry with them. And it came to pass, as he sat at meat with them, he took bread, and blessed it, and brake, and gave to them. And their eyes were opened, and they knew him; and he vanished out of their sight. And they said one to another, Did not our heart burn within us, while he talked with us by the way, and while he opened to us the scriptures? And they rose up the same hour, and returned to Jerusalem, and found the eleven gathered together, and them that were with them. Saying, The Lord is risen indeed, and hath appeared to Simon. And they told what things were done in the way, and how he was known of them in breaking of bread.

You never walk alone, dear Christian, but at all times in the grandest company. You have, no doubt, made the acquaintance of many most excellent men ; and while travelling together you have conversed piously, as Christians should. When you have done this, he who is greater than all has been with you. Where two or three believers speak together of the Lord, he is always near ; and the hearts, of a certainty, receive a blessing. But you have also often walked alone with him, in the bright morning of the new day and at night in darkness and gloom. In the scripture he has spoken to your heart, and you have taken courage to speak to him. He has resolved your doubts, and changed your lamentation into a song of joy. At times you have forgotten him, but still he has walked with you, and has never for one moment forgotten you. He often disappeared from your view ; but still he was near ; and he always revealed himself anew to you, either in the congregation of the brethren when you were hearing the word or partaking of the sacrament, or in the secrecy of your chamber when you read the word and bent the knee in prayer. — If you have a wife, or a husband, who loves the Lord, or if you live with other friends in

God, do not let Satan hinder you from speaking with one another concerning those things which came to pass in Jerusalem at the time of Easter. Let him who is the fulfilment of the scriptures, and who in these same sacred writings reveals himself to us, obtain a hearing among you. In other words, seek light and counsel in the Bible in regard to every concern of your soul; and he shall surely speak to you, and guide you into all truth. You shall see more and more clearly that Christ is that Sun of righteousness whose light, according to the eternal and loving purpose of God, was to flood the world after the multitude of beams more or less bright which had pierced the darkness during the times of the Old Testament. You shall see that this Sun must rise on the world in this way; that in him righteousness and mercy kiss each other, and that hence he ought to suffer and die. As God's eternal nature and will are, so is his eternal decree; as it was decreed, so it is written; and as it is written, so it *ought* to be, and so *it has come to pass.* And your heart shall, on occasion at least, burn within you. — If you walk alone, dear reader, remember that you are not alone, if you have the scriptures and believe them. Open your eyes, and see. Verily, the living Savior is with you. Do you not see him? Do you not believe that he is near, and that he sees and hears you? Walk with him; speak to him; pray to him, saying: "Abide with me, Lord. Abide with us; for it is toward evening, and the day is far spent!" He tarried with the two disciples in Emmaus; and in the evening he walked with them, though not in visible form, when they returned to Jerusalem. He will do likewise with us. Through the world's darkness we go, in company with the Invisible One, to the brethren in Jerusalem; — there we shall see him as he is. We thank thee, precious Savior, for this mercy; and we pray thee: Expound to us the scriptures, that our hearts may burn within us. Amen.

Abide with me! fast falls the eventide; The darkness deepens; Lord, with me abide! When other helpers fail, and comforts flee, Help of the helpless, O abide with me!
Swift to its close ebbs out life's little day; Earth's joys grow dim, its glories pass away; Change and decay in all around I see; O thou who changest not, abide with me!

177. Easter Monday. II.

O God, give us honest hearts. Amen.

Acts 10, 34–41. Then Peter opened his mouth, and said, Of a truth I perceive that God is no respecter of persons: But in every nation he that feareth him, and worketh righteousness, is accepted with him. The word which God sent unto the children of Israel, preaching peace by Jesus Christ: (he is Lord of all:) That word, I say, ye know, which was published throughout all Judæa, and began from Galilee, after the baptism which John preached; how God anointed Jesus of Nazareth with the Holy Ghost and with power; who went about doing good, and healing all that were oppressed of the devil: for God was with him. And we are witnesses of all things which he did, both in the land of the Jews, and in Jerusalem; whom they slew and hanged on a tree: Him God raised up the third day, and shewed him openly; not to all the people, but unto witnesses chosen before of God, even to us, who did eat and drink with him after he rose from the dead.

Jesus went about in Galilee and all the land doing good, and healing all that were oppressed. *Not one sought his assistance in vain.* He received all that came, of all sorts and conditions, and never once refused aid to one who needed it. Let all note this: *There is not one single instance in which Jesus failed to relieve misery when it came to him.* Grace and mercy shine forth in his every act. After his death and resurrection he is no longer in Galilee, or in the whole land of the Jews, only; but he is in all places where human hearts, of whatever race, long for him. For he loves all; he has redeemed all by his death on the cross, and he has healing and salvation for one and all. The preaching of peace through Jesus Christ unto the children of Israel is to be continued; but the glad tidings shall be proclaimed to all gentiles also; and himself is with his witnesses alway unto the end of the world. The apostles eat and drink with him after resurrection. In invisible form he is in their midst everywhere, and reveals himself whenever it pleases him to do so. After the ascension and the outpouring of the Spirit they see him no more; but do you think that he is not with them? In their preaching he manifests his power in glorious fashion, gives them victory everywhere, tears down the ramparts of Satan, and makes manifest through his disciples the sweet savor of his knowledge in every place. — Go out confidently, then, with the words of the Savior, ye his witnesses! You shall never, never go alone. Live all the time with him in faith; and preach his death and resurrection as something in which you have your life, as something which you have yourselves *experienced.* His peace shall obtain victory in your heart; and he shall manifest his victorious strength in his word, which you preach. Shall not he, who even in his lowly estate on earth healed all that were oppressed of the devil, send out his power from his throne of glory, and force the devil to retreat before the truth and life in the gospel of peace? Or, peradventure, he no longer desires to save man? "Jesus Christ is the same yesterday, and today, and for ever." (Hebrews 13, 8). God help us, that we may no longer be faithless, but believing!

O praise the Lord, all ye nations; praise him all ye people. For his merciful kindness is great toward us; and the truth of the Lord endureth for ever. Hallelujah! Amen.

Let every kindred, every tribe, On this terrestrial ball, To him all majesty ascribe, And crown him Lord of all.
O that with yonder sacred throng We at his feet may fall; Join in the .everlasting song, And crown him Lord of all!

178. Tuesday after Easter Day.

Lord, increase our faith. Amen.

Luke 24, 36–48. And as they thus spake, Jesus himself stood in the midst of them, and saith unto them, Peace be unto you. But they were terrified and affrighted, and supposed that they had seen a spirit. And he said unto them, Why are ye troubled? and why do thoughts arise in your hearts? Behold my hands and my feet, that it is I myself: handle me, and see; for a spirit hath not flesh and bones, as ye see me have. And when he had thus spoken, he shewed them his hands and his feet. And while they yet believed not for joy, and wondered, he said unto them, Have ye here any meat? And they gave him a piece of a broiled fish, and of an honey-comb. And he took it, and did eat before them. And he said unto them, These are the words which I spake unto you, while I was yet with you, that all things must be fulfilled, which were written in the law of Moses, and in the prophets, and in the psalms, concerning me. Then opened he their understanding, that they might understand the scriptures, and said unto them, Thus it is written, and thus it behoved Christ to suffer, and to rise from the dead the third day: And that repentance and remission of sins should be preached in his name among all nations, beginning at Jerusalem. And ye are witnesses of these things.

Jesus showed the disciples his hands and feet with the print of the nails by which he had been suspended to the cross, that they might make sure of its being he and none other. When he comes again we shall know him by these same prints. The Lord really has his wounds still, but in transfigured form. He is the same on the throne as on the cross, God and man in one person, the crucified and risen Savior. After death he might have resumed his body without its scars, had he wished it; but it was his will to show them to the Father and the angels, as well as to his accuser; and, as for us, we have reason to hold them dear; for they speak our cause before God. He that died for us, the same lives for us with the atoning and saving grace of his death.

In the meantime, our eye can not see him; for this is precisely the condition which God has fixed in regard to our salvation, that we must *believe* without having seen. "For we walk by faith, not by sight." But how, then, shall we find him, and be assured that we are with him, and that he is with us, and that it is he himself? For on this our life depends, and here we must not build on dreams, nor on human wisdom; here, if anywhere, it is necessary that we have a sure foundation under our feet. O that the Spirit might declare this truth to your heart! Pay attention, then, to that which you read in this gospel text. He sends his apostles, who were eye witnesses of his death and resurrection, out into the world to gather people to him; and he promises to be with them in this work. But they could no more than we point to the print of the nails and exhibit his scars to the eye; they could and should only *preach the gospel and baptize.* Herein his scars are plainly enough to be seen by the eye of faith. Where repentance and forgiveness are preached he is himself present and creates faith, as surely as he was with the ten disciples and brought conviction to them and caused them to believe. Let us not, as did the Pharisees, seek a sign from heaven; but let us hear the word and study the scriptures. Are not these all the signs that we need? They are precisely the right signs, certain, clear, and infallible. For the Lord himself is in them. Through them Jesus is in truth come to us with his death and resurrection, with peace and pardon. What more do you desire? By these means the Holy Spirit creates faith in your heart, if you do not stubbornly resist him. What more do you need? If you refuse to *believe, that* will be your condemnation. Whosoever believeth hath life in his name.

Precious Savior, thou art at the right hand of God and dost make intercession for us; and thou art here and dost reveal thyself to our heart. We thank thee for thy holy word and thy worthy sacraments; we will ask no other sign, and will seek thee in no other place. Nevertheless, thou knowest how hard a fight we still have against the unbelief in our heart. We pray thee, increase our faith, open the scriptures to us, give us a simple and childlike spirit, keep us by thy side, and give us grace to confess thee, and never to be offended by reason of thy cross. Amen.

He closed the yawning gates of hell; The bars from **heaven's high portals fell**; Let hymns of praise his triumphs tell; Hallelujah!
Lord! by the stripes which wounded thee, From death's dread sting thy **servants** free, That we may live, and sing to thee, Hallelujah!

---

179. Wednesday after Easter Day.

O God, let our hope of resurrection be grounded in the resurrection of Christ. Amen.

John 20, 1–10. The first day of the week cometh Mary Magdalene early, when it was yet dark, unto the sepulchre, and seeth the stone taken away from the sepulchre. Then she runneth, and cometh to Simon Peter, and to the other disciple, whom Jesus loved, and saith unto them, They have taken away the Lord out of the sepulchre, and we know not where they have laid him. Peter therefore went forth, and that other disciple, and came to the sepulchre. So they ran both together: and the other disciple did outrun Peter, and came first to the sepulchre. And he, stooping down, and looking in, saw the linen clothes lying; yet went he not in. Then cometh Simon Peter following him, and went into the sepulchre, and seeth the linen clothes lie, and the napkin, that was about his head, not lying with the linen clothes, but wrapped together in a place by itself. Then went in also that other disciple, which came first to the sepulchre, and he saw, and believed. For as yet they knew not the scripture, that he must rise again from the dead. Then the disciples went away again unto their own home.

The stone is rolled away, and the sepulchre is open; the Lord is not there; the linen clothes remain, and the napkin is wrapped together in a place by itself. Everything contradicts the assumption that enemies have despoiled the grave; nor is it possible that his friends have removed his body. — The grave is a tenement of death no more; nothing remains in it save the trappings of death. This is the grave of Jesus; but his grave is my grave. For whose sin did he die? It must have been for ours; for himself had none. It is, then, *our* death which he dies; but then it also is *our* grave in which he is buried. Does any one doubt that the eyes of Mary and Peter and John told them the truth; that the sepulchre was empty? That is a fact about which there can be no question, whether or no. But who can be supposed to have opened the grave and removed the body? The disciples could not have done it; for a watch had been set, and the stone had been sealed. Besides, such a thing would never have occurred to them; for they had no idea that he would, in fact, rise again from the dead. No; this is what has transpired, and to us it means eternal life: *He is risen; the grave is rent asunder; for the wages of sin has been paid, and death is swallowed up in life.* The scripture speaks true; and Jesus was in the right when he said that he would rise again on the third day. My grave still looks, to be sure, as though it were the tenement of death. The casket and the shroud and the napkin are there, and my body also, for a time; but my Jesus, who lay in the grave and arose again, has said: "I am the resurrection and the life; he that believeth in me, though he were dead, yet shall he live." (John 11, 25). The truth of this is evidenced to me by his open and empty sepulchre. My heart lives in Jesus; I may say that I feel, that the life which he gave, and which throbs in my innermost heart, is eternal and can not die. Nevertheless, that which is more sure and certain, a thousand times more certain than all things else, is his promise: "Because I live, ye shall live also." (John 14, 19). Because he is risen, we shall rise from the dead also.

Thou wilt shew me the path of life, O God; in thy presence is fulness of joy; at thy right hand there are pleasures for evermore. Give us grace to believe; give us the light of the Spirit, that we may have a true and living faith. Amen.

Jesus lives! thy terrors now Can no longer, death, appall me; Jesus lives! by this I know, From the grave he will recall me. Brighter scenes will then commence: This shall be my confidence.

Jesus lives! henceforth is death But the gate of life immortal; This shall calm my trembling breath, When I pass the gloomy portal. Faith shall cry, as fails each sense, "Lord, thou art my confidence."

180. Thursday after Easter Day.

Living Savior, reveal thyself to our heart. Amen.

John 20, 11-18. But Mary stood without at the sepulchre weeping: and as she wept, she stooped down, and looked into the sepulchre, and seeth two angels in white, sitting, the one at the head, and the other at the feet, where the body of Jesus had lain. And they say unto her, Woman, why weepest thou? She saith unto them, Because they have taken away my Lord, and I know not where they have laid him. And when she had thus said, she turned herself back, and saw Jesus standing, and knew not that it was Jesus. Jesus saith unto her, Woman, why weepest thou? whom seekest thou? She, supposing him to be the gardener, saith unto him, Sir, if thou have borne him hence, tell me where thou hast laid him, and I will take him away. Jesus saith unto her, Mary. She turned herself, and saith unto him, Rabboni; which is to say, Master. Jesus saith unto her, Touch me not; for I am not yet ascended to my Father: but go to my brethren, and say unto them, I ascend unto my Father, and your Father and to my God, and to your God. Mary Magdalene came and told the disciples that she had seen the Lord, and that he had spoken these things unto her.

The Lord had rescued Mary Magdalene out of the most wretched condition, into which she, by her sins, had plunged herself. He had saved her; had driven seven devils out of her. Now she was a new person, and she loved him with a living love. To her was given also the great honor and mercy of being the first to see him after his resurrection. Still, she had not as yet reached the perfection of saintliness. She clings too fondly to the earthly aspect of the Savior, though not, to be sure, in the same manner as the apostles. It is not probable that her mind was especially bent on seeing the Lord as a king, in order that she might reign with him; but her love still savoured somewhat of the senses, though we must by no means think of it as being in any way a carnal affection; and it had its roots in sight and sense, rather than in faith. "Tell me where thou hast laid him," she says, "and I will take him away." And Jesus says to her: "Touch me not; for I am not yet ascended to my Father." She was to see his holiness and greatness and divine majesty in a new light, and learn to say: "We know Christ no more after the flesh." Her love was in need of being purified; the Spirit of God must unite it with a holy reverence for the exalted Son of God. And yet, how gently does he not correct her! He speaks her name, "Mary;" and in the tone there is nothing but kindness. Then he adds only, "touch me not;" and her heart quakes with awe, and does penance.

It were to be wished that all Christians had a mind as zealous and pure as that of Mary Magdalene. The kind of carnality which Paul especially rebuked in the Corinthians, namely, envy, contentions, and heresies, is not the only one among us. There are various kinds of sensuality more secret and more dangerous. We are acquainted with it, and we know how it gnaws at the heart unless we fight against it with all our strength; but we also know and testify that the Spirit of God gives victory to the upright. *All* the old leaven *must* be purged out, and by the grace of God it *shall* be done; for Christ is dead and risen again for us, we are baptized into his death, we eat and drink his body and blood, and our life in him is spiritual and heavenly. Make no terms, brethren, with any sort of carnality in you; but have a pure bridal spirit toward our heavenly bridegroom. Love him of your whole soul with a holy devotion, proclaim his death and resurrection everywhere, and love one another tenderly of a pure heart! Then shall you have great peace.

Lord, chasten us, and cleanse us, and draw our mind to thee in heaven. Amen.

Now let the heavens be joyful, Let earth her song begin, Let all the world keep triumph, And all that is therein: In grateful exultation, Their notes let all things blend, For Christ the Lord hath risen, Our joy that hath no end.

----

181. Friday after Easter Day.

Lord, show us the excellence of our heritage, and strengthen our hope. Amen.

Psalm 16. Michtam of David. Preserve me, O God: for in thee do I put my trust. O my soul, thou hast said unto the Lord, Thou art my Lord: my goodness extendeth not to thee; but to the saints that are in the earth, and to the excellent, in whom is all my delight. Their sorrows shall be multiplied that hasten after another god: their drink offerings of blood will I not offer, nor take up their names into my lips. The Lord is the portion of mine inheritance and of my cup: thou maintainest my lot. The lines are fallen unto me in pleasant places; yea, I have a goodly heritage. I will bless the Lord, who hath given me counsel; my reins also instruct me in the night seasons. I have set the Lord always before me: because he is at my right hand, I shall not be moved. Therefore my heart is glad, and my glory rejoiceth: my flesh also shall rest in hope. For thou wilt not leave my soul in hell; neither wilt thou suffer thine Holy One to see corruption. Thou wilt shew me the path of life: in thy presence is fulness of joy; at thy right hand there are pleasures for evermore.

This psalm was fulfilled in Christ when he rose from the dead. But the head, which is raised up, will not let the members remain in the grave. As many as are united with Jesus through a living faith can sing this psalm as applying to themselves; and they shall thereby stir their soul to rejoice in the Lord. What are the riches and honors of the world worth as compared with the bliss of living in God? The human heart multiplies its sorrows when it hastens after other gods; but whosoever can say that "the Lord is the portion of his inheritance and of his cup," has received "an inheritance incorruptible, and undefiled, and that fadeth not away." Together with all the saints he shall have fulness of the purest joy in the presence of the Lord for evermore. — As surely as Jesus lives, all his believers shall live with him; as surely as he has entered heaven, we shall be gathered to him in the pleasant mansions at the right hand of God. Let us remember this, and praise the Lord, who gave us so goodly a heritage, and caused our lines to fall in pleasant places. His Spirit shall remind us of these things when we walk in darkness; at night, in the deepest darkness, he shall speak to us concerning them in the innermost chamber of the heart. Be assured that the Lord will maintain your lot, dear Christian. It is of his mercy that you can say: "The Lord is my portion; I have set the Lord always before me!" How shall you be moved, when *he* is at your right hand? Or how shall death be able to hold you fast, now that you are a member of the body of Christ? Be obedient to the Spirit of God; remember your hope! Train yourself to set the Lord always before you! Do not let unbelief, or a slavish spirit of fear, or the cares of this world, choke the joy which the Holy Ghost pours out in your innermost heart by showing you the path of life and reminding you of your goodly heritage.

Preserve me, O God; for in thee do I put my trust. Let me no more grieve thy Holy Spirit, whereby thou hast sealed me unto the day of redemption. Help me to be "rejoicing in hope, patient in tribu-

· lation, continuing **instant** in prayer." Let me not **lose** my goodly
heritage, but reach it, in heaven. Amen.

O Lord of heaven and earth and sea, To thee all praise **and glory** be;
How shall we show our love to thee, Who givest all?
Thou didst not spare thine only Son, But gav'st him for a world undone,
And freely with that blessed one Thou givest all.

182. Saturday after Easter Day.

*Give thanks unto the Lord; for he is good; for his mercy endureth for
ever. Amen.*

Psalm 118, 14-24. The Lord is my strength and song, and is become
my salvation. The voice of rejoicing and salvation is in the tabernacles of
the righteous: the right hand of the Lord doeth valiantly. The right hand
of the Lord is exalted; the right hand of the Lord doeth valiantly. I shall not
die, but live, and declare the works of the Lord. The Lord hath chastened
me sore: but he hath not given me over unto death. Open to me the gates
of righteousness: I will go into them, and I will praise the Lord; this gate
of the Lord, into which the righteous shall enter. I will praise thee; for thou
hast heard me, and art become my salvation. The stone which the builders
refused is become the head stone of the corner. This is the Lord's doing;
it is marvellous in our eyes. This is the day which the Lord hath made; we
will rejoice and be glad in it.

This psalm was sung at the time when the foundation of the
temple was laid in the days of Ezra, an account of which is given in his
book, Ezra 3, 10–13. Israel had been in exile; but the Lord had again
received them into favor, and had made them the corner stone of the
world's development. But it is *through Christ* that Israel is what it
is. He is the stone which was rejected, and which then was made the
chief stone of the corner. The Jews, the builders of God's kingdom,
despised him; but it was by the death which they caused him that he
became the substructure of his church, which is the habitation of God
among us and the tabernacle of life on earth. As the people of Israel
exulted when they had been delivered out of Egypt, while their enemies sank like lead into the deep waters; as they shouted aloud for joy
in the gate of the Lord at Jerusalem when they had returned from
Babylon; thus the church of Christ sings of victory and life and salvation through the death and resurrection of Jesus, by which death and
hell have gone down into an eternal grave, so that we never more shall
see them. To be sure, the voice of weeping still is mingled with the
voice of gladness, as in the days of Ezra; but the rejoicing shall prevail;
for "the glory of this latter house shall be greater than of the former,
saith the Lord of hosts." (Haggai 2, 9). — "Open to me the gates of
righteousness." The doors were opened to the court of the temple,
and the people streamed in with their joyful songs of praise. To us
the gates of righteousness are opened; the entrance to heaven itself
through the merit of Jesus; and we go in, and stand before his throne.
This we now do in faith; but later on we shall see that which we now

believe. This is the Lord's doing; it is marvellous in our eyes. Let us rejoice and be glad in him!

Can any others sing, as do the faithful: "I shall not die, but live, and declare the works of the Lord"? "Not die, but live." These words are a present to you from the Lord, faithful Christian. "I shall not die, but live, and declare the works of the Lord." This is the lot which the Lord has given you. The sickle of death mows down everything on earth; the throne and the cottage, the scholar and the clown, the virtuous and the vicious; but the church of Christ breasts the storm without being shaken, and lifts its golden spire toward heaven. And in this church is life, and the voice of rejoicing and salvation. When the eternal gates of death open to receive the unbelievers, the righteous shall enter their perfect and everlasting home of joy.

Lord, thou hast chastened me sore; but thou hast not given me over unto death. I will praise thee; for thou hast heard me, and art become my salvation. Save now, I beseech thee, O Lord; O Lord, send now prosperity. Thou art my God, and I will praise thee; thou art my God, I will exalt thee. Give thanks unto the Lord; for he is good; for his mercy endureth for ever. Amen.

Oh, bless the Lord, my soul! His grace to thee proclaim! And all that is within me join To bless his holy name.
Oh, bless the Lord, my soul! His mercies bear in mind! Forget not all his benefits! The Lord to thee is kind.

---

183. First Sunday after Easter. I.

Gospel Lesson, John 20, 19–23. Then the same day at evening, being the first day of the week, when the doors were shut where the disciples were assembled for fear of the Jews, came Jesus, and stood in the midst, and saith unto them, Peace be unto you. And when he had so said, he shewed unto them his hands and his side. Then were the disciples glad, when they saw the Lord. Then said Jesus to tnem again, Peace be unto you: as my Father hath sent me, even so send I you. And when he had said this, he breathed on them, and saith unto them, Receive ye the Holy Ghost: Whose soever sins ye remit, they are remitted unto them; and whose soever sins ye retain, they are retained.

It is entirely certain that Jesus has earned everlasting life for us all. He has in truth redeemed us all from sin and death and the devil, and gained for us eternal salvation. Now, if any man would reap the benefit and possess this salvation, he must come to Jesus and accept his grace, that he may, in reality, experience salvation, and live. For this also the Lord has made provision. He has given to us the ministry of reconciliation, and he sends his servants out into all the world with the word of salvation. "As my Father hath sent me, even so send I you." He was the messenger of his Father to carry out his purpose, and he brought about pardon and peace. The ministers of the word then do *his* errand, bringing forgiveness and peace to all who will repent. *In the word he is himself present with his atoning death and his resurrection.* As the crucified and risen Savior, about to ascend to his glory, he says: "Behold I am with you alway, even unto the end of the world." Note well that he says, "alway, even unto the end of the world;" hence not only with the apostles, but with their successors in the ministry. He does not stand in the midst of the ten apostles, only, pronouncing peace on them, but in the midst of every company of believers who are gathered together in his name; that is to say, gathered around his word and sacraments for edification in the faith. — When he pronounces peace it is not an empty word, but a divine reality which brings comfort and strength into every soul that is opened to receive it. The words of absolution are not the words of man, but are in very truth the words of the Lord himself; and they are, therefore, able to give that which they pronounce, namely remission of sins. It is *the Lord* who says to you that your sins are forgiven you. Must it not, then, be true? If you will but receive it in faith, you in truth have remission. The word of man may deceive, but the *word of God* never. Do you not hear *Jesus* say that he sends his servants, even as the Father had sent him? When a minister, then, who has the true word of God offers you the gift, it is your business to receive it as coming from Christ himself. If the word be there, the Lord is there with his gift; if it be the proper word, it contains the proper gift. Do not let it give you any concern whether the servant who brings you the gift be or be not a believer, if he do but have the true word of God; for it is not the faith of the minister, but the will and word of Christ which gives you the treasure. If the minister be one in whom I can have no confidence, I can not open my heart to him as my pastor, when I am struggling with difficulties, or torn with doubts, or assailed by temptations; but there is no reason why I may not through him receive absolution which shall be a blessing to my soul and assist me against sin and death. *God* shall judge the unbelieving and faithless servants; do not let *this* be your concern. But let it be *your* care, when you receive absolution, *that your heart may believe that which you hear,* may believe the words of forgiveness from the lips of the Lord. For then you have in truth that which the word promises you; while all who do not believe make God a liar; from which the Holy Spirit preserve us! Amen.

O faithful God, thanks be to thee, That thou forgiv'st iniquity, And helpest me in sin's distress, And dost my soul and body bless.

Now, Lord, us all thy Spirit give, Help us in holiness to live; Preserve to us, till life is spent, Thy holy word and sacrament.

---

184. First Sunday after Easter. II.

Speak, Spirit, in my heart, and say that Jesus is my life alway. Amen.

Epistle Lesson, 1 John 5, 4-12. For whatsoever is born of God overcometh the world: and this is the victory that overcometh the world, even our faith. Who is he that overcometh the world, but he that believeth that Jesus is the Son of God? This is he that came by water and blood, even Jesus

Christ; not by water only, but by water and blood. And it is the Spirit that beareth witness, because the Spirit is truth. For there are three that bear record in heaven, the Father, the Word, and the Holy Ghost: and these three are one. And there are three that bear witness in earth, the Spirit, and the water, and the blood: and these three agree in one. If we receive the witness of men, the witness of God is greater: for this is the witness of God, which he hath testified of his Son. He that believeth on the Son of God hath the witness in himself: he that believeth not God hath made him a liar; because he believeth not the record that God gave of his Son. And this is the record, that God hath given to us eternal life, and this life is in his Son. He that hath the Son, hath life; and he that hath not the Son of God, hath not life.

On the occasion of the baptism of Jesus the Spirit bare witness that he is the Son of God. But the water in which he was baptized — to suffer death, — and the water which flows from his side, together with the blood which he shed in death as an atonement for us; these two, the water and the blood, must be added, in order that he may be our Savior; and hence the Spirit and the water and the blood together bear witness that God has given us his Son for our Savior. The testimony of the *Spirit* can not be dispensed with; he is the principal witness. But the *blood and water* also are indispensable. (Note in this connection the words used by John in his Gospel 19, 34 and 35: "But one of the soldiers with a spear pierced his side, and forthwith came there out water and blood. And he that saw it bare record, and his record is true; and he knoweth that he saith true, that ye might believe.") If we did not have these three, the Spirit and the water and the blood, we could not know of a certainty that God has given his Son for us. But now that we have these three as ever living witnesses before the eye and ear of faith, *we through them have the full assurance that the Son of God died for us, and lives for us.* The voice of the *Spirit.* which gave testimony when Christ was baptized, still comes to our ears through the word which we have received of God. The *water* in which Jesus was baptized, and the water that flowed from his side, together with the blood; these we have in our baptism. Furthermore, we have the *blood* which he shed, together with his body, in the Holy Supper. He who does not believe this testimony of God must, it would seem, find it extremely difficult to answer the question, how it is possible that these three, the word and baptism and the sacrament of the altar, can have survived so long, and how they can have continued to exert such divine power among men. On the other hand, he that believes has the witness in himself that the Spirit has created a new life in him. — This life, dear Christian friend, is *life everlasting.* For your new nature, your sanctified mind, which loves God and the brethren, but which hates sin, and brings the body into subjection, and overcomes the world; what is this but Christ himself in you? Without seeing him you hold him fast by reason of these three witnesses; he is yours, and you love him with your whole heart; the Son of God is in you, and you in him. If you have this life, dear reader, you are truly blest; if you do not, you have no life at all. But come and hear; the three witnesses are still giving their testimony; **make** haste to hear it before it is too late! You must be born of God, and overcome the world, or you are lost.

Lord Jesus, open our eye and ear. Help us to believe; overcome our unbelief by the testimony of thy Spirit; and draw our heart to thee, that thou, thou mayest be our life. Amen.

I build on this foundation, That Jesus and his blood Alone are my salvation, The true eternal good: Without him, all that pleases Is valueless on earth: The gifts bestowed by Jesus Alone my love are worth.

---

185. Monday after First Sunday after Easter.

Lord Jesus, overcome our unbelief; give us grace to believe. Amen.

John 20, 24-31. But Thomas, one of the twelve, called Didymus, was not with them when Jesus came. The other disciples therefore said unto him, We have seen the Lord. But he said unto them, Except I shall see in his hands the print of the nails, and put my finger into the print of the nails, and thrust my hand into his side, I will not believe. And after eight days, again his disciples were within, and Thomas with them: then came Jesus, the doors being shut, and Jesus stood in the midst, and said, Peace be unto you. Then saith he to Thomas, Reach hither thy finger, and behold my hands; and reach hither thy hand, and thrust it into my side: and be not faithless, but believing. And Thomas answered and said unto him, My Lord and my God. Jesus saith unto him, Thomas, because thou hast seen me, thou hast believed: blessed are they that have not seen, and yet have believed. And many other signs truly did Jesus in the presence of his disciples, which are not written in this book: But these are written, that ye might believe that Jesus is the Christ, the Son of God; and that, believing, ye might have life through his name.

How dark the soul of Thomas while he walked in unbelief! Was the Lord, then, not risen from the dead, and did he not live? Was he not near? Were the thoughts true which Thomas harbored in his unbelieving heart? Many, alas, who hear the word and use the sacraments have much less faith than Thomas had, and know nothing whatever of the peace of Christ, although of a truth the Lord is in our midst with his gifts that bring salvation. The other disciples, who believed the testimony of them that had seen him after his resurrection, who *believed* without having seen; these disciples had the truth, and obtained the peace which he pronounced on them. Dear reader, if you should see Christ dying for you; if you should see him hang on the cross and die, and should see him after his resurrection with the print of the nails and the wound of the spear; if you should see him come to you with open arms, and should hear him call you in his own voice; would you then fall down before him and say with Thomas: "My Lord and my God"? Would you with all your heart surrender yourself to him, and serve him with all your soul? Would you rejoice in his love, turn with terror from your sin, believe his forgiveness, and trust confidently in his mercy? Let us hope so. Now, precisely in this manner he is near to you in his word, and yet you continue to live without peace in your heart! Verily it is his very voice which you hear in the preaching of the gospel, in absolution, and in the words of the sacraments. Do you dare to believe that your unbelief, which denies or doubt this, is truth, and that the Lord's own promise is a lie? What was right and true, the declaration of Jesus in regard to his resurrection, or the unbelief and denial on the part of Thomas ? What is right and true, the Lord's promise that he will be present in the midst of his own with his grace and peace unto the end, or your unbelief which denies this? Do you understand this, poor soul, that he still could reveal himself to our bodily eye, if he *would;* but he has decreed, that "blessed are they that have not seen, and yet have believed." Be satisfied to let the provisions in the Lord's gracious counsel for our salvation remain as they are. Believe without having seen, and you are saved. You may do it by the power of God in his word; for this word is the means by which the Spirit creates and preserves faith in us. — Away with this wretched unbelief, which makes the eternal and truthful God a liar! Yes, away with unbelief, which is a lie of the devil's own invention!

We beseech thee, merciful God, preserve us from the dead faith of the world, which takes thy grace in vain; and preserve us from the doubts of our own unbelieving heart, which refuse to let thee have full sway over us with thy living truth. Give us faith, the true and living faith which trusts in thy word, partakes of thy grace, confesses thy name, and mans the soul with courage in life and death. Amen.

I now have found the ground that ever Shall hold my anchor firm and fast; I can not be deceived, no never, For on my Savior it is cast; This ground unmoved and firm shall stay When heaven and earth have passed away.

---

186. Tuesday after First Sunday after Easter.

"Whom have I in heaven but thee? and there is none upon earth that I desire beside thee." God grant us this mercy. Amen.

Colossians 3, 1–6. If ye then be risen with Christ, seek those things which are above, where Christ sitteth on the right hand of God. Set your affection on things above, not on things on the earth. For ye are dead, and your life is hid with Christ in God. When Christ, who is our life, shall appear, then shall ye also appear with him in glory. Mortify therefore your members which are upon the earth; fornication, uncleanness, inordinate affection, evil concupiscence, and covetousness, which is idolatry; for which things' sake the wrath of God cometh on the children of disobedience.

To be united with Christ is the one thing needful. Vital Christianity is the communion of the heart with him. Then we have died with him, and have been raised again from the dead with him. Christ is the life of the true believers. He that does not live in Christ is no Christian. What sort of Christianity may that be which is not life? But what life could Christianity be, if it be not the life of Jesus Christ? Let none deceive himself with a vain or dead hope in Christ! For Christ has overcome death; he is the living God, who quickens all them that are his own, and gives them a living hope. As Christ is

16

in heaven, the heart of the faithful, which live in him, must likewise
be in heaven. "For where your treasure is, there will your heart be
also." "God has raised us up together, and made us sit together in
heavenly places in Christ Jesus." (Ephesians 2, 6). Mind and heart
have been set free and endowed with high aspirations. The soul's
longing reaches out beyond this life, and its goal is eternal communion
with God in perfect holiness. Then you are dead to the world, its
honors and pleasures, its riches and benefits, its poverty and misery,
its dogmas and ordinances, its nursery tales and its thraldom. And
the world regards you as lost and dead. The life which you live is the
life of Christ, and it is hid with Christ in God. As Christ it invisible
to the world, so also is his life in the faithful. Their faith in the Lord,
their hope and peace and joy in him, their love, their holy longing
after heaven, their zealous endeavors to keep their lives clean, their
self-denial and their resistance to the devil, their prayers in the sanctuary of the heart; in a word, *their life in God*, is wholly hid from the
world, which neither sees it nor understands it, but regards it as being
nothing more than an idle dream. The glory of the Christians is
covered over with troubles and poverty and afflictions and tears; nay,
with sin and *many infirmities.* — But Christ shall appear, then shall
you also appear with him in glory. Rejoice in this hope, and be not
led astray by reason of your afflictions in this world. Your members,
which are of the earth, are to be mortified; and herein the Lord as-
sists you by means of the cross. The evil lusts are the members and
joints of your old Adam, who by your conversion to the Lord has
been mortally wounded, but has not as yet been entirely annihilated.
They will seek to drag you down to the earth again; therefore mortify
them with the cross of Christ; mortify them, for Jesus' sake!

Lord Jesus, knowest thou me, that I live in thee, and thou in me?
Grant me this boon, most merciful Savior. "O take my heart and
soul and might, and fill them with thy heavenly light." Amen.

Not for any worldly pleasure Doth my thirsty spirit pine; Not the earth
with all its treasure Could content this soul of mine; For its Savior yearning
ever: I will leave my Jesus never.

From that living Fountain drinking, Walking always at his side, Christ
shall lead me without sinking Through the river's rushing tide, With the blest
to sing for ever: I will leave my Jesus never.

---

187. Wednesday after First Sunday after Easter.

Teach us, Lord Jesus, to go whither thou hast said, there to meet thee. Amen.

John 21, 1–6. After these things Jesus shewed himself again to the disciples at the sea of Tiberias; and on this wise shewed he himself. There were
together Simon Peter, and Thomas called Didymus, and Nathanael of Cana
in Galilee, and the sons of Zebedee, and two other of his disciples. Simon
Peter saith unto them, I go a fishing. They say unto him, We also go with
thee. They went forth, and entered into a ship immediately; and that night
they caught nothing. But when the morning was now come, Jesus stood on

the shore: but the disciples knew not that it was Jesus. Then Jesus saith unto them, Children, have ye any meat? They answered him, No. And he said unto them, Cast the net on the right side of the ship, and ye shall find. They cast therefore, and now they were not able to draw it for the multitude of fishes.

The Lord had told the disciples that he would shew himself to them i Galilee; and hence we now find them at the sea of Tiberias. Still, though he lives in them, and is in their thoughts and on their lips, they do not expect him to shew himself just now; and they therefore go a fishing. Even when he stands on the shore, and addresses them as "children," and bids them cast the net on the right side of the ship, they do not know him. For the apostles had not yet celebrated Pentecost. — Does not the same thing often occur in our case? He says to us: "I will meet you in the gospel, in the Gennesaret of holy baptism, at the holy communion table." We come to the tryst, and he is there, but we do not know him. He has said that he will shew himself to us in poor and despised Galilee; that is to say, he will meet us in his needy members on earth; and he leads us thither, and is there before us, and yet we do not see him, or do not see that it is he. — The apostles found happiness in obeying him. He had told them to go to Galilee, and they had gone; he found them there when he came, and they found him. He was their dearest treasure, their life. They could not fail to keep the appointment; and in the end they could not fail to know him. Let us follow them, and we shall have the same experience. Let us go and meet the Lord at the places which he has appointed; namely in the means of grace, on the path of self-denial at the foot of the cross. Should we do as the apostles did; that is, should we know him to be there, and yet forget it; should we expect him to make himself known to us, but not in the manner in which he had said; should we fail to recognize him at once; should our spirit be faint, and our eyes dim; — he will be with us for all that. He never fails to keep his appointment; he comes before we know it, and is at hand when we least expect it. And he makes himself known to us when it is necessary; reveals himself, not to our senses, but to our spirit; disciplines us, and confirms our faith. But do not forget that everything depends on our being upright, as were the disciples, and going to Galilee, as he has directed. There we shall find him. And the stranger on the shore, whom we dismiss with a brief "no, we have nothing," gives us a greater draught than we are able to draw. — Cast the net on the right side, brethren; cast the net on the right side of the ship!

Praise be to thee, Lord Jesus, for that thou art ever near to thy disciples, who are needy, and whose faith is so weak! Now we will in truth believe without having seen, and will ever thank thee, and serve thee, and never loose heart. Help us herein; of thy mercy grant us this blessing! Amen.

O God, our help in ages past, Our hope in years to come, Our shelter from the stormy blast, And our eternal home!
Under the shadow of thy throne Thy saints have dwelt secure; Sufficient is thine arm alone. And our defence is sure.

188. Thursday after First Sunday after Easter.

Teach us to say with all our heart: Not unto us, O Lord, not unto us, but unto thy name give glory. Amen.

John 21, 7–14. Therefore that disciple whom Jesus loved saith unto Peter, It is the Lord. Now when Simon Peter heard that it was the Lord, he girt his fisher's coat unto him, (for he was naked,) and did cast himself into the sea. And the other disciples came in a little ship; (for they were not far from land, but as it were two hundred cubits,) dragging the net with fishes. As soon then as they were come to land, they saw a fire of coals there, and fish laid thereon, and bread. Jesus saith unto them, Bring of the fish which ye have now caught. Simon Peter went up, and drew the net to land full of great fishes, an hundred and fifty and three: and for all there were so many yet was not the net broken. Jesus saith unto them, Come and dine. And none of the disciples durst ask him, Who art thou? knowing that it was the Lord. Jesus then cometh, and taketh bread, and giveth them, and fish likewise. This is now the third time that Jesus shewed himself to his disciples, after that he was risen from the dead.

John, the apostle of *love*, has the clearest vision, and is the first to recognize Jesus. His writings also bear witness to the depth of his knowledge of the Lord. The eye of love sees more clearly than any other. Peter, however, is at all times the most ardent and courageous. On the morning of Easter day he was the first to enter the sepulchre. The other five disciples who are in the ship quietly ply their vocation of drawing the net. This episode has been interpreted as illustrating the diversity of gifts with which the Lord's people are endowed. One has the tender love and the clear eye of John; another has the zeal and courage of Peter; while still others have their strength in the quiet, patient endurance with which they follow their humble vocations. — We have here also a picture of the work of the apostles and the whole church for the saving of souls, according to what the Lord himself said on the occasion of that former draught of fishes by Peter: "From henceforth thou shalt catch men." (Luke 5, 10).

However, what we especially want to impress upon one another as the lesson of this gospel is the declaration of John: "It is the Lord." It is *the Lord* who says: "Cast the net on the right side of the ship." The Lord has commanded all his disciples to cast the net of the word. The Lord sent the apostles out into the world; and the same Lord has sent you, who are now engaged in casting the net of the gospel out into the sea of humanity and down into the depths of the heart. You would not have been his witness, if the Lord had not issued this command to his church: "Go ye into all the world, and preach the gospel to every creature." It is the Lord who has made you one of his witnesses. — Furthermore, it is the Lord who makes the draught a successful one. When a minister of the word is given grace to add many converts to the number of the saints, the honor belongs not to him, but to the word of God, which he preaches. Let him beware of priding himself on his achievement; for it is not his own. Let him also beware of despising others who are engaged in the same work, but who seem not to be equally successful. It is possible that they may be working more patiently and faithfully, even though they do not draw a multitude of fishes to the shore. If the Lord were not with you in his word, you would accomplish nothing; when you do, "it is the Lord." When we lose heart let the spirit of John whisper into our soul: "It is the Lord." Then shall we gather courage anew. When we become slothful this word shall inspire us with fresh zeal; and when we are puffed up it shall humble us. Truly, it is *the Lord* who has given you your work, if you are a servant of Christ; and he is with you, and blesses you.

To the apostles of infidelity the world cries out: "Cast the net on the left side, on the banks of human reason, and draw many with you away from the faith." But is *this* of the Lord, do you think? These apostles want no Lord; they wish to be their own masters. They do not know that their inspiration comes from *their* Lord below.

Grant that we may hear thy voice, and know thee, Lord Jesus. Give us charity and wisdom and faithfulness in thy work, and give us grace to save many souls by means of thy word. Amen.

Baptize the nations; far and nigh The triumphs of the cross record: The name of Jesus glorify, Till every kindred call him Lord.
God from eternity hath willed, All flesh shall his salvation see; So be the Father's love fulfilled, The Savior's sufferings crowned thro' thee.

---

189. Friday after First Sunday after Easter.

O God, fill our heart with the love of Christ. Amen.

John 21, 15-19. So when they had dined, Jesus saith to Simon Peter, Simon, son of Jonas, lovest thou me more than these? He saith unto him, Yea, Lord; thou knowest that I love thee. He saith unto him, Feed my lambs. He saith to him again the second time, Simon, son of Jonas, lovest thou me? He saith unto him, Yea, Lord; thou knowest that I love thee. He saith unto him, Feed my sheep. He saith unto him the third time, Simon, son of Jonas, lovest thou me? Peter was grieved because he said unto him the third time, Lovest thou me? And he said unto him, Lord, thou knowest all things; thou knowest that I love thee. Jesus saith unto him, Feed my sheep. Verily, verily, I say unto thee, When thou wast young, thou girdedst thyself, and walkedst whither thou wouldest: but when thou shalt be old, thou shalt stretch forth thy hands, and another shall gird thee, and carry thee whither thou wouldest not. This spake he, signifying by what death he should glorify God. And when he had spoken this, he saith unto him, Follow me.

This surely is one of the grandest of gospel lessons. There is a wealth of edification in this colloquy between the Lord and Peter. There is a powerful appeal to the heart in the Lord's question: "Simon, son of Jonas, lovest thou me?" And what a loving reproof in the addition, "more than these?" The answer of Peter reveals to us the secret depths of his heart, especially when viewed in connection with his courageous declaration at Cedron. How much of instruction is there not in the connection between the Lord's question, "lovest thou me?" and the direction, "feed my lambs!" The Savior preaches a great penitential sermon by his thrice repeated question addressed to "Simon, son of Jonas." At the same time, the Lord is so lenient as to omit the words "more than these'" from the second question; and in the third he substitutes another word for "love," namely the one which Peter had used in making reply. There is a close relation between the humiliation of the apostle and his re-appointment as chief of the apostles. In the whole conversation *the hearts* meet and embrace each other in wonderful wise, with ever increasing tenderness. In the Lord we are impressed by the sublime love and wisdom of the divine teacher; and in Peter, by the humble, honest, reverent, and trusting spirit of the obedient disciple. How blessed thus to lay one's soul at the feet of Jesus, and be taken into his embrace! But how solemn a warning in that which the Lord adds in regard to the trials which love must undergo in trouble and affliction and self-denial unto death! May the Spirit of God expound this to your heart, dear reader. I will only ask you above all to hear and answer the Lord's question: *"Lovest thou me?"* This question is not addressed to Peter only. In his love the Lord addresses it to us all. If you could but apply it to your heart, you might by this means receive the greatest of all blessings, a soul filled with the love of God. "Lovest thou me?" the Lord asks you, because he loves you. If your dearest friend on earth speaks your name, so precious and sweet to him, and in tones of the most tender affection asks you: "Lovest thou me?" you rejoice in assuring him of your love, and the fire on the altar of your hearts burns the brighter. In the eternal love with which he desires to save your soul Jesus now asks you if you love him. You know that he does this because he loves you; you know that he prizes your love so highly that, in order to win it, he suffered death for you. Do you love him? Answer; answer at once! It is *Jesus* who asks: "Lovest thou me?" Blessed is he whose innermost heart is made to throb by this question, and who is able to make answer: "Lord, thou knowest all things; thou knowest that I love thee." O, that all the world were so blest as to be able to reply: "Yes, my heart burns with love of thee, my Lord Jesus!" But, alas, the greater number would not speak true, if they made this answer. Unhappy they who do not love him! I hope that you, dear reader, know the penitent spirit of Peter, and that you have his humble and true answer in your heart: "Lord, thou knowest all things; thou knowest that I love thee." Speak out as Peter did; answer the Lord honestly, and tell him that he has won your heart; then shall his love more and more become the very life of your soul.

We earnestly beseech thee, O God, and we can not let thee go, except thou hear us: Give us a heart full of the love of Jesus. Amen.

Oh, grant that nothing in my soul May dwell, but thy pure love alone! Oh, may thy love possess me whole, And be my treasure, and my crown! Strange flames far from my heart remove; May every act, word, thought, be love.

190. Saturday after First Sunday after Easter.

Lord, give me grace gladly to carry thy cross after thee. Amen.

John 21, 20–23. Then Peter, turning about, seeth the disciple whom Jesus loved, following; which also leaned on his breast at supper, and said, Lord, which is he that betrayeth thee? Peter, seeing him, saith to Jesus, Lord, and what shall this man do? Jesus saith unto him, if I will that he tarry till I come, what is that to thee? Follow thou me. Then went this saying abroad among the brethren, that that disciple should not die: yet Jesus said not unto him, He shall not die; but, If I will that he tarry till I come, what is that to thee?

"Follow me," says Jesus to Peter; meaning: Follow me in suffering and death. Then the Lord rises, and leaves the table; and Peter follows him. In like manner he shall follow him in dying on the cross. John also follows him. Peter then asks; either on behalf of John, in order that he also may know the fate which awaits him, or by reason of surprise and curiosity: "Lord, and what shall this man do?" Jesus, however, dismisses the question, and says that is a matter which he himself will dispose of. Was John, then, not to go the way of *the cross* in following the Lord? Certainly he was. There is no other way on which the Lord's footsteps may be followed. "If any man will come after me, let him deny himself, and take up his cross daily and follow me." "Whosoever doth not bear his cross, and come after me, can not be my disciple." But the cross is not the same for all. Peter has one kind, and John another. The Lord gives to each that which best fits his shoulders. He can, if it be his will, exempt his dearest friend from the death of the martyr, thereby exempting him from the martyr's crown also; or he can give him other sufferings and other honor equally great. The duty of each to take up *his own* cross is the very thing which Jesus here emphasizes by dismissing the question which Peter asks. Do not be dissatisfied and curious to learn whether others suffer less than you, or whether there be more honor connected with their cross than with yours; or *why* your path must be more narrow, or your strength less in proportion to the size of the cross. No believer has a cross which is too heavy or too light. None could afford to exchange it for any other. There is a self-willed and obstinate dissatisfaction, which murmurs against God and envies others; be careful not to let it gain a foothold in you. If you were permitted to make the exchange, you would soon discover that your neighbor's yoke does not fit your neck. Take up *your own* cross, and follow Jesus. There is an obedient devotion, which teaches us to suffer without complaint, to be grateful for everything, and gladly to bear the burden for others. *"Follow thou me,"* says the Lord. We will take this word with us, and then go and do it. In that case none of us shall want the conflict and the suffering of the cross; but neither shall its happiness and honor, its eternal blessing, be wanting.

Draw us after thee, Lord Jesus; thou knowest that it is our wish to follow thee, and thou knowest how reluctant our flesh is to bear the cross. Draw us after thee. Give us grace to walk in thy footsteps, and to bear our cross willingly and gladly, that thy name may be honored, and that the brethren may be strengthened. Amen.

Bane and blessing, pain and pleasure, By the cross are sanctified; Peace is there that knows no measure, Joys that through all time abide.

In the cross of Christ I glory, Towering o'er the wrecks of time; All the light of sacred story Gathers round its head sublime.

---

191. Second Sunday after Easter. I.

Lord Jesus, may we be of thy people. Amen.

Gospel Lesson, John 10, 11–16. I am the good shepherd: the good shepherd giveth his life for the sheep. But he that is an hireling, and not the shepherd, whose own the sheep are not, seeth the wolf coming, and leaveth the sheep, and fleeth: and the wolf catcheth them, and scattereth the sheep. The hireling fleeth, because he is an hireling, and careth not for the sheep. I am the good shepherd, and know my sheep, and am known of mine. As the Father knoweth me, even so know I the Father: and I lay down my life for the sheep. And other sheep I have, which are not of this fold: them also I must bring, and they shall hear my voice; and there shall be one fold, and one shepherd.

Of a certainty, he has given his life for us. Now, we had at one time belonged to him, but had sold ourselves to the devil. So the precious Lord and Savior determined to make us his own once more by purchasing us with his life and blood; and hence we now belong to him as his special and peculiar property, bought with a great price. But *who* are his sheep? He gave his life as a ransom for *all;* from which it follows that *all* might be his sheep. But are they? Alas, many will not be; and they refuse to be gathered into his fold. In our gospel lesson he mentions two marks by which they who belong to him may be known. The first is, that they *know* him; the second, that they *hear his voice.*

1) If you do not know him, you are not one of his sheep. There is between him and them an intimate acquaintance, even as there is between the Father and him. Is not this a truth to impress us with its gravity, as well as to give us the greatest joy? "I know mine, and am known of mine, even as I know the Father, and am known of the Father." How intimate the knowledge, and how close the relation! He knows them by name; he knows their condition and their needs, their longing and love and sorrow; knows each one of them as if he were the only one, and understands them better than they understand themselves. And the sheep know the Lord in faith. They do not see him, but they know him; know him better than they know any other; for they experience in their heart that he is love and mercy and life itself, holy and righteous, great and mighty, patient and faithful, and that in him the heart has all that it needs. They do not know the whole depth of his nature, and they do not know the full greatness of his grace; neither do all know him equally well; but each of them

knows him as his Lord and God, and gives himself to him, and trusts him with heart-felt confidence. It is not a superficial and slight acquaintance, but a daily, unceasing, confidential intercourse, a communion of life and heart in spirit and in truth. After a short acquaintance they have put his kindness, his faithfulness, and his patience to the test so often that they can say with truth that they know him, and in truth must say that he surpasses all knowledge.

2) The second mark is that they *hear his voice,* and *let him gather them into the fold.* The sheep follow the shepherd, and obey him. The sheep of Jesus answer to his call, and obey him; they are willing to receive chastisement and comfort and instruction from him, and they congregate where his word is to be heard. If you do not love the word of Jesus, it is certain that *you* are not of his fold. If you do not delight in them whose delight is in him, you are not of his fold. But come for all that; he calls you, and he will receive you.

Lord Jesus, thou great Shepherd of the souls; thou alone canst save from the wolf and from death. Let us be thine own, and do not surrender us to our own foolish devices. Call us to thee, and keep us in thy fold. Amen.

Shepherd of Israel, from above Thy feeble flock behold; And let us never lose thy love, Nor wander from thy fold.
Thou wilt not cast thy lambs away; Thy hand is ever near To guide them, lest they go astray, And keep them safe from fear.

---

192. Second Sunday after Easter. II.

Lord, make us acquainted with thy sufferings. Amen.

1 Peter 2, 21-25. For even hereunto were ye called: because Christ also suffered for us, leaving us an example, that ye should follow his steps: Who did no sin, neither was guile found in his mouth: Who, when he was reviled, reviled not again; when he suffered, he threatened not; but committed himself to him that judgeth righteously: Who his own self bare our sins in his own body on the tree, that we, being dead to sins, should live unto righteousness: by whose stripes ye were healed. For ye were as sheep going astray; but are now returned unto the Shepherd and Bishop of your souls.

You who are returned to the Lord are called to *endure suffering.* For Christ suffered for us, and we are to walk in these his footprints, not elsewhere. For the flesh it is a hard road to travel; but that which makes the flesh wince is the very best thing for the soul. — However, there is no virtue in suffering, if you do not endure it in the right spirit. Jesus suffered *patiently, uttering no complaint.* In this way only can suffering be said to be holy. But in order that we may be able to suffer in this way, we must above all know and believe in the *grace contained in the suffering of Christ.* He suffered for our sins, not for his own; and yet he did not murmur. How much more reason for us to endure suffering, and hold our peace, we who have so richly deserved to suffer! His *example* is striking; but that alone does not give us the needed strength. Another circumstance in connection with his suffering is the one which gives us strength to follow his steps: "His own self bare our sins in his own body on the tree." He took away our guilt by suffering our punishment. When we believe in him our suffering is, therefore, not a punishment under the lash of the judge, but a correction administered by a loving father. Understand this; and the sting which especially tempts to impatience is taken away, and in its place you will find that suffering soothes the soul. Christ took away also the power of sin; he sacrificed himself with our sin on his shoulders; the pure fire of his holy love, which consumed him, consumed our sins also; and hence in Christ you are dead from sin, and live in righteousness. His stripes are your healing. Faith knows this mystery, and possesses this grace. — Thus the Christians are able to shew forth the power of Christ's sufferings. But the greater number of those who call themselves Christians are such in name only ; and they neither will nor can suffer as Christians. — *Ye* are the ones whose lot it is to suffer, ye believers, who are returned unto the Shepherd of your souls. For even hereunto were ye called. Suffer patiently, and praise God, thereby giving proof that your Christianity is genuine.

God, give us this great mercy that we may suffer afflictions and thank thee for them. Amen.

Lead, kindly Light! amid th' encircling gloom, Lead thou me on; The night is dark, and I am far from home, Lead thou me on; Keep thou my feet; I do not ask to see The distant scene; one step enough for me.

I was not ever thus, nor prayed that thou Shouldst lead me on; I loved to choose and see my path; but now, Lead thou me on. I love the garish day, and spite of fears, Pride ruled my will. Remember not past years.

---

193. Monday after Second Sunday after Easter.

Prosper, O God, the work of thy word upon our hearts. Amen.

Psalm 23. A Psalm of David. The Lord is my shepherd; I shall not want. He maketh me to lie down in green pastures: he leadeth me beside the still waters. He restoreth my soul: he leadeth me in the paths of righteousness for his name's sake. Yea, though I walk through the valley of the shadow of death, I will fear no evil: for thou art with me; thy rod and thy staff they comfort me. Thou preparest a table before me in the presence of mine enemies: thou anointest my head with oil; my cup runneth over. Surely goodness and mercy shall follow me all the days of my life; and I will dwell in the house of the Lord for ever.

It was in one of the happy hours of his life that David wrote this psalm. The children of God have many dark hours; but the clouds roll away, and the upright again enjoy the bright sunshine. The strings of the heart are stretched until they seem ready to break; but this happens, in order that the joyful tones may thereafter sound with the greater clearness. In this psalm the Holy Spirit plays a grand anthem of praise on the harp of the psalmist.

The Lord, the strong and faithful God, is Israel's shepherd. And in the term Israel you are included, if you have the true faith. He cares for you, and gives you all good things; and hence you shall not want. He feeds, restores, leads, comforts, protects you. He is able and willing to do this; for you are one of the dearly purchased sheep of his hand.

1) Through the gospel and remission of sins he feeds and nourishes your soul, and he gives you the bread necessary for the sustenance of your body. His word and grace are the green pastures. 2) When you need it, and can bear it, he will give you great joy by allowing you to taste in advance something of the bliss of heaven. You shall have intervals of rest in the midst of your struggles; and in the heat of battle you shall be refreshed at the wells of water under the palm trees of Elim (Exodus 15, 27). This is what is meant by the "still waters." 3) He brings you back whenever you are about to be lost in the desert of sin and unbelief; he keeps you in the fear of him and in discipline; guides, admonishes, comforts, and instructs you by his Spirit, and is always at hand when you need him. You would soon plunge yourself into misery; but he hedges you in with tribulations and leads you in the paths of righteousness. That he will do this is vouched for by the everlasting name which he has made for himself in the revelation of his eternal nature through his works unto this day (Isaiah 63, 12). 4) The way leads through the valley of the cross; and none of God's children shall be exempt from pain and distress. It is their lot to bear many infirmities, and they are assailed by many temptations. They would soon lose heart, did not his rod and his staff comfort them. But when they are able to say, "thou art with me,"they walk through the darkness without despairing; for they know that they need fear no evil. 5) The strongest enemy is powerless to injure them that are in the fold of *Jesus*. Their shepherd is a wall of fire around them, within which they sit, secure from all danger, eating and drinking of a cup that runneth over, their heads anointed with the oil of gladness. "In quietness and in confidence shall be your strength." Happy are you, if Jesus is your shepherd! Only goodness follows you, and you shall inherit life in the house of the Lord for ever.

Lord Jesus, let me be of thy fold. My prayer is answered! Hallelujah! Amen. Thou hast bought me, and baptized me, and drawn my heart to thee.

The Lord's my shepherd, I'll not want; He makes me down to lie In pastures green; he leadeth me The quiet waters by.
Goodness and mercy all my life Shall surely follow me; And in God's house for evermore, My dwelling place shall be.

---

194. Tuesday after Second Sunday after Easter.

Give ear, O Shepherd of Israel, thou that leadest Joseph like a flock.

Ezekiel 34, 11-16. For thus saith the Lord God, Behold I, even I, will both search my sheep, and seek them out. As a shepherd seeketh out his flock in the day that he is among his sheep that are scattered; so will I seek out my sheep, and will deliver them out of all places where they have been scattered in the cloudy and dark day. And I will bring them out from the people, and gather them from the countries, and will bring them to their own land, and feed them upon the mountains of Israel by the rivers, and in all the inhabited places of the country. I will feed them in a good pasture, and upon the high mountains of Israel shall their fold be: there shall they lie in a good fold, and in a fat pasture shall they feed upon the mountains of Israel. I will feed my flock, and I will cause them to lie down, saith the Lord God. I will seek that which was lost, and bring again that which was driven away, and will bind up that which was broken, and will strengthen that which was sick: but I will destroy the fat and the strong; I will feed them with judgment.

In every part of his word we learn that the Lord takes pity on the wretched, but overthrows the proud of heart; and this is also evidenced by his whole life on earth. Hear this, ye poor sinners who are scattered and driven away by the devil. *Jesus* himself stands in the sight of all and declares: "Behold, I, even *I*, will both search my sheep, and seek them out." The places whither you have been scattered are the prison houses of sin. Zacchæus has allowed himself to be deceived and led away into the prison of coveteousness; the woman of Sychar, into unchastity; Saul, into self-righteousness; the prodigal son, into sensual lust; Onesimus, into false liberty. The proud and carnally minded shepherds, the Pharisees in Israel and the wordly minded clergy of every age, have lent their assistance as the loyal servants of the devil. Woe to such as these; for the Lord will require his flock at their hand. — Jesus *himself* is seeking you, poor sheep, who have been led astray. You belong to him. The devil has no title to you, even if you have surrendered to him; for Jesus has redeemed you with his blood, and you are his. He seeks each individual sheep, seeks them one and all with the loving desire to save them. He seeks you, that he may draw you to himself, into the good fold. He seeks that which is lost, brings back that which was driven away, binds up that which was broken, and strengthens that which was sick. Not one, not even the most utterly wretched, does he forget. When your conscience is troubled, and you tremble at the thought of death and the judgment, it is the voice of the shepherd calling to you and drawing you to him. Do answer the call; turn your heart to him, and ask of him to have mercy on you and give you true repentance. Come, then; by all means come, thou soul gone astray!

Gather, Jesus, thy sheep that are scattered here and there; gather them all into the good fold, feed them upon the mountains of Israel by the rivers, and protect them from the attacks of the wolf. Amen.

Savior, who thy flock art feeding With the shepherd's kindest care, All the feeble gently leading, While the lambs thy bosom share:
Never, from thy pastures roving, Let them be the lion's prey; Let thy tenderness, so loving, Keep them through life's dangerous way.

195. Wednesday after Second Sunday after Easter.

O Lord God of hosts, cause thy face to shine, and we shall be saved. Amen.

John 10, 23–30. And Jesus walked in the temple in Solomon's porch. Then came the Jews round about him, and said unto him, How long dost thou make us to doubt? If thou be the Christ, tell us plainly. Jesus answered them, I told you, and ye believed not: the works that I do in my Father's name, they bear witness of me. But ye believe not, because ye are not of my sheep, as I said unto you. My sheep hear my voice, and I know them, and they follow me: And I give unto them eternal life; and they shall never perish, neither shall any man pluck them out of my hand. My Father, which gave them me, is greater than all; and no man is able to pluck them out of my Father's hand. I and my Father are one.

Even as all who believe with childlike faith receive light to know the Lord, so we may say, on the other hand, that all who receive light to know Jesus believe in him. We have a Savior who is truth and love itself. If you see him with the eye of the spirit and hear his voice in your heart, he wins your confidence, and you commit yourself into his keeping with trust and love. When people do not believe in Jesus the reason is that they do not know him and do not hear his voice. Our hearts can not resist him, if the darkness of unbelief does not hide him from us. O, that all might open their eyes and see the Lord, incline the ear to hear his voice, and open wide the heart to receive the precious Savior! Then they would know of a certainty that he is the bountiful giver of life, the everlasting God, one with the Father, great in power, mighty to save. You that believe in him; you the sheep of his fold; you, at least, can not refuse to hear his voice and follow him! When the devil entices you with evil lusts and the seductions of the world, attend to the warning voice of the shepherd. Call to mind his life and his words while he was here on earth; and do not let the devil lead you wrong, but deny and renounce him. Your soul will, no doubt, at times be troubled by reason of temptations to sin and unbelief; but by means of his word and sacrament the Lord gives you comfort and peace, and exhorts you strongly to charity and good works. Every word of solace, every encouragement which your heart receives, every force and impulse urging you to that which is good, is his voice. This voice is in the word, out of which the Spirit takes it and causes it to be sounded in your soul. Nothing holy that is in you is of the flesh; your new life is created by his word, and lives and breathes in and of this word. Thus do you follow him, and thus does he save you. He says: "I give them eternal life; and they shall never perish, neither shall any man pluck them out of my hand." With these words he most wonderfully strengthens and quickens our hope of salvation. But in case that even this should not be sufficient to man our poor heart with courage and resolution, he adds: "My Father, which gave them me, is greater than all; and no man is able to pluck them out of my Father's hand. I and my Father are one." Shall not, then, the sheep of Jesus be *fully assured* of inheriting eternal life?

Lord, almighty and faithful God, may we be of thy fold. Draw us after thee, and establish our hearts in faith on thee unto the end. Blessed are thy sheep, thou good Shepherd! We earnestly beseech thee, draw us to thee, and let none pluck us out of thy hand. Amen.

We are thine, do thou befriend us, Be the guardian of our way; Keep thy flock, from sin defend us, Seek us when we go astray. Blessed Jesus, blessed Jesus! Hear, oh hear us, when we pray.

---

196. Thursday after Second Sunday after Easter.

Holy Spirit of God, give us ardent love in our hearts. Amen.

1 Peter 5, 1-5. The elders which are among you I exhort, who am also an elder, and a witness of the sufferings of Christ, and also a partaker of the glory that shall be revealed: Feed the flock of God which is among you, taking the oversight thereof, not by constraint, but willingly; not for filthy lucre, but of a ready mind; neither as being lords over God's heritage, but being ensamples to the flock. And when the chief Shepherd shall appear, ye shall receive a crown of glory that fadeth not away. Likewise, ye younger, submit yourselves unto the elder: yea, all of you be subject one to another, and be clothed with humility: for God resisteth the proud, and giveth grace to the humble.

They whom God has ordained elders and overseers in the churches, that is to say ministers of the word, shall "feed the flock of God." This calling of pastor is glorious; but it is one of great responsibility; for they shall render an account of the souls to the Lord, who bought them with his blood. Love is the great prince to whom everything belongs, and to whom all owe allegiance, and love alone can make the true pastor. The hireling has no care for the sheep. If God has ordained us overseers of the flock, and has given us love for his sheep, we are as careful of them as though they were our own. We willingly take the oversight of them, and care for them with joy and delight as for the beloved of Jesus Christ, whom he has bought with a price. If we in faith know his suffering, and in hope know his glory, we love him, and love the souls which he has redeemed with his blood and committed to our care. But how small is the number of the elders who take no thought of worldly gain, but solely of the welfare of the flock; and who in self-denying love gladly sacrifice everything for the eternal weal of the souls committed to their charge! Such pastors are the leaders of the church, not its rulers; they are the servants of God, who has placed them in their office; but they serve the church, and in the work of building it up they consume their strength. They are at the front in every good work, and lead the people in their battle with falsehood and sin; but they regard themselves as being the least of all, and to all they are an example in humility. God give us pastors of this class! At the same time, the congregations are not to sit in supercilious judgment on the pastors whom we have. Let them submit to the elders; for these are ministers in God's stead. Note that the word of God says. "*Submit* to the elders," and "be clothed with humility." Pray earnestly for one another that you may do this! We have the necessary grace to do so in the word and promises of God. Make use of this grace, and become every day less in your own eyes! This admonition is especially needful in our day. Pride and the desire to be lord over others assail us with more persistence than ever before. Now, let *all* submit to one another, all to one another! and let all be clothed and adorned with humility! May this admonition be followed, for Jesus' sake! Thus only can we expect to receive the crown of glory, that fadeth not away. — Give us to this end thy Holy Spirit, merciful God. Pour out the love of Christ into our hearts, and give us his spirit of humility. Amen.

O thou that hear'st when sinners cry, Though all my crimes before thee lie, Behold them not with angry look, But blot their memory from thy book. O may thy love inspire my tongue; Salvation shall be all my song, And all my powers shall join to bless The Lord, my strength and righteousness.

---

197. Friday after Second Sunday after Easter.

Isaiah 40, 9–11. O Zion, that bringest good tidings, get thee up into the high mountain; O Jerusalem, that bringest good tidings, lift up thy voice with strength; lift it up, be not afraid; say unto the cities of Judah, Behold your God! Behold, the Lord God will come with strong hand, and his arm shall rule for him; behold, his reward is with him, and his work before him. He shall feed his flock like a shepherd, he shall gather the lambs with his arm, and carry them in his bosom, and shall gently lead those that are with young.

God wants us to lift up our voice and cry out to the world: "Behold your God!" He wants this done, in order that people may wake up and give heed to that which the Lord does. For their sleep is heavy; Satan has hypnotized the souls. But the word of God is mighty to wake them up. Lift up thy voice, thou messenger in Zion; thou servant of the Lord, get thyself up on the heights, and shout to them that dwell on the earth. Fear not; for thou bringest good tidings, better than the message of Jonah to Nineveh. Thou art to announce the victory of the stronger over the strong, and the salvation of the souls by his mighty arm. Jesus has overcome the devil; and behold, here he is with the prize which his victory has secured; that is to say, with life and salvation for us lost sinners. Awake, ye people, and behold him. He has triumphed over death and hell, and now goes onward to extend his kingdom over all the earth. Awake; and you shall find him already at work in your heart on life's great miracle, your regeneration and sanctification. — He provides with great care for them that belong to him; heals and leads and carries them with the love of the faithful shepherd. The weak and timid lambs he gathers with his arm, and carries in his bosom. Do you hear this, you poor sinner? Your place is in the arm and bosom of the Lord.

at the heart of Jesus; there is your place, not under the feet of the
devil. — They that serve under Jesus in the church, feeding and caring
for his lambs, may count on his special guidance; for it is declared in
express words that he "shall gently lead those that are with young."
He provides a glorious heritage for them that are his own, using his
great might, in the service of his eternal love, for their salvation.
Their names are written in his hands with the nails by which he was
fastened to the cross. O, how zealous he is for their salvation! Lift
up your voice with strength, and let the good tidings be heard in
all the world! Fear not, and be not ashamed; but be partaker of the
afflictions of the gospel according to the power of God.

Lord Jesus, make thy witnesses fearless and zealous, and give
them strength to lift up the voice unto the cities of Judah, that they
who sleep may be awakened, and that the faithful may be strengthened. We thank thee, our divine Shepherd, for thy love toward us
unworthy sinners; and we know that thou wilt, according to thy promise, protect and keep us. Blessed be thy name. Amen.

Let the world despise and leave me; They have left my Savior, too;
Human hearts and looks deceive me — Thou are not, like them, untrue. Man
may trouble and distress me, 'Twill but drive me to thy breast; Life with trials
sore may press me, Heaven will bring me sweeter rest.

198. Saturday after Second Sunday after Easter.

Psalm 100. A Psalm of praise. Make a joyful noise unto the Lord, all
ye lands. Serve the Lord with gladness; come before his presence with singing.
Know ye that the Lord he is God: it is he that hath made us, and not we
ourselves: we are his people, and the sheep of his pasture. Enter into his gates
with thanksgiving, and into his courts with praise: be thankful unto him, and
bless his name. For the Lord is good, his mercy is everlasting; and his truth
endureth to all generations.

Three reasons are here given why we should come before the
presence of the Lord with thanksgiving and songs of joy. 1) The
Lord our God is *the true God;* beside him there is no God. He it is
whom we shall fear and love and trust with our whole heart. He is
Lord of all creation; and the gods of the heathen are nothing. Should
not we, then, who know him, make a joyful noise unto him, and let
our shouts of joy be heard in all the world? Is it not a great happiness
to know the one true God, and to have him for the God of our heart?
2) This great happiness is ours by reason of *his mercy alone.* "It is
he that hath made us, and not we ourselves, to be his people and the
sheep of his pasture." We would have been dwelling as servants in
a strange land, filling ourselves with husks as do the swine, if he had
not ransomed us and led us into his courts, the holy Chr'stian church.
Against our will he dragged us away from the land of lusts with its
satanical allurements, and led us onto the green pastures of his mercy.
3) This mercy is *everlasting.* We enjoy it every moment, we live of
his love all the time; and this shall never cease. His mercy is as

indispensible to our spiritual and to our physical life as is the air we breathe to our bodies. We live and move and have our being in the love of God; and we can rely on its enduring for ever. When we no longer enjoy it in faith we shall enjoy it at the wedding feast of the church in heaven. "Come, then, ye faithful, the Lord's chosen people; know that the Father is gentle and mild; call him with confidence Abba, your Father; rest in his arms with the faith of a child. Give thanks for the wonderful honor that ye his sons and his daughters for ever shall be!"

Proclaim it to all the world with shouts of joy that the Lord he is God, the fount of goodness and of life. Let the good tidings be proclaimed everywhere, in order that all peoples may thank him and bless his name!

O our God, give us this mercy, that we praise thee in this life and in the life to come. Loosen our tongue, that it may give thee thanks; and let thy great and gracious name be known and lauded throughout the world. Amen.

We'll crowd thy gates with thankful songs, High as the heavens our voices raise; And earth, with her ten thousand tongues, Shall fill thy courts with sounding praise.

Wide as the world is thy command, Vast as eternity thy love; Firm as a rock thy truth must stand, When rolling years shall cease to move.

---

199. Third Sunday after Easter. I.

Lord, teach us to understand that which thou shalt speak to us this day. Amen.

Gospel Lesson, John 16, 16–22. A little while, and ye shall not see me: and again, a little while, and ye shall see me, because I go to the Father. Then said some of his disciples among themselves, What is this that he saith unto us, A little while, and ye shall not see me: and again, a little while, and ye shall see me: and, Because I go to the Father? They said therefore, What is this that he saith, A little while? we cannot tell what he saith. Now Jesus knew that they were desirous to ask him, and said unto them, Do ye inquire among yourselves of that I said, A little while, and ye shall not see me: and again, a little while, and ye shall see me? Verily, verily, I say unto you, That ye shall weep and lament, but the world shall rejoice: and ye shall be sorrowful, but your sorrow shall be turned into joy. A woman when she is in travail hath sorrow, because her hour is come: but as soon as she is delivered of the child, she remembereth no more the anguish, for joy that a man is born into the world. And ye now therefore have sorrow: but I will see you again, and your heart shall rejoice, and your joy no man taketh from you.

"*A little while;* and again a little while." Our gospel lesson uses these words several times, and then concludes by making mention of a joy which shall be *without end.* In our present life we are happy one hour and sad the next. But in the midst of the rapidly shifting joys and sorrows of this life there gushes forth for the disciples of Jesus a current of joy which grows ever greater and stronger, and flows on through all eternity. — "A little while, and ye shall not see

17

me." This sounded strange and harsh in the ears of them to whom
it was addressed. In the beginning of our discipleship we feel little
else than the joy and wonder of walking with the Lord. He speaks
to us of tribulations; but we do not understand, and we turn a deaf
ear to him. Now, this can not last; the mortification of the flesh
can not be an altogether pleasurable sensation. Hours of sadness
must come; for we are to become like unto Jesus. He goes away
from us, and we are left in loneliness and sorrow. You then blame
yourself for your want of vigilance and for your disobedience; and
with good reason. Your soul is heavy, your devotion lacks warmth;
drowsiness and darkness are upon the heart. To be sure, this is not
exactly the unavoidable, but it is the usual experience of the disciples
of Jesus. Is, then, the joyous beginning to have this sad end? No,
thank God, dear reader; this is not the end. This is only the second
"little while." Whatever may transpire, do you keep together with the
brethren, continue to study the word and obey it! I have no doubt
that you wish to follow this advice; but I also know that you are
tempted to give up hope, and to leave the church and the society of
the brethren, which now seem to you to be the home of disappointment. Continue in the congregation of the brethren gathered around
the word of God; and the Lord will again let you see him; though
after a different manner, for he is dead and risen again. "Blessed are
they that have not seen, and yet have believed." The first sense of
exuberant happiness is gone; but you learn to *believe* the Lord's presence, and then you experience that he gives genuine peace and joy and
victory over sin. You hold fast the Invisible One as though you saw
him; but you do not ask to see, since it is the will of God that here
we shall walk in faith; but you do see him with the eye of faith, and
your sorrow has been turned into joy. — Nevertheless, do not feel assured that you are henceforth to experience no spiritual travail. The
words, "a little while," are used no less than seven times in our gospel
lesson. Whatever it may be your lot to endure, all your troubles
combined shall last but "a little while;" soon you see the Lord Jesus
face to face in eternal glory. "Ye shall be sorrowful, and ye shall weep
and lament." Thus saith the Lord to his disciples. The statement
is grave and impressive, yet there is comfort in it; for he adds: "Your
sorrow shall be turned into joy." On the other hand, when he says
that "the world shall rejoice," there is nothing but darkness and terror;
for the joy of which he speaks shall last but a little while, and then
be turned into endless lamentation.

"Lord my God, I long for the blessed happiness of peace; I cry
out for that peace which thy children enjoy, whom thou dost illumine
with thy words of comfort. If it please thee to give me peace and to
pour joy into my heart, the soul of thy servant shall be filled with song;
and shall praise thy name with warm devotion. But if thou withdraw
thy presence, as thou ofttimes dost, thy servant is too weak to follow
after thee; he can but fall on his knees and beat his breast; — for his
heart is not as it was yesterday, when thy light shone above his head,
and he was sheltered under the shadow of thy wings against all the
temptations that assailed him. When thy friend suffers afflictions in

the world it is one of the mercies which he receives from thy hand, no matter how great the measure of his affliction may be. Nothing happens on earth without thy counsel and thy prescience. It is expedient for me that thou dost *humble* me, in order that I may know that thy judgments are righteous, and that I may cast out of the heart all pride and conceit." (Kempis).

Lord Jesus, may thy Spirit support us in our faith and make us to understand that it is but for a little while that we do not see thee. Make us to rejoice in hope, to be patient in tribulation, continuing instant in prayer; grant us constancy, and make us partakers with thee in eternal bliss. Amen.

O mighty rock! O source of life, Let thy dear word, 'mid doubt and strife, Be so within us burning, That we be faithful unto death In thy pure love and holy faith, From thee true wisdom learning. Lord, thy graces on us shower! Be thy power Christ confessing, Let us win his grace and blessing.

---

200. Third Sunday after Easter. II.

Give us, O God, the spirit of true liberty and obedience. Amen.

Epistle Lesson, 1 Peter 2, 11–20. Dearly beloved, I beseech you as strangers and pilgrims, abstain from fleshly lusts, which war against the soul; Having your conversation honest among the gentiles: that, whereas they speak against you as evildoers, they may by your good works, which they shall behold, glorify God in the day of visitation. Submit yourselves to every ordinance of man for the Lord's sake: whether it be to the king as supreme; or unto governors, as unto them that are sent by him for the punishment of evildoers, and for the praise of them that do well. For so is the will of God, that with well doing ye may put to silence the ignorance of foolish men: As free, and not using your liberty for a cloke of maliciousness, but as the servants of God. Honor all men. Love the brotherhood. Fear God. Honor the king. Servants, be subject to your masters with all fear; not only to the good and gentle, but also to the froward. For this is thankworthy, if a man for conscience toward God endure grief, suffering wrongfully. For what glory is it, if, when ye be buffeted for your faults, ye shall take it patiently? but if, when ye do well, and suffer for it, ye take it patiently, this is acceptable with God.

You that believe in the Lord Jesus are not of the world, but have your true home in heaven; and this should be seen in you during the little while that you sojourn here in a strange land. Your heavenly descent, your saintly way of thinking, the truth and glory of your eternal calling, are to be manifested by saintly conduct in your earthly affairs and duties. While the children of the world strive to gather wealth, it is to be your object to become rich in good works and lay up treasures in heaven. While the spirit of the world causes people to covet power over others, it shall be your ambition that the spirit of Christ may make you submissive, as people who are truly free, and who have power to compel obedience from the rebellious flesh toward the dictates of the spirit. It is more and more becoming the fashion to pride one's self on being superior to governments and magistrates; and this is called "liberty." The Christians, however, have received power of God to resist the evil spirit of the age, and to submit themselves to every ordinance of man for the Lord's sake. The liberty of those who thirst after power is genuine slavishness and meanness; but the Christian submission to authority, on the other hand, is mastery over one's self and the world, and is true liberty. When the unbelievers deride you, Christian servants, on account of your obedience and respect toward your temporal masters, do you remember that it is Christ, not men, whom you serve; and make it your business to prove by your faithfulness and loyalty that you have learned to master yourselves and the world and the devil. But you will surely fall short and be caught in the world and the toils of the enemy, if you do not diligently and constantly watch and pray; for much grace is required, together with spiritual wisdom and a heavenly mind, in order to resist the alluring spirit of the age. It is, therefore, highly necessary that you take to heart the admonition of the apostle, and that you have the light of God's Spirit on the affairs of life. Never forget, dearly beloved, that you are strangers and pilgrims on earth; and never forget that you are here to serve the Lord in all things. Seek your glory with him, never on any account with men. Then shall they deride you for his sake, revile you *and him;* but he shall nevertheless be honored through you, and be glorified in the day of visitation; and you shall be glorified with him.

When thou makest us free, Lord Jesus, we are free indeed. We heartily beseech thee, give us this glorious freedom. Amen.

The powers ordained by thee, With heavenly wisdom bless; May they thy servants be, And rule in righteousness. O Lord, stretch forth thy mighty hand, And guard and bless our fatherland.

---

201. Monday after Third Sunday after Easter.

Lord Jesus, teach us to know thee. Amen.

John 14, 1–6 Let not your heart be troubled: ye believe in God, believe also in me. In my Father's house are many mansions: if it were not so, I would have told you. I go to prepare a place for you. And if I go and prepare a place for you, I will come again, and receive you unto myself; that where I am, there ye may be also. And whither I go ye know, and the way ye know. Thomas saith unto him, Lord, we know not whither thou goest; and how can we know the way? Jesus saith unto him, I am the way, and the truth, and the life: no man cometh unto the Father, but by me.

"In my Father's house are many mansions." In other words, there is room enough in heaven for all the friends of Jesus; and each of them shall there receive his own special measure of glory. They shall all be gathered there; and all shall have perfect bliss, but shall not have the same measure of glory. The splendor with which we shall shine in heaven shall be greater or less according to the gifts which we have received of God, and the manner in which we have used them. Some have the brilliance of the diamond, others of the ruby, and still others of the emerald; but all fit beautifully together. There is no envy in heaven, and no discordant note is heard in the song of praise before the throne of the Lamb.

Whosoever believes in Jesus, and continues in faith unto the end, can not be lost, but must and shall inherit salvation. For the heart of the believer clings to Jesus, and remains where he is; and thus Jesus takes the believer with himself to heaven. The Lord himself has gone through death and overcome it; but he did this for us. Himself is the life and the light which never can be quenched; and this he is for us who believe in him. "I am the way," he says. He is our bridge from death to life. He has thrown himself into the awful gulf of damnation; and over him we are thus carried home to the Father's house. "He is the living way, the great current on which the ship freighted with human lives is floated out into the sea of a blessed eternity." "I am the truth and the life." It is, therefore, not possible that any who is one with him in heart can be lost. He that has the Son has life already. No death can henceforth destroy him. And is not Jesus, in very truth, your life, your heart's delight and desire, dear Christian friend? We know the way, then, and have the life; and we are certain that we shall be gathered into the mansions of glory. For "we know that the Son of God is come, and has given us understanding to know the true God; and we are in him, in his Son, Jesus Christ, who is the true God and eternal life." — On the other hand, "he that hath not the Son of God hath not life." (1 John 5, 12). "We must, then, learn to regard and know the Lord Jesus as the one who always is and remains with us and in us, especially in the hour of death; nay, who is so near to us that he alone is in our heart. This I know when I fully and firmly believe in him as my Savior, who for me has gone through death to the Father, in order that he may receive me unto himself. When I have this faith I am on the right way which leads from this life to the next. For faith clings to Christ. Where he is it must be and remain also; and the stronger the faith is, the more secure do we walk along the way. To walk on the way simply means, then, to have a steadfast faith and to become all the time more fully assured of eternal life in Christ. When I continue in this faith to the end, and death then attacks and overcomes me, and my consciousness is lost, the journey has already been completed, I have reached the goal, and I begin the new life in the world to come." (Luther).

Lord Jesus, help us to hold thee fast in faith, and not to know any thing unto salvation save thee crucified. Amen.

Thou seest my feebleness; Jesus, be thou my power, My help and refuge in distress, My fortress and my tower.

Myself I cannot save, Myself I cannot keep; But strength in thee I surely have, Whose eyelids never sleep.

202. Tuesday after Third Sunday after Easter.

Lord Jesus, let thy word today kindle and strengthen faith in thee in our hearts. Amen.

John 14, 7–13. If ye had known me, ye should have known my Father also: and from henceforth ye know him, and have seen him. Philip saith unto him, Lord, shew us the Father, and it sufficeth us. Jesus saith unto him, Have I been so long time with you, and yet hast thou not known me, Philip? he that hath seen the Father; and how sayest thou then, Shew us the Father? Believest thou not that I am in the Father, and the Father in me? the words that I speak unto you I speak not of myself: but the Father that dwelleth in me, he doeth the works. Believe me that I am in the Father, and the Father in me: or else believe me for the very work's sake. Verily, verily, I say unto you, He that believeth on me, the works that I do shall he do also; and greater works than these shall he do; because I go unto my Father. And whatsoever ye shall ask in my name, that will I do, that the Father may be glorified in the Son.

Here we again have the assurance from his own lips that he is true God, one with the Father. "He that hath seen me hath seen the Father. Believest thou not that I am in the Father, and the Father in me? The Father that dwelleth in me, he doeth the works. Believe me that I am in the Father, and the Father in me." How could he speak thus, were he not one with the Father, true and eternal God? If Jesus Christ be the truthful teacher, he just as certainly is the true God. For he declares it in language which admits of no dispute; and it must be true, or he would be a liar. But in the latter case, how could he at the same time be the greatest of the world's wise teachers, as he is conceded to be even by the adherents of infidelity? And what explanation could be offered of the works which he did? How would you explain the wonders which he wrought in his disciples after his death and resurrection? It can not be denied that his disciples, after his ascension, did works which are greater than all that he did in his state of humiliation. During his life on earth he went about in Judea, and healed the sick, and raised the dead, and preached the word of life. These were works which proved that he was in the Father, and the Father in him. But since that time he has, through his disciples, created the world anew, and changed the whole form of the earth. From his place at the right hand of the Father he has sent the Holy Ghost, and has equipped his witnesses with power and grace to convert thousands, nay *countless* souls, and rescue them from death and the devil. How could the poor, unlearned, terrified and timid disciples have accomplished such results, if he had remained dead, and they had been left dependent on their own resources? It is impossible. The existence of the church, the life that it has lived and the deeds that it has done, are so conclusive of the divinity and resurrection of Christ, that *he* must indeed be stone blind who does not see that Christ is the Son of God, and that he hears the prayers of the faithful. He says that *himself* will do whatsoever we shall ask of the Father in his name. Every word is evidence that he speaks in the consciousness of being one with the Father. — How blessed are we who have so great and mighty a Savior! He has given us glorious promises, and he is able to fulfil them. Away with unbelief, the accursed lie!

Lord Jesus, thou true God; give us grace to believe in thee, and to pray with all confidence, nothing doubting. Give us the assurance of the Spirit in our hearts, for thy name's sake. Amen.

Approach, my soul, the mercy-seat, Where Jesus answers prayer; There humbly fall before his feet, For none can perish there.

Thy promise is my only plea, With this I venture nigh; Thou callest burdened souls to thee, And such, O Lord, am I.

---

203. Wednesday after Third Sunday after Easter.

Lord, make us glad with the comfort of thy word. Amen.

Psalm 126. When the Lord turned again the captivity of Zion, we were like them that dream. Then was our mouth filled with laughter, and our tongue with singing: then said they among the heathen, The Lord hath done great things for them. The Lord hath done great things for us; whereof we are glad. Turn again our captivity, O Lord, as the streams in the south. They that sow in tears shall reap in joy. He that goeth forth and weepeth, bearing precious seed, shall doubtless come again with rejoicing, bringing his sheaves with him.

The people of Israel had been delivered out of their Babylonian captivity; and though they had believed the promise and expected its fulfilment, their deliverance came to them in the nature of a surprise, and seemed to them such a glorious thing altogether that they were beside themselves with wonder and delight. But captivity and affliction again came upon them, as we read in the books of Ezra and Nehemiah. Now their cry once more is: "Turn again our captivity, O Lord, as the streams in the south." The heart of the psalmist is full of hope. The sower sows his seed with sweat and labor; there is a long drouth; the seed and the labor seem to have been wasted; the heart is held in suspense between hope and fear; the tears flow. O God, send rain, send rain from on high! And are we, then, after all, to have a bountiful harvest? Yes; the seed that is sown with sweat and tears shall be reaped with exultation and songs of joy. — This is the common experience of God's people, of the individual Christian, and of the Lord's church. Here on earth captivity and deliverance, lamentation and songs of joy, alternate; but they are followed at last by eternal bliss. — The Lord hath done great things for us. He has converted us, delivered us out of captivity, released us from the bondage of sin, and led us into the Canaan of his grace. What a change! What a wondrous change to be turned from death to life, from the power of Satan to God! We say with our whole heart: "The Lord hath done great things for us; whereof we are glad." However, there still are drawn swords round about us. And what is the situation now? The windows of heaven seem to be closed above the land. There falls no rain; the soul is parched with thirst in the fiery heat of spiritual trials. "I once *was* in the state of **grace**, *was* a child of God, tasted his life, lived in his love, had peace and joy, served the Lord willingly and hopefully. Now, alas, this happiness has fled. Again I am in captivity and sore trouble; the streams have run dry, the earth is parched, the seed dies." Thus sounds the complaint; but even in this there is hope and prayer, because the faithful Holy Spirit has not permitted the heart to sever itself from the word of God. Be of good cheer, dear friend, and fear not; you shall surely come again with rejoicing, bringing your sheaves with you. You long, and you pray; which proves that there is *faith* in your heart. And the Lord is the God who works wonders. The tears of *faith always* yield at last a bountiful harvest of joy. This never fails.

How long, O Lord, how long? Thou seest how I am assailed by unbelief. Have mercy, and turn again our captivity as the streams in the desert. Lord, may it please thee to do it quickly. Amen.

Judge not the Lord by feeble sense, But trust him for his grace; Behind a frowning providence He hides a smiling face.

His purposes will ripen fast, Unfolding every hour; The bud may have a bitter taste, But sweet will be the flower.

Blind unbelief is sure to err And scan his work in vain; **God is** his own interpreter, And he will make it plain.

---

204. Thursday after Third Sunday after Easter.

Lord Jesus, show us this great favor that we may hear thee pray. Amen.

John 17, 1–5. These words spake Jesus, and lifted up his eyes to heaven, and said, Father, the hour is come; glorify thy Son, that thy Son also may glorify thee: As thou hast given him power over all flesh, that he should give eternal life to as many as thou hast given him. And this is the life eternal, that they might know thee the only true God, and Jesus Christ, whom thou hast sent. I have glorified thee on the earth: I have finished the work which thou gavest me to do. And now, O Father, glorify thou me with thine own self, with the glory which I had with thee before the world was.

This Bible lesson is the first part of the pontifical prayer of Jesus; and there is nothing in the whole Bible which, for simplicity and depth, is more marvellous than this prayer.

In these five verses Jesus himself prays as the Savior of the world; that the Father will glorify him, in order that he may glorify the Father, and may give eternal life to all them whom the Father has given him. The hour was come; he was to suffer *death*, in order that he might be glorified, and that he might glorify the Father, and give us eternal life. He had power to lay down his life, and power to take it again. Herein is revealed the eternal, wise, and loving counsel of the holy Trinity in respect to the world; here we are met by a glory so overwhelming, and at the same time so gentle and gracious, that it melts the heart; here are righteousness and wisdom, and above all, love, so mighty that they draw unto themselves all whose eyes have been enlightened by the Spirit. "And this is life eternal." He that knows the one true God, who is revealed on earth by his only begotten

Son, our Lord Jesus Christ; he that knows the Father and the Son through the coming, the passion, the death, and the victory of the Son; knows him as a result of being enlightened by the Spirit, whom the Son after his ascension sends from the Father; he that knows God in such a way that the knowledge fills his heart, or that he knows him with the knowledge of love, even as the Son knows the Father; — he has life eternal. Love, which is stronger than death, is come to him, into his heart; he lives in Jesus, and Jesus in him. This is life eternal, *and this only*; but this is, in very truth, *eternal life*, "that they know thee — *know* thee, the only true God — the *only* — *only true God*, and *Jesus Christ, whom thou hast sent.*" How unutterably important is this! *This*, and this *only*, is life *eternal*, everlasting *life*. In order to give us this life, and thereby honor the Father, Jesus must through death enter into his glory; and this he *wishes* to do, and for this he *prays*. He is willing to accept this as a gift from the Father, though he is the only begotten Son, and as such had this glory before the world was. What a marvellous prayer this is! When we hear it every fiber in us is stirred to worship and thank him.

Blessed be thou, Lord Jesus, who didst renounce the use of thy glory, and didst pray the Father to glorify thee through the suffering of death, in order to translate us from death to life. Thou seest that we as yet understand but little of the depth and height of this truth; but give us, we pray thee, thy Holy Spirit, and shew us the Father, that we may in truth be possessors of life eternal. May we know thy love, which passeth knowledge. Glorify thyself in us, precious Savior; and glorify us with thee, that we in heaven may praise thy glory for ever and ever. Amen.

Jesus, priceless treasure, Source of purest pleasure, Truest friend to me: Long my heart hath panted Till it well-nigh fainted, Thirsting after thee. Thine I am, O spotless lamb! I will suffer naught to hide thee, Ask for naught beside thee.
In thine arms I rest me, Foes who would molest me Cannot reach me here; Though the earth be shaking, Every heart be quaking, Jesus calms my fear; Sin and hell, in conflict fell, With their heaviest storms assail me, Jesus will not fail me.

205. Day of Common Prayer. I.

Lord, let thy words chasten and humble us, and bring us to our knees before thy throne of grace. Amen.

Isaiah 55, 6–7. Seek ye the Lord while he may be found, call ye upon him while he is near. Let the wicked forsake his way, and the unrighteous man his thoughts: and let him return unto the Lord, and he will have mercy upon him: and to our God, for he will abundantly pardon.

Let these words ring in our hearts today, that we may keep them, follow them, and never more forget them: "Seek ye the Lord while he may be found, call ye upon him while he is near." It is the voice of his love calling to us; hear it, and it will draw your heart to him. When he says to us that we are to seek him, his word gives us power to do it; by virtue of this word we are then able to seek him, and to find him. He goes to meet you, and he gives you grace to come to meet him. Do not neglect it, and do not let the devil hold you bound with his fetters, from which the word of God sets you free. Call on the Lord while he is near. He it is who inspires you to pray. Today, as you *hear* this, there is a prayer to God in your soul; do not suppress it, but call upon him; he expects you, and has inclined his ear to you! You have many things about which to speak with him. You went astray in your youth, and walked without God. You went farther and farther, farther and farther, away from him. But *he* did not lose sight of you, nor did he forget you. He called to you many a time and oft, but you would not hear. Now he again calls out to you: Thou wicked man, forsake thy way, and return unto me! You are *wicked* as long as your heart flees from God. The depraved and vicious are not the only ones who are wicked; the term here includes all who love the world. Your way leads to eternal perdition; repent, therefore, and return unto the Lord! Do this for Jesus' sake; for his sake who died for you and reconciled you with God! Do not postpone it, but turn to the Lord now; go to him, and ask him to have mercy on you! Do it at once; for now he is near! Surely, you feel that you *should* do it. See how near he is; for this is his voice calling you to come. He will have mercy, and will abundantly pardon; you receive forgiveness for all your wickedness; he takes away your guilt; he teaches you to lay it where he has laid it; namely, on the Lamb; that you may be free and happy. The only thing required is that you return to him. If you do not turn to him, you are lost; your wickedness will carry you down to hell, whether you laugh and mock or no. Your conscience tells you that you are a miserable wretch and a fool, with your hardness and impenitent heart, as long as you remain a slave of Satan; and you understand that you are treasuring up unto yourself wrath against the day of wrath and the revelation of the righteous judgment of God. You have no excuse for continuing in your unrighteousness; for you may begin to seek the Lord; he draws you.

Lord, turn thou us, and we shall be turned! Draw us to thee, and do not let us go. We deplore and confess our wickedness; do thou have mercy on us, and pardon us, and lead us in the paths of righteousness for Jesus' sake. Amen.

A broken heart, my God, my king! Is all the sacrifice I bring: But thou, O Lord, will ne'er despise A broken heart for sacrifice.
Then will I teach the world thy ways; Sinners shall lears thy sov'reign grace; I'll lead them to my Savior's blood, And they shall praise a pardoning God.

---

206. Day of Common Prayer. II.

Lord, let thy word turn our hearts to obedience toward thee. Amen.

Matthew 3, 8-10. Bring forth therefore fruits meet for repentance: And think not to say within yourselves, We have Abraham to our father: for I say unto you, that God is able of these stones to raise up children unto Abraham.

And now also the axe is laid unto the root of the trees: therefore every tree which bringeth not forth good fruit, is hewn down, and cast into the fire.

Do not neglect to do sincere penance this very day; and let your life be evidence that you have turned to the Lord. Let none imagine that he is a Christian, merely because he belongs to a so-called Christian people, or because he uses the word of God and the sacraments, and leads a decent life. Neither must any comfort himself with the reflection that he did repent once upon a time, and that he no longer follows the multitude, but is one of the little flock. The Pharisees were very careful and exact in the observance of their worship and ordinances; but of true piety there was none whatever in their hearts. Do you bring forth fruits meet for repentance? Do you live in sincere humility, living faith, and true sanctification? Is Jesus your life, and do you walk honestly before your God? Do you practice self-denial and charity? We will not ask if you are perfect in these things; but we do ask in all earnestness if you live every day in genuine repentance, if you are a new creature in Christ, and if you *press on* toward perfection. Even the true Christians are deplorably weak; but they daily confess their sin with penitent heart, and pray for mercy. Many unregenerate persons, on the other hand, foolishly try to solace themselves with the infirmities of the Christians; and commit sin, in order that grace may the more abound. There is an immeasurable distance, however, between the upright man of the world and the weak Christian. The hearts of the unregenerate are strangers to God. They do not seek Jesus with heart-felt longing; for they neither know their sin nor feel their wretchedness. They love and seek their own, and mind the earthly things. The Christians, on the other hand, turn continually to God, seek him with sincere hearts, and strive all the time to live as he would have them live. They feel and regret their sin, and their only hope is the grace of God in Christ. Do not imagine that this is a matter of little importance. If you are a barren tree, the ax is laid to the root, and you shall be hewn down, and cast into the fire. The withered branches of the vine can neither bear fruit, nor have any value as building material; they are good for nothing but to serve as fuel. Repent, then; turn over a new leaf, and become a new man! O, that we might be able to impress on ourselves with all the emphasis which the gravity of the subject demands, how absolutely necessary this is! Do not postpone this; hear and follow the Lord's call now, *today!*

Ye believers, humble yourselves and do penance, one and all, for your own sins and for the sins of the church; and let it be seen in your lives that you have today had an audience with the Lord. Live hereafter, with greater care than heretofore, irreproachable and pure lives as God's blameless children in the midst of the wicked and perverse generation, among whom you shine as lights in the world. Let us all make this day a day of repentance! Let us all together prostrate ourselves before the throne of grace with sincere confession of our sins and earnest appeals for mercy! Give us to this end the power of thy Spirit, merciful God. Grant that we may bring forth fruits meet for repentance, **to** the glory of thy name and to the salvation of our souls. Amen.

Hasten, sinners, to be wise, Stay not for the morrow's **sun;** Wisdom if thou still despise, Harder is it to be won.

Hasten mercy to implore, Stay not for the morrow's **sun,** Lest thy season should be o'er Ere this evening's **stage be run.**

---

207. Saturday after Third Sunday after Easter.

Lord Jesus, grant us again the mercy, that we may hear thee pray. Amen.

John 17, 6–11. I have manifested thy name unto the men which thou gavest me out of the world: thine they were, and thou gavest them me; and they have kept thy word. Now they have known that all things whatsoever thou hast given me are of thee. For I have given unto them the words which thou gavest me; and they have received them, and have known surely that I came out from thee, and they have believed that thou didst send me. I pray for them: I pray not for the world, but for them which thou hast given me; for they are thine. And all mine are thine, and thine are mine; and I am glorified in them. And now I am no more in the world, but these are in the world, and I come to thee. Holy Father, keep through thine own name those whom thou hast given me, that they may be one, as we are.

Jesus here prays for us, his disciples; not for the world. To be sure, he prays for the world also, but not in this particular prayer. For there is an immense difference between the disciples of Jesus and the children of the world. The former are the Father's especial gift to the Son. Jesus says: "Thou gavest me them; thine they were, and thou gavest them me." Not until we are in heaven shall we fully understand exactly what is meant by this, that they were the Father's, and that he gave them to the Son; but even now we understand at least this much, that it is something unutterably precious and great. The disciples of Jesus are, then, chosen and set aside from the world. When the children of the world hear the word concerning the Father and the Son their souls are enveloped in darkness, and they do not understand what they hear. The disciples of Jesus, on the other hand, grasp the truth in their hearts, and keep it. It has become clear and sure to them that the Father sent his Son to be the Savior of the world; and they see the love which is herein revealed. They believe and confess that the Son is one with the Father; that in Christ the heart of God lies open before us; that Christ is the living way by which we have free access to the Father. These disciples of Christ are his dearly beloved treasures and the children of the Father. As the Father gave them to the Son, so they are again, through the Son, become the Father's own; "for all mine are thine, and thine are mine." For us, what infinite happiness and glory! And this grace belongs not only to the first disciples, but to all believers. For, in verse 20, Jesus says: "Neither pray I for these alone, but for them also which shall believe on me through their word." In consequence, the Father and Son are unspeakably great. glorious, and precious to them that

---

believe. The election of the faithful, their redemption, the love of the Father and the intercession of Christ for them, the light of the word and the gracious gift of faith; — all these things are more precious to the believers than gold to the miser; they rejoice in it, but at the same time it humbles their hearts as they remember that they are entirely unworthy to receive this great mercy. — What divine goodness in the care with which Jesus guards his disciples! "I am no more in the world, but these are in the world, and I come to thee. Holy Father, keep through thine own name those whom thou hast given me, that they may be one, as we are." This the Father *will surely do;* he has always heard the prayers of his Son. Hallelujah!

We thank thee for thy prayer, and for all things, Lord Jesus. We thank thee, heavenly Father, for thy unspeakably great gift. Blessed be the Holy Trinity for ever and ever! Amen.

Thou who art three in unity, True God from all eternity, Though daylight vanish into night, Yet shines on us thy heavenly light.

We praise thee with the dawning day, To thee at eve for mercy pray; With our poor song we worship thee Now, ever, and eternally.

Let God the Father be adored, And God the Son, the only Lord, And God the Holy Spirit be Adored through all eternity.

---

208. Fourth Sunday after Easter. I.

Come, heavenly Comforter, and explain to us the words of Jesus. Amen.

Gospel Lesson, John 16, 5–15. But now I go my way to him that sent me; and none of you asketh me, Whither goest thou? But because I have said these things unto you, sorrow hath filled your heart. Nevertheless I tell you the truth; It is expedient for you that I go away: for if I go not away, the comforter will not come unto you; but if I depart, I will send him unto you. And when he is come, he will reprove the world of sin, and of righteousness, and of judgment: Of sin, because they believe not on me; of righteousness, because I go to my Father, and ye see me no more; of judgment, because the prince of this world is judged. I have yet many things to say unto you, but ye cannot bear them now. Howbeit when he, the Spirit of truth, is come, he will guide you into all truth: for he shall not speak of himself; but whatsoever he shall hear, that shall he speak: and he will shew you things to come. He shall glorify me: for he shall receive of mine, and shall shew it unto you. All things that the Father hath are mine: therefore said I, that he shall take of mine, and shall shew it unto you.

Be not sorrowful because that Jesus is gone to the Father, and that we no more see him. Let it make you glad. For by his going through death and resurrection he has taken away our sins, won for us a righteousness entirely valid before God, and overcome the devil. From his place at the right hand of the Father he sends the Holy Spirit, who guides us into all truth, and who reproves the world of sin, and of righteousness, and of judgment.—In these last words the way of life is mapped out. The Comforter reproves the world of sin, *because they believe not on Jesus.* For the Savior has taken upon himself all the sin of the world; and hence the want of faith in him becomes the one sin which condemns. Unbelief is the sin which causes all other sins to be again imputed to the sinner. He that does not believe in Jesus despises the only means by which sin can be taken away, the Son of God, namely; together with his work of atonement. To show us this truth, to crush our hearts and make them penitent, is the work of the Spirit, without enlightenment by whom none can know the sin of unbelief.–Secondly, the Comforter reproves the world of *righteousness;* which righteousness consists therein, *that Jesus is gone to the Father,* and we see him no more. The obedience of Jesus, his suffering, his death, his resurrection; these, and nothing else, are the righteousness which suffices before God. Not that which the Spirit works in us, but that which Christ has done for us; not that which we can see and feel, but the going away of the invisible Savior to the Father, is the righteousness of the saints. We note two things in this connection; in the first place, that no work of man, but Christ *alone,* is our righteousness before God; and, secondly, that this righteousness is to be *believed* without being seen and felt; nay, in direct contradiction of that which is felt. At the very time when we feel nothing but sin and misery, the Spirit convinces us that we are justified before God through him who now is at the right hand of the Father, and who makes intercession for us. — Finally, the Spirit reproves, or convicts, the world of *judgment;* that is, that *the prince of this world is judged.* The devil lies when he represents to our conscience that, by reason of our sin, he still has some title to us, or power over us; for he is judged, and has lost this title and power. But he that will yet serve the devil is judged with him. He that chooses the devil as his master is with him under the judgment. This work of conviction was begun by the Comforter at the time of Pentecost, and he continues it until the end of time. He has overcome me with his truth, and by the persuasive power of his love he has forced conviction upon me. The world denies both sin and righteousness; but the word of God chastens me, and makes me to know my sin every day, and to believe his forgiveness. I am forced to be silent before him, and to surrender myself; and this chastening and victorious power of the Comforter over my soul through the gospel of Jesus is my blessed release from the bondage of the law and the flesh; for which reason I unceasingly pray him to bring my every thought and my whole soul into captivity to the obedience of Christ.

Holy Spirit, speak without ceasing to me and in me. Shew me the enormity of the sin of unbelief, and the perfect sufficiency of the righteousness of grace; and make me courageous in the war of the cross against the condemned prince of the world. Amen.

Come, Holy Spirit, heavenly dove, With all thy quickening powers; Kindle a flame of sacred love In these cold hearts of ours.
See how we grovel here below, Fond of these earthly toys; Our souls, how heavily they go, To reach eternal joys!

209. Fourth Sunday after Easter. II.

Lord, give me understanding, and I shall keep thy law; yea, I shall observe it with my whole heart. Amen.

Epistle Lesson, James I, 17–21. Every good gift and every perfect gift is from above, and cometh down from the Father of lights, with whom is no variableness, neither shadow of turning. Of his own will begat he us with the word of truth, that we should be a kind of firstfruits of his creatures. Wherefore, my beloved brethren, let every man be swift to hear, slow to speak, slow to wrath: For the wrath of man worketh not the righteousness of God. Wherefore lay apart all filthiness and superfluity of naughtiness, and receive with meekness the engrafted word which is able to save your souls.

There comes no evil from the Lord our God. All that is from above is good and perfect, bright and pure. As everything which God did at the creation was very good, so is that which he now does altogether good. There is no variableness in the Father of lights. By reason of sin there is in nature a constant alternation of day and night, light and darkness. The sun rises and sets; but the countenance of God remains unchanged above us, shining with a brilliancy in which there is no variation. Whether it is to be our salvation or our doom will depend on the manner in which we receive it. He has given to us all his only Son, who is himself light and life; and with him he has given us all good things. Among these glorious gifts in Christ the greatest is the word and grace of regeneration; for by this the soul is translated from the kingdom of darkness to the fellowship of Christ, and is brought to life from the dead. It was according to the perfectly free counsel of his own good will in Christ that he begat us anew with the word of truth. We have not chosen him, but he has chosen us; he caused his word to come home to our hearts, received us into his favor and made us his children, and created the new life in us. The congregation of the regenerated children of God is to him a kind of firstfruits of all his creatures; it is his treasure which he holds dear above all other creatures, visible and invisible. Even as the husbandman takes greater pleasure in the first fruit of the season than in the later harvest, so God holds his Son's bride more dear than he does his other creatures. For that which the Holy Spirit has wrought in the hearts of the faithful is God's most excellent and marvellous work. — As the word is the instrument used by the Spirit in bringing about this wonderful miracle, the regeneration of the human heart, so it also is the means employed by the Spirit for the preservation and growth of the new life. Let us, therefore, hear the word with willing soul, and keep it faithfully in the heart. O, that each of us might be especially swift to hear the word of God! Let none be slothful and slow to hear when the Lord speaks; and let every man be careful to avoid all those things which might interfere with the work of God in him. Otherwise we prevent the Spirit from making us partakers of the good and perfect gifts of God; and we miss some of those sunbeams of mercy of which we, especially in this cold age, stand in sore need. Wrath disturbs the mind. and makes it impossible for the word to

dispel the darkness; "all filthiness and superfluity of naughtiness"
covers the soul with slime, which shuts out the light of God's countenance in his word. But a Christian who keeps careful watch over
himself, who in patience resists temptation, and who walks his way
with meekness, can receive and keep the word, that it may perfect
the good work which it has begun in him. Then the end shall be the
salvation of the soul and an eternal thanksgiving in our long home in
heaven with the Father of lights.

Lord, make us swift to hear thy word. Grant that we may become its willing doers; and give us thereby more light and life in our
souls from day to day, until we see thee face to face. Amen.

God's word a treasure is to me, Through sorrow's night my sun shall be,
To faith a sword in battle; The Father's hand hath written there My title as
his child and heir, "The kingdom's thine forever;" That promise faileth never.

---

210. Monday after Fourth Sunday after Easter.

*Lord Jesus, give us grace to hear thy most holy words to the Father, in
that thou dost pray for us. Amen.*

John 17, 11–19. And now I am no more in the world, but these are in
the world, and I come to thee. Holy Father, keep through thine own name
those whom thou hast given me, that they may be one, as we are. While I
was with them in the world, I kept them in thy name: those that thou gavest
me I have kept, and none of them is lost, but the son of perdition; that the
scripture might be fulfilled. And now come I to thee; and these things I speak
in the world, that they might have my joy fulfilled in themselves. I have given
them thy word; and the world hath hated them, because they are not of the
world, even as I am not of the world. I pray not that thou shouldest take
them out of the world, but that thou shouldest keep them from the evil. They
are not of the world, even as I am not of the world. Sanctify them through
thy truth: thy word is truth. As thou hast sent me into the world, even so
have I also sent them into the world. And for their sakes I sanctify myself,
that they also might be sanctified through the truth.

The Father is holy; he is exalted above all creatures, and there is
in him no trace whatever of the impurity of the fallen world. *The
Son* is one with the Father, and is equally *holy;* as is also the third
person of the Trinity, *the Holy Ghost.* That which is to have communion with God must be holy; without holiness none can enjoy the
bliss which God gives. Therefore the faithful must be chosen out of
the world, sanctified to the Lord, cleansed by the Spirit, and kept unspotted in the purity of Jesus. In order that this may come to pass,
Jesus consecrated himself for us; that is, gave himself as a sacrificial
lamb for our sins. To sanctify a thing to the Lord God means to set
it apart, to give it and dedicate it as a sacrifice to him; as was done in
the case of the priests and the sacrifices in the Old Testament. (Exodus 29. Leviticus 22). Jesus consecrated himself for us; surrendered
himself wholly to God as a sacrifice and high priest for us. He laid
down his life for us, thus making his whole life and his death, his holy

will and obedience and work and suffering, ours. Of his own free will he delivered himself up to death in our stead. *"This is that* by means of which we are made holy: *That he hallowed himself for us.* It is a truth whose value is beyond all price. Briefly stated, it means that Christ is our priest and mediator, that on the cross he sacrificed himself to God the Father, and that by this sacrifice we are reconciled with God and have salvation. This is our chief article of faith and the source of all our comfort and riches as Christians." By this means they that are one with Christ are holy, even as he is holy; they no longer are of the world, but are separated from its sin, and consecrated to be kings and priests before God. This separation from sin and the world is something widely different from that which is affected by pharisaical self-righteousness while the heart is full of egotism and the things of this world. Jesus does not take his disciples out of the world before the time appointed of the Father; but he takes possession of their heart, and sends them out into the world to bear witness concerning him, and to consecrate themselves to the work of extending his kingdom. He prays to the Father that the word of truth, which contains and brings his self-sacrificing love, the power of his life and death, may so entirely fill their souls that they may be sanctified, and willingly give themselves as an offering to God, and die from all sin. And as he prays, so it *is* in truth with them that believe in Jesus. — Blessed are they who through the word and faith are one in God! Blessed are they when the world hates them and casts them off, blessed in their sufferings, blessed in their death! Heavenly Father, may we be of those whom thy Son didst receive from thee! Do not suffer us to reject thy mercy by loving sin, thus rushing headlong into perdition. Holy Father, sanctify us by the word, in the fellowship of Jesus, to thy service; make us to understand the full meaning of his passion and resurrection, that our whole life, our will and desire and all that is in us, may be devoted to thee. Draw our hearts to thee, that we may hate even the garment spotted by the flesh, and that we may not tolerate any sin in ourselves. We earnestly beseech thee in the name of Jesus: Sanctify us through thy truth; thy word is truth. Amen.

Holy Spirit, strong and mighty, Thou who makest all things new, Make thy work within me perfect, Help me by thy word so true, Arm me with that sword of thine. And the victory shall be mine.

---

211. Tuesday after Fourth Sunday after Easter.

Lord Jesus, allow us once more to hear thee pray for us. Amen.

John 17, 20–26. Neither pray I for these alone, but for them also which shall believe on me through their word; that they all may be one; as thou, Father, art in me, and I in thee, that they also may be one in us: that the world may believe that thou hast sent me. And the glory which thou gavest me I have given them; that they may be one, even as we are one: I in them, and thou in me, that they may be made perfect in one; and that the world

may know that thou hast sent me and hast loved them, as thou hast loved me.
Father, I will that they also, whom thou hast given me, be with me where
I am; that they may behold my glory, which thou hast given me: for thou
lovedst me before the foundation of the world. O righteous Father, the world
hath not known thee: but I have known thee, and these have known that thou
hast sent me. And I have declared unto them thy name, and will declare it:
that the love wherewith thou hast loved me may be in them, and I in them.

This text is so beautiful, and its every word so precious, that we
should keep it in our innermost heart, and rejoice in it as in a priceless treasure. Jesus prays for us also, who now live and believe in
him; and in the Father and the Son we are one with his apostles and
with all the saints. The love with which the Father is in the Son and
the Son in the Father, is in us also; and thus we are in the Son and in
the Father together with all them that believe. How blessed a truth
this is! "The glory which thou gavest me I have given them." Note
this: He has given us the glory which the Father gave him. By
reason of the fall in Adam we lost the glory of God; but we have found
it again; found, indeed, more than we lost. For the glory which the
Son received from the Father he has given us. We have it already,
though we do not see it; we do not need to see it, since Jesus has said
it. — Let me ponder this: Jesus has given me, a poor worm and a
wretched sinner, the glory which the Father gave him! Is it not
merely a dream? *Jesus in us, even as the Father in him!* Even though
it be supported by no evidence whatever in myself, I have his word
for it; and that is sufficient to dispel every dark doubt. In his early
childhood Jesus himself was unconscious of his glory; and yet, was
he not even then the Lord of glory? But now we have already begun
to feel in our hearts this divine glory. We know of a certainty that
Jesus loves us, and we know that we love him in return; we long
after him, rejoice in him, grieve because of our sins against him,
serve him, trust in him, live in him. There is in us a holy life
of love, which is not of the flesh, but of God; we love the
brethren, and have pity on our enemies. Is not this the image
and glory of God in Christ Jesus? What is it, indeed, but
that very love of which John says: "God is love; and he that
dwelleth in love, dwelleth in God, and God in him." Therefore Jesus
also says in our text: "Father, I will that they also, whom thou hast
given me, be with me where I am; that they may behold *my glory,*
which thou hast given me; *for thou lovedst me* before the foundation
of the world." When we reach the home to which he is gone before
us, and see that which we now believe, this glory in us shall become
perfect. Then we shall become like him, and look into this mystery
which now is but faintly reflected in our love toward the brethren:
into this depth of mercy, that *the Father has loved us, as he has loved
his only begotten Son.* Incredible as it seems, this is what Jesus says:
"Thou hast loved them, as thou hast loved me."
My God, what shall I say of this? I believe, and worship, and
live of this love. Lord Jesus, have mercy on thy people; there are
contentions and factions among those who are to be one in thee. Unite

in thyself as many of us as believe in thee. Let thy love knit us together and make us one in heart. Let our whole life be love. This
we ardently desire. Lord Jesus, let the love with which the Father
loved thee be in us; and be thou in us, thy poor, unworthy brethren,
for whom thou didst pay so great a price. Amen.

Praise to God, immortal praise, For the love that crowns our days!
Bounteous source of every joy, Let thy praise our tongues employ. All to
thee, our God, we owe, Source whence all our blessings flow.

---

212. Wednesday after Fourth Sunday after Easter.

Lord, open our eyes to see that which thou hast given us in thy gospel. Amen.

Romans 1, 16. 17. For I am not ashamed of the gospel of Christ: for it
is the power of God unto salvation, to every one that believeth; to the Jew
first, and also to the Greek. For therein is the righteousness of God revealed
from faith to faith: as it is written, The just shall live by faith.

There is no doubt that a time is near at hand in which the masses
and the wise men of the world will oppress the church and revile the
gospel as never before, and make it a shame to confess the faith.
Then we shall learn to understand the words of Paul, in Romans 10:
"If thou shalt confess with thy mouth the Lord Jesus, and shalt believe
in thine heart that God hath raised him from the dead, thou shalt be
saved. For with the heart man believeth unto righteousness; and
with the mouth confession is made unto salvation." Besides, it is
always the case, for that matter, that we are prone to be ashamed of the
gospel; for it takes away every merit of *ours;* and, furthermore, Christ
and his kingdom are in no wise glorious in the eyes of the world, but
are unto the Jews a stumbling block, and unto the Greeks foolishness.
Then the question is whether or not "the righteousness of God" is
regarded by us as a matter of grave importance. If we understand
that on it hinges our eternal fate, everlasting life or everlasting death,
and that the gospel alone can save our soul, we overcome the feeling
of shame, and esteem it an honor to suffer reproach with Christ. —
None but the righteous are able to stand before the righteous God;
where shall we, who are unrighteous, secure the righteousness which
will satisfy his demands? "That is easy enough," says the world; "I
do in all things as well as I can, and God can ask no more of me.
It would be foolish to worry on account of our sins when we do the
best we can." If this be so, then were Paul and Peter fools, to be consumed with anxiety for the safety of their fellows. And what shall
we say of God's own Son, who suffered unutterable agony and the most
bitter of deaths, in order that he might acquire righteousness for us?
It seems plain that Paul made no mistake when he declared that the
foolishness of God is wiser than the wisdom of men. — Righteousness
before God is not of our works, but of faith; it is a *righteousness by
faith alone.* In other words, it is the atonement of Jesus Christ, which
he brought about by his obedience, and which becomes ours when
we believe; it is not a *demand* of God on us, but a *gift* of God to us.

As it is a righteousness of faith only, and has no existence in us apart from faith; as it depends entirely on *faith*, and not on *works*, and belongs to the dispensation of faith, not the dispensation of the law, — therefore the apostle calls it "the righteousness of God from faith." Then again, it is a righteousness "to faith." For it is a gift to faith; to them that believe through the light and instruction of the gospel. The word creates faith in the heart, the faith which receives Christ and his righteousness, and by which man is justified and enabled to stand before God. Luther relates that he had gone through a long struggle in order to become righteous; he had fasted and prayed and almost destroyed his own life in hopes of finding peace; but it was all in vain. Then the Spirit of God taught him the meaning of this passage: "The just shall live by faith;" and he felt the pulsation of a new life in his heart. Then he understood that the righteousness which is valid before God is a gift of the grace of God in Christ, and is *imputed* freely to all poor sinners who believe, and that hence it is wholly and solely "'from faith to faith." "Then I at once felt that I had been born again, and had found an open door to paradise; and I now took an entirely new view of the precious word of God. While I had, in fact, hated the term 'God's righteousness,' it now became the greatest pride and joy and comfort of my heart; and to me this passage from Saint Paul became in very truth the gate to paradise." Luther is, to be sure, beyond question the greatest man who has trod the scene of history since the days of the apostles; but he is, of course, regarded as the merest tyro by the wise men of our times!

Help us, O God, to know sin and righteousness, death and life. Give us true faith, that we may never be ashamed of the gospel of Christ. Amen.

Thou sacred ardor, comfort sweet, Help us to wait with ready feet And willing heart at thy command, Nor trial fright us from thy band.

Lord, may thy power prepare each heart, To our weak nature strength impart, That as good warriors we may force, Thro' life and death, to thee our course!

---

213. Thursday after Fourth Sunday after Easter.

Lord, instruct us in the word of thy righteousness. Amen.

Philippians 3, 7-11. But what things were gain to me, those I counted loss for Christ. Yea, doubtless, and I count all things but loss, for the excellency of the knowledge of Christ Jesus my Lord: for whom I have suffered the loss of all things, and do count them but dung, that I may win Christ, and be found in him, not having mine own righteousness, which is of the law, but that which is through the faith of Christ, the righteousness which is of God by faith: That I may know him, and the power of his resurrection, and the fellowship of his sufferings, being made conformable unto his death; if by any means I might attain unto the resurrection of the dead.

If you, also, know the Lord Jesus Christ, and know that you have in truth been justified by faith in him, you must learn more and more to prize and praise the excellency of this knowledge. It is counted as having but little value by many in our times; even by many who have made a beginning in the true knowledge of it. When an apostle of infidelity parades his would-be-wise theories, they are at once ready to discard Christ and the gospel, faith and the righteousness which is of faith, the death and the life of the Son of God, with everything that can save from sin and Satan; and in its place they take up with some false and shallow ideas about their own wisdom and virtue, which end in hopelessness and despair. Paul learned to prize the grace of God in Christ more highly from day to day; and indeed it could not be otherwise, as he was all the time coming into closer fellowship with the Lord. A true scientist who studies the works of God in nature does not tire of it, but rejoices in every new discovery of new depths in the wisdom of God. Now, in Christ are hid all the treasures of wisdom and knowledge; in him are found the deep sources of life, the divine flood of love and righteousness. And the glorious feature of it is this, that in finding them we find exactly what the heart needs, true peace and the treasures of eternal bliss. Should not Paul, and we with him, zealously study these things, into which even the angels desire to look?

My own virtue from childhood is so absolutely worthless as a means of acquiring righteousness, and is such a paltry nothing in comparison with the merit of Christ, which he gives me precisely as though it were my own, that with Paul I do count all mine own righteousness but dung, and throw it away as foul uncleanness. Such a statement offends our reason and pride, and the whole world rises in revolt against it; but it is true for all that. My own righteousness is indeed filth, and I must throw it away. My whole heart follows after, if that I may be found in Christ, and in the righteousness which is of faith. Paul could not be without him. It is only in the power of Christ's resurrection that I can live the life of love; it is only in the fellowship of his sufferings that I am purified and made fit to dwell in the holy city. Jesus is my wisdom, my righteousness, my sanctification, my redemption. He *is* all this; *he* and none other. In myself I am altogether unrighteous and wretched; but in him I am righteous and blest. Shall not the truth be the truth? I live; yet not I, but Christ liveth in me. I live unto him who loved me, and gave himself for me. — Blessed be thou, Lord Jesus, who didst give me thy righteousness, and didst receive me into the fellowship of thy death and thy life. Let everything die in me which is not of thee, and let nothing but thy righteousness and love live in me. Sanctify me thereby wholly in spirit and soul and body, and let me be preserved blameless unto the coming of our Lord. Amen.

O love, how cheering is thy ray! All pain before thy presence flies: Care, anguish, sorrow, melt away, Where'er thy healing beams arise. O Jesus, nothing may I see, Nothing desire or seek but thee!
From all eternity, with love Unchangeable thou hast me viewed; Ere knew this beating heart to move, Thy tender mercies me pursued. Ever with me may they abide, And close me in on every side.

214. Friday after Fourth Sunday after Easter.

Dear Lord, let thy word create in our hearts a firm and living faith. Amen.

Hebrews 5, 5–10. So also Christ glorified not himself to be made an high priest; but he that said unto him, Thou art my Son, today have I begotten thee. As he saith also in another place, Thou art a priest for ever after the order of Melchisedek. Who in the days of his flesh, when he had offered up prayers and supplications, with strong crying tears, unto him that was able to save him from death, and was heard in that he feared; though he were a Son, yet learned he obedience by the things which he suffered; and being made perfect, he became the author of eternal salvation unto all them that obey him; called of God an high priest after the order of Melchisedek.

Our salvation through Christ stands firm as a rock. *God himself* has appointed him our high priest; his call is in due and proper form in accordance with the eternal counsel of God, and certified to by the oath of God himself. And it is the "glory" of Christ to be made an high priest for us. Shall the arrangement which *God* has made fail of its purpose? Does not our faith rest on a firm foundation? Do you think that Christ can fail to discharge with honor the duties of his office? Must not our salvation be a matter of the highest concern to God, since his Son, the only begotten, regards it as his glory to be our high priest? Our salvation rests on so sure a foundation that the gates of death are powerless against it; and the heaven prepared for us, our salvation and glory, is high above the devil's reach. Our high priest has performed his whole office and brought the sacrifice which was necessary as an atonement for our sin. As he had taken upon himself to be at once the sacrificing priest and the lamb to be sacrificed, he could not fail to make complete satisfaction for our sin; and there was not the slightest abatement of the claim, although he is the only begotten Son of the Father. He willingly charged himself with the duty of satisfying every demand of strict justice, and became obedient unto death, even the death of the cross. There never was any disobedience in him; and yet he learned through his suffering what it is to be obedient; he stood the test of obedience, experienced the sensation of obedience, and received the reward of obedience, which is victory over death and entrance into glory. And now he is our high priest at the right hand of the Father, and is, both by reason of his humiliation and by reason of his exaltation, the author of eternal salvation unto all them that obey him. For it is by reason of the suffering which he has undergone and the blood which he has shed as a sacrifice, and which he offers to God for our benefit, that we are justified and have continual and full forgiveness of sin. To *obey* him, however, means, above all things else, to *believe* in him. Bow your heart by the grace of the Spirit in submission to this word of truth, that the very Son of God is your high priest, who saves you by his blood; then you are obedient to him. Hereto we exhort and admonish one another. O, that you would *obey* him, who for your sake was obedient unto death! He was obedient and willing to accept the wrath of God, and you are not even obedient and willing to accept his grace! If the bridge were unsafe on which we are trying to lead you, you might decline to go even to heaven; but it is in fact built on the firm foundation of God's eternal decree, and on the office and the completed work of the Son.

Give us, O God, the light and the strength of thy Holy Spirit, that we may believe. Bend our will and intellect to sincere obedience in faith, that we may build on the strong rock of our salvation, the obedience of thy Son in suffering unto death. Amen.

Bold shall I stand in that great day, For who aught to my charge shall lay? Fully through thee absolved I am From sin and fear, from guilt and shame!

And when the dead shall hear thy voice, Thy banished children shall rejoice; Their beauty this, their glorious dress, — Jesus, thy blood and righteousness.

---

215. Saturday after Fourth Sunday after Easter.

Psalm 51, 10–19. Create in me a clean heart, O God; and renew a right spirit within me. Cast me not away from thy presence; and take not thy holy Spirit from me. Restore unto me the joy of thy salvation; and uphold me with thy free Spirit: Then will I teach transgressors thy ways; and sinners shall be converted unto thee. Deliver me from bloodguiltiness, O God, thou God of my salvation; and my tongue shall sing aloud of thy righteousness. O Lord, open thou my lips; and my mouth shall shew forth thy praise. For thou desirest not sacrifice, else would I give it: thou delightest not in burnt offering. The sacrifices of God are a broken spirit: a broken and a contrite heart, O God, thou wilt not despise. Do good in thy good pleasure unto Zion: build thou the walls of Jerusalem. Then shalt thou be pleased with the sacrifices of righteousness, with burnt offering, and whole burnt offering: then shall they offer bullocks upon thy altar.

Every believer is weak, and commits sin daily; and sometimes he does worse, and grieves the Spirit of God. Watch, then, dear Christians, and be on your guard. Never dally with sin; for the end may be eternal death. When you nevertheless fall, then accept correction from the Spirit of God, feel your sin with sincere regret, and go at once to Jesus with an honest confession; for this is the course followed by the true children of God. The heart suffers, and writhes in pain, and can not be still, before it has received the assurance from the Lord that the sin is forgiven. Then the joy of his salvation is restored, and with it the willing spirit which is necessary for the preservation of faith and the practice of holiness. When the Spirit bears witness with our spirit that we are the children of God; when our heart has righteousness, peace, and joy in the Holy Ghost; when we are sure that, in Christ, the Father is well pleased in us; — then we love him in return, and serve him in a willing spirit. In this wise only can we offer sacrifice pleasing to God, and stand fast in his grace.

He that himself has tasted the joy of God's salvation, and sits daily at his table, desires to bring others also to the Lord, and devotes his heart, his lips, and all that he has, to the Lord's service. When

Andrew had found Jesus he sought out his brother Simon, told him with joy of the discovery which he had made, and brought Simon also to the Lord. (John 1, 41–43). He that converts a sinner saves a soul from death, and hides a multitude of sins. (James 5, 20). Promise your God to confess him diligently, and to offer him holy fruit of your lips. But remember always that a heart which is humble, poor in spirit, broken and full of grief on account of your own sins and the sins of others, — that such a heart is the best sacrifice to God. Without this sacrifice he does not desire our words and deeds; but with it they are pleasing to him. With the prayers of the contrite heart for Zion and Jerusalem, with the loving prayers of the quickened spirit that the kingdom of God may come, our poor words and deeds are a sacred and pleasing frankincense ascending to the Lord in heaven. — Again we pray: "Create in me a clean heart, O God; and renew a right spirit within me. Cast me not away from thy presence; and take not thy Holy Spirit from me. Restore unto me the joy of thy salvation; and uphold me with thy free spirit." Keep me humble, and give me ardent love, that I may be a pleasing sacrifice to thee, and that I may consume my strength in thy service. Amen.

Love divine, all loves excelling, Joy of heaven, to earth come down! Fix in us thy humble dwelling, All thy faithful mercies crown. Jesus, thou art all compassion, Pure, unbounded love thou art; Visit us with thy salvation, Enter every trembling heart.

216. Fifth Sunday after Easter. I.

Lord Jesus, teach us to pray in thy name. Amen.

Gospel Lesson, John 16, 23–28. And in that day ye shall ask me nothing. Verily, verily, I say unto you, Whatsoever ye shall ask the Father in my name, he will give it you. Hitherto have ye asked nothing in my name: ask, and ye shall receive, that your joy may be full. These things have I spoken unto you in proverbs: but the time cometh, when I shall no more speak unto you in proverbs, but I shall shew you plainly of the Father. At that day ye shall ask in my name: and I say not unto you, that I will pray the Father for you: For the Father himself loveth you, because ye have loved me, and have believed that I came out from God. I came forth from the Father, and am come into the world: again, I leave the world, and go to the Father.

To pray in the name of Jesus is to pray in his service; or, which is the same thing, in his stead, together with him, for his cause, and trusting in his word and his merit. When I send my servant to a neighbor for something which he has promised me, the servant asks for it in my name. He must be in my service, say what I have commissioned him to say, and ask for that only which I have told him to ask for. But if the neighbor knows that the messenger comes from me, and if he wants to give me that for which I ask, he does not concern himself about the worthiness or the unworthiness of the servant. If the messenger has proof that he is commissioned by me, and if he knows that the neighbor is willing to give me the article for which

I ask, he does not doubt that he will receive it, even if the neighbor does not like him. You, dear Christian, who in baptism have been made a member of the kingdom of Christ, and who believe in him; you are of his household, in his service; you are wholly his child, and also the child of the Father, and you have his love and favor. Jesus has told you to go to the Father on his business. "Thus ye shall pray for me," he says: "Our Father who art in heaven; hallowed be thy name; thy kingdom come, etc. Tell the Father that I have said it; that you are under orders from me, and come about my business." How happy you would be, did you but understand and believe this as you should! All those things which Jesus has told us to ask for, such as all that which is contained in the Lord's Prayer, and everything which he has taught us to regard as necessary to salvation, we can ask in his name; — but not all those things which we may happen to think that we should like. Pray in simple faith, holding up before the Father that which Jesus has said; and do not doubt that for his sake you shall receive. Do not consider your own unworthiness, — although, for the matter of that, the Father is well pleased in you for Jesus' sake; — but remain a petitioner at the throne of grace until your prayer is answered, or until your faith has received the needful assurance. When you do this you pray in the name of Jesus, and you shall receive, and your joy shall be full. For he declares and affirms: "Verily, verily, I say unto you, whatsoever ye shall ask the Father in my name, he will give it you;'" and this promise is a draft on the Father, more safe than a government bond. When you own the bond you own the gold; but it is still more certain that you own those things which Jesus says that you may ask of the Father. All things needful to salvation and to the promotion of God's kingdom, as well as daily bread and the necessaries of life, are given you in the name of Jesus. Ask, and you shall receive!

Eternal thanksgiving and praise be to thee, dear Lord Jesus, with the Father and the Holy Ghost, for thy wonderful and precious promises! Heavenly Father, give us grace to believe and to pray in faith, for Jesus' sake. Amen.

Lord, teach us how to pray aright With reverence and with fear: Though dust and ashes in thy sight, We may, we must draw near.
Burdened with guilt, convinced of sin, In weakness, want, and woe, Fightings without and fears within, Lord, whither shall we go?
God of all grace, we come to thee With broken, contrite hearts; Give what thine eye delight to see, Truth in the inward parts.

217. Fifth Sunday after Easter. II.

Lord, give me understanding, and I shall keep thy law; yea, I shall observe it with my whole heart. Amen.

Epistle Lesson, James 1, 22-27. But be ye doers of the word, and not hearers only, deceiving your own selves. For if any be a hearer of the word, and not a doer, he is like unto a man beholding his natural face in a glass: For he beholdeth himself, and goeth his way, and straightway forgetteth what manner of man he was. But whoso looketh into the perfect law of liberty and continueth therein, he being not a forgetful hearer, but a doer of the work, this man shall be blessed in his deed. If any man among you seem to be religious, and bridleth not his tongue, but deceiveth his own heart, this man's religion is vain. Pure religion and undefiled before God and the Father, is this, To visit the fatherless and widows in their affliction, and to keep himself unspotted from the world.

The word of God is able to save your souls; but it must enter your hearts; and this is effected when you not only hear it, but *do* it. The desire and the strength to "*do*" must, it is true, be given you by the word itself; and doing must be preceded by hearing. When you "*hear*," however, you thereby receive the strength to "*do*;" and then it will be your fault if you will not do it. If you then obey the word, as far as the grace of God makes this possible, it works in you knowledge of sin, faith, regeneration, and sanctification. But if you neglect this obedience, you become merely a forgetful hearer, who learns to know neither himself nor God, and who has neither liberty nor peace, but remains in sin, and deceives his own self; the truth makes a certain impression on you, but it is not lasting. Therefore, dear friend, obey the word of God, live it, follow it, do it; for Jesus' sake! You understand, I hope, that we are not speaking of the mere *outward* "doing," but of the *heart's* obedience to the word of God. Let your conduct, inwardly and outwardly, in thought and in deed, conform to the word of God. You may safely do this; for the word will never lead you wrong. The Lord shall thereby give you wisdom which is worth having. You shall learn to know yourself, your sin and your need; and you shall learn to know the cure to be found in the gospel. You shall be permitted to look into the "perfect law of liberty;" that is, into the eternally sure and merciful counsel of God, that *whosoever believes shall be saved.* This law of the Spirit, which gives life in Christ Jesus, shall set you free from the law of sin and death. The life of love gives you liberty, and makes you to be blessed in your deed; — not blessed *by reason of* your deed, but blessed *in* your deed.

Our text closes with a two-fold lesson: 1) You who live the life in God, bridle your tongue! Is it not a piece of the devil's own cunning that even the children of God are careless about guarding their tongue, although this is a matter of the highest importance? 2) Ye doers of the word of God; do not forget that he wants you to serve him by serving his needy, lonely, and suffering children, the widows and the fatherless. It is as it should be that you worship God, and edify yourselves by hearing his word; but — read once more the last verse of our epistle lesson in connection with the first.

Lord, thou who dost work in us both to will and to do of thy good pleasure; prompt us to do that which thou dost command. Let it be our constant endeavor to live according to thy word, and always to do that which is pleasing in thy sight. Give us love in our hearts, and let holiness adorn us in our every word and deed. Amen.

God, my Lord, my King, thou art, Take possession of my heart; There thy blood-bought right maintain, And without a rival reign.
Show me what I have to do; Every hour my strength renew; Let me live a life of faith; Let me die thy people's death.

218. Monday after Fifth Sunday after Easter.

*Let the words of my mouth, and the meditation of my heart, be acceptable
in thy sight, O Lord, my strength, and my redeemer. Amen.*

Matthew 6, 5–8. And when thou prayest, thou shalt not be as the hypocrites are: for they love to pray standing in the synagogues and in the the
corners of the streets, that they may be seen of men. Verily I say unto you,
They have their reward. But thou, when thou prayest, enter into thy closet,
and when thou hast shut thy door, pray to thy Father which is in secret; and
thy Father, which seeth in secret, shall reward thee openly. But when ye
pray, use not vain repetitions, as the heathen do: for they think that they
shall be heard for their much speaking. Be not ye therefore like unto them:
for your Father knoweth what things ye have need of before ye ask him.

Prayer is a matter of the *heart;* the *heart* alone is able to pray.
The prayer which does not proceed from the heart is no prayer at
all. Do you imagine that mere idle words can be a prayer to the
Lord? In this Bible lesson Jesus teaches two things: 1) When you
pray, present yourself before God, and deal with him only; keep close
to him with all your thoughts and feelings. Let nothing else in the
world be in your mind; whether it be the beams in the ceiling, or the
stars in heaven; your daily business affairs, or your earthly joys and
sorrows, — unless, indeed, you happen at the time to be speaking of
them to the Lord. Neither shall you be thinking of the people who
surround you, nor of the eyes that see you; but you shall be alone
with your God, whether you are in your chamber or in the midst of
a congregation. The Pharisees prayed in order that they might be
regarded as pious men. You are guilty of the same hypocrisy when
you want people to know how diligently you pray, and when you
rejoice in being praised of men for the fervency and eloquence of
your prayer. — How, then? do the saints never have any irrelevant
thoughts in their mind during prayer? Yes, nearly always, alas; but
it grieves and humbles them, and they earnestly beseech God to give
them grace to pray with proper devotion. 2) Be not concerned about
the words in which your prayer is couched; and do not think that you
can move God, as you can move men, with eloquent phrases. Speak
straight from the heart, whether your words be many or few. It is
immaterial whether you often repeat a thought, because your heart is
so full of it that you can not do otherwise; as was the case with David
and Hannah; or you but breathe a few words, as did the publican. I
have heard long prayers which were so earnest from beginning to end
that they seemed not to contain a superfluous word; and I have heard
short prayers which laid the whole case before God in a few words.
But I have also heard long and idle prayers, from persons with a glib
tongue, and from persons who made up for their lack of words by
a constant repetition of God's name. The Lord does not prohibit the
use of *many* words; but he prohibits "vain repetitions"; and he forbids
us to think that God is to be moved by much speaking. "God is a
Spirit; and they that worship him must worship him in spirit and in
truth." What an abomination is that soulless, idle talk which people

sometimes call prayer! But how excellent a thing is true prayer; how strong to force its way into the heart of God, and how sweet and blessed for the hearts out of which it issues! "The best of all the hours we spend While here on earth above the sod Are those in which our way we wend In earnest prayer to meet our God." The Lord will and shall teach us this lesson.

Give us, O God, the Spirit of grace and prayer! Forgive us all the sins committed while praying to thee. Let thy Spirit work in us groanings that can not be uttered. Our own condition strikes us with terror when we appear before thee, thou holy God. Have mercy on us; and let us never more come to thee with idle words, but let us always pray in spirit and in truth. Amen.

Come, my soul, thy suit prepare, Jesus loves to answer prayer: He himself has bid thee pray, Therefore will not say thee nay.

With my burden I begin: Lord, remove this load of sin! Let thy blood, for sinners spilt, Set my conscience free from guilt.

---

219. Tuesday after Fifth Sunday after Easter.

Lord, open our eyes to see that which thou hast given us in thy word. Amen.

John 15, 7–11. If ye abide in me, and my words abide in you, ye shall ask what ye will, and it shall be done unto you. Herein is my Father glorified, that ye bear much fruit; so shall ye be my disciples. As the Father hath loved me, so have I loved you: continue ye in my love. If ye keep my commandments, ye shall abide in my love; even as I have kept my Father's commandments, and abide in his love. These things have I spoken unto you, that my joy might remain in you, and that your joy might be full.

The Lord says, John 16, 23: "Verily, verily, I say unto you, whatsoever ye shall ask the Father in my name, he will give it you." And here he says: "If ye abide in me, and my words abide in you, ye shall ask what ye will, and it shall be done unto you." These passages teach us that *prayer in the name of Jesus is prayer in the fellowship of Jesus.* He who is and abides in the Lord; he who lives in his love, for his kingdom, as did the apostle Paul, who says: "I live; yet not I, but Christ liveth in me;" — he is the one who can pray in the name of Jesus. This is a mercy beyond measure, and gives most precious peace to the soul. When we have it we take part in Christ's work for the salvation of men and the perfecting of his kingdom in glory; and we taste *his* own joy, the joy of divine love, in the salvation of sinners. Let none think that this is given to only a favored few of exceptional piety and learning. The Lord has not spoken these words for the benefit of his apostles only, but for us all who believe in him. All the faithful are branches of the vine; their life is the spirit and love of Christ. But we allow the devil to deceive us by reason of the infirmities of the flesh and the cares of this world, so that we do not see what God has given us in his Son. You, who believe, have in truth the spirit and love of Christ; his will is your will; your desire is that his kingdom may come; you are in him, and have his word in you. You are able to pray in the name of Jesus, and live in the joy of the Lord until it is full in you. However, you are like a man who has received the key to a vault containing immense wealth; but who does not believe that the key will fit the lock. Or you may be likened unto a man who has inherited a great and undisputed claim against the richest house in the world; but who makes no use of it, and dies of want because he does not believe that the claim has any value. It is the devil who deceives you, when you imagine that you can not pray in the name of Jesus. Ponder the word of the Lord in our text and in the gospel lesson of last Sunday, in connection with the Lord's Prayer; keep it in your heart; it all belongs to you since the time of your baptism; and the Spirit which it contains shall give you faith, and strengthen your faith.

Lord Jesus, give us the light and power of thy Holy Spirit, that we may pray in thy name and taste of thy joy. Lead us into thy death, to the foot of thy cross, that our pride and unbelief may die, and thy love reign in us. Thou hast loved us, as the Father hath loved thee! How astounding are these words: "As the Father hath loved me, so have I loved you!" They contain unutterable mercy; and do we still refuse to believe? Help us to believe, and teach us to pray; pour out thy love in our hearts by thy Holy Spirit, that we may keep thy commandments and abide in thy love. Amen.

Father, fix my soul on thee; Every evil let me flee, Nothing want beneath, above, Happy in thy precious love.
O that all may seek and find Every good in Christ combined! Him let Israel still adore, Trust him, praise him evermore.

---

220. Wednesday after Fifth Sunday after Easter.

Lord, let the Spirit make thy word sure in our heart. Amen.

1 John 5, 13–15. These things have I written unto you that believe on the name of the Son of God; that ye may know that ye have eternal life, and that ye may believe on the name of the Son of God. And this is the confidence that we have in him, that, if we ask any thing according to his will, he heareth us: And if we know that he hear us, whatsoever we ask, we know that we have the petitions that we desired of him.

It is the purpose of St. John to encourage us to believe and to pray with a trusting heart. If our hope were based on our own works, we never could be sure of our salvation; we all the time feel our imperfection, and would of necessity be all the time doubtful of reaching heaven. We would be continually asking ourselves: "Are you sufficiently pious to expect God to accept you? Do you worship God well enough to make him overlook your faults?" — Now, however, the Spirit has made it clear to us that we deserve nothing but eternal death, and that salvation by works is out of the question; but he has also taught us, thank God, that we are saved by the merit of Jesus, for his sake only, and for none other cause whatever. The Son of God has done the work and suffered death for us; his name is *Jesus*, and he has *saved* us; we have received the Son and the life, and all is finished. We do not deceive ourselves when we trust in him. Or do you think that his work also is imperfect; or that his blood is of too little value? Verily, he has fulfilled his office, and is an eternally sure foundation on which to build. God wishes us to know that we have life everlasting, and firmly to believe in the name of his Son. — It is a terrible lie, it is unbelief worthy of the devil, which rejects him who is truth and love itself!

With the prayer of the heart we reach out the hand of faith after the gifts of God in Christ; and the Holy Spirit has taught John to write this, in order that we may pray in full certainty of faith. When our heart desires enlightenment, faith, forgiveness of sin, love, purity, patience, meeknes; or when we pray for the extension of the church, the success of the word, and the coming of the kingdom; or when we ask God to give us daily bread and a contended mind, victory in temptations and a blessed death; in short, when we pray for anything whatsoever which Jesus has told us to pray for, or which God has commanded us to have, we ask something according to his will, and then himself is the author of the prayer in our heart. Then it is the Spirit of the Son in us which prays; and shall we, then, not receive that which we ask? It is the will of God to give it us; and he has created in us the wish to have it. He has already given us the gift in his Son; and he is now able to put us in possession of it, since we have a heart to receive it. Must not, then, our prayer have been heard? "We have the petitions that we desired of him," says the apostle; but God keeps them for us until the right time is come. Note this: "If we know that he hear us, whatsoever we ask, we know that *we have the petitions that we desired of him.*" John is not dreaming when he says that we *have them* already. A prayer from the heart according to the will of God never remains unanswered. Do have confidence in the word of God!

Make our will one with thy will, gracious God. Mortify our fleshly lust, and draw our hearts to thee. Assure us of thy fatherly grace and the certainty of our heritage, and help us to pray with child-like confidence in the name of Jesus. Amen.

Yea, indeed, he bids us pray. Promising to hear us, E'er to be our staff and stay, Ever to be near us. Ere we plead, will he heed, Strengthen, keep, defend us, And deliv'rance send us.

---

221. Ascension Day. I.

Thou hast ascended on high, thou hast led captivity captive; thou hast received gifts for men; yea, for the rebellious also; that the Lord God might dwell among them.

Gospel Lesson, Mark 16, 14-20. Afterward he appeared unto the eleven as they sat at meat, and upbraided them with their unbelief and hardness of heart, because they believed not them which had seen him after he was risen. And he said unto them, Go ye into all the world, and preach the gospel to every creature. He that believeth, and is baptized, shall be saved; but he that believeth not, shall be damned. And these signs shall follow them that believe: In my name shall they cast out devils; they shall speak with new tongues; they shall take up serpents; and if they drink any deadly thing, it shall not hurt them; they shall lay hands on the sick, and they shall recover. So then after the Lord had spoken unto them, he was received up into heaven, and sat on the right hand of God. And they went forth and preached everywhere, the Lord working with them, and confirming the word with signs following. Amen.

"Go ye into all the world, and preach the gospel to every creature." These are words of majesty. He commands these poor mendicants to go to all the principalities and kingdoms of the world, and to speak openly and confidently to all creatures, in order that all men may hear this preaching. This is a command so strong and mighty that its like has never before gone out into the world. Now, the word "gospel" means neither more nor less than glad tidings, or a message announcing something which one is glad to hear. "He that believeth and is baptized shall be saved; but he that believeth not shall be damned." "This is in truth a kind and comforting message, and can rightfully be called a 'gospel'. For this one word tells you that heaven is opened, hell closed, the sentence of God's wrath annulled, sin and death buried; while life and truth are let down into the very lap of all men, if they will but believe it. O, that we might fully understand the meaning of these words, 'believe' and 'be saved'! There is in these few letters a power which the world can not comprehend; for this preaching gives us grace and riches beyond measure; and this without any merit whatever on our own part, as we have done nothing to gain possession of these blessings, nor even so much as had any knowledge of them. Could the children of the world but believe it, they would come in great multitudes to praise and thank God that they had lived to hear a Christian sermon."

"There is not one of us but falls far short of having a perfect faith. For the grace and riches contained in the gospel are great beyond comprehension. The human heart can not help being terrified when it considers that the high and eternal King opens his heaven so wide, and pours out such a wealth of grace and mercy over my sins and misery, and over those of the whole world, and that this glorious gift is brought to us in and through the word only." Besides, we are always inclined to make our justification before God depend, in a measure at least, on our own works, thus placing obstructions in the way of faith. "If I am to believe, I must exclude from the consideration every work of mine, and I must not have the effrontery to come before God with my own merit. For *these two things can not be brought into harmony;* that is, we can not believe the grace of God for Christ's sake without our own merit, and at the same time hold that we are justified also by our own works. If we could ourselves earn salvation, we would have no need of Christ. When the children of the world nevertheless despise this doctrine and regard faith as being of but little account, the reason for it is that their sin causes them no uneasiness, and that they know nothing of the agony and terror experienced by a frightened conscience. But when death or some other horror overtakes them, they can find no means of escape; then they at once fall into the depths of despair, and learn that faith is something entirely different from what they had supposed; that it is not empty and soulless talk, nor an idle idea or opinion, but a dauntless courage, which is able to confide wholly in Christ in the teeth of sin and death and hell." (Luther). "He that believeth and is baptized shall be saved." This is eternally sure and true, and able to kindle and strengthen true faith in the heart; and it attracts us with the gentle and strong power of divine grace. Blessed be the Lord for the wise and great purpose of his love concerning us lost sinners! "But he that believeth not shall be damned." This is equally certain; for it is faith only that saves. Consider, my friend, that salvation is ready to your hand; you are baptized, and have access to the grace of God, and may believe. Will you, then, despite all this, walk in unbelief to eternal perdition? Will you throw away your only chance? The declaration is final: "He that believeth not shall be damned." Let none of us, dear readers, again call down upon himself the judgment of God's wrath.

Lord Jesus, send witnesses able to preach thy gospel in demonstration of the Spirit and of power, and let it create faith in the hearts everywhere. Amen.

Draw us to thee, Lord Jesus, And we will hasten on; For strong desire doth seize us To go where thou art gone.
Draw us to thee; nor leave us, Till all our path be trod; Then in thine arms receive us, And bear us home to God.

222. Ascension Day. II.

Lord Jesus, give us a childlike faith, and show us thy glory. Amen.

Acts 1, 1-11. The former treatise have I made, O Theophilus, of all that Jesus began both to do and teach, until the day in which he was taken up, after that he through the Holy Ghost had given commandments unto the apostles whom he had chosen. To whom also he shewed himself alive after his passion, by many infallible proofs, being seen of them forty days, and speaking of the things pertaining to the kingdom of God; and being assembled together with them, commanded them that they should not depart from Jerusalem, but wait for the promise of the Father, which, saith he, ye have heard of me: For John truly baptized with water; but ye shall be baptized with the Holy Ghost, not many days hence. When they therefore were come together, they asked of him, saying, Lord, wilt thou at this time restore again the kingdom to Israel? And he said unto them, It is not for you to know the times or the seasons, which the Father hath put in his own power. But ye shall receive power, after that the Holy Ghost is come upon you: and ye shall be witnesses unto me, both in Jerusalem, and in all Judæa, and in Samaria, and unto the uttermost part of the earth. And when he had spoken these things, while they beheld, he was taken up; and a cloud received him out of their sight. And while they looked stedfastly toward heaven, as he went up, behold, two men stood by them in white apparel; which also said, Ye men of Galilee, why stand ye gazing up into heaven? This same Jesus, which is taken up from you into heaven, shall so come in like manner as ye have seen him go into heaven.

When Jesus took his life again out of death, his body was transfigured; and thus he walked on earth during the forty days. He had been glorified, and was therefore invisible; but he could shew himself whenever he wished, could suddenly appear to the disciples behind closed doors, and then as suddenly disappear. But he still was on earth, and had not as yet begun the exercise of his power as ruler over all things. He had mounted two rounds on the ladder of his exaltation; but before going farther he was to reveal himself many times to his disciples, instruct them in regard to the kingdom of God, and prepare them to receive the Spirit. Today he mounts the third round. He now assumes dominion, and employs all power in heaven and on earth, that he may bestow on us the salvation which he had won, and thus lead us to eternal glory. That Christ "sitteth on the right hand of the Father" means that, with the Father, he possesses all power and glory. He, who is God and man in one person, and who died for the sins of the world, reigns for ever over all things. Daniel "saw in the night visions, and, behold, one like the Son of Man came with the clouds of heaven, and came to the Ancient of days, and they brought him near before him. And there was given him dominion, and glory, and a kingdom, that all people, nations, and languages, should serve him; his dominion is an everlasting dominion, which shall not pass away, and his kingdom that which shall not be destroyed." (Daniel 7). The sitting of Christ on the right hand of the Father means, then, his omnipresent omnipotence and power of dominion as the Savior of the world. — Nevertheless, we must hold fast the truth that the habitation of God in heaven, high above all creatures, is an actual place; but in an eternal and heavenly sense, and not according to our earthly conceptions of locality.

As the ascended Savior he sends us the Spirit, who establishes the kingdom of God within us, and thus gathers the church of the Lord on earth. It was not the eleven apostles only who were to receive the Holy Ghost, but all who should believe through their word. He has not promised supernatural gifts to all of us; for they are not necessary to salvation; but the light and power of the Spirit unto faith and regeneration he has promised to every one who will obey the truth. — Then, when all these have been gathered in, he shall come again; and then the kingdom of glory, which the disciples in a way longed after, and concerning which they inquired, shall arise in its celestial splendor, beautiful and blessed beyond the power of man to conceive. We, also, yearn for this consummation. May the Lord come quickly, and perfect his kingdom! In the mean time, let us *believe without having seen*, and patiently follow the way of the cross under the blessed protection of our exalted Lord.

Have you, dear reader, experienced on your heart the regenerating power of the Spirit? Is *your* eye directed upward, where dwells the bridegroom of the souls; and do *you* wait with longing for the time

when he shall come again? — Draw us after thee, Lord Jesus. Take
our hearts, and fill them with thy love. Give us, we earnestly beseech
thee, thy Holy Spirit, and let each of us be one in the army of thy witnesses. Amen.

Hail the day that sees him rise To his throne above the skies! Christ,
the lamb for sinners given, Re-ascends his native heaven.
There the glorious triumph waits; Lift your heads, eternal gates; He hath
conquered death and sin; Take the king of glory in!

---

223. Friday after Ascension Day.

Lord Jesus, bless us; even us do thou bless! Amen.

Luke 24, 50–52. Acts 1, 13–14. And he led them out as far as to Bethany,
and he lifted up his hands, and blessed them. And it came to pass, while he
blessed them, he was parted from them, and carried up into heaven. And they
worshiped him, and returned to Jerusalem with great joy. And when they
were come in, they went up into an upper room, where abode both Peter, and
James, and John, and Andrew, Philip, and Thomas, Bartholomew, and Matthew, James the son of Alphæus, and Simon Zelotes, and Judas the brother
of James. These all continued with one accord in prayer and supplication
with the women, and Mary the mother of Jesus, and with his brethren.

While in the act of *blessing* his disciples Jesus was carried up to
heaven. It is as one who dispenses blessings that he sits on the right
hand of God; it is *thus* that the disciples see him with the eye of faith,
and this is the picture of him on which our minds should dwell.
Then we have a true picture of him in our soul; for his hands are
lifted up day and night to bless the church. What does he do on his
throne of glory save to bless his people? He lifts up his hands to
intercede for us, and to protect us; and he gives us his Holy Spirit.
The priestly blessing of the fathers on their children was of great effect;
the words of blessing pronounced by Noah on Shem and Japheth
brought them good fortune, while his curse brought disaster to Ham;
the old and blind Isaac blessed Jacob, and thus made him a lord over
his brother; the blessing of Jacob made Judah the chief among his
brethren; — how great, then, must be the power of the blessing which
Jesus pronounces on his church! Through the Spirit, whom he sends
from the Father in the word and sacraments, he bestows upon us
heavenly gifts; life of his own life, celestial light, power which is
stronger than death, and a peace which passes understanding. For
the blessing of the Lord is not idle words, nor a meaningless motion
of the hand; when his hands are lifted up to bless they are full of
life and strength and every good gift, which they drop down into the
souls of those whom he blesses.

The fellowship in prayer among the disciples in Jerusalem is itself one of the results of the Lord's blessing. They all prayed with
one accord, and they continued without ceasing until they received the
Pentecost gift. Let us do likewise! Alas, we are in such sore need
of the fire of Pentecost, the baptism of the Spirit! But we may receive

it. Here we are, a gathering of disciples; and the Lord lifts up his hands to bless us, and we keenly feel the need of having the power of the Holy Ghost in greater measure. "Come, Holy Spirit, power divine, and fill this hungry heart of mine; Thou seest how in tears I stand, And ask a blessing of thy hand. In every need my comfort be; Refresh my soul, and strengthen me." Shall not the Lord, then, give us his Spirit? Let us, however, pray with one accord, and cling to his promise that he will send us the Holy Ghost; let us desire that only which he promises to give; and let us *continue in prayer* until we receive. Let these last days before Pentecost be a time of fellowship during which the whole church of God prays as with one voice!

Open our eyes, Lord Jesus, that in faith we may see thee as thou art in thy glory; in that thou dost bless us with thy wounded hands. Give us grace to pray with one accord and continually; and give us, O, do give us the Pentecost blessing, that we may receive the gift of love into our hearts, and joyfully confess thy name. Amen.

Him though highest heaven receives, Still he loves the earth he leaves; Though returning to his throne, Still he calls mankind his own.
See, he lifts his hands above! See, he shows the prints of love! Hark, his gracious lips bestow Blessings on his church below!

---

224. Saturday after Ascension Day.

Lord Jesus, give us thy Holy Spirit. Amen.

Psalm 110. A Psalm of David. The Lord said unto my Lord, Sit thou at my right hand, until I make thine enemies thy footstool. The Lord shall send the rod of thy strength out of Zion: rule thou in the midst of thine enemies Thy people shall be willing in the day of thy power, in the beauties of holiness from the womb of the morning: thou hast the dew of thy youth. The Lord hath sworn, and will not repent, Thou art a priest for ever after the order of Melchisedek. The Lord at thy right hand shall strike through kings in the day of his wrath. He shall judge among the heathen, he shall fill the places with the dead bodies; he shall wound the heads over many countries. He shall drink of the brook in the way: therefore shall he lift up the head.

"Sit thou at my right hand" means this: Rule in my strength over all things in heaven and on earth. "The Lord hath prepared his throne in heaven; and his kingdom ruleth over all." "This, 'sit thou at my right hand,' is at all times infinitely rich in comfort for the church of God. He that can but lay hold on and keep this one scripture passage in his heart rises superior to every haunting dread; and it is immaterial to him whether his enemies are many or few, strong or weak; he can look with perfect composure at their fury and their vain efforts. He says with Joh. Arndt: 'I know One who sits on the right hand of God; he is strong enough to prevail against all my enemies and all my distress'." (Hengstenberg). — The Lord has said to my Lord: "Sit thou on thy throne, until I make thine enemies thy footstool." *The Lord has spoken it*, and his statement is final. All his enemies shall either be laid *at* his feet, or be laid *under* his feet. Believe this, and you shall rule with him; or refuse to believe it, and it is true just the same. Addressing the Messiah the Psalmist declares: "The Lord shall send the rod of thy strength out of Zion; the throne of the ruler of heaven shall stand in the midst of the congregation, and thou shalt rule in the midst of thine enemies." — We see the enemies, and we hear the uproar made by the unbelievers; but who can see the throne of his omnipotence in their midst? Have no fear. The cause of truth triumphs through defeat only. Over the head of the *Crucified One* is written: "Jesus of Nazareth, King of the Jews;" and this writing remains, regardless of the fury of the high priests. He ruled in the midst of his enemies without their knowing it; and he does the same still. His enemies will all the time mock him in his members. We shall suffer with him, and reign with him. There always are enemies round about who seem to gain the victory; but he reigns in their midst; their noise and din only prove his victorious and ruling presence, even as the waters seethe and surge around the immovable rock.

He does not lack people when he needs them. In this Psalm they are likened to the dew of the morning. Only a few moments ago the earth was covered with a gray mist; but now the day is come, and on grass and leaf you see countless pearls, pure and brilliant, sparkling in the rays of the morning sun. They appear suddenly as by enchantment, but they had been fashioned and were there before we knew it. Thus it is with the Lord's people. At the proper time they appear in countless numbers, pure and fresh and sparkling in the light of the sun; that is, in the beauty of the Lord. They are nothing in themselves; he is their all. Without the sun there is no beauty in the dewdrop. They are willing, happy and cheerful, and young even in their old age; for he is not their *king* only, but also a *priest*, according to what the Lord hath sworn, who ever intercedes for us and puts on us garments of holiness. — Are you, dear reader, one of this multitude who now, while the church is in its state of lowliness, are making ready to share his glory on the day of his power? Is Christ the king of your heart? Is his merit your robe of honor, and his strength your armor? Woe to all who defy him! In the day of his wrath he shall strike down kings, the great and proud spirits who make war on his kingdom. He fills the land with dead bodies; pray God, our people be not among the chief sufferers! There are already many dead bodies, and there is much fatal poison in the atmosphere. Choose your place. To which camp do you belong?

Lord Jesus, rule in our hearts. Help us to believe in thy power and grace. Clothe us with thy purity, and arm us with thy righteousness. Thy power be our strength, thy merit our comfort, thy love our life; that we may be willing in thy service, and that we may fight manfully in thy army. Amen.

Hail him, ye heirs of David's line, Whom David Lord did call; The God incarnate, man divine, And crown him Lord of all!

Ye gentile sinners, ne'er forget The wormwood and the gall; Go, spread your trophies at his feet And crown him Lord of all!

225. Sixth Sunday after Easter. I.

Lord, let the Comforter come and bear witness in us. **Amen.**

Gospel Lesson, John 15, 26–16, 4. But when the comforter is come, whom I will send unto you from the Father, even the Spirit of truth, which proceedeth from the Father, he shall testify of me: And ye also shall bear witness, because ye have been with me from the beginning. These things have I spoken unto you, that ye should not be offended. They shall put you out of the synagogues: yea, the time cometh, that whosoever killeth you will think that he doeth God service. And these things will they do unto you, because they have not known the Father, nor me. But these things have I told you, that when the time shall come, ye may remember that I told you of them. And these things I said not unto you at the beginning, because I was with you.

Jesus Christ is to be preached in the world. The holy Ghost shall testify of him. The world shall have testimony concerning Jesus Christ; and the Holy Ghost is the witness; for he is the truth. His testimony is so convincing that even they who deny the truth of the Christian religion feel the sting of the truth in their hearts. He testifies through the written word, but also makes use of the faithful as his servants down through the ages in the office of bearing witness. The holy apostles, who were with Jesus from the beginning, are *eyewitnesses*. They speak that which they have seen, and which their hands have felt; and their testimony is mighty to put down all falsehood. The truth of the statement which Jesus makes, that, even as the Comforter testifies of him, so shall the apostles also bear witness, comes right home to us; for we ourselves hear them testify, and we feel the power of their testimony, and it has to us a value beyond price. Yet it is not the apostles only who bear witness by the Holy Spirit; but the same is true of *all* believers. The glory and affliction of being a witness belong to every Christian. He that believes in Jesus knows him; and shall testify of him to others by leading a Christ-like life. He is to be the image of Christ, his living and true presentment by the Holy Ghost. The Lord himself says: "Let your light so shine before men, that they may glorify your Father which is in heaven." And again: "By this shall all men know that ye are my disciples, if ye have love to one another." And the apostles exhort the saints to shine as celestial lights among the world's children of darkness. The Christian church shall fulfil its office as a witness, in part by a faithful administration of the means of grace, and in part by the saintly lives of its members. — Let, then, every one who by the grace of the Holy Spirit knows the Son and the Father testify at all times and places concerning that which he has experienced, and in his every word and deed confess Christ. Our likeness to the Savior is as yet far from being *perfect*; but if we are his disciples, the resemblance can not fail to be plainly visible; even an unfinished portrait by a master will clearly reveal the original. "If any man be in Christ, he is a new creature; old things are passed away; behold, all things are become new." Let the Spirit of God permeate your whole life and govern your conduct even in its minutest details. You shall live in holiness, suffer with patience, and not allow yourself to be led astray from the path of self-denial, though all the world entice and threaten you, and rob you of all that you have. This is not the old commandment which is weak through the flesh, but "the new commandment, which is true in him and in you; for the darkness is receding, and the true light shines already." — Heavenly Father, strengthen thy weak children. Give us life and grace to bear witness. Give us the great honor of being among Christ's witnesses, and of suffering for his name's sake. Keep us from all manner of hypocrisy; let our lips and our lives preach truth from the heart, and do thou bless the testimony to the coming of thy kingdom. Amen.

O Holy Spirit, enter in, Among these hearts thy work begin, Thy temple deign to make us; Sun of the soul, thou light divine, Around and in us brightly shine, To strength and gladness wake us. Where thou shinest, life from heaven There is given: We before thee For that precious gift implore thee.

---

226. Sixth Sunday after Easter. II.

Lord, give us thy Spirit. Amen.

Epistle Lesson, 1 Peter 4, 7–11. But the end of all things is at hand: be ye therefore sober, and watch unto prayer. And above all things have fervent charity among yourselves: for charity shall cover the multitude of sins. Use hospitality one to another, without grudging. As every man hath received the gift, even so minister the same one to another, as good stewards of the manifold grace of God. If any man speak, let him speak as the oracles of God; if any man minister, let him do it as of the ability which God giveth: that God in all things may be glorified through Jesus Christ, to whom be praise and dominion for ever and ever. Amen.

The Comforter, who glorifies the Lord Jesus, is the Spirit of *love;* and love is the life of the church of God. Love, however, rejoices in well-doing; it seeks not its own, but the happiness and welfare of others. The whole life of *Jesus* is love, and so should *our* life be. Then we would be truly happy! This is the will of God; and that we may lead such a life, he has bestowed upon each of us his gift of grace. In this life love must express itself through various services for the upbuilding of the whole church and its individual members. You must be actuated by *love;* the Spirit must lead you, or that which you do is nothing but dead works, which may have a form of godliness, but will be found mere hay and stubble in the fire of the coming day. — Minister one to another in fervent charity with the manifold grace of God! This is the sum and substance of the apostle's admonition in our epistle lesson. You and all that you have are the Lord's, as are also your brethren in Christ; and he has brought you together, that you may minister one to another and be of mutual assistance in working out your salvation. If you have a call to speak in the congregation, speak "as the oracles of God." Bear in mind always that the gospel which you speak is God's own word; teach it in its purity, according to the scripture; divide it rightly, according to the behoof of the souls; preach it with full confidence in its truth and effectiveness, and present it in a form worthy of its sacred character. Speak the word of God, and speak *as* the oracles of God. — If it be some other office which you have in the church or in the household, do your duty faithfully, and remember that it is the Lord whom you serve when you minister to his members. Do your work with the zeal of love, that God may thus be honored in all things. Never forget that as a Christian you are called to devote yourself to the exercise of charity throughout your whole life. While the world must hate and quarrel and tear asunder and cause all manner of sin, because it is in the service of the wicked spirit, you shall all the time love, bless, cover a multitude of sins, and call forth charity, thanksgiving and praise, for the glory of God and the happiness of man. The life of the church of God in the Spirit is beautiful and rich; but to the flesh, how bitter! It is nothing but self-denial, and cross and death. — Pour out this Spirit into our hearts, O God, that while we live we may lead a holy life in ministering charity, feel the comfort of life in the midst of our many afflictions, and rejoice in the knowledge that the end of all things is drawing nigh. Amen.

Grant that our days, while life shall last, In purest holiness be passed; Our minds so rule and strengthen That they may rise o'er things of earth, The hopes and joys that here have birth; And if our course thou lengthen, Keep thou pure, Lord, from offences Heart and senses; Blessed Spirit, Bid us thus true life inherit.

---

227. Monday after Sixth Sunday after Easter.

Lord, command that we love; and give us that which thou dost command. Amen.

John 15, 17–21. These things I command you, that ye love one another. If the world hate you, ye know that it hated me before it hated you. If ye were of the world, the world would love his own: but because ye are not of the world, but I have chosen you out of the world, therefore the world hateth you. Remember the word that I said unto you, The servant is not greater than his lord. If they have persecuted me, they will also persecute you; if they have kept my saying, they will keep your's also. But all these things will they do unto you for my name's sake, because they know not him that sent me.

A Christian does not make it his endeavor to be hated of the world; but he becomes an object of the world's hatred because he follows Jesus, and confesses his name. For the world hates Christ, and the testimony, and them that confess him. The distinctive feature of God's people is love, while the spirit of the world is hate and enmity. It is not possible that Christians, whose hearts are full of love, should desire the hatred of the world; on the contrary, they are sorry for the sake of those who hate them. They endeavor to be kind and patient in their dealings with all men; and they endure reproach and derision, and pray for their enemies. They seek also to choose the opportune time for the giving of their testimony, and they give it in a reverent manner, even when dealing with the most lowly of mortals. For they remember that all have been bought by Christ with a price, and they hope that the testimony concerning him will transform them into children of God. Neither do they regard themselves as too good to associate with the world; though they can not take part in, but must testify against and reprimand the world's sinful life. — It is no easy matter to walk thus among worldly-minded men. The faithful are themselves imperfect. They are tempted not only to neglect their duty as witnesses, but also to be hasty and injudicious; and they commit many blunders which injure their testimony. Thus their heart is grieved and their conscience wounded; and they blame *themselves* for the unbelief of the world. "If I were such a witness as I should be, they would repent; if I were a shining example of true love in my whole life, they would know Christ and come to him." We are sorry that the world hates us; but it is a comfort to reflect that the Lord himself was treated in the same way; and he has told us to bear this in mind. Let it only in truth be for his sake that we are hated, not on account of our own want of wisdom, and especially not by reason of hypocritical sanctimoniousness on our part! Let it be for the reason, that the Lord has chosen us; that we are like him; and that they do not know us, because they do not know him and the Father!

Give us, O God, the love of Jesus Christ in our hearts; that our whole life may bear witness that we are thy children, that we love one another, and that we walk in the light. Give us courage to proclaim thy truth, and give us joy in tribulations for Jesus' sake. Take pity on the world, and let our testimony bring many to repentance. Give us this grace, merciful God. Amen.

Through the night of doubt and sorrow Onward goes the pilgrim band. Singing songs of expectation, Marching to the promised land. Clear before us through the darkness Gleams and burns the guiding light; Brother clasps the hand of brother, Stepping fearless through the night.

---

228. Tuesday after Sixth Sunday after Easter.

Grant, O Lord, that our souls may wait upon thee. Amen.

Psalm 62, 1–8. Truly my soul waiteth upon God: from him cometh my salvation. He only is my rock and my salvation; he is my defense: I shall not be greatly moved. How long will ye imagine mischief against a man? ye shall be slain all of you: as a bowing wall shall ye be, and as a tottering fence. They only consult to cast him down from his excellency; they delight in lies: they bless with their mouth, but they curse inwardly. Selah. My soul, wait thou only upon God: for my expectation is from him. He only is my rock and my salvation: he is my defense: I shall not be moved. In God is my salvation, and my glory: the rock of my strength, and my refuge, is in God. Trust in him at all times; ye people, pour out your heart before him: God is a refuge for us. Selah.

David was able to bear witness that "many are the afflictions of the righteous; but the Lord delivereth him out of them all." (Psalm 34). How full of trouble was not his life even in his youth, when for a long time he was compelled to flee as a chased roe before Saul, and be in constant danger of his life! How sad was not the revolt of Absalom, and his miserable fate! And what grief was not brought upon David by his other children! But he emerged out of his troubles with a purified soul as the prize. *Thus* he became the sweet singer of Israel and the servant of the Lord to comfort and instruct us in our afflictions; and he could have become this in no other way.

"When one does not have God before his eyes, and does not turn to him in prayer, no stormy sea is as turbulent as is the human heart; for then terror, sorrows, and impatience follow hard upon one another, until the wretched soul sinks at last as a dismantled hull into the depths of despair." (Joh. Arndt). How sorely we need such instruction as that which the Holy Spirit through David gives us in this and other psalms! "Truly my soul waiteth upon *God;* he *only* is my rock and my salvation." Mark these two important lessons: 1) The soul must cling to God as its *only* Savior, and expect help from none other. When our enemies with wicked malice plan our destruction, and employ *all* their devil's cunning in tempting us to unbelief, the Lord is to be our *only* hope, the *only* source from which we are to look for help. All our thoughts and all our strength of soul must center in him. We must have no other God beside the true God. Learn well this *"only"* on which the psalmist lays so great a stress. 2) The Lord is a sure and safe refuge; and hence it is of no account, if the enemies be many and mighty. In order to strengthen his own faith and to cheer our hearts, the psalmist repeats again and again the assurance: God is my salvation, my rock, my glory; wait upon God, my soul; he is my expectation, my rock, my salvation; I shall not be moved; in him is my salvation and my glory; the rock of my strength, and my refuge, is in God. — He that knows these two lessons has help in every need. But they can not be learned to perfection all at once; wherefore God little by little increases the trials of his children, and thus brings them promotion in his training school. — The diseases of the souls under the Lord's care are many; and he is compelled to use many painful remedies in order to bring about a cure. If he did not, we would with self-willed perverseness hide our distresses in our own breast, and allow our disappointments and foolish desires and our sorrows to gnaw at our hearts, until our souls would be sick unto death. On the other hand, our afflictions teach us to pour out our hearts before God, and hopefully wait upon him.

Merciful God, we thank thee for all which thou dost in thy dealing with us; and we ask thee to chasten us and heal us. Teach us to hope in thee only, and to trust firmly in thee at all times. Amen.

Jesus Christ, my sure defense And my Savior, ever liveth; Knowing this, my confidence Rests upon the hope it giveth, Though the night of death be fraught Still with many an anxious thought.

Jesus, my redeemer, lives! I, too, unto life shall waken; He will have me where he is: Should my courage then be shaken? Should I fear? Or can the head Rise and leave its members dead?

229. Wednesday after Sixth Sunday after Easter.

Lord, open our eyes. Amen.

1 John 3, 1-6. Behold, what manner of love the Father hath bestowed upon us, that we should be called the sons of God: therefore the world knoweth us not, because it knew him not. Beloved, now are we the sons of God; and it doth not yet appear what we shall be: but we know that, when he shall appear, we shall be like him; for we shall see him as he is. And every man that hath this hope in him purifieth himself, even as he is pure. Whosoever committeth sin transgresseth also the law: for sin is the transgression of the law. And ye know that he was manifested to take away our sins; and in him is no sin. Whosoever abideth in him sinneth not: whosoever sinneth, hath not seen him, neither known him.

"This is the greatest and warmest love, which burns like a fiery furnace, that Jesus has loved us unto death on the cross, and been obedient to his Father, who gave him to us as our Savior. And not only do we *become* the sons of God, but we are also to be *called* and *known* by this title before God and his angels." When Missionary Ziegenbalg in Trankebar was translating the New Testament, and came to this passage, "we should be called the sons of God," his native assistants would not write it down, but substituted in its place the statement that "God will permit us to kiss his feet." However, God himself has written that "we should be called *the sons of God;*" and his words shall remain in force. He has elected us in Christ, and bestowed upon us the adoption of sons. He has regenerated us, given us his Spirit, and made us partakers of his divine nature; and thus our hearts belong to him in childlike faith and devotion. How great our glory shall be when we are perfected, and come into full possession of our inheritance, not even Saint John is able to say. "But we know that, when he shall appear, we shall be like him; for we shall see him as he is." And Paul says, 1 Corinthians 13, 12: "For now we see through a glass, darkly; but then face to face; now I know in part; but then shall I know even as also I am known." Here all is as yet but dimly visible, and love is kept down by the flesh. The clearest minds and the most noble hearts have the most fervent longing after more light and after deliverance from this body of death. The light and deliverance shall come; we shall reach a full understanding of the truth, and become like God in pure love. To "see him" is the bliss of heaven itself. "In thy presence is fulness of joy; at thy right hand there are pleasures for evermore." (Psalm 16, 11). — "And every man that hath this hope in him purifieth himself, even as he is pure." If any man hope for salvation, but do not purify himself from sin, his hope is vain. He that is in Christ can not endure the uncleanness of sin, but strives to attain perfect holiness. If we were not saved from sin, we would of necessity continue in it, and could not purify ourselves. On the other hand, if we were already without sin, it would be idle to talk about being purified. The world knows neither us nor the fountain in which we are cleansed; for it knows neither the Father nor the Son. But let us, by a holy life, prove to the world that we really have been saved from sin, and that we in truth have a living hope! "If the Father is to be known in the children, if our conduct is to be such, that it can endure the light, the flame of love must burn in us and be able to work miracles; we must glorify God by deeds of charity toward our enemies."

We thank thee for thy great love, heavenly Father. We heartily confess that we are not worthy of it. Enlighten us by thy Spirit, that with our whole heart we may believe in thee and thy Son, our Lord Jesus; that we may hold fast the hope of seeing thee in eternal bliss, and that we prepare for it by purging ourselves of all sin. O that we might become more like thee every day, and soon stand before thee face to face in heaven! Amen.

There is an hour of hallowed peace For those with care oppressed, When sighs and sorrowing tears shall cease, And all be hushed to rest.
'Tis then the soul is freed from fears And doubts that here annoy: Then they that oft had sown in tears Shall reap again in joy.

230. Thursday after Sixth Sunday after Easter.

Lord God, heavenly Father, quicken us by the Holy Spirit. Amen.

Isaiah 44, 1-5. Yet now hear, O Jacob my servant; and Israel, whom I have chosen: Thus saith the Lord that made thee, and formed thee from the womb, which will help thee; Fear not, O Jacob my servant; and thou, Jesurun, whom I have chosen. For I will pour water upon him that is thirsty, and floods upon the dry ground; I will pour my spirit upon thy seed, and my blessing upon thine offspring; and they shall spring up as among the grass, as willows by the water courses. One shall say, I am the Lord's; and another shall call himself by the name of Jacob; and another shall subscribe with his hand unto the Lord, and surname himself by the name of Israel.

This is another of those glorious promises which would make us rich and happy, did we but *believe* them. The Lord here speaks to the poor and thirsty. You are his "Israel," his "chosen servant," born of his Spirit, and fashioned to be his servant. It was God himself, and none other, who excited hunger and thirst in your soul, kindled the spark of faith, and created a new life in you. Your longing after God and your love for his children are not of flesh and blood, but of the Spirit of God. You feel parched, and you thirst after the water of life. Is this true of the world? No; your knowledge of sin, your longing after God, and your fervent desire to have a heart full of charity, are the work of the Holy Spirit in you. It is the Holy Spirit who moves your heart to breathe the prayer: "Come, rain from on high, and refresh the earth, that the work of Jesus may bring forth abundant fruit. Slake the thirst of our parched souls with the water of life proceeding out of the throne of God." And the Lord makes answer: ":Hear, my beloved, whom I have elected; my own, whom I have chosen for myself; I, who have made thee and will help thee, I will pour water upon him that is thirsty, and floods upon the dry ground; I will pour my spirit upon thy seed, and my blessing upon thine offspring." To whom

is this spoken, if not to the wretched, who thirst after the water of
life from on high? Why is it that you read this? Or, why has the
Lord given you this promise? Of a truth, it is *to* you that he speaks;
and you should pay attention. *He* has planted you; and *he* will care
for his tender shoots, and water them, that they may live and thrive.
They shall stand as willows by the water courses, and bear witness
that the Lord is faithful. He says this, in order that you may believe; and by this means he accomplishes his purpose. The Spirit
comes through his word; and *faith* in the heart is the secret of life.
Hear, then, O Jacob; and make answer: "It be to me according to
thy word!" When *he* says, that he has created you, and formed you
to be his child, and that he will help you; then you shall say: "I am
the Lord's," and subscribe with your hand unto the Lord, and surname yourself by the name of Israel. — Pentecost is near; and that
which the Lord has promised shall come to pass. Expect it with confidence; but do not anxiously inquire, whether or not you are to feel
the wondrous coming of the Spirit. Wait upon the Lord; he comes,
and kindles faith in the heart, working in secret, but with marvellous
power; but the sound of the Spirit may be heard, and the seed is scattered far and wide. Are not the promises of the Lord more to be
trusted than our sensations or our sight? And is not our unbelief our
great unhappiness? Bring into captivity every thought to the obedience of Christ! The Lord has spoken, and he shall do it; he shall
make his church to blossom, — through times of heavy trouble and
much tribulation. Fear not, thou worm Jacob; for thou art the Lord's,
and he shall bless thee. — Our God, our faithful and merciful God;
give us grace to believe thy word, for Jesus' sake. Amen.

Holy Ghost, with light divine, Shine upon this heart of mine! Chase
the shades of night away, Turn the darkness into day.
Let me see my Savior's face, Let me all his beauties trace; Show those
glorious truths to me, Which are only known to thee.

---

231. Friday after Sixth Sunday after Easter.

*Lord Jesus, excite the proper thirst in our soul, and refresh us with thy
Spirit. Amen.*

John 7, 37–40. In the last day, that great day of the feast, Jesus stood and
cried, saying, If any man thirst, let him come unto me, and drink. He that
believeth on me, as the scripture hath said, out of his belly shall flow rivers
of living water. (But this spake he of the Spirit, which they that believe on
him should receive: for the Holy Ghost was not yet given; because that Jesus
was not yet glorified.) Many of the people therefore, when they heard this
saying, said, Of a truth this is the Prophet.

Jesus must needs suffer and die, and make atonement for the
world, and break down the middle wall of partition between heaven
and earth, and in his transfigured human nature enter the glory of the
Father, before he could pour out the Holy Ghost. Now, however, all
this has come to pass, and the pouring out of the Spirit is begun. —

At the feast of tabernacles a priest brought water from the pool of Siloah in a golden bowl, and carried it into the inner court of the temple; and here he was received by the other priests with the blowing of trumpets, while all the people sang: "With joy shall ye draw water out of the wells of salvation." (Isaiah 12, 3). The priest thereupon carried the water to the altar and mixed it with the wine of the drink-offering; and then it was poured out, and ran through underground tubes into the brook Cedron, while the Levites, to the accompaniment of all manner of musical instruments, sang the great Hallelujah (Psalm 113–118). — Christ is our priest and our altar. The waters of Siloah represent the love of God, the life of Christ. This has passed through the altar, through the sacrificial fire, through the death of atonement, and flows out over the earth as living water to quench our thirst and heal the waters. (Ezekiel 47). Therefore the Lord cries out on the last great day of the feast of tabernacles: "If any man thirst, let him come unto me, and drink." The feast of tabernacles is a reminder of the journey through the wilderness; and this, again, is typical of our journey to the heavenly Canaan. Christ is the rock out of which gushes water to refresh the dry places of the earth. He stands in the midst of the church and shouts: "Come unto me, all ye that labor and are heavy laden, and I will give you rest." — Are you wretched and poor, and do you thirst after righteousness and love; come to Jesus; he has water to give you, and he invites you to come unto him. When you hear this, "if any man thirst, let him come unto me, and drink," you hear his own voice; it reaches *your* ear, because his invitation is meant for *you* also. But to come unto him, and drink, means the same as to *believe* in him. For he adds: *"He that believeth on me, out of his belly shall flow rivers of living water."* And, in John 4, 14 he says: "Whosoever drinketh of the water that I shall give him shall never thirst; but the water shall be in him a well of water springing up into everlasting life." *Believe* his love, and it shall enter your heart and be the guiding principle of your life. Think of the rivers of living water which flowed out of the apostles! But this was because of the fact that they believed. Dear friend; the Spirit is here, Christ is here, there is abundance of water, and you stand on the bank of the river; drink, and give the others to drink with you. *Believe* in him, and let your thought, your speech, your deed, be his love. — Help us to this end, merciful God; and give us the spirit of faith and love in Christ Jesus. Amen.

I heard the voice of Jesus say, "Behold, I freely give The living water: thirsty one, Stoop down and drink, and live." I came to Jesus, and I drank Of that life-giving stream; My thirst was quenched, my soul revived, And now I live in him.

---

232. Pentecost Eve.

Lord, give us grace to believe, and to hear thy promises. Amen.

Joel 2, 28–32. And it shall come to pass afterward, that I will pour out my Spirit upon all flesh; and your sons and your daughters shall prophesy, your old men shall dream dreams, your young men shall see visions: And also upon the servants and upon the handmaids in those days will I pour out my Spirit. And I will shew wonders in the heavens and in the earth, blood, and fire, and pillars of smoke. The sun shall be turned into darkness, and the moon into blood before the great and the terrible day of the Lord come. And it shall come to pass, that whosoever shall call on the name of the Lord shall be delivered: for in mount Zion and in Jerusalem shall be deliverance, as the Lord hath said, and in the remnant whom the Lord shall call.

Even as the Lord fulfilled this promise on that first day of Pentecost after his ascension, so he still continues to do it when we ask it of him in earnest prayer. And it is necessary that he should. The birth of Jesus, his life, his suffering and death, his victory, his resurrection, his ascension, and his seat at the right hand of the Father; furthermore, our knowledge, our worship, our baptism, our celebration of Holy Communion; — all these things profit us nothing, if the Holy Ghost do not gain access to our heart, and kindle in it a living faith. For Christianity is not knowledge and learning, nor virtuous conduct and good words, nor the habit of going to church and attending devotional exercises; but it is *the communion of the heart with the Lord*, which can be brought about only by the Holy Ghost. What God has done for us is all in vain; nay, becomes damnation to us, if we do not obey the Spirit. The eternal counsel of God's love, the sacrifice of his only begotten Son, the cross and blood of Christ, the most precious of all things in heaven and on earth, that which should become your eternal salvation — must needs become nothing but wrath upon you, if you do not receive the Holy Spirit. For the three persons of the godhead can not be separated; you can not have one without the other; not the Father without the Son, and not the Son without the Spirit. The three are one; and the *triune* God is the God of our salvation. Hence they are guilty of a grave error who hold that little children are saved by Christ without the gracious agency of the Holy Ghost. No; the Spirit must operate in babes as well as in adults, in order that they may be brought to Jesus. Do you imagine that some of the saved have the Father and Son only as their God of salvation, while others have all the persons of the Trinity? Such an idea would be absolutely without warrant. No; sons and daughters, the elders and the young men, servants and handmaids, adults and sucklings, all have need of the Holy Spirit; and he will come to all, if we will but receive him. On that first Pentecost day he was in a glorious manner poured out upon the apostles; and he shall continue to be poured out abundantly in these latter days. While we wait for this, we earnestly pray God to give us the light and gifts of the Spirit in such measure that we also may believe with living confidence, have love in our hearts, and attain our soul's eternal salvation. May this festival of Pentecost be richly blessed in our church and in all the world! Pray unceasingly for this blessing, ye Christians, with earnestness and faith. "I will pour out my Spirit upon all flesh," says the Lord. Do not let him go, except he do it! Shall we again live through the Pentecost season with its fire from on high, and not be warmed and set aglow? Sunshine and ιαιn cause dead bodies to become putrid and foul; but cause living plants to blossom and ripen.

We heartily beseech thee, O Lord, give us thy Holy Spirit, and create faith, hope, and charity in our soul. Bless this Pentecost for thy church. Make of us living witnesses in regard to victory over sin and death, and in regard to salvation in the name of Jesus, that many may repent, and live. Amen.

Come, Holy Spirit, God and Lord! Be all thy graces now outpoured On the believer's mind and soul, To strengthen, save, and make us whole.

Lord, by the brightness of thy light, Thou in the faith dost men unite Of every land and every tongue: This to thy praise, O Lord, be sung.

233. Whitsunday. I.

"Come, Holy Ghost, our God and Lord, To us thy gracious gifts impart; And kindle, by thy sacred word, The fire of love within our heart." Amen.

Gospel Lesson, John 14, 23–31. Jesus answered and said unto him, If a man love me, he will keep my words: and my Father will love him, and we will come unto him, and make our abode with him. He that loveth me not keepeth not my sayings: and the word which ye hear is not mine, but the Father's which sent me. These things have I spoken unto you, being yet present with you. But the comforter, which is the Holy Ghost, whom the Father will send in my name, he shall teach you all things, and bring all things to your remembrance, whatsoever I have said unto you. Peace I leave with you, my peace I give unto you: not as the world giveth, give I unto you. Let not your heart be troubled, neither let it be afraid. Ye have heard how I said unto you, I go away, and come again unto you. If ye loved me, ye would rejoice, because I said, I go unto my Father: for my Father is greater than I. And now I have told you before it come to pass, that, when it is come to pass, ye might believe. Hereafter I will not talk much with you: for the prince of this world cometh, and hath nothing in me. But that the world may know that I love the Father; and as the Father gave me commandment, even so I do. Arise, let us go hence.

God loved us first, and gave his Son for us. *Love* is of God; it is not of us, but of *God*. By faith, however, we receive it into our heart, and love him in return. God is love; and when we believe in him we build our faith on love itself. God has given us his love in Christ, and the Spirit gives us power to believe; and thus we are enabled to love God and keep his word. It is by reason of the coming of Christ, and his ascension, and the pouring out of the Spirit, that we, who had lost this love, can again come into possession of it and have true love in our heart. Each one of us, who are baptized unto Christ, has received his love into the heart. But we may either keep it, or reject it. The Spirit gives us grace to believe, but we also have power to resist him; and hence we Christians may then choose, whether or no we wish to have this love in the heart. Jesus says in our text: "If a man love me, he will keep my words." The fruit of love is hearty *obedience*. He that does not keep the words of Jesus must not think that he loves Jesus. But if any man love me, says Jesus, and keep my words, "my Father will love him;" that is, he will *delight* and be *well pleased* in him. For in his love God is *good* to all, but *fond* of his children; he is *kindly disposed* towards all, but in them that are good he is also *well pleased*. The Father loves you, if you love Jesus; you then are his joy and delight; you please him, and he rejoices in seeing you. Nor is this all. The Father and the Son will come unto you, and make their abode with you. When God has poured out his love in your heart by the Holy Spirit, he is in you, and nothing can separate you from him. Even two *human* beings who love each other may be said to live each in the heart of the other; and the two *hearts* are inseparably united. Let a whole world be between these two persons, and they yet are close together; for they live in each other. But in a fuller and deeper sense the triune God is with and in his children on earth. "For God *is* love." He who gave himself the name of Father in our hearts by sending us his Son; he who gave his life to save us, our most precious Lord Jesus; and he who placed us in the Savior's arms, the faithful Holy Ghost; — all three persons, the holy triune God, make the heart of the believer their temple, and fill it with their life. We must not suppose that God is inclosed in our heart; — the heaven and heaven of heavens can not contain him; — neither must we think that a part of God dwells in me and a part in others. In a manner which can not be expressed, by a miracle of the Spirit, by the power of his infinite love, he has made his abode with me and with all his children; and each one of us possesses his entire love, as though God loved him only of all the world. Even the love which God has given in our hearts, humble creatures and poor sinners as we are, is a great and wonderful thing. A Father loves each of his children as fondly, as though it were his only child. None of them owns a part only, but his whole heart. Praise be to God, who loves us with all his love, and has given it to us entire, and who thus lives in us, and we in him! Glorious Pentecost gift, which fills our souls with life, with peace and joy and hope, and is mighty to comfort us in all our distress and sorrow! Come, precious Holy Spirit, give light in our hearts, and teach us to know the Father and the Son. Take us, and place us in the arms of God, that we may accept his love, and live in it for ever. "Come, Holy Spirit, power divine, And fill this hungry heart of mine. Thou seest how in tears I stand And ask a blessing of thy hand. In every need my comfort be; Refresh my soul, and strengthen me." Amen.

Come, God Creator, Holy Ghost, And visit thou these souls of men; Fill them with graces, as thou dost Thy creatures make pure again.
For comforter thy name we call. Sweet gift of God most high above. A holy unction to us all. O fount of life, fire of love.

---

234. Whitsunday. II.

O God, Holy Spirit, give us thy celestial fire in our heart and on our tongue. Amen.

Acts 2, 1–11. And when the day of Pentecost was fully come, they were all with one accord in one place. And suddenly there came a sound from heaven, as of a rushing mighty wind, and it filled all the house where they were sitting. And there appeared unto them cloven tongues, like as of fire, and it sat upon each of them: And they were all filled with the Holy Ghost, and began to speak with other tongues, as the Spirit gave them utterance. And there were dwelling at Jerusalem, Jews, devout men, out of every nation under heaven. Now when this was noised abroad, the multitude came together, and were confounded, because that every man heard them speak in his own language. And they were all amazed, and marvelled, saying one to another, Behold, are not all these which speak Galilæans? And how hear we every man in our own tongue, wherein we were born? Parthians, and Medes, and Elamites, and the dwellers in Mesopotamia, and in Judæa, and Cappadocia, in Pontus, and Asia, Phrygia, and Pamphylia, in Egypt, and in the parts of Libya about Cyrene, and strangers of Rome, Jews and proselytes, Cretes and Arabians, we do hear them speak in our tongues the wonderful works of God.

The confusion of tongues at Babel, with the division into different languages, is typical of the rending asunder of the human race by reason of sin. It had been the will of God that the human family should be widely distributed upon the earth; and it had also been his will that they should form different nations, each with its distinctive features. As no two individuals are exactly alike, so every nationality is in some things different from all others; and these manifold differences between individuals and peoples would have existed, even if we had not sinned. But all would then have been linked together in peace and love; there would have been a perfect understanding and sympathy between all, and they would have dwelt together in a spirit of perfect unity. Now the bond has been broken. Men are become strangers, neither knowing nor understanding one another. Their minds go each its own way, and do not meet in harmony of thought and purpose. The nations are enemies, and destroy one another. *Love is dead and gone;* the image of God is lost. Man has risen in revolt against God; "the imagination of man's heart is evil from his youth," and so there is an end of the bond of unity and love.

Pentecost, however, is the reverse and the destruction of Babel. The tongues of fire from heaven are the living language which the Spirit teaches the saints, and which expresses the new life in their hearts; and this life is the life in the fellowship of love, fellowship with God in Christ, mutual fellowship with one another. When the Holy Ghost cleanses our hearts, he robs none of us of the individuality which God has given to each; but he sanctifies it, brings us into harmony with one another, and unites us as one in God. As many of us as are united with Christ are united with one another, and have all things in common; that is, each employs the talent entrusted to him for the edification of the whole church. — The differences of language shall never be abolished; but all shall be purified and transfigured into a higher unity. This glorious work has not yet been consummated; but the Spirit of God is prosecuting it unceasingly. The difficulties of language are being overcome, and the gospel is being preached throughout all the earth. All peoples shall hear the word of life in their own tongue, and all languages shall be filled with the everlasting truth. This was foretold in the miracle of Pentecost day, when men of all nations heard the apostles speak to them in their own tongue. When the church shall have been made perfect the saved of all the different nations shall together be one blessed and holy family; and all tongues shall unite in one grand harmony in the celestial language of love, in which the church shall sing the song of God and the Lamb.

Holy Spirit, gather our hearts to Christ, and gather all peoples, that there may be one fold, and one shepherd. Amen.

Holy Spirit! hear us On this sacred day; Come to us with blessing, Come with us to stay.
Come, as once thou camest To the faithful few Patiently awaiting Jesus' promise true.

---

235. Monday after Whitsunday. I.

Pour out thy love, O God, into our hearts by thy Holy Spirit. Amen.

Gospel Lesson, John 3, 16–21. For God so loved the world, that he gave his only begotten Son, that whosoever believeth in him should not perish, but have everlasting life. For God sent not his Son into the world to condemn the world; but that the world through him might be saved. He that believeth on him is not condemned: but he that believeth not is condemned already, because he hath not believed in the name of the only begotten Son of God. And this is the condemnation, that light is come into the world, and men loved darkness rather than light, because their deeds were evil. For every one that doeth evil hateth the light, neither cometh to the light, lest his deeds should be reproved. But he that doeth truth cometh to the light, that his deeds may be made manifest, that they are wrought in God.

Hear this, all people; hear it, all who have sorrow and grief: *God loves us all!* God, who is Lord of all things, does not want *any evil* to befall us; he loves us; and his purpose in regard to us is *good altogether.* Think of it: *God loves* the world. Hear *who* it is that loves: It is the everlasting, almighty God, *he* that "did whatsoever he pleased, in heaven, and in earth, in the seas, and all deep places." He *loves;* he is love. "The sun shines, the fire warms, *God loves."* He is kindly disposed towards us all; he gladly gives us everything that is good. He rejoices in our welfare, and does not want us to be unhappy. Hear also who the *objects* of his love are: He loves the world; *all men.* Not one is excluded; *all* are beloved of God. The good and the bad, the pious and the ungodly, you and I; we all can feel assured that God loves us. Think of this; repeat these words of Jesus aloud when you are by yourself, substituting "me" for "the world," thus: "For God so loved me, etc. Thus am I beloved of God, I and all mine, and every human being." — *Great* is the love of God; infinitely deep and high, and stronger than death. We were lost, and justice demanded the sentence of death on us; but God *so* loved the world, *that he gave his only begotten Son.* More than this could not be given. None other is so well beloved of God; there is none whom he holds so dear in his eternal love. Than the Son he could give us nothing greater. When I ponder it, and the Holy Spirit speaks of it to my heart, it becomes clear to me, that this gospel is not of men, but of God; for it never could have entered into the thought of man; — and I feel in my soul the joy of the love of God, a foretaste of eternal bliss. "He that spared not his own Son, but delivered him up for us all, how shall he not with him also freely give us all things?" — When God loves me so, who, then, shall be able to separate me from this love? — God's only begotten Son is delivered up to death on the cross. According to the decree of love he must be thus lifted up, even as the serpent in the wilderness; and thereby the demands of justice are satisfied. God gave us his Son as a sacrificial lamb; and the Jewish priests sacrificed him for the whole world. Now love can reign; we can believe it and accept it, rest secure in it, and enjoy it with all our heart. And nothing else is necessary to our salvation. Whosoever *believeth* in the Son shall not perish, but have everlasting life. For what is everlasting life but the love of God in Christ? This life *is given* us; and hence we can have nothing to do save to *believe* it. Have we any reason not to believe? Is not love truth? Is not unbelief falsehood? Is not the gospel light? — Keep this text in your thought, and ponder it in your heart; and the Spirit of God shall surely teach you to believe. It is something great which is to be believed, and faith itself is a great thing; but then, the Holy Ghost, who creates faith in us, is the omnipotent God. — Great is also that which follows, and which Luther expresses thus: "The important thing is not that I may receive crowns and kingdoms, which would leave me under the dominion of sin and death, but that I may be redeemed from death and hell, and be eternally saved. This it is which this gift shall accomplish, that the fire of hell is quenched, that the devil is cast under our feet, and that a terrified, sorrowful, and bruised heart may become a happy and quickened heart, with eternal life in place of eternal corruption and death."

Thanks, O God, for thy love; for thy unspeakably great gift! Give us the light of the Spirit to know it, and to belive; that we may not despise this salvation, but may be saved, and may taste thy love in the life eternal. Amen.

Thou strong defense, thou holy light, Teach us to know our God aright, And call him Father from the heart: The word of life and truth impart, That we may not love doctrines strange, Nor e'er to other teachers range, But Jesus for our master own, And put our trust in him alone.

---

236. Monday after Whitsunday. II.

Blessed is the man unto whom the Lord imputeth not iniquity, and in whose spirit there is no guile. Amen.

Acts 10, 42–48. And he commanded us to preach unto the people, and to testify that it is he which was ordained of God to be the Judge of quick and dead. To him give all the prophets witness, that through his name whosoever believeth in him shall receive remission of sins. While Peter yet spake these words, the Holy Ghost fell on all them which heard the word. And they of the circumcision which believed were astonished, as many as came with Peter, because that on the gentiles also was poured out the gift of the Holy Ghost: For they heard them speak with tongues, and magnify God. Ther answered Peter, Can any man forbid water, that these should not be baptized, which have received the Holy Ghost as well as we? And he commanded them to be baptized in the name of the Lord. Then prayed they him to tarry certain days.

All the prophets testify concerning our Lord Jesus Christ, that through his name whosoever believeth in him shall have remission of sins. *All the prophets;* — truly, a grand army of witnesses! Shall we not believe them? Are they all wrong, and testify to that which is not true, do you think? Ask the apostles also; their testimony is the same as that of the prophets. Hear, how they all with one tongue declare, that *as many as believe in Jesus* receive remission of sins through his name. All testify by the Spirit of God, that remission of sins is through the name of *him* who is the Judge of all. Truly, our God is very desirous that we should believe remission of our sins. When a man has been roused from his sleep, and sees his sin, he finds it no easy matter to believe. Some, to be sure, may in a short time receive the courage of faith; but in the case of others it is a slow process. The devil suggests all manner of doubt in the soul; for if we believe forgiveness of sins through Christ the devil has been defeated. God has, therefore, taken the greatest pains to force conviction upon us. Moses is a strong witness in regard to our sin. You believe him; and with good reason; for Moses is the servant of the Lord, and Jesus has himself certified to the truth of his testimony. But if you believe Moses when he testifies that you are a sinner, shall you not, then, believe *all the prophets of God,* Moses among the number, *and all his apostles, and the Son himself,* when they testify with one voice, that whosoever believes in Jesus Christ shall through his name receive remission of sins? You believe that he is the Son of God; you believe that he has taken away the sins of the world; you believe that he *is* the Savior of sinners, as his name declares; — *you believe in him,* and yet you doubt that your sins are forgiven you? Do you, then, not understand that your unbelief is hollow and empty, nothing but a lying contrivance of Satan? Do you not understand that with your unbelief you pit yourself against all the witnesses whom God has sent, and say to them: "I am not sure that you speak the truth!" Nay, you say to Jesus himself: "I do not know, whether or not thou hast the right to be called the Savior!" — Away with unbelief! You who know that you are a sinner, and who intend to sin no more; you who ask mercy for Jesus' sake, and who have none other Savior; remember this: *All the prophets bear witness, that in Jesus you have remission of sins.* Shall not the false preaching of the devil be put down? Shall not the word of God stand? It is glorious beyond belief; but it is true nevertheless. Or, is anything impossible with God? Rejoice: your sins are forgiven, and salvation is yours!

Praise be to thee, Lord Jesus, who didst baptize us unto thv name, and dost give us therein so great a mercy. Verily, thou hast taken our sins, and sacrificed thyself for our salvation. When thou hast taken our sins away, they are taken away indeed. Nothing can condemn us. We heartily thank thee; and we pray for grace to believe, and to serve thee for ever, our precious Lord and Savior. Amen.

Jesus, thou friend divine, Our Savior and our king, Thy hand from every snare and foe Shall great deliverance bring.
Sure as thy truth shall last, To Zion shall be given The brightest glories earth can yield, And brighter bliss of heaven.

---

237. Tuesday after Whitsunday.

Lord, gather us into thy fold, and lead us by thy hand. Amen.

John 10, 1–10. Verily, verily, I say unto you, He that entereth not by the door into the sheepfold, but climbeth up some other way, the same is a thief and a robber. But he that entereth in by the door is the shepherd of the sheep. To him the porter openeth; and the sheep hear his voice: and he calleth his own sheep by name, and leadeth them out. And when he putteth forth his own sheep, he goeth before them, and the sheep follow him: for they know his voice. And a stranger will they not follow, but will flee from him: for they know not the voice of strangers. This parable spake Jesus unto them: but they understood not what things they were which he spake unto them. Then said Jesus unto them again, Verily, verily, I say unto you, I am the door of the sheep. All that ever came before me are thieves and robbers: but the sheep did not hear them. I am the door: by me if any man enter in, he shall be saved, and shall go in and out, and find pasture. The thief cometh not, but for to steal, and to kill, and to destroy: I am come that they might have life, and that they might have it more abundantly.

The Lord himself is the shepherd of his church; but as the visible means of grace can not be immediately administered by the glorified Savior, he chooses out of the fold some to be shepherds for the others. "And he gave some, apostles; and some, prophets; and some, evangelists; and some, pastors and teachers; for the perfecting of the saints, for the work of the ministry, for the edifying of the body of Christ." (Ephesians 4). It is of this matter that he speaks in our text. "He that entereth by the door into the sheepfold is the shepherd of the sheep." Herein we learn these two lessons: 1) Only such as are themselves true members of the church can properly be pastors. A minister of the gospel who does not himself live in God, can not care properly for the souls. They only who come to the Father through Jesus, and live, all the time, of his love; who daily receive forgiveness; who daily appear before the throne of grace, and go out again to their work in the world with new strength; to whom Jesus is the way, the truth, and the life; — they only can be true shepherds, and can properly feed and care for his sheep. 2) Every true minister of the gospel must have been appointed to the work by the Lord, and not have forced himself into the sacred office. He must not only have entered the church by the right door; but he must also have entered the office of the ministry by the right door. The formal, orderly call in and through the church is necessary, because God is the God of good order, and every member of the congregation has his appointed work ; and this formal call is also highly necessary as a help and comfort in the temptations and difficulties of the work. But here we are especially concerned with the inner call, without which the other, after all, is of but little value to him. How shall we know this call? The answer is not difficult, but the self-examination is. If you can say with Peter, "Lord, thou knowest all things ; thou knowest that I love thee," if you have an imperative desire that you might serve the Lord in the office of the ministry; and if the circumstances of your life also point in the same direction, you may conclude that the Lord says to you: "Feed my sheep." Then, if you follow the call, you have entered in by the door; and the sheep will follow you, and know your voice. — The Lord himself is the door to the sheepfold. He is the door for *all*, because it is only *by reason of his merit and blood* that we can enter the kingdom of grace ; and he is the door for the *shepherds*, because it is *only by his love* that we are properly accredited and equipped for the office. — The Pharisees and all worldly-minded preachers and hypocritical exhorters are declared by the Lord to be thieves and robbers. He thereby strongly urges upon us the duty of a careful self-examination. They are thieves and robbers in so far as they gather unto themselves, and labor for worldly honor and filthy lucre ; while the true servants of Christ regard it as their highest glory to lead the souls to him. Blessed is every man who goes in and out through Jesus ! They shall have life, and have it abundantly. They shall themselves enjoy his abundant grace and his more than victorious love; and his life shall, therefore, reign in them; and they shall fill the hungry souls with the good things of his house.

Lord, give us shepherds who feed thy sheep on the good pastures ; and bless them, and preserve thy fold. Let us also be thine, and let us be members of thy church until our last hour, and in thee have life. Amen.

Lord of the church, we humbly pray For those who guide us in thy way, And speak thy holy word: With love divine their hearts inspire, And touch their lips with hallowed fire, And needful grace afford.

---

238. Wednesday after Whitsunday.

Lord, give us a thorough knowledge of sin and a living faith. Amen.

Acts 2, 22–28. Ye men of Israel, hear these words; Jesus of Nazareth, a man approved of God among you by miracles and wonders and signs, which God did by him, in the midst of you, as ye yourselves also know: Him, being delivered by the determinate counsel and foreknowledge of God, ye have taken, and by wicked hands have crucified and slain: Whom God hath raised up, having loosed the pains of death: because it was not possible that he should be holden of it. For David speaketh concerning him, I foresaw the Lord always before my face: for he is on my right hand, that I should not be moved: Therefore did my heart rejoice, and my tongue was glad; moreover also my flesh shall rest in hope: Because thou wilt not leave my soul in hell, neither wilt thou suffer thine Holy One to see corruption. Thou hast made known to me the ways of life; thou shalt make me full of joy with thy countenance.

The Holy Ghost speaks through Peter in words of earnestness to the Israelites and to us. His words stirred their hearts, and should stir ours also. Of his love for us God delivered up his Son for our sins; and him have we crucified with wicked hands. As long as we imagine that only others are guilty of the blood of the Son of God, we look on with composure; but when the truth comes home to us, that we ourselves are the perpetrators of the guilty deed, the matter assumes a different aspect. Though the Jews have the direct responsibility for having slain the Son of God, they are not alone in the matter; we also lent our assistance in the murder of the Lord of glory. For he died for sin; *our* sins, as well as those of the Jews, condemned and crucified him. — Ye men, whom God so loved that he gave his Son for you; how terrible a thing it is, that you with wicked hearts and bloody hands have crucified the only begotten of the Father! As many as obey the Spirit of God confess this with horror; but the children of the world refuse to admit that they have nailed the Son of God to the cross. If you would hear the word of God, and give heed to the voice of conscience, your guilt would be established in your own heart. Of a truth, you have, by your evil thoughts and words and deeds, scourged and mocked and crucified the Lord whose name you bear; and as long as you deny his divinity, or despise his mercy, and tread his blood under foot, you are in partnership with Caiaphas and Pilate, who condemned him.

Greater, however, than our greatest sin is the love of God. The most atrocious deed which heaven and earth have witnessed, — that the only begotten Son of God was crucified by his own people, — is, according to his determinate counsel, become our salvation. This is the height and the depth of love; the annihilation of death, and the life of humanity; the angels' song of praise, and the joy of all who are saved. By his death he pays the wages of sin, and thereafter he rises again in glory. Love is triumphantly victorious. "He was delivered for our offences, and was raised again for our justification." And now he sends us his Holy Spirit; bestows upon us through him the fruit of his work as the Savior, his grace which gives salvation; and creates in our heart the faith with which to receive his grace. Thus we are given a part in him, and live with him, — he takes delight in us, and all heaven rejoices in our happiness. Give him your heart; believe in him, and live in him!

Lord Jesus, precious Savior, living God; grant me this mercy, that I may believe in thee with a humble heart all my life, honor thee, and serve thee, and praise thy name in all eternity. Amen.

O deep abyss of love unbounded, Which all our sin hath swallowed up! Our wounds were healed, our foe confounded, When Jesus drank the bitter cup Of wrath, and shed his precious blood, That mercy might be had from God.

239. Thursday after Whitsunday.

Again we pray, Lord Jesus; pour out thy Spirit upon us. Amen.

Acts 2, 29–36. Men and brethren, let me freely speak unto you of the patriarch David, that he is both dead and buried, and his sepulchre is with us unto this day. Therefore being a prophet, and knowing that God had sworn with an oath to him, that of the fruit of his loins, according to the flesh, he would raise up Christ to sit on his throne; he, seeing this before, spake of the resurrection of Christ, that his soul was not left in hell, neither his flesh did see corruption. This Jesus hath God raised up, whereof we all are witnesses. Therefore, being by the right hand of God exalted, and having received of the Father the promise of the Holy Ghost, he hath shed forth this, which ye now see and hear. For David is not ascended into the heavens: but he saith himself, The Lord said unto my Lord, Sit thou on my right hand, until I make thy foes thy footstool. Therefore let all the house of Israel know asuredly, that God hath made that same Jesus, whom ye have crucified, both Lord and Christ.

That which the Son of God has done for us the Holy Ghost explains, and establishes it firmly in the hearts of the faithful. That Christ became a man, and suffered death, and rose again, and entered into his glory; that he made atonement for our sins, delivered us from the curse of the law, and gained for us eternal life; that he reconciled us to God, appeased his anger, and annihilated death; — all this is indisputable; "it is finished." It was foretold by David and all the prophets, because it had been determined in the counsel of God; and now it is presented in the gospel as an incontrovertible, accomplished fact. Now the prophecies are easy to understand; for they have been unwrapped out of their swaddling clothes. Now they are easy to believe; for their truth has been established by their fulfilment. Christ died, but is risen, and lives; the Holy Ghost came, and the church was founded; and in it we have the means of grace, the word and sacraments which Jesus has given us, with life and salvation for all them that believe.

We know this to be truth; for we have the testimony of the Holy Ghost in our hearts. He confirms the word in our experience; and he leads us into the fellowship of the Son of God, thus giving us knowledge of sin and grace, of death and life. But you are not saved by knowing these things and regarding them as true, if the Spirit do not establish their truth in your heart. Ask it of him in earnest prayer; he will not cast off one who says: "Lord, I believe; help thou mine unbelief!" Do not let him go, until you have the full assurance of the truth in your heart. This is not a matter to be regarded lightly; it is a question of eternal life or eternal death. We are dealing with the question of salvation from cruel death and the pit of hell, from the grievous corruption of your soul, and from the righteous wrath of God. Something more is needed than mere human learning and idle speculations. None save the Spirit of God can bring the truth and life into the heart, and there confirm the testimony of the scripture, so that we believe with that faith which is stronger than death and hell, because it is divine in its nature, and is founded on the truth of God. Dear friend, life is here, and light, and salvation; they are to be found in the word, in which is also the Spirit, who will bring them home to your soul. By his grace you may receive them, and arrive at certainty in regard to your salvation. If you do not as yet have this faith, then may God make you zealous to pursue it with all your heart! — Grant us this grace, merciful Lord Jesus. Proclaim the truth in such a way, that we accept it, and that we reach the full assurance of faith, the certainty that thou art God, and that we have life in thee. Let us experience in our souls the power of thy resurrection, that we may live in thee, and confess thy name alway. Amen.

Holy Spirit, all-divine, Dwell within this heart of mine; Cast down every idol-throne, Reign supreme, and reign alone.

See, to thee I yield my heart; Shed thy life through every part. A pure temple I would be, Wholly dedicate to thee.

---

240. Friday after Whitsunday.

God, let thy word bring our souls to conversion. Amen.

Acts 2, 37–42. Now when they heard this, they were pricked in their heart, and said unto Peter and to the rest of the apostles, Men and brethren, what shall we do? Then Peter said unto them, Repent, and be baptized every one of you in the name of Jesus Christ, for the remission of sins, and ye shall receive the gift of the Holy Ghost. For the promise is unto you, and to your children, and to all that are afar off, even as many as the Lord our God shall call. And with many other words did he testify and exhort, saying, Save yourselves from this untoward generation. Then they that gladly received his word were baptized: and the same day there were added unto them about three thousand souls. And they continued stedfastly in the apostles' doctrine and fellowship, and in breaking of bread, and in prayers.

"They were pricked in their heart." This is as it should be. If the word of God do not penetrate the heart, we have heard it in vain. What, then, did they feel? They felt their sin, and feared the wrath of God. This, also, is as it should be. He who does not feel his sin with "godly sorrow" does not have the true faith. — Many hear the story of the death of Jesus with hearts as unmoved, as though it did not in the least concern them. It is not until we feel in our soul the sharp sting of the declaration, "thou art the man," that the question, "what shall I do?" becomes one of vital interest to us, and that the ear is open to hear the word concerning remission of sins. The inevitable truth is, that he only who repents of his sin can believe the gospel. Man does not hearken to the message of mercy without having given heed to the voice exhorting him to do penance. Proclaim to the world that God is merciful; shout the message into the ears of men; preach it with the fiery eloquence of Peter, or with the impressive and loving voice of John, the "son of thunder;" give instruction with the clearness and power of the Spirit in regard to the value of Christ's grace, which brings salvation; and summon men to him in the heavenly and gentle words of the gospel, which seem almost irresistable; — it is all in vain; they do not hear, and will not come, although they may seem to hear, and to come nearer for a moment; they break away, and are lost, if they do not learn to know and repent of their sins. — You, on the other hand, who see that you deserve the wrath of God, and who now anxiously seek salvation; come, one and all, receive in the name of Jesus full forgiveness, and be comforted! You are baptized into Christ, and the promise is yours. It is the Holy Ghost who bends your heart in contrition on account of your sins; and he does it, in order that he may give you healing by means of the grace which Jesus has earned. Save yourself from this unbelieving generation! The Lord your God calls you; do not stand apart, but come here, and be a member of his church, and live with his people. When you sincerely repent of your sins, because they have offended your God; when it is your earnest purpose to avoid sin, and to live according to the word and commandments of God; when you are able to hear that the gospel is a good message, which you would gladly accept; then your conversion is genuine, and then you already have that which you desire; for the Lord your God has forgiven you all your trespasses. Believe what Jesus has done, and accept what he has given, and continue instant in the teaching of the apostles unto the end. Do not seek a sign; but *believe the word.*

Thus we are one with the apostolic church, and have all things in common with it; we sit at the same communion table, break the same bread, and pray the same prayers to the same heavenly Father. Praise God! Amen.

One, the light of God's own presence, O'er his ransomed people shed, Chasing far the gloom and terror, Brightening all the path we tread: One, the object of our journey, One the faith which never tires, One, the earnest looking forward, One, the hope our God inspires.

---

241. Saturday after Whitsunday.

Holy Spirit, kindle the fire of love in our hearts. Amen.

1 John 4, 9–12. In this was manifested the love of God toward us, because that God sent his only begotten Son into the world, that we might live through him. Herein is love, not that we loved God, but that he loved us, and sent his Son to be the propitiation for our sins. Beloved, if God so loved us, we ought also to love one another. No man hath seen God at any time. If we love one another, God dwelleth in us, and his love is perfected in us.

All that God does is love; and all creatures are witnesses that God loves. Blessed is he who sees it! But although the love of God is plainly to be seen in *all* his works, John speaks true when he says: "*In this* was manifested the love of God toward us, because that God sent his only begotten Son into the world, that we might live through him. *Herein* is love, that God sent his Son to be the propitiation for our sins." For all God's thoughts of love concerning us are brought to a focus, as it were, in his merciful decree, that his only begotten

Son should become man and redeem us with his blood. From the manger in Bethlehem, from the baptism in the Jordan, and especially from Gethsemane and Calvary, the love of God shines out with a brightness which illuminates all his works. "What is it sparkles in the blood From Jesus' riven side that flowed? The brightest beams of heavenly love, Which fall upon us from above. Now every hindrance which would stay Our faith in God is cleared away. Send doubt of whatsoever name Back to the devil, whence it came!" It is in Christ that God loves and blesses us. *Great*, high, deep, living, is this love; he that believes it will love God in return, and thus God dwells in us. You complain that you can not love God and the brethren. Of a truth, it is deplorable; for where love is wanting, all gifts are in vain, and all works are nothing. But have you overlooked that which John says in our text: *"Herein* is love, not that we loved him, but that he loved us, and sent his Son to be the propitiation for our sins?" Immediately before this he says: *"Love is of God."* Let the Spirit teach us this lesson! Let him teach us, that we are beloved of God, and that his love is come to us in the Son; that it is given us in him, in that he became man, and died for us, and we were baptized into his death, and hear his gospel, and partake of his Holy Supper. Let the Spirit explain this to us, in order that we may *believe* the love of God. This love is a blessed reality which envelops us; if we believe, it enters our hearts, and dwells in us. Believe in love as the nature of God and the gift of God; believe that God loves you in Christ, before you love him; then you believe that which is true, that which God himself has spoken; and then you shall taste his love, and shall love him for that he loves you. — Persist until this love is become your life! Make no mistake; this love is of God, and is his gift to all them that believe.

God, let thy love humble us and dwell in us. Do thou, who art rich in mercy and in the desire to make us happy, give us this love; let our hearts be full of it, and let it be the living force and moving principle in all that we do. Amen.

Lamb of God, I look to thee; Thou shalt my example be; Thou art gentle, meek, and mild, Thou wast once a little child.
Fain I would be as thou art; Give me thy obedient heart; Thou art pitiful and kind: Let me have thy loving mind.

---

242. Trinity Sunday. I.

Lord, let us experience the living power of thy word. Amen.

Gospel Lesson, John 3, 1-15. There was a man of the Pharisees, named Nicodemus, a ruler of the Jews: The same came to Jesus by night, and said unto him, Rabbi, we know that thou art a teacher come from God: for no man can do these miracles that thou doest, except God be with him. Jesus answered and said unto him, Verily, verily, I say unto thee, Except a man be born again, he cannot see the kingdom of God. Nicodemus saith unto him, How can a man be born when he is old? can he enter the second time into his mother's womb, and be born? Jesus answered, Verily, verily, I say unto thee,

Except a man be born of water and of the Spirit, he cannot enter the kingdom of God. That which is born of the flesh is flesh; and that which is born of the Spirit is spirit. Marvel not that I said unto thee, Ye must be born again. The wind bloweth where it listeth, and thou hearest the sound thereof, but canst not tell whence it cometh, and whither it goeth: so is every one that is born of the Spirit. Nicodemus answered and said unto him, How can these things be? Jesus answered and said unto him, Art thou a master of Israel, and knowest not these things? Verily, verily, I say unto thee, We speak that we do know, and testify that we have seen; and ye receive not our witness. If I have told you earthly things, and ye believe not, how shall ye believe if I tell you of heavenly things? And no man hath ascended up to heaven, but he that came down from heaven, even the Son of Man which is in heaven. And as Moses lifted up the serpent in the wilderness, even so must the Son of Man be lifted up: That whosoever believeth in him should not perish, but have eternal life.

By reason of our having lost the image of God we are, in our natural state, entirely unfit for the blessed fellowship of the Holy One in heaven. We do not love him; we have no joy in him; how could we, then, be happy with him in eternal glory? Even if it were possible that God could receive us into his heaven in our natural condition, we could not remain there and be happy. If we are to be saved, it is necessary that we again come into possession of the love which we have lost; that we become like-minded unto God, and thus have our joy in him.

To fall, and die, is something which we can do of our own strength, and in which the devil is glad to lend us his assistance; but to rise from the fall, and live again, is beyond our power; besides being an undertaking in which the devil would exert all his power against us. Life from the dead can be given by the Lord *only*. The love which has been quenched in our hearts can not be rekindled save by a torch from heaven. But the Lord is merciful; the whole blessed Trinity is engaged in the work of accomplishing this miracle. All which God does, is done in order that we may have everlasting life. The Father has sent his only begotten Son to us with this love; the Son has brought it into the human family, and has again made it the victorious power on earth; and *the Holy Ghost* creates faith in us, and thus enables us to receive this love into the heart. The life and work of Christ in his state of humiliation are completed, but have not passed away. He is here among us with his perfect life, his innocent death, his victorious resurrection; with his whole work of salvation, the annihiliation of sin and death, the life which he brought us, the life which he gained for us, the life everlasting, which is *love*. The great importance of the means of grace consists in this, that through them the Father and Son come to us with the gift of the Holy Ghost. In our *baptism* the triune God, the God of our salvation, comes to us, and *begets us anew*. Paul says: "As many as are baptized into Christ have put on Christ." And again: "Therefore we are buried with him by baptism into death; that like as Christ was raised up from the dead by the glory of the Father, even so we also should walk in newness of life." We are dead with Christ, but alive unto God through him. (Romans 6). It has pleased the Lord to use the water in connection with the word as the means of bringing about this miracle of grace. The same Lord Jesus, who once came and lay in a manger, wrapped in swaddling clothes, that he might *gain* for us life eternal, comes in his means of grace to our hearts, and *bestows* this life upon us. Therefore he says in our gospel lesson: "Except a man be *born of the water and of the Spirit,* he can not enter into the kingdom of God." And for the same reason it is declared, in 1 Peter 3, 21, that *"baptism doth also now save us."* Through the means of grace the Holy Ghost *extends* to us the treasure of grace, and works in us the *faith* by which we accept the gift. As it was the will of God that they who saw the brazen serpent should live, so it is his will that we should live by *faith.* Before the eye of the soul is the Lord Jesus, who was lifted up, and died for us, and was buried, and was raised again; and the Spirit enlightens this our eye, and enables us to believe in him. Through this faith, which trusts in the crucified and risen Savior in the means of grace administered by the church, his life of love then enters our hearts, and thus he abides in us, and we in him.

The new birth is a miracle which takes place in the hidden depths of the soul; but the new life springs forth, is known of the regenerated person himself, and is made manifest to others. — Do you, my dear reader, truly love God? Does Jesus with his love live in you? Do you long after him, rejoice in him, and gladly bend your will in obedience to his will? Do you pray that you may love him with your whole heart; and are you truly sorry that you do not love him as well as you ought? If so, you have, of a truth, been born again from above, and you are "partaker of the divine nature." — Let nothing else be as important to you as having this life in God. If you have that, you are saved; if you do not have it, you are lost. "Verily, verily, I say unto thee: Except a man be born again, he can not see the kingdom of God." These are the Savior's own words.

God, give us thy Holy Spirit, that we may have true faith, and that we may have the heavenly life of the love of Jesus in our hearts. Holy Spirit, make thy way into our hearts, and drive out darkness and death. Triune God, may we live in thee now and for evermore. Amen.

Come, Holy Spirit, come; Oh, hear my humble prayer; Stoop down and make my heart thy home, And shed thy blessing there.

Thy light, thy love impart, And let it ever be A holy, humble, happy heart, A dwelling-place for thee.

Let thy rich grace increase, Through all my early days, The fruits of righteousness and peace, To thine eternal praise.

---

243. Trinity Sunday. II.

Lord, teach us to believe, and to worship thy wisdom. Amen.

Epistle Lesson, Romans 11, 33–36. O the depth of the riches both of the wisdom and knowledge of God! how unsearchable are his judgments, and his ways past finding out! For who hath known the mind of the Lord? or who hath been his counsellor? Or who hath first given to him, and it shall be recompensed unto him again? For of him, and through him, and to him, are all things: to whom be glory for ever. Amen.

Do not lose heart, dear Christian, even if the outlook for the church does look dark; its cause is the *Lord's*, and the *Lord* shall lead his cause to victory. His wisdom is unsearchable. Of his ways we understand nothing, save that which it has pleased him to reveal to us; but in many cases it is expedient that he hides from us that which he does. We are too foolish to be consulted, and too little to understand the wisdom of God. He has, however, revealed to us enough to enable us to believe in him, and commit ourselves into his keeping.

It is a sad thing to see the Jews walking in blindness, and the multitude of the gentiles sitting in the darkness of idolatry; to see Christ rejected by men in greatest repute among Christian peoples, and to know that the true Christians among us are sadly wanting in faith and in love. He that has bowels of compassion can not avoid feeling "great heaviness and continual sorrow in his heart." — This is a sad state of affairs, to be sure; but do you imagine that it can embarrass God, or make him hesitate how to deal with us? Were Caiaphas and Pilate, who in their blindness and malice slew the Son of God, able to prevent him from accomplishing his gracious purpose as our Savior? Were they not, on the contrary, obliged to carry out his will? Or were the Jews able, by means of their unbelief, to prevent the extension of Christ's kingdom? On the contrary, their rejection of the gospel sent it out into all lands, and became the world's salvation! Do not doubt that God had foreknowledge of the unbelief and infidelity and atheism of our age, and that he has taken them into account in his plan for the perfecting of his kingdom. Men may think to build their tower of Babel *in opposition* to the Lord; but he interferes, and that which they do is made to *serve his purposes.* They built their tower on the plain of Shinar, against the Lord's command, in order that they might not be scattered; but the *Lord* "scattered them abroad from thence upon the face of all the earth." In our times men are collecting materials from the depths and the heights, from the secret places of nature and from the workshop of the human intellect, in order to build a tower which shall gather all people into one great temple of nature, and leave the church of Christ empty. It looks as if "nothing will be restrained from them, which they have imagined to do." (Genesis 11, 6). Have no fear; the Lord knows how to deal with the matter. "Of him, and through him, and to him, are all things." These three words, "of" and "through" and "to," you shall note well, dear Christian; they are grand words, and mighty against unbelief. — The gardener knows what he is doing when he cuts away the crown of the apple tree, although the children may think that he is destroying it. The church is the Lord's. Keep your peace, wait upon him, serve him and walk before his face; and little by little you shall see his wisdom, and with holy fear and joy give him your offering of worship and praise. If he again hide it all from your eyes, you shall still be able to believe and say: "To him be glory for ever!"

Let thy Spirit enlighten us, O God, that we may understand how thou hast concluded them all in unbelief, that thou mightest have mercy upon all. Let us see so much at least of thy counsel of love and justice, that we believe in thee with confidence, and gladly serve thee. Amen.

He built the earth, he spread the sky, And fixed the starry lights on high. Wonders of grace to God belong: Repeat his mercies in your song. He sent his Son with power to save From guilt and darkness and the grave. Wonders of grace to God belong: Repeat his mercies in your song.

244. Monday after Trinity Sunday.

Holy and merciful God, give us the light of the Spirit, that we may know thee in faith, that we may fear thee, and that we may become holy, as thou art holy. Amen.

Isaiah 6, 1–7. In the year that king Uzziah died, I saw also the Lord sitting upon a throne, high and lifted up, and his train filled the temple. Above it stood the seraphims: each one had six wings; with twain he covered his face, and with twain he covered his feet, and with twain he did fly. And one cried unto another, and said, Holy, holy, holy is the Lord of hosts; the whole earth is full of his glory. And the posts of the door moved at the voice of him that cried, and the house was filled with smoke. Then said I, Woe is me! for I am undone; because I am a man of unclean lips, and I dwell in the midst of a people of unclean lips: for mine eyes have seen the King, the Lord of hosts. Then flew one of these seraphims unto me, having a live coal in his hand, which he had taken with the tongs from off the altar; and he laid it upon my mouth, and said, Lo, this hath touched thy lips, and thine iniquity is taken away, and thy sin purged.

Holy is the Lord in his heavenly habitation, exalted high above all the earth and its littleness, — he is purity and perfect love, in eternal harmony with himself. *Holy* is the Lord in his revelation through the Son; he is absolutely unspotted, and there is a perfect unity in the will of the divine persons, even at the time when the Son was in the likeness of flesh, and suffered for our sins. *Holy* is the Lord in the work of the Spirit when he makes our hearts his dwelling place, regenerates us, and sanctifies us. "Holy, holy, holy, is the Lord of the hosts; the whole earth is full of his glory." This is seen and sung by the seraphims before his throne.

How, then, shall ungodly sinners be able to stand before him? Isaiah was a holy man; but when he saw the glory of the Lord he cried out: "Woe is me; I am undone, because I am a man of unclean lips!" And it is necessary that he be cleansed with a live coal from the altar, — a symbol of the grace of the Holy Spirit, which cleanses us through the sacrifice of Christ. The Spirit must assure the prophet that his sins are taken away. Not until that has been done does the prophet take heart to present himself before God, or become fit to serve him. Even the seraphim, these sinless and exalted angels of heaven, hide their faces and their feet before the Lord, when they move the posts of the door as they cry unto one another, saying: *Holy, holy, holy;* — how, then, shall we dare to appear before him? Wherewith shall we cleanse and cover ourselves before the eyes of the Holy One? Do you not feel how impossible it is that we should stand before him in our own righteousness, or in our natural condition, without having been born again? It is absolutely necessary that we cling to our heavenly high priest, and take shelter under the wings of his holiness. We must be born of the Spirit to a new and holy life in God, and be perfected in holiness by being renewed and cleansed from day to day. Praise be to thee, Lord Jesus, who didst come to us with both water and blood; and dost give us the Spirit, who clothes us in the garment of righteousness! Thou art my holiness; in thee I am of good cheer, and thou wilt not let me go, except thou hast taken away all my sin! I shall become perfect in holiness, and see the Lord of glory, and live!

O God, give us all, who ask thee, this grace by the Holy Spirit, for the sake of Jesus Christ. Give us vital piety and faith and holiness in our innermost heart. Amen.

Thee we adore, eternal Lord! We praise thy name with one accord;
Thy saints, who here thy goodness see, Through all the world do worship thee.
To thee aloud all angels cry, The heavens and all the powers on high:
Thee, holy, holy, holy king, Lord God of hosts, they ever sing.

---

245. Tuesday after Trinity Sunday.

Lord, teach us to know thy power and glory.

Matthew 28, 18–20. And Jesus came and spake unto them, saying, All power is given unto me in heaven and in earth. Go ye therefore, and teach all nations, baptizing them in the name of the Father, and of the Son, and of the Holy Ghost; teaching them to observe all things whatsoever I have commanded you: and, lo, I am with you alway, even unto the end of the world. Amen.

Christ is almighty God from everlasting; here, however, he speaks of his power as our high priest, prophet, and king. The whole world has been given him to save, and he has redeemed it through his death; whereafter the Father gave him a place at his right hand, and "there was given him dominion, and glory, and a kingdom." (Daniel 7, 14). All things are at his disposal in his work of extending the church by means of the word and sacraments; he can make use of all angels and spirits in heaven, and of all men and powers on earth. This we should bear in mind, in order that our faith may be strengthened. I wonder, if we have given due consideration to this glorious truth: "All power is given unto me in heaven and in earth." "All power," and all wisdom, and love, and righteousness, are in the service of the Christian church; and what, then, shall do it any injury? He who has dominion over *all things* for the benefit of the church is with his own alway, unceasingly, every hour, unto the end of the world. Therefore he is able

to command his disciples to go and make all the world subject to him.
1) They are to make *all people* his disciples; Christianize all nations.
Truly, a royal command; and it is obeyed! The whole mission work
of the church rests on this command of the Lord. Satan has all the
time furiously opposed it, — by means of persecutions, by the secular-
ization of the church, and by all manner of sects, which try to prevent
the conversion of the nations to the Christian faith. But his efforts
are vain; for no power can nullify the command of *Christ*: "Go ye
therefore, and teach all nations." 2) "Baptize them in the name of the
Father, and of the Son, and of the Holy Ghost; teaching them to
observe all things whatsoever I have commanded you." He can speak
in the name of the holy Trinity, and has control of the whole power
and revelation of God in word and deed. To be baptized into *the
name of the Father* is to be united with the Father of Jesus as his child.
Baptism into *the name of the Son* is to be received into his kingdom,
and to have part in his work of redemption. To be baptized into *the
name of the Holy Ghost* is to receive the Spirit into the heart, and become his habitation. "Baptize them," and "teach them;" by these
two means the kingdom of Christ is extended. Teach them to "observe *all things whatsoever* I have commanded you." Have not the
apostles done this? We need have no doubt whatever that they have
imparted to the church "all utterance and all knowledge;" and when we
teach that which they taught, we need not hesitate to declare that it is
the full and complete doctrine of Jesus Christ. But neither must we
forget to *"observe"* all these things. Even among the Christianized
nations the true disciples are apt to be *few*. The wheat is there; but the
tares are there in still greater abundance. There are many who confess
Christ, but few who follow after him. Let this grieve us; and let us
fulfil the command of Christ by taking upon our shoulders the sins of
our people, and praying, as he prayed, that they may be forgiven; and
let us, like Paul, Daniel, Nehemiah, Moses, and all the saints of old,
feel ourselves to be one with our people.

Our text brings out with clearness that the Father and Son and
Holy Ghost are three persons, but one God, as the church teaches.
God has revealed himself as the triune God, because that is what he
is in fact. And our faith *needs* just such a God. We could not do
without the Father; what would in that case become of our adoption
of sons, our right of inheritance, or of the prayer which Jesus has
taught us to address to "Our Father"? In like manner we need the
Son, our Savior and Lord, who is our only way to the Father. And
the Spirit is equally necessary; for who but the Spirit could lead our
hearts to Jesus, and teach us to cry Abba, Father? Blessed be the
triune God, the God of our salvation, the God of our strength and our
song! Amen.

To the great One in Three Eternal praises be, Hence evermore! His
sovereign majesty May we in glory see, And to eternity Love and adore.

322

246. Wednesday after Trinity Sunday.

Lord, turn our thougths heavenward. Amen.

1 Peter 1, 3–6. Blessed be the God and Father of our Lord Jesus Christ, which according to his abundant mercy hath begotten us again unto a lively hope by the resurrection of Jesus Christ from the dead, to an inheritance incorruptible, and undefiled, and that fadeth not away, reserved in heaven for you, who are kept by the power of God through faith unto salvation, ready to be revealed in the last time. Wherein ye greatly rejoice, though now, for a season, if need be, ye are in heaviness through manifold temptations.

All the faithful are the regenerated children of God, and have an everlasting inheritance awaiting them. We are strangers on earth, and we hasten heavenward. "A journey art thou, human life; thou art not the true life! Thou art alluring and seductive; and few are they that know thee. The majority of men trust in thee, instead of unmasking thee; they regard thee as their life, and thou dost rob them of the true life. Woe is me, wretched man that I am, if I do not see that life is eternal! Fly away, then, thou fleeting life; and we will flee from thee, ere thou dost flee from us! They that love thee are lead astray, and they that believe in thee are deceived; but they that hate thee are rich, and they that escape from thee are saved. Let us, then, not follow after the fleeting pleasures of this life; for if we do, we rejoice that the day of despair is coming; we eat, that we may have eternal hunger; and we drink, that we may thirst for evermore! Our pilgrimage is laborious; but as pilgrims we hasten homeward to find rest in our fatherland. Let us run, that we may reach our home! Let our love, our longing, the desire of our heart, be directed upward! Our fatherland is heaven, where our Father dwells. Let our watchword be: 'Vita — via!' (Life is a journey). May our souls be filled with thoughts and shapes of heaven! Let not our hearts cling to the gilded filth of this earth, to the dust under our feet. Let us sing with all our might: 'My soul thirsteth for God, for the living God; when shall I come and appear before God?' (Psalm 42, 2). 'I have a desire to depart, and be with Christ.' (Philippians 1, 23). Let us tread all sloth under foot, rid ourselves of all lukewarmness, and strive only to please *him* in whose presence we walk, and to come with an undefiled conscience out of our exile into the eternal and blessed home of our heavenly Father, from the visible to the invisible, from sorrow to joy, from that which passes away to that which endures for ever, from that which is of earth to that which is of heaven, from the regions of death to the land of the living, where we shall see the King, our Lord Jesus Christ, face to face in his glory." (Columban).

The *inheritance is safely reserved* in heaven; and through faith we are kept *secure* in every danger. Note what the Spirit of God says in our text: The inheritance is "reserved," and we are "kept." Can you doubt that your *inheritance* is safe? And shall not our hope be sure and immovable, when *we* are kept by the *power of God* through faith? The one who keeps us is *God,* who also has sealed us, and given us the Spirit as a pledge. Our trials last but a little while. **We hurry onward, and are rapidly approaching the goal!**

"My Jesus, kindle, I pray thee, thy light in my lamp, that I may see the holy of holies into which thou hast entered, thou great high priest of the good things of eternity. O, that I might there see thee for ever, desire thee, wait upon thee! Grant that we may love thee only, love thee with our whole heart, desire none but thee, have thee alone in our thoughts day and night. Occupy our whole heart with thy love; let us be wholly thine; let our spirit and mind and body be thy habitation, that thou, eternal love, mayest be the one object of our devotion. Nay, according to the measure of thy grace, fulfil in us also thy word, that 'many waters can not quench love, neither can the floods drown it.'" Amen.

Now let all the heavens adore thee, And men and angels sing before thee, With harp and cymbal's clearest tone; Of one pearl each shining portal, Where we are with the choir immortal Of angels round thy dazzling throne. No eye hath seen such sight, No ear heard such delight, Hallelujah! We raise the song, we swell the throng, To praise thee ages all along.

---

247. Thursday after Trinity Sunday.

Speak thy word to us, Lord Jesus; and purge us, that we may bring forth much fruit. Amen.

John 15, 1–6. I am the true vine, and my Father is the husbandman. Every branch in me that beareth not fruit he taketh away: and every branch that beareth fruit, he purgeth it, that it may bring forth more fruit. Now ye are clean through the word which I have spoken unto you. Abide in me, and I in you. As the branch cannot bear fruit of itself, except it abide in the vine; no more can ye, except ye abide in me. I am the vine, ye are the branches. He that abideth in me, and I in him, the same bringeth forth much fruit: for without me ye can do nothing. If a man abide not in me, he is cast forth as a branch, and is withered; and men gather them, and cast them into the fire, and they are burned.

All of us are branches of the tree of Adam; and all have been corrupted by his fall; the whole human family, root and branch, has the poison of sin coursing through its veins. We were thus doomed to eternal death. But there sprouts out of the tree one branch into which the poison does not penetrate. The only begotten Son of God becomes man, of the generation of Adam, but conceived by the Holy Ghost, and without sin. He was cut off by death, but then became a new tree, the second Adam, the true Noah, the founder of a new generation, which, like himself, is of the old, and yet is new. "He was cut off out of the land of the living;" yet when his soul is made "an offering for sin, he shall see his seed, he shall prolong his days." (Isaiah 53, 8. 10). By a new miracle of the Holy Ghost we are grafted into Christ, and made partakers of his life. By *nature* we are the children of Adam, born in sin and deserving of death; but we are *not* by *nature* branches of Christ; this we can become only by his Spirit.

He calls us through his gospel, and enlightens us by his gifts, and thereby creates faith in our souls, and causes our hearts to lay hold on Jesus. The vine of life is in the midst of us; and all we who are baptized are become its branches. But there are many who again sever their connection with the Lord; and these become dry branches, fit for nothing save to be cast into the fire.

Our life and salvation depend solely on the living *communion of our hearts with Jesus* in faith unto the end. No branch can bear fruit unto God of itself, except it abide in the vine. If we truly believe in him, the love which is in him flows into us, and reveals itself in our life as obedience toward God and charity toward our neighbor. Jesus says: "He that abideth in me, and I in him, the same bringeth forth *much* fruit." All do not bear an *equal* amount; but every branch on Jesus bears *much* fruit. Without him, no fruit; in him, much. Neither can any have love's *joy* in God, without having this life of Jesus, and nourishing it continually out of its fulness. The branches must receive their sap and strength from the vine *unceasingly*, if they are to live. If they are not nourished by him and purged by the husbandman, they must die. May we all carefully examine ourselves, and learn whether or not the love of Jesus reigns in our soul; may we with our whole heart strive to lay hold on this heavenly life!

Lord Jesus, grant that I may be a living branch in thee, and be purged daily to bring forth more and more fruit. Let me never wither, and become dry, and be cast out into the fire. From my soul I beseech thee: Lord Jesus, abide in me, and I in thee. Amen.

From Jesus naught shall ever part me; In faith I touch his pierced side
And hail him Lord, my God and Savior; Nor life nor death shall us divide.
O God, when tolls my parting knell, For Jesus' sake may all be well!

---

248. Friday after Trinity Sunday.

Lord our God, do thou expound the scripture to us.

Numbers 21, 5–9. And the people spake against God, and against Moses, Wherefore have ye brought us up out of Egypt, to die in the wilderness? for there is no bread, neither is there any water; and our soul loatheth this light bread. And the Lord sent fiery serpents among the people, and they bit the people; and much people of Israel died. Therefore the people came to Moses, and said, We have sinned, for we have spoken against the Lord, and against thee; pray unto the Lord, that he take away the serpents from us. And Moses prayed for the people. And the Lord said unto Moses, Make thee a fiery serpent, and set it upon a pole: and it shall come to pass, that every one that is bitten, when he looketh upon it, shall live. And Moses made a serpent of brass, and put it upon a pole: and it came to pass, that if a serpent had bitten any man, when he beheld the serpent of brass, he lived.

"As Moses lifted up the serpent in the wilderness, even so must the Son of Man be lifted up; that whosoever believeth on him should not perish, but have eternal life." The brazen serpent was *without venom*; but in appearance it was exactly like the venomous serpents.

It hung on the pole dead, and was a remedy against death. Even so is *he* who knew no sin made to be sin for us; that we might be made the righteousness of God in him. (2 Corinthians 5, 21). Bengel writes: "In like manner as the brazen serpent was a serpent without venom, but with healing against venomous serpents; so the Son of Man is the man without sin, but with healing against the old serpent." Another writer, Besser, says: "Jesus hangs on the cross, not in sinful flesh, but *in the likeness of sinful flesh*, bearing on his body our sins; and against the serpent bite of sin, which has inflicted on our nature a mortal wound, there is healing, in that sin is condemned and punished on the body of the Son of Man." In the words of Saint Augustine, "a serpent is nailed fast, in order that the serpent may have power no more." What does this mean? Death is nailed fast, in order that death may lose its power. Or, as Chrysostome puts it: "There is a serpent wounded, and a serpent healed; here death brings corruption, and death brings deliverance from corruption."

Were the unfortunates who had been mortally wounded in the wilderness obliged to run hither and thither, and to do many things in order to be healed, and live? How would it have been possible for them to do this? No, they were only to look upon the brazen serpent; that was all. God himself said: "*Every one* that is bitten, when he looked upon it, *shall live*." "And it came to pass, that if a serpent had bitten any man, when he beheld the serpent of brass, he lived." Every one without exception was permitted, nay commanded, to look upon the brazen serpent; and in no case did it fail, that when he did this, he lived. Thus God has commanded us all to believe, and has ordained that *whosoever* believes in the crucified Jesus shall have life everlasting. Only believe in him; nothing else whatsoever is required of you; nothing else can save you. God has given every sinner permission, nay orders, to believe. For all men; for you who have been wounded by the devil, whoever and whatever you may be; for each and all of you Christ is crucified; and it *shall come to pass* that *every one* that believes in him shall live. God has said it, and it can not fail to come true. Healing proceeds out of him unceasingly, through the word and sacraments, and is received by the faith of the heart. But this life of Jesus, which is given us through his death, and is our healing against death; what is that but the love in which he died for us, and vanquished death, and which thereby again belongs to us? What is it but the very life of God, in which we were created, but which we lost through the malice and the serpent bite of the devil?

Praise be to thee, Lord Jesus, who didst allow them to hang on the cross for us, and didst become the Son of Man, foreshadowed by the serpent of brass, and lifted up on the accursed tree! Give us grace to believe in thee, to feel thy life in our souls, and to live in thee for evermore. Amen.

Jesus, refuge of the weary, Object of the Spirit's love, Fountain in life's desert dreary, Savior from the world above:
O how oft thine eyes, offended, Gaze upon the sinner's fall! Yet, upon the cross extended, Thou didst bear the pain of all.

249. Saturday after Trinity Sunday.

Give us, O God, thy Spirit; and create in us new and pure hearts. Amen.

Ezekiel 36, 25–27. Then will I sprinkle clean water upon you, and ye shall be clean: from all your filthiness, and from all your idols, will I cleanse you. A new heart also will I give you, and a new spirit will I put within you; and I will take away the stony heart out of your flesh, and I will give you a heart of flesh. And I will put my Spirit within you, and cause you to walk in my statutes, and ye shall keep my judgments, and do them.

The heart of the children of the world clings to the things of this world. They love and trust in themselves, or in other men, or in riches and power; and if they have no temporal treasures and pleasures, they *pursue* them, and are unhappy because they do not have them. "For many walk, of whom I have told you often, and now tell you even weeping, that they are the enemies of the cross of Christ; whose end is destruction, whose God is their belly, and whose glory is in their shame, who mind earthly things." But the Lord has cleansed the faithful from *all* their "filthy idols." From *all!* If there be anything which you still love more than the Lord, your heart is not right before him. The life of the Spirit, the living stream of love, sweeps the idols away. Do believers, then, not love the gifts of God, such as wife, children, country, home? Yes; they love them and enjoy them *as being the gifts of God;* but the heart belongs to the Lord first and last, and "there is none upon earth that they desire beside him."

"The stony heart," of which the Lord here speaks, does not feel the correction which God administers, and is not willing to obey his commands. Some are *entirely* callous to the operation of the Spirit, and thus live in a feeling of absolute security, and hasten with closed eyes toward eternal perdition. Others *occasionally* have a sensation of unrest; and still others feel their conscience torturing them all the time; but they love the darkness more than the light, harden their hearts against God's call, and become more and more obdurate. — In regard to the children of God the case is an entirely different one. Their conscience is alive and tender; they feel the wrath of God and the love of God; they have that "godly sorrow," and they have joy in the Lord; they fear to do anything against his will, and they can find no peace until they have the assurance of his grace. They submit to his will, patiently accept correction from him, and strive in their conduct to please him, in opposition to their self-will and the lusts of the flesh. The pure and heavenly image of the Lord is stamped upon them with greater and greater clearness; the Spirit fashions them ever more closely after Jesus, the perfect model. In their conduct among *men* this new heart manifests itself in kindliness, in mercy, in love of peace, in meekness, and in all manner of goodness toward their friend and enemy.

Lord, grant that we may experience this miracle of a new creation, and that the new mind in us may increase "unto the measure of the stature of the fulness of Christ." Create in me a clean heart, O God;

and renew a right spirit within me. Help me to walk in thy ordinances, and to keep thy statutes. Amen.

Holy Ghost, with power divine, Cleanse this guilty heart of mine; In thy mercy pity me, From sin's bondage set me free.

Holy Ghost, with joy divine, Cheer this saddened heart of mine; Bid my many woes depart, Heal my wounded, bleeding heart.

---

250. First Sunday after Trinity. I.

Lord, anoint our eyes, that we may see what thou dost shew us. Amen.

Gospel Lesson, Luke 16, 19–31. There was a certain rich man, which was clothed in purple and fine linen, and fared sumptuously every day: And there was a certain beggar named Lazarus, which was laid at his gate, full of sores, and desiring to be fed with the crumbs which fell from the rich man's table: moreover the dogs came and licked his sores. And it came to pass, that the beggar died, and was carried by the angels into Abraham's bosom: the rich man also died, and was buried; and in hell he lift up his eyes, being in torments, and seeth Abraham afar off, and Lazarus in his bosom. And he cried and said, Father Abraham, have mercy on me, and send Lazarus, that he may dip the tip of his finger in water, and cool my tongue; for I am tormented in this flame. But Abraham said, Son, remember that thou in thy lifetime receivedst thy good things, and likewise Lazarus evil things: but now he is comforted, and thou art tormented. And beside all this, between us and you there is a great gulf fixed: so that they which would pass from hence to you cannot; neither can they pass to us, that would come from thence. Then he said, I pray thee therefore, father, that thou wouldest send him to my father's house: for I have five brethren; that he may testify unto them, lest they also come into this place of torment. Abraham saith unto him, They have Moses and the prophets; let them hear them. And he said, Nay, father Abraham: but if one went unto them from the dead, they will repent. And he said unto him, If they hear not Moses and the prophets, neither will they be persuaded, though one rose from the dead.

A rich man shall with difficulty enter into the kingdom of heaven. (Matthew 19, 23). A rich man is not condemned because of the fact that he is rich; but rich people are sorely tempted to worldliness and unbelief. The rich man in our gospel lesson is doomed to misery because he is *unbelieving, worldly-minded,* and *self-righteous.* His life is described in few, but extremely significant words: He was clothed in purple and fine linen, and fared sumptuously every day." Farther on we learn that he "received his good things in his lifetime," that he did not recognize the word of God as being sufficient unto salvation, and did not understand that *faith* is the way to life. — If you mind the earthly things, and flatter yourself that salvation, as a matter of course, belongs to you and to all decent people, you are the rich man's comrade, whether you have much or little of this world's good things. — Poverty and illness are heavy afflictions; and no man is saved merely *because* he has suffered here on earth. But these things may help us to hearken to the word of God, and may turn our hearts away from the world. Lazarus did not enter into bliss as a reward for his sufferings; but he inherited life *because he believed in the Lord.* This is indicated by the name Lazarus, which means one who *trusts in the Lord;* and, besides, we are told that he found rest in the bosom of Abraham, "the father of the faithful," and that he did not seek his good things in this earthly life. You are no Lazarus, and will not be saved, even though you suffer never so much; unless you have a believing heart, and endure suffering as a Christian, and have your treasure in heaven. But if you do this, your suffering is blessed, and your tears are a seed from which will spring a rich harvest.

There are in the world beyond the grave but two places; immediately after death the unregenerated lift up their eyes in hell, and the believers go straight to heaven; there exists no middle place, or neutral ground, as it were. The damned must suffer endless torment; they shall never escape from it, and shall never, in all eternity, receive any comfort; while the saved enjoy everlasting bliss, and shall never more fear any danger from sin, death, or devil. None shall pass from heaven to hell, nor from hell to heaven; nor shall any return to the earth. — The saved are in good company, and this augments their bliss. They know one another; Lazarus knows Abraham, and Abraham knows Lazarus; all the friends of God find one another there. They also know what is transpiring here on earth. Abraham, who died long before the time of Moses and the prophets, knows what these men have written, and its important bearing on our salvation. — The condition of the damned, on the other hand, is full of horror. They are "tormented in this flame," and receive not a single drop of water to cool the tongue. They are deprived of everything for which they wish; and feel everything which causes them torment. Their unhappiness infuriates them; they feel the eternal pain of hopeless despair, and suffer all the more by reason of companionship with their brethren from the earth, as it causes the flame of wickedness in them to burn the more fiercely. — All this our Lord Jesus distinctly teaches us in the gospel lesson of today, for our warning and our comfort; and the pictures which he presents before us are not overdrawn. How unutterably important is it not, therefore, to make good use of the time of grace! O, take the matter earnestly to heart; and consider, that wealth and splendor without the fear of God are wretchedness and terror; while the sufferings of the saints are not worth mentioning in comparison with the glory which shall be revealed in them.

Lord Jesus, give us earnestness in the concerns of our soul, and teach us to work out our salvation with fear and trembling. Help the rich to do good, and to lay up for themselves treasures in heaven; and help the poor to endure suffering patiently, as did Lazarus. Lord, save us from unbelief, and give us a blessed end. Amen.

Time is earnest, passing by; Death is earnest, drawing nigh: Sinner, wilt thou trifling be? Time and death appeal to thee.
O be earnest, do not stay; Thou mayest perish e'en today. Rise, thou lost one, rise and flee; Lo; thy Savior waits for thee.

251. First Sunday after Trinity. II.

God, give us thy love in our hearts. Amen.

Epistle Lesson, 1 John 4, 16–21. And we have known and believed the love that God hath to us. God is love; and he that dwelleth in love, dwelleth in God, and God in him. Herein is our love made perfect, that we may have boldness in the day of judgment: because as he is, so are we in this world. There is no fear in love; but perfect love casteth out fear; because·fear hath torment. He that feareth, is not made perfect in love. We love him, because he first loved us. If a man say, I love God, and hateth his brother, he is a liar: for he that loveth not his brother whom he hath seen, how can he love God whom he hath not seen? And this commandment have we from him, That he who loveth God love his brother also.

God is love. He who lives in hatred and anger is far away from God, and is a most unhappy person. He *must* repent, and receive a new·heart, if he is to become happy. But how blest are they who love God and the brethren! You surely have felt that the reflection of God's love, — the natural love between human beings, — is the noblest and best of all earthly good things, and delights the heart more than do honors and riches. How much greater, then, must be the divine love itself, or the sensation of having God's own blessed and heavenly life in the heart! — We have been created because God loves, and we are fashioned to receive this love into our hearts, and to enjoy its bliss. We lost this love at the time when we departed from God; but when the Spirit quickens us, our heart again thirsts after it, and absorbs it, and it thrills every fibre in us. *God is love;* and his kingdom on earth and in heaven is the kingdom of love. He that does not love God does not know him, and can not be his child. But if you long after God, and rejoice before him, and there is none on earth that you desire beside him, then is God in you. He loved you first, and you love him in return; your joy in him is his joy in you; and this is life eternal. Now, do you fear to meet him on the day of judgment? Do you now hide yourself from him, as did Adam after the fall? No; he has given his Son to be a propitiation for our sins; and these do not hereafter stand between us to hinder our love. Or, is there now any person whom you hate, and with whom you therefore would not like to have fellowship in heaven? The love in Jesus has made you kindly affectioned toward all men; it has awakened in you a new feeling toward the world, and has caused you to view all things in a new light. As all things live and move and have their being in God, even so has your heart also expanded, and there is rom in it for all. How great a thing is love; how rich, how mighty! He that loves is lord of all, independent of all, exalted above all, the servant of all. God is *love;* and he that dwelleth in love dwelleth in God, and God in him.

God, give us this most glorious and blessed of all things; give us this most noble, rich, beautiful, and pure life of love; and pour out the love of Christ in our hearts by thy Holy Spirit. Amen.

O God, thy grace and blessing give To us who on thy name attend, That
we this mortal life may live Regardful of our journey's end.
And when the awful signs appear Of judgment and the throne above, Our
hearts still fixed, we shall not fear, God is our trust, and God is love.

---

252. Monday after First Sunday after Trinity.

Lead us into thy sanctuary, O our God, and let us abide with thee alway. ***Amen.***

Psalm 73, 12–19. Behold, these are the ungodly, who prosper in the
world; they increase in riches. Verily I have cleansed my heart in vain, and
washed my hands in innocency. For all the day long have I been plagued,
and chastened every morning. If I say, I will speak thus; behold, I should
offend against the generation of thy children. When I thought to know this,
it was too painful for me, until I went into the sanctuary of God; then understood I their end. Surely thou didst set them in slippery places: thou castedst
them down into destruction. How are they brought into desolation as in a
moment! they are utterly consumed with terrors.

When the wicked prosper; when "there are no bands in their
death, and their strength is firm, and pride compasseth them about as
a chain, and their eyes stand out with fatness, and they speak wickedly
concerning oppression, and set their mouth against the heavens, and
their tongue walketh through the earth"; — then even the *pious* are
tempted to ask: "How doth God know? and is there knowledge in
the most High?" The prophet Jeremiah says: "Righteous art thou,
O Lord, when I plead with thee; yet let me talk with thee of thy judgments. Wherefore doth the way of the wicked prosper? Wherefore
are they happy that deal very treacherously? Thou hast planted them,
yea, they have taken root; they grow, yea, they bring forth fruit; thou
art near in their mouth, and far from their reins." (Jer. 12, 1. 2). The
believers of the time of the *Old* Covenant are not alone in finding it
hard to explain, why it is that the wicked blossom, while the saints
wither; the same question troubles us also. The fact, however, that
events do so shape themselves in this world points beyond the life
which now is to things eternal. Behind the curtain of visible things
there is another world, into which we have already entered; but our
natural eye does not see it. We all are, to be sure, children of this
world, and here our lot is cast for a little while; but we are children
of an invisible world also; each one of us belongs to, and has his
portion in, either heaven or hell; but it is only in the sanctuary of God
that we learn to understand this. The end of all the wicked who do
not repent is terrible; but it is not seen of men. The rich man died,
and was buried with proper honors, and was probably praised as one
whose virtues insured him salvation; — but he lifted up his eyes — in
hell! God is just, and sets the ungodly in slippery places. If they
enjoy riches and good health, *this* is at once God's mercy and his
judgment; if they are poor and wretched, *this* also is at the same time
a call from the God of mercy and a visitation inflicted by the God of
justice. But if they continue in sin, all things make for a more heavy

judgment upon them. — Do you abide with the Lord, my Christian friend! View his manner of dealing with us by the light of the word. Do not let your carnal mind, but the Spirit, control your feelings; then shall your heart not be tortured with envy by reason of the prosperity of "the foolish," but swell with tender mercy toward them on account of their misery in the midst of their apparent sumptuousness. Such has always been the nature and habit of God's children. "Whom have I in heaven but thee? and there is none upon earth that I desire beside thee. My flesh and my heart faileth; but God is the strength of thy heart, and my portion for ever." "I am continually with thee; thou shalt guide me with thy counsel, and afterward receive me to glory."

Give us godly hearts, that we may know thy ways, and that we may regard the suffering, poverty, and cross of Christ as greater riches than all the splendors of the world. Give us this light; give us this mind, for Jesus' sake. Amen.

Thou seest our weakness, Lord! Our hearts are known to thee: O lift thou up the sinking hand, Confirm the feeble knee! Let us in life, in death, Thy steadfast truth declare, And publish with our latest breath Thy love and guardian care.

253. Tuesday after First Sunday after Trinity.

Psalm 73, 23-28. Nevertheless, I am continually with thee; thou hast holden me by my right hand. Thou shalt guide me with thy counsel, and afterwards receive me to glory. Whom have I in heaven but thee? and there is none upon earth that I desire beside thee. My flesh and my heart faileth; but God is the strength of my heart, and my portion for ever. For, lo, they that are far from thee shall perish; thou hast destroyed all them that go a whoring from thee. But it is good for me to draw near to God: I have put my trust in the Lord God, that I may declare all thy works.

No matter how long the glory of the wicked may seem to last, be sure that it will have a miserable end. — We do not expect to see truth and right victorious while this world endures. We know very well that falsehood shall prosper, adorn itself with the name of truth, and tread the saints under foot as being the enemies of happiness. Nevertheless we find it hard to accept this state of facts; our heart is prone to become bitter, and our feet to turn aside from the path of faith and patience. However, the word of God gives us light and strength. It teaches us that the visible things pass away, but that the invisible are eternal, and that all the glory of the world is nothing as compared with our communion with God and the bliss of heaven. The bitterness of our temptation is the venomous thought: "How doth God know? and is there knowledge in the Most High? Can the God who governs in this way be a just God?" But when we go into the sanctuary of the word, and thence look over into heaven, and out upon the earth, we so far understand the purpose and will of God that we become contented and happy. It matters not that we suffer oppression; our rights and our happiness are absolutely secure. Through suffering we learn patience; through temptation we obtain victory. We have no reason, then, to feel sorrow except for them who let themselves be deceived by the devil. For it *is* sad that man, who was created to live in the love of God, and who is unhappy without him, regards his revelation as foolishness, and eternal life as a fable. You, who are a child of God, shall remain with the Lord alway; himself holds you with his right hand, with the power of his omnipotence. Think of this; it will strengthen your faith. He guides you with his counsel; then all is well, even if it be something else than you expected. Could you wish for anything better than to be led according to the counsel of *him* who is eternal wisdom itself? Thereafter he receives you into glory. To this you are chosen and anointed; what matters it, then, though you be mocked and oppressed by the world? Your portion is in heaven; your life is in God. What though your flesh and heart should fail, and you be in greater trouble than any other man? Love is the stronger, and does not die, nor relax its hold; God is ever the same, he in you, and you in him; how, then, can you perish? He remains the rock of your salvation, and your blessed portion. Your love of him is fostered and purified in temptation; and thus all things must work together for the good of them that love God.

Lord, let me ever remain with thee. Keep me with thy right hand, and be thou the portion of my heart for ever. Amen.

Now thank we all our God, With heart and hands and voices, Who wondrous things hath done, In whom his earth rejoices; Who from our mother's arms Hath blessed us on our way With countless gifts of love, And still is ours today.

---

254. Wednesday after First Sunday after Trinity.

Lord Jesus, grant us the grace of the Spirit to hear that which thou shalt speak to us. Amen.

Luke 12, 16–21. And he spake a parable unto them, saying, The ground of a certain rich man brought forth plentifully: and he thought within himself, saying, What shall I do, because I have no room where to bestow my fruits? And he said, This will I do: I will pull down my barns, and build greater; and there will I bestow all my fruits and my goods. And I will say to my soul, Soul, thou hast much goods laid up for many years; take thine ease, eat, drink, and be merry. But God said unto him, Thou fool! this night thy soul shall be required of thee: then whose shall those things be, which thou hast provided? So **is he** that layeth up treasure for himself, and is not rich toward God.

You know this parable of our Lord from your Bible History; and of course you are careful not to speak as did this rich husbandman. Now, every man who puts his trust in his riches; and feels secure, thinking that he has all which he can need, — is the man spoken of in this parable. It is a dangerous thing to have abundance. One imagines that he believes in God, and does not realize how strongly his heart is tied to the world. No doubt there are rich people whose heart is in the right place; but their number must be very small.

We do not fully understand how strong a hold our earthly possessions have on us. Without our knowing it the heart often is divided between them and God. It is, therefore, mercy on the part of the Lord, when he, as occasion demands, puts his hand on our worldly possessions, takes all or a part of them away from us, according to his knowledge of what we are able to bear; and teaches us to know, and sets us free from, our idolatrous trust in mammon. When everything shapes itself according to your wishes, when your wealth increases, when your moneys multiply, and you seem to have nothing but good fortune; it behooves you carefully to examine yourself, asking God to give you light and grace. For either you are one of the few whom wealth does not ruin, — in which case you surely will have trials of another kind; — or, you are one of those who have "received their good things in their lifetime," and who lay up treasures for themselves, and are not rich toward God. In the latter case the result is frightful. "Thou fool, this night thy soul shall be required of thee; then whose shall those things be, which thou hast provided?" "*This night*"; *this very night*, mark you! — "Woe unto them that join house to house, that lay field to field, till there be no place, that they may be placed alone in the midst of the earth! Therefore hell hath enlarged herself, and opened her mouth without measure; and their glory, and their multitude, and their pomp, and he that rejoiceth, shall descend into it." (Isaiah 5, 8. 14). — He, however, who is poor and dissatisfied; who is envious of the rich, and is full of cares; or who is idle, and lives on the earnings of others; such a one has no right to glory over the man of wealth; for he is himself the own brother of the unhappy husbandman of our text. — Let all the Lord's people hear and heed the words of the apostle, 1 Timothy 6, 10–12: "The love of money is the root of all evil; which while some coveted after, they have erred from the faith, and pierced themselves through with many sorrows. But thou, O man of God, flee these things; and follow after righteousness, godliness, faith, love, patience, meekness. Fight the good fight of faith, lay hold on eternal life, whereunto thou art also called, and hast professed a good profession before many witnesses." Lay not up for yourselves treasures on earth, brethren; but lay up treasures in heaven! Lay up treasures in *heaven;* for where your treasure is there will your hearts be.

Our God, do thou teach us to believe in thee with our whole heart, and to use our abundance in the exercise of charity toward the needy. Amen.

Help me to set mine house in order Betimes, and ever ready be, That when thou callest, I may answer, Lord, as thou wilt do unto me. O God, when tolls my parting knell, For Jesus' sake may all be well!

---

255. Thursday after First Sunday after Trinity.

God, incline my heart unto thy testimonies, and not to covetousness. Amen.

1 Timothy 6, 9–12. **But they that will be rich, fall into temptation, and** a snare, and into many foolish and hurtful lusts, which drown men in destruction and perdition. For the love of money is the root of all evil; which

while some coveted after, they have erred from the faith, and pierced themselves through with many sorrows. But thou, O man of God, flee these things;
and follow after righteousness, godliness, faith, love, patience, meekness. Fight
the good fight of faith, lay hold on eternal life, whereunto thou art also called,
and hast professed a good profession before many witnesses.

Nothing else destroys the heart like the love of money; nothing
else is so sure to kill man's every noble instinct, and bar love out of his
soul. It is a blessing to have enough to live on, and to escape worry
on that score; and it is right to work for it, and to manage in such
a way that one does not defraud anybody, nor live by the sweat of
others. To practice industry and economy is praiseworthy; but we
find it so easy to go beyond bounds. Generosity becomes lavish extra-
vagance, and thrift become covetousness. Let thrift beware lest it be
caught in this net. What a sad hallucination it is! A man covets
gold, in order that he may be happy; and thus he casts himself into
temptation and all manner of foolish lusts, which drown men in destruction and perdition. He labors to satisfy his thirst for riches, that
it may be well with him; while in reality he thereby fosters the root
of all *evil;* of sin, and disquietude, and heartlessness, and vexation, and
eternal misery. In this respect also the way of life is narrow; so narrow
that we can not get through without the assistance of the God who
works wonders. Every self-dependent man of honor and conscience
desires to have enough, and something to spare for the furtherance of
every good cause; but if it be his ambition to become rich, he errs
from the faith, becomes an idolator, and pierces himself through from
all sides with every manner of sorrow. God help us and save us from
this snare of Satan! Does not a Christian have something else than
these corruptible treasures after which to follow? Let the children of
the world, who know of nothing higher, covet earthly riches and its
sorrows; but you, O man of God, flee these things! Rather follow
after righteousness, godliness, faith, love, patience, meekness! These
are incorruptible wealth, and make you rich indeed. Let the unbelievers fight over the golden dross; do you fight the good fight of faith,
lay hold on eternal life, whereunto you are also called, and have professed a good profession before many witnesses! Do not forget that
you are in the Lord's army, and that you stand on the battle field in
the midst of a cloud of witnesses! Will you be false to your oath of
allegiance to Christ, and will you, instead of laying hold on your heritage of eternal life, chase the delusive phantom of earthly riches?

God, help us to run with patience and self-denial the race that is
set before us. Graciously deliver us from the temptation to covetousness, and keep us in faith unto the end. Make us zealous in our holy
covenant with thee, and make us strong to fight the good fight of
faith. Amen.

Watch against the devil's snares, Lest asleep he find thee; For, indeed,
no pains he spares To deceive and blind thee; Satan's prey oft are they Who,
securely sleeping, No good watch are keeping.
But, while watching, also see That thou pray unceasing, For the Lord
must make thee free, Strength and faith increasing, So to do service true: Let
not sloth enslave thee; Pray, and God will save thee.

256. Friday after First Sunday after Trinity.

God deliver us from the evil one. Amen.

Matthew 26, 21–25. And as they did eat, he said, Verily I say unto you, that one of you shall betray me. And they were exceeding sorrowful, and began every one of them to say unto him, Lord, is it I? And he answered and said, He that dippeth his hand with me in the dish, the same shall betray me. The Son of Man goeth as it is written of him: but woe unto that man by whom the Son of Man is betrayed! it had been good for that man if he had not been born. Then Judas, which betrayed him, answered and said, Master, is it I? He said unto him, Thou hast said.

The devil's most terrible and hideous piece of work, — that one of Jesus' own apostles betrayed the Lord, and then hanged himself, — was brought about through covetousness. So grewsome a deed could spring only from that most poisonous root. It is true, as Paul says, that "the love of money is the root of all evil." What glorious gifts has it not destroyed, and how many abominable things has it not begotten! Balaam was a most highly favored man of God; but he allowed himself to be seduced by the gold of Balak, and then led Israel astray into idolatry and whoredom and great wretchedness, and died a miserable death by the sword of wrath. (Read the account in Numbers 22–25, and 31, 8; and compare it with Revelations 2, 14). Other examples for our warning are the sons of Samuel, the servant of Elisha, Ananias, Saphira, and many others. We ministers of the gospel are sometimes charged with being especially addicted to covetousness; and there seems to be an impression that the "pious" are particularly fond of money. These accusations have not been dictated by love; and there probably is no more truth in them than there would be in decrying all the disciples of Jesus as rascally misers, merely because this was true in the case of Judas. But it is certain that Satan makes special efforts to lead the faithful, and more particularly the ministers of the gospel, into the snare of covetousness. He was able to catch one of the twelve apostles in his toils; let none among us, then, feel secure!

Our text shows us the terrible strength of the chain with which the devil had bound Judas. Jesus begins by saying that one of them shall betray him. Now, even this ought to have pierced Judas through marrow and bone; but though all the other apostles were "exceeding sorrowful," he was not affected. As this does not awaken in him horror of the way which he had determined to follow, the Lord declares in definite terms that he knows the betrayer; and then he adds the solemn and heart-wringing statement, that Judas must, to be sure, serve God's purpose, but that, as for him, "it had been good for that man if he had not been born." It is all in vain. The covetousness of Judas has given the devil such power over him that the tempter now fills his whole soul, and the Savior's warning has no other effect than to complete the hardening of his heart. Beware, Christian friends, of this horse-leach, which is never satisfied! (Proverbs 30, 15). Put it to death at once with its whole brood; else it shall not only devour the needy round about you, but shall drink your own heart's blood. Watch diligently, repent daily and thoroughly, obey the Spirit of God, remain all the time under the cross of Christ; so shall you be rid of the vice of covetousness, but become rich in noble deeds. — My God, "draw me to thee, and cure me of the terrible disease of covetousness; for no created thing can satisfy my hunger, or quiet my longing. Unite me with thee in the indissoluble bond of love; for in thee only can love find satisfaction, and without thee everything is sin and vanity." Amen.

God calling yet! — shall I not hear? Earth's pleasures shall I still hold dear? Shall life's swift passing years all fly, And still my soul in slumber lie? God calling yet! — I cannot stay; My heart I yield without delay. Vain world, farewell! from thee I part; The voice of God hath reached my heart.

---

257. Saturday after First Sunday after Trinity.

Revelations 2, 8–11. And unto the angel of the church in Smyrna write; These things saith the first and the last, which was dead, and is alive; I know thy works, and tribulation, and poverty, (but thou art rich) and I know the blasphemy of them which say they are Jews, and are not, but are the synagogue of Satan. Fear none of those things which thou shalt suffer: behold, the devil shall cast some of you into prison, that ye may be tried; and ye shall have tribulation ten days: be thou faithful unto death, and I will give thee a crown of life. He that hath an ear, let him hear what the Spirit saith unto the churches; He that overcometh shall not be hurt of the second death.

Struggles and trials all the time for every follower of Christ! Faithfulness unto the end, — and then *eternal* victory and glory! The devil hates us bitterly, and lies in wait for us with consuming anger. He brings heavy misfortune on the patient Job; he follows Paul everywhere, and buffets him; he makes the saints in Smyrna to suffer reproach and shame and tribulation. But the Lord, who loves us with a burning love, permits this, "that we may be tried," that thus our faith and patience may increase, and the lusts die. Jesus has gone before us through death, and has opened the way; but now he lives, and guards our every step. *He* knows your works, and values your unassuming faithfulness, which the world holds in derision. *He* sees your tribulation and poverty; — and this is the true riches; for the kingdom of heaven is yours. *He* keeps faithful watch over his sheep day and night; guides them by the leading-strings of love as by a mother's hand. Fear, then, none of those things which you shall suffer; the suffering is brief and light as compared with the glory; it is good and necessary as a preparation for heaven; it is Christ's own suffering, and shall never become greater than you can bear. *Be faithful unto death!* Let the heart belong entirely and for ever to the Lord. The devil employs his craftiness in the effort to entice you away from the Lord. He therefore tries to kindle the lusts in you, and to awaken unbelief, impatience, and other sins; but the Lord makes use of this to give you humility, that you may remain true to your first love for Jesus as the friend of sinners, and that the devil himself may thus become your servant, and that all those things which seem calculated to injure you may but benefit the new life in you. Be faithful, then! "God works in you both to will and to do of his good pleasure"; but for that very reason you must watch, and work out your salvation; — something which God has made it possible for you to do. Therefore it is in every way such a terrible thing that so many divorce their hearts from the Lord. They *might* have remained with him; and yet they have plunged themselves into perdition! — If you, dear reader, have been unfaithful, but now desire mercy; then do you return, and receive forgiveness, and remain with the Lord hereafter. Hear the voice of Jesus himself: "Be thou faithful unto death, and I will give thee a crown of life!" Does not your heart burn within you when you hear him address these words to you? Be faithful — faithful unto death — for my sake! He expects you to be willing to give your life for him. Do not fail him, then; himself will give you grace to be faithful, and will thereafter make you a partaker of his glory. In the words of Kempis, he shall "give you honor in place of shame, the palm of joy in place of sadness, an eternal throne in his kingdom in place of the most humble position on earth; there the fruit of your obedience shall be revealed, and there the bitterness of death shall bring happiness, and humble submission shall give you a crown of glory."

Tribulation and suffering for "ten days"; — victory and life for ever! Be faithful, brethren; let the whole heart be the Lord's for ever! The love of the Lord's bride be sacred and pure! — Lord Jesus, I feel thy celestial fire in my soul; but it burns feebly, and many things threaten to smother it. Do thou protect it, and let it burn more brightly every day unto my dying hour. Alas, I would be too weak to die for thee; and yet, Lord Jesus, by thy grace I would be able to do it in spite of my weakness. Amen.

Stand then in his great might, With all his strength endued; And take, to arm you for the fight, The panoply of God; That, having all things done, And all your conflicts past, Ye may o'ercome, through Christ alone, And stand complete at last.

---

258. Second Sunday after Trinity. I.

Lord, give us grace to follow thy heavenly call. Amen.

Gospel Lesson, Luke 14, 16-24. Then said he unto him, A certain man made a great supper, and bade many: And sent his servant at supper time to say to them that were bidden, Come; for all things are now ready. And they all with one consent began to make excuse. The first said unto him, I have bought a piece of ground, and I must needs go and see it: I pray thee have me excused. And another said, I have bought five yoke of oxen, and I go to prove them: I pray thee have me excused. And another said, I have married a wife, and therefore I cannot come. So that servant came, and shewed his lord these things. Then the master of the house, being angry, said to his servant, Go out quickly into the streets and lanes of the city, and bring in

338

hither the poor, and the maimed, and the halt, and the blind. And the servant said, Lord, it is done as thou hast commanded, and yet there is room. And the Lord said unto the servant, Go out into the highways and hedges, and compel them to come in, that my house may be filled. For I say unto you, That none of those men which were bidden shall taste of my supper.

"All things are now ready"; we have only to come. Everything needful for our salvation is prepared; we are only to receive it, and give thanks to God. The Savior is come, the sacrifice is slain, the blood has been carried to the altar, atonement has been made for sin, and eternal righteousness has been provided. And all this is offered and given to us in the word of God and in the sacraments. The Lord himself is there with his death and his life, his righteousness and his love. The Spirit is come, and has arranged the ministration of the gifts of life in God's household, keeps the house supplied with an abundance of the heavenly good things, and invites all with the urgent call of grace. He who accepts the invitation receives righteousness, peace and joy freely. Here is exactly what we need, that for which the heart hungers and thirsts. Here is fellowship with the only true God; here is holiness, and love, and liberty; here is comfort, and joy, and strength; here is the fountain of life, and here is the spring of salvation. Our paradise could not for ever be lost. There must somewhere be a haven of rest for the troubled human soul. Here, in the church of Christ, here at the great supper, is the home of the soul. Here is the remedy against sin and death; here life and salvation may be found. "Come; for all things are now ready."

They who were bidden first, however, made light of it. The Jews refused to believe in Christ. They wanted a *worldly* Savior; and so they rejected Jesus, with the gifts of the *Spirit* and the life eternal. God then sent the call of grace to us gentiles; but many of us do as did the Jews. They mind the earthly, and make light of the heavenly things; seek their happiness in the world, in fields and oxen, or in merchandise and money; in luxury and sensual pleasures, or in science and art. But he who chooses these things, and disdains the kingdom of heaven, loses both. Let us learn wisdom of the Spirit of God, and choose that good part, which shall not be taken away from us. Follow the call of God, give him your heart, repent, and believe in Jesus, accept his grace, and let the Holy Ghost pour out the love of God in your soul; then the heart is set free from the world; you no longer sacrifice it to the idols, and you are no longer the slave of corruptible things. For he who finds the treasure of heaven sells all things in order to possess this pearl. He who knows Jesus loves him of his innermost heart, and belongs to him with life and soul and all that he has. In return he receives all things as new and precious gifts from the heavenly Father's hand; and as the child of this Father he owns the bodily and spiritual, the earthly and heavenly things. Your secular affairs need not in any way shut you out from the kingdom of heaven; quite the reverse. It is the devil who thus turns everything upside down. When your work or business does not leave you time to turn to the Lord, this is as foolish and meaningless as though a poor man had no time to accept a valuable inheritance, because his time was fully occupied in begging and consorting with drunkards. — All things are ready; God sends us an earnest invitation, and gives us strength to accept it. None who stays away, and is lost, has any excuse. — And at all events, the house of the Lord shall be filled. If you will not take your place, he shall find another to fill it; and then there shall be no room for you. — Lord, draw us to thee, and give us part in the kingdom of heaven. Lord, thou knowest what power the things of this world have to stand in our way, and how easily we are deceived. Have mercy, and help us; help us to obey the call, and do not abandon us. Turn thou us, and we shall be turned; save us, and we shall be saved. Amen.

> God calling yet! — and shall I give No heed, but still in bondage live?
> I wait, but he does not forsake; He calls me still: — my heart, awake!
> Ah, yield him all: in him confide: Where but with him doth peace abide?
> Break loose, let earthly bonds be riven, And let the spirit rise to heaven!

---

259. Second Sunday after Trinity. II.

Help us, O God, to give heed to thy word concerning love. Amen.

Epistle Lesson, 1 John 3, 13-18. Marvel not, my brethren, if the world hate you. We know that we have passed from death unto life, because we love the brethren. He that loveth not his brother abideth in death. Whosoever hateth his brother is a murderer: and ye know that no murderer hath eternal life abiding in him. Hereby perceive we the love of God, because he laid down his life for us: and we ought to lay down our lives for the brethren. But whoso hath this world's good, and seeth his brother have need, and shutteth up his bowels of compassion from him, how dwelleth the love of God in him? My little children, let us not love in word, neither in tongue; but in deed and in truth.

"We know that we have passed from death unto life." Is there anything better which we could have done? We were the captives of death; this is now a thing of the past, and we have eternal life. My heart shouts with joy! Death is the greatest of evils; life is the highest good. Death is something most terrible, which I hate and dread with my innermost soul; while life is something most beautiful, on which my deepest desire is fixed, — and now I have passed from death unto life. What a blessed change it is! We *know* that this is true, says Saint John. He here teaches that God wants us to be sure of our new birth. It is the will of our heavenly Father that we shall be of good cheer, enjoy the life of love, and become rich in deeds of charity; but then we must *know* of a certainty that we are the children of life. He who feels uncertainty on this point is weak and vacillating, minds the things of the world, and is not willing to stake all on the Lord. — How, then, may we know that we are born of God? The answer is: Because *we love the brethren.* True life is love. It is love which is poured out in the hearts of the faithful; and they love that which God loves. He so loved us that his only begotten Son died for us. But in giving his life for us he gave it to us; and whosoever believes in him receives this life. We then love all men; but we find delight in the holy brethren, and are one with them in God. The hearts of the Christians are united in the love of Christ. If you have this brotherly spirit, you surely are one of the children of life. The natural man, who is dead in sin, may love his own, — in so far as this can be called love; — he may love his own kin, or those of like mind with himself; for this is to love one's self. But to love all men, with willing heart to do good to one's enemies, to pray for them, and bless them of one's innermost soul, and to love the children of God for the reason that they are the children of God, to love them because they love Jesus; in short, to "love the brethren," this is something which none can do, except he be born of God. — Now, if this love have begun in you, then do you practice it; and it shall increase, and with it your cheerfulness and peace shall increase also. Should hate and anger still stir in your soul, overcome them with prayer and the word of God, with the body and blood of Jesus; with intercession for your enemies, and with deeds of kindness toward them. Your heavenly Father will help you to do this. When you feel urged to do good, do not postpone it; follow the promptings of love, deny your indolent flesh, and live the life of the Spirit. Thus you make your sonship sure.

Alas, we poor fools; we boast of·our knowledge; but where is our love? Our speech is fair, but our hearts are cold. Woe be to us, if death reign in us after all! O thou God, who art rich in love, give us this most blessed gift of all, that we love one another. Thou who didst give us this gift in thy Son, pour it out in our hearts, that we practice it in our conduct, and that thy Spirit may give us the assurance that we have passed from death to life. Amen.

Whatever, Lord, we lend to thee, Repaid a thousand fold will be; Then gladly will we give to thee Who givest all,—
To thee, from whom we all derive Our life, our gifts, our power to give;
Oh, may we ever with thee live, Who givest all!

---

260. Monday after Second Sunday after Trinity.

Lord Jesus, let the word and the way of the cross become our hearts' dearest delight. Amen.

Luke 14, 25–33. And there went great multitudes with him: and he turned, and said unto them, If any man come to me, and hate not his father, and mother, and wife, and children, and brethren, and sisters, yea, and his own life also, he cannot be my disciple. And whosoever doth not bear his cross, and come after me, cannot be my disciple. For which of you, intending to build a tower, sitteth not down first, and counteth the cost, whether he have sufficient to finish it? Lest haply, after he hath laid the foundation, and is not able to finish it, all that behold it begin to mock him, saying, This man began to build, and was not able to finish. Or what king, going to make war against another king, sitteth not down first, and consulteth whether he be able with ten thousand to meet him that cometh against him with twenty thousand? Or else, while the other is yet a great way off, he sendeth an ambassage, and

·desireth conditions of peace. So likewise, whosoever he be of **you that** for-saketh not all that he hath, he **cannot** be my disciple.

We are not to consult flesh and blood when the Lord calls us to be his disciples; neither are we to let others, — parents, kindred, and friends, — make the calculation for us; but we shall take counsel with God, praying to him in simple faith, and meditating on his word. Then we choose "that good part." — In our text we hear that the Lord Jesus does not deceive any with promises of ease and comfort in this world. It is his will that all shall, to begin with, experience the cross and afflictions of their discipleship. The preacher who tries to attract his hearers by presenting to them the glory of God's kingdom, but who makes no mention of self-denial and tribulations, is not a true servant of the gospel. For men mind the earthly things, and take all things in a carnal sense, unless the glory of the kingdom is presented to them in the light of the cross. The good things which our Lord Jesus gives us are *spiritual* and *eternal*. In order that we may receive them, our mind must be estranged from the world; and in order that we may be able to enjoy them, our self-will and carnal lusts must die. Here we must renoun·e all things, carry the cross, follow after Christ, nay, give life itself; — and it is good for us to know this from the very start, in order that we may not begin our Christian life with foolish dreams concerning a bed of roses, and take fright when we feel the thorns.

Many wish to inherit glory with Jesus; but few are willing to follow him on the way of the cross. If it in truth is your purpose to be his disciple, you must be prepared to suffer, and to practice self-denial, as long as you remain on this earth. Not until you are in the world beyond shall you receive your heritage of glory. But bear in mind that under the cross you walk with Jesus; *there only* can you be in his company, and thus only can you become like unto him. Bear your cross, then, in the strength of the Lord! As we shall hear his word concerning self-denial, cross, and death, so likewise shall we hear his word concerning grace and strength from the Lord. And if we give heed to the word of the cross of Christ, we hear at the same time the word of his power. — The heaviest cross is carried, not by those who really hear the word of the cross, but by the slothful man, who says: "There is a lion without; I shall be slain in the streets." (Proverbs 22, 13).

Lord Jesus, draw us after thee. Grant that we may become acquainted with thy suffering in our own flesh; give us grace to rejoice in our tribulations, to glory in them, and praise thee for them. Do not allow us to be frightened away by the law of self-denial, nor by the cross which must be borne by thy holy brotherhood; but give us courage and strength out of thy love, which is stronger than death. Amen.

Jesus, I my cross have taken, All to leave, and follow thee; Destitute, despised, forsaken, Thou from hence my all shalt be. Perish every fond ambition, All I've sought, or hoped, or known; Yet how rich is my condition! God and heaven are still my own.

261. Tuesday after Second Sunday after Trinity.

Lord, give us the spirit of wisdom and revelation in the knowledge of thee. Amen.

Isaiah 49, 5. 6. And now, saith the Lord that formed me from the womb to be his servant, to bring Jacob again to him, Though Israel be not gathered, yet shall I be glorious in the eyes of the Lord, and my God shall be my strength. And he said, It is a light thing that thou shouldest be my servant to raise up the tribes of Jacob, and to restore the preserved of Israel; I will also give thee for a light to the gentiles, that thou mayest be my salvation unto the end of the earth.

This servant of the Lord, the Savior of the tribes of Jacob, and the light of the gentiles, is none other than our Lord Jesus Christ. This text is that which Simeon had in mind when he saw the infant Savior. The Spirit of Christ in the prophets dwelt in him, and he repeats this text in this form: "Mine eyes have seen thy salvation, which thou hast prepared before the face of all people; a light to lighten the gentiles, and the glory of thy people Israel."

Christ was to "raise up the tribes of Jacob;" that is, the Jewish people. But though he was formed for this work from his mother's womb, and though his judgment was with the Lord, yet he must say: "I have labored in vain; I have spent my strength for nought, and in vain." This is at once cause for sorrow and cause for joy. It is a sad thing for Israel. Alas, the children of Abraham, "who are Israelites; to whom pertaineth the adoption, and the glory, and the covenants, and the giving of the law, and the service of God, and the promises; and of whom as concerning the flesh Christ came;" God's chosen and peculiar people, — these are scattered to the winds, and refuse to be gathered by their own King! But it is fortunate for us, as we the sooner receive that salvation which they have rejected. When they that are bidden make light of the invitation to the supper, it is sent to the halt and the blind and the maimed in the streets and lanes and hedges; and the last become the first, and the first the last. — Furthermore, it is comforting to us to hear our Lord Jesus himself complain of having labored for nought; — in vain, and yet not in vain! It is good for us that the Lord himself has been thus tried. A true servant of the Lord has sorrow by the reason of the obstinacy of his people, and is zealous for their salvation. He labors, and invites, and calls, and urges them, and intecedes for them before God; and can not understand why they will persist in serving Satan. He feels that he should be able to compel them to hear the word of life, but all that he does seems to be in vain; he labors for nought; they will not repent and believe. But then the Lord says: "It is a light thing that thou shouldest be my servant to raise up the tribes of Jacob; I will also give thee for a light to the gentiles, that thou mayest be my salvation unto the end of the earth." This is to be the final result of his work of salvation; and all his servants labor in this work. He accomplishes it through them at the very time when it seems to them that their labor is in vain. Nothing whatever which is done for the Lord is in vain; every thought which you think, every effort which you make in the cause of love and truth, is of God. How, then, can it go for nought? Your want of wisdom may be an obstacle in the way; but the Lord has taken this als· into account; and he does wisely that which you do foolishly. There is no danger of loss by reason of the good which you do; the danger lies in that which you neglect. Be zealous, and rejoice; the honor of the Lord is advanced by your efforts; and the grace of Christ, which brings salvation, shall make its way unto the end of the earth. — In this faith do thou make us diligent to do thy work, Lord Jesus. Amen.

To comfort and to bless, To find a balm for woe, To tend the lone and fatherless, Is angels' work below.

Oh, hearts are bruised and dead, And homes are bare and cold, And lambs, for whom the Shepherd bled, Are straying from the fold!

---

262. Wednesday after Second Sunday after Trinity.

Lord Jesus, draw the thoughts and the longing of our hearts to thee. Amen.

Luke 9, 57–62. And it came to pass, that, as they went in the way, a certain man said unto him, Lord, I will follow thee whithersoever thou goest. And Jesus said unto him, Foxes have holes, and birds of the air have nests; but the Son of Man hath not where to lay his head. And he said unto another, Follow me. But he said, Lord, suffer me first to go and bury my father. Jesus said unto him, Let the dead bury their dead; but go thou and preach the kingdom of God. And another also said, Lord, I will follow thee; but let me first go bid them farewell which are at home at my house. And Jesus said unto him, No man, having put his hand to the plough, and looking back, is fit for the kingdom of God.

You must not seek in Jesus the things of earth, but those of heaven. He is Lord of heaven and earth; but for our sake he became the poorest of all; and we must learn of him to renounce everything in the world, if we are to enjoy the good things of his kingdom. He tells us this at once; but if we are of the truth, he does not cast us off for not being able at once fully to understand him. Is it not a most deplorable thing that riches and covetousness prevent so many from coming to the Lord? Is it not a surprising illusion of the senses; or, I should rather say, a sad *illusion of the heart*, that these things, which Jesus regards as being of such little account, and which we know to be corruptible, are held in such high regard by us, and have such a power over our hearts? Come to him, and let him teach you to seek the good things which are eternal; and you shall be set free from mammon, and be its master! No matter how weak you may be, he shall not cast you off, if you will but hear him, obey him, and receive from him that sacred poverty which is the true riches of the soul. Do this, for the sake of your eternal salvation!

To this man, who declares that he will follow him whithersoever he goes, the Lord speaks of his poverty; for he sees that as yet the man's zeal is carnal, but that his character is not without a certain groundwork of honesty. To another man the Lord says: "Follow me. Let the dead bury their dead; but go thou and preach the kingdom of God;" — for he saw that the man's heart was bound up in his earthly home. This same is true in respect to the man who wanted to follow the Lord, but wished first to bid them farewell which were in his house. This spirit of Demas must be cast out, if we are to be saved; for with it we would perish in the destruction of Sodom. How many are there not who, having put their hand to the plow, and looked forward for a time, have thereupon lost sight of the goal, looked back, entangled themselves with worldly affairs, and lost their courage! Thus it is with him who steps aside from his post to sip the pleasures of this world; he loses more and more that purity of mind which is most precious in the sight of Jesus. — "Work out your own salvation with fear and trembling; for it is God which worketh in you both to will and to do of his good pleasure." (Philippians 2, 12. 13). "Love not the world, neither the things that are in the world! If any man love the world, the love of the Father is not in him. For all that is in the world, the lust of the flesh, and the lust of the eyes, and the pride of life, is not of the Father, but is of the world. And the world passeth away, and the lust thereof; but he that doeth the will of the Father abideth for ever." (1 John 2, 15–17).

Lord Jesus, do thou never suffer the riches or joys of the world to prevent us from following thee, nor to entice us away from thee. Draw us to thee, and keep us with thee to our last hour. Amen.

Savior, draw away our heart From all pleasures base and hollow; Let us there with thee have part, Here on earth thy footsteps follow; Fix our hearts beyond the skies, Whither we ourselves would rise.

---

263. Thursday after Second Sunday after Trinity.

O thou Spirit of God, let us hear thy word with close attention. Amen.

Acts 13, 38–41. Be it known unto you therefore, men and brethren, that through this man is preached unto you the forgiveness of sins: And by him, all that believe are justified from all things, from which ye could not be justified by the law of Moses. Beware, therefore, lest that come upon you, which is spoken of in the prophets; behold, ye despisers, and wonder, and perish: for I work a work in your days, a work which ye shall in no wise believe, though a man declare it unto you.

No man can be justified by the law; no sin can be taken away by the law; there neither is nor can be forgiveness for any man who trusts in the works of the law. But in Jesus Christ is remission of all sins, and for all sinners. The law demands punishment, and Christ grants mercy for every transgression. He has done all the work, suffered all the punishment, fulfilled all righteousness. Therefore the announcement is: "Come; for all things are now ready." None has sins so foul that they can not be washed away by the blood of the Son of God; none has sins so many that they outweigh the merit of the Son of God. None is so corrupt that Jesus can not heal him; none has fallen so low that Jesus can not raise him up. In

Jesus there is a remedy for *every* evil; in him *only*, and in none other.
Could you search through heaven, you would find none other able
to take away your sin; for *there is no other Savior.* Come, then, to
him with everything that oppresses your conscience; *he* takes it all
away! — For this he became man; for this he died; for this he went
with his own blood into heaven, and makes intercession for us; that
we might have full forgiveness of sin, and everlasting life in his name.

We here learn that "forgiveness of sins" and "justification" are
essentially one and the same thing; as is taught with equal clearness in other Bible passages also. What is meant by being *justified?*
Answer: When I believed, God had mercy on me; he "imputed to
me the righteousness of Christ, acquitted me of sin and its punishment,
and regards me in Christ, as if I had never sinned." — Thus I stand
without fear under my great high priest, and joyfully say with Saint
Paul: "Who shall lay anything to the charge of God's elect? It is
God that justifieth. Who is he that condemneth? It is Christ that
died, yea rather, that is risen again, who is even at the right hand of
God, who also maketh intercession for us." (Romans 8, 33. 34). All
is given me of pure grace, without any work or merit on my part.

Our Bible lesson is the conclusion of Paul's first recorded
sermon, and gives us the substance of all that he spoke and wrote:
Justification by faith in Christ for Jew and gentile. He finds it necessary, however, to add a warning to the Jews; and let it be a warning
to us also: "Behold, ye despisers, and wonder, and perish," etc. The
Lord wrought a work with the Jewish city and people which they
would not believe when it was declared to them in advance. This
work stands complete before our eyes. Let us beware, then, lest we
also in unbelief despise his love, tread under foot his grace, which
brings justification, and call down upon ourselves his angry judgment!

Merciful God, make us to see our sin, and draw us by thy call
of grace. Do not abandon us; for Jesus' sake, do not abandon us
to sin and unbelief; but give us conversion, and make us righteous
in his blood. Amen.

Blest is the man to whom the Lord Imputes not his iniquities, He pleads
no merit of reward, And not on works, but grace relies.
How glorious is that righteousness That hides and cancels all his sins!
While a bright evidence of grace Through his whole life appears and shines.

264. Friday after Second Sunday after Trinity.

*Grant, Lord, that we may fear thee, and understand the proper order of
thy grace. Amen.*

Acts 13, 44-49. And the next sabbath day came almost the whole city
together, to hear the word of God. But when the Jews saw the multitudes,
they were filled with envy, and spake against those things which were spoken
by Paul, contradicting and blaspheming. Then Paul and Barnabas waxed bold,
and said, It was necessary that the word of God should first have been spoken
to you: but seeing ye put it from you, and judge yourselves unworthy of everlasting life, lo, we turn to the gentiles. For so hath the Lord commanded us,

saying, I have set thee to be a light of the gentiles, that thou shouldest be
for salvation unto the ends of the earth. And when the gentiles heard this
they were glad, and glorified the word of the Lord: and as many as were
ordained to eternal life, believed. And the word of the Lord was published
throughout all the region.

The Jews of Antioch "put from themselves the word of God, and
judged themselves unworthy of everlasting life;" *therefore* they were
rejected. We here learn why men are lost. "God will have all men
to be saved, and to come unto the knowledge of the truth" (1 Timothy
2, 4); but they put from them his grace, and reject the only Savior.
The statement, in verse 46, that God wished to save them, but that
they themselves rejected the word and salvation, teaches us to understand verse 48, which says that the gentiles believed, "as many as
were *ordained* to eternal life." This can not, then, by any possibility
be construed to mean that God has ordained some to be saved *and*
others to be damned; it is clear, in regard to the lost, that they are
lost for the reason that they themselves put from them the life which
God has prepared for them, and which he urges them to accept. But
when they who are saved are said to have been *ordained* to eternal
life, this points back to God's eternal decree in Christ as the cause
of our salvation, and is a source of strength to our faith and hope.
It was not today, or yesterday, that the Lord decided to call you,
dear Christian; it was decreed in the counsel of his love before the
world was. He determined, not only to redeem us all by his only
begotten Son; but he ordained you, that is, every believer, to become
partaker of this salvation. He knew you from everlasting; and he
saw that you would accept his call, repent, and believe, and keep the
faith unto the end; and "whom he did foreknow, he also did predestinate to be conformed to the image of his Son, that he might be
the firstborn among many brethren. Moreover whom he did predestinate, them he also called; and whom he called, them he also justified; and whom he justified, them he also glorified." (Romans 8, 29-
30). Do hear this: Whom he called, and whom he justified, *them he
also glorified.* Be, then, sure of this in faith! While we, on the one
hand, hold fast the truth that God does not will the death of any
sinner, but the conversion of all; and while all are to be told that
they are created for salvation, that a place is prepared for each of
them at the great supper, but that they are lost, if they do not turn
to the Lord; — we declare, at the same time, to every believer: Your
salvation rests on an eternal decree; on the immutable counsel of
God's good pleasure and will; and no man shall be able to separate
you from the love of God in Christ Jesus.

Lord, teach us to believe, and to build our hopes on thy grace
alone; that we may be strengthened in our faith, obtain victory in
every temptation, and finally reach a place at thy table in heaven.
Amen.

My God is reconciled, His pardoning voice I hear; He owns me for his
child, I can no longer fear; With confidence I now draw nigh, And Father,
Abba Father! cry.

265. Saturday after Second Sunday after Trinity.

Lord God, give us grace by thy Spirit to hear thy glorious word. Amen.

Isaiah 55, 1–5. Ho, every one that thirsteth, come ye to the waters, an·. he that hath no money; come ye, buy and eat; yea, come, buy wine and milk without money, and without price. Wherefore do ye spend money for that which is not bread? and your labor for that which satisfieth not? Hearken diligently unto me, and eat ye that which is good, and let your soul delight itself in fatness. Incline your ear, and come unto me: hear, and your soul shall live; and I will make an everlasting covenant with you, even the sure mercies of David. Behold, I have given him for a witness to the people, a leader and commander to the people. Behold, thou shalt call a nation that thou knowest not; and nations that knew not thee shall run unto thee, because of the Lord thy God, and for the Holy One of Israel; for he hath glorified thee.

Here, in our Lord Jesus, in his church, is to be had everything which the soul needs: water to refresh us, wine to strengthen us, milk to nourish us. 1) If you thirst after God, he is to be found here; if you thirst after forgiveness of sins, this is the place where it is to be had; if you thirst after righteousness and love, after holiness and light and peace, all these are here; here are the waters of life. "If any man thirst," says Jesus, "let him come unto me, and drink. He that believeth on me, out of him shall flow rivers of living water." (John 7, 37. 38). 2) If you feel weak and weary and ill, he cries out to you, saying: "Come to me, *all* ye that labor, and are heavy laden, and I will give you rest." Even though you be on the point of going down, he shall strengthen you, that you may "mount up with wings as eagles; run, and not be weary; walk, and not be faint." (Isaiah 40, 31). "The kir~'lom of God is righteousness, peace, and joy in the Holy Ghost." You shall receive of comfort and joy all that you need, and can bear; and with it you shall receive the desire and the strength to fight the good fight of faith unto the end. The Holy Spirit bears witness with your spirit, that you are a child of God, and strengthens you mightily with the gladness of hope. 3) In the sincere milk of the word and in the heavenly gifts of the Holy Supper there is sufficient nourishment for your inner life. Here is food for your mind, that you may grow in the knowledge of God and in heavenly wisdom; and for your heart, that you may increase in charity, and in . fitness for all which is good.

Everything is to be had *for nothing*. This is what is here meant by "buying"! *Nothing* is the price which you are required to pay for the good things of God's house. It is clear, then, that all who will may come, and buy. For we all have nothing; we all have lost our possessions, and have nothing for which to buy. Or do you still, perhaps, make an effort to count out money; to make payment with prayers, tears, works, sufferings? These are but coins of lead; and you spend them in places where there is no bread; in the house of the bondmen, and of the ministers of the letter, not of the spirit. No; in reality you have nothing. Come, then, just as you are, and enter the kingdom of grace, where Christ is the ruler, and all are free; where forgiveness of sins is the law of the covenant, and the hearing of the word is the rule of life. "Lo, every one that thirsteth, come; and whosoever will, let him take the water of life freely!" So says the Lord; and if you hear it, you taste the love and grace and peace of God, and have eternal life. Incline your ear, and come unto Jesus; hear, and your soul shall live!

Give us grace to do this, merciful God. We confess with sorrow, that we are hard of hearing when thou dost proclaim thy gospel of life. Dear Lord, have mercy, and open our ears by thy Holy Spirit, that we may receive life and strength of the abundance of thy house. Amen.

He that drinks shall live forever; 'Tis a soul-renewing flood: God is faithful; God will never Break his covenant in blood, Signed when our redeemer died, Sealed when he was glorified.

---

266. Third Sunday after Trinity. I.

O God, teach us to know thy lovingkindness. Amen.

Gospel Lesson, Luke 15, 1-10. Then drew near unto him all the publicans and sinners for to hear him. And the Pharisees and scribes murmured, saying, This man receiveth sinners, and eateth with them. And he spake this parable unto them, saying, What man of you, having a hundred sheep, if he lose one of them, doth not leave the ninety and nine in the wilderness, and go after that which is lost, until he find it? And when he hath found it, he layeth it on his shoulders, rejoicing. And when he cometh home, he calleth together his friends and neighbors, saying unto them, Rejoice with me; for I have found my sheep which was lost. I say unto you, that likewise joy shall be in heaven over one sinner that repenteth, more than over ninety and nine just persons, which need no repentance. Either what woman having ten pieces of silver, if she lose one piece, doth not light a candle, and sweep the house, and seek diligently till she find it? And when she hath found it, she calleth her friends and her neighbors together, saying, Rejoice with me; for I have found the piece which I had lost. Likewise, I say unto you, there is joy in the presence of the angels of God over one sinner that repenteth.

When we consider how infinitely small we are in comparison with the almighty God, we wonder what possible difference it could make to him if he were to lose one of us. The wealth of a shepherd is reduced by a hundredth part, when he loses one sheep out of his flock of one hundred; but would God be made less rich by losing you or me? Consider, how infinitesimal a part we are of all his riches! Or could my absence cause any break in the circle of the saved around his throne? Would the heavenly chorus be incomplete without my voice? Certainly, God is as rich and blessed without us as with us; and yet he loves us so well, that he would not lose us for any price. To be sure, there is no sorrow in heaven when a man is lost; for there can be no sorrow there. But there is joy in heaven over every sinner who is saved. The reason for this is God's infinite love for us in Christ. Infinitesimally small as we are in comparison with God, and wretched as we are become by reason of our deep fall, we nevertheless are of great value in the sight of God, according to his mercy in creating, redeeming, and sanctifying us; for we are created in the image of God, and are the flower of all his creatures. We have been redeemed by the life and blood of the Son to be his own peculiar people; and God the Holy Ghost has made us his temple. It has pleased the holy triune God to love me, and to give me his heart from everlasting; therefore I also am formed to love, and to receive his life in my heart. It is, then, the most malicious delight of the devil to destroy us; while it is God's highest delight to save us.

"Then drew near unto Jesus *all* the publicans and sinners for to hear him;" and he never cast one of them out. He never repulses any poor sinner. His enemies intend to speak ill of him; but in reality they glorify his office as the Savior: "This man receiveth sinners, and eateth with them." He has left his blessed hosts of heaven, and is come to the earth to save us. He speaks of a shepherd who leaves the ninety and nine sheep, and goes into the wilderness after the one which is lost, until he find it, when he lays it on his shoulders, rejoicing, and carries it home; and of a woman who sweeps the house, and seeks diligently till she find her lost piece of silver; and then he adds: "Likewise joy shall be in heaven over one sinner that repenteth." He thereby proves to us that the greatest desire of his heart is our salvation. He diligently seeks him who has gone astray; he willingly receives the penitent sinner; he gladly saves each and all who let him find them. Let all hear this! Do you still live in sin? — Jesus seeks you, and will bring you back; you need no longer wander homeless in the desert; stop, and hearken to the voice of your heavenly Shepherd! If you are penitent, Jesus accepts you, rejoicing. Believe his love and mercy; it is a thousand times greater than your sin; greater than you are able to believe. — Shall he seek us with such ardent longing, and we still run from him into the arms of the devil? Should we not rather run to him like frightened sheep, pursued by death and the devil, and throw ourselves into his arms, which are stretched out to save us? — Lord Jesus, we are so blind and so wicked. Draw us to thee, and make us to see thy love. Do this, that thy ardent love may overcome, melt, and heal our hearts. Amen.

Thou hast promised to receive us, Poor and sinful though we be; Thou hast mercy to relieve us, Grace to cleanse and power to free. Blessed Jesus, blessed Jesus! We will early turn to thee.
Early let us seek thy favor, Early let us do thy will: Blessed Lord and only Savior! With thy love our **bosoms fill**. Blessed Jesus, blessed Jesus! Thou hast loved us — love us still.

---

267. Third Sunday after Trinity. II.

Help us in the name of the Lord, who made heaven and earth. Amen.

Epistle Lesson, 1 Peter 5, 6-11. Humble yourselves therefore under the mighty hand of God, that he may exalt you in due time: Casting all your care upon him, for he careth for you. Be sober, be vigilant; because your adversary the devil, as a roaring lion, walketh about, seeking whom he may devour; whom resist, steadfast in the faith, knowing that the same afflictions are accomplished in your brethren that are in the world. But the God of all grace, who hath called us unto his eternal glory by Christ Jesus, after that ye have suffered a while, make you perfect, stablish, strengthen, settle you. To him be glory and dominion for ever and ever. Amen.

When God smites us, his purpose is to make us humble. Let us, then, humble ourselves under his mighty hand! None can escape this hand; but if we humble ourselves under it, it will lift us up, and save us. If you acknowledge *his* righteousness and *your* guilt, and receive without complaint correction from his hand as something which you have richly deserved; you shall surely receive grace to believe in his mercy toward you, and shall learn to cast all your care upon him. There is not one among us who would not become conceited and puffed up, did not the Lord discipline him with afflictions and temptation; his happiness as a child of God would intoxicate him, and then the devil would cause him to stumble, and plunge him into despair. It is a good thing that the Lord lays his heavy hand upon us, though it seem to bring sorrow rather than joy. Then pride and self-confidence die; the sober and humble spirit is preserved; faith increases; humility thrives, and the spirit's holy trust in God; the bond of brotherly love between you and all the saints is strengthened; Aaron and Hur support the hands of Moses while Joshua defeats Amalek. Understand this, dear brethren; humble yourselves, and cast all your care upon him; for he cares for you. There is the closest connection between these two things, to "humble one's self" and to "cast all one's care upon the Lord." — The apostle calls him "the God of all grace;" a name which is worth remembering. *He,* the God of all grace, *called* you to be partakers of the salvation which cost the life of his Son; and he will with equal diligence prepare and fashion you for this glory; stablish, strengthen, settle you. If you wish to watch and stand steadfast in the faith, his gracious discipline shall enable you to do it. Then shall the devil flee from you. But if you choose the other alternative, you shall be like helpless sheep in the power of the ravenous wolf. You who lack both wisdom and vigilance; what does your poor strength amount to against the prince of hell and his army? If, however, you have been *humbled* by the *chastening* grace of the Lord, and continue to put your *trust* in our strong God; then shall the devil be shamed, but the Lord have honor, and you have salvation, for evermore.

God of all grace, keep us from pride and carnal self-confidence; give us vigilant, humble, and pious hearts, which trust in thee with childlike confidence. Strengthen us in suffering, and establish us, with all our brethren in the faith, in thy fellowship unto the end. Amen.

Still to the lowly soul He doth himself impart, And for his temple and his throne Chooseth the pure in heart.
Lord, we thy presence seek, May ours this blessing be: Give us a pure and lowly heart, A temple meet for thee!

268. Monday after Third Sunday after Trinity.

Faithful God, keep us; do not let us go away from thee. Amen.

Luke 15, 11-16. And he said, A certain man had two sons: And the younger of them said to his father, Father, give me the portion of goods that falleth to me. And he divided unto them his living. And not many days after the younger son gathered all together, and took his journey into a far country, and there wasted his substance with riotous living. And when he had spent all, there arose a mighty famine in that land; and he began to be in want. And he went and joined himself to a citizen of that country; and he sent him into his fields to feed swine. And he would fain have filled his belly with the husks that the swine did eat: and no man gave unto him.

In this younger son the Lord pictures the heathen and publicans, who have gone far away from God. But it is also a picture of the apostate Christians. How sad it is that a man will discard the glory which he has as a child of God, and choose instead the wretched pleasures of the world! He wastes *all* that he had of heavenly riches; he throws away his peace and joy in the Lord; he loses the most glorious treasure which is to be had in heaven or on earth, the life of love in God. The Spirit of God deserts him; and thus the light in his understanding is put out, and he walks in darkness. He casts away his trust in God, and his privilege and comfort as a child of the heavenly Father; the gracious gift of prayer; the precious right to pour out the heart before the Lord, and receive help in every danger and trouble; the songs of praise and thanksgiving; the divine service, the joyful communion of the saints, and the brotherly spirit; the life in holiness and honor, and the desire for that which is pure and true; — in short, he casts away everything which the child of God possesses. — He *wastes* all his substance. That is, he either plunges into wickedness at once; or he gradually becomes lukewarm, and cold, insensible to correction by the Spirit, worldly-minded, and careless; thus losing the life in God. Then he seeks to satisfy himself with the pleasures of the world; but all the children of the world without exception suffer hunger, and have nothing which satisfies. Selfishness consumes; love alone gives. Love is the only thing which satisfies the craving of the soul. The world does not have this love; and therefore it can not appease our hunger. Alas, how wretched is the man of the world even in the midst of his riches and splendors! What a sad bargain it is when one of God's children exchanges the glory of his estate of grace for the hollow happiness to be found in carnal pleasures! Look at him; he was pure and comely, and enjoyed existence among the angels and other children of God in the rich house of the Father; — and now he walks among the swine, greedy for the husks which the greedy swine want for *themselves*, and being consumed by his own lusts. — Watch, then, ye Christians, and fall not from grace! Do not, under any circumstances, leave our heavenly Father's house! We beseech and adjure you: Walk in the light, and abide in the Son and Father! Never let yourselves be deceived by the hollow and miserable world!

Heavenly Father, hold us fast to thee; preserve us in the state of grace, and keep us from the evil way of the prodigal son. This we pray with our whole heart. Amen.

Other refuge have I none; Hangs my helpless soul on thee; Leave, ah! leave me not alone, Still support and comfort me. All my trust on thee is stayed; All my help from thee I bring; Cover my defenceless head With the shadow of thy wing!

---

269. Tuesday after Third Sunday after Trinity.

Lord, bring the prodigal sons back to thee. Amen.

Luke 15, 17–24. And when he came to himself, he said, How many hired servants of my father's have bread enough and to spare, and I perish with hunger! I will arise and go to my father, and I will say unto him, Father, I have sinned against heaven, and before thee, and am no more worthy to be called thy son: make me as one of thy hired servants. And he arose, and came to his father. But when he was yet a great way off, his father saw him, and had compassion, and ran, and fell on his neck, and kissed him. And the son said unto him, Father, I have sinned against heaven, and in thy sight, and am no more worthy to be called thy son. But the father said to his servants, Bring forth the best robe, and put it on him; and put a ring on his hand, and shoes on his feet: And bring hither the fatted calf, and kill it; and let us eat, and be merry: For this my son was dead, and is alive again; he was lost, and is found. And they began to be merry.

Worldly-minded men are not "themselves"; they sleep and dream. When the Son of God conquers the heart, and rouses it out of the sleep of sin, man "comes to himself." Then he sees that he is far away from God, and feels that he is wretched; and if he be a fallen Christian, he thinks with pain of his former happiness, and longs to return to the Father's house. Here we note especially two things: 1) He who wakes up, and repents, will acknowledge his sin before the Lord, and his unworthiness to be called a child of God. 2) He will arise, and go to his Father, humble himself, and confess his sin. Without these two things there can be no true conversion. A man may feel the unhappiness of sin, and yet not humble himself before God; or he may see that he is far away, and yet not return to the Father.

However, the principle lesson which the Lord Jesus wishes to teach us in this text is, that *God receives the penitent sinner with open heart and arms*, pardons him, and with all the heavenly host rejoices over the return of the child that was lost. While you are yet a great way off, he sees you; he has long been waiting for you, and looking down the road in hopes of your return. And now he has tender compassion, and makes haste to meet you; his desire to pardon you is infinitely greater than your desire to come and receive his forgiveness. Even before you have had time to make your confession, he has pardoned you, and forgotten your disobedience. And now, as you in deep humility speak with your Father, confessing your guilt and asking his forgiveness, he causes you to be clothed with the perfect righteousness of Christ, gives you the pledge of the Holy Spirit that you are his son and heir, and gives you grace to guard your feet, or to lead a saintly life, and increase in holiness even in the midst of sin and temptation. All this he gives you through the prophets and apostles, who have brought us the word and the sacraments from the Lord; and through his ministers, who in every age preach the gospel. For faith is created *by means of the word*; it is only through the means of grace in the church that the Spirit performs his office for the justification, regeneration, and sanctification of sinners. This is *life from the dead.* There is no greater change than this. Have you experienced it? Have you known the mercy and grace of the Father? Is your soul a living one in God? Do you have your home with him? Do not stay away; come, and throw yourself into the arms of the Father!

Heavenly Father, most merciful God, draw to thee them that are far off, and keep with thee all them that have been found. Amen.

Come, ye sinners, poor and needy, Weak and wounded, sick and sore; Jesus ready stands to save you, Full of pity, love, and power; He is able, He is willing: doubt no more.

---

270. Wednesday after Third Sunday after Trinity.

Lord Jesus, let thy word chasten and humble us. Amen.

Luke 15, 25–32. Now his elder son was in the field: and as he came and drew nigh to the house, he heard music and dancing. And he called one of the servants, and asked what these things meant. And he said unto him, Thy brother is come; and thy father hath killed the fatted calf, because he hath received him safe and sound. And he was angry, and would not go in: therefore came his father out, and entreated him. And he, answering, said to his father, Lo, these many years do I serve thee, neither transgressed I at any time thy commandment; and yet thou never gavest me a kid, that I might make merry with my friends: But as soon as this thy son was come, which hath devoured thy living with harlots, thou hast killed for him the fatted calf. And he said unto him, Son, thou art ever with me, and all that I have is thine. It was meet that we should make merry, and be glad: for this thy brother was dead, and is alive again; and was lost, and is found.

The Lord addresses this parable to the Pharisees, who murmured because he received sinners; and his purpose is to correct their pride and self-righteousness. They had all the rights of children of the household; none of the good things of God was denied them. (Romans 9, 4. 5). But they did not know the joy in the Lord, and did not understand how he could have any love for lost sinners who repented. Self-righteousness and self-exaltation make men blind to the glorious grace of God, and close the heart to the joy of love.

If you also, who read this, have no knowledge of the joy of the Lord in the communion with his children, it is to be hoped that you will let him discipline you for your pride and self-complacency. Without that "godly sorrow" there can be no joy in God. "Lo, these

354

many years do I serve thee, neither transgressed I at any time thy commandments." These are the words of unblushing self-righteousness. As a rule, men would now hesitate to speak in that way; it is rather their habit to say, that they are sinners, to be sure; but — many will add, that they are not aware of their having transgressed any commandment of God; while others will express the same idea in terms more equivocal. But the striking and sad fact is, that few, or none, will admit that he is the self-righteous man whom the Lord rebukes in our text. Can it be that I am such a man? Or, may the Lord possibly mean you? Let each of us pray for grace to know himself; for pride and self-righteousness hide in the depths of the heart, and disguise themselves as humility and piety. It is surprising how slow we are to know ourselves, and how much of the wickedness of our corrupt nature may be found in even experienced Christians, without our being aware of it. It is an easy matter to say, that persons whose Christianity *consists* merely in reading and hearing the word of God, taking part in mission work, associating with Christian people, and leading blameless lives, can have no true joy in God; but it is less easy for one to increase in humility every day, and always to remain true to his first love for our Lord Jesus. It is not easy; but by the grace of God it is possible. None who lacks this joy in the Lord can lay the blame on God. If you say, that he never gave you a kid, that you might make merry with your friends, you thereby pronounce judgment on yourself; for he makes answer, and with truth: "Son, thou art ever with me, and all that I have is thine."

We, who have the word of God dwelling richly among us, must acknowledge that a bountiful table is spread before us all the time, and that we have full permission to regale ourselves with all that we need in order to live and be happy. Neither shall the Holy Spirit fail to administer correction, if we will but heed it. It is the Lord's purpose to rouse and humble you also by the word which he has spoken. Lay it to heart whoever you may be; and especially do you hear it, you who *were* one of God's happy children, but *are* one of them no longer; — humble yourself, and return to the Father! Accept correction, and let yourself be humbled, and you shall again be joyful in God, and love his children. This shall not fail.

Merciful God, enlighten us by thy Spirit, that we may know ourselves, and our sin, and may have an ever increasing joy in thy lovingkindness. Preserve us from the terrible and dark spirit of Jonah, which complains of thy mercy; and give us hearts able to rejoice with sinners who are saved. Amen.

O thou before whose presence Naught evil may come in, Yet who dost look in mercy Down on this world of sin; Oh, give us noble purpose To set the sin-bound free, And Christlike, tender pity, To seek the lost for thee.

271. Thursday after Third Sunday after Trinity.

Lord, give us a living knowledge of sin, a living faith, and a saintly life. Amen.

Matthew 9, 9–13. And as Jesus passed forth from thence, he saw a man, named Matthew, sitting at the receipt of custom: and he saith unto him, Follow me. And he arose, and followed him. And it came to pass, as Jesus sat at meat in the house, behold, many publicans and sinners came and sat down with him and his disciples. And when the Pharisees saw it, they said unto his disciples, Why eateth your Master with publicans and sinners? But when Jesus heard that, he said unto them, They that be whole need not a physician, but they that are sick. But go ye and learn what that meaneth, I will have mercy, and not sacrifice: for I am not come to call the righteous, but sinners to repentance.

Matthew was called to follow Jesus as one of his apostles, and was to go out with the preaching of the word; we are called to follow him as disciples who receive his instruction, and walk in his steps, yet without leaving our earthly vocation. *"Follow me,"* he says to us. "Follow me in obedience to the Father, in humility and love and self-denial, in truth and purity, in holiness and patience; become like unto me in mind and conduct, in your every relation toward God and man." He has left us an example, that we should follow his steps. Our Christianity is a falsehood and a delusion, if we do not follow Jesus. Now, dear reader; do you follow the Savior? Is it your care above all things to walk with him, and be like him? Does your failure to follow him as you ought give you pain; and do you improve from day to day? All believers follow Jesus, though even the best among them fall far short of his perfection. "He has many *followers* in his obedience and suffering, but no companions." Are you one of those who follow Jesus?

We begin to follow Jesus when we come to know our sin, and when we find healing in his wounds; and we continue to follow him when we desire and believe in his pardoning grace. They that be whole need not a physician. Only such as suffer, and are troubled by their sins, come to Jesus, and abide with him. The physician is for the sick; Jesus is for sinners. They who make the sacrifice for themselves, and need no mercy, will never become the Savior's disciples; for he is the servant of mercy, and the king of mercy; and they only who submit themselves to the law of mercy are citizens of his kingdom. When you see yourself as a lost sinner, and Jesus standing in your stead before God, you place yourself under him, and use him as your shield; and *then you also follow him.* By faith in his name you receive his Spirit, and live his life. He who has his righteousness in the wounds of Jesus, healing in his blood, salvation in his grace, life in his love, will surely also have his delight in following the Savior, and will have strength to do this in free obedience. But he who does not know Jesus as the Savior of lost sinners, and does not live every day of his grace, is and remains in bondage, outside of the fellowship of God's children, and without childlike obedience and true holiness. Rejoice, you needy sinner, who have no healing save in the wounds of

Jesus! He has drawn you to him, and draws you after him to that place, where you shall be perfectly pure and holy.

Lord Jesus, give us humble, believing, and willing hearts; and let it be seen in all our conduct, that we are thy followers. Precious Savior, grant us this blessing. Amen.

Lord, to thee I now surrender All I have, and all I am; Make my heart more true and tender, Glorify in me thy name. Let obedience, To thy will be all my aim.

272. Friday after Third Sunday after Trinity.

Draw us unto thee, thou merciful friend of sinners. Amen.

Luke 7, 36–50. And one of the Pharisees desired him that he would eat with him. And he went into the Pharisee's house, and sat down to meat. And, behold, a woman in the city, which was a sinner, when she knew that Jesus sat at meat in the Pharisee's house, brought an alabaster box of ointment, and stood at his feet behind him weeping, and began to wash his feet with tears, and did wipe them with the hairs of her head, and kissed his feet, and anointed them with the ointment. Now when the Pharisee which had bidden him saw it, he spake within himself, saying, This man, if he were a prophet, would have known who and what manner of woman this is that toucheth him; for she is a sinner. And Jesus, answering, said unto him, Simon, I have somewhat to say unto thee. And he saith, Master, say on. There was a certain creditor which had two debtors: the one owed five hundred pence, and the other fifty: And when they had nothing to pay, he frankly forgave them both. Tell me, therefore, which of them will love him most? Simon answered and said, I suppose that he to whom he forgave most. And he said unto him, Thou hast rightly judged. And he turned to the woman, and said unto Simon, Seest thou this woman? I entered into thine house, thou gavest me no water for my feet: but she hath washed my feet with tears, and wiped them with the hairs of her head. Thou gavest me no kiss: but this woman, since the time I came in, hath not ceased to kiss my feet. My head with oil thou didst not anoint: but this woman hath anointed my feet with ointment. Wherefore I say unto thee, Her sins, which are many, are forgiven; for she loved much: but to whom little is forgiven, the same loveth little. And he said unto her, Thy sins are forgiven. And they that sat at meat with him began to say within themselves, Who is this that forgiveth sins also? And he said to the woman, Thy faith hath saved thee: go in peace.

He who takes offence because Jesus receives sinners is still a stranger to the Savior's way of thinking. Nothing pleases the Lord more than to dry the tears of penitent sinners. The distress of sinners is *his* distress; their pain is *his* pain. Let the afflicted hear and keep this truth, and pay no heed to the voice of the devil, which seeks to entice and frighten him away from the Lord. When nothing has power to keep the sinner away from Jesus; when his own need drives, and the Lord's goodness draws him, and causes him to come and kiss the Savior's feet; — then it is exactly as it should be. The woman who was diseased with an issue of blood did precisely the right thing when, in spite of the trepidation of her heart, she pushed her way through the throng of people, and touched the hem of the Savior's garment. It was entirely proper of Zacchaeus to surmount every obstacle, in order that he might see Jesus. The Lord was exceedingly well pleased when the woman of Canaan persisted in crying out to him: "Lord, help me!" It is a beautiful thing in the sight of the Lord that this sinful woman in our text takes heart to enter the Pharisee's house, wash the feet of Jesus with her tears, wipe them with the hair of her head, kiss them, and anoint them with ointment. The merciful heart of the blessed and holy Savior is stirred with tender love, which comforts and heals the woman's soul. There is no joy equal to the joy of Jesus over the salvation of a sinner. He who in his time of need by reason of his sins has learned to know this love, which brings salvation, and who experiences this love *every day*, is not offended because of the Lord's mercy toward other lost sinners; but worships it, and loves more and more on account of the many sins which have been forgiven him and others.—We bless thee, Lord Jesus, for thy great mercy, which takes away all our sins. May it fill our souls with holy joy, and cause us to be glad together like children on account of thy love for sinners. Grant that by thy Holy Spirit I also may hear thee say to me: "Thy faith hath saved thee; go in peace." Amen.

Jesus sinners doth receive! Let the lost and sorrowing hear it; Though in sin and shame they grieve, And Jehovah's anger merit, Here's what can their woe relieve: Jesus sinners doth receive.

---

273. Saturday after Third Sunday after Trinity.

Psalm 103, 8–14. The Lord is merciful and gracious, slow to anger, and plenteous in mercy. He will not always chide: neither will he keep his anger for ever. He hath not dealt with us after our sins, nor rewarded us according to our iniquities. For as the heaven is high above the earth, so great is his mercy toward them that fear him. As far as the east is from the west, so far hath he removed our transgressions from us. Like as a father pitieth his children, so the Lord pitieth them that fear him. For he knoweth our frame; he remembereth that we are dust.

Last Sunday we heard of God's great joy in the salvation of sinners. It humbled us, and it raised us up, to learn that no shepherd can seek one of his lost sheep, and no poor woman one of her lost pieces of silver, as diligently as the Lord seeks sinners who have gone astray. Tomorrow we will be met by the demand: "Be ye merciful, as your Father also is merciful." Thus he surrounds us with words of mercy. The Bible lesson just read is, then, especially appropriate on this day. The Lord wishes to force upon us the truth, that he is the God of tender mercy. It is his will that his gospel of mercy shall fill our souls, in order that our lamentation may be turned into thanksgiving, and our sighs into songs of praise. When Moses for the second time went up to Sinai, after the idolatry of the people had broken the covenant and its tables, the Lord introduced his declaration in regard to the just punishment of sin with these words: "The Lord, the Lord God, merciful and gracious, longsuffering, and abundant in goodness and truth, keeping mercy for thousands, forgiving iniquity and transgression and sin." (Exodus 34, 6. 7). Even on *Sinai* he proclaims himself the God of *mercy!* In Nineveh he reveals a mercy so great that his own prophet is angered by it and says: "I pray thee, O Lord, was not this my saying, when I was yet in my country? Therefore I fled before unto Tarshish; for I knew that thou art a gracious God, and merciful, slow to anger, and of great kindness, and repentest thee of the evil." (Jonah 4, 2). "As the heaven is high above the earth, so great is his mercy toward them that fear him." This makes even our greatest sins shrink into nothingness. The distance from earth to heaven can not be measured. The distance is the same from the highest mountain and the deepest valley; the difference is infinitesimal, because heaven is so high! In like manner, though your sins rise mountain high, the mighty grace of the Lord can take them away as easily as it can take away the least of the weaknesses of the saint who is nearest perfection. What does the power of men, or angels, or devils, amount to as against the Lord's all-powerful mercy? — "As far as the east is from the west, so far hath he removed our transgressions from us." What can this mean but that he has removed them so far from us, that they never more can harm us? But how can they have been removed to such a distance? *He* has done it; he laid them on his Son, and the Son has carried them so far from us.

Lord God, our heavenly Father, how shall we thank thee for thy mercy! Teach us the lesson by thy Holy Spirit; teach us to fear thee, to believe in thee, to love thee, and to praise thee for evermore. Amen.

Come, ye weary, heavy-laden, Lost and ruined by the fall; If you tarry till you're better. You will never come at all. Not the righteous, Sinners, Jesus came to call.

---

274. Fourth Sunday after Trinity. I.

Heavenly Father, give us one mind with thee. Amen.

Gospel Lesson, Luke 6, 36-42. Be ye therefore merciful, as your Father also is merciful. Judge not, and ye shall not be judged: condemn not, and ye shall not be condemned: forgive, and ye shall be forgiven: give, and it shall be given unto you; good measure, pressed down, and shaken together, and running over, shall men give into your bosom. For with the same measure that ye mete withal, it shall be measured to you again. And he spake a parable unto them: Can the blind lead the blind? shall they not both fall into the ditch? The disciple is not above his master: but every one that is perfect shall be as his master. And why beholdest thou the mote that is in thy brother's eye, but perceivest not the beam that is in thine own eye? Either how canst thou say to thy brother, Brother, let me pull out the mote that is in thine eye, when thou thyself beholdest not the beam that is in thine own eye? Thou hypocrite! cast out first the beam out of thine own eye, and then shalt thou see clearly to pull out the mote that is in thy brother's eye.

Our heavenly Father shows us mercy unceasingly, **though it** often *seems* to be otherwise. His bowels yearn with compassion **on** us day and night. No mother feels such tenderness for her sick child as does the Lord for us miserable sinners. And he wants to pour out **this mercy** in our hearts, that we may be minded toward one another **as he is** toward us. We are to be merciful to friends and enemies, **to the** wicked and the good, so that we "rejoice with them that do rejoice, and weep with them that weep." Our gospel lesson mentions four things wherein our mercy shall manifest itself. 1) *Judge not;* judge **not,** but be kind to one another in every thought and word. Charity bears all things, endures all things, interprets everything as leniently as possible, "excuses and speaks well of others, and puts the most charitable construction on all their actions." Endeavor to do this at all times and toward all persons; this is God's will and his gift to us in Christ, and it is a great mercy. He who has this mind has a clear eye, which sees the good and the beautiful where others do not; and he is able to lead the erring ones on the right way; for his love shines into their souls, and "covers a multitude of sins." He who does *not* judge is the man who is *able* to judge; for he can distinguish between falsehood and truth, and help others to judge themselves; while those who have no mercy, and who are censorious, are themselves blind, and lead others into an ever thickening darkness. 2) *Condemn not;* condemn not, but draw the erring ones to you, and save them. When it becomes your duty to correct the wicked, and tell them that they are on the road to perdition, if they do not repent, be careful to do it with pity and love. Put yourself in their place, pity their unhappy condition, and relieve them. If everything which bewails the number and the misery of the wicked were but genuine mercy, things would wear a different appearance among us. Brethren, do not condemn the unconverted, but save them. 3) *Forgive;* forgive, and ye shall be forgiven; forgive with willing heart whatsoever man sin against you. If we harbor hate and revenge in our soul, the wrath of God rests upon us; for then we are no longer in the kingdom which is called the kingdom of grace. No matter what wrong your neighbor may do you, take it before the Lord; — not with an evil heart which demands revenge; for in that case you will not find your way to God; but in compassion, asking God to forgive and bless him who has wronged you; then you imitate our Lord Jesus, and then mercy shall prevail. 4) *Give;* give, and it shall be given unto you; give with cheerful heart and open hand, not that you may be called generous, nor that you may be rewarded of God or men; but in such a way as not to let the "left hand know what the right hand doeth."

Go now, ye Christians, and do these things willingly and gladly! Let your whole life be mercy. Here also the important thing is this: Go and *do* it! Then shall you also with each passing day gain a clearer understanding of that which the Lord says in regard to the "mote" and the "beam." It shall be your constant care to cast out first the beam out of your own, and then the mote out of your brother's eye; and you shall make good progress. — Heavenly Father, give us.

---

we heartily beseech thee, a clear eye and a merciful heart. Let it be seen in our every act, that we are thy children. Amen.

Vain are our fancies' airy flights, If faith be cold and dead; None but a living power unites To Christ, the living head; Faith must obey our Father's will, As well as trust his grace: A pardoning God requires us still To perfect holiness.

275. Fourth Sunday after Trinity. II.

Give us, O God, a sure and living hope. Amen.

Epistle Lesson, Romans 8, 18–23. For I reckon that the sufferings of this present time are not worthy to be compared with the glory which shall be revealed in us. For the earnest expectation of the creature waiteth for the manifestation of the sons of God. For the creature was made subject to vanity, not willingly, but by reason of him who hath subjected the same in hope; because the creature itself also shall be delivered from the bondage of corruption into the glorious liberty of the children of God. For we know that the whole creation groaneth and travaileth in pain together until now. And not only they, but ourselves also, which have the first fruits of the Spirit, even we ourselves groan within ourselves, waiting for the adoption, to wit, the redemption of our body.

In this world the children of God are to *suffer*. Let us familiarize ourselves with this truth, in order that in the midst of tribulations we may rejoice in hope. The church of God, and with it the whole creation, is in travail. However, it lasts but a little while, and is not worthy of mention in comparison with the eternal glory which awaits us. Now our soul is fettered by the flesh, and weighed down by its infirmities; but then it shall freely develop all its faculties, and have dominion over all things. Now it is a prisoner in this tenement of death; then it shall receive a glorified body like unto that of Christ. Now we are all the time burdened by our sins; then we shall be pure as the angels of heaven. Now our sight is dim and obscured; then we shall see all things more clearly than did Adam before the fall. Now we are, as it were, riveted to one spot on this earth; then we shall be exalted above all worlds, more untrammeled and free than thought itself. — Sickness, and sorrow, and poverty, and old age, and death; in short, everything which sin has brought upon us, shall then be exchanged for light and life and joy, eternal youth and beauty. The form of the present world shall pass away; but creation itself shall not be annihilated. If it were to be utterly destroyed, Paul could not have used the expressions which we have before us in our text. Creation shall not be destroyed, but glorified, regenerated, and renewed on that day when heaven and earth shall pass away. (Matthew 19, 28).

"The earnest expectation of the creature waiteth for the manifestation of the sons of God;" and the whole creation groans with us, and waits for redemption. From this we may with certainty draw these two lessons: 1) That which we wait for is something *unspeakably glorious;* for it is the *deliverance of all creation* "from the bondage of corruption into the glorious liberty of the children of God." By reason of *our* sin all things are made subject to the fear of death. We hear this in the cry of the animals, in the sough of the forest, in the splash of the waters. All things flee from death; and yet all things must die. But this law shall be repealed; death shall be annulled, and all shall become life and songs of praise — to the eternal joy of the church triumphant. 2) We may know *for certain* that these things will come to pass. The *waiting and groaning* of creation give us the assurance that there are for us and for it redemption from death, and life everlasting. If there were no such thing as liberty, the prisoner would not sigh for it; if there were no light above the earth, the plant germs down in the darkness would not send their shoots upward. The groanings in us and in all creation are a sure witness, that although sin has made us the prisoners of death, life itself is everlasting. When infidelity declares that all things shall remain as they are, under the law of corruption, and that our bodies shall for ever disappear in death and the grave, it feels in its own heart that this is not true. The whole creation, and all that is in us, says: No; corruption is not eternal; corruption is corruptible; but creation and our bodies shall be transfigured unto eternal glory through our Lord Jesus Christ.

With the holy apostle, then, we "reckon that the sufferings of this present time are not worthy to be compared with the glory which shall be revealed in us." Merciful God, let us be found among thy children with the firstfruits of the Spirit. Help us to look forward to the glory in heaven, and to rejoice in it in the midst of all sufferings. Amen.

My Father's house on high, Home of my soul, how near At times, to faith's foreseeing eye, The golden gates appear.
Ah! then my spirit faints To reach the land I love, The bright inheritance of saints, Jerusalem above!

---

276. Monday after Fourth Sunday after Trinity.

God give us holiness and charity. Amen.

John 8, 1–11. Jesus went unto the mount of Olives. And early in the morning he came again into the temple, and all the people came unto him; and he sat down, and taught them. And the scribes and Pharisees brought unto him a woman taken in adultery; and when they had set her in the midst, they say unto him, Master, this woman was taken in adultery, in the very act. Now Moses in the law commanded us that such should be stoned: but what sayest thou? This they said, tempting him, that they might have to accuse him. But Jesus stooped down, and with his finger wrote on the ground, as though he heard them not. So when they continued asking him, he lifted up himself, and said unto them, He that is without sin among you, let him first cast a stone at her. And again he stooped down, and wrote on the ground. And they which heard it, being convicted by their own conscience, went out one by one, beginning at the eldest, even unto the last: and Jesus was left alone, and the woman standing in the midst. When Jesus had lifted up himself and saw none but the woman, he said unto her, Woman, where are those thine accusers? hath no man condemned thee? She said, No man, Lord. And Jesus said unto her, Neither do I condemn thee: go, and sin no more.

In the sight of Jesus, the merciful Savior of sinners, nothing is more detestable than uncharitable judgments. He that exalts himself, and wields the sharp lash of the law on his neighbor, is the exact reverse of that which Jesus was. This applies not only to those who without charity condemn others as gross sinners, but also to those who boldly presume to decide whether their neighbors are or are not true Christians. — Humility, charity, and kindliness are pleasing to the Lord; but he detests pride and heartlessness, which assume the garb of pious zeal, or make a pretense of being interest in the salvation of souls. — Men are won by love and confidence, but are repelled by distant assumption of superiority. Have you not even so much love as is required to understand this? You do not help any one to examine himself by your looking on him with suspicion; but by believing him to be a better man than he really is you might induce him to reflect on his condition.

"Moses in the law commanded us, that such should be stoned; but what sayest thou?" They hold forth that which Moses had written; and then, for once, Jesus writes something. I imagine that he wrote that which Moses has recorded in Leviticus 19, 18: "Thou shalt love thy neighbor as thyself; I am the Lord." They knew that the Lord had mercy on sinners; and now they hoped to find an opportunity to use his mercy as a weapon against him. See with terror what pride leads to, dear reader! They seek to make of the Lord's *mercy* toward poor sinners a halter for *himself.* They argue in this wise: If he condemns her, he loses the favor of the sinners; if he acquits her, we can charge him with having disregarded the law." They did not see that they themselves were treading under foot the law of love, with which they were acquainted, and that they were more to be condemned than was this guilty woman. Then the Lord speaks words which pierces their conscience like a fiery dart: "He that is without sin among you, let him first cast a stone at her." The place becomes too close for them, and they all go out. All of them without one exception! Here is something which we do well to ponder! — Jesus has not repealed the law, but confirmed it, and here he makes the scribes and Pharisees feel its sting. He never approves of sin, but condemns it; and we may hope that some of them in this case also admitted the justice of his decision, and never afterward passed sentence on others. And the woman? When the others had gone away, Misery and Mercy were alone together. Jesus had judged her accusers; but he does not condemn her. He says to her: "Go, and sin no more." Let us bear in mind that this woman had been taken in adultery, and that she does not come to the Lord of her own accord in her soul's need. He does not say that her sins are forgiven her; but neither does he condemn her. Is there not herein a lesson which you might do well to learn?

Lord Jesus, forgive us our want of charity; and do thou make right the wrong which we thus have done. Lord, give us humility and charity; give us in our souls that love which thou hast. Amen.

Lord, if thou thy grace impart, Poor in spirit, meek in heart, I shall as my master be, Clothed with humility:
Simple, teachable, and mild, Changed into a little child, Pleased with all the Lord provides, Weaned from all the world besides.

---

277. Tuesday after Fourth Sunday after Trinity.

Lord Jesus, give us charity. Amen.

Matthew 5, 38–42. Ye have heard that it hath been said, An eye for an eye, and a tooth for a tooth: But I say unto you, That ye resist not evil: but whosoever shall smite thee on thy right cheek, turn to him the other also. And if any man will sue thee at the law, and take away thy coat, let him have thy cloke also. And whosoever shall compel thee to go a mile, go with him twain. Give to him that asketh thee, and from him that would borrow of thee turn not thou away.

"Whosoever shall smite thee on thy right cheek, turn to him the other also." These words the Lord himself explained in the house of Caiaphas. When one of the officers struck him in the face, Jesus said: "If I have spoken evil, bear witness of the evil; but if well, why smitest thou me?" He loved his enemy, and wished to save him. It is our duty to put ourselves in our neighbor's place, and deal with him in the manner which best serves his interest, even if it be directly contrary to our inclination. Rather than quarrel you should let your enemy keep everything which is yours. Of what account is all your property as compared with charity or the value of your neighbor's soul? As you must be careful to wrong no man yourself, so also must you guard against helping others to do wrong. It is your duty to refuse your neighbor that which you could wish him to refuse you under the same circumstances; for instance, money to spend for strong drink, or a loan to be expended in riotous living, or in a useless business venture. But this is a matter which requires the exercise of holy earnestness, charity, and self-denial. The matter would be disposed of without difficulty, if it could be settled by merely saying: "I might be willing to turn to him the other cheek also, if it were not for the fear of exasperating him; I would not hesitate to let him keep the cloak, if love did not forbid me to help him to do wrong; I would gladly go two miles with him, could I do it without encouraging him in his wickedness; and I would be more than willing to give and lend, were I not afraid that I might thereby tempt him to do wrong." It is easy enough to indulge in this kind of talk; but it is mere idle vaporing, unless you at the same time prove your sincerity by self-sacrificing deeds of charity toward your neighbor. While you do not keep the Lord's command by merely obeying it in its literal sense, it is equally certain that a charitable impulse in the heart will, as a rule, be followed by the corresponding act, and that it never can fail to come to the surface. Your love may impel you to refuse money to a drunken reprobate; but in that case it will also move you to do something better for him. — Are you sure that the temporal and eternal welfare of your enemy is more dear to you than are your worldly belongings and your ease and comfort? Do you cheerfully take upon yourself labor and trouble in order to serve one who persecutes you with malice? This is mercy; practice it. Live thus; it is a glorious life. It is a life in liberty; a rich, a strong, an honored life, even though you be the least, the most needy, and the most humble of all men; for the love which ministers to the wants of others is the true greatness of life. None but Jesus can teach it. None can learn it save he only who daily throws himself at the feet of the Savior, and receives pardon for his sins. Such a one really does learn the lesson; though, to be sure, he must spend his whole life in learning it to perfection.

We heartily pray thee, O Lord, give us thy love in our hearts; let our whole life be love. Amen.

Redeemer, come! I open wide My heart to thee; here, Lord, abide! Let me thy inner presence feel, Thy grace and love in me reveal; Thy Holy Spirit guide us on, Until our glorious goal be won. Eternal praise and fame We offer to thy name.

---

278. Wednesday after Fourth Sunday after Trinity.

Again we pray thee, O Lord, give us thy love in our heart. Amen.

Matthew 5, 43–48. Ye have heard that it hath been said, Thou shalt love thy neighbor, and hate thine enemy: But I say unto you, Love your enemies, bless them that curse you, do good to them that hate you, and pray for them which despitefully use you, and persecute you; that ye may be the children of your Father which is in heaven: for he maketh his sun to rise on the evil and on the good, and sendeth rain on the just and on the unjust. For if ye love them which love you, what reward have ye? do not even the publicans the same? And if ye salute your brethren only, what do ye more than others? do not even the publicans so? Be ye therefore perfect, even as your Father which is in heaven is perfect.

Jesus says that we are to love our enemies; and his Christians must, therefore, do it. His words give strength to do that which they command. If you do not love your enemy, you are not a disciple of Jesus, and must not call yourself by his name. — Now, the lite of love in the heart declares itself through acts of charity. Your love is not genuine, unless both your heart and your hand are in it. A good impulse which dies without having borne fruit is of no account; and a good deed which does not spring out of the heart has no value. In the case of Jesus and his disciples there is truth in all things, truth in the heart, and truth in the deeds. When he says "love," he speaks of a vital and active love. He adds: "Bless them that curse you," that is, proffer them, with words of blessing, heavenly good things when they, with evil heart and evil words, pour out evil upon you. "Pray for them which despitefully use you, and persecute you;" intercede for them, as Christ did on the cross; speak of them to your heavenly Father, and receive of him grace and peace for them, that you may be gathered with them in heaven. Exercise charity with equal willingness toward the wicked and the good, toward enemies and friends. God "maketh his sun to rise on the evil and on the good, and sendeth rain on the just and the unjust." In this matter they all stand side by side; all are first, and all are last. When a special promise is attached to that which we do for God's children, as something which we have done for the Lord himself, and which shall be remembered in heaven (Matthew 25, 40. Luke 16, 9. 1 Timothy 6, 17–19), this applies to just such works as are done in the spirit of the Lord, which loves all, and blesses all, has pity on the evil and the good, and does not think of the reward.

Only the children of God, who know the love of the Father, are able to love their enemies. On the other hand it is equally true, that only they who practice this love can know the heavenly Father, and become his children. Obey the words of Jesus, my soul; then shall the impossible become possible, and every difficulty be made clear. — Lord God, our heavenly Father, give us thy Holy Spirit, and make us perfect as thou art perfect. Thou seest that we are still far away. Have mercy on us, and pour out thy love in our hearts, for Jesus' sake. Amen.

Finish, then, thy new creation, Pure and spotless let us be; Let us see thy great salvation, Perfectly restored in thee, Changed from glory into glory, Till in heaven we take our place, Till we cast our crowns before thee, Lost in wonder, love, and praise.

---

279. Thursday after Fourth Sunday after Trinity.

Give us, O God, thy Holy Spirit with the love of Jesus Christ. Amen.

1 Corinthians 13, 1–7. Though I speak with the tongues of men and of angels, and have not charity, I am become as sounding brass, or a tinkling cymbal. And though I have the gift of prophecy, and understand all mysteries, and all knowledge; and though I have all faith, so that I could remove mountains, and have not charity, I am nothing. And though I bestow all my goods to feed the poor, and though I give my body to be burned, and have not charity, it profiteth me nothing. Charity suffereth long, and is kind; charity envieth not; charity vaunteth not itself, is not puffed up, doth not behave itself unseemly, seeketh not her own, is not easily provoked, thinketh no evil; rejoiceth not in iniquity, but rejoiceth in the truth; beareth all things, believeth all things, hopeth all things, endureth all things.

Let it be our ardent desire that we may have charity; and let us not give up striving for it, until it is ours. Charity is more to be desired than are all things else. It eclipses everything in heaven and on earth; it is eternal, and shall never fail, but shall unfold its glory and beauty in the perfect world to come. Faith and hope shall cease when we see God as he is; but charity remains, and shall then burn with a brighter flame for ever. For God is charity, or love; and love is the bliss eternal.

How poor is he who is without love; and how rich he who loves, even though he in other things be the poorest of all men! How empty is a life without love, but how full and beautiful with it! Love makes of the beggar a prince, of the cottage a palace; and our perishable belongings it transforms into everlasting riches. Without it all that you have is nothing. Your money, your jewels, your knowledge, your works; without love they have no value. But if you love, and use your talents in the service of love, all are beautiful and good, and bring forth blessed fruit. Let love live and reign in you, and you have all things, you are independent of all, and the servant of all. Love all with the love of Christ, and you shall feel continual sorrow while you are on earth, but shall still live a blessed life. "Many waters cannot quench love, neither can the floods drown it; if a man would give all the substance of his house for love, it would utterly be contemned." (Solomon's Song 8, 7). — How shall we with sufficient emphasis urge upon one another the importance of having charity? How shall we praise it as it deserves? Let the apostle speak; his words need no interpretation; but let the Holy Ghost impress them on our soul, and let us keep them and ponder them all in our heart: "Charity suffereth long, and is kind; charity envieth not; charity vaunteth not itself, is not puffed up, doth not behave itself unseemly, seeketh not her own, is not easily provoked, thinketh no evil; rejoiceth not in iniquity, but rejoiceth in the truth; beareth all things, believeth all things, hopeth all things, endureth all things." — Do you not feel a burning desire that you may have charity? If you do, a spark has already been kindled in you. Go, then, and do that which the apostle says; then shall the sacred fire burn in your heart, though trouble and temptations will at times cause it to burn with but a feeble flame. Do this; for charity is worth it!

Merciful God, give us thy Holy Spirit, that we may have charity. Make us to see our love of self, and let it humble us; and pour out the love of Christ in our heart. Do this, O God, by thy Holy Spirit. Amen.

Come, O come, thou quickening Spirit, Thou forever art divine: Let thy power never fail me, Always fill this heart of mine; Thus shall grace, and truth, and light, Dissipate the gloom of night.

280. Friday after Fourth Sunday after Trinity.

Holy Spirit of God, let thy word become truth in our heart. Amen.

Romans 14, 7–13. For none of us liveth to himself, and no man dieth to himself. For whether we live, we live unto the Lord; and whether we die, we die unto the Lord: whether we live therefore, or die, we are the Lord's. For to this end Christ both died, and rose, and revived, that he might be Lord both of the dead and living. But why dost thou judge thy brother? or why dost thou set at nought thy brother? for we shall all stand before the judgment seat of Christ. For it is written, As I live, saith the Lord, every knee shall bow to me, and every tongue shall confess to God. So then every one of us shall give account of himself to God. Let us not therefore judge one another any more: but judge this rather, that no man put a stumbling-block or an occasion to fall in his brother's way.

The faithful do not belong to themselves, but wholly and entirely to the Lord. He died for us, and overcame sin and death; and his victory belongs to them that believe in him. Christ is eternal Lord of all things; and there is no restraint whatever upon his will. But he became man; and of his own free will he took upon himself the penalty and pain of sin and death in order to break these fetters. This he brought about, and united us with himself through baptism; and thus we are no more the bondmen of sin, but the freedmen of Christ, able to *love him* and *live unto him* of our whole heart. He who in unbelief lives without Christ is the slave of his own self-will, and lies when he boasts of his liberty. He, on the other hand, who believes in Christ is subject to him, and is therefore free. His heart obeys the law of love, and therefore has liberty; for his will is the will of the Lord. The believers are not, to be sure, entirely rid of their self-will, but it has been brought into subjection; they master it, and mortify it. Dear reader, do you live this life of liberty? Christ, the Son of God and the judge of all things, has of a truth redeemed you from the bondage of sin; and it is equally true and certain that through your baptism you have a right and access to the kingdom of love. It is likewise certain that the Spirit has the will to create faith in your soul; and *on this* everything depends. The grace is given you; let now your eye be open to see, and your hand to receive, the gift. *You* are in the house of God, and the life is *yours;* you also have knowledge of it, and feel the need of it. Do you, then, let the Spirit enter your soul! — and the change will take place; you are set free from the devil's witchcraft, and have liberty and a new life. These are not idle words; — blessed is he who learns this by experience!

Then we "live unto the Lord," serve one another, and build his church. "As he is, so are we in this world." Independent of all, and masters of all, we are the servants of all. In lowliness we esteem others better than ourselves; and we judge no man, but bear one another's infirmities, and wash one another's feet. When we die we die also "unto the Lord." It is a death in his fellowship, and to his honor; we go to our home, and the brethren are strengthened in the faith. In this light we see one another, and walk together, and bend the knee with one another, and confess the glory of the Lord; until we all, the strong and the weak, perfected in love, stand before him on that day, not to be judged, but to receive our crown. — Lord Jesus, draw us to thee, unite us with thee, and give us thy life, in order that we may be one in thee, and may reveal thy glory to the world, and be without fear on the judgment day, to the glory of thy name. Amen.

O Son of God, we wait for thee, We long for thine appearing, We know thou sittest on the throne, And we thy name are bearing. Who trusts in thee may joyful be, And see thee, Lord, descending, To bring us bliss unending

281. Saturday after Fourth Sunday after Trinity.

Lord God, give us the delight and strength of love, for Jesus' sake. Amen.

James 5, 19. 20. Brethren, if any of you do err from the truth, and one convert him, let him know that he which converteth the sinner from the error of his way shall save a soul from death, and shall hide a multitude of sins.

When men sin both against God and against you, do not let this subdue your love; "be not overcome of evil, but overcome evil with good." Let it grieve you that they are so unhappy; acquaint yourself with their condition, and feel love's sorrow on account of their misery. They who live in sin are the slaves of their lusts, bereft of peace and liberty; and this would have been your condition also, if the Lord had not found means to save you through the call of grace. They are eternally lost, if they do not repent; — can this fail to touch your heart? To be sure, it is their own fault that they serve the devil; but it is the Lord's mercy alone that you are saved. Certainly, Satan reigns in the hearts of the wicked; but it is also certain that God has no pleasure in the death of the sinner, but wants him to repent and live. The heart has heretofore been closed tight against his word; but by the grace of the Holy Ghost it may be possible to find some crevice; a thread may be found which leads through the labyrinth of the soul to a quiet chamber in which the word of God can make itself heard. Seek to find this crevice, this thread; it will be worth your trouble. God shall prosper your effort; and then you save a soul from eternal death. Here it is well to have a sharp eye and a thorough knowledge of the human soul; but this is not given to all; and the one thing of greatest importance is to have love. Love is said to be blind; and there is some truth in the saying; for love is slow to see the faults of others. But at the same time love, nay love *only*, has sight; for nothing else can find the way to your neighbor's heart. Love is said to be weak, but it is strong; so strong that you regard it as a mere trifle to bear even the great faults of others. It is strong, persistent, and enduring, and does not give up the fight before the neighbor's soul has been won. Elijah prayed in the name of righteousness for drought and rain, and his prayer was answered. Yet he was but a man, subject to the same law with us. Shall God, then, not hear your earnest and persistent prayer in the name of love for the salvation of an erring soul which he has loved unto the death on the cross? O, that our hearts were full of love! If we did but have love, we would be richly blessed co-workers with the Lord, save many soul from death, and "hide a multitude of sins."

Merciful God, again we pray thee to give us true love in our heart, for Jesus' sake. Amen.

And of thy mercy now bestow True Christian faith on me, O Lord! That all the sweetness I may know Which in thy holy cross is stored; Love thee o'er earthly pride or pelf, And love my neighbor as myself; And when at last is come my end, Be thou my friend, From satan's wiles my soul defend.

282. Fifth Sunday after Trinity. I.

Lord Jesus, help us to give heed to thy words of instruction. Amen.

Gospel Lesson, Luke 5, 1-11. And it came to pass, that, as the people pressed upon him to hear the word of God, he stood by the lake of Gennesaret, and saw two ships standing by the lake: but the fishermen were gone out of them, and were washing their nets. And he entered into one of the ships, which was Simon's, and prayed him that he would thrust out a little from the land. And he sat down, and taught the people out of the ship. Now when he had left speaking, he said unto Simon, Launch out into the deep, and let down your nets for a draught. And Simon, answering, said unto him, Master, we have toiled all the night, and have taken nothing: nevertheless, at thy word I will let down the net. And when they had this done, they inclosed a great multitude of fishes: and their net brake. And they beckoned unto their partners, which were in the other ship, that they should come and help them. And they came, and filled both the ships, so that they began to sink. When Simon Peter saw it, he fell down at Jesus' knees, saying, Depart from me; for I am a sinful man, O Lord. For he was astonished, and all that were with him, at the draught of the fishes which they had taken: And so was also James and John, the sons of Zebedee, which were partners with Simon. And Jesus said unto Simon, Fear not; from henceforth thou shalt catch men. And when they had brought their ships to land, they forsook all, and followed him.

Out of the wealth of instruction contained in this gospel we will to-day treasure up in our heart the following two lessons: 1) That *men may be caught for the kingdom of God*, be led to Jesus, believe in him, and continue in the faith, is God's loving purpose in all that he does; and all the events of our life are shaped to serve this end. The *will* of God is that you shall save others, in order that there may be a saved human race. He wants us to come out of the darkness of sin into the light of his grace; to receive again the wisdom which we have lost; that we may know his love, and love him with holy joy. It is his will that we shall again have dominion over all creatures, and that all the forces of nature shall willingly obey our command. But the way of salvation is humility and penitence from beginning to end. When Peter and his partners toil all the night, and take nothing, this is a part of God's plan to make them fishers of men. When Jesus *begins* by giving them the bread *of life*, and then fills their ship, we understand what important object the Lord has in view; and when the great draught of fishes causes Peter to fall down in astonishment and fear at the feet of Jesus, we see what the Lord's purpose was in working this miracle. Let us understand that the Lord knows all which happens to us; that his purpose is to promote our eternal welfare, make us efficient workers for the kingdom, and allow us to labor on in our earthly vocation with the things of heaven before our eyes.

2) *At the Lord's word we shall let down the net.* We are not to trust in our own skill, but are to expect everything as a result of his blessing; *expect it with certainty*, but only according to his gracious

promise, and as an undeserved gift from his hand. Why must Peter toil all the night, and take nothing? He is to learn that the Lord rules in all things, and especially in the work of catching men, to which Peter is now called. He is to know of a certainty that the word which the Lord commands him to preach accomplishes that whereto it is sent; he is to learn to trust in the Lord, and commit all things into his hand! *"At thy word* I will let down the net;" that is, I will do it in *obedience* to the Lord, and *trusting* in him. We are to do all our work unto the Lord. Whatsoever he says unto you, do it gladly, and without question, whether you be a magistrate, or a teacher, or a master, or a servant; and whether it promise to pay, or seem useless. Lend the Lord your ship, and he shall return it to you full of fishes. Let down the net at his word, and at the proper time you shall have a great draught. All are not called to be apostles or teachers; but still it is the duty of all to labor for the salvation of souls. Live in the Lord; do your work in his service; follow Jesus in humility, love, self-denial, and patience; confess his name by the word and sacraments, and by holiness in all your speech and conduct; — then shall you catch men. Thus we, together with the apostles and the whole church, draw the net, and lift the souls into the ship to our Lord Jesus.

Grant us this grace, dear heavenly Father. Help us to say from our heart: Lord, at thy word I will let down the net. Take from us all carnal self-confidence, and give us the childlike and simple faith of the lowly of heart. Lord Jesus, we commit ourselves to thee. Do thou in mercy take me and all that is mine, and make use of me for the furtherance of thy kingdom, for the salvation of souls. Amen.

Spread, oh, spread, thou mighty word! Spread the kingdom of the Lord, That in earth's remotest bound Men may hear the joyful sound.
Tell them how the Father's will Made the world, and keeps it still, How his only Son he gave, Man from sin and death to save.

---

283. Fifth Sunday after Trinity. II.

Holy God, sanctify us in heart and deed by thy holy word. Amen.

Epistle Lesson, 1 Peter 3, 8–14. Finally, be ye all of one mind, having compassion one of another; love as brethren, be pitiful, be courteous: Not rendering evil for evil, or railing for railing; but contrariwise blessing; knowing that ye are thereunto called, that ye should inherit a blessing. For he that will love life, and see good days, let him refrain his tongue from evil, and his lips that they speak no guile: Let him eschew evil, and do good; let him seek peace, and ensue it. For the eyes of the Lord are over the righteous, and his ears are open unto their prayers: but the face of the Lord is against them that do evil. And who is he that will harm you, if ye be followers of that which is good? But and if ye suffer for righteousness' sake, happy are ye: and be not afraid of their terror, neither be troubled.

If you wish to gather souls for Christ, live according to this epistle lesson. He who thus walks confesses Christ unceasingly, magnifies his name, and leads souls to him. And for himself also he has the joy of the true life and the blessings of the cross. The peace of God reigns in his heart; he experiences the Lord's help in every trouble, and he is grateful for it all. "He that will love life, and see good days," let him speak and do that which is good. The Lord himself says: "He that loveth his life shall lose it." "Life" and "life" are two different things. The life which we are to love is the fellowship with God; while the life which we are to hate is the life in carnal and sensual lusts. The Lord himself shall be our life; we shall love him with such devotion that everything else which we love must pale and disappear before him, our soul's delight, even as the stars are blotted out when the sun rises. Then he will fill our hearts with heavenly joy, and make our lives full and rich. For this Christ has taught us to pray in the Third Petition of the Lord's Prayer. As the blessed angels in heaven praise God and serve us, so shall we gladly serve one another and praise the Lord. This is the life which we shall love. Be ye, then, Christian brethren, *all of one mind;* be *all* likeminded according to Christ, that you mind the same thing, have the same love, being of one accord, of one mind. Regard yourselves as nothing, and adorn yourselves with humility. In the humble souls love increases; without humility the brotherly spirit can not thrive. Have *compassion* one of another; for are you not members one of another? And when one member suffers all the members suffer with it. *Love* ye as brethren; for "by this shall all men know that ye are my disciples, if ye have love one to another." (John 13, 35). "See that ye love one another with a pure heart fervently," and show this in being *courteous*, and having active sympathy with all. Do not close your hand to the necessities of others, but practice heartfelt *mercy*, even as you are the children of mercy. Let it never be said of the faithful that they are slow to give, and that it is better to seek assistance from others; but let experience ever teach people that none shall knock in vain at the door of a Christian. *Render not evil for evil;* but love your enemies, do good to them that hate you, heap coals of fire on their head. *Bless* them that curse you; carefully consider their case; consider how unhappy they are, and do not forget how great and undeserved a mercy you have obtained. Even as your Father in heaven makes his sun to rise on the evil and on the good, so also shall your heart and tongue and hand do good to all, so that the curse hurled against you by the wicked may return from you as a blessing upon them. This is happiness; this is life! And God bestows this great mercy on you!

Give us now the mind and strength of thy Holy Spirit, merciful God. Give us a loving and saintly mind; and let all our conduct please thee, and be a blessing to mankind. Amen.

I love thy Zion, Lord! The house of thine abode, The church our blest Redeemer saved With his own precious blood.
I love thy church, O God! Her walls before thee stand, Dear as the apple of thine eye, And graven on thy hand.

284. Monday after Fifth Sunday after Trinity.

Lord Jesus, draw us to thee. Amen.

John 1, 35-42. Again the next day after John stood, and two of his disciples; and looking upon Jesus as he walked, he saith, Behold the Lamb of God! And the two disciples heard him speak, and they followed Jesus. Then Jesus turned, and saw them following, and saith unto them, What seek ye? They said unto him, Rabbi, (which is to say being interpreted, Master,) where dwellest thou? He saith unto them, Come and see. They came and saw where he dwelt, and abode with him that day: for it was about the tenth hour. One of the two which heard John speak, and followed him, was Andrew, Simon Peter's brother. He first findeth his own brother Simon, and saith unto him, We have found the Messias, which is, being interpreted, the Christ. And he brought him to Jesus. And when Jesus beheld him, he said, Thou art Simon the son of Jona: thou shalt be called Cephas, which is by interpretation, A stone.

John has here with his inspired pen described his first meeting with Jesus. "Behold the Lamb of God!" He and Andrew heard this remark by John the Baptist, and they followed the Lord. He who hears the word of repentance, and feels his sin with sorrow, will also hear the gospel, and follow the Lamb of God. Jesus at once turns to them and speaks to them, helps them to voice their longing, and invites them to come to him. Happy men! But we; where shall we hear the voice of the Baptist calling to repentance? Where shall we find the Lord Jesus? "I know a house in which my Savior dwells, his holy church, the city of God (Psalm 46, 5). Often have I said to him with burning heart: 'Master, where dwellest thou?' And he has answered: 'Come and see!' And I came, and saw where he dwelt; and now, while I live, I will sing with David, Psalm 65, 4: 'Blessed is the man whom thou choosest, and causest to approach unto thee, that he may dwell in thy courts; we shall be satisfied with the goodness of thy house, even of thy holy temple.' 'Come and see!' Do not stand far away, you who inquire after the Lord and his habitation. We pray you, and press you to come in. Do come and see!" (Besser). — The two who had found the Messias could not let the sun go down before finding Simon, Andrew's brother, who like them thirsted after the water of life. They could not sit rejoicing at the fountain, and let him perish with thirst in the desert. The Lamb of God makes missionaries of his followers. Both of these men go out; and Andrew "first findeth his own brother Simon," and with glad voice cries out to him, "We have found the Messias!" and then bring him to Jesus. Then there is joy in the presence of the angels of God, when one brother brings the other to the Savior. And "Jesus beheld him," and saw that this was the man whom in the counsel of the Father he had ordained to be his instrument in founding the church of the Pentecost. "Thou art Simon, the son of Jonas." Jesus knew what Simon was; a man warmhearted, but carnally minded; honest, but easily tempted. And he saw what he would be able to make of him: "Thou shalt be called

Cephas, which is by interpretation, A man of rock;" or, in Greek, *Peter.* The truth which Peter confessed: "Thou art Christ, the Son of the living God;" this truth is the rock, and therefore he is called Peter. — How did the Lord find you, dear reader? And how have you been since he found you? Who brought you to him; and whom have you brought to him? What has the Lord said to you? What was your name; and what name did you receive of him?

"I am a great sinner; this is the only name I have of which to be proud when I hear the sentence of the law. But Jesus is become my Savior, and has borne my iniquity; there I now have a beautiful name written in the book of life." Blessed be thy name, Lord Jesus!

O make thy church, dear Savior, A lamp of burnished gold, To bear before the nations Thy true light as of old; O teach thy wandering pilgrims By this their path to trace, Till, clouds and darkness ended, They see thee face to face.

285. Tuesday after Fifth Sunday after Trinity.

Lord, reveal to us thy glory. Amen.

Matthew 16, 13-19. When Jesus came into the coasts of Cæsarea Philippi, he asked his disciples, saying, Whom do men say that I, the Son of Man, am? And they said, Some say that thou art John the Baptist; some, Elias; and others, Jeremias, or one of the prophets. He saith unto them, But whom say ye that I am? And Simon Peter answered and said, Thou art the Christ, the Son of the living God. And Jesus answered and said unto him, Blessed art thou, Simon Bar-jona: for flesh and blood hath not revealed it unto thee, but my Father which is in heaven. And I say also unto thee, That thou art Peter; and upon this rock I will build my church; and the gates of hell shall not prevail against it. And I will give unto thee the keys of the kingdom of heaven: and whatsoever thou shalt bind on earth, shall be bound in heaven; and whatsoever thou shalt loose on earth, shall be loosed in heaven.

Jesus is the Christ, the Son of the living God, true and everlasting God; and the Son of Man, true man of the race of Adam. This is the faith and confession of the church. Such a faith can not be born in the heart save by the Spirit of God; and it is an unmistakable seal of membership in the church. "None can say that Jesus is the Lord, but by the Holy Ghost." We may regard him as the greatest teacher, the wisest sage, and the foremost founder of a religion; but to believe in him as "the true God and eternal life" is something which none can do, but by the Holy Ghost. He who knows himself as a lost sinner, and believes that Jesus Christ, God and man, died for us, and lives for us; he is enlightened of God, and is a blessed man. The Holy Ghost does not create loose opinions or dry views, but a positive conviction in regard to the Inconceivable One, and a hearty trust in the Invisible One; moving the soul to give itself to him, rely on him, and confess him in life and death.

The church is not built on the person of Peter, who in himself was weak; but on the truth that Jesus, the Son of Man, is the Christ.

the Son of the living God; and as the truth is immovable, the church stands immovable against all the power of hell. Remain on this rock, dear soul, and have no fear, even though there be violent storms on every hand. The sword of temporal power and the pen of the great intellects are alike powerless in their attack on the camp of God. "God is in the midst of her; she shall not be moved; God shall help her, and that right early." (Psalm 46, 5). By the grace of the Spirit we also shall remain in the camp. If the accuser could gain control of our conscience, we were undone; but we have an advocate with the Father, Jesus Christ the righteous; and we have the office of forgiveness of sins among us, and we walk in light before God. You have access to him at all times with the petition: "Forgive us our trespasses, as we forgive those who trespass against us." And when your sin becomes especially heavy to bear, when you again feel the venomous fang of the serpent, you must make use of the power which the Lord gave to Peter and the whole church, to absolve from sin; and you must go to the communion table, from which point you have the clearest view of the Savior on the cross (John 3, 14. 15); so shall you be healed, and remain one of his quickened people. Through these seemingly little and insignificant things, absolution and the holy Supper, the Lord strengthens our souls to such a degree that Satan with all his anger and all his mighty power is put to shame. The rock of our salvation, Christ, is sure.

Lord Jesus, give us the light of the Spirit, that we may believe in thee unto righteousness, and confess thee unto salvation. Amen.

Yea, as I live, Jehovah saith, I do not wish the sinner's death, But that he turn from error's ways, Repent, and live through endless days.
What ye shall bind, that bound shall be; What ye shall loose, that shall be free; For unto you the keys are given To ope or close the gates of heaven.
They who believe, when ye proclaim The joyful tidings, in my name, That I for them my blood have shed, Are free from guilt and judgment dread.

286. Wednesday after Fifth Sunday after Trinity.

Grant, O Lord, that we hear thy word. Amen.

Exodus 4, 10–15. And Moses said unto the Lord, O my Lord, I am not eloquent, neither heretofore, nor since thou hast spoken unto thy servant: but I am slow of speech, and of a slow tongue. And the Lord said unto him, Who hath made man's mouth? or who maketh the dumb, or deaf, or the seeing, or the blind? have not I the Lord? Now therefore go, and I will be with thy mouth, and teach thee what thou shalt say. And he said, O my Lord, send, I pray thee, by the hand of him whom thou wilt send. And the anger of the Lord was kindled against Moses; and he said, Is not Aaron the Levite thy brother? I know that he can speak well. And also, behold, he cometh forth to meet thee; and when he seeth thee, he will be glad in his heart. And thou shalt speak unto him, and put words in his mouth: and I will be with thy mouth, and with his mouth, and will teach you what ye shall do.

God will, in the first place, have you to know of a certainty that he has appointed you to your work. In the next place he will

have you to know your own utter inability. And, lastly, he will
have you to feel full confidence in him.

1) Who can doubt that God appointed Moses to be the liberator of
Israel, David to be king and psalmist, Peter and Paul to be apostles,
John the Baptist and Elijah to be voices calling people to repentance,
Mary to be the mother of Jesus, Eunice to be the teacher of Timothy,
Mark to be an evangelist, Luther to be the reformer? But do you
think that the great are the only ones of whom the Lord has had
foreknowledge? What is great, and what is little to him? Every
good and useful work on earth is the Lord's; and when he has disposed your life in such a way that you have by fair means become
a master, or a servant, or a magistrate, or a farmer, or whatever
you may be, assuming that you have a useful and honest vocation;
do not doubt that the Lord prepared your work for you, and you
for the work. Confess the sins of your youth, which have influenced
your life, and they are forgiven. Moses also sinned, at this time in
awakening the Lord's anger, and previously, when he took upon
himself to slay the Egyptian; but notice how the Lord even then
directed the course of his life. There is glorious comfort in the conviction that the Lord has appointed me to my work, and led me to
the place where he would have me.

2) Here Moses has an entirely different opinion of himself from
that which he had forty years earlier when he assumed to himself
the office of being his brother's savior. How widely different
from the ambitious men, who insist on being leaders! He who prides
himself on his ability is of no account. That everything depends
on the Lord is a truth which is spoken with ease and learned with
difficulty; but which it is necessary to learn nevertheless. Moses
was educated as an Israelite and in all the learning of Egypt; yet
he must take a course of forty years' training in the wilderness.
David was a pious and splendidly equipped young man; and still
he was compelled to undergo a long term of hard discipline; and
Peter had learned but little of the great lesson when he had toiled
all night in vain. O, that we might have a living knowledge of the
truth that of ourselves we are fit only to disturb and tear down;
and that we might thus learn not to shut out the Lord's power by
confidence in our own strength!

3) Moses, however, does wrong to decline, because of his own
weakness and the magnitude of the work, to that which the Lord called
him. Should he not have been ready at once when the Lord spoke
to him? However, the charge was so stupendous that hardly any
other man than Moses would have dared, with humble heart and for
God's sake only, to undertake it. Who has been about the Lord's
business, and has not felt that it is the nature of the flesh to make
a man timid when he should have his strength in the Lord *only*?
In this way God teaches us this spiritual law, 2 Corinthians 12, 10:
"For when I am weak, then am I strong." It is really true that you
yourself are utterly incapable; but it is also true that in Christ you
are able to do all things to which the Lord calls you. "Who maketh
the dumb, or deaf, or seeing, or blind? have not I, the Lord? Now

therefore go, and I will be with thy mouth, and teach thee what thou shalt say."

Lord, keep us from going when thou dost not send us; but give us grace to go willingly when thou dost call us. Teach us that thy strength is made perfect in weakness. Amen.

God calling yet! — shall I not rise? Can I his loving voice despise, And basely his kind care repay? He calls me still: can I delay?
God calling yet! — and shall he knock, And I my heart the closer lock?
He still is waiting to receive, And shall I dare his Spirit grieve?

---

287. Thursday after Fifth Sunday after Trinity.

Lord Jesus, reveal thyself to us through faith. Amen.

Acts 26, 12–18. Whereupon as I went to Damascus, with authority and commission from the chief priests, at midday, O king, I saw in the way a light from heaven, above the brightness of the sun, shining round about me and them which journeyed with me. And when we were all fallen to the earth, I heard a voice speaking unto me, and saying in the Hebrew tongue, Saul, Saul, why persecutest thou me? it is hard for thee to kick against the pricks. And I said, Who art thou, Lord? And he said, I am Jesus whom thou persecutest. But rise, and stand upon thy feet: for I have appeared unto thee for this purpose, to make thee a minister and a witness both of these things which thou hast seen, and of those things in the which I will appear unto thee; delivering thee from the people, and from the gentiles, unto whom now I send thee, to open their eyes, and to turn them from darkness to light, and from the power of Satan unto God, that they may receive forgiveness of sins, and inheritance among them which are sanctified by faith that is in me.

"I am Jesus whom thou persecutest," says the Lord to Saul. Is it not, then, the church which Saul persecutes? Certainly; but here we are again told that the Lord and his disciples are one. Wrong *them*, and you wrong *Jesus;* do good to *them*, and you do good to *him*. As Paul now becomes a servant of Christ, the Lord himself is in and with him also. That which Paul does is the Lord's doing; that which he suffers is the suffering of Christ; that which he accomplishes is the honor of God. He is *chosen* to be a minister of the gospel; the Lord *appears* to him, and calls him; and the Lord *goes with him*, and delivers him.

Every servant of the Lord has from his mother's womb, nay from eternity, been "made," or *chosen*, for this office. He, or she, was created and equipped for the position as pastor of that church, missionary at that station, or teacher in that school; or for the calling of a mother, as Jochebed and Eunice; or to be the wife of a missionary, as Priscilla. A wise master always selects the proper material. Let this truth encourage, gladden, and comfort you. — To Paul the Lord says: "I have made thee a minister and a witness of me." The apostles had seen the Lord with their own eyes, and their hands had felt him. Herein their case is different from ours. But in *faith* we also have found him; to us also he has appeared, thus enabling us to bear witness concerning him. He who can not of his own experience *witness* of eternal life in the Son of God is not a fit person to be a minister of the gospel. He only who has himself found mercy can properly preach the word of mercy. He who does not *know* our Lord Jesus can not truly praise his glory. The power is in the word itself; but this must be rightly divided. Let us preach it with full confidence in the power of the Lord, which it contains. As a minister of the word of God shall be certain of his call, so shall he also be sure that the word which he preaches, as the word of the Lord, is mighty and living, and accomplishes the Lord's purpose. He shall preach it *in faith.* He must not doubt that it opens the eyes of the blind, and causes them to turn from the power of Satan unto God. Such a minister can go confidently to his work; the Lord shall save him from the fury and anger of the devil. "Greater is he that is in you, than he that is in the world." Even yet many a furious persecutor becomes a zealous confessor.

Blessed be thou, Lord Jesus; thy name will we praise and confess unto the end of the earth. Amen.

Then let us sing of Jesus, While yet on earth we stay, And hope to sing of Jesus Throughout eternal day:
For those who here confess him He will in heaven confess. And faithful hearts that bless him He will forever bless.

---

288. Friday after Fifth Sunday after Trinity.

Lord, enlighten us by thy Spirit. Amen.

Ephesians 3, 5–12. Which in other ages was not made known unto the sons of men, as it is now revealed unto his holy apostles and prophets by the Spirit: that the gentiles should be fellowheirs, and of the same body, and partakers of his promise in Christ by the gospel: whereof I was made a minister, according to the gift of the grace of God given unto me by the effectual working of his power. Unto me, who am less than the least of all saints, is this grace given, that I should preach among the gentiles the unsearchable riches of Christ: and to make all men see what is the fellowship of the mystery, which from the beginning of the world hath been hid in God, who created all things by Jesus Christ: to the intent that now unto the principalities and powers in heavenly places might be known, by the church, the manifold wisdom of God, according to the eternal purpose which he purposed in Christ Jesus our Lord: in whom we have boldness and access with confidence by the faith of him.

According to an eternal purpose God has redeemed the world, both Jew and gentile, by his only begotten Son; and it is in accordance with the same purpose that he leads peoples and individuals. The whole history of the church (and the history of the world as well) is a revelation of God's purpose in Christ. When he first lets the gentiles go their own ways, and then accepts them, but hardens the hearts of the Jews, yet without casting off his people; when he sends the gospel to the Orient and the Occident, to the frozen North and to the lands farthest south, everywhere with life and light and healing for the souls; this is a revelation of his eternal purpose in Christ. And when the word of the cross, which is to the Jews a stumblingblock, and to the Greeks foolishness, transforms the world, overthrows the temples of idolatry, drives out devils, teaches men to lead saintly lives and die blessed deaths, and also to dwell happily in their earthly fatherland; when he for these purposes employs the most humble instruments, chooses the foolish things of the world, and things which are despised, and things which are not, to bring to nought things that are; when he leads the church and its individual members to the goal by ways past finding out, down into the deep in order to lift them up, and into the midst of death in order to give them life;—all these things reveal the same eternal purpose in Christ, and glorify him in *heaven* and on *earth.*—God has created all things *by* Jesus Christ, and *to* him. All things which are, and everything that comes to pass, are for the sake of Christ's office as the Savior; and all are to reveal the glory of God in the church. Even the principalities and powers in heavenly places serve this purpose, and thus gain a deeper insight into the eternal nature of God, into the infinite depths of his wisdom and mercy, into the unity of the Father and Son and Spirit, and into the connection between the works of creation and redemption and sanctification. We have "boldness to enter into the holiest by the blood of Jesus, by a new and living way, which he hath consecrated for us, through the veil, that is to say, his flesh" (Hebrews 10,19.20); and thus we even in this life begin to stand before the throne day and night. Paul is overwhelmed by the greatness of God's mercy to man, and is sensible of being less than the least of all saints, altogether unworthy to preach the unsearchable riches of Christ. If Paul was less than the least, what shall we say of ourselves?

He pardons all thy sins; Prolongs thy feeble breath; He healeth thine infirmities, And ransoms thee from death.

Then bless his holy name, Whose grace hath made thee whole, Whose loving-kindness crowns thy days: Oh, bless the Lord, my soul!

---

289. Saturday after Fifth Sunday after Trinity.

Psalm 119, 41–50. Let thy mercies come also unto me, O Lord; even thy salvation, according to thy word. So shall I have wherewith to answer him that reproacheth me: for I trust in thy word. And take not the word of truth utterly out of my mouth; for I have hoped in thy judgments. So shall I keep thy law continually for ever and ever. And I will walk at liberty: for I seek thy precepts. I will speak of thy testimonies also before kings, and will not be ashamed. And I will delight myself in thy commandments, which I have loved. My hands also will I lift up unto thy commandments, which I have loved, and I will meditate in thy statutes. Remember the word unto thy servant, upon which thou hast caused me to hope. This is my comfort in my affliction: for thy word hath quickened me.

It is good to dwell with the Lord in his word, always to hope in his mercy, and in all affliction trust in his salvation. "If God be for us, who can be against us?" At his altar none can injure you. He who can answer them that reproach him, that he has trusted in the word of the Lord, has an impenetrable shield against their attacks. And when they mock, saying, "where is your God, where is now your God?" and it is as a sword in our bones; and when God hides his face from us also, and lets us experience something of that which Christ felt in his great passion; — then it is good to be able to say: "Lord, I trust in *thy word;* I await the fulfilment of thy promise."

So it is also when everything goes against one, and he finds life full of trouble. How countless are the ills to which flesh is heir! Your only, or, it may be, your favorite child dies, perhaps under peculiarly sad circumstances; or it suffers a fate which gives you even deeper pain. Your good and faithful husband is struck down with disease, and your heart is heavy; but your loving care is rewarded, and he recovers for a time only to become hopelessly demented as a result of overwork. You had worked your way to independence, and are suddenly ruined by coming to the rescue of a friend. You have labored, and have built up a prosperous and beloved church, and "Christian" robbers come and destroy it for you. — Ye sons of men, put your trust *in the word of the Lord,* and it shall be with you as with Peter; he toiled all the night, and caught not a fish, yet in the morning his ship was filled. Hold your peace, and have patience, and hope in the Lord! When you are compassed about with distresses he shall bring relief, enabling you to walk at liberty, and to sing with Job: "Blessed be the name of the Lord!" If you can not now rejoice in the word of the Lord, yet the word can comfort you; and if *you* do not *now* understand what the Lord does, bear in mind that *he* understands it, and you likewise shall understand it hereafter. He wounds in order to heal, and he takes in order to give. Believe in him, and give yourself to him; then shall all that you lose be gained, even that which to you seems to be lost irretrievably. He *shall do it,* even though your faith be most deplorably weak.

"All my trust is in thee, O Lord, now and at all times. Thou art my comfort; thy word and voice the joy of my heart in my every affliction." Help me to say this in truth, for Jesus' sake. Amen.

Lord, I believe; but thou dost know My faith is cold and weak; Pity my frailty and bestow The confidence I seek. Yes, I believe; and only *t*hou Canst give my soul relief: Lord, to thy truth my spirit bow; "Help thou mine unbelief!"

---

290. Sixth Sunday after Trinity. I.

Lord Jesus, expound to us thy holy word. Amen.

Gospel Lesson, Matthew 5, 20–26. For I say unto you, That except your righteousness shall exceed the righteousness of the scribes and Pharisees, ye shall in no case enter into the kingdom of heaven. Ye have heard that it was said by them of old time, Thou shalt not kill: and whosoever shall kill shall be in danger of the judgment: But I say unto you, That whosoever is angry with his brother without a cause, shall be in danger of the judgment: and whosoever shall say to his brother, Raca, shall be in danger of the council: but whosoever shall say, Thou fool, shall be in danger of hell fire. Therefore, if thou bring thy gift to the altar, and there rememberest that thy brother hath ought against thee, leave there thy gift before the altar, and go thy way; first be reconciled to thy brother, and then come and offer thy gift. Agree with thine adversary quickly, whiles thou art in the way with him; lest at any time the adversary deliver thee to the judge, and the judge deliver thee to the officer, and thou be cast into prison. Verily I say unto thee, Thou shalt by no means come out thence, till thou hast paid the uttermost farthing.

The righteousness of the Pharisees was an *external* righteousness. The better ones among them kept the law "to the best of their ability," and imagined that this made them righteous before God. The others were careful to make themselves seen of men; prayed at the street corners, and gave alms, that they might have glory of men, while they at the same time robbed widows and orphans. Though the more sincere among the Pharisees were men who in a way did much for God, and were zealous in his cause, their righteousness was of no account. For the law of the Lord deals with the heart; so that none can escape its condemnation save the man who is perfect in holiness within and without. The law of the Lord demands charity out of a pure heart, and of good conscience, and of faith unfeigned. The least uncharitableness, even though it be but a passing impulse; the least spark of anger, or selfishness, or any other wrong feeling, is sufficient utterly to destroy your righteousness; for "whosoever shall offend in one point, he is guilty of all." It takes but one break of the thread to lose all the beads on the string. The law of the Lord is perfect, as is the Lord himself; and your life must be absolutely blameless in every detail, else the law can not pronounce you righteous before God.

Is any man, then, perfect in holiness? There has dwelt but one such on earth, our Lord Jesus Christ. But he lived *for us;* and God counts this for righteousness to all who believe in him. For the Son of God had no need to keep the law, and to suffer the punishment of transgression for himself; but he did it for us. If you believe, it is yours; God has so ordained from eternity, and revealed it on earth before the law of Moses. The holy demand of the law is satisfied, the works are done, and nothing is wanting; the righteousness which exceeds that of the Pharisees has been given you. He who believes this grace of God in Christ, need have no fear; he "shall not come into condemnation, but is passed from death unto life."

As Christ, then, is my righteousness, shall I in my life and conduct discard the law of God? On the contrary, the law is now once more written into the heart. The man who understands the final demand of the law, who is sensible of his want of righteousness, who believes in Christ, and who dies from the law, now finds it possible to do that which he never could do while he was under the law, and regarded himself as righteous; — he keeps the law, he loves God and his neighbor, and leads a holy life. This life, however, which has in truth been kindled in him, is still imperfect by reason of the flesh. It can not enable him to stand before God; but neither does he need it for this purpose; for by faith he is already a child of God and heir to the kingdom of heaven. In the mean time he is thus sanctified unto perfect purity in the day of Christ. — "O Lord, thy blood and righteousness The treasures are which I possess; With them shall I before thee stand, And have a place at thy right hand." Give us this grace by thy Holy Spirit, merciful God. Let this lesson be life and truth in us. Amen.

The law is good; but since the fall Its holiness condemns us all: It dooms us for our sin to die, And has no power to justify.

To Jesus we for refuge flee, Who from the curse has set us free, And humbly worship at his throne, Saved by his grace through faith alone.

---

291. Sixth Sunday after Trinity. II.

Lord, make us partakers of the grace of thy death and resurrection. Amen.

Epistle Lesson, Romans 6, 3-11. Know ye not, that so many of us as were baptized into Jesus Christ were baptized into his death? Therefore we are buried with him by baptism into death; that like as Christ was raised up from the dead by the glory of the Father, even so we also should walk in new-ness of life. For if we have been planted together in the likeness of his death, we shall be also in the likeness of his resurrection: Knowing this, that our old man is crucified with him, that the body of sin might be destroyed, that henceforth we should not serve sin. For he that is dead is freed from sin. Now if we be dead with Christ, we believe that we shall also live with him: Knowing that Christ, being raised from the dead, dieth no more; death hath no more dominion over him. For in that he died, he died unto sin once: but in that he liveth, he liveth unto God. Likewise reckon ye also yourselves to be dead indeed unto sin, but alive unto God through Jesus Christ our Lord.

This truly is a grand lesson, a power unto faith and sanctification. Learn this epistle lesson well, and heed its instruction; and sin can never have dominion over you. You are righteous, and alive, and free, and strong in Christ. Christ dies no more; and neither shall you, who by baptism are united with him, if you believe. Death has no more dominion over Christ; neither has it dominion over you who believe. Loehe writes: "If one died for all, then have all died. All believers are dead in Christ; in him they have been punished for their sins, for which they have in him fully atoned. Their union with him in faith makes them all partakers of his suffering and death. But if they be counted like him in his death, they are like him also in his resurrection: in faith they already live the life of the resurrection. And even as the glory of Christ shone in his resurrection; as he by his resurrection was acquitted of all that which men had brought to his charge, and for which they had condemned him; and as God justified him by raising him from the dead; so are all believers, in that he rose again, absolved from all sin, even as they all were punished in his death. A blessed exchange between us sinners and him, who died and rose again in our stead! It is a marvellous truth, which never entered the thought of man, a truth which no man could understand or have courage to accept, did not the Spirit of God in his mercy enlighten us. There is no truth more sure, or which has a more firm

foundation; but alas, it does not find a foothold and take root among
men. Yet all the world and its wisdom is as nothing compared with
this truth; and if *this* truth were not, what would then be? This is our
salvation: I in them, and they in me. Jesus all things in all; wisdom,
righteousness, holiness, redemption. We in him, as partakers in all
that he has." Then ponder this epistle lesson well, word for word, and
ask the Spirit of God to give you light. — We pray thee, merciful God,
give us the grace of the Spirit to understand the word, to believe it,
and to show it obedience. Amen.

My faith looks up to thee, Thou Lamb of Calvary, Savior divine; Now
hear me while I pray, Take all my guilt away, Oh, let me from this day Be
wholly thine.

May thy rich grace impart Strength to my fainting heart, My zeal inspire;
As thou hast died for me, Oh, may my love to thee Pure, warm, and change-
less be, A living fire.

---

292. Monday after Sixth Sunday after Trinity.

Lord, teach us to believe thy righteous grace. Amen.

Romans 3, 23-28. For all have sinned, and come short of the glory of
God; being justified freely by his grace, through the redemption that is in
Christ Jesus: whom God had set forth to be a propitiation through faith in
his blood, to declare his righteousness for the remission of sins that are past,
through the forbearance of God; to declare, I say, at this time, his righteousness: that he might be just, and the justifier of him which believeth in Jesus.
Where is boasting then? It is excluded. By what law? of works? Nay: but
by the law of faith. Therefore we conclude that a man is justified by faith
without the deeds of the law.

How many glorious assurances God has given in his word in regard to the justification of sinners; assurances to comfort and
strengthen our hearts! When I believed in Christ I was "justified";
that is to say, God imputed to me the merit of Christ, and adjudged
me to be righteous, as though I had never sinned. This was the
exact opposite of what I had deserved; for I have sinned, and am deserving of eternal punishment. Yet God revealed *his righteousness* by
forgiving instead of punishing; for Christ had suffered the penalty, and
has atoned for us by his blood. God's righteous judgment was executed on him instead of on us. This is the law of faith, given in the
eternal counsel of God: 1) Christ stands in the place of all men; and
hence his atoning blood is for all, and means that all have suffered
death for their sins. 2) Whosoever believes is one with Christ, and
is for his sake declared of God to be righteous, so that none can lay
anything to his charge, and nothing can condemn him. — God makes
manifest his righteousness in that he punishes sin, leaving not one
transgression unpunished. Even that which through the centuries he
has endured with much longsuffering has yet been avenged according
to the strict rule of justice; the chastisement was upon Christ; for him,
who knew no sin, God has made to be sin for us; and he has paid to
the uttermost farthing. Then again, God manifests his righteousness

in that he declares all them to be righteous who accept the merit of Christ. How could it be otherwise, since Christ is wholly righteous? He who still persists in accusing and condemning the faithful will have to do with the righteous God himself; for he denies and insults the justice of God. But if any believer takes credit to himself for his justification, as though his faith were something which he had given himself, or as though faith were a virtue deserving of reward; such a one violates the law of faith, and places himself again under the condemnation of the law of works. Let this, then, be our steadfast faith and the sure rock of our salvation: We are "justified freely — freely — by his grace through the redemption that is in Christ Jesus."

Gracious God, give us the light of thy Holy Spirit, that we from the bottom of our hearts may acknowledge that we have sinned, and come short of the glory of God; and let the Spirit make known to us the blessed law of grace and truth, our justification by faith in the blood of Jesus; that we may believe in it with all our heart, find comfort therein, and thus be eternally saved. Amen.

There is a fountain filled with blood Drawn from Immanuel's veins; And sinners, plunged beneath that flood, Lose all their guilty stains.
The dying thief rejoiced to see That fountain in his day; And there have I, as vile as he, Washed all my sins away.

---

293. Tuesday after Sixth Sunday after Trinity.

God, renew our hearts according to thy holy law. Amen.

Matthew 5, 17-19. Think not that I am come to destroy the law, or the prophets: I am not come to destroy, but to fulfil. For verily I say unto you, Till heaven and earth pass, one jot or one tittle shall in no wise pass from the law, till all be fulfilled. Whosoever therefore shall break one of these least commandments, and shall teach men so, he shall be called the least in the kingdom of heaven: but whosoever shall do and teach them, the same shall be called great in the kingdom of heaven.

God's law, the law of love, can not be abolished or changed; for God is unchangeable, and love is ever the same. He was, and is, and shall be, love; and what should he then command us to do if not to love? Or could we be blessed, do you think, if we did not love him with all our heart? No; there is no life for us mortals save in loving fellowship with God. — Can it be, then, that Christ came to destroy the law? Impossible! Our Savior must *fulfil and establish* it. The law is not to be changed, but we; not the demands of love are to be taken away, but everything in us which is contrary to love.

Christ fulfils the law, establishes the law; in the first place, by living a life in perfect love, and obeying to the letter its every command; and as God has ordained that Christ shall be *in our stead*, he counts it as *our* fulfilment of the law. Note the marvellous confirmation of the law by Christ: The Son of God becomes man, and dies, that the law may be fulfilled; as was done in Bethlehem, on Calvary, and wherever he spent a part of his life on earth in the form of a servant

It is finished, and is now extant as an accomplished fact; and I can stand without fear before all who may wish to accuse me as a transgressor. Christ has fulfilled the law to the letter; and I have done it through him. — It is an incredible mercy that the Son of God is become my servant to fulfil the law; but the eternal love of God has so ordained, and it is *a fact.* Blessed be his name! In the second place, Christ fulfils and establishes the law by writing it anew in my heart by the Spirit of faith. The love wherewith he loved us is in us, and he in us (John 17, 26); and what is love but the fulfilment of the law? Now that we of his grace alone have received so rich a blessing, and are the children of God and heirs to eternal life, absolved from the demands and the curse of the law, because all is finished in Christ; should we not love him who loved us first? Should not our faith work by love? Having been made free from the law, we now do that which the law demands : We truly love God; and in that wherein we still fall short we shall increase gradually as the flesh dies, until we once more bear the perfect image of God in the state of glory beyond the grave. — In this manner Christ came to fulfil the law *for* us and *in* us.

Holy and righteous God, teach us to know the gravity and rigor of thy law, that we may see our sin and be truly penitent. Teach us also to believe in Christ's fulfilment of the law for us, that we may receive the adoption of sons, and may have the law written in our hearts. Pour out thy love in our hearts by the Holy Spirit, for Jesus' sake. Amen.

Create my nature pure within, And form my soul averse to sin; Let thy good Spirit ne'er depart, Nor hide thy presence from my heart.
Though I have grieved thy Spirit, Lord, His help and comfort still afford; And let me now come near thy throne, To plead the merits of thy Son.

---

294. Wednesday after Sixth Sunday after Trinity.

Let the truth of thy word, O God, permeate us and sanctify us. Amen.

Psalm 15. A Psalm of David. Lord, who shall abide in thy tabernacle? who shall dwell in thy holy hill? He that walketh uprightly, and worketh righteousness, and speaketh the truth in his heart. He that backbiteth not with his tongue, nor doeth evil to his neighbor, nor taketh up a reproach against his neighbor. In whose eyes a vile person is contemned; but he honoreth them that fear the Lord. He that sweareth to his own hurt, and changeth not. He that putteth not out his money to usury, nor taketh reward against the innocent. He that doeth these things shall never be moved.

The doctrine of our justification by faith alone is the sun which gives sinners life and light, on their journey, and when they come to die. This sun must not be obscured by doctrines of human invention. No work of ours whatsoever must be introduced in connection with the merit of Christ. The scripture distinctly teaches that man is justified by faith only; and this truth and none other can give us certainty in our hope of salvation, as the work of Christ is alone perfect.

Justification, however, by which God adjudges to all who believe the full right to salvation, is nevertheless inseparably connected with a man's regeneration and renewal, whereby he is made fit for communion with the holy God. In the first place it is the upright only who *come* to Christ; for they who wish to hide, and to continue in their sin, and to give God at the most a divided heart, can never believe in spirit and in truth and never *receive* grace, but will continue in their unrighteousness under the wrath of God. Then again, none can *continue* in the estate of grace without leading a life as before the face of God. "If we walk in the light, as he is in the light, we have fellowship with one another, and the blood of Jesus Christ, his Son, cleanseth us from all sin." And, finally, it is the nature of faith to quicken us, and open the heart to the love of God; thus causing all who continue in faith to lead holy lives, hate sin, and serve the Lord. The believer trusts solely in the grace of God, and becomes all the time more firmly grounded in this fundamental truth of the gospel that "the just shall live by faith"; but this grace urges and impels him to walk in newness of life.

Our Psalm draws a beautiful picture of the life of the saints. "Lord, who shall abide in thy tabernacle? who shall dwell in thy holy hill?" This impressive question awakens the yearning of the soul after the blessed fellowship of the Lord. The answer is given in verses 2 and 3, in which it is set forth what a righteous man *does*, and what he will *not* do. He walks uprightly; he is the same within and without. He *works* righteousness, or deals with all men according to God's commandments; and he speaks the truth in his heart. He backbites no man, does no evil to any man, and brings no reproach upon his neighbor. The statement as to what he *will* and what he will *not* do is continued in verses 4 and 5: He measures men according to their relations with God. In his eyes the vile person is contemned, be he never so distinguished; but he honors the man who fears the Lord, no matter how lowly his estate in the world; and in obedience to God he is a man of his word. He does not lay up treasures on earth, nor can he by any means be induced to wrong any man. — Let all this help us to examine ourselves.

Blessed the people which dwells in the Lord's holy hill! Blessed the man who abides in his tabernacle; the billows of death shall never move him! Give us this grace, O God, for Jesus' sake. Amen.

Glorious things of thee are spoken, Zion, city of our God; He whose word cannot be broken, Formed thee for his own abode: On the rock of ages founded, What can shake thy sure repose? With salvation's walls surrounded, Thou may'st smile at all thy foes.

---

295. Thursday after Sixth Sunday after Trinity.

Lord, let my soul live, and it shall praise thee; and let thy judgments help me. Amen.

James 2, 10–17. For whosoever shall keep the whole law, and yet offend in one point, he is guilty of all. For he that said, Do not commit adultery, said also, Do not kill. Now if thou commit no adultery, yet if thou kill, thou art become a transgressor of the law. So speak ye, and so do, as they that shall be judged by the law of liberty. For he shall have judgment without mercy, that hath shewed no mercy; and mercy rejoiceth against judgment. What doth it profit, my brethren, though a man say he hath faith, and have not works? can faith save him? If a brother or sister be naked, and destitute of daily food, and one of you say unto them, Depart in peace, be ye warmed and filled; notwithstanding ye give them not those things which are needful to the body; what doth it profit? Even so faith, if it hath not works, is dead, being alone.

"The law of liberty"; what is it? The eternal purpose and the fixed order of love and grace concerning our salvation by faith in Christ alone; this love, which Christ fulfilled, and poured out in our heart, and which the Spirit has made a living fact in us, — is "the law of liberty." He who does not through faith know and feel that, being dead and buried with Christ, he is free from the compulsion of the law; and that, having been raised again with Christ from the dead, he has been quickened in love; he does not know the law of liberty, nor understand what it is. He, on the other hand, who is united with Christ through a living faith sustains a new relation to both God and man. The former commandment, which *made* love a matter of compulsion under the law, is become a new commandment of love, *a law of liberty.* If any man say that he has faith, but know not love, his faith is dead and of no account, and he is the slave of sin.

Among those who expect to be saved there are many who dwell in the house of bondage, labor in their own strength, rely on their works, and do not understand that this road is impassable. They should be able to see that the holy demand of the law is perfect love; that the least transgression of one commandment violates the law in its entirety, destroys their whole effort to make themselves righteous, and brings upon them the curse of all their sins; but they do not grasp it. — Others expect to be saved through faith; but they imagine that they have the faith which saves, when they hold it to be true that there is a God, and that Jesus is the Son of God. But alas, what can empty words and idle opinions avail against sin, death, and devil? — No, faith alone justifies; by faith only, not by the law, is a man saved. But the faith which brings salvation works by love. (Gal. 5, 6). Therefore James says, 2, 17. 19. 20, that "faith, if it have not works, is dead, being alone. Thou believest that there is one God; thou doest well; the devils also believe, and tremble. But wilt thou know, O vain man, that faith without works is dead?" — He, on the other hand, who truly believes, and thus in faith flees from his sin to Christ, and receives the righteousness of Christ, and his victory over the devil, his life and love, liberty and salvation in the Son of God; — this man has the faith which brings salvation, and shall of a certainty inherit the kingdom of God. Whom the Son makes free is free indeed; he is Abraham's seed, and heir according to the promise. There is a wealth of life and power in true faith. This faith works unceasingly to make free from the guilt of sin, and to keep the conscience unfettered. But it is equally tireless in the active practice of charity, in giving thanks to the Lord, and doing mercy toward men. God preserve us from deceiving **ourselves** in bondage under the law, or in a faith which is dead!

We pray thee, merciful God; give us thy Holy Spirit. Create by him true faith in our hearts; and increase it, and make us active in every good work. Amen.

If you cannot cross the ocean, And the heathen lands explore, You can find the heathen nearer, You can help them at your door. If you cannot give your thousands, You can give the widow's mite; And the least you do for Jesus Will be precious in his sight.

---

296. Friday after Sixth Sunday after Trinity.

I will pay my vows unto the Lord now in the presence of all his people.

Isaiah 58, 5–8. Is it such a fast that I have chosen? a day for a man to afflict his soul? is it to bow down his head as a bulrush, and to spread sackcloth and ashes under him? wilt thou call this a fast, and an acceptable day to the Lord? Is not this the fast that I have chosen? to loose the bands of wickedness, to undo the heavy burdens, and to let the oppressed go free, and that ye break every yoke? Is it not to deal thy bread to the hungry, and that thou bring the poor that are cast out to thy house? when thou seest the naked, that thou cover him; and that thou hide not thyself from thine own flesh? Then shall thy light break forth as the morning, and thine health shall spring forth speedily; and thy righteousness shall go before thee: the glory of the Lord shall be thy reward.

There be many in our times who worship no God but their stomach and politics; and then again, there are others, who worship God with prayer and song and with the reading and hearing of his word; who associate with believers, abstain from profanity, cards, dancing, and the like, live quietly and decently, and regulate their conduct by that of the true Christians; — and whose whole Christianity consists in these things, though they may perhaps at times feel moved by an impressive sermon, and may occasionally feel the touch of the Spirit of God. The piety which consists merely in things such as these is at the best a sorry affair; but the worst of it is that these people by this sort of religion rob themselves of eternal salvation.

True Christianity is the heart's fellowship with the God of love; and causes us to love one another in the Lord, and to live all our life in charity. Not that we already are wholly love; but that love governs all our conduct, is the mainspring and life of all our work, and more and more purges out of us the old leaven. — Go, then, ye Christians, who have tasted the heavenly gift, and who live of it all the time; go, and become rich in deeds of charity. Loose them that are in bondage, break the yoke and undo the burden of the oppressed, help the wretched by the gospel and the grace of the Spirit; pass none by in his soul's misery, and help your neighbor in his bodily need also. Give bread to the hungry, clothe the naked, and make the homeless welcome: — they all are your brethren, of your own flesh and blood. Ye believing brethren: wherefore so slow and slothful in the exercise of charity? Is not this true religion to help the fatherless and the widows? Do it quickly, and do it abundantly; God shall give the will and the strength. You stand at the fountain; draw for triend and stranger, and scatter the blessings of life and thanksgiving and praise round about you. Then shall your light break forth as the morning, and your health shall spring forth, and your righteousness shall go before you, and the glory of the Lord shall be your reward. Your life in grace shall increase, you shall grow all the time into a clearer knowledge of God, and become stronger in all that is pure and true and good. And the blessing of the Lord shall rest on all that you do.

O God, kindle love in us by thy Holy Spirit. Let this sacred flame burn brightly in our soul, that we may become rich in fruits of love, and that thus much thanksgiving may ascend to thee unceasingly from those who give and from those who receive. Do, Lord God, kindle this flame of love in us, for Jesus' sake. Amen.

Thou, Lord, hast brethren here below, The partners of thy grace, And wilt confess their humble names Before thy Father's face.
Thy face, with reverence and with love, We in thy poor would see; Oh, may we minister to them, And in them, Lord, to thee.

---

297. Saturday after Sixth Sunday after Trinity.

Lord, incline my heart unto thy testimonies, and not to covetousness. Amen.

Isaiah 58, 9-11. Then shalt thou call, and the Lord shall answer; thou shalt cry, and he shall say, Here I am. If thou take away from the midst of thee the yoke, the putting forth of the finger, and speaking vanity: And if thou draw out thy soul to the hungry, and satisfy the afflicted soul; then shall thy light rise in obscurity, and thy darkness be as the noon day: And the Lord shall guide thee continually, and satisfy thy soul in drought, and make fat thy bones: and thou shalt be like a watered garden, and like a spring of water, whose waters fail not.

God is rich; he always has sufficient to give. And he is ready to do it; he takes delight in blessing us, and making us happy, and satisfying our heart with good things. If a man will but bow to the will of God, renounce his unbelief, live of God's mercy, and practice it toward others, he shall have the Lord's blessing abundantly, draw water out of the wells of salvation, pour out more and more freely for the benefit of friend and enemy, and his own soul shall have sweet solace and refreshment. In that case, if you pray, you shall receive; for then the Lord's will is your will, and you pray for that which is good for yourself and others. As it is the *Lord's* delight to satisfy and refresh, so it is also *your* delight and joy to feed the hungry and comfort the afflicted. The church is the home of love and mercy. There are all manner of sick and needy persons under the porches of Bethesda, in ordei that we may exercise mercy; but there also is divine healing in the pool of Bethesda, since the Son of God came, and sacrificed himself on the altar from whose foot the water gushes forth; and therefore we never need stand helpless in the presence of one another's distress.

Our text has precious promises for the people of love. Your obscurity and darkness shall be as the noon day; that is to say, all that is most evil shall be turned into good. The Lord shall guide you *continually*, every hour, today and hereafter, every moment and unceasingly, through your whole life, and beyond the gates of death. The thought fills my soul with exultation. "He shall satisfy thy soul in drought, and make fat thy bones." When your heart is tired, and your bones ache; when your strength is dried up, and you wither and bear no fruit; God, who has a heaven full of everything that you need, shall satisfy your soul, and give strength to your bones, and make you to be a blessing. You shall be like a watered garden, and like a spring whose waters do not fail. The mouth of the Lord has said it; believe it, and you shall *not* be deceived! — Bear in mind: You are not to be rich in charity first, in order that you may believe and accept God's blessing. No; in the midst of your sinful need, do you *believe God's love* as being pure grace, and *exercise* this love. This is the way of life from the first hour to the last.

Give us, O God, thy Holy Spirit, that we may know thee, believe in thee, and live in thee. "Send us thy Spirit from above to fill our hearts with burning love." Do this for Jesus' sake. Amen.

Lord, be mine this prize to win; Guide me through a world of sin, Keep me by thy saving grace, Give me at thy side a place. Sun and shield alike thou art; Guide and guard my erring heart; Grace and glory flow from thee; Shower, O shower them, Lord, on me!

298. Seventh Sunday after Trinity. I.

Lord, let thy blessing be upon us. Amen.

Gospel Lesson, Mark 8, 1–9. In those days the multitude being very great, and having nothing to eat, Jesus called his disciples unto him, and saith unto them, I have compassion on the multitude, because they have now been with me three days, and have nothing to eat: and if I send them away fasting to their own houses, they will faint by the way: for divers of them came from far. And his disciples answered him, From whence can a man satisfy these men with bread here in the wilderness? And he asked them, How many loaves have ye? And they said, Seven. And he commanded the people to sit down on the ground: and he took the seven loaves, and gave thanks, and brake, and gave to his disciples to set before them; and they did set them before the people. And they had a few small fishes: and he blessed, and commanded to set them also before them. So they did eat, and were filled: and they took up of the broken meat that was left seven baskets. And they that had eaten were about four thousand: and he sent them away.

These people were gathered around the Lord, and heard him. — His Christians are with him always. As many as believe are ever with him, and he with them. He is with us not only in the sense in which God is present everywhere with his omnipotence, and sustains and directs all things; but he is with us in his sacred word as our Savior and the king of our heart, as the God of love and mercy who gives us of his Spirit, and is himself our meat and our life.

These people in our text ate of gifts provided by the Lord's power to work wonders. We also live of his blessing. We receive both our spiritual and our bodily sustenance from his hand; and he prepares our food for us in many wonderful ways, even as he in a wonderful way converts it into blood and muscle and bone in our bodies. He satisfies the wants of the wicked and the good; but the faithful receive his gifts in another spirit than do the unbelievers; they "sanctify all things by the word of God and prayer"; and in these earthly things they partake of the love which is of heaven and eternity. Thus the children of God live all the time of the Lord's miracles, even though their food is provided for them by the ordinary process of nature. We sit every day among the four thousand, and have nothing ourselves, but are fed by the Lord, take of his hand that which he has blessed, divide it among us all, and have enough, nay seven baskets left over.

Did these people have reason to fear any want? So neither shall we take thought for meat and drink and raiment. The Lord cared for them, before they thought of caring for themselves. "I have compassion on the multitude," said he; and he thought of the length of time they had been with him, and of what would happen to them, should he send them away fasting. He is full of kindness and compassion, and knows what we need. Is he not able, think you, to provide us with all things necessary? The account before us is written, that we may have faith in him, and be rid of all anxiety; and with the same end in view the Spirit of God has caused to be recorded for our benefit the story of Elijah, and of the widow in Sarepta, and that which Jesus in his sermon on the mount said in regard to the flowers of the field and the fowls of the air. How happy you might be, would you but allow the Lord to care for you! However, no matter how weak your faith may be, he will always give you all that you need, nay more.

Now, how shall we *use* the gifts of God? In the first place we shall partake of them with joy and thanksgiving. Receive them of God as pledges of his love, and *enjoy them before his face;* it pleases him to see your happiness. Be fond of his good gifts for the sake of the giver; let them cause you to give him your heart so entirely, that you may be able to thank him for the loss and the chastisement, should he again take them from you. In the next place, we shall cheerfully divide with others, set food before the hungry, and never fear that there may not be enough. You shall do every day that which the disciples did on the occasion spoken of in our gospel lesson.

Lord Jesus, let us ever be with thee, live continually of thy wonders, and fear no want, but believe in thee, and receive thy gifts with joy and thanks, and give with generous hand to all who need. Amen.

Through each perplexing path of life Our wandering footsteps guide; Give us each day our daily bread, And raiment fit provide. Oh, spread thy covering wings around, Till all our wandering cease, And at our Father's loved abode, Our souls arrive in peace!

299. Seventh Sunday after Trinity. II.

Lord, thou hast loosed my bonds; lead me in thy paths. Amen.

Epistle Lesson, Romans 6, 19–23. I speak after the manner of men, be-cause of the infirmity of your flesh: for as ye have yielded your members serv-ants to uncleanness and to iniquity, unto iniquity; even so now yield your members servants to righteousness, unto holiness. For when ye were the serv-ants of sin, ye were free from righteousness. What fruit had ye then in those things whereof ye are now ashamed? for the end of those things is death. But now being made free from sin, and become servants to God, ye have your fruit unto holiness, and the end everlasting life. For the wages of sin is death; but the gift of God is eternal life, through Jesus Christ our Lord.

Unconverted persons are the slaves of the devil, and yield their members to be his instruments. He makes use of them as servants to his uncleanness and unrighteousness; and they do things in the dark of which they would be ashamed even in the eyes of men. They do not bear in mind that God sees all things; and they do not feel how deplorable it is that their precious soul, which should be the temple of the Holy Ghost, is the dwelling place of Satan, and that their mem-bers, which God has gloriously fashioned to be instruments of good, are employed in the service of iniquity. But "the end of those things is death"; that is to say, eternal perdition and separation from God. They who serve the prince of death receive their reward of him; and he has nothing but death with which to reward them. Doleful service, and dreadful reward! In the mean time the devil deceives his servants with dreams of splendor, and teaches them to declaim about liberty. — Now, if the slaves of sin serve the devil in all uncleanness and in-iquity, shall not the faithful serve the Lord in all holiness and truth? Your whole conduct shall bear witness that you have been made free from sin, and are become a servant of God. The rightousness in your heart shall hold sway over all your members. Your eyes shall never more be used in the service of lust, your ears shall close themselves against uncleanness and falsehood, your tongue shall speak only that which is good and true, and your hands shall always do justice and mercy. Then though your members shall be weak and expiring, they yet are imperishable. Your pure eyes shall see God in eternal light; your tongue, which now speaks the Lord's praise, shall sing the song of the Lamb in heaven; your hands, which here have been used in chari-table service,shall pick the fruits off the tree of life in the new Jerusalem. All is pure grace. You are made free from sin; this is grace. You are the servant of God; this is grace. You shall reap in due season, if you faint not; what is this but the grace of God? In the Lord's house everything is liberty, everything is grace, none is a hireling, all are children, all is a free gift of mercy, and all is received as such. Without are the servants of self-righteousness as well as the slaves of vice. Death is the "wages," that is the reward and pay, of sin; "but the gift of God is eternal life through Jesus Christ our Lord." This last is *not* a re-ward, but a gift of *mercy*.

God, give us thy Spirit. Where he is, there is liberty, there is love, there is holiness. Give us these gifts, we heartily beseech thee, mercifully hear us, for Jesus' sake. Amen.

These lively hopes we owe To Jesus' dying love: We would adore his grace below, And sing his power above.

Dear Lord, accept the praise Of these our humble songs, Till tunes of nobler sound we raise With our immortal tongues.

---

300. Monday after Seventh Sunday after Trinity.

Lord, in thy light let us see light. Amen.

Psalm 37, 1–6. A Psalm of David. Fret not thyself because of evildoers, neither be thou envious against the workers of iniquity: for they shall soon be cut down like the grass, and wither as the green herb. Trust in the Lord, and do good: so shalt thou dwell in the land, and verily thou shalt be fed. Delight thyself also in the Lord; and he shall give thee the desires of thine heart. Commit thy way unto the Lord; trust also in him, and he shall bring it to pass: and he shall bring forth thy righteousness as the light, and thy judgment as the noonday.

Heed these words. Do not envy others their good fortune, and do not fret yourself because of the happiness of evildoers; for they shall soon be cut down like the grass, and wither as the green herb. Trust in the Lord; build on him with *full* confidence; let nothing induce you to leave this immovable rock. "Ye who fear the Lord, trust in the good unto eternal joy and mercy. Look to the generations of old: Who hath believed in the Lord, and been deceived? Who hath abided in the fear of the Lord, and been forsaken? or who hath called to him, and been despised of him?" Do good to them that vex you; then you have gained a victory over the devil, who wanted to shake your trust in God, and make you also a thorny bramble. — Dwell in the land, and verily thou shalt be fed. Do not let your heart cling to any spot of earth, nor do you allow this to become a cause of unseemly strife; remember Abraham and Lot. But neither should you leave your paternal acres, merely because they require labor of you. Dwell with God, and enjoy his faithful care. Let this be your rule, not to be moving restlessly from place to place, unless the Lord clearly indicates it as his will; for it is a great comfort to know: Here God has placed me, and here I live on his bounty. — In the following verses the Holy Spirit points out how we may without fail secure to ourselves a life of happiness: Delight thyself also in the Lord, and he shall give thee the desires of thine heart. His will, your will; his love, your joy. "Where shall I find comfort in my sore need and distress? Shall I ever be happy and satisfied? Yes; all that is necessary is this, that you make your will conform to the will of Jesus." Commit thy way unto the Lord; trust also in him; and he shall bring it to pass. This is a glorious command and promise. Do like the child that is being taken through a dark room: Clasp the arms tightly around the Fathers neck, and feel safe. Commit your way, your all to the Lord. Let the troubles and difficulties of your life fall upon him: all the mountains of care weigh-

ing on your heart; commit all to the Lord, and he shall take everything on his shoulders, and carry you and all your burdens. He shall
bring forth your righteousness as the noonday. It shall be *made plain*
that he does not forget his own, when they walk in darkness. "Even
here he shall justify them before the face of all men; but the promise
shall be fulfilled in its entirety on that day, when the saints shall shine
as the sun and as the stars of heaven for ever and ever." Dear reader,
obey now the words of the Psalmist, and be happy!

Help us, Lord, to trust in thee, and to find delight and rest in thy
will. How blessed were we, could we but with childlike confidence
commit ourselves to thee. Help us to do it, dear Lord God. Help us
to commit our way unto thee, and to believe, nothing doubting, that
thou shalt bring it to pass. Amen.

What our Father does is well: Shall the willful heart rebel, If a blessing
he withhold In the field, or in the fold? Is he not himself to be All our store
eternally?

What our Father does is well: Though he sadden hill and dell, Upward
yet our praises rise For the strength his word supplies. He has called us
sons of God: Can we murmur at his rod?

---

301. Tuesday after Seventh Sunday after Trinity.

Let the beauty of the Lord our God be upon us. Amen.

1 Kings 17, 12–16. And she said, As the Lord thy God liveth, I have not
a cake, but a handful of meal in a barrel, and a little oil in a cruse: and, behold, I am gathering two sticks, that I may go in and dress it for me and my
son, that we may eat it, and die. And Elijah said unto her, Fear not; go, and
do as thou hast said: but make me thereof a little cake first, and bring it unto
me, and after make for thee and for thy son. For thus saith the Lord God
of Israel, The barrel of meal shall not waste, neither shall the cruse of oil fail,
until the day that the Lord sendeth rain upon the earth. And she went, and
did according to the saying of Elijah; and she, and he, and her house, did eat
many days. And the barrel of meal wasted not, neither did the cruse of oil
fail, according to the word of the Lord, which he spake by Elijah.

This widow believed the words of the Lord spoken to her by Elijah; therefore she did according to the saying of Elijah, and experienced the fulfilment of his promise. She took the last meal and oil
that she had, and made thereof a cake for Elijah, in order that she
might thereafter prepare food for herself and son out of the barrel and
cruse, in which nothing remained. She may possibly as yet have been
without a living knowledge of sin, and it may not have been awakened
in her until the death of her son; or it may be that her heavy trials
were means by which the Lord gave her a more hearty penitence and
a deeper knowledge of self; — be this as it may, we see at least that
even here, on this occasion of her first meeting with the prophet, she
bows to the word of God with humble faith in his power and providence, and gives a beautiful proof of her faith by her charity and hospitality. Let us, dear Christians, learn a lesson of this widow. We

have not only one, but many promises in which the Lord says that he will provide for us all things needful. "Take no thought; your heavenly Father knoweth that ye have need of all these things. He who doth feed the fowls, and clothe the lilies, shall he not feed and clothe you?" "He that delivered up his own Son for us all, shall he not with him also freely give us all things?" Thus God himself speaks to us through his Son and his apostles; and we know that he is greater than Elijah. If you have but little, do not doubt that it shall be enough; do not hesitate to take of it, and divide with others who are in need of it; and it shall surely suffice and last till the rain come again with plenty. Our times, with the prevalent system of doing business and living on borrowed money, certainly have peculiar difficulties; but faith in the holy, living God is able to overcome them. Beware of contracting debts; and do not consume what the Lord has not given you. But beware still more of penuriousness; you do not need much for yourself, but you need much to invest at interest with the Lord.

Even as this widow was forced to marvel and smile every day when she drew on her unfailing supply of meal and oil, so shall it be in your case also. You shall see the wonders of the Lord in this, that the supply of meal in your barrel, water in your well, milk in your jar, and money in your purse, does not fail. Or have you not had occasion to wonder at the way in which the Lord provides for you? Do not angel hands set a table before you every day? You have gone to your table many thousand times, and had many of the brethren as your guests, and yet there is food remaining; and I am ready to risk something on the prophecy that, no matter how long you live, your loaf will outlast your life. — It may be that the widow in our text gradually came to regard the Lord's miracle as a simple matter of course; until she was recalled to herself by the death of her son and by the miracle of bringing him back to life. Salt and fire also are among the necessities of our existence.

Lord, again we pray thee, teach us to accept our bread from thy hand, to serve it out to others, and to partake of it ourselves with joy and thanksgiving. Amen.

Wait on the Lord, my heart, in meekness And cheerful hope; be thou content To get whate'er thy Father's kindness And all-discerning love hath sent; Doubt not that all thy wants are known To him who chose thee for his own.

---

302. Wednesday after Seventh Sunday after Trinity.

Lord, teach us to believe in thy goodness and mercy. Amen.

Psalm 145, 14–21. The Lord upholdeth all that fall, and raiseth up all those that be bowed down. The eyes of all wait upon thee; and thou givest them their meat in due season. Thou openest thine hand, and satisfiest the desire of every living thing. The Lord is righteous in all his ways, and holy in all his works. The Lord is nigh unto all them that call upon him, to all that call upon him in truth. He will fulfil the desire of them that fear him: he also will hear their cry, and will save them. The Lord preserveth all them that love him: but all the wicked will he destroy. My mouth shall speak the praise of the Lord; and let all flesh bless his holy name for ever and ever.

"Great is the Lord, and greatly to be praised; and his greatness is unsearchable. The Lord is gracious, and full of compassion; slow to anger, and of great mercy. The Lord is good to all; and his tender mercies are over all his works." His goodness attracts all creatures to him. As the flowers all turn toward the sun, so do the eyes of all turn to the Lord. As the children stand around the mother, and eye her hand, so all creatures stand around the Lord, and wait upon his bounteous hand. The wicked only, together with the devils, turn away from the Lord. They live of his bounty; but they receive it with evil and cold hearts, and do not give him thanks. The heart of the Lord is as full of kindness to us, as his munificent hand is full of good gifts. As a spring pours out its water year after year and century after century, and yet has as copious a supply as ever, so the goodness of the Lord is from everlasting to everlasting. Take of it, and enjoy it; drink, and give others to drink with you. It is his great delight to do us good, to cheer our hearts, and to satisfy our desire. "Fear thou not; let not thine hands be slack. The lord thy God in the midst of thee is mighty; he will save, he will rejoice over thee with joy; he will rest in his love, he will joy over thee with singing." (Zeph. 3, 16. 17). — "But why, then, is he often so hard with me? Or how shall I draw in abundance out of his fountain when I see it empty before my eyes? It often seems to me that he makes sport of me most unmercifully, gives me something of which I am fond, and then robs me of it at the moment when I love it most dearly; leads me forward, but only to make me more sensible of my loss when he thrusts me back again; shows me a good way out of a difficulty, and then closes it before me when I am about to make use of it." My dear friend; do not find fault with God, but with your own sin and unbelief. If you needed nothing more than temporal happiness, the Lord would give you this in abundance; if it were a good thing for you to become great and rich and to fare sumptuously every day, you might complain of the Lord, who does not bring this about. But such things would not be good for you. If you had free scope, you would lose everything; but if the Lord be allowed to have command, — the command over your heart also, — you shall eternally possess and enjoy all things. When he denies you an earthly wish, or seems to deal harshly with you, he does this either that you may repent, or, if you are already his child, that you may die to the things which are corruptible, and live in those which are of heaven. No; the stream of God is not empty; it is full of water. That branch of it also which contains temporal blessings runs full at your feet; and there would be nothing to prevent you from taking what you need, and giving to others also, were you not wanting in the faith of the widow of Sarepta! Seek *this faith* first of all, and God shall give it you. God is good to all; and his tender mercies are over all his works. This is most certainly true.

This truth do thou establish in our hearts, merciful God, for Jesus' sake. Amen.

The Lord is never far away, Forsakes his people never, He is their re-
iuge and their stay, Their peace and trust forever; And with a mother's watchful love He guides them wheresoe'er they rove: To God all praise and glory!

---

303. Thursday after Seventh Sunday after Trinity.

Teach us, O God, to make the proper use of thy exceeding great riches.

2 Corinthians 9, 8–11. And God is able to make all grace abound toward you; that ye, always having all sufficiency in all things, may abound to
every good work: (As it is written, He hath dispersed abroad; he hath given
to the poor: his righteousness remaineth for ever. Now he that ministereth
seed to the sower both minister bread for your food, and multiply your sown,
and increase the fruits of your righteousness;) being enriched in every thing
to all bountifulness, which causeth through us thanksgiving to God.

When the pious Francke, the founder of the Orphans' home in
Halle, had just begun his work of giving bodily and spiritual assistance to all manner of poor children, he sat one day talking with his
wife about means of obtaining the wherewithal for the prosecution of
the work. Being in perplexity he opened the Bible which lay before
him, and his eyes fell on these words: "And God is able to make all
grace abound toward you; that ye, always having all sufficiency in
all things, may abound to every good work; as it is written: He hath
dispersed abroad; he hath given to the poor; his righteousness remaineth for ever." "*Yes*," said he to himself, "*God* is able to do it;
and he will do it." Shortly afterward, when a letter was brought to
him, he thought: Here is a contribution, no doubt. His heart was
happy, and he opened the letter; alas, it was from a poor father who
complained that he and his family were in bitter want, and on the
verge of starvation. With heavy heart Francke laid the letter aside,
and repeated the words of scripture: "God is able to give you abundantly to every good work." But the passage would not comfort him.
He then entered his chamber, and reminded the Lord of his promise,
wrestling like Jacob with the Almighty; and came out to his wife with
a face radiant with happiness. He now saw his way clear, and it did
not fail him.

Let it be your sorrow, dear reader, that there is so much of distress in
the world; but do not let it be an idle sorrow of which nothing comes.
Of a truth, "God is able to make all grace abound toward us; that we,
always having all sufficiency in all things, may abound to every good
work." It is "God" who is to do it; he is "able"; he is rich enough
to give us all things. He does it of his "grace"; and thus your sin shall
not hinder him. God is rich in his omnipotence; and thus he never
lacks the power to help. He is rich in mercy; and thus he never lacks
the will. He is rich in munificence, and never tires; and thus you shall
always have a sufficiency for yourself, and "abound to every good
work." Sow diligently; no other field is so fertile as that of beneficence, no other seed so prolific as that of mercy. Even here there
spring up out of it a thousand prayers of gratitude from the hearts of

them that give and them that receive; the hearts are strengthened, and made happy, and knit together in love, and the blessing of God is upon them. And in the next world you shall find your acts of charity springing up into an eternal harvest of joy.

Thanks be to God for his unspeakable gift! Thou who didst give us thine only Son, how shouldst thou not with him also freely give us all things? We heartily beseech thee, pour out the love of Jesus Christ in our hearts by thy Holy Spirit. Amen.

O may this bounteous God Through all our life be near us, With ever joyful hearts And blessed peace to cheer us; And keep us in his grace, And guide us when perplexed, And free us from all ills In this world and the next.

All praise and thanks to God, The Father, now be given, The Son, and Holy Ghost, Who reign in highest heaven, The one eternal God, Whom earth and heaven adore; For thus it was, is now, And shall be evermore.

---

304. Friday after Seventh Sunday after Trinity.

Lord, establish our hearts in righteousness and mercy before thy face. Amen.

Psalm 37, 21—26. The wicked borroweth, and payeth not again: but the righteous sheweth mercy, and giveth. For such as be blessed of him shall inherit the earth; and they that be cursed of him shall be cut off. The steps of a good man are ordered by the Lord; and he delighteth in his way. Though he fall, he shall not be utterly cast down: for the Lord upholdeth him with his hand. I have been young, and now am old; yet have I not seen the righteous forsaken, nor his seed begging bread. He is ever merciful, and lendeth; and his seed is blessed.

When this word of God declares that the wicked borroweth, and payeth not again, such men are especially meant as are careless about fulfilling their obligations, and contract debts without taking thought of the question whether or not they will be able to pay them. There is herein also a solemn warning to all Christians against all sorts of business and money entanglements by which they put themselves in the way of becoming swindlers. Do not live beyond your means. Let husband and wife agree that by the mercy of God they will avoid getting into debt. Let the man not demand more than he provides; and let the wife keep house in accordance with their income. I say this by way of friendly advice to all young women. Do not doubt that you will succeed, if you make the effort with prayer and earnestness. God always gives us a sufficiency, if we are frugal and generous; that is to say, generous with that which is our own; not generous, like the unfaithful steward, with that which belongs to others. And let it be said to the men: Fill your wife's hand with the fruits of your honest labor. Do not dabble in business for which you have neither the means, nor the requisite knowledge, and whereby you may easily come to grief, and make it necessary for others to pay your debts. You may not intend to defraud anybody; but if you go into such speculations that you find yourself unable to fulfil your obligations, this statement applies to your case also: "The wicked borroweth, and payeth not again." God's children, however, should on no account lay themselves open to such a charge. — "They that will be rich fall into temptation and a snare, and into many foolish and hurtful lusts, which drown men in destruction and perdition." (1 Tim. 6, 9). But they that fear the Lord, and practice justice, and do good, shall never want; they shall always have abundance, that they may be "ever merciful, and lend, and their seed be blessed." There is no blessing in the wealth which is acquired by stinginess, penuriousness, and usury; but neither is there any stability in the wealth which comes easily as a result of unsound and reckless undertakings. He, on the other hand, who with sincere piety plies his vocation, and supports himself honestly and faithfully, and does good; his steps shall be established by the Lord; he shall "inherit the earth, and delight himself in the abundance of peace." "Mark the perfect man, and behold the upright; for the end of that man is peace."

Preserve us, O God, from the snares of the world, and from the temptations and allurements of our own flesh. Mercifully prosper us in our vocation, that we always may have a sufficiency, and may abound to every good work. Give us a holy abhorrence of all fraud and injustice, and a holy desire to do good toward all men. May we and all who are of our household be a blessing. Amen.

Peace, prosperity, and health, Private bliss, and public wealth, Knowledge, with its gladdening streams, Pure religion's holier beams; Lord, for these our souls shall raise Grateful vows and solemn praise.
As thy prospering hand hath blest, May we give thee of our best, And by deeds of kindly love For thy mercies grateful prove; Singing thus through all our days Praise to God. immortal praise.

305. Saturday after Seventh Sunday after Trinity.

Lord, enlighten us, and establish our hearts in thy word. Amen.

Proverbs 30, 5-9. Every word of God is pure: he is a shield unto them that put their trust in him. Add thou not unto his words, lest he reprove thee, and thou be found a liar. Two things have I required of thee; deny me them not before I die; remove far from me vanity and lies; give me neither poverty nor riches; feed me with food convenient for me; lest I be full, and deny thee, and, say, Who is the Lord? or lest I be poor, and steal, and take the name of my God in vain.

Man was created with wisdom in his soul, and therefore it is a man's duty to be wise, But — we are all become fools; none knows God and his glorious works (Romans 3, 11). "The natural man receiveth not the things of the Spirit of God." Who and what is he, the great and eternal God, who created and upholds all things? "Who hath ascended up into heaven, or descended? who hath gathered the wind in his fists? who hath bound the waters in a garment? who hath established all the ends of the earth? what is his name, and what is his son's name, if thou canst tell?" No; of my own wisdom I can not tell; but the word of God has taught me the answer. "Every word of God is pure;" it is a clear glass, in which I see him reflected, and know him in so far as he opens my eyes. It is there I learn that the great almighty God has loved me, and that his Son Jesus Christ became man in order to save us. In this word I have a safe shield against falsehood and death. He, however, who does not believe understands nothing of this, and has no weapon against the devil. — In the word of God only can our soul find wisdom and strength; do not seek elsewhere, neither add anything to his words. Mix no alloy of human doctrine with the heavenly truth of God's word; this the Lord does not tolerate, as you thereby ruin yourself and others. Pray as did Agur: 1) "Remove far from me vanity and lies. 2) Give me neither poverty nor riches; feed me with food convenient for me."

1) Let the word of God govern your thoughts, your views in matters of faith, your purposes and plans, your words and deeds. Let the divine truth be the prop that sustains all your undertakings; think and do everything in humility and the fear of God according to the word of the Lord.

2) Guard against poverty; gather up the fragments, that nothing be lost; live contentedly and frugally, and do not use more than God has given you. Work with zeal and spirit; be industrious like the ant, and wise like the bee. At the same time, beware of desiring riches; for how hardly shall a rich man enter the kingdom of God! The temptations of poverty are great; but those of riches are greater. God shall deliver you from both. His word is a shield unto them that put their trust in him; for it teaches us to know the almighty Father in the Son, our Lord Jesus; and it gives us sonship with him in this world and in the next.

God, teach us to know the purity of thy word, and its power against the cares of this world and of mammon, as well as against all falsehood and every dogma of human invention. We heartily pray thee: Remove far from me vanity and lies. Give me neither poverty nor riches; feed me with food convenient for me. Amen.

Thy everlasting truth, Father, thy ceaseless love, Sees all thy children's wants, and knows What best for each will prove; And whatsoe'er thou will'st, Thou dost. O King of kings, What thy unerring wisdom chose, Thy power to being brings.

Thou everywhere hast sway, And all things serve thy might; Thy every act pure blessing is, Thy path unsullied light. When thou arisest, Lord, What shall thy work withstand? When all thy children want thou giv'st, Who, who shall stay thy hand?

---

306. Eighth Sunday after Trinity. I.

Lord, enlighten us, and lead us in the paths of truth. Amen.

Gospel Lesson, Matthew 7, 15–21. Beware of false prophets, which come to you in sheep's clothing, but inwardly they are ravening wolves. Ye shall know them by their fruits. Do men gather grapes of thorns, or figs of thistles? Even so every good tree bringeth forth good fruit; but a corrupt tree bringeth forth evil fruit. A good tree cannot bring forth evil fruit, neither can a corrupt tree bring forth good fruit. Every tree that bringeth not forth good fruit is hewn down, and cast into the fire. Wherefore by their fruits ye shall know them. Not every one that saith unto me, Lord, Lord, shall enter into the kingdom of heaven; but he that doeth the will of my Father which is in heaven.

It is of the highest importance to have the pure doctrine of God's word, without any admixture of falsehood and error. For false doctrine is poison to the soul; and if it enter the heart, it will kill our spiritual life. The pure word of God is mighty to regenerate us, and mighty to keep us in that living fellowship with the Lord, which causes us to grow into spiritual perfection. The gospel of Christ is "the power of God unto salvation to every one that believeth." When the light of God's holy love in the law and the gospel shines in your face, and by the operation of the Spirit, who is in it, enters your soul, you are humbled and bowed down in a heart-felt knowledge of sin; and then a living faith is kindled in you, and drives out the powers of darkness, and makes your heart a dwelling-place of the Holy Ghost. And when the same faithful Spirit makes all the time more clear to you the demands of the law and the gift of the gospel, and keeps the flesh under the discipline of the law, but preserves the spiritual life in the liberty of grace, then the new man is nourished and increases by the sincere milk of the word. But false doctrine; lies in the guise of truth; half truths; law without gospel, or gospel without law; the jumbling together of law and gospel, or the dissolving of both; rationalism and human precepts intermixed with the sacred truth of the word; — these things can not effect true conversion and a living faith; they do not guide the seeking soul rightly, nor nourish the life of grace; but their effect is either carnal security in sin, or spiritual bondage, or spiritual levity.

This is a question of eternal life or death; and hence the matter is one of the *highest* importance. The pure doctrine of God's word is the sun which shines on us, gives us warmth and life, and causes us to bring forth fruits of righteousness. It is more than important to have the word of God pure and undefiled; it is more than *very* important; it is of the very *highest and greatest* importance; there is nothing else so precious as the holy word of God. For this reason Jesus has taught us in the Lord's prayer to ask this blessing in the very first petition.

How, then, shall teachers and hearers learn to distinguish between truth and error? The holy scripture is the touch-stone on which all doctrine and life shall be tested. A doctrine which is taken from the Bible, and confirmed by the Bible, is true and pure; while that which is found wanting when put to this test is false. If any teach that Jesus is not the Son of God and true God, you know that such a teacher is a liar; for the Bible declares that Jesus is God's only begotten Son, and true God from eternity. If any teach that man is by nature good, but only somewhat weak, this is false doctrine; for scripture says that we are evil. If any teach that baptism is *merely* a bath in water, and a sign of the purification of the heart, you know from the Bible that he is in error; for it is written that baptism is "the washing of regeneration, and renewing of the Holy Ghost," that by it we "put on Christ," and that it "saves us." If any teach that man is justified by the law and its works, repudiate him as a false teacher; for scripture says that "by the deeds of the law there shall no flesh be justified." Or if any teach a scheme of faith without conversion and without sanctification, we have but to turn to the Bible to find that he is a liar. And thus with every article of the Christian faith. But if there be any who *seems* to teach the truth, but who leads an ungodly life, you shall beware of his example and carefully examine his teaching; for there may be poison in his fine words.

Holy Father, sanctify us through thy truth; thy word is truth. Amen.

Let thy holy word instruct us; Guide us daily by its light; Let thy love and grace constrain us To approve whate'er is right, Take thine easy yoke. and wear it, Strengthened with thy heavenly might.

Taught to lisp the holy praises Which on earth thy children sing, Both with lips and hearts unfeigned, May we our thank-offerings bring; Then with all the saints in glory Join to praise our Lord and King.

---

307. Eighth Sunday after Trinity. II.

Lord God, heavenly Father, give us the Spirit of truth, the Spirit of adoption, in our hearts. Amen.

Epistle Lesson, Romans 8, 12–17. Therefore, brethren, we are debtors, not to the flesh, to live after the flesh. For if ye live after the flesh, ye shall die: but if ye through the Spirit do mortify the deeds of the body, ye shall live. For as many as are led by the Spirit of God, they are the sons of God. For ye have not received the spirit of bondage again to fear; but ye have received the Spirit of adoption, whereby we cry, Abba, Father. The Spirit itself beareth witness with our spirit, that we are the children of God: And if children, then heirs; heirs of God, and joint-heirs with Christ; if so be that we suffer with him, that we may be also glorified together.

Glorious estate of grace! Children of God, free from the guilt of sin, free from the dominion of the fleshly lusts, free from death; — everywhere surrounded by God's love; heirs of eternal life! But let none deceive himself, and imagine that he is in this estate, when he it not. Let none dream that he is a child of God, while he continues to live after the flesh. How can he be a child of God who lives in anger and enmity, uncleanness, drunkenness, gluttony, covetousness, or other such deeds of the flesh? How shall he who is made free, and is dead to sin, live any longer therein? However, while none must dream of sonship and the right of inheritance with God, except he have a true and living faith in our Lord Jesus; the faithful shall, on the other hand, have the full assurance that they are children of the heavenly Father. Our sonship may be known in this, that we have a new and childlike mind which is of heaven, and that God's own Spirit bears witness with our Spirit. If I were not born of God, I could not have the mind and spirit of a child of God; for of myself I am carnal, sold under sin. This spirit of a child of God expresses itself in a determined struggle against the lusts of the flesh, in grief because of them, and victory over them; and furthermore in simple and trusting prayer to God, to whom we from our innermost soul cry, Abba, Father; thus praying the Lord's Prayer from the bottom of our hearts. I pray to God not reluctantly, but gladly. (I here speak of my inner man, not of the flesh; not of the "law of sin in my members, warring against the law of my mind"). I do not stand trembling with a bad conscience before the righteous God; but happy and of good cheer in Christ, I speak to him in regard to the extension of his kingdom, and in regard to my own sin and distress and all my concerns, and praise him for his ineffable mercy. In harmony with this testimony of the Spirit in me, *the Spirit himself* testifies for me through the word and sacraments. The word of God confirms itself to my heart as being true and living; and I find my own inner man reflected in the word. Or, to express the same idea in other words, the Spirit in the word, with his demands and promises, is identical with the Spirit in my new life. The Spirit that dwells in me is the Spirit of faith and charity and hope; and this is precisely the Spirit in the word and sacraments. The Spirit in my heart is the Spirit of purity and of adoption to sonship, which wars against the flesh, and overcomes it, and cries, Abba, Father; and this is the very same Spirit that is in the word. Nay, it is through the word and sacraments that I have received the Spirit; he has permeated and sanctified my spirit, and given it of his divine nature; and thus it is the very Spirit of God that bears witness in me and with me, that I am a child of God. Blessed sonship, giving free access to the Father! Blessed hope of life, to be followed by heavenly glory!

Give us grace, then, dear heavenly Father, to lead saintly lives, and to suffer with patience in the fellowship of our Lord Jesus. Let thy Spirit bear witness with us in life and death that we are thy children; and let our life and our death bear witness before all the world that thy Spirit dwells in us, and gives us the assurance that there awaits us a heavenly heritage of glory. Amen.

O Holy Ghost, thou precious Gift, Thou Comforter unfailing, O'er Satan's snares our souls uplift, And let thy power availing Avert our woes and calm our dread: For us the Savior's blood was shed: We trust in thee to save us.

---

308. Monday after Eighth Sunday after Trinity.

Lord, guide us on the right way to the life everlasting. Amen.

Matthew 7, 12–14. Therefore all things whatsoever ye would that men should do to you, do ye even so to them: for this is the law and the prophets. Enter ye in at the strait gate: for wide is the gate, and broad is the way, that leadeth to destruction, and many there be which go in thereat: Because strait is the gate, and narrow is the way, which leadeth unto life; and few there be that find it.

Our own will must die, our flesh and blood be mortified. First they must receive their mortal hurt in our regeneration; and thereafter they must every day be nailed more firmly to the cross. For the unbridled thoughts of our self-conceit are wholly opposed to the truth, and the carnal desire of our wilfulness is directly contrary to charity.

Your own opinion of yourself is a flat contradiction of the word of God; and your own will is the exact reverse of the holy will of God. You think that there is no God; or that, if there be one, he is either careless, and winks at everything; or cruel, and thirsts for our blood. You think concerning yourself that you are righteous, if you only do your best; and you imagine that salvation is sensual enjoyment. Your delight is in the earthly things, and your will is selfishness and evil inclinations. Such thoughts are lies, and such a will is sin; therefore the old man must die, and both thoughts and will become new. The teaching of the word concerning the living, holy, just, and yet unutterably loving and merciful God; concerning your sin and unrighteousness; concerning the grace of God in Christ, and justification by faith; concerning the mystery of the new birth, and the work of the Spirit in the sanctification of the faithful; — in short, the truth in Christ, must be apprehended by you in such a way that you accept it with willing heart, and hold it fast in life and death, knowing in your soul that it is more sure than all things else. And that to which your carnal mind is an entire stranger must become true in you, and govern your life and conduct; this namely, to love God above all things, and your neighbor as yourself. To know one's self as wicked and lost; to bend thought and will in submission to the word of God; to receive mercy for everything, and to believe without seeing; to lose righteousness and piety and life, in order to become righteous and have life and salvation in Christ; to know nothing and have nothing of one's self, but to have all things in Jesus; — this is the strait gate which few find. And in daily repentance to live of God's grace alone; to deny one's own will, and joyfully practice charity for his sake, in spite of the resistance of the flesh; always to mortify one's wilfulness, and patiently follow the Lord, and carry the cross; — this is the narrow way which few find. Do you follow this way, dear reader? God himself works in us both to will and to do; and thus the impossible becomes possible by his grace. — Or do you walk with the many on the broad way to destruction? Do it no more! Quit the broad way now, for Jesus' sake!

Lord God, thou who hast opened to us the gate of life in thy Son, our Lord Jesus; lead us through this gate, that he may become to us the way, the truth, and the life. Amen.

Onward therefore, pilgrim brothers! Onward, with the cross our aid! Bear its shame and fight its battle, Till we rest beneath its shade! Soon shall come the great awaking, Soon, the rending of the tomb, Then, the scattering of all shadows, And the end of toil and gloom.

---

309. Tuesday after Eighth Sunday after Trinity.

Let the pure doctrine of thy holy word shine like the sun among us. Amen.

Romans 4, 1–8. What shall we then say that Abraham, our father as pertaining to the flesh, hath found? For if Abraham were justified by works, he hath whereof to glory; but not before God. For what saith the scripture? Abraham believed God, and it was counted unto him for righteousness. Now-to him that worketh is the reward not reckoned of grace, but of debt. , But to him that worketh not, but believeth on him that justifieth the ungodly, his faith is counted for righteousness. Even as David also describeth the blessedness of the man, unto whom God imputeth righteousness without works, saying, Blessed are they whose iniquities are forgiven, and whose sins are covered. Blessed is the man to whom the Lord will not impute sin.

That man is justified by faith, without the works of the law, is the most important article of our creed; and it is absolutely necessary that we hold it fast in our fight against sin, death, and devil. Let the grand words of scripture which we have just heard strengthen our faith and gladden our heart. — "Abraham believed God, and it was counted unto him for righteousness." In his comments on the Epistle to the Romans Besser writes: "Abraham grasped the promise of mercy in Christ with sincere faith, and the judgment of God concerning him was: 'Because of his faith he is counted righteous in my sight.' God gives grace only; and when I accept grace only, I am justified. That in which Abraham excelled was this, that he neither looked back for works by which he might have merited the promised great reward, nor looked forward for works by which he might supplement the grace offered him, but simply 'believed on him that justifieth the ungodly.' Then he was so entirely stripped of all his own, so entirely without reliance in his own strength, that God could deal with him according to his riches of his grace, and count his faith unto him for righteousness. Note this carefully. — Although the faith of Abraham, by which he placed himself in the right relation toward God, is a spiritual act, wrought by the Holy Ghost and pleasing to God, still it is not a perfect act, as Abraham is still in the flesh. To be sure, he gave God all honor, rejoiced in him, and trusted in him; but he did not do these things in a degree worthy of the majesty of God. Strictly speaking, then, his faith was not his righteousness, but was *counted* unto him for perfect righteousness, for the reason that God was pleased with it for Christ's sake. 'Christian righteousness,' says Luther, 'depends, firstly, on faith, which accords to God the honor belonging to him; and secondly, on this, that God counts such a faith unto us for righteousness. For as faith is weak and imperfect, — even the strongest faith, such as that of Abraham, having all sorts of infirmities, — the second part is necessary, namely that God counts our faith unto us for righteousness, and does not impute to us our other sins, but pardons them, and takes them away, as though not one of them had been committed; and this not for our sake, for any worthiness, merit, or work on our part, but for the sake of Christ, in whom we believe. A Christian is therefore both a righteous man and a sinner; he loves and worships God, and at the same time he may be angry and vexed with him. — But, say you, how is it possible that I can be righteous, and yet be a sinner? Well, your sense and knowledge of your sin are good signs; therefore you shall not despair, but rather thank God. Go to Christ; he is the true physician; this is his name. He can and will heal the bruised hearts, and give poor sinners salvation. Do not, on your life, follow the prejudices of your own reason, which would have you to believe that the

Lord is at war with needy sinners. Mortify and sacrifice your reason which gives you such a suggestion ; but believe in him, and cry to him, and you shall become holy and righteous. Then you praise God, and confess that he is very God, the just and merciful. Whatever sins you may still have, they are, then, not imputed to you, but are forgiven for Christ's sake. His perfect righteousness is yours, and your sins are his.' "

O God, imprint this blessed article of faith indelibly on our soul ; and let us be of those blessed people whose transgressions are forgiven, and in whose spirit there is no guile. Amen.

Blest is the man to whom the Lord Imputes not his iniquities, He pleads no merit of reward, And not on works, but grace relies.

From guile his heart and lips are free, His humble joy, his holy fear, With deep repentance well agree, And join to prove his faith sincere.

How glorious is that righteousness That hides and cancels all his sins! While a bright evidence of grace Through his whole life appears and shines.

---

310. Wednesday after Eighth Sunday after Trinity.

Lord, let thy word penetrate to the very marrow of our bones. Amen.

Ezekiel 3, 17–21. Son of Man, I have made thee a watchman unto the house of Israel: therefore hear the word at my mouth, and give them warning from me. When I say unto the wicked, Thou shalt surely die; and thou givest him not warning, nor speakest to warn the wicked from his wicked way, to save his life; the same wicked man shall die in his iniquity; but his blood will I require at thine hand. Yet if thou warn the wicked, and he turn not from his wickedness, nor from his wicked way, he shall die in his iniquity; but thou hast delivered thy soul. Again, When a righteous man doth turn from his righteousness, and commit iniquity, and I lay a stumblingblock before him, he shall die: because thou hast not given him warning, he shall die in his sin, and his righteousness which he hath done shall not be remembered; but his blood will I require at thine hand. Nevertheless, if thou warn the righteous man, that the righteous sin not, and he doth not sin, he shall surely live, because he is warned; also thou hast delivered thy soul.

It is our *duty* to say to the unconverted : "You are on the way to eternal death. We dare not fail to warn you; for in that case we would be responsible for the loss of your soul. *If you do not repent,* you can not be saved. Your life in the service of sin leads you to hell; and you must by no means imagine that you will be saved. The devil will hold you in fancied security, and give you hope; but the word of God makes it plain that you must come to grief in eternity. How should the *righteous* God spare the obstinate sinners? He would then be unjust, as they are! Or how can the ungodly and worldly-minded be received into his *holy* heaven? In that case heaven would become the home of wickedness! Understand this, that it is the devil, not God, who gives you hope of salvation in the midst of your impenitence. Bear in mind that this hope is false, and will rob you of eternal happiness! Alas, man you who were created for heavenly glory and eternal life in communion with God; will *you* for the sake of a little sordid and unclean enjoyment, lasting but a short time, plunge yourself into endless misery? *You shall be cast into everlasting fire,* if you do not betimes turn to the Lord your God!"

This shall be said to you with all the emphasis and clearness possible; else we were false prophets and the servants of the devil. But it is not to be said as a mere matter of duty; even a hireling in the house of God might do that much. But it shall be spoken out of a heart which cares for you, and feels sincere pity for you; out of *his* love who gave his life and blood for you. When I put myself in your place, as you are weighed down with the fetters of Satan, and drag your heavy way as fast as possible to perdition, approaching ever nearer to the verge of the eternal pit without seeing it, blind to your misery and a stranger to your God, who loves you, and has a heaven full of salvation for you; — my bosom burns, and I can not hold my peace. I am forced to cry out: "Repent; turn to the Lord! Go no farther on that way; stop, for Jesus' sake, and save your soul! Do you not see the danger? Do you not feel that you are unhappy? Wait upon the Lord, hear his voice, and return to your God." — I will take you out of the devil's power; by means of the word of life I will set you free from the enchantment, tear you by the power of the Spirit out of the assassin's hands, and carry you to Jesus, and place you in his arms. — Repent, and you shall be saved; come, and remain on the path of righteousness, and you shall live!

I should myself be lost, did I not warn you. You must die in your iniquity, and be eternally lost, if you do not repent; but the Lord would require your soul at my hand, if I did not warn you; and what could I answer him? Do turn to the Lord, and continue on the path of righteousness, that you may live!

Lord, thou great and good Shepherd of Israel; give us a heart after thee, give us of thy Spirit the mind of a true shepherd and the tongue of a true prophet. Lord, convert and save the erring, for the sake of Jesus Christ; and keep the righteous from falling again into sin. Amen.

Rescue the perishing, care for the dying, Snatch them in pity from sin and the grave; Weep o'er the erring ones, lift up the fallen, Tell them of Jesus, the mighty to save. Though they are slighting him, still he is waiting, Waiting the penitent child to receive; Plead with them earnestly, plead with them gently: He will forgive, if they only believe.

311. Thursday after Eighth Sunday after Trinity.

Lord, let thy word of truth light us onward on the true way of faith. Amen.

1 John 4, 1–4. Beloved, believe not every spirit, but try the spirits whether they are of God: because many false prophets are gone out into the world. Hereby know ye the Spirit of God: Every spirit that confesseth that Jesus Christ is come in the flesh, is of God: And every spirit that confesseth not that Jesus Christ is come in the flesh, is not of God: and this is that spirit of antichrist, whereof ye have heard that it should come; and even now already is

ut in the world. Ye are of God, little children, and have overcome them: because greater is he that is in you, than he that is in the world.

"Beware of false prophets," says the Lord. And here the apostle admonishes us, saying: "Believe not every spirit, but try the spirits whether they are of God; because many false prophets are gone out into the world." Love is kindly and trusting; it thinks no evil; it believes all things, and hopes all things, and puts the most charitable construction on everything; but at the same time it is watchful, and sensitive as the eye, against that which is false and wicked. And how very necessary this is! We must by no means think ourselves secure; but be alive to the fact that the shafts of falsehood are everywhere whistling about our ears. The devil allows himself no rest; wherever the word of God is preached he is always on hand to pour his venom into the hearts, sometimes as one who appeals to our reason, and sometimes as our sympathetic friend. And, unfortunately, he does not lack servants; there are many enough who are more than willing to do his errands.

In our text the Holy Ghost gives us a sure token by which we may know the antichrists: "Every spirit that confesseth not that Jesus Christ is come in the flesh is not of God." That is to say; he is a false prophet who does not teach that Jesus Christ is true God and true man in one person. On the other hand, "every spirit that confesseth that Jesus Christ is come in the flesh is of God." That is: He who teaches, and confirms it by his life, that Jesus is the Son of God is a servant of God; for "no man can say that Jesus is the Lord, but by the Holy Ghost."

Usually the antichrists have sought to disguise themselves in the garb of one who imitates Christ; and they always profess to teach the true Christian religion in a new and purified form. In our times they come forward with shameless impudence, and openly deny the Father and the Son, and have the effrontery to call *this* advanced Christianity! 'The old faith is obsolete, away with it; away with that old trumpery! The new age needs a new faith." Now, you know, dear Christians, what manner of spirit this is. It is fortunate that Saint John has given us an unmistakable mark by which the antichrists may be known. Everything which wants to do away with the old articles of faith, "the dogmas," as they call them; the doctrine concerning the Son of God, and the atoning power of his blood; — is in truth the voice of the antichrist. — These people imagine that the future is theirs; and in a sense this is but too true. We do not expect good and bright times. Nevertheless, John says: "Ye are of God, little children, and have overcome them; because greater is he that is in you, than he that is in the world." The victory shall, then, be yours at the last. "Be ye therefore wise as serpents, and harmless as doves;" be kind and charitable, but watchful and earnest. Walk in the light everywhere as children of light. Have no fellowship with the antichrists!

O God, let thy light and thy truth be with us; let them guide us to thy holy hill and thy habitations Keep us on the evil day; help us to stand steadfast against all the assaults of falsehood, and always to speak the truth in love. Amen.

Oh, keep us in thy word, we pray; The guile and rage of Satan stay; Unto thy church grant, Lord, thy grace, Peace, concord, patience, fearlessness.

A trusty weapon is thy word, Thy church's buckler, shield and sword; Lord, let us by this word abide, That we may seek no other guide.

312. Friday after Eighth Sunday after Trinity.

God, remember thy congregation, which thou hast purchased of old; the rod of thine inheritance, which thou hast redeemed. Amen.

Micah 3, 5-12. Thus saith the Lord concerning the prophets that make my people err, that bite with their teeth, and cry, Peace: and he that putteth not into their mouths, they even prepare war against him: therefore night shall be unto you, that ye shall not have a vision; and it shall be dark unto you, that ye shall not divine; and the sun shall go down over the prophets, and the day shall be dark over them. Then shall the seers be ashamed, and the diviners confounded: yea, they shall all cover their lips; for there is no answer of God. But truly I am full of power by the Spirit of the Lord, and of judgment, and of might, to declare unto Jacob his transgression, and to Israel his sin. Hear this, I pray you, ye heads of the house of Jacob, and princes of the house of Israel, that abhor judgment, and pervert all equity. They build up Zion with blood, and Jerusalem with iniquity. The heads thereof judge for reward, and the priests thereof teach for hire, and the prophets thereof divine for money; yet will they lean upon the Lord, and say, Is not the Lord among us? none evil can come upon us. Therefore shall Zion for your sake be plowed as a field, and Jerusalem shall become heaps, and the mountain of the house as the high places of the forest.

The nation is unhappy which has covetous, lying teachers and unjust magistrates. Such teachers and rulers are in themselves a punishment from God, and they call down upon the people new judgments of his wrath. When people have the pure word of God, and will not hear it; when they have a good and just government, and yet are dissatisfied; God sends them false prophets and wicked magistrates. Under the lash of these hard masters it may happen that the people humble themselves; but as a rule there is awakened in them a servile mind or a spirit of rebellion. Worse, however, than a bad government are the false teachers with their lies, which are deadly poison to the souls. When people are not disciplined by earnest teachers with the unadulterated word of God, the result will be the springing up and increase of unbelief and wordliness with their accompaniment of contentions, bitterness, strife, envy, sensuality, and lasciviousness; and with it all the most dreadful feeling of security, and under these circumstances a nation is sick unto death. The threats uttered by the Lord in our text have been fulfilled to the letter on the Jewish people, as a warning to us.

Though a worldly-minded clergy and unjust magistrates are

God's scourge on a people, this does not in any sense justify their wickedness. Even if they have been sent as a punishment for the wickedness of the people, they have no excuse. It were well, if we ministers and teachers would seriously consider, that there exist no men more wretched than the spiritual hirelings, who for money and favor sell their convictions, nay the divine truth itself, and with it the temporal and eternal welfare of the souls whose salvation the Lord has committed to their charge. Alas, many a servant of the Lord, who started out with the ardor of youth and holy zeal, has had his earnestness and vigor choked by the cares of this world. Let us all watch and be on our guard against ourselves, and let none think that he is beyond the reach of this temptation. This feeling of security may be that "peace" of which the prophet speaks in our text. But all who wish to remain faithful shall surely receive the requisite mercy from the Lord. "I am full of power by the spirit of the Lord, and of judgment, and of might, to declare unto Jacob his transgression, and to Israel his sin." As compared herewith, what are gold and honor, private gain and popular favor? Here are truth and right and the eternal salvation of the souls. Come, now, to our assistance, you believers! Let us strengthen one another, and lift one another's hands toward heaven. For the sake of God and your own salvation, fight and pray for us and with us, and be obedient to the word of God, that we may give an account with joy; not with grief, for this is not expedient for you.

Fill us, O God, with the power of thy Spirit, that we may march with victorious strength against the unbelief of the multitude and against the whole army of Satan. Lord, in mercy chasten us for our sins, that we humble ourselves; but do not take from us the joy and comfort of thy word and Spirit. Be gracious unto us, and bless our people, for Jesus' sake. Amen.

Those haughty spirits, Lord, restrain, That fain would o'er thy Christians reign, And e'er bring forth some fancies new, Devised to change thy statutes true.

And, as the cause and glory, Lord, Are thine, not ours, do thou afford Us help and strength and constancy; With all our heart we trust in thee.

---

313. Saturday after Eighth Sunday after Trinity.

God, open our hearts, and open our eyes, that we may know thee in Christ. Amen.

1 Timothy 6, 13-21. I give thee charge in the sight of God, who quickeneth all things, and before Christ Jesus, who before Pontius Pilate witnessed a good confession; that thou keep this commandment without spot, unrebukeable, until the appearing of our Lord Jesus Christ: which in his times he shall shew, who is the blessed and only Potentate, the King of kings, and Lord of lords; who only hath immortality, dwelling in the light which no man can approach unto; whom no man hath seen, nor can see: to whom be honor and power everlasting. Amen. Charge them that are rich in this world, that they be not highminded, nor trust in uncertain riches, but in the living God

who giveth us richly all things to enjoy; that they do good, that they be rich in good works, ready to distribute, willing to communicate; laying up in store for themselves a good foundation against the time to come, that they may lay hold on eternal life. O Timothy, keep that which is committed to thy trust, avoiding profane and vain babblings, and oppositions of science falsely so called; which some professing have erred concerning the faith. Grace be with thee. Amen.

"No man hath seen God at any time; the only begotten Son, which is in the bosom of the Father, he hath declared him." There is none other God than the God who has revealed himself in Christ; and there is no revelation of the true God, but in him. It is therefore of the utmost importance that we have the article of faith concerning Christ pure and undefiled. But it is equally important to accept this confession, preserve and keep it, believe it, and willingly obey it. For even if you have the teaching of Christ, and hold it to be true, God can not reveal himself to your soul, if you do not yield obedience to the truth; but if you in your heart obey the truth, God therein reveals himself to your spirit, and the light of eternity illumines you. Then you learn to know him to whom none can come but through the Son; you then have found the blessed and only Potentate, from whom all life and all power come; nay then you live in him, and he in you. He who does not believe in Christ does not know God; and they who do not know God in Christ dispute about who and what he is, or deny his existence, and declare their independence of every god; and yet they serve their own idol with the most abject servility of heart. They say that they are free; and they do not know that they are the slaves of corruptible things, and sacrifice their all on the altars of their false gods. He, on the other hand, who believes in Christ believes in the true and living God, knows him, has power over all idols, and is able to use all things to the glory of heaven. — Let the faithful show that they know the glorious God of love, and serve him! Let them show that they are the children of the heavenly Father, and are like him! Let the holy faith prove itself in their holy life, and bring forth fruit which is good in the sight of God and man! None but believing Christians can do that which is truly good; but neither can any be a true believer without doing good deeds. Use your belongings for the benefit of your neighbor, become rich in good works, and lay up for yourself a treasure in heaven!

Merciful and everlasting God, help us to believe in thee in Christ, to serve thee, and live our whole life in thee. Make us free from the world, and teach us to make it our servant in the work of reaching heaven. Amen.

Grant my mind and my affections Wisdom, counsel, purity, That I may be ever seeking Naught but that which pleases thee. Let thy knowledge spread and grow, And all error overthrow.

Lead me to green pastures, lead me By the true and living way; Shield me from each strong temptation, That might lead my heart astray; And if e'er my feet should turn, For each error let me mourn.

314. Ninth Sunday after Trinity. I.

Instruct us, Lord Jesus, thou heavenly wisdom. Amen.

Gospel Lesson, Luke 16, 1–9. And he said also unto his disciples, There was a certain rich man, which had a steward; and the same was accused unto him that he had wasted his goods. And he called him, and said unto him, How is it that I hear this of thee? give an account of thy stewardship; for thou mayest be no longer steward. Then the steward said within himself, What shall I do? for my lord taketh away from me the stewardship: I cannot dig; to beg I am ashamed. I am resolved what to do, that, when I am put out of the stewardship, they may receive me into their houses. So he called every one of his lord's debtors unto him, and said unto the first, How much owest thou unto my lord? And he said, A hundred measures of oil. And he said unto him, Take thy bill, and sit down quickly, and write fifty. Then said he to another, And how much owest thou? And he said, A hundred measures of wheat. And he said unto him, Take thy bill, and write fourscore. And the lord commended the unjust steward, because he had done wisely: for the children of this world are in their generation wiser than the children of light. And I say unto you, Make to yourselves friends of the mammon of unrighteousness; that, when ye fail, they may receive you into everlasting habitations.

In so far as he was unjust, this unfaithful steward is an example for our *warning;* but in so far as he was wise and resolute, he is still more an example for our *instruction and humiliation.*

In respect to the first point the parable teaches: *Remember that you shall give an account.* You have, to be sure, been made ruler over all that you have, things bodily and things spiritual; still nothing is yours, but all the Lord's; and you must use it according to his will, to his honor, and to the true benefit of yourself and your neighbor. Bear in mind that the time is short, and the responsibility heavy. Let the outcome of this faithless steward's wicked way rouse you betimes, that these words may not at last sound in your ears like the crack of doom: "Give an account of thy stewardship; for thou mayest be no longer steward."

In respect to the second point the parable teaches: *Be wise, and be quick to use your time and all that you have for the promotion of your eternal welfare.* This is the leading thought in the parable. See how wise and resourceful the children of the world are in their generation; how they make use of every opportunity, and how they sacrifice name and reputation, nay justice and conscience, in order to secure earthly advantages. Should not you, then, the children of *light,* be still more zealous to win the treasures of *eternity?* But the men of the world shame you! The unjust steward had but a little time remaining in which he could freely make disposition of the property committed to his charge; but he knew how to turn this short respite to his advantage. He treated his lord's debtors in such a way as that he might not be without friends when he was forced to leave the service. — The right use of the *earthly things* is the principal lesson which Jesus through this parable wants to teach his disciples. "Make to yourselves friends of the mammon of unrighteousness; that, when ye fail, they may receive you into everlasting habitations." Use the temporal things, to which there always adheres some measure of unrighteousness, and by which so many are robbed of true happiness; use them without stint in giving to your fellow mortals, whom Jesus has bought with his blood; with the simple trust that they are, or will become, children of God; for what you do unto them you do unto Jesus himself, and these perishable things are turned into eternal treasures of love and the bliss of fellowship in heaven.

The wisdom of Jesus as a teacher is incomparable. He teaches us to transform the mammon of unrighteousness into eternal and heavenly treasures. The mammon of unrighteousness! The name accurately expresses the thing; but Christ teaches us to use even this mammon in such a way that it is changed into true, precious, blessed wealth; and this he lets the unjust steward teach us by his example! To the world, what foolishness!

Lord Jesus, give us the wisdom and miraculous power of love; and let our whole life and all that we have be devoted to its service. Give us, needy paupers that we are, this wealth; and give us poor fools this wisdom. Amen.

As a shadow life is fleeting; As a vapor so it flies: For the bygone years retreating, Pardon grant, and make us wise;
Wise that we our days may number, Strive and wrestle with our sin; Stay not in our work nor slumber Till thy holy rest we win.

---

315. Ninth Sunday after Trinity. II.

God of Israel, be thou the God of our heart. Amen.

Epistle Lesson, 1 Corinthians 10, 6–13. Now these things were our examples, to the intent we should not lust after evil things, as they also lusted. Neither be ye idolaters, as were some of them; as it is written, The people sat down to eat and drink, and rose up to play. Neither let us commit fornication, as some of them committed, and fell in one day three and twenty thousand. Neither let us tempt Christ, as some of them also tempted, and were destroyed of serpents. Neither murmur ye, as some of them also murmured, and were destroyed of the destroyer. Now all these things happened unto them for ensamples: and they are written for our admonition, upon whom the ends of the world are come. Wherefore let him that thinketh he standeth take heed lest he fall. There hath no temptation taken you but such as is common to man: but God is faithful, who will not suffer you to be tempted above that ye are able; but will with the temptation also make a way to escape, that ye may be able to bear it.

" 'Be not idolaters,' says the apostle, and points to the warning example of the Israelites who 'sat down to eat and drink, and rose up to play.'

What does this 'eat and drink and play' have to do with the question of idolatry? In Exodus 32, from which chapter the passage is taken, the eating and drinking and playing had, to be sure, some connection with idolatry; for it was at the feast in honor of the golden calf that they ate, drank, and played. But when Paul wishes to warn against idolatry, would it not have been more reasonable to have made reference to the first seven verses of that chapter, in which an account is given of the golden calf itself and the sacrifice offered to it? Why does he emphasize this circumstance, that they *ate, drank, and played?* Well, there is a good reason for it. I have in mind the festivals of the living God in the Old Testament, when people were happy, and ate, and drank, and sang, and played in honor of the Lord. And, then again, I have in mind our festivals, Christmas and Easter and Pentecost, when people also eat and drink and enjoy themselves. They then appeal to the accounts in the Old Testament as a justification of their banquets and drinking bouts and games. 'There is no idolatry in it; they do only that which was done of old to the honor of God.' And yet by this means people are led astray!

It is true that the early Christians were in the habit of congregating and 'breaking bread' together, and allowing body and soul to rejoice in the living God. But these feasts were different from those in vogue among the Christians of the present day. Joy in the living God is not the modern fashion on festival occasions; say what you will, your conscience recognizes the distinction. Your eating and drinking degenerates into riotous living; and then you do not eat and drink as before God. You do not converse about the goodness of God and the love of Christ; but you forget God, and take his holy name in vain. And then, your sports, your songs and dances! I would on no account deny to any the right to indulge in innocent pleasure; but do not pretend that our customary sports and games are of an innocent character! — You commit *sin;* and this sin is the pleasure to which you look forward with joyful anticipation! You will not, I hope, seriously pretend to compare yourselves with the first Christians and the pious Israelites. In your hearts you will finally be forced to admit that you serve *the devil* on the festivals of *the Lord;* for God can have no pleasure in them. Then you are idolaters, and the words of Paul fit your case, when he says, in the first verse of our text, that 'these things were our examples.' Pray read the whole chapter, and weigh it well for your own good." (Loehe).

Merciful God, give us holy earnestness. Teach us to enjoy thy gifts with Christian temperance, and to have our joy in praising thee, and in having compassion on the needy. Amen.

No sinful word, no deed of wrong, No thoughts that idly rove, But simple truth be on our tongue, And in our heart be love.
And grant that to thine honor, Lord, Our daily toil may tend: That we begin it at thy word, And in thy favor end.

---

316. Monday after Ninth Sunday after Trinity.

God, avert from us the covetousness of the wicked; and give us the mercy of the righteous. Amen.

Proverbs 11, 23–25. The desire of the righteous is only good: but the expectation of the wicked is wrath. There is that scattereth, and yet increaseth·

and there is that withholdeth more than is meet, but it tendeth to poverty. The liberal soul shall be made fat: and he that watereth shall be watered also himself.

The word of God does not conceal from us that he who does good of an affectionate heart receives an abundant reward of the Lord in return, either in his own person or in his posterity; while he who accumulates illgotten wealth accumulates distress and misery for his children. It is a natural law that wealth insures against want, and that a great inheritance makes the children rich; but back of this is the other and deeper law that the blessing of God makes rich, and that our acts of charity are our children's best inheritance and safest livelihood. What is the fortune of the richest of the rich as compared with the Lord's ownership of earth and sea and air? Money and bonds will not satisfy hunger; they must be turned into food; and no rich man owns as much as the products of even one little country for a single year. The children of the rich, who divide their parents' infinitesimal little fraction of the perishable things of this earth, are wretchedly poor as compared with the children of the merciful man, who have access to all God's possessions, and who receive all that they need of his bounty. If you would become rich, and make your children rich; if you would have more than enough, whether you have much or little according to the world's way of measuring it, — and if you have an abundance with which to help others; then do you lend at interest to the Lord! As he lives, he shall pay you.

The word of God also says: "Let not thy left hand know what thy right hand doeth." And it tells of a widow who gave a farthing, which was more than the great sums given by the rich. He who gives much, *in order that* he may receive much in return, does not stretch out his hand to give, *but to take*. All depends on the heart. The heart opens, and the heart *closes* the hand, and it is to the attitude of the heart that reference is made when the Bible says: "He which soweth sparingly shall reap also sparingly; and he which soweth bountifully shall reap also bountifully. For God loveth a cheerful giver." Lord, be gracious unto us. Make of us liberal souls, which bless, and refresh, and become as an early rain. Amen.

That man in life wherever placed, Hath happiness in store, Who walks not in the wicked's way, Nor learns their guilty lore.
That man shall flourish like the trees Which by the streamlets grow; The fruitful top is spread on high, And firm the root below.

---

317. Tuesday after Ninth Sunday after Trinity.

O God, make us partakers of the heavenly riches of thy grace and love. Amen.

Luke, 12, 32–37. Fear not, little flock; for it is your Father's good pleasure to give you the kingdom. Sell that ye have, and give alms: provide yourselves bags which wax not old, a treasure in the heavens that faileth not, where no thief approacheth, neither moth corrupteth. For where your treasure is, there will your heart be also. Let your loins be girded about, and your lights burning; and ye yourselves like unto men that wait for their lord, when he will return from the wedding; that, when he cometh and knocketh, they may open unto him immediately. Blessed are those servants, whom the lord, when he cometh, shall find watching: verily I say unto you, that he shall gird himself, and make them to sit down to meat, and will come forth and serve them.

"It is your Father's *good pleasure* to give you the kingdom." He takes pleasure in it; it is his most earnest desire; it is his delight to save you, and he longs to have you with himself. Be of good cheer, then, thou little flock. Be willing to endure poverty and want on earth; beware of loving mammon; your heart possesses a much greater treasure, which you shall surely enjoy; for it is the Father's *good pleasure* to give you the kingdom. "This is a grand expression, sweet and strengthening to our poor and unbelieving heart, which so easily grows despondent. Shall not the almighty Father be able to bring about that which is the good pleasure of his will? You are, then, rich, and have treasures which no thief can reach, neither moth corrupt. Sell, then, that you have. This does not mean that you are to hold an auction, and turn all your property into money, and give it away; this would not necessarily bring you nearer the kingdom. But in your heart you shall sell that you have; let the heart rid itself of every earthly encumbrance. And give alms with hearty pleasure, whether you have much or little; be ready and willing to relinquish it all. Thus you have your treasure in heaven; thus your heart possesses that which God has given you in Christ, the glory of the kingdom of heaven. The hands of the poor are 'bags which wax·not old.' If we delight in filling them, we lay up treasures in heaven. But the treasures of heaven possessed by the heart, what are they but the living God himself, the heavenly fulness of love? Where your treasure is, there will your heart be also. As the bees in the flowers, thus our hearts in Christ. The heart of the Christian lives and is bound up, not in chests and storehouses; not in moneys and chattels; not in fine clothes and ornaments; not in house and farm, nor in family and friends; not in honors and high reputation; not in art and science, nor in any good things whatsoever of this earth; but in heaven, in the life eternal, in Jesus Christ."

Lord, teach us to gird about our loins; and to kindle our lights, and keep them burning. In mercy loose our hearts from all the treasures of the world. Be thou our life, our delight, and our salvation; and make us rich in charity and mercy. Amen.

Thine forever! Oh, how blest They who find in thee their rest; Savior, guardian, heavenly friend, Oh, defend us to the end.
Thine forever! Thou our guide, All our wants by thee supplied, All our sins by thee forgiven, Lead us, Lord, from earth to heaven.

318. Wednesday after Ninth Sunday after Trinity.

Prosper, O God, the work of our hands. Amen.

2 Thessalonians 3, 7-13. For yourselves know how ye ought to follow us: for we behaved not ourselves disorderly among you; neither did we eat any man's bread for nought; but wrought with labor and travail night and day, that we might not be chargeable to any of you: Not because we have not power, but to make ourselves an ensample unto you to follow us. For even when we were with you, this we commanded you, that if any would not work, neither should he eat. For we hear that there are some which walk among you disorderly, working not at all, but are busybodies. Now them that are such we command and exhort, by our Lord Jesus Christ, that with quietness they work, and eat their own bread. But ye, brethren, be not weary in well doing.

The *burden* of our earthly labor, which is a curse pronounced on man in punishment of sin, yet has, by the wisdom and mercy of God, been turned into a blessing for us Christians. "Idleness is the parent of vice." If you labor in your vocation in a Christian frame of mind, the labor helps to subdue the flesh, and strengthen the spirit; tame the sensual lusts, and rouse to action the noble powers of the soul; banish gloomy and wicked thoughts, and give nourishment to joy and hope; while at the same time it seasons your food, gives you sound sleep, and is the best medicine in the world. You do not realize how good a thing God has given you in your hard labor. You should hold on to it with both hands, be tirelessly faithful in your vocation, rejoice in it, and thank God for it.

The important thing, however, is to do your work with *faith* in your heart. You are a child of God, you who believe; and everything that you have under your charge belongs to him; you are in his house and in his service all the time. While your son is a child you give him freely that which he needs; and so when he performs any service for you, he claims no reward, but serves you willingly and gladly. In like manner you and I are in the house of the Lord our God. We have received everything of his fatherly kindness, and of this we live; all things are ours, and we control as many of them as is expedient for us. Thus we are to labor in our vocation, and bear our day's burden, not in order that we may earn our bread of our heavenly Father, but that we may do his will, and fill our place among his children in a way pleasing to him and useful to men; not as bondmen, but in a grateful and happy spirit as children who, by reason of their rights as such in Christ, have all the good things of the Father's house, and live in the hope of eternal glory.

Heavenly Father, give us a childlike faith and obedience in all things, and make our hard labor easy by thy grace in our dear Lord Jesus. How wisely and well hast thou ordered all things! Even the curse which we brought upon ourselves thou hast turned into a blessing for thy needy children. May we always remain with thee, dear heavenly Father, and eat, drink, work, and rest in thy house as thy children, and thank thee heartily for all things. And when at last the evening is come, and our strength has been exhausted, do thou give us that rest which remains to the people of God; let us then enter into thy joy in heaven. Amen.

Come unto me, when shadows darkly gather, When the sad heart is weary and distressed, Seeking for comfort from your heavenly Father, Come unto me, and I will give you rest.

Large are the mansions in thy Father's dwelling, Glad are the homes that sorrows never dim; Sweet are the harps in holy music swelling, Soft are the tones which raise the heavenly hymn.

---

319. Thursday after Ninth Sunday after Trinity.

Speak to us, Lord Jesus, and create in us through thy word hearts full of charity.

Luke 6, 31–35. And as ye would that men should do to you, do ye also to them likewise. For if ye love them which love you, what thank have ye? . for sinners also love those that love them. And if ye do good to them which do good to you, what thank have ye? for sinners also do even the same. And if ye lend to them of whom ye hope to receive, what thank have ye? for sinners lend to sinners, to receive as much again. But love ye your enemies, and do good, and lend, hoping for nothing again; and your reward shall be great, and ye shall be the children of the Highest: for he is kind unto the unthankful, and to the evil.

Love is the parent of that holy wisdom which knows how to use the earthly things in such a way that they become *eternal* riches. Love understands the wonderful art of transforming perishable things into treasures outlasting the universe. Self-love and penuriousness, which flatter themselves on being wise in the matter of keeping and increasing their possessions, are in fact bad economy, and lose everything. So it is also with the ambitious and self-righteous, who expect *spiritual* benefit as a reward of their acts of charity. Love is the only thing which can save and preserve your goods. Love your neighbor; do to him as you would that he should do to you. Put yourself in his place, and consider carefully what would, in that case, be to your benefit; and then let sincere sympathy move you to help him. Then shall you become truly rich in eternity. — Alas, how little we do for one another; how much for ourselves, and how little for others! And how little of that which we seem to do for one another is done in true love, out of a holy heart, and unselfishly! Therefore much of the little which we do is done in vain. No true act of charity is barren of results; each one of them brings forth blessed fruit in eternity. But the seed sown for the sake of the reward is wasted, nay it is in itself dead. May God give us his love in our hearts that we may love in spirit and in truth; love all, even our most bitter enemies, and do good to them with the holy joy of love! None of us fully understands the great value in heaven and on earth of every deed of charity which springs out of this pure and divine fountain. None can calculate the value of even the smallest genuine deed of true love. — "Jesus, who didst give me

27

an open ear, do thou also stretch out to me thy strong hand, that I
may live hereafter as a true Christian in the spirit of holiness."
Dear Lord, have mercy on us in our great poverty of spirit; give
us love, and make us rich in deeds of charity. Again we pray, give
us above all things love, for Jesus' sake. Amen.

Thou givest the Spirit's holy dower, Spirit of life, and love, and power,
And dost his sevenfold graces shower Upon us all.
For souls redeemed, for sins forgiven, For means of grace and hopes of
heaven, What can to thee, O Lord, be given, Who givest all?
We lose what on ourselves we spend, We have, as treasure without end,
Whatever, Lord, to thee we lend, Who givest all.

---

320. Friday after Ninth Sunday after Trinity.

Lord Jesus, give us grace to receive thy divine words into our heart. **Amen.**

Luke 16, 10-13. He that is faithful in that which is least, is faithful also
in much: and he that is unjust in the least, is unjust also in much. If therefore
ye have not been faithful in the unrighteous mammon, who will commit to
your trust the true riches? And if ye have not been faithful in that which is
another man's, who shall give you that which is your own? No servant can
serve two masters; for either he will hate the one, and love the other: or else
he will hold to the one, and despise the other. Ye cannot serve God and
mammon.

These words of our Lord put the use of the things of earth in a remarkable light, and show how very important it is to use these things
properly. That which the Lord calls the "least" plainly is the same
as that which he afterward calls the "unrighteous mammon," and
then speaks of as "that which is another man's." With these three
designations he places the proper valuation on our earthly belongings, and tells us how we are to regard them. The earthly things are
"that which is least," and are so to be regarded by us. To the children
of the world these things are much the most important, nay everything. To the healthy human heart worldly goods are "that which
is another's"; the heart is not made for mammon, but for something
infinitely more high and noble. To us also mammon is, then, to be
"that which is another's"; it is to have no place in our heart. When
the unrighteous mammon is to you "that which is least" and "that
which is another man's," you have dominion over it, and do not serve
it, but use it in your service. Then you can be "faithful" in these
things; that is to say, wise as the unjust steward in last Sunday's
gospel lesson, and as righteous as he was unrighteous. If you do not
regard and use mammon in this way, but cling to it with your heart,
and serve it, and esteem it something glorious; if you do not use the
earthly things in doing good, but abuse them in covetousness or sinful
luxury; you are at the same time unfaithful in the use of the *spiritual,*
imperishable things which the Lord began to give you; namely, wisdom, knowledge of God, love, joy, and the other gifts of the Spirit;
and if you continue in this way, you will lose them entirely. You be-

come a *slave of mammon*, and can not be a *servant of God*. You have
been unfaithful in that which is another's; your heart has possessed
itself of something which did not belong to it, and is thereby become
the slave of corruptible things; how can you, then, be fit to have holy
dominion over all things in love's heavenly fellowship with the eternal
God? — Dear brethren, take the words of precious wisdom in our
text with you, and make them a part of your life and conduct. We are
all the time dealing with these earthly things, and our faithfulness
herein is a measure of our ownership of the things of heaven.

Lord Jesus, let me never become a slave of mammon; but give
me grace to use that which is another man's in such a way that thou
canst give me that which is my own: Love and all the unperishable
treasures which thou, my God, hast destined me to have. Amen.

Breathe, O breathe thy loving spirit Into every troubled breast; Let us
all in thee inherit, Let us find thy promised rest. Take away the love of sinning,
Alpha and Omega be; End of faith, as its beginning, Set our hearts at liberty.
Come, almighty to deliver, Let us all thy life receive; Come to us, dear
Lord, and never, Never more thy temples leave! Thee we would be always
blessing, Serve thee as thy hosts above, Pray, and praise thee without ceasing,
Glory in thy precious love.

---

321. Saturday after Ninth Sunday after Trinity.

Lord, give us grace to believe these words. Amen.

Genesis 4, 3–11. And in process of time it came to pass, that Cain
brought of the fruit of the ground an offering unto the Lord. And Abel, he
also brought of the firstlings of his flock, and of the fat thereof. And the
Lord had respect unto Abel, and to his offering: But unto Cain and to his
offering, he had not respect. And Cain was very wroth, and his countenance
fell. And the Lord said unto Cain, Why art thou wroth? and why is thy countenance fallen? If thou doest well, shalt thou not be accepted? and if thou doest
not well, sin lieth at the door. And unto thee shall be his desire, and thou
shalt rule over him. And Cain talked with Abel his brother: and it came to
pass, when they were in the field, that Cain rose up against Abel his brother,
and slew him. And the Lord said unto Cain, Where is Abel thy brother?
And he said, I know not: Am I my brother's keeper? And he said, What hast
thou done? the voice of thy brother's blood crieth unto me from the ground.
And now art thou cursed from the earth, which hath opened her mouth to receive thy brother's blood from thy hand.

If we had seen Cain and Abel bringing their offerings, one of
these offerings would probably in our eyes have seemed as good as the
other. "For man looketh on the outward appearance, but the Lord
looketh on the heart." Deeds have their value according to the person
who performs them. Therefore it is written: "The Lord had respect
unto *Abel* and to his offering; but unto *Cain* and to his offering he
had not respect." No matter how much good you do, if your deeds
are not done in love, they are not good in the sight of God; he has
no respect unto you, and therefore he has no respect to your works.

After the offering Cain became more wicked than he had been.

He had been without warmth and life and charity; he became bitter
and angry, and his countenance fell. Here is a lesson, especially for
the benefit of parents and teachers. See to it that the young people
willingly and gladly take part in the divine services, in holy Communion, in the mission work; *willingly* and with glad heart; for if they do
it unwillingly, they are made worse by it, and close their hearts wholly
against the Spirit of God.

Yet the gracious God spoke kindly to Cain, admonishing him and
offering him mercy, and wished to arm him against the devil; but Cain
would not. With what infinite patience God seeks the sinners who
have gone wrong! The soul of Cain also was precious to the Lord.
Therefore he seeks to terrify him, and humble him, and raise him up:
"Cain, beware; be on thy guard; sin lieth in wait for thee at the door;
and how unhappy thou wilt be, should it out-wit you. But the sin
which thou dost so much desire shall not rule over thee, but be ruled
over by thee." This was at once a *warning* and a *promise*. "*Thou
must not* let sin rule over thee; nor *shall* it." If Cain had received this
word of God into his heart, he would have put the devil to shame.
But *Cain does not believe the word of God;* therefore his offering is not
acceptable; he becomes a fratricide, and he bears the brand of God's
curse on his soul. *Cain does not believe the word of God.* This account
should be read of all the world, that all men may learn that Cain, *Cain,*
rejects the word of God, *does not believe it!* This was the *real crime*
of Cain. It was *this* which led him to hate his brother and slay him,
and then with evil conscience and scowling face to answer the Lord:
"I know not! Am I my brother's keeper?" and then go his way with
the Lord's curse upon him!

God, help us to believe thy word, that we may love thee, and bring
ourselves and our possessions to thee as an acceptable offering. Give
us also grace to love one another, serve one another, and stand united
as one man with thy word as a weapon and shield against the devil
and the seductive power of unbelief. Amen.

Fierce is our subtle foeman: The forces at his hand, With woes that none
can number, Despoil the pleasant land; All they who war against them, In
strife so keen and long, Must in their Savior's armor Be stronger than the
strong.

---

322. Tenth Sunday after Trinity. I.

God, make us partakers of the heavenly riches of thy grace and love. Amen.

Gospel Lesson, Luke 19, 41-48. And when he was come near, he beheld
the city, and wept over it, saying, If thou hadst known, even thou, at least in
this thy day, the things which belong unto thy peace! but now they are hid
from thine eyes. For the days shall come upon thee, that thine enemies shall
cast a trench about thee, and compass thee round, and keep thee in on every
side, and shall lay thee even with the ground, and thy children within thee; and
they shall not leave in thee one stone upon another; because thou knewest
not the time of thy visitation. And he went into the temple, and began to cast
out them that sold therein, and them that bought; saying unto them, It is

written, My house is the house of prayer: but ye have made it a den of thieves. And he taught daily in the temple. But the chief priests and the scribes and the chief of the people sought to destroy him, and could not find what they might do: for all the people were very attentive to hear him.

That which the Lord foretold concerning Jerusalem has been fulfilled to the minutest detail. As the people of Israel "knew not the time of their visitation," but crucified the Son of God, who came to save them, it was necessary that the judgment of wrath should come upon them, and destruction fall upon them as an armed man. For God is just, and punishes without respect of person all that despise his mercy. Jerusalem and the Jews shall be a powerful warning to us; for they are a living and striking illustration of the truth that God is not mocked, but that every man shall reap that which he has sown. Let the judgment on Jerusalem and the dispersion of the Jewish people unto this day teach you that the word of God is true, and that his righteous wrath falls surely and heavily on the obdurate.

Above all, however, our gospel lesson shows that the Lord's heart is full of tender mercy toward his people; and this, again, may in a two-fold manner serve for our edification.

1) God *will not* have the sinner to be destroyed and die. There is in his heart something which revolts against the thought, and which cries out with loud voice to all the earth and into the soul of every prodigal son: "Repent! This I pray thee with burning heart, with my tears and my blood! Turn to me, and live!" The tears of Jesus over the obdurate city and his words of infinite sadness, "if thou hadst known, even thou, at least in this thy day, the things which belong unto thy peace," show us beyond contradiction that justice makes the punishment of the impenitent unavoidably necessary; but they also show us with at least equal clearness that God does everything for our salvation, and that the death of a sinner is therefore wholly the sinner's own fault. These tears and sighs of pain give us the assurrance that Jesus most ardently desires to receive sinners. Had Jerusalem, soiled by sin and torn by Satan though it was, but given heed to the Lord's call, and sought mercy at his feet, he would have taken it to his heart, washed it with his tears and blood, and brought it to the Father; and what rejoicing would there not then have been in heaven! — The Lord still is what he was; he has the same loving heart toward you and me and all.

2) The friends of Jesus must grieve with him over the unhappy fate of the Jewish people. Jesus wept over them; and Paul could wish himself accursed from Christ, if they might thereby be saved; should not, then, their unhappy condition grieve us? Shall we look without concern on the affliction of the daughter of Zion? Shall we not weep over the deep abasement and misery of this glorious chosen people of God? The children of Abraham, Isaac, and Jacob; the people of whom Christ was, he who is God exalted for evermore; — these people are his most bitter enemies, and curse the God of glory, whose mission it was to bless them, and to make them a blessing to all the earth. And in place of the heavenly heritage of the first-born son, of love and

the life eternal, they have chosen mammon and worldly wisdom, and have sold themselves to those things which are not of God. The joy of their heart is ceased; their dance is turned into mourning. The crown is fallen from their head; their heart is faint, their eyes dim. The mountain of Zion is desolate; foxes walk upon it. But hast thou, O Lord, utterly rejected thy people? Is there no more hope for them? There is hope. We will not let thee go; we will weep and pray day and night for Israel. — Lord Jesus, help us to weep as thou didst weep over thine own people. Amen.

O that the Lord's salvation Were out of Zion come, To heal his ancient nation, To lead his outcasts home! Let fall thy rod of terror, Thy saving grace impart; Roll back the veil of error, Release the fettered heart.

Let Israel, home returning, Her lost Messiah see; Give oil of joy for mourning, And bind thy church to thee.

---

323. Tenth Sunday after Trinity. II.

Come, Holy Ghost, and give us thy gifts. Amen.

Epistle Lesson, 1 Corinthians 12, 2–11. Ye know that ye were gentiles carried away unto these dumb idols, even as ye were led. Wherefore I give you to understand, that no man speaking by the Spirit of God calleth Jesus accursed: and that no man can say that Jesus is the Lord, but by the Holy Ghost. Now there are diversities of gifts, but the same Spirit. And there are differences of administrations, but the same Lord. And there are diversities of operations; but it is the same God which worketh all in all. But the manifestation of the Spirit is given to every man to profit withal. For to one is given, by the Spirit, the word of wisdom; to another the word of knowledge, by the same Spirit; to another faith, by the same Spirit; to another the gifts of healing, by the same Spirit; to another the working of miracles; to another prophecy; to another discerning of spirits; to another divers kinds of tongues; to another the interpretation of tongues: But all these worketh that one and the selfsame Spirit, dividing to every man severally as he will.

Every man who speaks by the Spirit of God exalts Jesus, and proclaims his exellence. If any man say that he has the Spirit of God, and do not with word and deed confess that Jesus Christ is God's only begotten Son, that man is a liar, and the Spirit of God does not speak through him. But whosoever calls Jesus Lord, and exalts his divine grace and power, and lives in his precepts, and walks in the light; this man has the Holy Ghost; for he can learn this of no other teacher. Here is the keynote by which the Spirit of God is known. The love of the pure and lowly Savior is in his believers. He is their only hope, and they belong to him; they live by him, and in him, and for him.

This one and the selfsame Spirit gives impulse to the diverse gifts of the Christians, even as one and the selfsame mind of a man directs the several members of his body. Every believer has his special gifts and his special service to perform in God's kingdom. The church in Corinth was exceedingly rich in gifts, but was therefore also exposed to many temptations. For, the greater the gifts, the greater the temptations; — temptations to pride, and to contentions, and to opening the door to false spirits. For this reason Paul writes, and gives the Corinthians the above mentioned general rule for the discerning of spirits, and teaches them to serve one another in love and humility with the different gifts. — Our churches also have received their several talents; the gifts have not ceased in the church, but are given it to profit withal. Here are the word of wisdom, and the word of knowledge, and prophecy, and faith; and there may on occasion be the power of working wonders, if the Lord see fit, and it be profitable. If we would but be faithful and make the proper use of that which he has given us, the great diversity of gifts would even now more gloriously appear. But we let the spirit of the world subdue us and prevent the best use of our gifts. The cares of this world hover like swarms of locusts over our hearts, shut out the sun, and devour the growing grain. God help us in these evil times! May the spirit of love unite us, and that condition be brought about in fact concerning which it has been written: "How beautiful shall be the church of God, and how lovely in his sight, when all hearts are united in the one mind and desire to love God and continue to increase in charity!" In this case how wonderfully the diverse gifts of the Spirit would thrive! Are you working for this object, dear reader? In what way are you making use of your talent to this end? Let me remind you that the virtue known as *humility* is of the very highest possible importance in causing charity and peace to flourish under one and the selfsame Spirit. O, that we might in the love of Christ bend our every energy and consume our strength for the increase of the church, and adorn all our conduct with his holy humility! Then the gifts would increase and be multiplied. This we earnestly ask of thee, merciful God; grant us this favor for Jesus' sake. Amen.

O make the deaf to hear thy word, And teach the dumb to speak, dear Lord, Who dare not yet the faith avow, Though secretly they hold it now.
Shine on the darkened and the cold, Recall the wanderers to thy fold, Unite all those who walk apart, Confirm the weak and doubting heart.

---

324. Monday after Tenth Sunday after Trinity.

Lord, we will keep thy statutes; O forsake us not utterly. Amen.

Isaiah 5, 1–7. Now will I sing to my well-beloved a song of my beloved touching his vineyard. My well-beloved hath a vineyard in a very fruitful hill: and he fenced it, and gathered out the stones thereof, and planted it with the choicest vine, and built a tower in the midst of it, and also made a winepress therein: and he looked that it should bring forth grapes, and it brought forth wild grapes. And now, O inhabitants of Jerusalem, and men of Judah, judge, I pray you, betwixt me and my vineyard. What could have been done more to my vineyard, that I have not done in it? wherefore, when I looked that it should bring forth grapes, brought it forth wild grapes? And now, go to; I will tell you what I will do to my vineyard: I will take away the hedge thereof, and it shall be eaten up: and break down the wall thereof, and it shall be trodden down: And I will lay it waste: it shall not be pruned nor digged: but there shall come up briers and thorns: I will also command the clouds that they rain no rain upon it. For the vineyard of the Lord of hosts is the house of Israel, and the men of Judah his pleasant plant: and he looked for judgment, but behold oppression; for righteousness, but behold a cry.

"What could have been done more to my vineyard, that I have not done in it?" says the Lord in regard to Israel; and must the same thing not be said of us? He has planted us to be his church, and fenced us in with his almighty power and fidelity, bestowed upon us rich and beautiful gifts, given us the light of his word, appointed watchmen among us, and chastened us according to our need and strength; — what could have been done more to us, that he has not done? He delivered up his only Son to die for us; and all paths on which he led us were paths of mercy and salvation. "What could have been done more to my vineyard, that I have not done in it? Wherefore, when I looked that it should bring forth grapes, brought it forth wild grapes?" Yes; why are we evil, and bring forth evil fruits? Of a truth, it is deplorable. Here grow hatred and falsehood, deceit and injustice, idolatry and covetousness, enmity and contentions, gluttony and drunkenness and lasciviousness; and they who avoid these things look calmly on, and say and do nothing; or they take hold with the wrong hand, because they are wanting in love. Alas, love is wanting; but why? After his ineffable grace and mercy toward us the Lord might well "look for judgment, but behold oppression; for righteousness, but behold a cry!" His love should have knit our hearts together, and embellished us all with the beautiful fruits of the Spirit; but behold, we are cold and divided, and agree only in love of self; resembling indeed the like poles of a magnet, which repel each other. Therefore the Lord must remove the candlestick from us, except we repent. He says: "I will lay my vineyard waste, and there shall come up briers and thorns." He has done this with the people of Israel, though they were the choicest vine which he had planted. Their city is a waste, and the people scattered to all the winds. These conditions now obtain before our eyes, and serve as a warning to us. — Let our scripture lesson impress upon us these two things, between which there is an intimate connection: 1) God has given us abundantly all grace and every gift, that we lack nothing needful to faith and holiness. 2) If we do not bring forth better fruit than heretofore, he will take the light from us; and we deserve this judgment. — We pray thee, merciful God, help us to see and hear, in order that we may escape destruction. Wake us, and let the Holy Spirit be victorious. This is yet the prayer of all the upright. Have mercy on our people. Drive out the evil spirit, thou strong and faithful, longsuffering and merciful God; and let the Spirit of grace and peace obtain victory in us and among us, for Jesus' sake. Amen.

Send forth thy heralds, Lord, to call The thoughtless young, the hardened old, A scattered homeless flock, till all Be gathered to thy peaceful fold.
Send them thy mighty word to speak, Till faith shall dawn and doubt depart, To awe the bold, and stay the weak, And bind and heal the broken heart.

325. Tuesday after Tenth Sunday after Trinity.

Lord, give us the obedience of faith, and enlighten us in the mystery of grace. Amen.

John 8, 21–27. Then said Jesus again unto them, I go my way, and ye shall seek me, and shall die in your sins: whither I go, ye cannot come. Then said the Jews, Will he kill himself? because he saith, Whither I go, ye cannot come. And he said unto them, Ye are from beneath; I am from above: ye are of this world; I am not of this world. I said therefore unto you, that ye shall die in your sins: for if ye believe not that I am he, ye shall die in your sins. Then said they unto him, Who art thou? And Jesus saith unto them, Even the same that I said unto you from the beginning. I have many things to say and to judge of you: but he that sent me is true; and I speak to the world those things which I have heard of him. They understood not that he spake to them of the Father.

With profound sorrow Jesus tells these people how unhappy they are in that they do not believe in him. Every word expresses the grief of tenderest love; by which means he attempts to rouse them to repentance. But how terrible is the wickedness of the impenitent! They understand very well what he means when he says: "Whither I go ye cannot come." Yet they wickedly construe his words to mean that he may perhaps intend to kill himself. It is a suggestion worthy of the devil himself. They know that self-murder is the most awful crime which a man can commit; and yet they speak in this way of the Son of God! How the devil much have rejoiced in their speech! In spite of their poisonous tongue, however, the Lord is no less loving and meek than before; he seeks only to win them, and again and again he proclaims to them the truth that without faith they must die in their sins. — All who are to be saved must *believe* in *him*. For he is one with the Father, the only true God. We can not come to the Father but through *the Son*, and that by *faith*. But whosoever believes in him does in fact come to the Father through the Son. He *is* that which he speaks; and he who receives and keeps *the word*, — that is, *believes it*, — thereby comes into the fellowship of the Son and the Father. Mark that Jesus here says: *I am "even the same that I said unto you."* If you receive my word into your soul, I myself am therein, and abide in you; *I am that I am;* I am from the beginning, and remain for ever the same; the living God from above, the Blessed One, who came to the world in order to draw you with me to heaven. — The Jews understood not that he spake to them of the Father; *for they would not believe*, but would continue in their sins. Do you, dear friend, understand the Lord's speech? Has it entered your heart, and thus made him to become your life?

Lord Jesus, I catch a glimpse of thy glory, and see more and more of it, as gradually I receive grace to obey thee, and to hold fast thy word in childlike faith. Give me ever new grace thereto, most merciful Savior, blessed Son of God! Amen.

Thou my faith increase and quicken, Let me keep thy gift divine; Howsoe'er temptations thicken, May thy word for ever shine As my guiding star through life, As my comfort in my strife.

326. Wednesday after Tenth Sunday after Trinity.

Lord, be gracious unto us, and save us. Amen.

Isaiah 1, 2–6. Hear, O heavens; and give ear, O earth; for the Lord hath
spoken: I have nourished and brought up children, and they have rebelled
against me: The ox knoweth his owner, and the ass his master's crib: but
Israel doth not know, my people doth not consider. Ah sinful nation, a people
laden with iniquity, a seed of evildoers, children that are corrupters! they have
forsaken the Lord, they have provoked the Holy One of Israel unto anger,
they are gone away backward. Why should ye be stricken any more? ye will
revolt more and more. The whole head is sick, and the whole heart faint.
From the sole of the foot even unto the head there is no soundness in it; but
wounds, and bruises, and putrifying sores: they have not been closed, neither
bound up, neither mollified with ointment.

The heavens and earth and all things therein bear witness against
the impenitent, and accuse them on account of their obstinacy. The
whole creation was, to be sure, corrupted by our fall, but not in the
same manner as we, who have departed from the divine laws. The
other creatures are not in the same measure refractory; and do not,
as we do, consciously and of their own free will close their eyes and
heart to the Lord. Man is most highly endowed, and man is most
deeply corrupted; man should know God most clearly, and obey him
most willingly; but no other creature is become in the same degree a
stranger to God, and none other resists him with as much obstinacy.
"Hear, O heavens, and give ear, O earth; for the Lord hath
spoken: I have nourished and brought up children, and they have
rebelled against me!" Stirring and impressive though these words
be, men remain deaf to them. They were spoken to the Jews; they
are spoken to us. They applied to them; they apply to us. Alas, they
apply with almost as much force to our case as to that of the Jews!
But heaven and earth hear them, and yet we hear them not!— Read
slowly and with deliberation that which the Lord further says: "Ah
sinful nation, a people laden with iniquity, a seed of evildoers, children
that are corrupters; they have forsaken the Lord, they have provoked
the Holy One of Israel unto anger, they are gone away backward!"
These are words to stir us to our innermost depths; and yet the many
disdain them now, as did the Jews of old. How have we profited by
the Lord's many words and deeds of love and correction? He has
shown us the goodness of a father a thousand times over; and now he
follows it up with discipline. Some few repent, and are "as a cottage
in a vineyard," or as fruit remaining after the harvest. In the case of
the many all correction also is in vain. "Why should ye be stricken any
more? Ye will revolt more and more." How terrible a thing it is
that even the chastisement but increases the evil!— God thereupon
describes to us our true condition, holding up to our view our deep,
gaping, and foul wounds, for the humiliation of the individual and the
people: "The whole head is sick, and the whole heart faint. From the
sole of the foot even unto the head there is no soundness in it; but
wounds, and bruises, and putrifying sores; they have not been closed,

neither bound up, neither mollified with ointment." Behold yourself, my reader, and behold your people as in a glass! As the word of God and faith are rejected, the people become more diseased, and the judgment is more near. But, alas, this is not understood! "The ox knoweth his owner, and the ass his master's crib; but Israel doth not know, my people doth not consider."

Turn thou us unto thee, O Lord, and we shall be turned; renew our days as of old. Hast thou utterly rejected us? Art thou very wroth against us? Give us repentance, most merciful God, and save us for Jesus' sake. Amen.

Hasten, sinners, to return, Stay not for the morrow's sun, Lest thy lamp should fail to burn, Ere salvation's work is done.
Hasten, sinners, to be blessed, Stay not for the morrow's sun, Lest perdition thee arrest Ere the morrow is begun.

---

327. Thursday after Tenth Sunday after Trinity.

Shew us thy mercy, O Lord, and grant us thy salvation. Amen.

Isaiah 29, 10–14. For the Lord hath poured out upon you the spirit of deep sleep, and hath closed your eyes: the prophets and your rulers, the seers hath he covered. And the vision of all is become unto you as the words of a book that is sealed, which men deliver to one that is learned, saying, Read this, I pray thee: and he saith, I cannot; for it is sealed: and the book is delivered to him that is not learned, saying, Read this, I pray thee: and he saith, I am not learned. Wherefore the Lord said, Forasmuch as this people draw near me with their mouth, and with their lips do honor me, but have removed their heart far from me, and their fear toward me is taught by the precept of men: Therefore, behold, I will proceed to do a marvellous work among this people, even a marvellous work and a wonder: for the wisdom of their wise men shall perish, and the understanding of their prudent men shall be hid.

When a man resists the Spirit of God, and will not repent, although he hears the word of God, and knows its power; he comes to feel more secure, is more obdurate, sleeps more soundly, and walks more blindly, than do the heathen. I once heard a clergyman say that he had for a time been weighed down by contrition on account of his sins; but that he now regarded this as a species of madness, or as a nervous disease, of which he had been cured! "God speaketh once, yea twice, yet man perceiveth it not." God sends chastisements, shakes the sinner out of his sleep, and puts the words of repentance into his soul. "Lo, all these things worketh God oftentimes with man, to bring back his soul from the pit, to be enlightened with the light of the living." (Job 33, 29. 30). But as man will not repent God pours out upon him the spirit of deep sleep, and closes his eyes, that he can not see those things which are most clear, and can not be rid of his scales by any word of God however full of force; but goes in the happiness of insanity or in the gloom of despair with Saul and Judas to eternal perdition.

As it is with the individual, so it is with the peoples. There is a sort of mutuality of responsibility between members of the same people, as is the case between children and parents. We know that the Lord will rescue the upright out of the destruction of a corrupt people; but we here speak of people in their collective capacity as a nation. When the Lord repeatedly visits a people with a spiritual awakening, and the people each time sink down again into callousness, into a soulless worship of God, into worldliness and unbelief, God will at last abandon them to the hardness of their hearts, take from them the little which remains of their spiritual understanding, and turn their wisdom into foolishness. "They are drunken, but not with wine; they stagger, but not with strong drink." The candlestick is moved away entirely. Heretofore the intercessions of the poor and despised Christians had supported the whole structure; but this is now a thing of the past, and the carcase lies ready for the ravens. As yet our people have not reached this stage, and God grant that they never may! But the spirit of the antichrist is extremely busy among us; and many shut their eyes to the light of truth.

Lord, teach us to know the time of our visitation, and to understand the things which belong unto our peace. Have mercy on us and on our people. Make thy face to shine upon us, for Jesus' sake. Amen.

Jesus, merciful Redeemer, Rouse dead souls to hear thy voice; Wake, oh, wake each idle dreamer Now to make the eternal choice!
Mark we whither we are wending; Ponder how we soon must go To inherit bliss unending, Or eternity of woe.

---

328. Friday after Tenth Sunday after Trinity.

Lord Jesus, let us experience the power of thy name to bring salvation. Amen.

Acts 4, 8–12. Then Peter, filled with the Holy Ghost said unto them, Ye rulers of the people, and elders of Israel, if we this day be examined of the good deed done to the impotent man, by what means he is made whole; be it known unto you all, and to all the people of Israel, that by the name of Jesus Christ of Nazareth, whom ye crucified, whom God raised from the dead, even by him doth this man stand here before you whole. This is the stone which was set at nought of you builders, which is become the head of the corner. Neither is there salvation in any other: for there is none other name under heaven given among men, whereby we must be saved.

The name of Jesus Christ had healed the lame man, with the result that "he, leaping up, stood, and walked, and entered with them into the temple, walking, and leaping, and praising God." This name shall heal all sinners who believe in him. There is none other, nor any other thing whatever, that can save us poor lost and condemned men. Only the name of Jesus is able to bring about this gracious miracle of miracles. Some have sought salvation in the law, some in their name of Christians and in the mere outward use of baptism and the Lord's supper, some in their penitence and tears, some in their prayers and religious exercises; but none has found it in any of these things

Peace and life are to be had only in Jesus Christ, in heart-fellowship
with him through faith. — "There is none other name under heaven
given among men, whereby we must be saved." It was necessary
that salvation be *"given"*; it must of necessity be a *gift* of God, and
Jesus was given us; the only begotten Son of God became man and
our Savior. *"Jesus,"* Savior, was and is his precious name. It is the
name above every name, and contains God's love for us, our deliverance from all evil, and our eternal salvation. By this name *only* must
we be saved; and all who are so happy as to know him wish to be
saved by him, and by none other; and they also know in the deepest
recesses of the heart that they can be saved by none other. But by
this name we *must* be saved. You *ought* to be saved in the name of
Jesus; and you *shall* be, if you believe in him. As surely as the lame
man was healed, so surely shall you be saved by this name. For it
is full of saving power and blessed life for poor sinners. As the lame
man by the power of Jesus' name entered into the temple, leaping,
and walking, and praising God, so shall you, by the power of this name
to forgive sin and to quicken you, praise God and serve him in his
church here on earth, and bless him for ever in the heavenly temple
of glory. There is salvation in *none but Jesus;* and there is *nothing
but salvation* in Jesus. Then let our watchword be: Only bliss, and
this only in the name of Jesus.

Precious Savior, give us thy Holy Spirit; so that we heartily believe in thee, experience the power of thy grace to save us, and confess thee with confidence and joy. May none of us through unbelief
reject the mercy unto salvation contained in thy precious name. Amen.

Jesus! only name that's given Under all the mighty heaven, Whereby man,
to sin enslaved, Bursts his fetters, and is saved.
Jesus! Name of wondrous love! Human name of God above! Pleading
only this, we flee, Helpless, O our God, to thee.

---

329. Saturday after Tenth Sunday after Trinity.

Psalm 51, 1–9. Have mercy upon me, O God, according to thy lovingkindness; according unto the multitude of thy tender mercies blot out my transgressions. Wash me thoroughly from mine iniquity, and cleanse me from my
sin. For I acknowledge my transgressions; and my sin is ever before me.
Against thee, thee only, have I sinned, and done this evil in thy sight; that
thou mightest be justified when thou speakest, and be clear when thou judgest.
Behold, I was shapen in iniquity, and in sin did my mother conceive me. Behold, thou desirest truth in the inward parts; and in the hidden part thou shalt
make me to know wisdom. Purge me with hyssop, and I shall be clean: wash
me, and I shall be whiter than snow. Make me to hear joy and gladness; that
the bones which thou hast broken may rejoice. Hide thy face from my sins,
and blot out all mine iniquities.

The sin with Bathsheba and against Uriah was not the only one
which David felt; he confesses: "Behold, I was shapen in iniquity;
and in sin did my mother conceive me." A true knowledge of sin
does not see the sinful acts only but is sensible of the deep depravity

of the heart, and finds therein a terribly poisonous fountain out of which flow all sinful acts. In the heart are lies, and hate, and unchastity, and covetousness, as the plant is hid in the seed; and this poison has permeated us, and made the heart evil from our childhood. "For out of the *heart*," says Jesus, "proceed evil thoughts, murders, adulteries, fornications, thefts, false witness, blasphemies." — The Lord so arranged it that David saw Bathsheba, and that he was, by means of the visit of Uriah to his home, prevented from hiding his sin. If the Spirit can in no other way bring us to a knowledge of sin, the Lord permits the hidden lust of the heart to come out into the light, in order that we may be moved to humble ourselves, and to sue for mercy. Let none, however, dally with sin, and do that which is evil in order to learn contrition, and to prove the truth of God's word! Quench the spark that it may not burst forth into a fierce flame! Ask God to keep you from the dreadful way of David; and be on your guard against the evil enemy, who lies in wait at the door. God will not fail so to shape your life that you shall taste the bitterness of sin, if you be upright and will obey his Spirit. And this sense of sin is absolutely necessary; he who does not feel his sin with sorrow, and recognize the justice of God's judgments, can not know the sweet and blissful peace of his mercy. — Note the prayer and confession of David. They are not words proceeding out of a cold heart, but the piercing cry of a heart on fire and pleading for mercy. It is not a dull admission that he has the human frailties common to all; but it is a contrite soul's deep and true confession that he is a malefactor from his birth. He is not done with the matter as soon as he has spoken his prayer and confession, but it is of inexpressible importance to him to receive mercy and be made clean. "Wash me thoroughly from my sin; purge me with hyssop, and I shall be clean; wash me, and I shall be whiter than snow." Have you also, dear reader, this prayer in your heart? Have you likewise given to God the true sacrifices, a broken spirit and a broken and a contrite heart? Humbly pray God to give you the true spirit of contrition, and say in the words of Asaph: Feed me, O Lord, with the bread of tears, and give me tears to drink in great measure.

Lord God, we do not have the deep humility of David; but we feel our depravity and guilt with contrition and sorrow. Truly, I am wretched and wicked; cleanse me and heal me, O God, for Jesus' sake. Amen.

To thee may raise our hearts and eyes, Repenting sore with bitter sighs,
And seek thy pardon for our sin, And respite from our griefs within.
For thou hast promised graciously To hear all those who cry to thee,
Through him whose name alone is great, Our Savior and our advocate.

330. Eleventh Sunday after Trinity. I.

Lord, make us lowly of heart. Amen.

Gospel Lesson, Luke 18, 9–14. And he spake this parable unto certain which trusted in themselves that they were righteous, and despised others;

Two men went up into the temple to pray; the one a Pharisee, and the other a publican. The Pharisee stood and prayed thus with himself: God, I thank thee that I am not as other men are, extortioners, unjust, adulterers, or even as this publican: I fast twice in the week, I give tithes of all that I possess. And the publican, standing afar off, would not lift up so much as his eyes unto heaven, but smote upon his breast, saying, God be merciful to me a sinner. I tell you, this man went down to his house justified rather than the other: for every one that exalteth himself shall be abased; and he that humbleth himself shall be exalted.

God grant that this gospel lesson today may make us in truth lowly of heart! However, it is our habit to feel sure in advance that we are not Pharisees; and so the Lord's words of correction make no impression on us. Nevertheless, assuming that you are not a Pharisee, but a humble Christian, there still is something of the Pharisee in you; for our nature is proud and self-righteous, and we each and all still have flesh and blood. See yourself reflected in the words of the Lord today, and let yourself be humbled. Perhaps you may, after all, be one of the Pharisees! But if you will permit the word to enter your heart, it shall bring you as a needy sinner to your knees at the Lord's feet.

The great fault of the Pharisee is that he *does not come into the presence of God.* His mouth, to be sure, speaks with God; but his heart is far away from him. This is heard in his speech; he does not speak of the relations between God and himself, but makes a comparison between himself and other men. I do not mean to say that it always is wrong to institute such a comparison; for God has presented these two men to us, in order that we may see ourselves in them. We must, however, at all times do it in the sight of the Lord! The Pharisee did not know the righteousness of God, and did not see the holy eye which saw him; he knew no law but that of self-love; — he had knowledge of, but still he did not know God's commandment of love, — and therefore he seemed to himself to be righteous. In reality he is evil; he is proud, selfish, conceited, vainglorious, and without mercy; but, for himself, he does not doubt that he is a good and pious man, very near absolute perfection. Deplorable blindness! But such is *man;* are you aware of it? The Pharisee thanks God that he is not as other men are, sinful and wretched, but fears God and is blameless according to the law; and yet he is in fact worse than others, and defiles the holy law of God by his self-appointed worship. But it is dangerous to tell him so. Jesus did it, in love laying bare the sins of the Pharisees; and therefore they became his sworn enemies, and were of the opinion that they had the best of reasons for it. Words fail to express in how strong a network of lies and self-deceit the devil entangles the poor self-righteous and proud human heart. For God's sake, pray the Lord to enlighten you! Perhaps you are "pious," and hold yourself aloof from the world because you are too good for it; or you are not and will not be one of the "pious," because you regard yourself as better than such Pharisees. I exhort you, whoever you may be, to pray the Lord to give you light and to make you humble. Whether you are one of the "pious" or not, you may be a Pharisee; and you are one, in fact, if *your heart* do not all the time pray the prayer of the publican.

The Pharisee did not ask mercy, and did not receive mercy; but the publican stood before God, and knew his sin, and sued for mercy, and received forgiveness. The publican did not compare himself with others; God's presence was so vivid to him that he knew of none but the Lord and himself. Had he compared himself with other men, he would have said: I am the greatest of all sinners. His penitence is earnest, and his prayer sincere. You and I do not have as deep a sense of sin as he had, nor are we as strong in prayer. But if you with upright heart acknowledge yourself to be deserving of the wrath of God, and sincerely sue for mercy, and have the earnest purpose to renounce all sin; then you shall, like the publican, go "down to your house justified." You never become too good to pray: "God be merciful to me a sinner." Take note, however, of this comfort in the midst of your sorrow on account of your pitiful Christianity: As long as the prayer of the publican continues ever to rise from your heart, you continue to be one of God's children, whom he has taken into favor and justified. — Give us, O Lord, this humility, this longing for mercy, this gift of prayer, and this righteousness. Amen.

To thy temple I repair; Lord! I love to worship there, When within the veil I meet Christ before the mercy-seat.
From thy house when I return, May my heart within me burn; And at evening let me say, "I have walked with God today."

---

331. Eleventh Sunday after Trinity. II.

Lord, give us humility and true faith; so that thy gospel may save us. Amen.

Epistle Lesson, 1 Corinthians 15, 1-10. Moreover, brethren, I declare unto you the gospel which I preached unto you, which also ye have received, and wherein ye stand; by which also ye are saved, if ye keep in memory what I preached unto you, unless ye have believed in vain. For I delivered unto you first of all that which I also received, how that Christ died for our sins according to the scriptures; and that he was buried, and that he rose again the third day according to the scriptures; and that he was seen of Cephas, then of the twelve: After that, he was seen of above five hundred brethren at once; of whom the greater part remain unto this present, but some are fallen asleep. After that, he was seen of James; then of all the apostles. And last of all he was seen of me also, as of one born out of due time. For I am the least of the apostles, that am not meet to be called an apostle, because I persecuted the church of God. But by the grace of God I am what I am: and his grace which was bestowed upon me was not in vain; but I labored more abundantly than they all: yet not I, but the grace of God which was with me.

Here we learn what is the sum and substance of the gospel; namely, that *Christ died for our sins, and was buried, and rose again the third day.* Herein is healing for the poor heart weighed down by sin. Christ took our sins upon himself, and died for them in our stead;

witness of which is borne by the whole Old Testament also, from the promise concerning the seed of the woman, and the story of the blood of Abel, to John the Baptist, who points to Jesus, saying: "Behold the Lamb of God, which taketh away the sin of the world." Death, which we deserve by our sins, has been suffered; a fact testified to by all scripture. Is not this a message of joy, the true gospel? Our sin and death are buried and have disappeared in the grave of Jesus. That Jesus died and was buried is established beyond controversy. It came to pass exactly as the scriptures had foretold; not one passage only, but all scripture; for this truth is the subject matter of the whole Bible. His resurrection also is established by incontrovertible evidence; and this likewise according to the prophecy of the scriptures. The risen Savior was seen so clearly and so often that the unbelieving disciples *were compelled* to believe. On one occasion he was seen of above five hundred brethren at once, of whom the greater part were living at the time when Paul wrote this. The gospel of your redemption from sin and death, of your Savior's victorious atonement and atoning victory, of the resurrection of our precious Lord from the dead, is not uncertain; it is sure, and you may build on it with your soul's full confidence. Do it, and you shall be saved by this faith. No matter *who* you have been, or *what* your heart and conduct may have been, you shall be saved, if you believe. For the death of Jesus Christ, — a death which his resurrection turned into a victory, a victory over sin and death and the kingdom of the devil, — is a full redemption for all and a ransom for all possible sins. Therefore *all* who know their sin have *all* their sins wiped out by faith in him. Paul had been a persecutor, a blasphemer, a scoffer, and here he calls himself "one born out of due time"; and yet he had received mercy. Can you doubt that Paul had received pardon for all his sin? Do you doubt that Paul is saved, and that he now dwells with our Lord Jesus in heaven? Now, *why* was he saved? Do you think that it was by reason of his being a highly gifted preacher and a zealous apostle? Or was it because he labored more than the others? or because he suffered and strove more than any other for the gospel? No; his *glory* in heaven is the greater by reason of these things and by reason of his great humility; — for "he that shall humble himself shall be exalted;" — but *salvation* itself is his by means of the heart's simple *faith* in the gospel. A lost sinner, he found his only comfort in the truth that Jesus bare our sin. The discipline of grace preserved him in his humility, and the comfort of grace kept him in this faith unto the end. You and I, dear Christian friend, hope only in the grace of God through the blood of Jesus; we shall as surely be saved; for the gospel shall not fail. Shall the promise of God fail any who believes it? Nevermore; it can not be!

God, give us humble and believing hearts, for Jesus' sake. Amen.

The Gospel shows the Father's grace, Who sent his Son to save our race:
Proclaims how Jesus lived and died That man might thus be justified.
May we in faith its tidings learn, Nor thanklessly its blessings spurn:
May we in faith its truth confess, And praise the Lord our righteousness.

332. Monday after Eleventh Sunday after Trinity.

Lord, teach us to worship thee in spirit and in truth. Amen.

Isaiah 1, 10–15. Hear the word of the Lord, ye rulers of Sodom; give ear unto the law of our God, ye people of Gomorrah: To what purpose is the multitude of your sacrifices unto me? saith the Lord: I am full of the burnt offerings of rams, and the fat of fed beasts; and I delight not in the blood of bullocks, or of lambs, or of he goats. When ye come to appear before me, who hath required this at your hand to tread my courts? Bring no more vain oblations: incense is an abomination unto me; the new moons and sabbaths, the calling of assemblies, I cannot away with: it is iniquity, even the solemn meeting. Your new moons and your appointed feasts my soul hateth: they are a trouble unto me; I am weary to bear them. And when ye spread forth your hands, I will hide mine eyes from you; yea, when ye make many prayers, I will not hear: your hands are full of blood.

Do not neglect the word of God, as many do; but use it at home and in the church, and pray and sing to the Lord. He who despises the word of God has no weapon against the devil. He who neglects divine service and the Holy Supper, and ceases to read his Bible every day, will find that his spiritual life wastes away and dies. He who does not daily call upon the name of the Lord, pray, praise, and give thanks, will be overwhelmed and ruined by the cares and riches of this world. — But "God is a spirit; and they that worship him must worship him in spirit and in truth."

1. Your worship of God is not only useless, but wicked and abominable, if you lead a wicked life, and serve the devil. Did the Lord delight, think you, in the sacrifices and the burnt offerings of the rulers of Sodom and the people of Gomorrah? To him your donations and your hymns of praise are vain oblations and an abominable incense. He who is a Sunday saint, but is at other times evil, angry, bitter, and covetous; let him hear the word of the Lord: "It is iniquity, even the solemn meeting!" He who is strict in the observance of sabbaths and festivals, and seldom, if ever, neglects a religious meeting, but who struts about in complacent self-sufficiency, and despises others; let him hear the words of the Lord: "Your new moons and your appointed feasts my soul hateth; they are a trouble unto me; I am weary to bear them. When ye come to appear before me, who hath required this at your hand, to tread my courts?" Let us not bring unto the Lord the offering of Cain! Hate is murder; and it is a terrible thing to clasp bloody hands together in prayer to the Holy One in heaven!

2. When you read and hear the word of God, and when you pray, see that you stand in a devotional spirit before the Lord your God. "Keep thy foot when thou goest to the house of God, and be more ready to hear, than to give the sacrifice of fools." Strive earnestly to give your whole mind to it when you are in the congregation of the brethren, and when you pray in your own chamber. People do not present themselves unwashed and unkempt before princes. Put on your best attire when you go to meet your God; that is to say, collect your thoughts, ponder the importance of the matter, attune your soul

to a solemn mood, and forget the whole world. And when you hea
the word of God, or when you speak with him, do not let your hear,
go wandering hither and thither; it would be in the highest degree
discourteous and offensive, if you should, when admitted to an audience
with an earthly ruler, look about you and speak to others while he
addressed you. The Lord never fails to be present when we meet
together to hear his word, or when we read and pray in the secrecy
of our chamber. "Put off thy shoes from off thy feet; for the place
whereon thou standest is holy ground." By the grace of God you
shall succeed in concentrating your thoughts and feelings on him when
you stand before his face; then the observance of divine worship is
a blessed thing, and the Bible and prayer become pearls of great price.

3. Do not on any account join a church for the purpose of making
a good appearance before God and man, nor in order to deserve the
reward of godliness; nothing else is as detestable as hypocrisy and
self-righteousness. Use the means of grace for the edification of your
soul. This we all sorely need.

Lord, give us piety, humility, a devotional spirit, and eager hunger
and thirst after the spiritual power of the word. Amen.

Savior, if of Zion's city I, through grace, a member am, Let the world
deride or pity, I will glory in thy name. Fading is the worldling's pleasure,
All his boasted pomp and show; Solid joys and lasting treasure None but
Zion's children know.

---

333. Tuesday after Eleventh Sunday after Trinity.

Lord, give us grace to hear and obey thy call. Amen.

Matthew 21, 28-32. But what think ye? A certain man had two sons;
and he came to the first, and said, Son, go work today in my vineyard. He
answered and said, I will not; but afterward he repented, and went. And he
came to the second, and said likewise. And he answered and said, I go, sir;
and went not. Whether of them twain did the will of his father? They say
unto him, The first. Jesus saith unto them, Verily I say unto you, That the
publicans and the harlots go into the kingdom of God before you. For John
came unto you in the way of righteousness, and ye believed him not; but the
publicans and the harlots believed him: and ye, when ye had seen it, repented
not afterward, that ye might believe him.

"The publicans and the harlots go into the kingdom of God before you"; that is to say, they enter the kingdom, while you do *not*.
Let us, dear brethren, not allow this judgment to fall on us! We will
put the devil to shame, and become the blessed spoil of Christ. It is
our wish that publicans and harlots may be cleansed and sanctified,
and enter the kingdom of heaven; but neither will we remain without,
where are the dogs, and sorcerers, and idolators, and whosoever loveth
and maketh a lie. What, then, shall we do? We shall obey the word
of the Lord, and go work in his vineyard. Let us who hear and
read the word of God, who come together to be edified by it, and to
confess it; who are church-goers and communicants; who are called,

and who wish to be, Christians; — let us go and *do that which the Lord says!* The world has a habit of finding fault with the conduct of the Christians, and comforts itself in its sins by accusing them of hypocrisy, pride, and covetousness. Let this cause us to examine ourselves, and to cultivate a holy earnestness in our faith and life. Let us not shut our ears against the accusation; there may be some truth in it for our correction. Then the world shall see that we have a living Savior who purifies unto himself a peculiar people, zealous of good works, and able to stop the mouth of them that mock him. Go work in the Lord's vineyard; that is, in his kingdom on earth, the Christian church! To enter this vineyard is to repent and believe; but to work in it is to do all things in faith, to the honor of God and the good of man. Publicans and harlots *believed* John the Baptist, took his preaching of repentance to heart, confessed their sin, and came to Jesus. Thereafter they walked in newness of life, and served him. The important thing is to believe the word of God. The obedience of the heart; the acquiescence of the heart in the declarations, "you are a lost sinner," and "Jesus has saved you from sin and death and devil"; — this obedience of the heart is followed by obedience in word and deed, causing you to live for the Lord; and then you work in his vineyard. Do all things in the consciousness that you belong to him, and that he has a right of ownership in all men, as he has bought them with a price; and make the salvation of their souls, and their temporal welfare, and their healing, and comfort, and happiness, the object of your work; and it shall be said of you: "And he answered and said, I go, sir; and went out." Remember that Christ served us unceasingly in obedience to the word of the Father, and that you thereby are become his own, free from sin and the law, a child of God, and heir of salvation. Be therefore, in return, zealous to serve others in love, obedient and happy always and everywhere before the face of the Lord. Help us to do this, merciful God. Make us obedient under the discipline of thy word, that we may have knowledge of our sin; and help us to believe thy gospel, that we may enter into the true liberty of grace. Make us rich in charity, that we may become a blessing to the world. Amen.

Lord, to thee I make confession: I have sinned and gone astray, I have multiplied transgression, Chosen for myself my way. Now I see my grievous error, And my heart is struck with terror.

Yet, though conscience' voice appall me, Father, I will seek thy face; Though thy child I dare not call me, Yet receive me to thy grace: Do not for my sins forsake me, Do not let thy wrath o'ertake me.

---

334. Wednesday after Eleventh Sunday after Trinity.

Lord, instruct me, and teach me, and guide me with thine eye. Amen.

1 John 1, 8–2, 2. If we say that we have no sin, we deceive ourselves, and the truth is not in us. If we confess our sins, he is faithful and just to forgive us our sins, and to cleanse us from all unrighteousness. If we say that we have not sinned, we make him a liar, and his word is not in us. My little

children, these things write I unto you, that ye sin not. And if any man sin, we have an advocate with the Father, Jesus Christ the righteous: and he is the propitiation for our sins: and not for our's only, but also for the sins of the whole world.

There is probably not one of my readers who will declare in so many words: "I have no sin," or: "I have not sinned"; but there may be some who do not repent of and confess their sin. And this is equivalent to denying it. You thereby make God a liar; you make him a sinner. He, on the other hand, who confesses his sin honors the Lord's truth and receives forgiveness. For the Lord says that we are sinners, but promises mercy to the penitent; and he is the *faithful* God, and can not fail to redeem his promise. His *faithfulness* insures us forgiveness; and so does his *justice.* "He is *faithful* and *just* to *forgive* us our sins, and to cleanse us from all unrighteousness." For through Jesus we have paid our debt; and it is, then, justice in God to cancel it. If we let truth be truth, accept as final that which God says, and confess our sins, we are in Christ; and with him before us we have in the *justice* of God a safe guarantee of our salvation. Here, under the wings of Christ's mercy, is also our power of *sanctification;* here are kindled in us love of God and hatred of sin. Under the cross of Christ flow the water and blood which cleanse both body and soul. Shall he who is justified from sin continue to live in sin? Certainly not. And yet even the saints would be guilty of lying, should they deny that they have sin. The more nearly perfect you are in holiness, the more painfully acute is your feeling of sinfulness. To which we may add that the saints also may at times fall into grievous sins. Then they bitterly repent of it; and so they should; for they have done a great wrong. But God caused John to write this, in order that the devil might not gain the mastery over us. Your Savior is, after all, your advocate with the Father; and he is the propitiation for the sins of the world, for every sin of whatever kind or degree. Return to God; place yourself once more under our high priest; confess, pray, and believe; — his atoning blood, which is your advocate in heaven, surely carries greater weight than does even the worst of your transgressions. What business has Satan with you anyhow? "Who shall lay anything to the charge of God's elect? It is God that justifieth. Who is he that condemneth? It is Christ that died, yea rather, that is arisen again, who is even at the right hand of God, who also maketh intercession for us." "If we walk in the light, as God is in the light, we have fellowship one with another, and the blood of Jesus Christ his Son cleanseth us from all sin." — Come, all men; confess everything, receive forgiveness for everything, and praise the faithfulness and justice of God in Christ!

Give us light, O Lord; teach us to know our sin, and teach us to know thy grace which justifies. Do not suffer us to harbor a feeling of carnal security; but humble us every day, that we may have our comfort in the blood of Christ only. Keep us from falling, and do not let us remain in sin; but help us to increase in holiness, and man us with fearless hearts in life and death. Amen.

Ah, hide not for our sins thy face; Absolve us through thy boundless grace: Be with us in our anguish still, Free us at last from every ill; That so with all our hearts we may Once more our glad thanksgivings pay, And walk obedient to thy word, And now and ever praise thee, Lord.

---

335. Thursday after Eleventh Sunday after Trinity.

Lord, speak to our hearts of the greatness of thy mercy. Amen.

Romans 5, 12–16. Wherefore, as by one man sin entered into the world, and death by sin; and so death passed upon all men, for that all have sinned: For until the law, sin was in the world: but sin is not imputed when there is no law. Nevertheless, death reigned from Adam to Moses, even over them that had not sinned after the similitude of Adam's transgression, who is the figure of him that was to come. But not as the offence, so also is the free gift. For if through the offence of one many be dead, much more the grace of God and the gift by grace, which is by one man, Jesus Christ, hath abounded unto many. And not as it was by one that sinned, so is the gift: for the judgment was by one to condemnation, but the free gift is of many offences unto justification.

There is a resemblance between Adam and Christ: Adam sinned and died, and *all* men sinned and died in him. Christ suffered death, and rose again, and was justified; and this is the death and resurrection of *all* men, and is righteousness for all. The circumstance that death reigned from the time of Adam to Moses, while there were no positive enactments of law, shows that the sin and guilt of Adam were the sin and guilt of all; for what other transgression of the law was there during that time but that of Adam? We all were in Adam; and by his fall we fell, and became subject to death. But we are likewise all raised again in Christ, and have again received life, if we will but believe. — Nevertheless, there is in respect to two phases of the matter a great *distinction*: 1) The grace of Christ is so *exceeding great* that nothing can be compared with it. 2) The offence of Adam is one, and judgment on it one; while the *grace of Christ* is for many offences, for that of Adam and for all which have been added since the time when the law was given.

Of a truth there is in the world much sin of many kinds. We all are transgressors from our birth, with a wicked nature and a disobedient heart. The whole race is corrupted and poisoned and permeated with wickedness. We all are guilty of the transgression of Adam, as though each of us had committed it in his own person. Even though we be unable to see this with our darkened understanding, the word of God and our own conscience declare it with such emphasis as to make doubt impossible. Superadded to this are the countless transgressions in the life of every human being. Multiply the number of transgressors by the number of the transgressions of each, and who shall read the product? And then, every transgression is full of the poison of hell, and some of them are terrible in their enormity. Yet the grace of God in Christ is much greater than all the world's transgressions together. For, declares the Spirit of God through Paul, the grace of God, and the gift by grace, which is by one man, Jesus Christ, hath *much more* abounded unto many, than have the offence and death; — *much more* abounded, and *abounded unto many*. And later he says: "Where sin *abounded*, grace did much *more abound.*" Such mercy has God given us, and with such words he wants to help us to believe. Do not, then, hereafter humor Satan, who will have you to doubt on account of your imperfections; but obey the word of God, and rejoice in the hope of the glory of God. Christ lives, and makes intercession for you; shall you not, then, be saved by his life? Or can it be that your sin, after all, outweighs the life and death of the Son of God, and that your death is stronger than the righteousness of God? Is it possible that your unbelief is true, and the word of God a lie? — Nay, Lord, I am put to shame, and I surrender to your gospel from heaven; give me the necessary grace hereto by thy Spirit. The depravity of my heart, my obduracy and insensibility, my unbelief and worldliness, which always present themselves as obstacles in the way of faith; these, together with all my wicked deeds and my corrupt nature, are outweighed a thousand times by thy free gift of grace, Lord Jesus. Blessed be thy name. Amen.

Let not conscience make you linger, Nor of fitness fondly dream; All the fitness he requireth Is to feel your need of him; This he gives you; 'Tis the Spirit's rising beam.

Lo! th'incarnate God ascended Pleads the merit of his blood; Venture on him, venture wholly, Let no other trust intrude: None but Jesus, Can do helpless sinners good.

---

336. Friday after Eleventh Sunday after Trinity.

Psalm 32, 1-5. Blessed is he whose transgression is forgiven, whose sin is covered. Blessed is the man unto whom the Lord imputeth not iniquity, and in whose spirit there is no guile. When I kept silence, my bones waxed old, through my roaring all the day long. For day and night thy hand was heavy upon me: my moisture is turned into drought of summer. Selah. I acknowledged my sin unto thee, and mine iniquity have I not hid. I said, I will confess my transgressions unto the Lord; and thou forgavest the iniquity of my sin. Selah.

"When I kept silence, my bones waxed old"; that is, when I would not confess my sin, I was without peace and happiness. This was the situation of David from the time of his fall until Nathan came to him. I wonder, if it be not the case with many among us. At times they more or less distinctly feel in their conscience the wrath of God; but they are too proud, too thoughtless, too worldly-minded, to humble themselves and seek mercy; and thus they gradually come to feel more and more secure. — "I acknowledged my transgressions; and thou forgavest the iniquity of my sin." Forgiveness follows confession; you no sooner lay your sins before God, and pray for mercy, than he forgives you. He answers before you have found time to finish speaking. While you are still trying to say: "God be merciful to me a sinner," he makes reply: "I have put away thy sin; thou shalt not die." For who other than God himself has produced in your soul the

confession of sin? Shall he, then, deny the prayer himself has inspired? Shall that stream of mercy which from God's heaven is poured
out upon all humanity, in order that it may open and refresh the hearts,
fail in the case of the very persons who thirst after it? Away with
the lies of Satan! Away with the fancied security which denies, or
defends, or excuses sin, and causes a man to say: "I am no better;
I *can* not help it; I am no worse than God made me; I am, at any
rate, better than many others." Away also with the denial of God's
mercy, in which the heart says: "I dare not as yet believe that my sin
is forgiven; I *can* not believe it; I do not as yet feel it, and I will
not deceive myself with a dead faith." Beware of the devil's cunning;
that you do not on account of your own feelings charge God with
being a deceiver, and with saying that which he does not mean, and
with making promises which he does not keep! It always is entirely
safe to trust in the word of the Lord. Dear timid soul, make honest
confession of your sin; tell the Lord what you are and what you have
done, how you feel and what you want; speak out before him, and
plead for mercy; but do not be afraid that you may forget to say everything that you should; the prayer of the publican was not a long one.
When you thus pray, you may feel assured *that your sin is forgiven*
you. At the moment when you confess your sin Jesus possesses you
of his own merit, and you are a blessed child of God.

Help us all, merciful God, to confess our transgressions and receive forgiveness for the iniquity of our sin. Our guilt is and always
will be too heavy for us to carry. Let thy Spirit enlighten us, that
we may repent, and believe, and be saved in our Lord Jesus Christ.
Amen.

Eternal Spirit, by whose breath The soul is raised from sin and death,
Before thy throne we sinners bend; To us thy quickening power extend.
Jehovah! Father, Spirit, Son! Mysterious Godhead! Three in One!
Before thy throne we sinners bend; Grace, pardon, life, to us extend!

---

337. Saturday after Eleventh Sunday after Trinity.

Psalm 119, 169–176. Let my cry come near before thee, O Lord: give me
understanding according to thy word. Let my supplication come before thee:
deliver me according to thy word. My lips shall utter praise, when thou hast
taught me thy statutes. My tongue shall speak of thy word: for all thy commandments are righteousness. Let thine hand help me: for I have chosen thy
precepts. I have longed for thy salvation, O Lord; and thy law is my delight.
Let my soul live, and it shall praise thee; and let thy judgments help me. I
have gone astray like a lost sheep: seek thy servant; for I do not forget thy
commandments.

Prayers by the saints, like that before us, the Lord has caused to
be recorded for our sakes; he has wished to teach us that *we are to
come to him*, and to shew us *how* we are to pray. When you have gone
astray, and discover that you are lost, you shall not surrender to the
devil, but cry to God; and he shall come to your aid. At all times
when you are unhappy, you are not to keep the burden weighing down

your heart, but "in all your need and distress call upon the name of the Lord, pray, praise, and give thanks." When God gives you joy keep it in your heart, and increase it by praising the Lord; but do not keep your sorrow; for God's sake do not bury your gloomy thoughts in your soul! God does not wish it; he says: "Be careful for *nothing;* but in *every* thing by prayer and supplication with thanksgiving let your requests be made known unto God." God help us to do this; then shall we sing more songs of praise, and understand better the music of rejoicing. — Our Bible lesson teaches us especially three things in regard to the prayer of the seeking soul: 1) Your prayer shall express your longing and lamentation with a humble cry to God. "Let my *cry* come near before thee." "Let my *supplication* come before thee; *deliver* me according to thy word." "*I have longed* for thy salvation." "I have gone astray like a lost sheep; seek thy servant" 2) Your prayer must keep close to the Lord's word and promise. "Give me understanding *according to the word.*" "Deliver me *according to thy word.*" "Thou hast taught me thy statutes." "Thy law is my delight." The whole of this long psalm lauds *the word* of God. Believe that which he promises; incline your heart to his testimonies, not according to wisdom of your own invention, but *according to that which the mouth of the Lord hath spoken.* 3) Your prayer must include the promise that you will *praise* God and *obey* him. "My lips shall utter praise." "My tongue shall speak of thy word." "Let my soul live, and it shall praise thee." "Seek thy servant; for I do not forget thy commandments."

Lord, teach me thus to pray; and "quicken me according to thy lovingkindness! Thy word is true from the beginning; and every one of thy righteous judgments endureth for ever. I rejoice at thy word as one that findeth great spoil. I hate and abhor lying; but thy law do I love. Seven times a day do I praise thee because of thy righteous judgments. Great peace have they which love thy law; and nothing shall offend them." "Make thy face to shine upon thy servant; and teach me thy statutes." Amen.

Bowed down beneath a load of sin, By Satan sorely pressed, By wars without and fears within, I come to thee for rest.
Be thou my shield and hiding place, That, sheltered near thy side, I may my fierce accuser face, And tell him, thou hast died.

---

338. Twelfth Sunday after Trinity. I.

Let my lips declare the judgments of thy mouth. Amen.

Gospel Lesson, Mark 7, 31–37. And again, departing from the coasts of Tyre and Sidon, he came .nto the sea of Galilee, through the midst of the coasts of Decapolis. And they bring unto him one that was deaf, and had an impediment in his speech; and they beseech him to put his hand upon him. And he took him aside from the multitude, and put his fingers into his ears, and he spit, and touched his tongue; and looking up to heaven, he sighed, and saith unto him, Ephphatha, that is, Be opened. And straightway his ears were opened, and the string of his tongue was loosed, and he spake plain. And he

charged them that they should tell no man: but the more he charged them,
so much the more a great deal they published it; and were beyond measure
astonished, saying, He hath done all things well: he maketh both the deaf to
hear, and the dumb to speak.

"His *ears were opened*, and *the string of his tongue was loosed*, and
he spake plain." Notice that *first* his ears were opened, and *then* the
string of his tongue was loosed. The inability to speak is caused by
inability to hear. Deaf-mutes usually have perfect organs of speech,
but can not use them, because they can not hear. The reason why
there are so many who are spiritually dumb is that so many are spiritually deaf. They have a glib tongue; are able to commend and cen-
sure, to attack and defend, and to choose their words wisely and well;
and still their tongue is tied: They can not praise the Lord, nor re-
count his wonders. The fact that we have received the gift of speech,
this glorious gift, which is possessed by no other creature on earth,
evidences the Lord's goodness to us, and proclaims his wisdom. That,
however, which this most marvellous gift itself proclaims many who
have it are unable to proclaim; in so far they are dumb. They have
nor heart nor tongue to speak any divine truth for the glory of the
Lord. Nor can they, therefore, speak in a way to edify others. When
the divine life is not in our heart, neither can it be on our tongue; for
out of the abundance of the heart the mouth speaketh.

First, then, the love of God in Christ must enter our hearts. By
nature we all are evil and dead. Life and light must come from without; that is to say, from God. And this comes to pass when we *hear
his word;* hear the truth and love in Christ, spoken to us through his
gospel. When the ear of the soul is opened, and it actually hears the
truths of the gospel, then we learn to speak, and to praise God. The
Spirit of life then abides in us, and causes our tongue to speak the
language of the regenerated and purified heart. Let the Lord take
you aside by yourself alone; let him put his finger, — that is, the power
of his word unto salvation, — into your ears, and let him touch your
tongue with the juice of his mouth; let him sigh and make intercession for you; place yourself under the mercy of him, your high priest,
and hear his "Ephphatha"; so shall you learn to "speak plain". Then
shall you sing, and heaven and earth sing with you, concerning that
which the Lord has done: "He hath done all things well; he maketh
both the deaf to hear, and the dumb to speak." Let this blessed miracle befall many, many among us, merciful God. Give us grace so
to hear the words of thy Spirit that they may abide in us. "Blessed
the soul that hears the Lord speak in the heart, and receives the word
of comfort out of his mouth! Blessed the ears which hearken to that
which the Spirit of God softly whispers, and do not incline to the noisy
and confused voices of this world!" — Give us grace to use this excellent gift, our tongue, for the purpose of speaking thy praise. Give
us this happiness through Jesus Christ. Amen.

Ye nations round the earth, rejoice Before the Lord, your sovereign King;
Serve him with cheerful heart and voice, With all your tongues his glory sing.
The Lord is God, 'tis he alone Doth life and breath and being give; We
are his work, and not our own, The sheep that on his pastures live.

339. Twelfth Sunday after Trinity. II.

"Glorious Lord, thyself impart; light of light, from God proceeding."

Epistle Lesson, 2 Corinthians 3, 4–9. And such trust have we through Christ to God-ward: not that we are sufficient of ourselves to think any thing, as of ourselves; but our sufficiency is of God: who also hath made us able ministers of the new testament; not of the letter, but of the spirit: for the letter killeth, but the spirit giveth life. But if the ministration of death, written and engraven in stones, was glorious, so that the children of Israel could not steadfastly behold the face of Moses for the glory of his countenance; which glory was to be done away; how shall not the ministration of the Spirit be rather glorious? For if the ministration of condemnation be glory, much more doth the ministration of righteousness exceed in glory.

It is a thing glorious beyond measure to preach the gospel of Jesus Christ. This ministration is glorious by reason of its origin; for it has been given us by the King, our blessed Savior himself. It is *his* own work which we do when we preach the word. Who is not glad to serve the greatest and best master? Who does not esteem it as an honor to be the personal representative of such a master? Let the ministers of the word of God not forget that they are "ambassadors for Christ"; that it is God himself who by them speaks to the souls. — This ministration is glorious by reason of the subject-matter with which the word deals. The gospel of our Lord Jesus Christ is truth, spirit, and life; it has its source in God's own heart, in his eternal love and divine wisdom, revealed to us in the birth and death of the only begotten Son, and sealed by his resurrection. It is the sun which shines on humanity, and gives light and warmth to the hearts. Without this sun everything in us would be dead and desolate. This gospel is the celestial music which again draws the heart heavenward; it is the strong life-line which the Lord throws about the souls, and with which he drags them out of the jaws of death. Moses was obliged to put a vail over the glory shining in the face of the Lord; we make every effort to reveal the glory of the Lord which shines upon the earth from the face of Christ. For that which we preach in the gospel is not the God of terrors, but our merciful heavenly Father; not wrath, but grace. — This ministration is glorious by reason of its purpose, which is the eternal salvation of the souls. Its object is none other than the creation of life from the dead. *Life from the dead;* could anything be more glorious? It glorifies the Lord; it magnifies the name of Jesus; mention, if you can, anything more beautiful than this. It makes love victorious, and satisfies justice; it leads men back to the place where they rightfully belong, the throne of God; it delivers them from the power of the devil; and translates them into the kingdom of light, and finally into eternal bliss. The ministration of the letter wrote the law of love in stones, the ministration of the spirit writes it in the hearts.

What a grave responsibility! "And who is sufficient for these things?" Let every man acknowledge in his heart that of himself he is not sufficient; nay, that he is not able to think even one thought as he should! Then, however, the Lord's "Ephphatha" shall open his ears and anoint his tongue.

Lord Jesus, expound thyself to us; that the glory of thy face may beam upon the church in the words and the lives of thy servants. Amen.

Shall we, whose souls are lighted With wisdom from on high, Shall we to men benighted The lamp of life deny? Salvation, O salvation! The joyful sound proclaim, Till each remotest nation Has learned Messiah's name.

---

340. Monday after Twelfth Sunday after Trinity.

Know that Jesus Christ is our God, and that there is no other Savior.

Matthew 15, 29–31. And Jesus departed from thence, and came nigh unto the sea of Galilee; and went up into a mountain, and sat down there. And great multitudes came unto him, having with them those that were lame, blind dumb, maimed, and many others, and cast them down at Jesus' feet; and he healed them: Insomuch that the multitude wondered, when they saw the dumb to speak, the maimed to be whole, the lame to walk, and the blind to see: and they glorified the God of Israel.

Search the world and see, if you can find any other like our Lord Jesus! Search among the ancient Egyptians, the Greeks, the Romans; search among the Hindoos, Arabians, and Persians; among the sages of the past and the present; among the mighty intellects, the great and the good among men. Search among the angels, if you can, among the princes of heaven; ascend into the high, or descend into the deep, there is none like Jesus. *He, he is the only one who can and will save us.* His power and mercy are equal. Of none other can it be said, as it is said of him: "Himself took our infirmities, and bare our sicknesses." "Great multitudes came unto him, having with them those that were lame, blind, dumb, maimed, and many others, and cast them down at his feet; *and he healed them.*" He is more to us than any other is or could be; he alone is just what we need. We are sinners; he is the Savior of sinners. We are sick; he is the physician of the sick. We are unrighteous; he is our righteousness. We are the captives of death; he is the destroyer of death. He has a remedy for your every ailment. You are wretched in body and soul; Jesus heals them both. He takes away your guilt, and cleanses your soul; he destroys the poison which is the cause of all your trouble, and you are made pure and well for ever. "He forgiveth all thine iniquities, and healeth all thy diseases; he satisfieth thy mouth with good things: so that thy youth is renewed like the eagle's." — Then again, he turns not one away who seeks healing at his hands. None, no not one, is so wretched, so evil, so wicked, but that he shall receive, if he come to Jesus and ask help of him. Note this well: Jesus never has cast off any man, not one, who came to him, and wished to be saved. His whole life certifies to the truth of what himself says: "Him that cometh to me I will in no wise cast out." How blessed and happy are we, who have such a master! I have found him whom my soul sought.

whom my soul loveth; my Savior and Physician, my King and God, my life and my heaven! All is well; and all that is in me praise his holy name Hallelujah!

Draw us all to thee, Lord Jeuss; thou hast room for us all. Heal us, and save us; so shall we rejoice, and serve one another before thy face, and give praise to the Father, who with thee and the Holy Ghost is one true God from everlasting. Amen.

At even, ere the sun was set, The sick, O Lord, around thee lay; Oh, in what divers pains they met! Oh, with what joy they went away!

Once more 'tis eventide, and we, oppressed with various ills, draw near; What if thy form we cannot see? We know and feel that thou art here.

---

341. Tuesday after Twelfth Sunday after Trinity.

Lord, let my thoughts, words, and deeds please thee. Amen.

Matthew 12, 33-37. Either make the tree good, and his fruit good; or else make the tree corrupt, and his fruit corrupt: for the tree is known by his fruit. O generation of vipers! how can ye, being evil, speak good things? for out of the abundance of the heart the mouth speaketh. A good man out of the good treasure of the heart bringeth forth good things; and an evil man, out of the evil treasure, bringeth forth evil things. But I say unto you, That every idle word that men shall speak, they shall give account thereof in the day of judgment: for by thy words thou shalt be justified, and by thy words thou shalt be condemned.

Let truth, charity, goodness, and purity dwell in your heart, and they will of necessity cause you to speak good things. As every tree brings forth fruit after its kind, so every man speaks according to the nature of his heart. If the heart be evil, bitter, unclean, worldly, selfish; so will the speech be also. There are, to be sure, many degrees of wickedness in the hearts; but there is nothing truly good in an unregenerate man, and he can not speak the holy words of love. Above all, then, see to it that you have a new heart, which after God is created in righteousness and true holiness. Even men can judge from your words what it is that dwells in you; especially the saints, who have the Spirit of God. But even though men might be mistaken in you, the Lord always knows exactly what you are; and your speech always reveals something of the quality of your heart. The spirit which dwells in you is in your words, and it will in some way affect the spirit of them that hear you, and will, when it meets a kindred soul, fructify it, and cause it to grow, and to strike its roots deep, and appear in the person's life. If the spirit in that which you say does not at once strike the right kind of soil in the one to whom you speak, yet it may after repeated trials in the course of time fasten itself to his heart and strike root. Thus the word is a great power in the world; so great that there is no greater. Let it be a good spirit which iives in you, and brings forth your words.

Even if you have the Holy Spirit in your soul, his light in your understanding, his purity in your heart, his peace in your conscience :

so that you are justified by your words; — do you still keep careful watch over yourself, and guard your tongue; for your evil nature is all the time struggling to come out into the light, and the devil rejoices in putting evil words into the mouth of the saints. The sins of unchastity, anger, covetousness, impatience, and the like, stir in you; and if you are not on your guard, they will flow out over your lips. Your tongue, as Saint James expresses it, "defileth the whole body, and setteth on fire the course of nature." Certainly the Lord may thus humble his children, and in that way benefit them; but the damage done to others by an unbridled tongue is something which you can not prevent. Always keep in mind, then, these words from the Lord's own lips. "I say unto you, that every idle word that men shall speak, they shall give account thereof in the day of judgment." Strive earnestly to benefit your neighbor by everything that you say; let this be your *constant endeavor!* Let *everything* which you speak be true and pure and good. In this way you may bring forth much good fruit; you may thus scatter many blessings among men. Do it! — Mercifully help us, O God, always to speak words of truth and charity, to honor thee and edify our neighbor. Keep us from all evil speech; let wicked words neither be uttered by us, nor find their way into our soul. Amen.

I lay my sins on Jesus, The spotless Lamb of God; He bears them all, and frees us From the accursed load. I bring my guilt to Jesus, To wash my crimson stains White in his blood most precious, Till not a spot remains.

---

342. Wednesday after Twelfth Sunday after Trinity.

Lord, open our ears, that we may hear thy word. Amen.

Isaiah 29, 17–19. Is it not yet a very little while, and Lebanon shall be turned into a fruitful field, and the fruitful field shall be esteemed as a forest? And in that day shall the deaf hear the words of the book, and the eyes of the blind shall see out of obscurity, and out of darkness. The meek also shall increase their joy in the Lord, and the poor among men shall rejoice in the Holy One of Israel.

"If any man be in Christ, he is a new creature; old things are passed away; behold, all things are become new." In the sacred language of the prophets this idea is expressed thus: "Lebanon shall be turned into a fruitful field, and the fruitful field shall be esteemed as a forest." This also suggests to our minds these words of the apostle: "The creature itself also shall be delivered from the bondage of corruption into the glorious liberty of the children of God." Sin has changed man and all creation; grace again transforms man's heart, and makes all things new. Jesus has brought the strength to effect this transformation, and he exercises it by the gospel in his church. "The words of the book," the divine teachings of holy writ, are able to find a way into our hearts, which by nature are closed against the truth. For the Spirit of the Lord is in the word, and his "Ephphata" has power to work miracles. The word itself opens our ears to hear and receive it; and it also contains and brings life, and thus quickens us. The Spirit of the word anoints our eyes; so that we, who are blind, see. And the Lord is himself with us in the word; so that we therein see him, and have him. "God's own word, our Holy Bible is our only source of light; life on earth would be without it nothing but a hideous night." Have you, dear friend, experienced this illuminating and quickening power of the word of God? Have you therein heard the Lord's "Be opened"? If so, you have learned that the meek increase their joy in the Lord, as they come to hear the words of the book more and more distinctly; and that the poor among men rejoice in the Holy One of Israel. "Even though all the world go wrong, Jesus shall not fail us, nor his covenant be broken." Soon everything which resists the Spirit of God shall for ever be done away with; "for the terrible one is brought to naught, and the scorner is consumed, and all that watch for iniquity are cut off."

God, have mercy on us, and give us thy Spirit. Explain thy word to us, and let us experience its power. Help us to be obedient to thee, that thou mayest reveal to us more and more of the mysteries of thy grace, and mayest sanctify us more and more through thy truth. Amen.

Thrice blessed word of God, Gift or a Father's love, Which holy prophets wrote, Moved by the Holy Dove:

Within thy pages fair, What hidden treasure lies! Sweet lessons for the young, Deep wisdom for the wise.

Therefore with grateful hearts, O Trinity divine, We magnify thy name, For this blest gift of thine.

---

343. Thursday after Twelfth Sunday after Trinity.

Lord enlighten us, that we may understand how wonderful are thy testimonies.

1 Corinthians 2, 9–13. But, as it is written, Eye hath not seen, nor ear heard, neither have entered into the heart of man, the things which God hath prepared for them that love him. But God hath revealed them unto us by his Spirit: for the Spirit searcheth all things, yea, the deep things of God. For what man knoweth the things of a man, save the spirit of man which is in him? even so the things of God knoweth no man, but the Spirit of God. Now we have received, not the spirit of the world, but the Spirit which is of God; that we might know the things that are freely given to us of God. Which things also we speak, not in the words which man's wisdom teacheth, but which the Holy Ghost teacheth; comparing spiritual things with spiritual.

No; these things have not entered into the heart of man; that much is certain. Human wisdom and invention never could have devised that which the word of God teaches us in regard to the salvation in Christ and the glory awaiting the faithful. This counsel of wisdom, which brings about such a glorious unison between love and justice, and which turns our deep fall into the highest salvation, by means of the incarnation, death, and resurrection of the only begotten Son; this conception of eternal mercy, which destroys wrath, and fills heaven with saved human beings; — how could these things have originated elsewhere than in the own heart of God? "The natural man receiveth not the things of the Spirit of God; for they are foolishness unto him; neither can he know them, because they are spiritually discerned." How, then, could these things have their origin in man? Ask a worldly-wise philosopher whether the biblical plan of salvation seems reasonable to him; whether he would have evolved such a plan out of his own intellect! That, however, which has not entered into the heart of man, and which is and shall be hid from the carnally minded, God has revealed to his believers, and makes it known to each of them in ever increasing measure. The treasures of the kingdom of heaven have been given us by Jesus in the means of grace in his church. The mysteries of grace are revealed in the apostolic word; but the worldly-minded can not discern that which is spiritual; the good things of the house of God, which have power to make a man eternally rich and happy, are before their eyes; yet they do not see them. The gospel is sounded in their ears; but even as one who is wholly without musical sense hears the grandest harmony without apreciating any of its beauties, so the worldly-minded person understands nothing of that which is the substance of the gospel. None but the Spirit of God can teach us to understand the word of God, and to know what God has given us in this gospel. Follow these three rules: 1) Read and hear the word diligently and with a mind open to conviction. 2) Pray without ceasing that the Holy Ghost may enlighten you; and hold fast his promise to do this (Luke 11, 9-13). 3) Obey the word with honest heart, in so far as you understand it. If you do this, you shall surely receive new light in your soul, and see your own distress and misery; but you shall also see the glory which is given us in Christ. — Holy Spirit, illumine our hearts; we earnestly ask of thee this favor in the name of Jesus. Amen.

Unnumbered choirs before the shining throne Their joyful anthems raise, Till heaven's glad halls are echoing with the tone Of that great hymn of praise, And all its host rejoices, And all its blessed throng Unite their myriad voices In one eternal song.

344. Friday after Twelfth Sunday after Trinity.

Heal me, O Lord, and I shall be healed; save me, and I shall be saved. Amen.

Matthew 8, 14-17. And when Jesus was come into Peter's house, he saw his wife's mother laid, and sick of a fever. And he touched her hand, and the fever left her: and she arose, and ministered unto them. When the even was come, they brought unto him many that were possessed with devils: and he cast out the spirits with his word, and healed all that were sick: that it might be fulfilled which was spoken by Esaias the prophet, saying, himself took our infirmities, and bare our sicknesses.

The prophecy which is here fulfilled by the *work of Jesus in healing* the sick is found in the 53rd chapter of Isaiah, and treats of the Lord's *suffering* for our sin. Here we learn that sin is the cause of all our sickness, and that the effect disappears with the cause. For that which the prophet says concerning the taking away of *sin* the evangelist declares to have been fulfilled by the healing of the *sick* and the casting out of evil spirits. — Furthermore we here learn that in all that he did Jesus was the *suffering* Savior. When he heals the sick he enters into their condition and feels their pain as though it were his own. He makes their sickness his own, and suffers it with them, and thus takes it away. For this reason he sighs when confronted by the deaf-mute; and for this reason he weeps at the grave of Lazarus. During the whole of his life on earth he is the Lamb which taketh away the sin of the world; all the time he was afflicted with suffering; and all that he does is done as a propitiation and atonement for our transgressions. "Him who knew no sin, God hath made to be sin for us"; the iniquity of us all was laid on him, and he was made to bear it, and was made acquainted with grief. Therefore it is written also that he was in all points tempted like as we are, yet without sin.

As a result the righteous wrath of God is taken away, and the power of the evil spirits is broken; so that all who believe in Jesus shall have perfect health for evermore, and shall be rid of all evil. Every defect shall be cured, all bands be loosed, all darkness disappear; all sorrows shall be turned into bliss, every sigh and lamentation be changed into songs of praise. Yet a little while you shall feel the burning fever; yet a little while you shall be tormented by the evil spirits, and with all the saints suffer under the buffetings of Satan; yet a little while you shall be afflicted by corruption and the infirmities of the flesh. But it is only for a little while; and these things befall you, in order that you may be *like Jesus* in his humiliation, and thereafter in glory; that you may be purged, and then shine as the sun in the kingdom of your heavenly Father; that you may know what it is from which you have been delivered, and prize salvation the more highly. Furthermore, God employs this means of fitting you to be his ambassador to others, and enabling you of your own experience to "speak a word in season to him that is weary." *You are saved, and shall be saved unto eternal glory.* It is no longer the chill and the fever of death which courses through your members, even though it may seem so to you; and you are no longer in bondage under the evil enemy; but are the freedman of Christ and the quickened child of God the Father. For Jesus took away your death, and gave you life in his word. Since you hear this word, and accept this mercy, you shall reign with him in the life eternal. Believe this in your heart; *for hc has done it.* The death which you feel is nothing but life; it is life which struggles in you, and destroys death. Let your sole care be that you may have true faith in your heart. Let the weary labor which the Lord performed, the long suffering which he endured, the great price which he paid, make us zealous for our salvation; and let the sense of our deep distress without him impel us to come to him, and to bring with us all who are of our household, leaving not one behind!

Lord Jesus, open our ears to hear thy voice, and our eyes to see thy power. Heal us, Lord; and teach us to lay all our griefs and sorrows on thee, even as thou didst take them, and carry them. Cast the wicked spirits out of our hearts and our homes; and grant us grace

29

to serve thee and thine, to follow thee, and to bear one another's burdens. Amen.

O Savior Christ! our woes dispel, For some are sick, and some are sad, And some have never loved thee well, And some have lost the love they had; And some are pressed with worldly care, And some are tried with sinful doubt; And some such grievous passions tear That only thou canst cast them out.

345. Saturday after Twelfth Sunday after Trinity.

Psalm 142. Maschil of David; A Prayer when he was in the cave. I cried unto the Lord with my voice: with my voice unto the Lord did I make my supplication. I poured out my complaint before him: I shewed before him my trouble. When my spirit was overwhelmed within me, then thou knewest my path: in the way wherein I walked have they privily laid a snare for me. I looked on my right hand, and beheld, but there was no man that would know me: refuge failed me; no man cared for my soul. I cried unto thee, O Lord: I said, Thou art my refuge, and my portion in the land of the living. Attend unto my cry; for I am brought very low: deliver me from my persecutors; for they are stronger than I. Bring my soul out of prison, that I may praise thy name: the righteous shall compass me about; for thou shalt deal bountifully with me.

Do not, dear Christian, shut your sorrows up in your own breast; but lay your soul bare before God, and pour out your heart to him in words of prayer. The devil is a dumb spirit, who wants to tie our tongue, that we may not be able to "cry unto the Lord"; and he is a proud spirit, who wants to make our heart stubborn, that we may not "with our voice make supplication unto the Lord." I am sure that you have some acquaintance with this dark cavern in which the soul sits silent, and broods on its own misery, reproaches God and all men, and refuses admittance to every thought of comfort. Our Psalm instructs us to break this unhappy silence. 1) You are not the only one who eats the bread of tears. On the contrary; *all* who have true piety receive their share. David was brought so very low, and felt so despondent, that his spirit was overwhelmed within him. He had a sense of being so entirely alone and forsaken in his distress that his refuge failed him, and no man cared for him. When the saints have this experience, they become like unto Christ; for on him these words were fulfilled to the letter. 2) *Humble yourself* before the Lord. Than this nothing is, I might say, more important. There is nothing to which the devil has a stronger dislike; nothing which so decidedly promotes your peace. Know that you *deserve* punishment; and then sue for mercy. Note the words of our Psalm: "With my voice unto the Lord did I make supplication." 3) You must learn to believe *in the Lord;* to renounce every form of idolatry, that the Lord, *the Lord* alone, may be your God. "My flesh and my heart faileth; but God is the strength of my heart, and my portion for ever." (Psalm 73, 26). 4) *He* "knoweth your path," and cares for you. His eye watches over you, and his ear is open to your complaint. "Can a woman forget her

sucking child, that she should not have compassion on the son of her
womb? yea, they may forget, yet will I not forget thee, saith the Lord."
(Isaiah 49, 15). 5) In this way your complaint shall *soon come to an
end.* "For his anger endureth but a moment; in his favor is life;
weeping may endure for a night, but joy cometh in the morning"
(Psalm 30, 5). He shall bring your soul out of prison, and you shall
praise his name; and the righteous shall praise the Lord for your
deliverance. — Now, follow the instruction of David: Cry unto the
Lord with your voice; make your supplication to the Lord; pour out
your complaint before him; shew before him your trouble. Cry to
the Lord, saying: "Thou art my refuge and my portion in the land of
the living; attend unto my cry, and bring my soul out of prison!" The
Spirit of God shall himself loose your tongue; and when you have
brought everything to the Lord in humble prayer, your sorrow shall
become joy, and your lamentation a song of praise.

Lord, help us hereto by thy Holy Spirit. Bring my soul out of
prison, that I may praise thy name; the righteous shall compass me
about; for thou shalt deal bountifully with me. Amen.

O thou. from whom all goodness flows, I lift my heart to thee; In all my
sorrows, conflicts, woes, Dear Lord, remember me!
When on my aching, burdened heart My sins lie heavily, My pardon speak,
new peace impart; In love, remember me!

346. Thirteenth Sunday after Trinity. I.

Lord, teach us to know mercy, and to practice it alway. Amen.

Gospel Lesson, Luke 10, 23-37. And he turned him unto his disciples, and
said privately, Blessed are the eyes which see the things that ye see: for I tell
you, that many prophets and kings have desired to see those things which ye
see, and have not seen them; and to hear those things which ye hear, and have
not heard them. And, behold, a certain lawyer stood up, and tempted him,
saying, Master, what shall I do to inherit eternal life? He said unto him, What
is written in the law? how readest thou? And he answering said,Thou shalt
love the Lord thy God with all thy heart, and with all thy soul, and with all thy
strength, and with all thy mind; and thy neighbor as thyself. And he said unto
him, Thou hast answered right: this do, and thou shalt live. But he, willing
to justify himself, said unto Jesus, And who is my neighbor? And Jesus answering said, A certain man went down from Jerusalem to Jericho, and fell among
thieves, which stripped him of his raiment, and wounded him, and departed,
leaving him half dead. And by chance there came down a certain priest that
way; and when he saw him, he passed by on the other side. And likewise a
Levite, when he was at the place, came and looked on him, and passed by on
the other side. But a certain Samaritan, as he journeyed, came where he was:
and when he saw him, he had compassion on him, and went to him, and bound
up his wounds, pouring in oil and wine, and set him on his own beast, and
brought him to an inn, and took care of him. And on the morrow when he
departed, he took out two pence, and gave them to the host, and said unto him.
Take care of him; and whatsoever thou spendest more, when I come again. I

will repay thee. Which now of these three, thinkest thou, was neighbor unto him that fell among the thieves? And he said, He that shewed mercy on him. Then said Jesus unto him, Go, and do thou likewise.

The lawyer in our text knew very well what God will have us to do; and the opportunity to do it was given him, but he *did not make use of it.* So it was also in the case of the priest and the Levite. They had just attended the temple service in Jerusalem; and then they had come face to face with an instance of that crying distress which appeals to the feeling of mercy; but they shut their hearts, and passed by, *and did not do* that which they knew to be their duty. They did not do what they could to get to heaven; but they did what was possible to insure their own damnation. God placed the afflicted man in their path; but they turned aside, and did not go to the home of love. — Before relating the parable the Lord says to the lawyer: *"this do"*; and after having told it he says: *"Go, and do thou likewise."* That which the Spirit of God wants to impress upon us today is these words, *"this do"; "this do."* — The priest and the Levite has *performed* their service in the temple, kept the Sabbath, and made their prayers and sacrifices. They had for so long a time read and heard the commandment of love without obeying it that they were satisfied with merely observing the outward form of religion. The lawyer, on the other hand, seems to have felt less safe. His knowledge of the law and his conversation with Jesus indicate that something better was stirring in him; though the immediate purpose of his questioning was to tempt the Lord. What his fate came to be we do not know; but we hope that he went his way, and *did* like the Samaritan; in which case he now is in heaven. How, then? Does the word of God promise us heaven in return for our good deeds? By no means. The case is this: If any one honestly desire to *do* the will of God, this desire has been created in him by God himself; and when he continues therein, and earnestly examines himself according to the law of love, he sees with ever greater clearness these two things: 1) That which he does is nothing more than his bounden duty. 2) He does not do this duty of a pure heart and in holy love, as he should. Neither does he, as did the lawyer, stop short at the second table of the law; but recognizes that his foremost duty is to love *God* with his whole heart. He learns that he is a sinner; and this knowledge is not mere information in regard to man's wicked nature and wicked deeds, but a matter of *living experience.* Then he becomes a man mortally wounded, who is saved, not by the priest and the Levite, but by the Samaritan; one who can not be quickened by the law, but by the merciful Lord Jesus. Thus he receives life and salvation; and now his delight is in doing good, but his righteousness and hope are in the merit and blood of Jesus. — Go now at once, and do this; love God with all your heart, and your neighbor as yourself. The afflicted are in your path, in order that you may find *God.* Do as did the Samaritan! Is this not right and proper? Let love take root in your heart, be on your tongue, and bring forth fruit in your actions. If you, like the Samaritan, take your neighbor with you, he shall receive you in the everlasting habitations: "but if you pass him by, like the priest and the Levite, he shall be an obstacle in your path, and shut you out from heaven." "Blessed are the merciful; for they shall obtain mercy." Dear reader, go, and *do* this! Lord Jesus, give us to this end thy Holy Spirit; give us, we pray, thy Holy Spirit. Amen.

Let none hear you idly saying, "There is nothing I can do," While the souls of men are dying, And the master calls for you. Take the task he gives you gladly, Let his work your pleasure be; Answer quickly when he calleth, — "Here am I, send me, send me."

---

347. Thirteenth Sunday after Trinity. II.

Gracious God, give us the Spirit of faith. Amen.

Epistle Lesson, Galatians 3, 15–22. Brethren, I speak after the manner of men; Though it be but a man's covenant, yet if it be confirmed, no man disannulleth, or addeth thereto. Now to Abraham and his seed were the promises made. He saith not, And to seeds, as of many; but as of one, And to thy seed which is Christ. And this I say, that the covenant, that was confirmed before of God in Christ, the law, which was four hundred and thirty years after, cannot disannul, that it should make the promise of none effect. For if the inheritance be of the law, it is no more of promise: but God gave it to Abraham by promise. Wherefore then serveth the law? It was added because of transgressions, till the seed should come to whom the promise was made; and it was ordained by angels in the hand of a mediator. Now a mediator is not a mediator of one, but God is one. Is the law then against the promises of God? God forbid: for if there had been a law given which could have given life, verily righteousness should have been by the law. But the scripture hath concluded all under sin, that the promise by faith of Jesus Christ might be given to them that believe.

God promises to Abraham and his seed the Land of Canaan for ever; but this land is the *new, transfigured earth* with heavenly glory and salvation; and the seed of Abraham is *Christ in his church,* the communion of all the faithful, Jews and gentiles. *Faith, faith alone,* is the means which God has fixed as necessary in the case of every one who is to be partaker of the inheritance. The "promises" are God's *covenant,* his immutable will, to which nothing can be added, and from which nothing can be subtracted by any man. None must imagine that since God himself afterward gave the law, he is fickle, and has changed his will already established; as though the law *together with* faith, or the law *instead of* faith, were to give us the inheritance. "God is not a man, that he should lie; neither the son of man, that he should repent." The law has not been added in order to change or annul the given covenant; though it certainly is the word of God, the word of the one and the same God, given by "a mediator," namely Moses, who is not a mediator of one; who stood not only in man's stead to receive the law, but also in God's stead to give the law to man. On the contrary, the law is given to confirm the promise; the law multiplies our transgressions, and shews us our sin, thus making it clear that faith

alone can save. — This is an unutterably precious truth, the very
doctrine of life and the sun of salvation, which dispels the darkness and
lifts the burden of unbelief and bondage. It has pleased God to establish this covenant; *this* is his eternal will and his last testament: Every
one of whatever people who believes in Jesus Christ shall inherit the
glory and salvation of the children of God. And it has pleased him
to give *me* the "baptism into Christ," and let *me* learn this gospel, in
order that even *I* may believe. He has also shewn me my sin, and
driven me to Christ; so that I know nothing unto salvation, save his
cross and blood. What, then, shall now condemn me? — Neither
will we, then, brethren, bring the law and our own works into the
covenant of God. We have learned to know that everything in us is
sin according to the law; and we see this more clearly every day. Our
experience is, then, in perfect harmony with all the scripture, and
declares that *faith alone, Christ alone, grace alone,* is the sinners'
way to salvation. Is not this the faith and confession of your heart? This
faith the Holy Ghost has created in you; and where he is there is
liberty. "We are no longer under a schoolmaster. For ye are all the
children of God by faith in Christ Jesus. For as many of you as have
been baptized into Christ have put on Christ. There is neither Jew nor
Greek, there is neither bond nor free, there is neither male nor female;
for ye are all one in Christ Jesus. And if ye be Christ's, then are ye
Abraham's seed, and heirs according to the promise." (Verses 25–29).
— Blessed be God, who has made this covenant, and given it to us!
Now none need be in doubt concerning his salvation; for everything
which is our own has been excluded, and the inheritance is given us
in the gospel. Lord, help us to believe the truth and the mercy of
God. Amen.

Where'er the greatest sins abound, By grace they are exceeded; Thy helping hand is always found With aid, where aid is needed: Thy hand, the only
hand to save, Will rescue Israel from the grave, And pardon his transgression.

348. Monday after Thirteenth Sunday after Trinity.

Good Holy Spirit, give us the liberty in Christ. Amen.

Romans 7, 1–6. Know ye not, brethren, (for I speak to them that know
the law,) how that the law hath dominion over a man as long as he liveth?
For the woman which hath a husband is bound by the law to her husband,
so long as he liveth; but if the husband be dead, she is loosed from the law
of her husband. So then if, while her husband liveth, she be married to another man, she shall be called an adulteress: but if her husband be dead, she
is free from that law; so that she is no adulteress, though she be married to
another man. Wherefore, my brethren, ye also are become dead to the law
by the body of Christ; that ye should be married to another, even to him who
is raised from the dead, that we should bring forth fruit unto God. For when
we were in the flesh, the motions of sins, which were by the law, did work in
our members, to bring forth fruit unto death. But now we are delivered from
the law, that being dead wherein we were held: that we should serve in newness
of spirit, and not in the oldness of the letter.

When Christ was here in his state of humiliation, he was under the condemnation and dominion of the law (Gal. 4, 4; 3, 13); by his obedience unto death, however, the power of the law to judge and its right to reign have been destroyed; by his death he is set free from the law. But it was for us that the Son of God was born under the law, and was made a curse, so *his* liberty from the law is *our* liberty. This blessing is enjoyed by the faithful. They are baptized into the death and resurrection of Christ, and are thus united with him as he died, and united with him as he again lives. Without Christ they were under the law, bound to keep it, and cursed for ever. But now, that they are one with Christ (Eph. 5, 30–32), they are by his death loosed from the law, in like manner as a woman is loosed from her husband when death has parted them.

This liberty of the faithful from the law is a very excellent thing. In the first place, there is no obligation resting on them to keep the law, in order that they may be justified before God. Satan can not accuse them of any transgression of the law. Christ has fulfilled the law perfectly, and this is counted as having been done by them that believe in him; he has suffered the whole punishment, and thus they have suffered it also. They are free from the law which says: "Keep the commandments, and thou shalt be justified." They are free from it as completely, as the woman is loosed and free from her husband when death separates her from him. The law has nothing whatever to do with the question of my right to salvation. I was a transgressor, and my life is still imperfect; but this can no more condemn me. It no more affects my right to salvation, than it affects the right of my Lord Jesus; for I am no longer under the dominion of the law, but have by my baptism entered the house of the precious bridegroom of my soul; and in that house there is a dispensation entirely different from the law's command, "do this, and thou shalt live." — In the second place, the believers have a free and happy conscience, and serve God and all men with joy and delight in the new life of the Spirit. They do not flee from God, but to him; and do his will, not as bondmen, but as children. Herein they are not, however, perfect, as they are in respect to their righteousness in Christ. All Christians do not have so clear a conception of their state of grace that they know how excellent is the liberty in which they live; and neither is the truth equally clear at all times to the same person. The sins which cling to him obscure his vision, and give the devil occasion to tempt him. He is tempted to put on again the yoke; — but then the sun of mercy shines out once more, the soul is with its bridegroom; and the prize of victory, the spirit of liberty, is won. That which Paul here teaches is a matter of the greatest importance. While an earnest man clings to his own righteousness, he has the fear of death in his heart; for his good works are nothing but the forced obedience of the slave. But when you understand what grace is, and believe yourself quickened with Christ, and know that you are free, and the spirit in you cries out Abba, Father; then you bring forth fruit before God unto eternal life. The Spirit of Christ, which makes us free from the law, writes the law in our hearts.

God, teach us this through living experience, by thy Holy Spirit,
for Jesus' sake. Amen.

Thou, O Christ, art all I want; More than all in thee I find: Raise the
fallen, cheer the faint, Heal the sick, and lead the blind. Just and holy is thy
name; I am all unrighteousness: False and full of sin I am; Thou art full of
truth and grace.

349. Tuesday after Thirteenth Sunday after Trinity.

God, let the light of the gospel shine into our hearts. Amen.

Galatians 3, 5–11. He therefore that ministereth to you the Spirit, and
worketh miracles among you, doeth he it by the works of the law, or by the
hearing of faith? Even as Abraham believed God, and it was accounted to
him for righteousness. Know ye therefore, that they which are of faith, the
same are the children of Abraham. And the scripture, foreseeing that God
would justify the heathen through faith, preached before the gospel unto Abraham, saying, In thee shall all nations be blessed. So then they which be of
faith are blessed with faithful Abraham. For as many as are of the works of
the law, are under the curse: for it is written, Cursed is every one that continueth not in all things which are written in the book of the law to do them.
But that no man is justified by the law in the sight of God, it is evident: for,
The just shall live by faith.

All the unregenerated are under the law; and in so far as they
hope to be saved, it is through their own works. To some it is a light,
to others a grave matter. Some imagine that they keep the law, and
feel safe; others strive to keep it, but are wearied and troubled. Some
feel sure that they have faith, but say to themselves: What can it
profit, when my works are not perfect? Others work like slaves in
the effort to believe and to bring forth the fruits of faith. To some
the most important thing is to hear, to read, to pray, and to shun the
pleasures of the world; others seek to do right and justice and practice
mercy. All these lack knowledge of the law's last demand and true
meaning, and all are under the condemnation of the law. Dear friends,
"wherefore do ye spend money for that which is not bread? and your
labor for that which satisfieth not?" How do you read the law? and
how do you understand Saint Paul? Look at yourself in the law of
love as in a glass, and see that you are a lost and condemned sinner;
and *let the law drive you to Christ!* This is God's purpose with the
law. As long as you are your own savior, either alone or with the
help of Christ, you remain under the curse. When you die from yourself, and are quickened in Christ; when you learn to rest on faith, and
not on the law; you are blessed with faithful Abraham. "Christ hath
redeemed us from the curse of the law, being made a curse for us;"
and this redemption belongs to every one that *believes.* The law has
nothing to do with you in the matter of your justification before God.
The handwriting that was against you is nailed to the cross; the tables
of stone have disappeared. You are as far from the court of the works
of the law, as the east is far from the west. Do you never hereafter
bring your works into the work of Christ; but let him alone be and

remain your righteousness. Go forward, now, in the Spirit, become ever less in yourself, and let Jesus be your only glory! Then are you a child of Abraham, and inherit his blessing. You are wholly righteous, and there is no condemnation in you. Your conscience is cleansed of *dead* works to serve the living God. You love him, who loved you first, and you gladly do his will. The holy commandment of the law is written on the tables of your heart. — Hear this, all you who desire to be saved: No man is justified before God by the law. All scripture bears witness that every one who trusts in the works of the law is cursed; all scripture testifies that *the just shall live by faith*. Come, and incline your heart to this blessed teaching! The Spirit himself shall work it in you; and when you obey him, you shall experience his blessed and mighty power against sin and death and devil.

Merciful God, enlighten us with the gifts of thy Holy Spirit, lead us into the blessed liberty of faith, and bring about mighty works in us, to the glory of thy name. Amen.

Savior! all my sins confessing, Gracious hear me when I cry; Give, through faith, the promised blessing, Freely, fully justify.

By thy holy Spirit's leading, Bring me to thy bosom nigh, In thy blessed footsteps treading, Soul and body sanctify.

Thus, the days of conflict ended, In the mansions of the sky, Whither, Lord, thou art ascended, With thyself, me glorify.

---

350. Wednesday after Thirteenth Sunday after Trinity.

Lord, awaken us, and create faith in our hearts. Amen.

Acts 16, 25–34. And at midnight Paul and Silas prayed, and sang praises unto God: and the prisoners heard them. And suddenly there was a great earthquake, so that the foundations of the prison were shaken: and immediately all the doors were opened, and every one's bands were loosed. And the keeper of the prison awaking out of his sleep, and seeing the prison doors open, he drew out his sword, and would have killed himself, supposing that the prisoners had been fled. But Paul cried with a loud voice, saying, Do thyself no harm; for we are all here. Then he called for a light, and sprang in, and came trembling, and fell down before Paul and Silas, and brought them out, and said, Sirs, what must I do to be saved? And they said, Believe on the Lord Jesus Christ, and thou shalt be saved, and thy house. And they spake unto him the word of the Lord, and to all that were in his house. And he took them the same hour of the night, and washed their stripes; and was baptized, he and all his, straightway. And when he had brought them into his house, he set meat before them, and rejoiced, believing in God with all his house.

Paul and Silas were thrown into prison in the first European city which they visited; but they were happy, and sang joyful praises unto the Lord. The body in the dark, cold prison, but the spirit free; such is the fate of the church in the world. In this way the church does its work, which is to save souls, and gather them into the kingdom. Luke

458

does not tell us what effect the songs of praise by Paul and Silas, and the miracle which accompanied them, had on their fellow-prisoners, but mentions the keeper of the prison. This man had but now made their feet fast in the stocks, and he was, no doubt, one who slept soundly in sin. Now, however, he awakes. First he would have killed himself; for according to the Roman law he was liable to suffer death in the place of the escaped prisoners. Afterwards, when he hears the voice of Paul, learns of the miracle which had been wrought, and looks the apostle in the face, he feels the presence of the living God, and his own life in sin is presented to his view. He knows his unrighteousness, and quakes before the wrath of God. He then brings the apostles out, and asks them: "Sirs, what must I do to be saved? How shall I be able to make restitution for all the wrong which I have done? How shall I with deeds of charity toward all whom I have maltreated make sufficient atonement for all my guilt? What sacrifice shall I bring, in order that the wrath of God may be appeased? Ye are the servants of God, and can tell me what to do!" Paul and Silas answer with one voice, saying: "Believe on the Lord Jesus Christ, and thou shalt be saved, and thy house. This is all which thou shalt do." Marvellous scheme of salvation, which never could have been conceived in the human brain! Glorious gospel which snatches sinners out of the power of Satan, and creates light and peace and life in the soul! *"Believe on the Lord;"* but where is he to be found? Notice what the Spirit teaches us on this point in our text. "Believe on the Lord Jesus," say the apostles; and they spake the word of the Lord to them, and baptized them. Hence the Lord Jesus, on whom we are to believe, is in *the word* and in *baptism.* When they believed the *word,* and were *baptized,* they believed in *God.* Being baptized into Christ they believed his gospel; and *then there was nothing more to do.* — Go thou, and do likewise, dear reader! Believe on him in the word and in baptism; on him who died and rose again; then are you saved, — and your *whole* house shall follow you. Note this also! Thus it was in the case of the keeper of the prison. Ask as he did, and you shall receive the same answer; and the joy shall spread from the prison to your heart and house, as it did to the heart and house of the prison-keeper. "What must I do to be saved?" "Believe on the Lord Jesus Christ, and thou shalt be saved, and thy house." Now is the time. Ask; ask, and hear, and believe, and give thanks to God! Is it not a grand thing, even for us, that the apostles crossed over to Macedonia?

Lord Jesus, wake us all, and give us a living desire to be saved and a thorough knowledge of our sin; and give us grace to believe on thee, with all our household. Amen.

Lord Jesus Christ, in thee alone My only hope on earth I place; For other comforter is none, No help have I but in thy grace. There is no man nor creature here, No angel in the heavenly sphere, Who in my need can succor me; I cry to thee, In thee I trust implicitly.

351. Thursday after Thirteenth Sunday after Trinity.

"He that toucheth you toucheth the apple of his eye."

Zechariah 3, 1–5. And he shewed me Joshua the high priest standing before the angel of the Lord, and Satan standing at his right hand to resist him. And the Lord said unto Satan, The Lord rebuke thee, O Satan; even the Lord that hath chosen Jerusalem rebuke thee: is not this a brand plucked out of the fire? Now Joshua was clothed with filthy garments, and stood before the angel. And he answered and spake unto those that stood before him, saying, Take away the filthy garments from him. And unto him he said, Behold, I have caused thine iniquity to pass from thee, and I will clothe thee with change of raiment. And I said, Let them set a fair mitre upon his head So they set a fair mitre upon his head, and clothed him with garments. And the angel of the Lord stood by.

Joshua the high priest represents the whole people of Israel. It was a "brand plucked out of the fire;" that is to say, just now barely and with difficulty saved from the wrath of God. The "angel of the Lord" is Christ, who defends the wretched people against Satan. The "filthy garments" are their sins, of which Satan accuses them. The "change of raiment" is the righteousness which they receive of the Lord, and which gives them courage to lift their heads with hope. — Are not all who have been converted "brands plucked out of the fire"? Have not all been the children of wrath, and nearer then we are aware to the fire of perdition? Have not all the faithful been plucked out of the godless world; and is it not by the wonderful grace of God alone that we are saved? The faithful "sit together in heavenly places," and stand ever before God in Christ (Eph. 2, 6. Hebr. 12, 22 sqq.); but Satan is at hand to accuse them. This is shown clearly by the Book of Job. In these latter days "the accuser of the brethren" has been cast out to wreak all his furious anger on the earth (Revelations 12, 9 sqq.). His power is, to be sure, already broken (Luke 10, 17–19); but he still is permitted to act as our accuser; and he goes about, and gathers up our sins, and places himself with them at our side, when we stand before God. Unhappy we, did we not have the advocate that we have! (1 John 2, 1. 2). In our Bible lesson Israel has just been plucked out of the fire. We are instructed in regard to the justification of a penitent sinner. The soul is before God, but is clothed with many sins, "filthy garments." How impossible for it to pass muster! Even if there were but one spot on you, one single little blemish; or if only one unclean desire had stirred in you; this would yet be enough to condemn you. How, then, shall you be able to stand before God with your many and great sins? — However, praise be to God! The "angel," God's messenger, our Lord Jesus Christ, has authority and power to say: "The Lord rebuke thee, O Satan! Thou hast no more any right to accuse this man, whom God hath chosen and called and saved. I, Jesus, have been in the fire of wrath, and plucked him out of it; shall I, then, not defend him?" The sinner stands before the angel's face in filthy garments; the penitent man does not hide his sin; but confesses it, and comes to the Lord "just as I am." Then the Lord says to his servants: "Take away the filthy garments from him." "David said unto Nathan, I have sinned against the Lord. And Nathan said unto David, The Lord also hath put away thy sin; thou shalt not die." "Behold, I have caused thine iniquity to pass from thee, and I will clothe thee with change of raiment." "Bring forth the best robe, and put it on him," and "set a fair mitre upon his head." It is done as he commands; and while his stewards in the gospel serve him, and deal out to the souls forgiveness of sins, he stands by, and defends them against Satan, and guides them with his eye. For this reason it is that we can sing: "I will greatly rejoice in the Lord, my soul shall be joyful in my God; for he hath clothed me with the garments of salvation, he hath covered me with the robe of righteousness." "Who shall lay anything to the charge of God's elect? It is God that justifieth. Who is he that condemneth? It is Christ that died, yea rather, that is risen again, who is even at the right hand of God, who also maketh intercession for us." Go thy way, thou pardoned sinner; be of good cheer by reason of the comfort of forgiveness and the defence by our heavenly advocate; keep your garments pure, and walk in the ways of the Lord! Help us, O God, that we sin not! But when we sin, do thou chasten us; and forgive us for the sake of thy Son's blood; and let the Spirit remind us that we have an advocate in heaven, Jesus Christ the righteous; so that we preserve a free and good conscience, and obtain victory over the accuser of the brethren. Amen.

Still for us his death he pleads, Prevalent, he intercedes, Near himself prepares our place, Harbinger of human race.
There we shall with thee remain, Partners of thy endless reign, There thy face unclouded see, Find our heaven of heavens in thee.

---

352. Friday after Thirteenth Sunday after Trinity.

Lord, give us a living knowledge of sin and a living faith in thee. Amen.

1 Timothy 1, 12–16. And I thank Christ Jesus our Lord, who hath enabled me, for that he counted me faithful, putting me into the ministry; who was before a blasphemer, and a persecutor, and injurious: but I obtained mercy, because I did it ignorantly in unbelief. And the grace of our Lord was exceeding abundant with faith and love which is in Christ Jesus. This is a faithful saying, and worthy of all acceptation, that Christ Jesus came into the world to save sinners; of whom I am chief. Howbeit for this cause I obtained mercy, that in the first Jesus Christ might shew forth all longsuffering, for a pattern to them which should hereafter believe on him to life everlasting.

It is not an unusual thing to hear from the children of God a statement like this: "I am the chief of all sinners; none other can be as wretched and as corrupt as I." If you are *sincere* in saying this, and it is not mere idle words, a great miracle of grace has been wrought in you by the Spirit of God. For we are by nature blind to our own defects, and see the mote in a brother's eye, but not the beam in our own. He only who stands before God, and sees himself clearly in the light of his holy law, is so humble of heart that he can say with the apostle : "I am the chief of sinners;" "I am less than the least of all saints" (Eph. 3, 8). Many may have this feeling at certain times in their life; but I fear that only a few of us have in fact this measure of piety. The many dissensions and the discord obtaining among us indicate neither humility nor a thorough knowledge of sin. Let Paul be a pattern for our correction. Let us, as he did, enter the presence of God, and stand in the clear light of his countenance; and we shall become little in our own eyes, and forget to find fault with those who stand at our side.

However, the Holy Ghost has written this Bible text for the comfort of all those who grieve because of the magnitude of their transgressions. The law condemns you, but Jesus does not. *For this very purpose* he is come into the world, *that he may save sinners.* Will he fail to carry out the purpose for which he came, do you think? "This is a *faithful* saying, and *worthy of all acceptation.*" Do hear how the Holy Ghost in Paul bears witness, and wants to help us to believe. But if you think that your sin is great, he has foreseen this also, and presents Paul to you for a pattern. Paul says truly that he was the chief among all sinners. It does not only seem so to him, but he is fully conscious of *being that which he says.* Yet he obtained mercy; and shall not you, then, also obtain mercy? He had blasphemed, persecuted, and reviled Jesus, and breathed out threatenings against him. "Lord, I have heard by many of this man how much evil he hath done to thy saints" (Acts 9, 13). He says that he "did it ignorantly in unbelief;" but he does not offer this as an excuse. On the contrary; it was his own fault that he was so blind. Nevertheless, he can now accept mercy because of this; and he says that mercy is extended to him as chief of sinners, in order that all others, *all other great sinners,* may know, that there is mercy for them also. If the chief of all sinners actually has obtained mercy, your sin can not by any possibility be so great that mercy can not take it away. There is not in the world one sinner who asks forgiveness, and does not receive it. For the mercy of the Lord is *great beyond all measure;* "as the heaven is high above the earth, so great is his mercy toward them that fear him." Jesus never has cast off any penitent sinner; and never shall.

To the God of grace and mercy be praise and honor for evermore! Amen.

As the shepherd seeks to find His lost sheep that from him strayeth, So hath Christ each soul in mind, And for its salvation prayeth; Fain he'd have each wanderer live: Jesus sinners doth receive.

Come, then, all by guilt oppressed, Jesus calls, and he would make you God's own children, pure and blest, And to glory he would take you; Think on this, and well believe Jesus sinners doth receive.

---

353. Saturday after Thirteenth Sunday after Trinity.

Lord, cleanse us and keep us in the covenant with thee. Amen.

Ezekiel 16, 9–14. Then washed I thee with water: yea, I throughly washed away thy blood from thee, and I anointed thee with oil. I clothed thee also with broidered work, and shod thee with badgers' skin, and I girded thee about with fine linen, and I covered thee with silk. I decked thee also with ornaments, and I put bracelets upon thy hands, and a chain on thy neck. And I put a jewel on thy forehead, and earrings in thine ears, and a beautiful crown upon thine head. Thus wast thou decked with gold and silver; and thy raiment was of fine linen, and silk, and broidered work: thou didst eat fine flour, and honey, and oil: and thou wast exceeding beautiful, and thou didst prosper into a kingdom. And thy renown went forth among the heathen for thy beauty: for it was perfect through my comeliness, which I had put upon thee, saith the Lord God.

As it was the custom of oriental princes at their own expense to robe and deck their brides with ornaments for the wedding, so the Lord cleansed and decked Israel to be his bride. By its system of sacrifices Israel was washed of its sins; through its religious service it was clothed in glory; and it was crowned a queen among the peoples with power and honor. — The true bride of the Lord is the *spiritual* Israel, the Christian church. In our text the prophet describes the purification and adornment of every Christian. You have sprung from sinful seed, and are unclean from your birth, and must confess with David: "Behold, I was shapen in iniquity; and in sin did my mother conceive me." You were "cast out in the open field," and were in a wretched condition like the man in the desert of Jericho; and no eye would have pitied you, had not Jesus come. But "I saw thee," he says, "and I said unto thee, when thou wast in thy blood, Live! Yea, I sware unto thee, and entered into a covenant with thee, saith the Lord God, and thou becamest mine." And he "washed you with water;" he washed you in baptism with the water and blood from his side; and you received forgiveness of sins and a new life. And he "anointed you with oil;" he gave you his Spirit, and made you a king and priest before God. He "clothed you also with broidered work, with fine linen and silk, and decked you also with ornaments;" he gave you his righteousness and all manner of spiritual gifts, charity, humility, patience, mercy, peace, joy, meekness, temperance. "Christ loved the church, and he gave himself for it; that he might sanctify and cleanse it with the washing of water by the word, that he might present it to himself a glorious church, not having spot, or wrinkle, or any such thing; but that it should be holy and without blemish" (Eph. 5, 25–27). The 45th Psalm sings of the theme in this wise: "Upon thy right hand did stand the queen in gold of Ophir. Hearken, O daughter, and consider, and incline thine ear; forget also thine own people, and thy father's house; so shall the king greatly desire thy beauty; for he is thy Lord; and worship thou him. . . . The king's daughter is all glorious within; her clothing is of wrought gold. She shall be brought unto the king in raiment of needlework; the virgins, the companions that follow her, shall be brought unto thee. With gladness and rejoicing shall they be brought; they shall enter into the king's palace." Such purity and glory did you receive in your baptism, dear Christian; and all the believers stand thus arrayed before God in the righteousness of Christ. "For thy beauty was perfect

through my comeliness, which I had put upon thee," saith this our
Lord Jesus. Israel was a faithless bride to him; — be thou faithful
unto the end!

Lord, give us hereto thy grace. Good Holy Spirit, faithful guide,
care for us, and guard us, and keep us with the bridegroom of our
souls, until thou dost conduct us to the wedding feast in heaven. This
we pray thee of our innermost heart. Lord Jesus, do thou never take
thy Holy Spirit from me. Amen.

Rejoice, all ye believers, And let your lights appear! The evening is advancing, And darker night is near; The Bridegroom is arising, And soon he
draweth nigh; Up! pray, and watch, and wrestle! At midnight comes the cry.
The watchers on the mountain Proclaim the Bridegroom near; Go meet
him as he cometh, With hallelujahs clear. The marriage-feast is waiting, The
gates wide open stand; Up, up, ye heirs of glory! The Bridegroom is at hand.

---

354. Fourteenth Sunday after Trinity. I.

Lord, make us clean, and let us live and praise thee. Amen.

Gospel Lesson, Luke 17, 11-19. And it came to pass, as he went to Jerusalem, that he passed through the midst of Samaria and Galilee. And as he
entered into a certain village, there met him ten men that were lepers, which
stood afar off: and they lifted up their voices, and said, Jesus, Master, have
mercy on us. And when he saw them, he said unto them, Go shew yourselves
unto the priests. And it came to pass, that, as they went, they were cleansed.
And one of them, when he saw that he was healed, turned back, and with a
loud voice glorified God, and fell down on his face at his feet, giving him
thanks: and he was a Samaritan. And Jesus answering said, Were there not
ten cleansed? but where are the nine? There are not found that returned to
give glory to God, save this stranger. And he said unto him, Arise, go thy
way: thy faith hath made thee whole.

We are all lepers by birth. "Who can bring a clean thing out
of an unclean?" But we who live here in the church with the word
and sacraments have all been cleansed also; and should we have allowed the leprosy to take hold on us again, the Lord is near, so that
we can cry to him: "Jesus, Master, have mercy on us." He who
sees that he is unclean, and feels that he is diseased, will thus cry out.
Then the Lord makes reply: "Go, and be cleansed. Believe my
word; believe in the cleansing power of my blood, and you are clean.
You may then come with confidence among my saints, sit at my
Supper, and appear before my Father in heaven." We must do like
these ten men, who went away in accordance with the Lord's word
before they had been made clean; went away *in faith*, and believed
his word, and were confident that they would be cleansed because he
had said it; went to shew themselves as having been cleansed, even
while they yet saw and felt their uncleanness. He who sees his sin, and
is sensible of being sick and wretched, lost and condemned, shall hear
the word of the Lord: "I have cleansed you with the washing of water
by the word;" "ye are clean through the word which I have spoken

unto you." He shall then believe the word, and he is in truth cleansed; he is accepted of God, is justified, has remission of sins; and none can accuse and condemn him. Let all the Jewish priests and most malicious enemies of Christ, all the pious and all the wicked, all spirits and angels, see one who *believes* the Lord's word, "I have cleansed thee with water and blood, and thou art clean;" and they shall confess that it is true. For as the Lord speaks so it is; and he who believes, to him belongs the blessing. — Thereafter you shall go to him, and thank him. In this way only can you preserve your purity; with Jesus only can the one who has been cleansed remain clean. The nine are to warn us, and the one to encourage us. Come back to the Savior again and again unceasingly, and give him thanks! Never forget what he has done for you! There are indeed not many who, when they have just been cleansed, forget to render thanks; but when some time has elapsed they come to regard the grace of God as a matter of course; and then they easily forget to praise the Lord. It is therefore necessary that you see your daily sins with ever increasing clearness, and feel how glorious a thing it is to receive forgiveness all the time. Never, never let the blood of Jesus, nor the precious water of baptism become things of little value in your eyes; and never neglect to give thanks for them. Sing a new song always in praise of the old, yet ever new, nay ever more great, more sweet, more rich, grace of God! "Bless the Lord, O my soul; and all that is within me, bless his holy name! Bless the Lord, O my soul, and forget not all his benefits; who forgiveth all thine iniquities; who healeth all thy diseases; who redeemeth thy life from destruction; who crowneth thee with lovingkindness and tender mercies!" Happy child of God; bless the Lord now, this hour, and next hour, today, tonight, tomorrow morning, unceasingly, while you live; prostrate yourself at the feet of Jesus, giving him thanks for ever and ever! This is his will, and your salvation. Satan must not be allowed to prevent it!

Blessed be thou, Lord Jesus, who didst atone for all my sin with thy holy and precious blood! Blessed be thou for the gospel, which brings salvation, for the cleansing water of baptism, and for the healing strength of thy holy Supper! Blessed be thou for the grace of the Spirit, which kindled the spark of faith in my soul, and created in me a new and holy life. Preserve my faith, and increase it; and let nothing seduce me to separate myself from thee, thou only lover of my soul in time and in eternity. Amen.

My soul, now bless thy maker! Let all within me bless his name, Who maketh thee partaker Of mercies more than thou dar'st claim. Forget him not, whose meekness Forgiveth all thy sin; Who healeth all thy weakness, Renews thy life within; Whose grace and care are endless, Who saved thee through the past; Who leaves no sufferer friendless. But rights the wronged at last.

He shows to man his treasure Of judgment, truth, and righteousness, His love beyond all measure, His yearning pity o'er distress; Nor treats us as we merit, But lays his anger by; The humble, contrite spirit Finds his compassion nigh; Far as the heavens above us, As break from close of day, So far, since he doth love us, He casts our sins away.

355. Fourteenth Sunday after Trinity. II.

Lord God, give us the holy Spirit of liberty. **Amen.**

Epistle Lesson, Galatians 5, 16–24. This I say then, Walk in the Spirit, and ye shall not fulfil the lust of the flesh. For the flesh lusteth against the Spirit, and the Spirit against the flesh: and these are contrary the one to the other: so that ye cannot do the things that ye would. But if ye be led of the Spirit, ye are not under the law. Now the works of the flesh are manifest, which are these; Adultery, fornication, uncleanness, lasciviousness, idolatry, witchcraft, hatred, variance, emulations, wrath, strife, seditions, heresies, envyings, murders, drunkenness, revellings, and such like: of the which I tell you before, as I have also told you in time past, that they which do such things shall not inherit the kingdom of God. But the fruit of the Spirit is love, joy, peace, longsuffering, gentleness, goodness, faith, meekness, temperance: against such there is no law. And they that are Christ's have crucified the flesh with the affections and lusts.

To "walk in the Spirit" is, then, the opposite of being "under the law." The apostle contrasts "the Spirit" with "the flesh"; and he also speaks of walking in the Spirit as contrary to being in bondage under the law. Be not deceived, however. They who are not under the law are not without the law. The carnally minded would like to be without the law; but they have its judgment in their conscience, whether they know it or not; and in reality they all are in bondage under the law. They are not the children of the Spirit. The spiritually minded, on the other hand, who are free from bondage, cherish and obey the law of love. The law condemns the works of the flesh, and is an object of hatred to the carnally minded; but against the fruit of the Spirit there is no law, and there is no enmity between the law and the spiritually minded.

The believer knows that the commandment of love is pure and just. He believes that Christ has fulfilled it for him; and through this faith the Holy Ghost gives him the new life of love in his soul. That which Christ has done has been given me, I know, in my baptism, and is counted exactly as if I had done it myself. By this means I am righteous and saved, and free from every demand of the law, and from the condemnation of the law; nay, in this respect the law no more has any existence for me, but is nailed to the cross, and is dead and gone. In this faith in the love of God, however, I love God with all my heart, and love all men, even my worst enemies. Through the gospel God has given me his love, and thus written his law in my heart. "The law of the Spirit of life in Christ Jesus hath made me free from the law of sin and death. "For what the law could not do, in that it was weak through the flesh, God sending his own Son in the likeness of sinful flesh, and for sin, condemned sin in the flesh; that the righteousness of the law might be fulfilled in us, who walk not after the flesh, but after the Spirit." (Romans 8, 2–4). At the same time we still have the flesh, which causes our conduct to be marred by weaknesses and imperfections. When the apostle says that "the *flesh* lusteth against the Spirit, . . . so that ye cannot do the things that *ye* would," we understand that the believers shall humbly acknowledge the lusts of the flesh as their own. That which the *flesh* lusts after, that which *you yourselves* desire, is to be renounced. I must not forget that I, the selfsame individual who loves God with holy love, I have in my self-will, in my flesh, such hideous things as adultery, fornication, uncleanness, etc.; which have, however, thank God, been crucified. I must *suffer* these things, in order that I may learn humility and self-denial; but I *must not follow* them to be their slave; I must mortify the flesh with the affections and lusts. On the other hand, let us come forward with the fruits of the Spirit! Let the roots of the heart strike deeper every day into the love of God! Let us walk more and more in the free, happy spirit of the child; and let it bear more abundant fruit in all heavenly virtues! Grant us this grace, merciful God, through Jesus Christ. Amen.

Spirit of adoption! Make us overflow With thy sevenfold blessing, And in grace to grow.

Into Christ baptized, Grant that we may be Day and night, dear Spirit, Perfected by thee!

356. Monday after Fourteenth Sunday after Trinity.

Psalm 6. To the chief Musician on Neginoth upon Sheminith. A Psalm of David. O Lord, rebuke me not in thine anger, neither chasten me in thy hot displeasure. Have mercy upon me, O Lord; for I am weak: O Lord, heal me; for my bones are vexed. My soul is also sore vexed: but thou, O Lord, how long? Return, O Lord, deliver my soul: Oh save me for thy mercies' sake. For in death there is no remembrance of thee: in the grave who shall give thee thanks? I am weary with my groaning; all the night make I my bed to swim; I water my couch with my tears. Mine eye is consumed because of grief; it waxeth old because of all mine enemies. Depart from me, all ye workers of iniquity: for the Lord hath heard the voice of my weeping. The Lord hath heard my supplication; the Lord will receive my prayer. Let all mine enemies be ashamed and sore vexed: let them return and be ashamed suddenly.

The sore trouble in which we here find David was occasioned by his persecutions suffered at the hands of his enemies. For the saints of God recognize that there is an intimate connection between sin and trouble. Their spiritual distress may be caused by some special act of wickedness, or it may be the result of some earthly affliction, as poverty, sickness, the death of a dear one, the loss of property, the malice of other men, the tongue of slander, and the like; and in many cases they do not know with certainty, whether that which they feel is "godly sorrow," or "sorrows of the world;" and this uncertainty increases their fear. — Jesus has suffered the punishment for all our sins; and hence it is not the anger of the judge, but of the Father, which disciplines the faithful. Yet all suffering, being a result of sin, has another meaning to *their* conscience than it has to that of the world. We therefore, in this psalm and elsewhere in the scriptures, hear how the greatest of heroic souls fear, and tremble, and weep like children. Furthermore, the truly pious do not have the callous hearts of unbelief, but a quickened sense of good and evil. None has found suffering so bitter as did our Lord Jesus; none has felt more sorrow and shed more tears than he; — the bravest and strongest champion against death and hell.

This psalm and similar passages of scripture are of great assistance to such as are in spiritual trouble; for here they find expressed that which their own hearts have felt, and learn how to lay their troubles before God. Not all the saints of God are as sorely tried as was David, who several times in the course of his life "made his bed to swim all the night" with his sweat and tears; for he was to learn to sing songs of lamentation, in which each of us finds his own misery expressed; and to sing songs of joy, in which the heart of the whole church throbs with exultation. But at some time or other in his life as a child of God every man must taste *something* of the bitterness of death. Then he is conscious of nothing but the wrath which punishes. God appears in his eyes as the strange and stern master in Egypt appeared to the sons of Jacob; so that he remembers his sins. He withers and is consumed. The happy days of grace and the light of life have disappeared. He *was* happy and full of bliss; but this *is passed away.* And yet the soul cries out to God, who seems all anger: "Have mercy upon me, O Lord; save me for thy mercies' sake." It is the true nature and distinguishing mark of the saints *that they bow before God, and always fly to him.* Then the soul groans and cries out: "O Lord, rebuke me not in thine anger, neither chasten me in thy hot displeasure!" "O Lord, heal me; for my bones are vexed. My soul also is sore vexed; but thou, O Lord, how long? Return, O Lord, deliver my soul! I am thine, Lord Jesus; thy property which thou hast brought with a price. Thou must, thou must have mercy! Do with me what thou wilt; but surrender me not to the power of the devil and the darkness of death. Thou hast created me, and bought me to the glory of thy name; and *this* is my salvation. Thou canst not and wilt not desert me!" — And the Lord saves in truth; "unto God the Lord belong the issues from death." Note how the psalmist closes his lamentation with shouts of *joy.* Wait upon the Lord; commit your way unto him with "hope against hope;" and you shall surely sing — though it may not be until a long time after your "O Lord, how long," which has been the motto of some of the pious children of God throughout their whole life — you shall surely sing at last: "The Lord hath heard my supplication; the Lord will receive my prayer." "Away, then, ye false and terrifying accusers, ye spirits and powers, which threaten me with anger and punishment and death, and would imprison my happy and victorious life as in a hell!" Come, thou Spirit of life, my comforter in every trouble, and teach me to sing songs of thangsgiving before God. Amen.

Come, Holy Comforter, Thy sacred witness bear In this glad hour; Thou who almighty art, Now rule in every heart, And ne'er from us depart, Spirit of power!
Jesus, our Lord, descend; From all our foes defend, Nor let us fall; Let thine almighty aid Our sure defence be made; Our souls on thee be stayed; Lord, hear our call!

357. Tuesday after Fourteenth Sunday after Trinity.

"Heal me, O Lord, and I shall be healed." **Amen.**

John 5, 2–9. 14. Now there is at Jerusalem, by the sheep market, a pool, which is called in the Hebrew tongue Bethesda, having five porches. In these lay a great multitude of impotent folk, of blind, halt, withered, waiting for the moving of the water. For an angel went down at a certain season into the pool, and troubled the water: whosoever then first after the troubling of the water stepped in, was made whole of whatsoever disease he had. And a certain man was there, which had an infirmity thirty and eight years. When Jesus saw him lie, and knew that he had been now a long time in that case, he saith unto him, Wilt thou be made whole? The impotent man answered him, Sir, I have no man, when the water is troubled, to put me into the pool: but while I am coming, another steppeth down before me. Jesus saith unto him, Rise, take up thy bed, and walk. And immediately the man was made whole, and took up his bed, and walked: and on the same day was the sabbath. Afterward Jesus findeth him in the temple, and said unto him, Behold, thou art made whole: sin no more, lest a worse thing come unto thee.

All the miracles of Jesus manifest his glory, and strengthen our faith. To us he is then a present Savior; and we experience his power on ourselves. That which he did he does; that which we read in regard to the sick whom he healed agrees with our own experience. Even if it be a spiritual healing, it is no less true; but, for the matter of that, it is he who by healing and quickening them gives *our bodies* also the power to live for ever.

The story in our text may greatly edify the earnest reader. Bear in mind that this hospital is called *Bethesda* (the house of mercy); which vividly reminds one of the church of Christ; that it is by the market for *the sheep which are to be sacrificed;* that it has five porches; that under these are a *great multitude of sick persons;* that they are *blind, halt, and withered;* that it is *water* in which they are healed; that *it is an angel,* a messenger of God, who troubles the water; that the sick need aid to get into·the pool; etc. Let me call special attention to but one of these sick men, and to Jesus. Clearly, this man is the most wretched of all, or at least one of the most wretched. *Him* Jesus saves. He has been waiting for help a long, long time; and has almost lost the last remnant of hope. He has been abandoned by everybody. Jesus asks him: "Wilt thou be made whole?" and thus quickens his dormant longing. Why does God let some men be sick for so long a time? Is it because they are greater sinners than others? By no means; it is for the purpose of teaching them humility. In the case of some he for this purpose employs sickness; in the case of others some other means. We have often seen that sin and sickness go together; and the Lord calls our attention to this truth when he says: "Behold, thou art made whole; sin no more, lest a worse thing come unto thee." — Here we see, then, that *Jesus can help, and does in fact help the most abjectly wretched of men;* if we do but admit our guilt and feel our helplessness. *The Lord* speaks first. He comes first; he is the author, and he is the finisher of our salvation. When he has opened our ears to hear him, he again speaks to us; and in his words is *life;* through them he gives us the *faith* which receives this new life. Jesus said "rise"; and this word raised the impotent man from his bed. It entered his heart, and made him believe that he should rise; and as soon as he *believed* it he was able to do it. Have not you also had this experience, dear reader? When your soul, in sin and trouble, heard the words of Jesus, "I save you; I took away your sin; you shall inherit eternal life; rise, and walk with God;" — you received a new life, rose up, and praised the Lord. Or, if you have not *had* this experience, give heed now to that which the Lord says. Is it your wish that Jesus may save you from sin and sickness, and make you whole in soul and body for ever? If this be your wish, hear his words to you: " Rise, and walk." Obey them; do this; the word itself gives you the required strength. Go thy way, then, and "sin no more, lest a worse thing come unto thee."

Precious Savior, thou art the Lord who healeth me. Let me know thy healing power until I become perfectly whole in the life eternal. Amen.

O Savior Christ! Thou too art Man; Thou hast been troubled, tempted, tried; Thy kind, but searching glance can scan The very wounds that shame would hide.

Thy touch has still its ancient power; No word from thee can fruitless fall; Hear in this solemn evening hour, And in thy mercy heal us all.

---

358. Wednesday after Fourteenth Sunday after Trinity.

Teach me thy way, O Lord, that I may walk in thy truth. Amen.

2 Timothy 2, 19–22. Nevertheless the foundation of God standeth sure, having this seal, The Lord knoweth them that are his. And, Let every one that nameth the name of Christ depart from iniquity. But in a great house there are not only vessels of gold and of silver, but also of wood and of earth; and some to honor, and some to dishonor. If a man therefore purge himself from these, he shall be a vessel unto honor, sanctified, and meet for the master's use, and prepared unto every good work. Flee also youthful lusts: but follow righteousness, faith, charity, peace, with them that call on the Lord out of a pure heart.

The holy church of God, built on Christ as the chief stone of the corner, and the doctrine of truth which it possesses, can not be overthrown by any teachers of falsehood. As the devil came to Eve in paradise, so his prophets come into the church, mingle with the saints, and try to keep themselves from being known for what they are. But as the inscription on a seal stands sure, has its specific meaning, indicates to whom it belongs, and prevents fraud; so the church of God stands sure, having this seal: 1) "The Lord knoweth them that are his;" so that none shall be able to steal in among them without being known of the Lord. He has already judged and separated the liars from the others, and we need have no fear; they shall neither overthrow the foundation, nor destroy them that have the seal of the living God in their foreheads. 2) "Let every one that nameth the name of Christ depart from iniquity." All the Lord's people strive after sanctification. None of them can live in deceitfulness, pride, carnal lusts, covetousness, gluttony, conceit, lust of power, a partisan spirit, or other manner of uncleanness. This is written for the admonition of the Christians, that they may examine themselves; and as a testimony for the world.

We must not allow ourselves to be led wrong by the circumstance that there are vessels of wood as well as vessels of gold in the great house; for here on earth it can not be otherwise. In the external church organization are two classes of men, with many differences within each class. Our text, however, does not speak further of the vessels of dishonor. — If you know before God that you walk in the truth, you are a vessel to honor, can endure the fire of purification; and neither shall you flee from it, but endure hardness as a good soldier of Jesus Christ. "Study to show thyself approved unto God." *Study to do this!* Be thoroughly in earnest in striving to shew yourself *approved of God.* "Remember Jesus Christ," and walk in his steps. If we be dead with him, we shall also live with him; if we suffer, we shall also reign with him (Verses 3. 8. 11. 12. 15). Keep yourself undefiled by the vessels of dishonor; do not cultivate spiritual fellowship with them that serve the flesh; so shall the Lord sanctify you, and use you unto his honor, to the edification of the church, and to every good work. "*Follow* righteousness, faith, charity, peace, with all them that call on the Lord out of a pure heart." *Follow* these things. *Follow* them; not slowly, not in a lukewarm way, but zealous and fervent in spirit! *Follow* these things; then shall the Lord deliver you from every evil work, and preserve you unto his heavenly kingdom; to whom be glory for ever and ever! Amen.

Behold the sure foundation stone Which God in Zion lays, To build our heavenly hopes upon, And his eternal praise.
Chosen of God, to sinners dear, And saints adore the name; They trust their whole salvation here, Nor shall they suffer shame.

359. Thursday after Fourteenth Sunday after Trinity.

Psalm 103, 1–5. A Psalm of David. Bless the Lord, O my soul; and all that is within me, bless his holy name. Bless the Lord, O my soul, and forget not all his benefits: Who forgiveth all thine iniquities; who healeth all thy diseases; who redeemeth thy life from destruction; who crowneth thee with lovingkindness and tender mercies; who satisfieth thy mouth with good things; so that thy youth is renewed like the eagle's.

When you awake in the morning let your first thought be that the Lord is good; and let the first impulse of your soul be to give him thanks. During the day, when you work or rest; in the evening, when you seek your repose; in the watches of the night, give thanks to the Lord. Ye Christians old and young; how is it with your Christianity? How will you be able to join in the anthem of praise sung by the saints before the throne, if you here have dissatisfied minds, or are at least slow to praise the Lord? It is well that you know and regret your sin; nay, this is an unavoidable necessity. It is well that you are tried in diverse temptations; for this is the lot of the saints on earth; they must carry the cross, and feel its weight. But it is not well that sorrow is victorious, and the tongue of praise is silent. He that humbles himself receives mercy. The Lord chastens, but comforts also. The needy and meek shall delight themselves in the abundance of peace. There is an immeasurable difference between the soul whose keynote is a wail of complaint and the soul in whose cry of distress is resignation, victory, and hope. Why is your life so poor in songs of praise and joy? Because your penitence is so shallow. You bewail your condition; but your wailing is a complaint against God, and an accusation against the church or the brethren; and there is in it little or nothing of true humility. What is it makes it possible for *David* to sing such grand songs of *praise?* It is the deep *penitence* of his heart. Why does his cry of distress end in thanksgiving and praise? Because even his songs of mourning celebrate the righteousness of God. Humble yourself, and believe the mercy of God; humble yourself, I beg, and believe his words of mercy; then shall goodness and mercy follow you all the days of your life; and how can you, then, fail to give thanks? Be simple and honest before the Lord; be one of those of whom David speaks in Psalm 89, 15–18, where he says: "Blessed is the people that know the joyful sound; they shall walk, O Lord, in the light of thy countenance. In thy name shall they rejoice all the day; and in thy righteousness shall they be exalted. For thou art the glory of their strength; and in thy favor our horn shall be exalted. For the Lord is our defence; and the Holy One of Israel is our king." Blessed is he whose heart is full of harpstrings, giving a beautiful sound in praise of the Lord. You may be thus blessed, dear reader; for he forgiveth all thine iniquities, and healeth all thy diseases; redeemeth thy life from destruction, and crowneth thee with lovingkindness and tender mercies. Shall not all that is within you bless his name?

Lord God, I confess my sin, my odious ingratitude; and I earnestly beseech thee, give me grace to humble myself and to believe. Give me victory over the pride and unbelief of my wicked heart. Give me this great mercy, that I may praise thee all my life; that of my whole heart I may thank thee and praise thee for all things. Amen.

O Father ever glorious, O everlasting Son, O Spirit all victorious, Thrice Holy Three in One, Great God of our salvation, Whom earth and heaven adore, Praise, glory, adoration, Be thine for evermore. Amen.

---

360. Friday after Fourteenth Sunday after Trinity.

Holy Father, sanctify us through thy truth. Amen.

1 Peter 1, 14–19. As obedient children, not fashioning yourselves according to the former lusts in your ignorance: But as he which hath called you is holy, so be ye holy in all manner of conversation; because it is written, Be ye holy; for I am holy. And if ye call on the Father, who without respect of

persons judgeth according to every man's work, pass the time of your sojourning here in fear: forasmuch as ye know that ye were not redeemed with corruptible things, as silver and gold, from your vain conversation received by tradition from your fathers; but with the precious blood of Christ, as of a lamb without blemish and without spot.

The least taint of leprosy made an Israelite unclean, and caused his exclusion from the people. The least of sins which rules over you excludes you from God's Israel; and every one who is to enter the perfect sanctuary of heaven must be wholly cleansed from all sin. The Father is holy; and the children must be holy. The Son is holy; and the blood wherewith he cleanses you is that of a lamb without blemish and without spot. The Spirit who dwells in the faithful is none other than the very Holy Ghost. You have been bought with a great price; and precious and pure you must be. The evil from which you were delivered was something terrible; and "a burned child fears the fire." He is righteous; and you call upon him as your Father; he does not, as did Eli, wink at the wickedness of his children. If, then, you be one of Christ's believers, you live no more in sin; for you have been washed, justified, and sanctified by the blood of Jesus and by the Spirit of God. But as you for all that, while you are in the flesh, have sin and evil desires, you must continually mortify them, that you may become ever more holy in all your conversation. God will give you both the desire and the strength to do this. When he says, "Be ye holy; for I am holy," your heart makes reply: "Cleanse me, O Lord; sanctify me wholly, merciful God!" And your prayer is answered; so that the power of sanctification is given you. Use it, and increase in purity and piety day by day. Your hatred of sin and your love of God should be stronger today than yesterday; your patience greater, your mercy more tender, your gratitude more warm, all your conduct more like that of the Lord Jesus. If you be a child of God, let it be seen of angels and men. See that you be distinguished from the world by a truly saintly life. "Come out from among them, and be separate, saith the Lord, and touch not the unclean thing; and I will receive you, and will be a Father unto you, and ye shall be my sons and daughters, saith the Lord Almighty. Having therefore these promises, dearly beloved, let us cleanse ourselves from all filthiness of the flesh and the spirit, perfecting holiness in the fear of God!" (2 Cor. 6, 17–7, 1).

Lord God, who dost work in thy saints both to will and to do of thy good pleasure; grant us grace; grace to work out our own salvation with fear and trembling, and to receive the desire and the power of holiness from thee in the word and sacrament; so that we may increase daily in the likeness of thy image. Holy Lord God, sanctify us wholly in spirit and soul and body. Amen.

By the baptismal stream, Which made me thine, By the dear flesh and blood, Thy love made mine, Purge thou all sin from me, That I may nearer be, Nearer to thee!
Surely it matters not What earth may bring, Death is of no account, Grace will I sing. Nothing remains for me, Save to be nearer thee, Nearer to thee!

361. Saturday after Fourteenth Sunday after Trinity.

Psalm 139, 13–18. For thou hast possessed my reins: thou hast covered me in my mother's womb. I will praise thee; for I am fearfully and wonderfully made: marvellous are thy works: and that my soul knoweth right well. My substance was not hid from thee, when I was made in secret, and curiously wrought in the lowest parts of the earth. Thine eyes did see my substance, yet being unperfect: and in thy book all my members were written, which in continuance were fashioned, when as yet there was none of them. How precious also are thy thoughts unto me, O God! how great is the sum of them! If I should count them, they are more in number than the sand: when I awake, I am still with thee.

Truly the Lord has fashioned man wonderfully and gloriously. Deep is the great sea, deeper still the depths of space; but yet more deep is the spirit of man. Our body is curiously and beautifully fashioned. The eye, the ear, the tongue, all members great and small; with what marvellous nicety have they not been formed! Could any human ingenuity have invented and adjusted the processes of respiration, digestion, or any other of the vital functions? And yet what is all this as compared with the wonders of the *soul*, the spirit, which God breathed into us from the beginning? Here are understanding and memory with their ever increasing powers; the will, which no force can bend, but which can bend itself, when it is in a healthy state; the conscience, this heavenly witness; the heart, which can give itself, can love, can receive into itself the love divine, and be united with God in liberty most glorious and bonds most beautiful. All this hast thou, O God, designed from eternity; and thy thoughts and thy will wrought me curiously in secret, in my mother's womb. — As thou hast wonderfully wrought me, so thou dost wonderfully lead me, in ways which not I, but thou, my God, hast found. I am fallen, and my form has been disordered; but thou dost heal me, and lead me in the paths of salvation; thou hast destined me to eternal life, and thou dost give me this life. Thou dost care for me in all things; nothing befalls me without thy counsel; never for one day, for a single moment, dost thou abandon me. "O Lord, thou hast searched me, and known me. Thou understandest my thoughts afar off. Thou compassest my path and my lying down, and art acquainted with all my ways. Thou hast beset me behind and before, and laid thine hand upon me. The darkness hideth not from thee; but the night shineth as the day."

This will we ponder, dear reader! We must marvel at the wisdom and power of the Lord, and his infinite goodness toward us; it follows us always; shall we not always praise it? In his arms we fall asleep at night, and in them we awake in the morning. When we go to rest, and when we rise from our couch, we are with the Lord; we are near him always with soul and body. We dwell in the Lord's house, we eat at his table; with him we labor, and with him we rest; with him we live, and with him we die. Blessed every man who knows thee, O Lord! Thy mercy is in the heavens; and thy faithfulness reacheth unto the clouds. Thy righteousness is like the great mountains; thy judgments are a great deep. How excellent is thy lovingkindness, O God! therefore the children of men put their trust under the shadow of thy wings. Blessed be thy glorious name for ever! Amen.

Plenteous grace with thee is found, Grace to cover all my sin; Let the healing streams abound; Make and keep me pure within. Thou of life the fountain art, Freely let me take of thee: Spring thou up within my heart, Rise, to all eternity.

362. Fifteenth Sunday after Trinity. I.

Lord, speak to us, and help us to hear thy word. Amen.

Gospel Lesson, Matthew 6, 24–34. No man can serve two masters: for either he will hate the one, and love the other; or else he will hold to the one, and despise the other. Ye cannot serve God and mammon. Therefore I say unto you, Take no thought for your life, what ye shall eat, or what ye shall drink; nor yet for your body, what ye shall put on. Is not the life more than meat, and the body than raiment? Behold the fowls of the air: for they sow not, neither do they reap, nor gather into barns; yet your heavenly Father feedeth them. Are ye not much better than they? Which of you by taking thought can add one cubit unto his stature? And why take ye thought for raiment? Consider the lilies of the field, how they grow; they toil not, neither do they spin: and yet I say unto you, That even Solomon in all his glory was not arrayed like one of these. Wherefore, if God so clothe the grass of the field, which today is, and tomorrow is cast into the oven, shall he not much more clothe you, O ye of little faith? Therefore take no thought, saying, What shall we eat? or, What shall we drink? or, Wherewithal shall we be clothed? (For after all these things do the gentiles seek:) for your heavenly Father knoweth that ye have need of all these things. But seek ye first the kingdom of God, and his righteousness; and all these things shall be added unto you. Take therefore no thought for the morrow: for the morrow shall take thought for the things of itself. Sufficient unto the day is the evil thereof.

Our Lord Jesus speaks thus to us, dear brethren, in order to strengthen our hearts to resist the temptations of covetousness and worldly cares, that whatever our earthly lot and portion, we may be happy and praise God. Covetousness and worldly cares vex, torture, and kill the inner life, if we give them room. God does not want this to be our fate. He cares for us with most tender and mighty love. Therefore he says: "Take no thought" for these things! Alas, why will you worry? Do not borrow trouble! And he repeats the instruction: "Therefore take no thought" for your life, nor yet for your body! With the strongest reasons he demonstrates to us, in the first place, that all our worry is *unnecessary;* and in the next place, that it also is *unprofitable.*

We have *no cause* to feel concern in regard to that which is necessary for the support of this life; for the life itself is the Lord's, and shall he not, then, sustain it as long as he deems it expedient? Life itself is more than meat; shall he, then, who gave the greater, not give the lesser also? Here we are reminded of that which Paul says: "He that spared not his own Son, but delivered him up for us all, shall he not with him also freely give us all things?" Then again, shall he who feeds the fowls and clothes the lilies forget us? Do you think that he will care for the least of his creatures, and not for the greatest? for the fowls so far beneath us in the scale, and for the grass which withers in a day or two; but not for us, whom he has created and redeemed to live for ever? Shall the fowls and the grass praise him, and we be consumed by the cares of this life? Furthermore, he is our *Father;* and we are his children; and he has taught us to pray: "Our Father, who art in heaven." Shall not the *heavenly Father* care for his children? An earthly father considers what his children need, knows that it is his duty to provide it, and does not forget any of them. Shall not *he*, of whom all fatherly kindness is, remember all his children, and provide them with all things needful? There is strength and comfort unspeakable in these words: "Your heavenly Father knoweth that ye have need of all these things." Your *Father*, your Father *in heaven* knows what you need, *knows* it well; knows your wants, and does not forget you; knows that you have such need of *all* these things that you can not be without them. If you were heathens, you might with some reason feel anxiety; but you are the own *children of the heavenly Father*, the sons and daughters of the Father in heaven.

However, if you stubbornly disobey the Lord, and insist on taking thought for these things, *what does your worry accomplish?* Are you not troubling yourself to no purpose? Do you by this means add one cubit to your stature, or prolong your life? Is your heart enlarged or your life made more rich by your cares? No; but your trouble is increased, and may become so heavy as to crush you entirely. Every day will bring us labor and trials; and it were well for us to learn this truth; — and sufficient unto the day is the evil *thereof*. He who adds to this evil the cares of riches, or the fears of future poverty, will have a load so heavy that it will crush him. He takes a cubit from his stature.

Lord God, heavenly Father, help me to seek first thy kingdom, and thy righteousness. Give me a childlike trust in thee; give me a contented mind; and prosper me in my vocation. Give me neither poverty nor riches; but feed me with food convenient for me. Lord, thou knowest our hearts and our temptations; have pity, and satisfy us early with thy mercy, that we may rejoice and be glad all our days. Amen.

Thou on the Lord rely, So safe shalt thou go on; Fix on his work thy steadfast eye, So shall thy work be done. No profit canst thou gain By self-consuming care; To him commend thy cause; his ear Attends the softest prayer.

---

363. Fifteenth Sunday after Trinity. II.

Lord, give by thy word the power of the Spirit. Amen.

Epistle Lesson, Galatians 5, 25–6, 10. If we live in the Spirit, let us also walk in the Spirit. Let us not be desirous of vain glory, provoking one another, envying one another. Brethren, if a man be overtaken in a fault, ye which are spiritual restore such a one in the spirit of meekness; considering thyself, lest thou also be tempted. Bear ye one another's burdens, and so fulfil the law of Christ. For if a man think himself to be something, when he is nothing, he deceiveth himself. But let every man prove his own work, and then shall he have rejoicing in himself alone, and not in another. For every man shall bear his own burden. Let him that is taught in the word communicate unto him that teacheth in all good things. Be not deceived; God is not mocked: for whatsoever a man soweth, that shall he also reap. For he that soweth to his flesh, shall of the flesh reap corruption; but he that soweth to the Spirit, shall of the Spirit reap life everlasting. And let us not be weary in well doing: for in due season we shall reap, if we faint not. As we have therefore opportunity, let us do good unto all men, especially unto them who are of the household of faith.

They that "*live* in the Spirit" shall "*walk* in the Spirit." The life *must* of necessity come into view, and the fruit of the Spirit *appear*. The spiritual freedmen are constrained by love to serve one another. "Though I be free from all men, yet have I made myself servant unto all." All that I have is the Lord's for the edifying of the church. — Let us give heed to the admonition of the holy apostle to bear one another's burdens! There is great need of it.

Each of us needs indulgence and the assistance of the brethren to wash his feet. We all admit this; but forget it in real life, when others are overtaken in a fault. Why is this? The reason appears when you note how the apostle speaks of "vain glory" in connection with "envying," and how in encouraging charity and patience he warns against "thinking one's self to be something." He who is desirous of vain glory, and thinks himself to be something, is not like the meek Savior, and can not bear the burdens of others. Such a one flatters himself that he is humble and loving and zealous for the brethren; and does not understand that he is merely looking with complacency on his own picture of himself. He sees the faults of others, and thinks: "That is something which I neither do, nor could do." And he excludes the erring one from the kingdom of God. What would have been the fate of Peter after his offence in the court of Caiaphas, and afterward in Antioch, had you been his judge? You forget that Jesus said to the woman taken in adultery: "Neither do I condemn thee; go, and sin no more." You forget the parable of the mote and the beam. You do not understand what it means to feel the weight of the sins of others, and to remove it; which you can do, not by making atonement, but by making intercession for them. You are able to pronounce others wanting in the godly life, but are unable to live this life yourself. Verily, God has the greatest abhorrence of such spiritual bloodthirstiness; he does not recognize as his children such executioners of other people's souls. You think yourself to be something, and call yourself spiritual; but you are carnal, and deceive yourself. Do prove your *own* work; this *every* man should do, says the apostle; but he does not instruct you to prove the work of others. If you must see their sin, take it upon yourself, as Daniel and Nehemiah took upon themselves the sins of their people; and confess it to the Lord as your own sin. Bear with your weak brother, and endure the suffering of love on account of his sin. Then Jesus endures you and him; the blood of Jesus cleanses you both, and you practice the blessed art which only love understands, that of "hiding a multitude of sins." Brethren, ponder this epistle lesson, and follow its golden precepts.

Help us, O God, to go the way of humility and charity. Help us to bear one another's burdens, and so fulfil the law of Christ. Help us, O God, to sow to the Spirit, and of the Spirit reap life everlasting. Amen.

The law of God is good and wise, And sets his will before our eyes; Shows us the way of righteousness, And dooms to death when we transgress.

To those who help in Christ have found And would in works of love abound, It shows what deeds are his delight, And should be done as good and right.

---

364. Monday after Fifteenth Sunday after Trinity.

Lord, give me a whole heart and a right spirit. Amen.

1 Kings 18, 17–21. And it came to pass, when Ahab saw Elijah, that Ahab said unto him, Art thou he that troubleth Israel? And he answered, I have not troubled Israel; but thou and thy father's house, in that ye have forsaken the commandments of the Lord, and thou hast followed Baalim. Now therefore send, and gather to me all Israel unto mount Carmel, and the prophets of Baal four hundred and fifty, and the prophets of the groves four hundred, which eat at Jezebel's table. So Ahab sent unto all the children of Israel, and gathered the prophets together unto mount Carmel.

Our Lord Jesus said to his disciples: "Ye cannot serve God and mammon." In like manner Elijah spoke to Israel: "How long halt ye between two opinions? If the Lord be God, follow him; but if Baal, then follow him!" We are always prone to fall into this unhappy habit of being half-hearted and fickle; and that which is written concerning this matter is for the warning of us all. We are tempted not by the heathen gods, but rather by the riches and honors of the world; not by gods of wood and stone, but by pride and lust of power in worldly or in spiritual guise; not by Baal, but by the golden calf; not by the prophets of the groves, but by the company of Korah (Numbers 16). Be on your guard, brethren; walk in earnestness and fear! It is to the *children of God* that Jesus speaks of this matter; and the sermon of Elijah is addressed to *Israel*. The heart of the unregenerate belongs to the idols; but yours is to belong *wholly and entirely* to the Lord. If you have riches, you shall be none the less poor; and if poverty be your lot, you shall be none the less rich for all that. If God give you power and honors, you must with even more abject humility lie in the dust at his feet; and if you be servants, your royal glory shall prove itself in cheerful obedience and in praise and thanks to God. Do not let the spirit of the world, which always desires to enjoy temporal pleasures and make the heart to trust in fleeting things, obtain power over you; but *believe in the Lord;* hold fast the Invisible One, as though your eyes saw him. Let *him be your God;* that is to say, *trust in him* with full confidence, put all the faith of your soul in him, and never make flesh your arm. *Love him with all your mind,* that he may be your supreme good, your joy and delight, the king of your heart, whom you would not for any earthly consideration desert, or grieve, or offend; *fear* him from the bottom of your heart, and be of nothing so much afraid as of stirring him to anger. Is he not the true God? Is he not willing and able to care for his own? Is it not a glorious thing that he wants to possess our undivided heart, and that he has a jealous affection for us poor, miserable mortals? Shall not *you,* who have begun to know him, and feel his life in you, keep a jealous watch against every form of idolatry which assails you with temptation? Should not *you* be entirely on the Lord's side with a holy ardor surpassing even that of Elijah himself? You know that he answered by fire from heaven; and when the people saw it they said: "The Lord, he is the God; the Lord, he is the God." You shall give yourself with all that is yours as an offering to the Lord; and he shall kindle in you a fire better than that which he sent down to Elijah. It shall consume your sacrifice and lick up all the water round about; that is, you shall consume your strength and all that you have in the service of charity, and nothing shall be able to quench your love. But there are strange doings in the world; they who worship idols boast in their own hearts of their piety; while they whose God the Lord is never cease to deplore before him the idolatry which they find in their hearts. The first are their own saviors; these have Jesus as their Savior.

God, thou knowest how the flesh and the world entice and tempt us; how the spirit of the age threatens to ensnare us; so that we are easily drawn hither and thither, and halt between two opinions. Save us, faithful God; let our hearts be wholly thine. Amen.

So let our lips and lives express The holy Gospel we profess: So let our works and virtues shine, To prove the doctrine all divine.
Thus shall we best proclaim abroad The honors of our Savior God; When his salvation reigns within, And grace subdues the power of sin.

---

365. Tuesday after Fifteenth Sunday after Trinity.

Give me, O God, an eye single and clear. Amen.

Matthew 6, 19–23. Lay not up for yourselves treasures upon earth, where moth and rust doth corrupt, and where thieves break through and steal: But lay up for yourselves treasures in heaven, where neither moth nor rust doth corrupt, and where thieves do not break through nor steal: For where your treasure is, there will your heart be also. The light of the body is the eye: if therefore thine eye be single, thy whole body shall be full of light: but if thine eye be evil, thy whole body shall be full of darkness. If therefore the light that is in thee be darkness, how great is that darkness!

Every man must have something or other as his treasure; the soul holds to something, either the corruptible or the eternal. It is foolishness to rest one's heart on the things of earth; for every earthly good passes away. When a man has labored hard, and secured it, and wants to enjoy it, it proves to be motheaten, and brings nothing but sorrow and disappointment; when he thinks that he has it safe, he finds that it has been stolen. The more your heart gathers of earthly riches and splendor, the poorer do you become; a burning thirst tortures your soul, and you have nothing with which to satisfy it. Alas, what a wretched thing is man's idolatrous love of earthly treasures! It is a deplorable blindness, which darkens his whole existence, and shuts him out from the eternal light. We regard the temporal things as the truly real, as though they could satisfy the eternal craving of our hearts; while they are in fact only shadows of the true treasures of life. If we be wise, we have these earthly good things without owning them; or rather, without allowing our hearts to cling to them. We are free from them, and masters of them, and able to turn them into deeds of charity.

We need an eye which is single. Worldly-minded men also want the things of heaven; but "their eyes do not look right on." They wish to enjoy the world, and to have heaven before them; but the eye which receives the images of different objects at the same time sees nothing clearly; the heart which is divided between God and mammon is in darkness.

Ye Christians, who have been enlightened by the Spirit of God and have caught a glimpse of heaven; keep your hearts free from the curruptible things. The Lord, the living God, be your God; and the eternal heritage of glory be your treasure! Let your whole heart be with Jesus! See him ever more clearly with the eye of faith, and give yourselves to him more and more with living confidence and love! "My son, attend to my words; incline thine ear unto my sayings: Keep thy heart with all diligence; for out of it are the issues of life. Let thine eyes look right on, and let thine eyelids look straight before thee." (Proverbs 4, 20. 23. 25).

Help me, O God; the things of this world are always before me, and threaten to obscure my vision. Give me a good, single, clear eye; so that I give myself wholly to thee, use all the earthly things in the service of charity, and lay up treasures in heaven. Grant us, O God, this mercy, for Jesus' sake. Amen.

Well for him who all forsaking, Walketh not in shadows vain, But the path of peace is taking Through this vale of tears and pain!
O that we our hearts might sever From earth's tempting vanities, Fixing them on him for ever, In whom all our fulness lies!

---

366. Wednesday after Fifteenth Sunday after Trinity.

Give us, O God, light and the desire to find and buy the pearl of great price. Amen.

Matthew 13, 44-46. Again, the kingdom of heaven is like unto treasure hid in a field; the which when a man hath found, he hideth, and for joy thereof goeth and selleth all that he hath, and buyeth that field. Again, the kingdom of heaven is like unto a merchant man, seeking goodly pearls; who, when he had found one pearl of great price, went and sold all that he had, and bought it.

The hidden treasure is the riches of God's mercy; that is, righteousness, peace, and joy in the Holy Ghost. Christ is in the means of grace in the church, with the fruit of his death and resurrection, forgiveness of sins and eternal love; but hidden from our reason and the mind of the natural man. But when the Holy Spirit enlightens us, we find the treasure and keep it in our heart. Christ becomes more precious than all others to us; and the gospel with its blesesd contents becomes so dear to us that our heart is willing to sell everything in order to possess it. Everything else which you value, as, for instance, your wife or husband, your home, your good health, your friends; everything which seemed good to you, and shed luster on your life, disappears like the stars before the light of the sun. You still have these earthly things; you keep your home; you live with your family and kindred; you enjoy your good health, if God preserves it; you ply your vocation, and love your country; but nothing of all these things is now your dearest treasure. There is One dwells in your heart; and for *his* sake you are willing to leave everything else. In him wife and children and all earthly blessings come to have a new meaning; they are, I might say, of less and of greater value than before. You rejoice in all these things, and thank him for them; and you can part with them all, if it be his will, — *lose* them you can *not*, as long as you do not lose him. You can do without everything else; he remains as dear as ever to you. You may feel sorrow because of what you have lost; but in the midst of your sorrow you can be happy. Your Savior alone is indispensable to you; to lose *him* would be to lose your heart and life.

Some there are who seem to find this treasure without having sought it. It falls in their way, and they hide it; they receive the word into the heart as soon as they hear it, and go and practice the required self-denial. Others *seek* with patience after life and peace, — and find God. And a glorious find it is; a *"pearl of great price,"* a gem of the highest value, pure and beautiful and precious above all other precious stones combined! God moves with us in different ways; to some faith is given early, to others late. But all who find the Lord deny themselves for his sake. Note this lesson, dear reader; there is admonition in it: He will and shall have your undivided love. At the same time there is comfort in it also. To "sell all" means to practice self-denial. The Lord speaks of "selling," because it is something which costs all Christians a struggle. Do not lose courage, even if you feel that it is a costly transaction. Pray for the light of the Spirit, that you may see the excellence of the treasure; and for grace to believe the presence of the Savior whom you do not see, and to taste, in so far as you can bear it, the "joy of his salvation." Howbeit, we all understand, I hope, that the "buying" of which the Lord here speaks is the "buying without money and without price."

"O thou eternal Light, who dost transcend all created light; fill my whole heart. Cleanse, gladden, enlighten, and quicken my spirit and all its powers, that I may cling to thee with grateful and joyous devotion. O, when shall come the happy time in which thou shalt satisfy me with thy presence, and become my all in all!"

O Zion, hail! bright city, now unfold The gates of grace to me! How many a time I longed for thee of old, Ere yet I was set free From yon dark life of sadness, Yon world of shadowy naught, And God had given the gladness, The heritage I sought.

---

367. Thursday after Fifteenth Sunday after Trinity.

Lord, come and dwell in our hearts. Amen.

Romans 8, 5–11. For they that are after the flesh do mind the things of the flesh; but they that are after the Spirit, the things of the Spirit. For to be carnally minded is death; but to be spiritually minded is life and peace: Because the carnal mind is enmity against God; for it is not subject to the law of God, neither indeed can be. So then they that are in the flesh cannot please God. But ye are not in the flesh, but in the Spirit, if so be that the Spirit of God dwell in you. Now if any man have not the Spirit of Christ, he is none of his. And if Christ be in you, the body is dead because of sin; but the Spirit is life because of righteousness. But if the Spirit of him that raised up Jesus from the dead dwell in you, he that raised up Christ from the dead shall also quicken your mortal bodies by his Spirit that dwelleth in you.

No Christian should be able to read this Bible lesson without being impelled by it to institute an earnest and thorough self-examination. To be *carnally* minded is death; if I have this mind, I live in enmity against God and in antagonism to his law. But if I be *spiritual*, the Spirit of God, the Spirit of Christ is in me; and Christ himself is then my life. To no Christian can it be a matter of indifference, whether he be a child of death or of life; whether God be his enemy or his friend. — How shall I know, then, whether I am carnally or spiritually minded? "They that are after the flesh do mind the things of the flesh;" their thoughts and desires are contrary to God and his law; they feel no sorrow and pain on account of sin; and Jesus, the Savior of sinners, is a stranger to them; neither do they know his humble, holy, and loving spirit. Their mind is filled with the lust of the eyes, the lust of the flesh, and the pride of life; their care is that they may have power, honor, riches, sensual pleasure, or that they may seem to be righteous, and may boast of their virtues. On the other hand, "they that are after the Spirit mind the things of the Spirit." To them God's grace and favor and the soul's salvation are more important than all things else; so that this is their first thought and concern. They willingly submit to the law of God, feel that their flesh is evil and corrupt, and acknowledge that their life is sinful, and that they deserve death. But the Spirit of Christ in them works faith in his blood; so that they, being baptized into his death and resurrection, always seek him, on the cross and on the

31

throne, and receive grace. — If you are, then, subject to the law of God, and confess your sin with honest heart; if Christ is your right-eousness, and his death and resurrection your hope; if you love him, and always pray for grace to do his will; — this is the work of the Spirit in you, and you are not carnal, but spiritual. Now, let the Spirit himself make you sure of this, and cause you to taste the life and peace of God's grace. Never mind the *how* and the wherefore of this miracle, that "Christ is in you;" but rejoice in it, and be glad to walk the way of self-denial in his strength. You live no more after the flesh; but still the flesh lives in you; now you shall be made aware of its enmity against Christ, and mortify it every day. — It seems a little thing to be a Christian; but it is great beyond measure! "Christ in you, the hope of glory!"

Lord Jesus, save me from the deceitfulness of the flesh; give me thy Spirit, and let me have no peace but in thee. Come, Lord, dwell in me, and let my whole life become pleasing to thee and the Father. Amen.

How blessed, from the bonds of sin, And earthly fetters free, In single-ness of heart and aim Thy servant, Lord, to be! The hardest toil to undertake With joy at thy command, The meanest office to receive With meekness at thy hand!

Thus may I serve thee, gracious Lord! Thus ever thine alone, My soul and body given to thee, The purchase thou hast won: Through evil or through good report Still keeping by thy side, By life or death, in this poor flesh Let Christ be magnified!

---

368. Friday after Fifteenth Sunday after Trinity.

Lord our God, give us the light and joy of the Spirit.

Romans 8, 28–32. And we know that all things work together for good to them that love God, to them who are the called according to his purpose. For whom he did foreknow, he also did predestinate to be conformed to the image of his Son, that he might be the firstborn among many brethren. Moreover, whom he did predestinate, them he also called: and whom he called, them he also justified: and whom he justified, them he also glorified. What shall we then say to these things? If God be for us, who can be against us? He that spared not his own Son, but delivered him up for us all, how shall he not with him also freely give us all things?

This is the voice of a soul which is filled with joy; a song of victory in the very midst of every manner of danger and trouble. Too often we complain with David: "How long wilt thou forget me, O Lord? for ever? How long shall I take counsel in my soul, having sorrow in my heart daily?" — God grant that the spirit of gladness in our Bible lesson might enter our poor hearts, that we also, in spite of all our distress, may sing: "Who shall separate us from the love of Christ?" — We are of those who "love God," if we daily resign our-selves to him, and ask of him grace to deny ourselves, but do his pleasure; "for this is the love of God, that we keep his command-ments." We are called according to God's eternal purpose in Christ, and have obeyed the call. Therefore the glorious comfort contained in our Bible lesson belong to us also. *We know that all things work together for our good. We know this.* We do not *see* it; neither do we comprehend it; but *in faith we "know it."* *"All things"* — so our text plainly says — *all* things; good fortune and bad fortune, nay sin, and temptation, and danger, and death; *all things work together for our good;* they help to encourage us, humble us, strengthen us, purify us. In Romans 5, 3–5, Saint Paul speaks of the benefits of tribulations; and Saint James says 'that we shall "count it all joy when we fall into divers temptations." When it seems to us that we do not love God, are not called to glory, and that everything goes against us rather than for us; this also must be for our good. Do not forget that *"all* things" promote our welfare. The eternal love of God in Christ embraces us and all our ways. Before the world was he knew us, and ordained us in Christ to be brought low and to be exalted, to lose all things and die, and to possess all things and live. In the Son he loves us eternally; of this love he gave us the Son for our Savior, reconciled us with himself, and made us the brethren of the only begotten of the Father. And that which he has begun he shall perform; so that we shall be glorified as surely as we have been called and justified. Whom he *has* called and justified, *"them he also glorified."* "What shall we then say to these things?" Are we to sigh and complain? Yes, on account of our unbelief we may! But at the same time we shall say: *God is for us* and with us; *he* is our friend, our Father; God the Almighty is on our side; "who can be against us?" Who or what can harm us? *Our* cause is in all these things *his;* must not, then, all things make for our benefit? Why are you sad, despondent Christian? Is not everything well? Hear what the apostle further says: "He that spared not his own Son, but delivered him up for us all, how shall he not with him also freely give us all things?" The *"Only Begotten"* was not in God's eye too precious to be sacrificed for us; him God delivered up *for* us all, for our benefit, for our reconciliation, when we were enemies, — how impossible, then, that he should deny us anything which our welfare demands! How utterly impossible! How should it come to pass that he should not with him also freely give us all things? "With him" we have already received all things; for is he not the beloved Son of the Father, and are not all things his; all mercy, all salvation, all victory, all treasures, the heart of God, and everything in heaven and on earth? Him we *have* received, *that* we might become partakers of all these blessings; *how,* then, shall God not with him freely give us all things? It could not by any possibility be otherwise; my unbelief is silenced and must pale into nothingness before the clear light of the Spirit of truth. — Ponder our text, speak of it with God in your chamber, and remind him of his promise; and you will come to say with Paul Gerhard: "If God be for me, let whatsoever will be against me; in the joy of prayer I shall tread it under foot. If God be willing to hear me, and if the Father love me, the devil and all his hosts can do me no injury." — Merciful God, give us this faith and courage. Amen.

Who puts his **trust** in God most just Hath built his house securely; He
who relies on Jesus Christ, Heaven shall be his most surely. Then fixed on
thee my trust shall be, Whose truth can never alter; While mine thou art, not
death's worst smart Shall make my courage falter.

---

369. Saturday after Fifteenth Sunday after Trinity.

Psalm 34, 1–10. I will bless the Lord at all times: his praise shall continually be in my mouth. My soul shall make her boast in the Lord: the
humble shall hear thereof, and be glad. O magnify the Lord with me, and let
us exalt his name together. I sought the Lord, and he heard me, and delivered me from all my fears. They looked unto him, and were lightened; and
their faces were not ashamed. This poor man cried, and the Lord heard him,
and saved him out of all his troubles. The angel of the Lord encampeth
round about them that fear him, and delivereth them. O taste and see that
the Lord is good: blessed is the man that trusteth in him. O fear the Lord,
ye his saints: for there is no want to them that fear him. The young lions
do lack and suffer hunger: but they that seek the Lord shall not want any
good thing.

It is one of my gravest offences that I have not always blessed
the Lord for all things, but have often spent much of my time in complaining of my lot. Now, a Christian dwells all the time in the Lord's
house, inhales his love every moment, receives without ceasing full
forgiveness of sin, is given help in every need; and nothing which
may mar his true happiness can ever befall him. The eye of the Lord
watches over him; and the ear of God is open to hear his prayer; the
Spirit sighs in him, and the power of God delivers him out of all
tribulations. A ladder to heaven is before him always, as before Jacob
in Bethel; and hosts of angels are encamped round about him, as
around Elisha in Dothan. He that touches a child of God touches
the apple of the Lord's eye (Zech. 2, 8). — Even if it seems to you,
dear Christian, that much evil befalls you, it is nevertheless certain
that "goodness and mercy shall follow you all the days of your life."
David does not in our text speak to the "young lions," or, in other
words, to the noble and brave, but to "the poor man"; and farther
on he says, in verse 19: "Many are the afflictions of the righteous;
but the Lord delivereth him out of them all." Paul, who knows that
"all things work together for good to them that love God," has but a
short time before said: *"Wretched man that I am!* who shall deliver
me from the body of this death?" All who seek the Lord have the
sense of being wretched; for they know their sin, and accept chastisement for it. But in fact they are blessed; and God will have us to *believe this fact,* believe the word of God; and praise him for salvation,
though we do not see it. In doing which we shall see it. Therefore it
is written: "Taste and see that the Lord is good; blessed is the man
that trusteth in him." Again we hear *who* it is that sees the Lord's
goodness; *it is the man that trusteth in him.* "They looked unto him,
and were lightened; and their faces were not ashamed. This poor
man cried, and the Lord heard him, and saved him out of *all* his

troubles." You do not understand how blessed an effect your troubles have in making you whole and promoting your happiness. They are useful beyond measure, even if they do have their origin in your sins.

My purpose is and shall be this: "I will bless the Lord at all times; his praise shall continually be in my mouth." By his grace my innermost heart shall always be happy and well satisfied in my God; so that my life shall make for the honor of his name and the edifying of his church. — Lord, for this in thee we trust; grant us this mercy by thy Holy Spirit, for Jesus' sake. Amen.

Thou art my portion, O my God! Soon as I know thy way, My heart makes haste to obey thy word, And suffers no delay.
I choose the path of heavenly truth, And glory in my choice; Not all the riches of the earth Could make me so rejoice.

---

370. Sixteenth Sunday after Trinity. I.

Lord Jesus, speak to us; thou hast the words of eternal life. Amen.

Gospel Lesson, Luke 7, 11-17. And it came to pass the day after, that he went into a city called Nain; and many of his disciples went with him, and much people. Now when he came nigh to the gate of the city, behold, there was a dead man carried out, the only son of his mother, and she was a widow: and much people of the city was with her. And when the Lord saw her, he had compassion on her, and said unto her, Weep not. And he came and touched the bier: and they that bare him stood still. And he said, Young man, I say unto thee, Arise. And he that was dead sat up, and began to speak. And he delivered him to his mother. And there came a fear on all: and they glorified God, saying, That a great prophet is risen up among us; and, That God hath visited his people. And this rumor of him went forth throughout all Judæa, and throughout all the region round about.

On this earth we carry one another to the grave; it is one continuous funeral which no man can stop. A thousand times the heart of the parent has said: "I will not place my son on the bier; you shall not carry him out to the grave!" In vain! The whole earth is a cemetery, and the whole human race a funeral procession. We do not only *follow* to the grave them that are dead; we carry death in ourselves, and hasten onward to our own grave. These eyes, this tongue, these hands, shall rot; decompose; return to dust, in the bowels of the earth, or in the depths of the sea. That which is most closely joined together must be put asunder. You surrender your place to another, and he in his turn to still another; and soon you are as completely forgotten as a blade of grass whose place knows it no more. This is the death of the *body;* but there is also a death of the *soul,* namely when man is separated from God through sin and unbelief. Every one who does not in his heart believe in Jesus is dead while he lives; and is on the way to eternal death. Here such a man has a darkened understanding which knows not Christ; and his heart is cold toward God, having neither love's longing after him, nor joy in him. And in the next world such a man is for ever shut out from light and life. Nothing is more terrifying than pitchy darkness; but eternal death is that "outer darkness"; that is to say, eternal misery and gloom and despair.

This we men have brought upon ourselves by our revolt against God; and there is none can save himself or others. Behold, however; the procession of death coming out of the gate of Nain is met by a procession of life, Jesus and his disciples. And *Jesus* is able to change its character, making them that went forth in sorrow and tears return with joy and songs of praise. He goes all the time at the head of his company of disciples, the holy Christian church, and subdues death, and adds to the number of his people; and they turn back to Nain, to the earth which has been created anew and made beautiful for ever. For as many as believe in Jesus Christ have been quickened from the dead; their understanding has been enlightened, and their heart awakened; they love God, and live in the fellowship of love with him. They "have passed from death unto life," and need have no fear of the death eternal. When their body dies, it is but a sleep, out of which Jesus gloriously wakes them; his members can not remain in death. They are nourished by his ever living body and blood, and are the temple of the Holy Ghost; how, then, can they be doomed to die? "No," says Luther, "Christ shall in a moment gather all who are dead, call them forth with a word out of dust and ashes, air and water; and, as Paul puts it, in 1 Thessalonians 4, 14, *bring* them with him as the head its members, a countless multitude of the faithful, and *translate them from death and misery into eternal life.* He shall, as Isaiah says, 25, 8, *wipe away the tears from off their faces,* that they may with eternal joy and praise and honor for ever and without ceasing laud and exalt him, their Lord and Redeemer. This we must learn to believe, in order that we may have comfort in every sorrow and in the agony of death; so that we, — should we come to the point where, like this widow of Nain, we see nothing but death and corruption, nay if we be in the jaws of death, and be placed in our coffin, as was her son, and be carried out to the grave, — may still have the unshaken faith that in Christ we have life and victory over death. For faith in Christ must be so constituted, or must at least try to learn the lesson taught in Hebrews 11, 1, that it *may grasp and hold fast the evidence of things not seen,* nay even that which seems to be contradicted by the things seen. Thus Christ will have this widow to believe and hope life, in that he says '*weep not*'; although she and all the world, according to their sense and reason, must entirely despair of life. For he wants to teach us by experience that of us and in us there is nothing *but* corruption and death, while of him and in him is nothing but life, which swallows up both our sin and death. Nay, the more of misery and death there is in us, the greater wealth of comfort and life shall we find in him, if we do but in faith cling to him; to which he encourages and exhorts us by his word as well as by this example."

Lord Jesus, give us the light and the gifts of the Spirit to believe and to hold fast to thee, that thou mayest give us eternal life. Save us, Lord, from cruel death; save us from eternal perdition. Amen.

Since thou from death didst rise again, In death thou wilt not leave me; Lord, thy ascension soothes my pain, No fear of death shall grieve me: For thou wilt have me where thou art, And thus with joy I can depart, To be with thee for ever.

---

371. Sixteenth Sunday after Trinity. II.

Heavenly Father, give us thy Spirit in Christ Jesus. Amen.

Epistle Lesson, Ephesians 3, 13–21. Wherefore I desire that ye faint not at my tribulations for you, which is your glory. For this cause I bow my knees unto the Father of our Lord Jesus Christ, of whom the whole family in heaven and earth is named, that he would grant you, according to the riches of his glory, to be strengthened with might by his Spirit in the inner man; that Christ may dwell in your hearts by faith; that ye, being rooted and grounded in love, may be able to comprehend with all saints, what is the breadth, and length, and depth, and height; and to know the love of Christ, which passeth knowledge, that ye might be filled with all the fulness of God. Now unto him that is able to do exceeding abundantly above all that we ask or think, according to the power that worketh in us, unto him be glory in the church by Christ Jesus, throughout all ages, world without end. Amen.

The love of Christ passes all knowledge. It embraces the whole world, causing him to die for all men; it flows like the *broadest* stream of mercy over all the earth; and it endures from everlasting to everlasting, so that its *length* is infinite. It descends into the *deepest depth*, suffers death itself, and has mercy on the most wretched of men; and it sits on the throne *on high*, and leads us to eternal glory. It is the will of the Father to give us grace by his Holy Spirit, that in this love of Christ we may be *rooted and grounded* through faith. The Spirit illumines us; so that we believe this love, and have the assurance in our hearts that God loves us in Christ with a love which is victorious over sin and death, and which is so infinite and so mighty that we surrender to it with our whole heart. We are made fast to it with the deepest roots of our nature; so that nothing can separate us from it. The union is so strong and intimate, and all is so entirely of and through God, that we dare ask men and angels: "Who shall separate us from the love of Christ? We are more than conquerors through him, *through him* that loved us! For I am persuaded, that neither death, nor life, nor angels, nor principalities, nor powers, nor things present, nor things to come, nor height, nor depth, nor any other creature, shall be able to separate us from the love of God, which is in Christ Jesus our Lord." (Romans 8). He then dwells in our hearts by faith; and we *know* this love, which passes all knowledge. Do the words of the apostle terrify you; and do you think: Alas, I am far, far away from this glorious estate? In that case you must humble yourself, and ask the God of love, who spared not his Son, to give you his Holy Spirit; and he shall do it. Humble yourself, but do not lose heart. If you know that you are a lost sinner, and believe that Jesus died for all the world, and pray that your heart may be cleansed in his blood, you are in truth received into the communion of the saints; you are embraced in God's eternal love, are already his child in Christ, and a branch of the vine of life. It is God himself who has brought this about; and he shall continue to do exceeding abundantly above all that you ask or think. Do you not believe that his love is great beyond your power to understand? Do you not believe that his mighty power can overcome everything which resists him in you and about you? "Yes; but dare I have this faith? Dare I for my own part take this comfort to my heart?" Are you not to believe that which is true? Has not God given his Son for you? Have you not been baptized into his death and resurrection? Has not his Spirit made you to see your sin? Or have you done this yourself? Does not the Spirit groan in you, and do you not thirst after his love? He loves you infinitely better than you can love him; and the fact that he dwells in you is the only thing which has taught you to cry after the living God. O, that he might enlighten us by his Spirit and thus make us to *believe;* so that the power of Christ in us may be victorious and prove itself in patience and joy and the praise of the Lord! Grant us this grace, merciful heavenly Father, for Jesus' sake. Amen.

Now I am thine, for ever thine: O save thy servant, Lord! Thou art my shield, my hiding-place; My hope is in thy word.

Thou hast inclined this heart of mine Thy statutes to fulfil; And thus, till mortal life shall end, Would I perform thy will.

---

372. Monday after Sixteenth Sunday after Trinity.

Jesus, thou Lord of life, give us the grace to believe in thee, and to love thee. Amen.

John 11, 1–13. Now a certain man was sick, named Lazarus, of Bethany, the town of Mary and her sister Martha. (It was that Mary which anointed the Lord with ointment, and wiped his feet with her hair, whose brother Lazarus was sick.) Therefore his sisters sent unto him, saying, Lord, behold, he whom thou lovest is sick. When Jesus heard that, he said, This sickness is not unto death, but for the glory of God, that the Son of God might be glorified thereby. Now Jesus loved Martha, and her sister, and Lazarus. When he had heard therefore that he was sick, he abode two days still in the same place where he was. Then after that saith he to his disciples, Let us go into Judæa again. His disciples say unto him, Master, the Jews of late sought to stone thee; and goest thou thither again? Jesus answered, Are there not twelve hours in the day? If any man walk in the day, he stumbleth not, because he seeth the light of this world. But if a man walk in the night, he stumbleth, because there is no light in him. These things said he: and after that he saith unto them, Our friend Lazarus sleepeth; but I go, that I may awake him out of sleep. Then said his disciples, Lord, if he sleep, he shall do well. Howbeit Jesus spake of his death: but they thought that he had spoken of taking of rest in sleep.

"Lord, behold, he whom thou lovest is sick." These are beautiful words; words expressive of pain, but still more of hope and trust.

In this manner we also should speak to the Lord concerning our dear ones who are sick. Tell him your fears and troubles with genuine trust in his power and mercy. "Lord, behold, he whom thou lovest is sick." This was all the message which they sent; having done which they had placed all their trouble on him. — "This sickness is not unto death." This was the glorious reply which Jesus made; and these words also apply to all the diseases of all the friends of Jesus. — In the mean time Lazarus died, nevertheless. What must they then have thought of Jesus? What doubts must have crossed one another in their minds, do you think? Because Jesus loved them he waited two days, that Lazarus might die and be buried. He loves us; and *therefore* he allows us to be tortured with gloomy thoughts, to suffer, and to die; yet his purpose in all things is to give us life and salvation. "Our friend Lazarus sleepeth," says Jesus. A black woman who had received the gift of faith was asked, if she had seen Missionary Kitchen recently; and she answered: "The fever attacked him; he said, 'I go to God'; and he fell asleep." "O, is Kitchen dead?" "Dead, sir? No; Father Kitchen can not die. He fell asleep; and he sleeps until the voice of the Son of God wakes him. Mister Kitchen does not die, but he sleeps." This is the echo of the words of Jesus: "Our friend Lazarus sleepeth; but I go, that I may awake him out of sleep." Now that Lazarus lay in the grave, it was the "day" for Jesus to go again into Judæa.

Dear reader; shall we not love him? If you do, no sickness which you have is unto death, but unto the honor of God and his Son. He shall try you with afflictions, and remain away from you longer than seems right to you; nay, he may let you wither and die; but he does this, in order that everything in you which is of sin and death may be destroyed. He shall have no difficulty in awakening you; and you shall rise again in perfect health. Let us only be able to say of you with truth: "Lord, behold, he whom thou lovest is sick!"

Lord Jesus, I know that thou lovest us all with an ardent desire to save us. Give me, then, grace to love thee, that thou mayest say of me: "My Father will love him, and we will come unto him, and make our abode with him." Come into our hearts and houses, thou Lord of life, that when we or our loved ones are sick, we may say to thee: "Lord, behold, he whom thou lovest is sick." And let us then hear thy answer: "This sickness is not unto death, but for the glory of God, that the Son of God might be glorified thereby." Amen.

A slumber I know, in Jesus' name, A rest from all toil and sorrow; Earth tenderly takes my weary frame, To sleep till the blissful morrow; In heaven my soul with God abides, Forgotten are cares and trials.

O Savior, when darkens life's last day, And death in his bonds me keepeth, Come unto my bed, in mercy say: The child is not dead, but sleepeth. Then grant me thy grace, that I arise To praise thee in life eternal.

373. Tuesday after Sixteenth Sunday after Trinity.

Lord, increase our faith. Amen.

John 11, 20-27. Then Martha, as soon as she heard that Jesus was coming, went and met him: but Mary sat still in the house. Then said Martha unto Jesus, Lord, if thou hadst been here, my brother had not died. But I know, that even now, whatsoever thou wilt ask of God, God will give it thee. Jesus saith unto her, Thy brother shall rise again. Martha saith unto him, I know that he shall rise again in the resurrection at the last day. Jesus said unto her, I am the resurrection, and the life: he that believeth in me, though he were dead, yet shall he live: and whosoever liveth and believeth in me shall never die. Believest thou this? She saith unto him, Yea, Lord; I believe that thou art the Christ, the Son of God, which should come into the world.

There was mourning in the house of Martha. The two women had buried their brother, and been left to weep over their bereavement. Worst of all, they were assailed by unbelief; and the soul was like a storm-tossed sea. "Why did the Lord not come? Is he also faithless? Could he also be one of those friends who fail when trouble comes. Impossible! Why, then, did he not come? He had said: 'This sickness is not unto death.' Yet our brother is now dead. We can, then, no longer trust in *that which Jesus says!* Yet, after all, there *can* be no guile in his mouth. Nevertheless, Lazarus is dead!" — The Jews could give them no comfort; it was necessary for the Lord himself to come. He sometimes appears in one of his servants, but his own real presence is necessary; for *he* alone can loose the bonds of the soul, even as he alone can deliver the body from death. He came to Bethany; and the words of Martha show us what thoughts were struggling for mastery in her. They are the selfsame thoughts which cause my own sick heart to waver between submission to the Lord and accusation against him, between belief and unbelief. The words of the Lord, however, light up the heart, humble, comfort, heal, and quicken. Jesus says not only that Lazarus "shall rise again"; but he adds: *"He that believeth in me, though he were dead, yet shall he live; and whosoever liveth and believeth in me shall never die."* And now he has given me also faith. I am certain that Jesus is the Son of God; that he died for my sins, and rose again for my justification; that he is the Lord of life and death; that in baptism he has made me a member of himself, and that in the holy supper he gives me his own body and blood. Himself gives me the grace of the Spirit to believe and to gain victory in the fight against unbelief. We have, then, brethren, the life eternal in us. He who said, that Lazarus should rise again, also said: *"Whosoever believeth in me shall never die."* The last is as certainly true, as was the first. Do you not already feel that your heart clings to him, and that his love holds you fast? Yet, we do not build our hope of life on our feelings, but on his eternally true and faithful promise. Though I die, yet my soul is with him; and he shall resurrect my body also. Whether here or yonder, Christ is my life; and that which he has said remains in force for ever: "He that believeth in me, though he were dead, yet shall he live; and whosoever liveth and believeth in me shall never die." Blessed be thy name, Lord Jesus! Grant us grace to believe in thee with our whole heart. Amen.

, I shall see God with these eyes, Shall behold my blessed Savior; I, the selfsame, shall arise, In my flesh see God for ever; Then shall wholly disappear Frailties that oppress me here.
What now sickens, mourns, and sighs, Christ with him to glory bringeth; Earthly is the seed and dies, Heavenly from the grave it springeth; Natural is the death we die, Spiritual, our life on high.

---

374. Wednesday after Sixteenth Sunday after Trinity.

Lord, take us also with thee into the grave of Lazarus. Amen.

John 11, 33–38. When Jesus therefore saw her weeping, and the Jews also weeping which came with her, he groaned in the spirit, and was troubled, and said, Where have ye laid him? They said unto him, Lord, come and see. Jesus wept. Then said the Jews, Behold, how he loved him! And some of them said, Could not this man, which opened the eyes of the blind, have caused that even this man should not have died? Jesus therefore, again groaning in himself, cometh to the grave. It was a cave, and a stone lay upon it.

Two words form the most noteworthy sentence in this Bible lesson. They have been set apart as a separate verse; and this verse, John 11, 35, is the shortest in the whole Bible, and at the same time one of the greatest. *"Jesus wept."* Here he wept at the grave. Shortly after this he wept over Jerusalem, and then again during his spiritual agony in Gethsemane. The Son of God waters with his tears our cemeteries, our pleasure-grounds, and our paths to glory. His tears at the grave of Lazarus prove to us his human heart, his brotherly spirit, and his friendly feeling toward us. When you mourn the death of a dear one, you have the sympathy of Jesus. You need not fear to weep; besides which you know that your tears have been consecrated by his tears; you know that he likewise has wept, and has been tried in the same sorrow. You know that he has made atonement for the sin which still taints your sorrw by reason of your self-love and the weakness of your faith; but you know also that your tears are of an entirely different nature from the tears of the unbelievers. In the sorrow of unbelief are hopelessness and bitterness against God; in the sorrow of faith is a feeling of bitterness against sin and death, but submission to the will of God and the hope of a blessed reunion. — That which is here recorded concerning Jesus is precious beyond the power of words to express. *"He groaned in the spirit, and was troubled,* and said, Where have ye laid him? They said unto him, Lord, come and see! *Jesus wept."* Always when death has come home to me, and taken away one of my dear ones, I have been stirred to thorough anger against this "king of terrors," and have felt deep sorrow on account of our grievous offence, which has given cruel death power over us. Away with it! Let it be utterly destroyed; let it be sent back to the devil, from whom it came! It would be vain for me to cry out, and weep, and curse sin and death; but the Son of God has taken upon himself our sorrows; and he does not weep in vain; it is not in vain that he groans in the spirit against death, which reigns on the earth. For he takes sin, and buries it; and by his resurrection he promises us that death shall be for ever destroyed; and hence I *no longer* cry and weep in vain against sin and death. Lord Jesus, we thank thee for that thou didst weep! Teach us the meaning of thy tears, and grant that in them we may find healing. Amen.

Be thou my consolation And shield when I must die; Remind me of thy passion, When my last hour draws nigh. Mine eyes shall then behold thee, Upon thy cross shall dwell, My heart by faith enfold thee: Who dieth thus, dies well.

---

375. Thursday after Sixteenth Sunday after Trinity.

Lord Jesus, reveal to us thy glory. Amen.

John 11, 39-45. Jesus said, Take ye away the stone. Martha, the sister of him that was dead, saith unto him, Lord, by this time he stinketh: for he hath been dead four days. Jesus saith unto her, Said I not unto thee, that, if thou wouldest believe, thou shouldest see the glory of God? Then they took away the stone from the place where the dead was laid. And Jesus lifted up his eyes, and said, Father, I thank thee that thou hast heard me. And I knew that thou hearest me always: but because of the people which stand by I said it, that they may believe that thou hast sent me. And when he thus had spoken, he cried with a loud voice, Lazarus, come forth. And he that was dead came forth, bound hand and foot with graveclothes: and his face was bound about with a napkin. Jesus saith unto them, Loose him, and let him go. Then many of the Jews which came to Mary, and had seen the things which Jesus did, believed on him.

These are the words of omnipotence which Jesus speaks: "Lazarus, come forth!" Nothing can resist them. The body of Lazarus had by this time lain in the grave four days, and decomposition had begun; but in obedience to the Lord's command the soul returned, death retreated, and the body was again quickened. He speaks to the dead, and awakes him as out of sleep. God, who gave life, has power to take it away, and power to give it anew; and this power he has given to his Son. From everlasting the Son is with the Father, and equally omnipotent; but in his state of humiliation he has left the use of his omnipotence in the hands of the Father, and asks the Father's consent to every miracle. His will always coincides with the will of the Father; for which reason his prayer always is answered. By this obedience unto death the Son of Man has received the "uttermost parts of the earth for his possession," and shall on the last day awake us all from the dead. My brother who has fallen asleep in the Lord shall, as well as the dead brother of Martha, hear the voice of the Son of God, and come forth before my very eyes. Or, if I also die before the coming of the Lord, I shall myself be awakened by this voice, and the angels shall be my servants. — "Said I not unto thee, that, if thou wouldest believe, thou shouldest see the glory of God?" With these words Jesus sustained Martha when she was about to sink; her faith was victorious, and she saw the Son of God glorified. Could we also but *believe*, we should see his glory! We would in faith ask of him new life for one another, spiritual revivals through the name of Jesus. We would see that it is the word of the Lord which brings about everything great and good on earth; and we would see that the graves of the faithful are chambers in which to sleep, and that their decomposing bodies are seed springing forth to the glorious harvest of the great day. Thank God, our struggling faith shall obtain victory through his grace, and all our sickness shall make for the honor of God; for sorrow and death must flee before the voice of our Lord Jesus.

Lord, we pray thee, increase our faith, and make us to see thy glory. This we beseech of thee: Give us thy Spirit, strengthen our weak faith, and open our eyes to see thy glory. Amen.

These eyes shall see him in that day, The Lord that died for me: And all my rising bones shall say, Lord, who is like to thee! If such the views which grace unfolds, Weak as it is below, What raptures must the Church above In Jesus' presence know!

---

376. Friday after Sixteenth Sunday after Trinity.

"They that sow in tears shall reap in joy."

Romans 5, 1–5. Therefore being justified by faith, we have peace with God through our Lord Jesus Christ; by whom also we have access by faith into this grace wherein we stand, and rejoice in hope of the glory of God. And not only so, but we glory in tribulations also: knowing that tribulation worketh patience; and patience, experience; and experience, hope; and hope maketh not ashamed; because the love of God is shed abroad in our hearts by the Holy Ghost, which is given unto us.

In vain the devil accuses the faithful on account of the sin and weakness which still cling to them; they stand in grace unceasingly, are clothed with the righteousness of Christ, and thus they all the time have peace with God. The apostle does not here speak of the *feeling* of peace in their hearts, but of God's relation to them, that he no more condemns them or casts them off, but is to them a God of peace and a merciful Father in Christ. Rejoice, then, in the midst of your afflictions, dear Christian; you dwell continually in "a peaceable habitation, and in sure dwellings" with the Almighty. To have him as your enemy is terrible; but to be his child of grace is bliss; for "if *God* be for us, who can be against us?" — In Christ faith has access to the heart of God. He has taught us to pray to "our Father," and has given us the spirit of children; so that by his blood we have boldness to enter into the holiest, and find help at all times. Glorious estate of grace! Yet our rejoicing is in the hope of the glory *to come*. For this very reason, however, no tribulation can rob us of our joy; on the contrary, we glory in tribulations also. It has been said concerning woman, that she "is in pain from the day on which she becomes a mother"; and this can be said with still more truth of a Christian: The world persecutes him, and God disciplines him; and he has labor and vexation and danger and fear every day. Herein we glory, however; for "tribulation worketh patience." It does not only *demand*, but *"worketh"* patience; and "patience worketh experience." It teaches us to suffer without complaining, and to have brave hearts, and to gain the victory. It consumes our pride and our despondency, and gives our faith the stamp of experience. Saint James says: "My brethren, count it all joy when ye fall into divers temptations; knowing this, that the trying of your faith worketh patience. But let patience have her perfect work." We glory in everything with which our enemies would injure us; for it must serve to injure and destroy our sin only, and to strengthen our hope of glory. — Cause and effect here work beautifully in a circle: *Hope* causes *tribulation;* tribulation, *patience*; patience, *experience*; experience again, a stronger hope. Christ has taken away my sin; God has bound me to himself in an eternal covenant of peace; he who can not lie has from ages eternal promised me everlasting life. — Give us, O God, faith unfeigned; and shed abroad thy love in our hearts by the Holy Ghost. Let our hope wax strong, and sustain us in our tribulations, that we may emerge from them with the genuine stamp of experience; and give us at last the heritage of glory. Amen.

When darkness and when sorrows rose And pressed on every side, The Lord has still sustained my steps, And still has been my guide.
Here will I rest, and build my hopes, Nor murmur at his rod; He's more than all the world to me, My health, my life, my God!

377. Saturday after Sixteenth Sunday after Trinity.

Psalm 116, 1–9. I love the Lord, because he hath heard my voice and my supplications. Because he hath inclined his ear unto me, therefore will I call upon him as long as I live. The sorrows of death compassed me, and the pains of hell gat hold upon me: I found trouble and sorrow. Then called I upon the name of the Lord: O Lord, I beseech thee, deliver my soul. Gracious is the Lord, and righteous; yea, our God is merciful. The Lord preserveth the simple: I was brought low, and he helped me. Return unto thy rest, O my soul; for the Lord hath dealt bountifullly with thee. For thou hast delivered my soul from death, mine eyes from tears, and my feet from falling. I will walk before the Lord in the land of the living.

If Israel must love the Lord, because he had delivered them out of their Babylonian captivity, and guided them back to their own country; should not we love him, we whom he "hath delivered from the power of darkness, and hath translated into the kingdom of his dear Son"? If they must shew forth his praises, his grace and righteousness and grace and mercy, and thank him for deliverance out of great trouble; how much more should we do it! God has shown you, dear Christian, so much mercy, that you must feel impelled to prostrate yourself before him with praises and thanksgiving for ever. You deserved death and hell for evermore; and now you have received as your portion a heritage in heaven, and have already begun to taste the sweetness of eternal life, love, peace, and joy in God. You walked in darkness and spiritual death, and did not want to come out into the light; but the Lord called you so long and so urgently that you awoke; and he led you in before his face in the land of the living. How faithfully does he not follow you with his Spirit, and from how many temptations and dangers has he not delivered you! He hears your voice, and inclines his ear to your cry; he keeps you, and helps you, and shall fulfil his good work in you. You may lean with confidence on his mercy and faithfulness. — We will, then, love the Lord always, and call upon him with thanks and praise as long as we live. Who is like unto thee, Lord Jesus; to deliver the needy when he crieth; the poor also, and him that hath no helper? Who is like thee, strong, and faithful, and kind, and loving; beautiful, and a joy to the soul? "Grace is poured into thy lips"; and "thy name is as ointment poured forth." Nothing in heaven and on earth is so sweet. I was needy; thou didst save me. I am needy; thou dost save me. What shall I render unto thee for all thy benefits toward me? I will offer to thee the sacrifice of thanksgiving, and take the cup of salvation, and call upon the name of the Lord. O Lord truly I am thy servant; I am thy servant, and the son of thine handmaid; thou hast loosed my bonds. Of my heart I love thee, precious God; but I earnestly beseech thee to quicken my love. Let all that is within me love thee, and praise thy holy name; let "my bowels sound like an harp" to thy glory. In the Savior's name. Amen.

Thou art my hiding-place, O Lord! On thee I fix my trust, Encouraged by thy holy word, A feeble child of dust. I have no argument beside, I urge no other plea; And 'tis enough the Savior died, The Savior died for me.

---

378. Seventeenth Sunday after Trinity. I.

Lord, heal us, and teach us. Amen.

Gospel Lesson, Luke 14, 1-11. And it came to pass, as he went into the house of one· of the chief Pharisees, to eat bread on the sabbath day, that they watched him. And behold, there was a certain man before him, which had the dropsy. And Jesus, answering, spake unto the lawyers and Pharisees, saying, Is it lawful to heal on the sabbath day? And they held their peace. And he took him, and healed him, and let him go; and answered them, saying, Which of you shall have an ass or an ox fallen into a pit, and will not straightway pull him out on the sabbath day? And they could not answer him again to these things. And he put forth a parable to those which were bidden, when he marked how they chose out the chief rooms; saying unto them, When thou art bidden of any man to a wedding, sit not down in the highest room; lest a more honorable man than thou be bidden of him; and he that bade thee and him come and say to thee, Give this man place; and thou begin with shame to take the lowest room. But when thou art bidden, go and sit down in the lowest room; that when he that bade thee cometh, he may say unto thee, Friend, go up higher: then shalt thou have worship in the presence of them that sit at meat with thee. For whosoever exalteth himself shall be abased; and he that humbleth himself shall be exalted.

The Spirit of God warns us against being like unto the proud Pharisees, who employed the sabbath in tempting Jesus. How, then, shall we keep the sabbath day holy? The Lord employed it in *deeds of mercy* and in *teaching the word.* The world makes of Sunday a day on which to indulge the flesh; the Pharisees used the sabbath to strengthen themselves in self-righteousness, and to judge others; but Jesus spends the day in services of love, causing much thanksgiving to ascend to God. "If thou draw out thy soul to the hungry, and satisfy the afflicted soul; then shall thy light rise in obscurity, and thy darkness be as the noon day. If thou turn away thy foot from the sabbath, from doing thy pleasure on my holy day; and call the sabbath a delight, the holy of the Lord, honorable; and shalt honor him, not doing thine own ways, nor finding thine own pleasure, nor speaking thine own words; — then shalt thou delight thyself in the Lord; and I will cause thee to ride upon the high places of the earth, and feed thee with the heritage of Jacob thy father; for the mouth of the Lord hath spoken it" (Isaiah 58, 10. 13. 14). "Pure religion and undefiled before God and the Father is this, to visit the father-less and widows in their affliction, and to keep himself unspotted from the world" (James 1, 27). This is the right way to use the day of rest. Call on one who is sick, or sad, or a widow; on one who has gone astray spiritually, or on a brother who suffers. First go to your chamber and pray the Lord to give you charity. Take the word of God with you, above all in your own heart. Hear the story of the afflicted, and put yourself in his place; enter into his circumstances, take upon your soul his infirmities, and apply to his soul the healing ointment of the word. Whatsoever you may do more for him, the Lord will teach you, and give you the necessary strength. — However, if Sunday is to be a day of *charitable deeds*, it must first of all be to us a *day of rest.* Our soul shall always have rest in the word of God; this is "the one thing needful" (Luke 10, 42); blessed is he who with Mary choses "that good part"! Jesus calls to himself all them that labor and are heavy laden; but he is in his word; and Sunday and the other days of rest are appointed, in order that we may devote them especially to the study of this word. Do not neglect the word of God; do not remain away from the divine service except for the most urgent reasons. Many stay away from church for almost no reason at all; and are absent as often as present. It gives me great pain to observe that very many of our young people after their confirmation become strangers to the church. What must be the fate of such as despise the word of God; the only means by which they might cleanse their way? Defenceless against the devil, they must soon become his prey. If parents and masters gave this matter proper thought, they would be diligent church goers; if for no other reason, that they might draw the young people with them to the house of God. But when the old people are careless about going to church, the young follow their example; and then the descent of both into wickedness is rapid. Do not, I beseech you, neglect the services in the church! This prayer comes from the heart; do you take it to heart! Promise the Lord that you will come to meet him at the appointed time; and keep the promise! Let it be as much a matter of course that you go to church on Sunday as that you go to your work on other days, and to the table when you are called. Go with simple heart to meet the Lord; and fix your eyes on him, who looks on you; then shall you forget the imperfections of the preacher, and in the spiritual fellowship of the saints, as less than the least of all, feel that the hands of the heavenly High Priest are lifted over you to bless you. For *the public church service is the solemn audience of the congregation with Christ.* We come to him in company as his people with petitions and thanks; and he comes to us in the word and sacraments with grace and blessing. As a whole people gathered in the presence of their king, praying, and rendering thanks, and receiving his blessing, the Christian church stands in its Sunday service before the Lord Christ. Will *you* remain away, dear brother? Or is it possible that you can come in the spirit displayed by the Pharisees in our gospel lesson? Believe the truth, that the Lord is there; and accept his love with humble soul. Go out with joy in the service of love, and bring the blessing of the divine service to those who were prevented from coming.

Lord God, give us humble hearts; that we gladly hear thy word, and keep it as our greatest treasure. Give us therein rest for our souls, and power to mortify the lusts of the flesh, and to practice deeds of charity. Give us at last part in that rest which remains to thy people. Amen.

Thine earthly sabbaths, Lord, we love; But there's a nobler rest above: To that our laboring souls aspire, With ardent hope and strong desire.
O long-expected day, begin! Dawn on these realms of woe and sin! Fain would we leave this weary road, And sleep in death, to rest with God.

---

379. Seventeenth Sunday after Trinity. II.

Lord Jesus, make us like minded unto thee. Amen.

Epistle Lesson, Ephesians 4, 1–6. I therefore, the prisoner of the Lord, beseech you that ye walk worthy of the vocation wherewith ye are called, with all lowliness and meekness, with longsuffering, forbearing one another in love; endeavoring to keep the unity of the Spirit in the bond of peace. There is one body, and one Spirit, even as ye are called in one hope of your calling; one Lord, one faith, one baptism, one God, and Father of all, who is above all, and through all, and in you all.

All believers are united with the Lord Jesus, and knit together by his love. They walk the same narrow path to the same glorious goal. Strangers on earth, they hasten toward heaven. One hope comforts and strengthens them all; the hope, namely, that they shall dwell together in the same house of the Father in the land beyond the sky. They all serve the same master, to whom the hearts of all belong; and all have the same faith, which is created by the Spirit, and which rests on the only true God, as it is founded on the word of forgiveness and salvation for Jesus' sake only. All are baptized with one baptism, the baptism in the name of the triune God. He is the God of their heart; and thus they all are children of the Lord in heaven, and pray to him as to their Father. His omnipotence and mercy cover them all together; the Son's life of love courses through and controls them all, as the brain controls the movements of the body; and the Spirit which sanctifies, sevenfold yet one, lives in them all. They all are nourished by the same spiritual meat, the gospel and the body and blood of the glorified Savior; they all stand before the same mercy seat; and all fight the same fight under the same standard, the cross of Christ. Neither time nor space separates them. We who now live sit at the Supper with the apostles in Jerusalem the same night in which Jesus was betrayed; and Paul belongs to us as much as to the church in Ephesus.

What an admonition is there not herein! Do not violate this precious and holy unity, but endeavor to keep it in the bond of peace. There is *nothing* whatever which *Jesus* himself more ardently desires than that his disciples may dwell together in the fellowship of love. How earnestly does he not pray that all who shall believe on him through the word of the apostles may be one, as the Father in him, and he in them, that the world may know the love of God (John 17); hence that they may not only be one in spirit, but that there may be an outward and visible unity before the eyes of all men. How earnestly does he not exhort them to prove to the world their discipleship; and what an example of humility and forbearance does he not present to them by washing their feet; even the feet of Judas, though well aware of his perfidy! In like manner do *all the apostles* beseech the faithful to walk worthy of the vocation wherewith they are called, with all lowliness and meekness, with longsuffering, forbearing one another in love.—Do not, then, separate, but keep together, and forbear one another. Punish sin, and purge out the old leaven; but do not go from one another, and do not disrupt the body of Christ. Hear also the old fathers; they weep, and pray that the brethren may continue speaking the truth in love. Alas, this admonition is much needed in our age! True humility seems to have disappeared; and there are sects without number! Dear brethren, make the *earnest endeavor* to keep the unity of the Spirit in the bond of peace! *Endeavor to do this, for Jesus' sake!* What must the world think of you, if you, who formerly dwelt together in brotherly unity, now go each his own way? How do you honor the name of the Lord? Or how shall you in this way stand against the hosts of darkness, which are wise enough to present an unbroken front in the fight against the church of God? Do not go and divide yourselves up into factions; but when the time comes in which the world shall cast you out, do you stand together, and the Lord shall lead his people. — Lord Jesus, unite thy believers; and resist the devil, who would cause dissensions among us. Help us to obey thee, and walk in thy lowliness and love. Let none of us grieve thy Holy Spirit by rending asunder thy body; but give us grace to be united, and to wash one another's feet in the spirit of humility and meekness. Amen.

The Church's one foundation Is Jesus Christ her Lord; She is his new creation By water and the word; From heaven he came and sought her To be his holy bride, With his own blood he bought her, And for her life he died. Elect from every nation, Yet one o'er all the earth, Her charter of salvation One Lord, one faith, one birth; One holy name she blesses, Partakes one holy food, And to one hope she presses, With every grace endued.

380. Monday after Seventeenth Sunday after Trinity.

Psalm 84, 1–7. How amiable are thy tabernacles, O Lord of hosts! My soul longeth, yea, even fainteth, for the courts of the Lord; my heart and my flesh crieth out for the living God. Yea, the sparrow hath found a house, and the swallow a nest for herself, where she may lay her young, even thine altars, O Lord of hosts, my King and my God. Blessed are they that dwell in thy house: they will be still praising thee. Selah. Blessed is the man whose strength is in thee: in whose heart are the ways of them: who passing through the valley of Baca make it a well: the rain also filleth the pools. They go from strength to strength; every one of them in Zion appeareth before God.

The "courts of the Lord" were, during the time of the old covenant, the tabernacle, and afterward the temple; but the true courts of the Lord are the Christian church. Without God I am in the world like a sparrow or a swallow which has no nest. In the house of God, however, the holy church, I have shelter and protection, peace and joy. And the more I know of the glory of this house, the more do I long for it, until I come out of the courts into the wedding hall itself, out of the church militant on earth into the church triumphant in heaven. "My soul *longeth*, yea, even *fainteth* for the courts of the Lord"; while at the same time "my heart and my flesh crieth out to the living God." In the words of Joh. Arndt: "My poor soul, this frightened little bird, has found its right house and its right nest, even thine altars; but had I not found this beautiful and glorious house of God, I must needs have gone astray, and been homeless for ever. I had been as a sparrow alone upon the housetop, and like a turtledove which has lost its mate." This is a beautiful and striking figure: "The sparrow hath found a house, and the swallow a nest for herself, where she may lay her young, even thine altars, O Lord of hosts, my King, and my God." I and mine and all the friends of God have been received into the house of the Lord of hosts as our King and our God; and there we dwell while our exile lasts. Must not, then, the valley of tears be made a well, and the rain also fill the pools? Even though we must for a *long time* sow the seed with *tears*, the harvest of joy shall be all the more glorious. To be sure, the song of tears and dark valleys is always heard among the saints on earth; and it were well for us to learn this! Nevertheless we say: "Blessed are they that dwell in thy house; they will be still praising thee. Selah." — All is well, if but God be our *strength;* that is, if our heart do but trust in him *only*, and *confidently* lean on him without fainting :

and if he but be our *King* who reigns in our heart, our God whom we *love*, fear, and trust above all things! Lord, grant us this mercy. "O Lord God of hosts, hear my prayer; give ear, O God of Jacob. For a day in thy courts is better than a thousand. I had rather be a doorkeeper in the house of my God, than to dwell in the tents of wickedness. For the Lord God is a sun and shield; the Lord will give grace and glory; no good thing will he withhold from them that walk uprightly. O Lord of hosts, blessed is the man that trusteth in thee."

Pleasant are thy courts above, In the land of light and love; Pleasant are thy courts below, In this land of sin and woe. O, my spirit longs and faints For the converse of thy saints, For the brightness of thy face, For thy fulness, God of grace!

Happy souls! their praises flow Even in this vale of woe; Waters in the desert rise, Manna feeds them from the skies; On they go from strength to strength, Till they reach thy throne at length, At thy feet adoring fall, Who hast led them safe through all.

---

381. Tuesday after Seventeenth Sunday after Trinity.

Psalm 42, 1-5. As the hart panteth after the water brooks, so panteth my soul after thee, O God. My soul thirsteth for God, for the living God: when shall I come and appear before God? My tears have been my meat day and night, while they continually say unto me, Where is thy God? When I remember these things, I pour out my soul in me: for I had gone with the multitude; I went with them to the house of God, with the voice of joy and praise, with a multitude that kept holyday. Why art thou cast down, O my soul? and why art thou disquieted in me? Hope thou in God; for I shall yet praise him for the help of his countenance.

True Christians have a deep and imperative longing to commune with God in their hearts. They *can not* do without him; no substitute whatever will satisfy them. Their soul thirsts and pants after God himself, the living God. They must speak with him out of their heart daily, and satisfy themselves with his word; and when the church has its meeting with him they always find it necessary to be present. The thirsty man needs no command to drink. Instinct teaches the infant to find the mother's breast. True Christians need no ordinances to compel them to go to church; but by reason of the temptations of the flesh and the devil, that is nevertheless a good commandment of the Lord which says: "Remember the sabbath day to keep it holy." Even the devil knows that a diligent use of the word of God is more necessary than all things else; therefore he especially tempts us to neglect the word, and can not endure to have us sit still and hear what Jesus speaks to us. For this reason the Lord introduces this particular commandment with his emphatic "Remember!" It is a precious command, which is in harmony with the inner law in every sanctified soul. He who can go on day after day without the word of God is surely dead, and his heart is more dark than that of a heathen; and he who does not care to attend divine service, and to partake of the Lord's supper, has no part in the kingdom of heaven. When in the darkness of temptation the Lord is lost to sight by the believer, the soul is made to bend like a bulrush, or it becomes like a stormy sea. If he did not have the word, he would despair; the word keeps *hope* alive: "Hope thou in God; for I shall yet praise him for the help of his countenance." — I know not what is worse; either those terrible thoughts of unbelief, which deny God, and are like a "sword in my bones"; or the sense of fear before God as the just judge, the waves and billows of whose wrath go over the soul (verse 7). Yet the upright receive help for evermore. "The Lord will command his lovingkindness in the daytime, and in the night his song shall be with me, and my prayer unto the God of my life" (v. 9). He who panteth after him, as the hart after the water brooks, and who therefore eats the bread of tears all the day long, shall yet close his complaint at last with the song of hope in praise of his victory over the powers of darkness. "Why art thou cast down, O my soul? and why art thou disquieted within me? Hope thou in God; for I shall yet praise him, who is the health of my countenance, and my God." Yet the *word* was and is the light and comfort, the shield and weapon of all saints.

The word they still shall let abide, Nor thanks be due them for it; The Lord of hosts is by our side, Grants us his gifts and Spirit; And though they take our life, Goods, honor — children, wife, Yet, when their worst is done, They still have nothing won: The Kingdom ours remaineth.

---

382. Wednesday after Seventeenth Sunday after Trinity.

That brethren dwell together in unity is as the dew of Hermon, and as the dew that descended upon the mountains of Zion.

Philippians 2, 1-4. If there be therefore any consolation in Christ, if any comfort of love, if any fellowship of the Spirit, if any bowels and mercies, fulfil ye my joy, that ye be likeminded, having the same love, being of one accord, of one mind. Let nothing be done through strife or vainglory; but in lowliness of mind let each esteem other better than themselves. Look not every man on his own things, but every man also on the things of others.

If, says Paul to his dear Philippians, there be among you these good things, consolation in Christ, comfort of love, the fellowship of the Spirit, bowels and mercies; then do ye increase therein more and more! The world *must* live in strife; for the spirit of pride and self-love rends asunder and scatters. But ye, who are Christ's, ye have received the Spirit of love and lowliness; and wherever this prevails, it knits the hearts together in the same mind and in the same judgment; walk in this Spirit, and ye fulfil my joy.

The times become steadily more perilous, as the end approaches (2 Tim. 3, 1); but there always shall remain a brotherhood among whom love is law. If we have in some measure learned by experience how good and how pleasant it is for brethren to *dwell* together in unity (Psalm 133), let us fulfil the joy of the apostle. What do I say? of the apostle? Yes; but still more the joy of *our Lord and Savior!* Let us walk in *lowliness* of mind, that each esteem other better than themselves; and in *love,* that we look not every man on his own things. For the sake of your lowly Savior, esteem others better than yourself! Examine yourself; learn to know the pride of your heart, and mortify it with the mind of Jesus! Live not unto yourself, but unto Christ; look on the good of others; please your brethren for their good; that is to say, study to practice charity always, and increase therein! This is the sure bond of union between God's people, which prevents us from dividing into sects and parties. There is but one Father and one family of children, one Lord and one kingdom of light, one head and one body, one house and one household; shall we not, then, endeavor to stand together, shudder at the thought of dismemberment, and abhor all manner of factions? Is it not God's own command that we shall present ourselves as *one* body? (Eph. 4; 1 Cor. 1, 10). Has not Christ redeemed us with his blood, in order that we may be *one* in him? (Eph. 2, 16; John 17, 21). Every founder of a sect acts in direct opposition to the heart of God and the cross of Jesus; dismembers, as far as in him lies, the body of Christ, and scatters the people whom Christ gathered about him at the Supper the same night in which he was betrayed. When Satan succeeds in causing dissensions among us; so that the Christian people, who in every place should present themselves as the one body of Christ, are divided into parties which will not be united; then the Spirit of God is grieved, and the church presents a sad picture of that God whose unity in love his children should make manifest to all the world. (John 17, 23). Is it, then, to be wondered at that the apostle says: *Fulfil ye my joy* by living with one another in the undisturbed fellowship of love?

Lord Jesus, give us thy lowly and loving mind, and keep us united with the bond of perfectness. We earnestly beseech thee, prevent the devil from henceforth causing dissensions among thy people; and unite all that can be united in the truth. Have mercy on us; have mercy, Lord Jesus. Amen.

One, the strain that lips of thousands Lift as from the heart of one; One the conflict, one the peril, One, the march in God begun: One, the gladness of rejoicing On the far eternal shore, Where the one almighty Father Reigns in love for evermore.

---

383. Thursday after Seventeenth Sunday after Trinity.

Lord, today we again pray thee: give us humility and charity. Amen.

Matthew 20, 25–28. But Jesus called them unto him, and said, Ye know that the princes of the gentiles exercise dominion over them, and they that are great exercise authority upon them. But it shall not be so among you: but whosoever will be great among you, let him be your minister; and whosoever will be chief among you, let him be your servant: even as the Son of Man came not to be ministered unto, but to minister, and to give his life a ransom for many.

Help us, O God, to understand and practice the lesson here taught us! It is a heavenly lesson, which the carnal mind is utterly unable to grasp; but to the spirit it is the word of wisdom. In the world the great is great, the mighty is mighty, and the ruler rules; but in the kingdom of Christ the least is the greatest, the weakest is most mighty, and the servant of all is the chief of all. This is the mystery of *humility*, as strange to the natural man as a sealed book, but revealed to the saints of God. If you be a disciple of Christ, you have begun to understand and practice this lesson; but you have done nothing more than to make a beginning, and most zealously seek the revelation of the mystery. There is nothing which the Lord said a greater number of times than this: "Whosoever shall exalt himself shall be abased; and he that shall humble himself shall be exalted." If you wish to become great, *strive to become one of the least; not* in pretended, but in hearty and true lowliness of mind. Let your worldly condition be that which God has ordained, whether honored or obscure; but whatever you may be, *you must not wish to become great;* but your wish shall be to *regard* yourself and to *be* in truth the servant of all. This is the true dignity of love; a dignity as far from the vainglorious greatness of the world as the heaven is far from the earth. If you are to be chief, you must not, like the sons of Zebedee, ask to sit on the right and the left hand of the Lord in his glory, nor must you, like Diotrephes (3 John 9), love to have preeminence among men; but you must become the servant of the brethren, in duty bound to minister to them all. What a dignity, and what a kingly estate of liberty, to be the servant of all, never to be prevented by anything from practicing charity! "Free from all men," says Saint Paul, "yet have I made myself servant unto all; for the love of Christ constraineth us." Alas, I am as yet far, far from the rank of "chief"; but do thou reach out after this dignity, O my soul! Jesus will have you to be like him. "The Son of Man came not to be ministered unto, but to minister, and to give his life a ransom for many." The better you learn in the distress occasioned by your pride and love of self to apply to your heart the comfort of these gospel words, the more fully will the *admonition* which they contain become truth in your life and conduct, and thus cause you to descend to lower depths of humility, and to ascend to a higher rank in the kingdom of God. — Lord Jesus, give us thy mind, and shed abroad thy love in our hearts. Let us come near to thee, that the spirit of pride may depart far from us. Give us light to understand thy ministering life on earth; that we may live in the power of thy redemption, establish love and peace, and devote ourselves wholly to the service of one another. Grant us this mercy, precious Lord and Savior. Amen.

How shall we show our love to thee, Thou living God most high, But loving this thy family, For which thou deignedst to die?
If thou for me such love didst bear, Shall I not love again? For all are objects of thy care; Thy love doth all sustain.

384. Friday after Seventeenth Sunday after Trinity.

Lord, chasten us, and give us truth in our heart of hearts. Amen.

Mark 7, 6–13. He answered and said unto them, Well hath Esaias prophesied of you hypocrites, as it is written, This people honoreth me with their lips, but their heart is far from me. Howbeit, in vain do they worship me, teaching for doctrines the commandments of men: For laying aside the commandment of God, ye hold the tradition of men, as the washing of pots and cups: and many other such like things ye do. And he said unto them, Full well ye reject the commandment of God, that ye may keep your own tradition. For Moses said, Honor thy father and thy mother; and, Whoso curseth father or mother, let him die the death. But ye say, If a man shall say to his father or mother, It is Corban, that is to say, a gift, by whatsoever thou mightest be profited by me; he shall be free. And ye suffer him no more to do ought for his father or his mother; making the word of God of none effect through your tradition, which ye have delivered: and many such like things do ye.

"This people honoreth me with their lips, but their heart is far from me." This is true of those who go to church, read their prayers, partake of holy communion, and lead decent lives; yet are dead, and ignorant of their danger, and have knowledge neither of sin nor of grace, and will not admit the necessity of repentance and a new birth. Dear reader, hear these words of the Lord, and examine yourself in their light! There are thousands of such among us; and they rob themselves of eternal salvation. Even among those who are regarded as patterns of piety there are doubtless many whose judgment is pronounced in these words: "They honor me with their lips, but their heart is far from me." They associate with believers, receive "the brethren" in their houses, and have a way of speaking with unction and of looking devout, but they are without the daily knowledge of sin and the grace of the blood of Jesus, which cleanses from sin. Neither do they know that charity which "seeketh not her own," and which "beareth all things, believeth all things, hopeth all things, endureth all things"; but they are severe in pronouncing judgment on those whom they call the children of the world; give short measure; are willing to profit at the expense of others; drive hard bargains, and make it unpleasant to have any dealings with them; are blind to the faults of their own set, and fairly shine with self-complacency. Such people are the greatest pest of the church; the upright must suffer, and the name of God is blasphemed for their sake. Let none think that truly pious men are like those above described, and let none cast a stone at his brother; but rather let each examine himself as in the sight of God! — These words of the Lord are for the admonition of us all. You know that your flesh is a snare always, and that out of it come many evil things. You must watch, and obey the Spirit, if your life is to please God and be for the edification of man. Shun all hypocrisy as the worst of Satan's belongings; and exterminate all falsehood in *yourselves!* I do not advise you to abstain from using the word of God and from doing good until you shall be able to do it in a perfectly proper spirit; but I must say to each one of you: *Lay to heart the word* of God, and *obey* it; obey it *as the word of God*, in the fear of God and with honest heart; and set men a good example! Let them see that it is *charity* which speaks and acts in you; the charity which never is petty, but generous and rich; never censorious, but high-minded and merciful; and bear in mind that your conduct must bear witness of Jesus!

Help us, O God, that our hearts may fear thee, and that we may in truth honor thee. Grant us grace to live in true holiness, in holy charity; that they who revile our good conversation in Christ may be put to shame, and repent, and praise thee. Amen.

Whate'er we do, where'er we go, Let love our sonship prove: Our lives the fire celestial show, Our thoughts and words be love.

O deign to send the love of thee From highest heaven above; For then our life thy praise shall be, When all our life is love.

385. Saturday after Seventeenth Sunday after Trinity.

Psalm 119, 97–105. O how love I thy law! it is my meditation all the day. Thou, through thy commandments, hast made me wiser than mine enemies: for they are ever with me. I have more understanding than all my teachers: for thy testimonies are my meditation. I understand more than the ancients; because I keep thy precepts. I have refrained my feet from every evil way, that I might keep thy word. I have not departed from thy judgments: for thou hast taught me. How sweet are thy words unto my taste! yea, sweeter than honey to my mouth! Through thy precepets I get understanding: therefore I hate every false way. Thy word is a lamp unto my feet, and a light unto my path.

Is the word of God so dear to *you* also? Is *it* your greatest treasure and your highest delight? Stop and think of it! Is the word of God sweeter to your taste than all things else? Is it more precious to you than gold? Alas, many read newspapers, while their Bible is covered with dust! They have time enough for balls and banquets; but they often are too busy to go to church, and when they do go it is not for the purpose of hearing what the Lord has to say to them. They do not know that they slight and despise the most sacred thing which God has given us. They do not know that they walk in darkness; for the darkness has made them blind. — However, if you have tasted of the heavenly gift, and been made partaker of the Holy Ghost, and have tasted the good work of God, and the powers of the world to come; you then love the word, and would not lose it for anything in the world. "God's own word, the Holy Bible, is our only source of light; all our life would be without it nothing but a hideous night. For this book on all its pages shews the Father's tender love in the Son who died to save us, lead us to our home above." Yet I am sure that you wish to love the word of God better than you do; and here are two means by which you shall accomplish this result: 1) *Meditate on the word of God all the day.* When you are not obliged to occupy your thoughts with the work imposed on you by your worldly vocation, let them busy themselves with the word of God; and though you must think on other things, do not forget that God is present, — even as when good children play in the presence of their parents. I have known young people who always carried a copy of the New Testament, and employed every vacant hour in reading it; and I have known men who never tired of searching the scriptures; — and their faces had something of the glory of Tabor. Read thoughtfully and in regular order, and compare the different passages; and make use also of the assistance which the Spirit offers you in the works of pious commentators. Now, do not say that you have neither the inclination nor the opportunity to do this. You have begun to love the word of God, have you not? Do not, then, sin by neglecting this love; but cultivate it, and overcome your natural resistance and sloth by means of the word. 2) *Walk faithfully in the light of the word,* hate every false way, and keep the Lord's precepts. *Act in all things according to the word;* make no step but in the light which this word gives. Undertake nothing without having inquired, if it have the sanction of God's word, and be pleasing to the Lord. Do without any hesitation that which he says; but *never* do that which he hates. Then shall you see your sin, and become needy and hungry, and come to love the gospel of mercy. — Our Bible lesson opens to us this double door into the sanctuary of the word. Come, enter, and behold the glory of the Lord, and drink of his well of gladness! — Grant us this great favor, merciful God! Enlighten us by thy Spirit, help us to study thy word in a devout spirit, and make it our holy desire to live according to thy precepts. Amen.

How shall the young secure their hearts, And guard their lives from sin? Thy word the choicest rules imparts To keep the conscience clean.
'Tis like the sun, a heavenly light, That guides us all the day; And through the dangers of the night A lamp to lead our way.

---

386. Eighteenth Sunday after Trinity. I.

Holy Spirit, write the law of love in our hearts by faith in our Lord Jesus Christ.

Gospel Lesson, Matthew 22, 34-46. But when the Pharisees had heard that he had put the Sadducees to silence, they were gathered together. Then one of them, which was a lawyer, asked him a question, tempting him, and saying, Master, which is the great commandment in the law? Jesus said unto him, Thou shalt love the Lord thy God with all thy heart, and with all thy soul, and with all thy mind. This is the first and great commandment. And the second is like unto it, Thou shalt love thy neighbor as thyself. On these two commandments hang all the law and the prophets. While the Pharisees were gathered together, Jesus asked them, saying, What think ye of Christ? whose son is he? They say unto him, The Son of David. He saith unto them, How then doth David in spirit call him Lord, saying, The Lord said unto my Lord, Sit thou on my right hand, till I make thine enemies thy footstool? If David then call him Lord, how is he his son? And no man was able to answer him a word; neither durst any man, from that day forth, ask him any more questions.

"Thou shalt love." What a beautiful commandment! What is better than love? It is the greatest thing of all; and there is no salvation but in it; as it is written: Love God above all things, and thy neighbor as thyself; *this* do, and *thou shalt live* (Luke 10, 27. 28). And what a *just* commandment this is! That which the Lord himself has given us, and which alone can make us happy, *he must want* us to have; and he gave us his love from the beginning, and without it we are unhappy men. In it is embraced everything that is good; and all his commandments are therefore but reflections of this one great, holy, and righteous law of love. But, alas, we have lost the love which he gave us; and the commandment can not return it to us; but can only reveal our poverty, and condemn our unrighteousness. And there we stand, unhappy, with the holy commandment over us; it demands of us that which we have received, but have ourselves thrown away; that which we *must* have in order to be happy, but of which we have entirely stripped ourselves. There we stand, lost and condemned; and the commandment can not help us. For it can only demand; and can give nothing whatever. We *must* have love, but there is none in us; we must love, but can not! There is, then, nothing for us but to die and be lost on account of this beautiful and righteous commandment! Is there not after all some way in which my heart can be made to give up its resistance, and come again into agreement with the law; so that the holy commandment, the loving will of my God, can once more become *my* will and the desire of *my* heart? Is there no commandment of the law by way of which I might return to the great commandment? Is there no commandment which I could begin to keep, and thus by degrees reach the higher level of the great commandment of love? Foolish questions! Can one who is evil do that which is good? Can the Ethiopian change his skin, or the leopard his spots? (Jer. 13, 23). No; all the commandments of the law demand love, while not one of them can give us a spark of it. However, praise be to God; *he* has given us something more than the law: He has given us the gospel concerning his only Son; by which means the Holy Ghost can *beget us anew,* bring our hearts over onto the side of the divine law, and make this to become life and truth *within* us. The Son of David is the Lord of David; the man Jesus Christ is the only begotten Son of God, true God from everlasting to everlasting. In him love has returned to the world. He is himself the fulfilment of the great commandment; and he is this for us, in our stead. God has thus ordained. He counts that which Christ does as having been done by us; and it is finished. Christ has fulfilled the law for me, has loved with a perfect love, been obedient in all things, submitted to the will of the Father even unto the death of the cross; and thus I have received pardon for my transgressions, and that *title* to salvation which is contained in the proviso of the law: Keep the law, and thou shalt live. Christ has kept it for me; and thus I have kept it. The Holy Ghost gives me grace to believe this; so that I live and die trusting in the vicarious atonement of Jesus. Thus I am in Christ; and then he also is in me. His love has entered my heart; and now we may

therefore speak of keeping the several commandments; — not in order that we may learn to fulfil the great commandment, but *because* this commandment now *is* in our hearts, and we in it. For now *my heart* has its being in the great commandment; and this is in my heart. Now we can and shall practice love by obedience to all the commands of the Lord; so that love of self, hate, covetousness, and all the lusts of the flesh, which still are in us, may die and be destroyed, in order that we may at last sit in the midst of the heaven of love. — We do not, then, in any sense make void the law through grace, but rather establish the law by the very means of the gospel. "The law was given by Moses, but grace and truth came by Jesus Christ." Love, the eternal and immovable, the heavenly and immutable law, truth itself, which *shall* and *must* be realized in us, confronts us in Moses as the law of works with its requirements and commands; but it thus never becomes truth in us; for it can only make us to see our unhappy condition, and be our "schoolmaster to bring us unto Christ." Through Jesus, on the other hand, love is become *grace;* and thus it enters our hearts. God's loving purpose concerning the world, the truth itself, is in and through Christ from eternity; and through the gospel it becomes in us the truth of faith. — Have you, dear reader, had this experience? Is the law of love your great commandment, dear and sweet and blessed? Do you understand Saint John, who writes not a new commandment, but one old, and yet new, which is true in God and in us? (1 John 2, 7. 8.). Then you have begun to know the *joy* of love and the *sorrow* of love. Now, make diligent use of the power which God has given you; obey the Spirit of God; hear the voice of Christ, and he will take you to his heart. There your sin and distress and pain shall die. Amen. God grant us this mercy. Amen.

Jesus, thy boundless love to me No thought can reach, no tongue declare: Unite my thankful heart to thee, And reign without a rival there. Thine wholly, thine alone I am; Be thou alone my constant flame.

---

387. Eighteenth Sunday after Trinity. II.

Give us, O God, the living hope of the humble hearts. Amen.

Epistle Lesson, 1 Corinthians 1, 4-8. I thank my God always on your behalf, for the grace of God which is given you by Jesus Christ; that in every thing ye are enriched by him, in all utterance, and in all knowledge; even as the testimony of Christ was confirmed in you: so that ye come behind in no gift; waiting for the coming of our Lord Jesus Christ: who shall also confirm you unto the end, that ye may be blameless in the day of our Lord Jesus Christ.

Though Paul wrote this epistle to the Corinthians with a *sad* heart, because there was so much wickedness in the church, yet he begins this way: "I thank my God *always* on *your* behalf." — In like manner we also will *thank our God always* for his mercy in Christ. The numerous infirmities of the church must never for one moment interrupt our thanksgiving. It is the most bitter fruit of your unbelief and pride that you do not give thanks all the time. Always, when I turn my eyes in that direction, I see through Jesus on the cross into the heart of God, full of mercy toward us. Nor do we at any time come behind in divine instruction; the word of God dwells in us richly. Through the enlightenment of his Spirit all scripture also is opened to me; I walk nowhere in darkness; Christ shines out everywhere in the Old and New Testaments. Though I do not understand clearly all the details, and though I feel that the whole is infinitely more deep than I am able to see; I yet have "all knowledge"; that is, the key to it all and the necessary light for my whole life. Others in our church have more light; and it is the common property of us all. — The testimony of Christ is not on our lips merely; the Holy Ghost has written it in our hearts. And he does not write faintly on the surface, but burns the truth into the soul. Wherein, then, do we come behind? "Alas," you say, "how sad is the condition of the church!" It is true; and you have the right to make the complaint; — if it be *love* which burns in you by reason of the offences given, and if you weep with Paul, moved by the mercy of Christ. In that case, however, you certainly also shall with Paul, in the fellowship of the same Lord, rejoice because of God's great mercy toward us, and with longing and joy wait for the coming of our Lord. The pure eye looks upon that which is pure, and rejoices in every virtue which appears; but acquiesces in the arrangement that the tares and wheat are to grow together until the harvest. You are weighed down by the sin in yourself and in the church; you shall find deliverance; you shall become perfect in holiness, and the church shall be purified and stand an undefiled bride at the Lord's side. This *hope* dwelt in the church at Corinth, in spite of all its imperfections; and it dwells in us also. The children of the world cling to that which is of earth; the children of God, to that which is of heaven. There is in truth a church of God among us, which waits and yearns for the second coming of Christ; and you may be as sure of his coming as though you already saw him; and you may be equally sure that he "shall also confirm you unto the end, that ye may be blameless in the day of our Lord Jesus Christ." "God is faithful, by whom ye were called unto the fellowship of his Son Jesus Christ our Lord." Is not this something to strengthen us and to humble us? Must you not hereafter thank and praise God always? Repent, all the ends of the earth, and be ye saved; but do ye also repent, ye believers. I say it with emphasis: *Repent, ye believers, and become as children; for of such* is the kingdom of heaven.

Give us, O God, the humble and grateful spirit of faith; and confirm us in the truth unto the end, for Jesus' sake. Amen.

Abide, our Strength and Refuge, With us till life's last hour. That world and Satan never Our weakness overpower.
Abide, O faithful Savior, Among us with thy love; Grant steadfastness, and help us To reach our home above.

388. Monday after Eighteenth Sunday after Trinity.

Enlighten us, our God, that we may praise thy mercy. Amen.

Ephesians 1, 3-7. Blessed be the God and Father of our Lord Jesus Christ, who hath blessed us with all spiritual blessings in heavenly places in Christ: according as he hath chosen us in him before the foundation of the world, that we should be holy and without blame before him in love: having predestinated us unto the adoption of children by Jesus Christ to himself, according to the good pleasure of his will, to the praise of the glory of his grace, wherein he hath made us accepted in the beloved: in whom we have redemption through his blood, the forgiveness of sins, according to the riches of his grace.

We also bless God for that he has made us partakers of "the glory of his grace." We also, dear brethren in the Lord, are among those whom he has "blessed with all spiritual blessings in heavenly places in Christ;" and he has chosen even us in him before the foundation of the world, "that we should be holy and without blame before him in love; having predestinated us unto the adoption of children by Jesus Christ to himself, *according to the good pleasure of his will*, to the praise of the glory of his grace, wherein he hath made us accepted in the beloved." He has given us his only Son, and by his death redeemed us from death and devil; received us into his fellowship; forgiven us our sins; created in us a new heart; given us spiritual light; and keeps us by his power until we reach the appointed end, eternal salvation. *All* believers are embraced in this "good pleasure" of God "which he hath purposed in himself," that Jews and gentiles, as many as accept the call, shall be gathered together in one house, and be glorified in heavenly glory. Nay, all believers already "sit together in heavenly places" (Eph. 2, 6); for we stand before the throne together with an "innumerable company of angels, and the spirits of just men made perfect" (Hebrews 12, 22. 23). Is it not in the house of God, in his service, before his face, together with the blessed angels, that we live and do all our work? And is it not the life of heaven which stirs in us with love and peace and joy in the Holy Ghost? But "we walk by *faith*, not by sight." We *see* that we are on earth; but we *believe* that we are embraced by the love of God; sustained by his eternal purpose to save us, and by his divine power; surrounded by angels and beatified human spirits as being of the same household; — and is not that which *God says* more certain and true than that which we *see?* It is, a thousand times! Then blessed be the God and Father of our Lord Jesus Christ, who has chosen us, and saved us; and called us with an holy calling, not according to our works, but according to his own purpose and grace, which was given us in Christ Jesus before the world began! My God, I am deeply sensible of my own unworthiness; but it was the good pleasure of thy will to predestinate me unto the adoption of children by Jesus Christ to thyself. I will, then, by this grace serve thee with all my soul; do thou help me by thy Holy Spirit. Amen.

No good in creatures can be found, But may be found in thee; I must have all things, and abound, While God is God to me.
O that I had a stronger faith To look within the veil, To credit what my Savior saith, Whose word can never fail!

389. Tuesday after Eighteenth Sunday after Trinity.

God Holy Spirit, enlighten us with thy gifts. Amen.

Ephesians 1, 8–14. Wherein he hath abounded toward us in all wisdom and prudence; having made known unto us the mystery of his will, according to his good pleasure which he hath purposed in himself: that in the dispensation of the fulness of times, he might gather together in one all things in Christ, both which are in heaven, and which are on earth; even in him: in whom also we have obtained an inheritance, being predestinated according to the purpose of him who worketh all things after the counsel of his own will; that we should be to the praise of his glory, who first trusted in Christ. In whom ye also trusted, after that ye heard the word of truth, the gospel of your salvation: in whom also, after that ye believed, ye were sealed with that holy Spirit of promise, which is the earnest of our inheritance, until the redemption of the purchased possession, unto the praise of his glory.

To gather, to *gather together* is the good pleasure of the Lord. Understand that it is the nature of love, and hear what the apostle says on this subject; and you will pray for grace to gather together, but have a dread of rending asunder. It is God's *good pleasure* from eternity that he "might gather together in one all things in Christ, both which are in heaven, and which are on earth." The fulness of time is come, the dispensation has been established, and the gathering together is in progress; one church has been built, with one gospel, and one baptism, and one communion table; one Spirit unites Jews and gentiles in one body, whose head is Christ. Even as all things in heaven and earth are created by him, and by him all things consist, so all things are by him reconciled unto God, who has made peace through the blood of his cross (Col. 1, 16–20). While the angels in heaven had no need of redemption, as they did not fall, yet the love of God in Christ is their bliss also; so that they also have been included in the same dispensation. Christ is the head of the church of thrones, and of principalities, and of the Jews and gentiles who have been saved. We also have obtained an inheritance in him. God, "who worketh all things after the counsel of his own will," has foreordained that there now shall be a gathering into his kingdom here among us; and he has predestinated us, who hear and believe, to partake of this salvation. For this reason we also have received the Holy Ghost as earnest. Every believer clings to God in Christ; can not let him go; expects salvation at his hands; worships him with childlike fear and confidence; and has his peace and joy in him, saying in his heart: "Heavenly Father, I bless thee for the salvation in the blood of thy Son; help me to believe until my last hour, and to bless thee for evermore!" This is the voice of the *Spirit*, not the voice of flesh and blood. The longing after God, and the joy in God's love are the earnest of our salvation; and he who has given you this earnest money can not deceive you. He is himself the seal with which you are sealed; can it, then, fail to be valid? Believe in him, have faith in him, and you shall receive the inheritance. "Inheritance" it is called; and in truth it is an *inheritance* with Jesus, and mercy altogether; faith, and the earnest, and purification, and sanctification, all is grace only. Do not let your sins and imperfections create any doubt in you; for the grace in the blood of Christ is the one thing on which everything depends.

Praise be to thee, God the Father, God the Son, and God the Holy Ghost! Enlighten us, that we may know the excellence of our inheritance. Give us grace to gather together and unite in Christ, from far and near, and to approach ever nearer to perfect holiness. Amen.

Welcome, O my Savior, now! Hail! my portion, Lord, art thou! Here, too, in my heart, I pray, Oh, prepare thyself a way!
And when thou dost come again, As a glorious king to reign, I with joy may see thy face, Freely ransomed by thy grace.

---

390. Wednesday after Eighteenth Sunday after Trinity.

I rejoice at thy word, as one that findeth great spoil.

Romans 8, 1-4. There is, therefore, now no condemnation to them which are in Christ Jesus, who walk not after the flesh, but after the Spirit. For the law of the Spirit of life in Christ Jesus hath made me free from the law of sin and death. For what the law could not do, in that it was weak through the flesh, God, sending his own Son in the likeness of sinful flesh, and for sin, condemned sin in the flesh: that the righteousness of the law might be fulfilled in us, who walk not after the flesh, but after the Spirit.

Frivolous, carnal, and self-righteous persons do not know that they are condemned; and thus they are able to remain unmoved when they read words of life such as these, full of celestial fire. It is an easy matter for them to comfort themselves, as they do not feel the sting of sin, and the devil does not assail the faith which is dead. He, on the other hand, who feels that he is himself carnal, sold under sin, and that he ought to die; and who thus is dumb before his accuser, and is condemned by his own conscience; — such a one finds it not so easy to repeat that which Paul says in our text. However, if the Spirit succeed in teaching him this lesson, it becomes a song of praise in his heart. To him who feels no condemnation, and has no knowledge of the fight of faith, there is nothing but condemnation; but to him who feels his sin, and leans on Christ alone, "there is no condemnation" whatever. Here you must learn to forget yourself and all that you are and do and feel, and look to Christ only, who has condemned sin in the flesh; so that it can no more condemn you, nor hold sway either in your conscience or your life. For Christ took upon himself our flesh, and fulfilled the law, and bore the curse; and unto *him*, the selfsame Christ, you are baptized, you hear *his* voice in the gospel, and of *his* body and blood you partake in holy Com-munion. Pharisees and shallow Christians may be able to find comfort in their own feelings; but he who is sincerely conscious of the sin and death in his own members wants Christ himself, who died and rose again, sits on the throne, and reigns in the midst of the church by means of the word and sacraments. When you yourself have nothing except that which can condemn you, and yet feel that you can not deliver yourself up to be condemned, but must on your life find salvation; then the Spirit teaches you to believe, and thus, in the words of Luther, moves you to "go out of yourself and into Christ, and belong to him, as one who has been baptized into him, and is a partaker of his body and blood. Thus you rid yourself of sin and an evil conscience, of death and devil; so that you can say that you know neither death nor hell. Let death first consume my Lord Jesus Christ; let hell swallow my Savior; if sin, or law, or conscience, can condemn, let them direct their accusations against the Son of God! If they can prevail against him, I will let them condemn and destroy me also. But since the Father and Christ still live, I also remain alive; for I know that I am in Christ, even as Christ is in the Father." (John 14, 20). Commit yourself, then, into the hands of your Savior; he has made all things ready, and all is given *you* in the gospel. The important thing is to *be in Christ;* on which point Paul says, Gal. 3, 27: "As many of you as have been baptized into Christ have put on Christ." You do not believe it, and you urge your objections. You say that it is the world which puts its trust in Christ as he is found in the sacraments. You are mistaken. The world does not in any sense trust to *Christ* in the word and sacraments. In so far as they trust to anything, it certainly is not to *Christ* in the means of grace, but rather to their own deed in making use of word and sacraments. By their unbelief they reject the living Savior in the means of grace. You, however, who heartily desire him, shall by the Spirit of God be taught to believe; and then behold, you are made free from the law of sin and death!

Good Holy Spirit, help us in this most important of all concerns. Teach us, and guide us, that Jesus may be to us the way, the truth, and the life. Amen.

To God the only wise, Our Savior and our King, Let all the saints below the skies Their humble praises bring. 'Tis his almighty love, His counsel and his care, Preserves us safe from sin and death, And every hurtful snare.

---

391. Thursday after Eighteenth Sunday after Trinity.

Lord Jesus, light of our life, come and abide in us. Amen.

1 John 2, 4–11. He that saith, I know him, and keepeth not his commandments, is a liar, and the truth is not in him. But whoso keepeth his word, in him verily is the love of God perfected: hereby know we that we are in him. He that saith he abideth in him, ought himself also so to walk, even as he walked. Brethren, I write no new commandment unto you, but an old

commandment, which ye had from the beginning. The old commandment is the word which ye have heard from the beginning. Again, a new commandment I write unto you; which thing is true in him and in you, because the darkness is past, and the true light now shineth. He that saith he is in the light, and hateth his brother, is in darkness even until now. He that loveth his brother abideth in the light, and there is none occasion of stumbling in him. But he that hateth his brother is in darkness, and walketh in darkness, and knoweth not whither he goeth, because that darkness hath blinded his eyes.

"Darkness" means spiritual ignorance and blindness, malice and wickedness, and, finally, affliction, terror, and distress. Saint John speaks of the darkness of ignorance and wickedness, and of deceit and hatred, which holds sway in all hearts in which Jesus does not dwell. A terrible night of death came upon the earth when man fell. Love and the knowledge of God were extinguished in our soul, and were replaced by the blindness and wickedness of hell. Now, however, it is again true in the church of God that "the darkness is past, and the true light now shineth." What light is this? What should it be but Jesus Christ, the true God? And what is God but love? He that says he is in the faith and grace of Jesus Christ, and harbors hatred and malice, is a liar; he is in darkest darkness; he turns the kingdom of Christ into the kingdom of the devil. If you comfort yourself in the thought of Christ, while you at the same time are angry with your neighbor, you are in a sad and terrible condition. God help you out of the darkness before it is too late! For you walk in darkness, and know not whither you go. "He that loveth not his brother abideth in darkness," says the same apostle, in 3, 14; and in our text he declares: "He that saith he abideth in him ought himself also so to walk, even as he walked." Can any earnest Christian read this without being humbled and made to confess that he still, alas, is far, far from being that which he ought? Yet, there is comfort also in these words: "*I ought* also so to walk, even as he walked." Yes, this is my bounden duty, as my own innermost heart also tells me. The old commandment, "love ye one another," is become a new commandment in you; and can there, then, in all the world be any man whom you hate? "No, by the love of Christ I pray for every man, and wish him well; and I can not give up the fight before having learned this lesson." This, my friend, is not darkness, but light. God's commandment, "*Thou shalt love,*" is through Jesus become truth in you; you give it your assent; your knowledge and will coincide with it; you keep his commandments; you are in the kingdom of light; you are in Jesus, and he in you. Walk now in love; that you may shed abroad light more pure, more beautiful, more abundant, day by day! — God of love, grant us this mercy in Jesus Christ Amen.

Deluded souls that dream of heaven, And make their empty boast Of inward joys and sins forgiven, While they are slaves to lust!
Vain are our fancies' airy flights, If faith be cold and dead; None but a living power unites To Christ, the living Head;
A faith that changes all the heart, A faith that works by love; That bid all sinful joys depart, And lifts the thoughts above.

392. Friday after Eighteenth Sunday after Trinity.

Lord, give unto us the spirit of revelation in the knowledge of thee. Amen.

Galatians 2, 19–21. For I through the law am dead to the law, that I might live unto God. I am crucified with Christ: nevertheless I live; yet not I, but Christ liveth in me: and the life which I now live in the flesh, I live by the faith of the Son of God, who loved me, and gave himself for me. I do not frustrate the grace of God: for if righteousness come by the law, then Christ is dead in vain.

Here we again have one of those divine scripture passages which, when we examine it, seems to transcend all the others in glory. — In Romans 7, 1–13, Paul has explained how he through the law was dead to the law, that he might live unto God. Worldly-minded and self-righteous men do not feel the condemnation of the law; even as a dead body does not feel the surgeon's knife. But the penitent sinner knows that the law works wrath, and revives sin; so that sin, taking occasion by the commandment, slays him. *In this way only* can the soul learn to give heed to the gospel of faith; namely this: Christ is crucified for you, and thus you are crucified; the law's demands have been fulfilled; the punishment has been borne; the accursed death has been suffered, suffered with entire willingness, without sin and without complaint; Christ truly died, not without cause, but as one wholly guilty, the object of God's righteous anger. All this for you; can it have been done in vain? And now you are baptized into his death (Rom. 6, 3; Gal. 3, 27), and are through faith united to him; so that his death and his life are yours. Thus you are dead to the law, and justification by the law must, therefore, be entirely out of the question; but thus you are also raised up with Christ, that you may live the life of Christ unto God. He has bestowed on you that love wherewith he loved unto death; he who gave himself *for* you has given himself *to* you; and the Spirit has given you faith, through which you receive him, and live in him. You are dead to sin, but living unto God; for Christ lives in you. Thus saith the gospel; — what do you think of it? Is not Christ in truth crucified and risen again; and have you not been baptized into his death and resurrection? Are you going to defeat the arrangement which God has made: His death to be your death; his life, your life? "Alas, I can not find his life in me," say you? I answer: *Faith* does not lay hold on that which we find in ourselves, but on that which God has done for us, and speaks to us. "The life which I now live in the flesh," says the apostle, "I live by the faith of the Son of God, who loved me, and gave himself for me." "We must, therefore," as Luther says, "when dealing with the righteousness of the Christians, pay no regard to ourselves; else, no matter how we take it, the gospel could apply to none but saints, who fulfil the deeds of the law. No; I must fix my eyes on nothing but Jesus Christ, the crucified Savior, who rose again from the dead. For if I turn my eyes from Christ, I am undone." "Learn to say confidently and fearlessly: I am Christ; not personally, but in the sense that the righteousness, the victory, and the life of Christ are mine. For Christ says: I am this needy sinner; that is to say: His sin and death are my sin and death; through faith he clings to me, and I dwell in him." — Help us, O God, to believe with childlike confidence, and in all our life to praise thee for thy infinite mercy. Amen.

This I believe — yea, rather, Of this I make my boast, That God is my dear Father, The Friend who loves me most; And that, whate'er betide me, My Savior is at hand, Through stormy seas to guide me, And bring me safe to land.

393. Saturday after Eighteenth Sunday after Trinity.

Psalm 102, 1–14. Hear my prayer, O Lord, and let my cry come unto thee. Hide not thy face from me in the day when I am in trouble; incline thine ear unto me: in the day when I call, answer me speedily. For my days are consumed like smoke, and my bones are burned as a hearth. My heart is smitten, and withered like grass; so that I forget to eat my bread. By reason of the voice of my groaning, my bones cleave to my skin. I am like a pelican of the wilderness; I am like an owl of the desert. I watch, and am as a sparrow alone upon the housetop. Mine enemies reproach me all the day; and they that are mad against me are sworn against me. For I have eaten ashes like bread, and mingled my drink with weeping, because of thine indignation and thy wrath: for thou hast lifted me up, and cast me down. My days are like a shadow that declineth; and I am withered like grass. But thou, O Lord, shalt endure for ever, and thy remembrance unto all generations. Thou shalt arise, and have mercy upon Zion: for the time to favor her, yea, the set time, is come. For thy servants take pleasure in her stones, and favor the dust thereof.

In temptations it seems to the believer that God has entirely deserted him, and is deaf to his prayer. He never before stood in such need of God as now; and never had God seemed to be so far away. The cry of his soul dies away without having reached the ear of God. He *must* have help, and at once: "Make haste to help me, Lord; fear is on every hand, I sink in the deep mire"; — but there is no reply! "Alas, was this to be my lot? I had thought that my life was to be bright and full, that my strength was to increase, my heart to remain young in the Lord; but my days have fled, and I am become old, they are consumed like smoke; my bones are brittle, and my heart, my heart is smitten, and withered like grass." — In the bright seasons of our life of faith we feel love's fellowship with God and the brethren; but in temptations we are cut off and alone We are left to be mocked by the venomous spirits of evil, and are not sensible of the delightful bond of brotherly union with the children of God. "How happy *was* I when in the company of God's saints! Then I was in Bethany and on Zion; nay I was lifted up to heaven by the mercy of the Lord; I was blessed, and I was a blessing to others. But I kept not the grace which I had, nor made I the right use of it; I exalted myself, and thus I lost my place in the beautiful family circle of God's children. Formerly I was with the Lord when I fell asleep, and when I awoke; now I lie at night trembling with fear. I am like a pelican of the wilderness; I am like an owl of the desert." You, dear brother, may perhaps fear that this sorrow in you is nothing but that "sorrow of the *world*." If it were, you would not lament in this way; you would not thus pour out your complaint before the Lord. You do not belong to the devil; you belong to our Lord Jesus. There are two things which you shall do: In the first place you shall confess that you have neglected to be faithful and vigilant; and you shall humble yourself, and say: "I will bear the Lord's anger; for I have sinned against him." The Spirit of God shall help you herein; he has indeed done it already. In the second place, you shall continue to pray for mercy, and cling to the promises of God. This also the Spirit of God works in you. The Lord hears you, even if you do not perceive that he answers. The whole word of God declares that he delights in mercy. When we ask mercy of him this is, therefore, a prayer according to his will; and we know that we then "have the petitions that we desired of him" (1 John 5, 14. 15). "He will regard the prayer of the destitute, and not despise their prayer. This shall be written for the generation to come; and the people which shall be created shall praise the Lord. For he hath looked down from the height of his sanctuary; from heaven did the Lord behold the earth; to hear the groaning of the prisoner; to loose those that are appointed to death." (Psalm 102, 17–20). You shall, then, receive strength to wait and suffer, and in the midst of the darkness to have hope; and God shall shame the devil, but give you double your former glory; to declare the name of the Lord in Zion, and his praise in Jerusalem. — Have mercy, Lord; save us, pardon us, and heal us; and when we shall sit in darkness, be thou our light. Help us against hope to believe in hope, and never to grow faint. Amen.

In the weary hours of sickness, In the times of grief and pain, When we feel our mortal weakness, When all human help is vain, By thy mercy, O deliver us, good Lord!

In the solemn hour of dying, In the awful judgment day, May our souls, on thee relying, Find thee still our rock and stay By thy mercy, O deliver us, good Lord!

---

394. Nineteenth Sunday after Trinity. I.

Blessed is he whose transgression is forgiven, whose sin is covered.

Gospel Lesson, Matthew 9, 1–8. And he entered into a ship, and passed over, and came into his own city. And, behold, they brought to him a man sick of the palsy, lying on a bed: and Jesus seeing their faith, said unto the sick of the palsy, Son, be of good cheer; thy sins be forgiven thee. And, behold, certain of the scribes said within themselves, This man blasphemeth. And Jesus knowing their thoughts, said, Wherefore think ye evil in your hearts? For whether is easier, to say, Thy sins be forgiven thee; or to say, Arise, and walk? But that ye may know that the Son of Man hath power on earth to forgive sins, (then saith he to the sick of the palsy,) Arise, take up thy bed, and go unto thine house. And he arose, and departed to his house. But when the multitudes saw it, they marvelled, and glorified God, which had given such power unto men.

"Son, be of good cheer; thy sins be forgiven thee." This declaration Christ has not taken with him away from the earth; in that case we were undone. What did I say? taken with him from the earth? As though Christ had left us! No; as these are living words, which never pass away, even so our Lord Jesus himself is here among us with these his words unto the end of time. When we preach in his name repentance and forgiveness of sins, so that the penitent soul believes and finds peace in the blood of Jesus, it is the Lord himself who declares: "Son, be of good cheer; thy sins be forgiven thee." If he were not present to let his divine voice be heard through us, our preaching would not have power to drive sin and the devil out of the hearts of our hearers. Let every minister of the gospel bear in mind that the Lord is with him when he rises to preach; that he may "speak as the oracles of God." In like manner the Lord is with the words of forgiveness of sins in baptism and the Lord's supper; — while to them who feel themselves weighed down by their sins, and are unable to apply to their hearts the comfort offered them when they hear or read the gospel addressed to all, he has given the rite of absolution; through which we give the anxious soul which confesses its sin, and prays for mercy, assurance of full forgiveness by the word of God. When David confessed his sin, Nathan said: "The Lord also hath put away thy sin; thou shalt not die." This was the own word of God; and who can doubt that it came true? When Jesus said to the man sick of the palsy, "Thy sins be forgiven thee," were they not in truth forgiven? And the word is equally true when spoken to you in absolution; for it is the very word which Jesus spoke, God's own word, which he has given his church the office of proclaiming to poor sinners; and in which himself is present, though unseen; — unseen, because we are to be saved by *faith*. Or is it not true that he gave his disciples this commission: "Go ye into all the world, and preach the gospel to every creature"? And again: "Whose soever sins ye remit, they are remitted unto them; and whose soever sins ye retain, they are retained"? Do *all*, then, who receive absolution come into possession of forgiveness of sins? We say that it all depends on faith. He that does not believe is condemned already; for he makes God a liar. They who in their hearts despise the grace of God, and covet the world only; and they whose hearts refuse the gift, and who with the scribes in our text declare absolution by men to be blasphemy; — these certainly do not come into possession of the forgiveness which the words of absolution contain. For the very reason that *faith* alone can accept the grace of God, and that it is a most dangerous thing to refuse this great gift from the Lord, and deny this divine truth unto salvation; therefore we are vitally interested in giving one another instruction on this point, and by the revelation of the truth encourage one another to believe. If you do not as yet feel your sin with regret and pain, I beseech and exhort you by the love of Jesus to repent, and to come unto the knowledge of the truth. For he who does not know his sin with at least that degree of godly sorrow which *impels* him to go to Jesus and seek mercy, such a one has no life at all, but belongs to either the Pharisees or the Sadducees or the thoughtless multitude. If, on the other hand, you are sensible of your sin, and pray for mercy, you must not look about you in the domain of your own works or feelings in order to become a believer and find peace; but let yourself be brought to Jesus like the man sick of the palsy, and receive the comfort of forgiveness in the word which he has spoken, and which is preached to you by his servants. You do not believe that the word which we preach is the word which was spoken by his lips? Whence comes, then, this word of forgiveness which has been, and is, and will be heard in his church unto the end? From whom does it proceed? "Well," say you, "the message may come from *him;* but it may not be addressed to *me.*" Let me ask you one question: "Who is the author of your soul's prayer for mercy? Dare you say that it is any other than he? And yet you dare assert that he may have forgotten you, or that he may refuse to hear your prayer of which he is himself the author! Such unbelief surely is the height of foolishness and falsehood. Let me ask you another question: Of the many who came to Jesus with their burden of sin can you mention one who was turned away? Why, then, should he refuse to help you? Himself declares: "Him that cometh to me I will *in no wise* cast out." Yet you dare think that he may cast you out? Away, terrible unbelief, which contradicts the very words of truth itself! — Thank God, the truth shall remain the truth; our Lord Jesus is present in his own word with forgiveness of sins for every needy soul; and on this word we will take our stand, and bid defiance to sin and death and the kingdom of Satan. In the word of Jesus, and in nothing else whatever, will we put our trust, and let him be in the right in all things.

Do thou help us to do this, Lord Jesus; thou knowest the unbelief of our hearts. Hold us fast; draw us to thee; give us the grace of thy Holy Spirit to believe in thee, and to find rest in thy word of truth. Amen.

By servant thine thou say'st to me: "My child, thy sin's forgiven thee! Depart in peace, and sin no more, And e'er my pard'ning grace adore."
Yea, Lord, we bless the wondrous grace That granteth us this joyful peace; It is through Jesus' precious blood That we enjoy the heavenly good.

---

395. Nineteenth Sunday after Trinity. II.

Lord God, give us today by the word new zeal and new strength. Amen.

Epistle Lesson, Ephesians 4, 22–28. That ye put off, concerning the former conversation, the old man, which is corrupt according to the deceitful lusts; and be renewed in the spirit of your mind; and that ye put on the new man, which after God is created in righteousness and true holiness. Wherefore putting away lying, speak every man truth with his neighbor: for we are members one of another. Be ye angry, and sin not; let not the sun go down upon your wrath: neither give place to the devil. Let him that stole steal no more: but rather let him labor, working with his hands the thing which is good, that he may have to give to him that needeth.

Paul writes this exhortation to believers who are sealed with the Holy Ghost. Even they, then, still have such sins as these. Let no wicked man, however, comfort himself with this reflection. For the wicked will not put away that which is evil. When they rejoice at the sins of the saints it is the devil's joy, springing out of their love of sin. To the children of God, on the other hand, who grieve by reason of the evil still remaining in their flesh, and who fear that they may not be true Christians, it shall be a source of comfort that Paul finds it necessary to write thus to the holy church at Ephesus.

Let us also, then, obey the admonition of the apostle to put off the old man, and put on the new. No garment is so thoroughly moth-eaten and so full of filth and vermin as is the old man here spoken of. In these foul rags the unconverted are clothed; but without knowing it, because their lusts make them blind. You Christian, however, have put off the hideous garment; yet you must continue still to drag it with you; and the devil wants to make you put it on; but do you stamp it under foot, and put down the promptings of the flesh! If the soul stricken with palsy be healed by the grace of forgiveness, it must arise, and walk in newness of life; when the prodigal son has been received into the house of the father, and the best robe has been put on him, he must stay there, and wear it, and keep it clean, and consort no more with harlots. O with what zeal the regenerated children of God should follow after holiness! And the pure conversation proceeds *from within*. They have received a new mind, which, being born of God, is altogether holy; but in this they must be continually *renewed*. As there is a constant renewal of matter in a living body, some of the old being all the time replaced by the new; so it is also in the case of a living Christian. Of the Spirit of God he is ever receiving new light and new strength, and is being purged of the sin which still dwells in him; thus he has every day a *new desire* after that which is good. Many who at one time were filled with holy fire became cold, because they neglected this renewal of the mind. It gives the bounding freshness of youth to young and old; so that "they shall mount up with wings as eagles; they shall run, and not be weary; and they shall walk, and not faint."
— Out of this renewal of *mind* proceeds holiness of life. Let the devil and his people do all the lying; for love and lying can by no possibility be yoked together. And let them have all the bitterness; for love and bitterness will not intermix. When you are overcome by the temptation to anger, and persist in it, you grieve the Spirit of God; can neither pray nor give thanks, but are palsied of both heart and hand. Is it not solemnly impressive that the apostle combines these two things: "Let not the sun go down upon your wrath," and "Neither give place to the devil"? In Cain and Saul the devil found lodgment by their wrath; in Absolom and Ahithophel, by their greed

of power; in Judas, by his covetousness; in you he must never find a place by any means whatever! *The Lord* shall keep you. "Of him, and through him, and to him, are all things." — Merciful and faithful God, work in us to will and to do; and sanctify us wholly in spirit and soul and body. Amen.

Cleanse our hearts from sinful folly, In the stream thy love supplied, Mingled stream of blood and water, Flowing from thy wounded side; And to heavenly pastures lead us, Where thine own still waters glide.

---

396. Monday after Nineteenth Sunday after Trinity.

Psalm 130. Out of the depths have I cried unto thee, O Lord. Lord, hear my voice; let thine ears be attentive to the voice of my supplications. If thou, Lord, shouldest mark iniquities, O Lord, who shall stand? But there is forgiveness with thee, that thou mayest be feared. I wait for the Lord, my soul doth wait, and in his word do I hope. My soul waiteth for the Lord more than they that watch for the morning; I say, more than they that watch for the morning. Let Israel hope in the Lord: for with the Lord there is mercy, and with him is plentous redemption. And he shall redeem Israel from all his iniquities.

God's good Holy Spirit does not tire of pointing out to us the only and safe way out of our troubles: We must confess our sins, humble us before the Lord, and confidently expect his gracious help. "This psalm," says Hengstenberg, "teaches us that the church of God must not complain nor lose heart in her suffering; but pray her merciful Lord and Savior to forgive her sins, and remit their well deserved punishment; and confidently believe that he has the will to do it and truly does it. This is the royal road by which we attain fearlessness in trouble, and escape from suffering into the state of joy." Especially do we here learn to *wait and hope, wait and hope* for the Lord's help, and never cease humbly to pray in faith and hope, even though for a long time we hear no answer. In this waiting and hoping are included two things: 1) We have a hearty *longing* and *yearning*, and say: "Lord, make haste to help me!" This lesson is readily learned when we are in distress, when we cry out of the depths, when the waters threaten to engulf us. 2) We *confidently expect the Lord to save us;* we cling to his promise, and have the assurance in our heart that the help will come in due season. This is, alas, more difficult; and none can learn it save by the Holy Ghost. That we may learn it, he has caused this and many similar psalms to be written. By means of words such as these he gives humility, faith, and comfort to the upright hearts; so that they not only learn *what* they *are to do* in their affliction, but also receive grace *to do it.* At the time of the Diet at Augsburg, when Luther made his home at Coburg, he was often in such sore spiritual distress that he himself says: "I have been in deep agony of spirit, the like of which you will, I hope, never feel; I should not wish any man to have the experience which I have had." At this time of trial he often sang the psalm before us; and it so mightily strengthened him that he was able to write: "And were the world with devils filled, all eager to devour us, our souls should not yield to fear; for on our side we have One who can easily and quickly fell them all." — It is the way of our Lord to postpone helping us, when it seems to us, that if he loved us, and were aware of our distress, he should come at once to our assistance; and then it is the way of Satan to whisper into our soul: "There is no God to hear and deliver you." But then, thank God, it is the way of the Holy Spirit to keep us in the word and faith, and say to the soul: "Let Israel hope in the Lord; for with the Lord there is mercy, and with him is plenteous redemption. And he shall redeem Israel from all his iniquities." In the greatest need the *one* thing to do is to *wait* with humble faith for the Lord, and continue to *expect mercy and salvation of him; this,* and nothing else; *of him,* and of none other. None who has waited for the Lord has ever been made ashamed. — To wait for the Lord, and to hope in the Lord, he shall give you the strength *by the power of his word!*

Out of the depths I cry to thee, Lord, hear me, I implore thee! In grace thine ear incline to me, My prayer let come before thee! If thou remember each misdeed, If each should have its rightful meed, Lord, who can stand before thee?

Like those who watch for midnight's hour To hail the dawning morrow, I wait for thee, I trust thy power, Unmoved by doubt or sorrow. So thus let Israel hope in thee, And he shall find thy mercy free, And thy redemption plenteous.

---

397. Tuesday after Nineteenth Sunday after Trinity.

"Unto thee, O God, do we give thanks, unto thee do we give thanks; for that thy name is near thy wondrous works declare."

Lamentations 3, 22–33. It is of the Lord's mercies that we are not consumed, because his compassions fail not. They are new every morning: great is thy faithfulness. The Lord is my portion, saith my soul; therefore will I hope in him. The Lord is good unto them, that wait for him, to the soul that seeketh him. It is good that a man should both hope and quietly wait for the salvation of the Lord. It is good for a man that he bear the yoke in his youth. He sitteth alone and keepeth silence, because he hath borne it upon him. He putteth his mouth in the dust; if so be there may be hope. He giveth his cheek to him that smiteth him: he is filled full with reproach. For the Lord will not cast off for ever: but though he cause grief, yet will he have compassion according to the multitude of his mercies. For he doth not afflict willingly, nor grieve the children of men.

The Lord does you no evil. He smites you because he loves you, and wants to prepare you for eternal happiness. *If you be converted,* the afflictions with which he visits you will cause you to heed his word and obey his call. Thousands who are in heaven would have been in hell, had not their tribulations taught them obedience to the word of God. That man who was sick of the palsy would not have been prepared to receive absolution, had he not been suffering with a painful disease; nor would David have been able to speak of

the bliss of those on whom God had bestowed favor, had he not

previously felt the hand of the Lord heavy upon him. It was not for

his own pleasure that the Lord put the hollow of Jacob's thigh out

of joint; nor was it without a purpose that he let sorrow visit the

house of Jairus. The saved in heaven thank God that he brought

them out of their sleep by laying on them the sharp lash of affliction;

and who shall say that the sorrow which now oppresses you may not

become a blessed aid in the hand of God for your conversion? As

you live, this is at all events the Lord's purpose. — If you be a be-

liever, it should not be necessary for me to assure you that the cross

is a blessing; but alas, we are slow to learn to thank God for our

tribulations. Know, then, that the adversity and sorrow which you

have are the very best things that can befall you, and that the Lord's

great mercy has sent them to you. By this means you are humbled

and become like Jesus; by this means your heart is loosed from the

world; by this means you are taught to pray, and to have patience,

hope, and confidence in God; by this means you are sanctified, and

prepared to enjoy the bliss of heaven. "We must through much

tribulation enter into the kingdom of God"; and none is become

great before the Lord except through humiliations. Through what

deep waters were not such men as Jeremiah and David compelled

to go in order to become the comforters of the church of God; in

order that they might be able to sing the pilgrims across the dark

valleys on to Jerusalem! — What should I do in my great distress

and anxiety, if thou, O Lord, didst not strengthen me with thy holy

word? If I do but reach the haven of safety at last, what care I

how many severe storms I must encounter on the voyage! — Thou,

Lord, art my portion; what more do I desire? If thou do hide thy

face, I will wait and hope; and thou shalt change my lamentation to

songs of praise, and gird me round with eternal joy. Blessed be thy

name! Amen.

Whate'er the burden be, The cross upon me laid, Or want or shame, I

look to thee: Be thou, O Christ, my aid.

And let thy sorrows cheer My soul when I depart: Give strength to cast

away all fear, Console, sustain my heart.

Since thou hast died for me, Help me to trust thy grace, That thou wilt

take me up to thee, Where I shall see thy face.

398. Wednesday after Nineteenth Sunday after Trinity.

God, give us to see something of the depth of thy mercy. Amen.

Micah 7, 18–20. Who is a God like unto thee, that pardoneth iniquity,

and passeth by the transgression of the remnant of his heritage? he retaineth

not his anger for ever, because he delighteth in mercy. He will turn again,

he will have compassion upon us; he will subdue our iniquities: and thou wilt

cast all their sins into the depths of the sea. Thou wilt perform the truth

to Jacob, and the mercy to Abraham, which thou hast sworn unto our fathers

from the days of old.

This is the glorious issue of the judgments of God which were proclaimed to Israel by the prophet Micah. Such was the issue in the case of Israel: "Who is a God like unto thee?" The name *Micah* means: Who is like unto Jehovah? But that glory of our God at which the prophet marvels is his infinite *mercy*. In righteous anger he chastises us to make us penitent, in order that we put away our sins, and come over on his side; and then he "pardoneth iniquity, and passeth by transgression," and "retaineth not his anger for ever, because he delighteth in mercy." "As the heaven is high above the earth, *so great* is his mercy toward them that fear him." *So great* is his delight in mercy that he gave his only begotten Son in order to have compassion upon us and save us. Must we not say in wonder and worship: "Lord, who is like unto thee?"—"He will turn *again*, he will have compassion upon us," says the prophet. He will "again" have compassion; let the troubled soul take note! If you *now* feel his anger, take notice that he says he will "turn *again*." There is to be a change; the matter shall take a new turn, and have another issue. "He will have compassion." Our iniquities are as enemies resisting us; they accuse us, attack our conscience, and want to kill us; but he will have compassion, and subdue them. Every time that old sins and evil desires and all manner of infirmities rise against us, *he* shall place his foot on their neck, and give us victory over them. "Into the depths of the sea shalt *thou*, Lord God, cast all the sins of thy people. *Thou, thou* canst hide them; thou canst cast them into eternal oblivion; *thou* only. *I* will confess them, nor hide one of them from thee." — This is the right way, brethren! Come to God with all the sin of which you have knowledge; and it is engulfed at once in the bottomless sea of mercy. You shall *lay bare* your sin before him; he shall take it away and *hide* it. And do you think that the sin which has been drowned in these depths shall hereafter burn in your conscience? Can Satan kindle anew the spark which has been quenched in this great sea? Impossible! When he causes you to tremble in fear of eternal perdition he is practicing the art in which he is the great master, that of lying. But God is true, and his words shall stand: "I, even I, am he that blotteth out thy transgressions for mine own sake, and will not remember thy sins." (Isaiah 43, 25). Your sin is not only forgiven, but eternally forgotten. — Thy oath, O God, can never fail; thou hast delivered us out of the hand of our enemies, and we shall serve thee without fear, in holiness and righteousness, all the days of our life. Do also, we pray thee, "*turn again*" soon, and "perform the truth to Jacob, and the mercy to Abraham." Amen.

Grant us, dear Lord, from evil ways True absolution and release; And may we more than in past days Increase in purity and peace.
Thy pardon give, and give us joy, Sweet fear and sober liberty, And loving hearts without alloy, That only long to be like thee.

399. Thursday after Nineteenth Sunday after Trinity.

Psalm 25, 1–11. A Psalm of David. Unto thee, O Lord, do I lift up my soul. O my God, I trust in thee: let me not be ashamed; let not mine enemies triumph over me. Yea, let none that wait on thee be ashamed: let them be ashamed which transgress without cause. Shew me thy ways, O Lord; teach me thy paths. Lead me in thy truth, and teach me: for thou art the God of my salvation; on thee do I wait all the day. Remember, O Lord, thy tender mercies and thy lovingkindness; for they have been ever of old. Remember not the sins of my youth, nor my transgressions: according to thy mercy remember thou me, for thy goodness' sake, O Lord. Good and upright is the Lord: therefore will he teach sinners in the way. The meek will he guide in judgment, and the meek will he teach his way. All the paths of the Lord are mercy and truth unto such as keep his covenant and his testimonies. For thy name's sake, O Lord, pardon mine iniquity; for it is great.

"Gold is tried in the fire, and acceptable men in the furnace of adversity. Believe in him, and he will help thee; order thy way aright, and trust in him. Ye that fear the Lord, wait for his mercy; and go not aside, lest ye fall. Ye that fear the Lord, believe him; and your reward shall not fail. Ye that fear the Lord, hope for good, and for everlasting joy and mercy. Look at the generations of old, and see; did any ever trust in the Lord, and was confounded? or did any abide in his fear, and was forsaken? or whom did he ever despise, that called upon him? For the Lord is full of compassion and mercy, long-suffering, and very pitiful, and forgiveth sins, and saveth in time of affliction." (Ecclesiasticus 2, 5–11). You, dear friend, who call upon the name of the Lord may feel sure that he shall lead your cause to a glorious issue. This you may expect with as much confidence as though you already saw it. He who has loved you from eternity, and has given you his only begotten Son; he who is love and mercy and truth without end; could he be the God of your perdition, calamity, and ruin? Impossible! He must, then, be the God of your salvation, as David here calls him. Wait for his salvation in all manner of need; whether it be of the soul, fear and sorrow by reason of sin; or it be of the body, poverty, sickness, and danger; — wait upon him, and hope in him; he is as *willing* as he is *mighty* to help you. If the end be not that which *you* had hoped for, it is because the Lord makes it much more glorious; and if he do not come when it seems to *you* that he should, he comes at the proper time; for he is much wiser than you, even as he loves you better than you love yourself. He places you in the fiery crucible, in order that he may give you more resplendent glory. It is an unalterable law that *"none that wait on the Lord shall be ashamed."* "But," say you; "how about my *sins?"* You must confess them, and pray him to forgive them. David is not speaking of angels. He says: "Remember not the sins of my youth, nor my transgressions." "For thy name's sake, O Lord, pardon my iniquity; for it is great." *"According to thy mercy* remember thou me for thy goodness' sake, O Lord!" *"Good* and *upright* is the Lord; therefore he will teach *sinners* in the way." Take your soul to him out of your sins, and believe his forgiveness; then you are in his covenant; and, as he lives, *all his paths are mercy and truth unto you!*—Lord, keep my soul, and deliver me; let me not be ashamed; for I put my trust in thee. Let integrity and uprightness preserve me; for I wait on thee. Redeem Israel, O God, out of all his troubles. Amen.

Thou on my head in early youth didst smile, And though rebellious and perverse meanwhile, Thou hast not left me, oft as I left thee; On to the close, O Lord, abide with me!

I need thy presence every passing hour; What but thy grace can foil the tempter's power? Who like thyself my guide and stay can be? Through cloud and sunshine, O abide with me!

---

400. Friday after Nineteenth Sunday after Trinity.

Romans 5, 6–11. For when we were yet without strength, in due time Christ died for the ungodly. For scarcely for a righteous man will one die; yet peradventure for a good man some would even dare to die. But God commendeth his love toward us, in that, while we were yet sinners, Christ died for us. Much more then, being now justified by his blood, we shall be saved from wrath through him. For if, when we were enemies, we were reconciled to God by the death of his Son, much more, being reconciled, we shall be saved by his life. And not only so, but we also joy in God, through our Lord Jesus Christ, by whom we have now received the atonement.

In this text we again have one of those pearls of great price which, when carefully examined, seem to transcend all others. For us, weak, helpless, and ungodly men, Christ died in due time. "For us"; that is to say, *in our place, for our benefit.* It is done; it had been promised, and it is finished. For us, who were without strength, but were thoroughly depraved, and wicked, and strangers to God; for us, the ungodly, the Son of God died. He *died* for us, sacrificed himself on the cross, gave himself as a ransom for us. Scarcely for a righteous man will one die; yet Christ died for us ungodly men. Peradventure some might be willing to die in the stead of their best friend and benefactor; but Christ died for his enemies. *Thus has God loved us, and proved his love.* Could he have done more to "commend" it? Could he have given us better proof that he loves us? Shall this not assure us of our eternal salvation, lead us to commit ourselves wholly to God, melt our heart, cause us to fall down and worship before his throne, make us certain that we are in the state of grace, and make us fearless in the face of the accusations brought against us by sin and Satan? Christ shed his blood for us, when we were dead in sin and altogether ungodly; being now justified by his blood, shall we not, now that God is well pleased in us, escape wrath through *him*, through his life and his intercession for us? He wished to save us, when we were ungodly; shall he not wish to save us now that we are his beloved? He was willing to *die* for us then; can it be that he is unwilling to be our advocate and *intercede* for us now?

Behold, how sure is our salvation! We were the *enemies* of God; the wrath of God was upon us; then he gave his Son to *die for us,* and reconciled us to himself. Now we are friends, and his Son *lives for us.* On the one hand, *enmity* and the Son's *death* for his enemies; on the other, *friendship* and the Son's *life* for his friends. "For if, when we were enemies, we were reconciled to God by the death of his Son, much more, being reconciled, shall we be saved by his life." Nor can Christ be lost to us by death. An earthly father may die, leaving a bereaved family behind; but Christ dies no more. We were reconciled to God by his death; much more, says Paul, *much more* shall we be saved by his life. We might have thought that he would not be willing to die for us, — as, thank God, he has done; — but it is not possible for us to think that he will not live for us. — Has not God given us a firm rock on which to build our faith? And this is for us all, *let us but believe.* For Christ died for us *all.* Shall we with Paul glory in God through our Lord Jesus Christ, by whom we *have received* reconciliation; or shall we glory in ourselves; or shall we still doubt, and all the time complain that God does not give us a sufficiency of grace and light to enable us to believe? — Lord God, we are ashamed of our unbelief. Thou knowest how difficult it is for us to learn that Christ died for us; to learn this, which to our reason and senses seems utterly impossible: "The Son of God died for us, and lives for us." Nevertheless, we thank thee; we praise thy infinite love, and will praise it for ever and ever, world without end. Help us to do this. Amen.

Do we pass that cross unheeding, Breathing no repentant **vow, Though** we see thee wounded, bleeding, See thy thorn-encircled brow?

Yet thy sinless death has brought us Life eternal, peace, **and rest; Only** what thy grace has taught us Calms the sinner's stormy breast.

---

401. Saturday after Nineteenth Sunday after Trinity.

Psalm 63, 1-7. O God, thou art my God; early will I seek thee: my soul thirsteth for thee, my flesh longeth for thee in a dry and thirsty land, where no water is; to see thy power and thy glory, so as I have seen thee in the sanctuary. Because thy lovingkindness is better than life, my lips shall praise thee. Thus will I bless thee while I live; I will lift up my hands in thy name. My soul shall be satisfied as with marrow and fatness; and my mouth shall praise thee with joyful lips: when I remember thee upon my bed, and meditate on thee in the night watches. Because thou hast been my help, therefore in the shadow of thy wings will I rejoice.

Notice how David "thirsteth for God," and *rejoices;* how he is happy, and praises God in the midst of most grievous afflictions. Such psalms as this he sang in the desert, when he fled before his son Absalom. Will not you also aspire to this glorious state; that your longing for God may grow more intense, as your troubles increase, and your joy in praising him become greater, as your cross becomes more heavy? "To David every spring of human comfort had run dry; but he thirsted the more after the well of salvation. This is the true mark of God's children. When the children of the world wander in the desert even the last remnant of longing for God dies in their soul; while the children of God thirst for him more and more in proportion to the sufferings through which he leads them. By this rule each of us may test the condition of his soul." — "All thy waves and thy billows are gone over me. Yet the Lord will command his lovingkindness in the daytime, and in the night his song shall be with me" (Psalm 42, 7. 8). "Alas," say you, "point out to me the wicket into the holy land, and give me the key which will open its gates!" If you earnestly desire to gain admittance, you are near the gate; and the Spirit, the true and faithful, shall guide you. David mentions the way when he declares his longing "to see thy power and thy glory, so as I have seen thee in the sanctuary." If we have· and use the Lord's word and sacraments, there is no doubt that the Lord himself is here with grace and life. Had David "seen him" with his *bodily* eyes, do you think? No; he *believed* his presence, because he had the Lord's own promise; and thus it was that he saw the Lord. That God who had brought the Israelites out of Egypt, and planted them in Canaan, and given them the law, and kept his covenant with them; him David saw in the holy of holies in the tabernacle, where it was pitch dark to the eye, and where none but the high priest was permitted to enter. Let the Holy Spirit reveal to you your sin; *it* is real, but can not be seen without the light of the Spirit; and let him teach you, as he taught David, to see our Lord Jesus Christ, who is just as truly present among us in his means of grace, — Christ, who destroyed death, founded the church, preserves it unto the end, and mercifully pardons you for all your sins. Let the Spirit teach you thus to see him; then *he* becomes your God, glorious to you, as he is the Glorious One in fact; and the Spirit shall knit your heart more closely to him through many tribulations. — I pray and beseech you by the burning love of Jesus Christ, let nothing, *nothing in all the world*, keep you away; but come in, and learn to "rejoice in the shadow of the Lord's wings!" Bring this to pass, O God, by thy Spirit, for Jesus' sake. Amen.

Soon shall I pass the gloomy vale, Soon all my mortal pow'rs must fail;
O may my last expiring breath His lovingkindness sing in death.
Then let me mount and soar away To the bright world of endless day;
And sing, with rapture and surprise, His lovingkindness in the skies.

---

402. Twentieth Sunday after Trinity. I.

Lord Jesus, let thy Holy Spirit teach us what is meant by the wedding garment, and clothe us with it. Amen.

Gospel Lesson, Matthew 22, 1–14. And Jesus answered and spake unto them again by parables, and said, The kingdom of heaven is like unto a certain king, which made a marriage for his son, and sent forth his servants to call them that were bidden to the wedding: and they would not come. Again he sent forth other servants, saying, Tell them which are bidden, Behold, I have prepared my dinner; my oxen and my fatlings are killed, and all things are ready: come unto the marriage. But they made light of it, and went their ways, one to his farm, another to his merchandise: and the remnant took his servants, and entreated them spitefully, and slew them. But when the king heard thereof, he was wroth: and he sent forth his armies, and destroyed those murderers, and burned up their city. Then saith he to his servants, The wedding is ready, but they which were bidden were not worthy. Go ye therefore into the highways, and as many as ye shall find, bid to the marriage. So those servants went out into the highways, and gathered together all, as many as they found, both bad and good: and the wedding was furnished with guests. And when the king came in to see the guests, he saw there a man which had not on a wedding garment: and he saith unto him, Friend, how comest thou in hither, not having a wedding garment? And he was speechless. Then said the king to the servants, Bind him hand and foot, and take him away, and cast him into outer darkness: there shall be weeping and gnashing of teeth. For many are called, but few are chosen.

The kingdom of heaven, or the church of Christ, is the kingdom of grace in this world and the kingdom of glory in the world to come. It is likened unto the marriage of a king's son, because it surpasses everything else in splendor. In this kingdom we are re-united with God, and receive that which the soul needs; righteousness, peace and joy, love, life and salvation. We, who are baptized and use the word of God and the Lord's supper; we are guests at the wedding. Now all depends on our having the wedding garment; if we are without this garment, we shall be cast into outer darkness, into eternal despair and misery. How unspeakably important, then, to have the wedding garment!

What we need is the *righteousness* and *purity* which can avail us before God. He that is righteous and holy in the sight of God has this wedding garment. Now, "Christ Jesus of God is made unto us wisdom, and *righteousness*, and *sanctification*, and redemption"; and as many as have been baptized into Christ, and believe in him, have put on Christ (Galatians 3, 26. 27). Christ is himself our wedding garment; Christ himself, the Savior of sinners, who died for us, and lives for us, and through the means of grace in the church imparts his *righteousness* and *holiness* to every one that believes. It is often said, and with truth, that the wedding garment is nothing else than the righteousness of Christ; but in this case the "righteousness of Christ" is his whole grace unto salvation, which presents us *righteous* and *undefiled* before the sight of God. He who is to stand before God must have put on the Lord Jesus Christ, and trust only to his merit. As the hymn has it: "Nothing in my hand I bring; Simply to thy cross I cling; Naked come to thee for dress; Helpless, look to thee for grace." Then I am, in the words of Isaiah, 61, 10, "clothed with the garments of salvation, and covered with the robe of righteousness, as a bride adorneth herself with her jewels." He who has put off his own righteousness, and who has no hope but in the merit of Christ; he has put on the wedding garment. Then he has also been born again and sanctified; in Christ he not only has *remission* of sins, but

34

he has also been *cleansed*; he is not only counted pure in the sight
of God by the mercy of the Father for Christ's sake, but has also
received the pure and holy mind of Christ, and becomes every day
more pure in spirit and soul and body. According to that merciful
decree of God which scripture calls justification, he is in Christ absolved from every charge against him, and can stand without fear
before the bar of divine justice; but by reason of the indwelling of
the Spirit of Christ, and the resultant purity of mind and conduct, he
is also fit to dwell with God and enjoy his eternal bliss. The merit
of Christ covers him; the purity of Christ adorns him. Now, do you
understand what the wedding garment is? Blessed is he who is able
to say with Paul: "For Christ I have suffered the loss of all things,
and do count them but dung, that I may win Christ, and be found
in him, not having mine own righteousness, which is of the law, but
that which is through the faith of Christ, the righteousness which is
of God by faith." Of these David sings: "Lord, who shall abide in thy
tabernacle? who shall dwell in thy holy hill? He that walketh uprightly,
and worketh righteousness, and speaketh the truth in his heart."
These belong to the church, which Christ "loved, and gave himself for it; that he might sanctify and cleanse it with the washing
of water by the word." Blessed is he who can say to the Savior:
"Thou art my precious garment, the great treasure of my heart. Thy
righteousness is my eternal wedding jewel." Help us thereto, O
Lord, by thy good Holy Spirit. Amen.

Zion hears the watchmen singing, Her heart with heavenly joy is springing, She wakes, she rises from her gloom; For her Lord comes down all-glori-
ous, The strong in grace, in truth victorious, Her star is risen, her light is
come! All hail, incarnate Lord, Our crown and our reward! Hail! Hosanna!
The joyful call we answer all, And follow to the nuptial hall.

403. Twentieth Sunday after Trinity. II.

*Lord, let thy word wake us, and make us to walk wisely and circum-
spectly always. Amen.*

Epistle Lesson, Ephesians 5, 15–21. See then that ye walk circumspectly,
not as fools, but as wise, redeeming the time, because the days are evil. Wherefore be ye not unwise, but understanding what the will of the Lord is. And
be not drunk with wine, wherein is excess; but be filled with the Spirit; speaking to yourselves in psalms and hymns and spiritual songs, singing and making
melody in your heart to the Lord; giving thanks always for all things unto
God and the Father in the name of our Lord Jesus Christ; submitting yourselves one to another in the fear of God.

The sky becomes more dark, and the path more dangerous;
there are pitfalls on either hand, and a secret snare at every footstep.
Infidelity and false doctrine, worldliness and stupid carelessness,
pride and sectarianism are stronger temptations now than ever before;
"the days are evil." "See then that ye walk circumspectly!" Do not
allow yourself to be enticed hither and thither! Remain in the

narrow path of lowliness and self-denial. Become ever less in your own eyes; believe in Christ; let your heart be full of his love, your life abound in his virtues! "Redeem the time"; do not neglect to make use of that which can promote the salvation of your soul; grasp the precious hours of grace, and use them, that you may have fruit thereof!

In order that we may thus walk circumspectly and wisely, our epistle lesson commends to us these four rules: 1) "Be not drunk with wine; but be filled with the spirit." The brethren of Nabal and Elah and Ben-hadad in the matter of gluttony and drunkenness are many among the children of the world; but you, who fear God, must shun excesses. Enjoy the gifts of God in such a way that you may always be in a fit condition for worship and prayer. Never drunk with wine; but all the time more happy, brave, hearty, and zealous; more entirely filled with the Spirit. (Acts 2, 4. 15). If you have begun to taste the love of God, then do you watch and pray and do good, and drink of the river of his pleasures, of the fountain of life in his word and sacraments (Psalm 36, 9. 10). 2) "Sing and make melody in your heart to the Lord"; and if you have the gift of song, make use of it for the delight of others. "If any be afflicted, let him pray; if any be merry, let him sing!" Do it; it is a natural and healthy impulse. The Israel of old was a people of song; should not this be even still more true of the new Israel? God has given our Lutheran church a rich treasure of grand hymns; learn them, and sing them while at your work and in your home. Keep close to the brethren always, that they may kindle the fire in you, and you in them. Rake the embers apart, and they die; heap them together, and they glow. 3) "Give thanks always for all things unto God." That which God gives you is altogether good, and altogether undeserved. There is absolutely nothing for which you do not owe him thanks. All is included in the name of Jesus Christ; you receive it for his sake; and the purpose of everything which befalls you is to carry to completion his work as your Savior. Give thanks, then, in "*all things*"; and in return give them *all* to God with humble gratitude. This rule, also, is one to be honored in the observance! 4) "Submit yourselves one to another in the fear of God." Let the contemplation of God's holiness and greatness and mercy cause you to become less than the least in your own eyes, in honor preferring one another. "Ye younger, submit yourselves unto the elder. Yea, all of you be subject one to another, and be clothed with humility." (1 Peter 5, 5). — He that does these things walks circumspectly, as the wise, understanding what the will of the Lord is. — God, give us grace thereto according to thy promise in Jesus Christ our Lord. Amen.

O God, thou faithful God, Thou Fountain ever-flowing, Without whom nothing is, All perfect gifts bestowing; A pure and healthy frame O give me, and within A conscience free from blame, A soul unhurt by sin.

404. Monday after Twentieth Sunday after Trinity.

Psalm 8. O Lord, our Lord, how excellent is thy name in all the earth! who hast set thy glory above the heavens. Out of the mouth of babes and sucklings hast thou ordained strength, because of thine enemies; that thou mightest still the enemy and the avenger. When I consider thy heavens, the work of thy fingers; the moon and the stars, which thou hast ordained; what is man, that thou art mindful of him? and the son of man, that thou visitest him? For thou hast made him a little lower than the angels, and hast crowned him with glory and honor. Thou madest him to have dominion over the works of thy hands: thou hast put all things under his feet: all sheep and oxen, yea, and the beasts of the field; the fowl of the air, and the fish of the sea, and whatsoever passeth through the paths of the seas. O Lord, our Lord, how excellent is thy name in all the earth!

The holy bard of Israel glorifies the mercy and goodness of the Lord toward man; this is one thought of the psalm before us.* The Lord, who is so great, and has set his glory above the heavens in such a way that even babes must praise him, — to the shame of blind and infatuated scoffers and infidels; — he has appointed little man to have dominion over all his works, and put all things under his feet.

Excellent is the name of the Lord in all the earth! Consider the splendor of the heavens; it is *the name of our Lord* which you see written in these lines and curves of countless jewels. When you know that nearly all these points of light are mighty suns, they speak to you, saying: Infinitely *great* is the Lord of hosts. When they look down upon you with their wondrously gentle and kindly light, they declare that the Lord is *good*; and when the mists roll away, and the stars reappear, each in the place in which it was seen by Abraham and Moses, they proclaim the unchangeable *truth* of the Lord. The universe is a crown of heavenly orbs; and how incomparably more grand than the crown of an earthly king! What then, shall we say of the inconceivable goodness of God, in that he has made man to have dominion over all his works? Man, know your littleness, and your greatness! Know the Lord and his mercy, and become humble; so shall you become great! From the beginning he created man in his own image, and said: Have dominion over all things, in the height and in the depth. By the fall we lost our glory; but it has been given us again in Christ; and in him we shall attain to supreme dominion over all things. One outgrowth of the Christian religion is an intellectual culture which has enabled man to penetrate deep into the secrets of nature, and harness its forces, and compel them to do his will; and yet, how much more shall humanity see when it has been made perfect, and how like a king shall it be then in its relations to all things! God, the glory of whose name shines forth in all his works, did not only give us an intellect above all other creatures, when he breathed life into us from the beginning; but he has given

---

* According to Matthew 21, 16; Hebrews 2, 6–9 and 1 Corinthians 15, 27 this Psalm treats first of our Lord Jesus Christ.

to us *fallen* creatures his Son, and in him renews us to be his children, and fashions us into a church which is flesh and bone of the only begotten Son of God. This I remember when I consider the greatness of the Lord in all the earth and his splendor in the heavens; and then I sink down at his feet with the fear of the humble and sinful creature before the infinitely glorious and holy One, but with the trust of a child in my heavenly Father, and say: "O Lord *our* Lord, how excellent is thy name in all the earth!"

Before Jehovah's awful throne, Ye nations, bow with sacred joy: Know that the Lord is God alone; He can create, and he destroy.

His sovereign power, without our aid, Made us of clay, and formed us men; And when like wandering sheep we strayed, He brought us to his fold again.

We are his people, we his care, Our souls and all our mortal frame: What lasting honors shall we rear, Almighty Maker, to thy name?

---

405. Tuesday after Twentieth Sunday after Trinity.

Ephesians 2, 13–22. But now, in Christ Jesus, ye who sometimes were far off, are made nigh by the blood of Christ. For he is our peace, who hath made both one, and hath broken down the middle wall of partition between us; having abolished in his flesh the enmity, even the law of commandments contained in ordinances; for to make in himself of twain one new man, so making peace; and that he might reconcile both unto God in one body by the cross, having slain the enmity thereby; and came and preached peace to you which were afar off, and to them that were nigh. For through him we both have access by one Spirit unto the Father. Now therefore ye are no more strangers and foreigners, but fellowcitizens with the saints, and of the household of God; and are built upon the foundation of the apostles and prophets, Jesus Christ himself being the chief corner stone; in whom all the building, fitly framed together, groweth unto an holy temple in the Lord: in whom ye also are builded together for an habitation of God through the Spirit.

Without Christ the law is a wall of partition between the Jews and gentiles, and sin a wall of partition between God and both of them; but *in Christ* both are reconciled to God, and united with each other. God's holy, eternal, and immutable law no more stands as a threat between God and Israel; for Christ has fulfilled both its demands and its judgment. "In his flesh," — his work of atonement in his human nature and his humiliation, — he "abolished even the law of commandments contained in ordinances." "He blotted out the handwriting of the ordinances that was against us, which was contrary to us, and took it out of the way, nailing it to his cross." As he has atoned for the sin of the whole *world*, Jews and gentiles now have free access to God.

Paul everywhere teaches that Jesus Christ as our Savior himself is in the words of the gospel. "*He* is our peace," he who abolished the enmity; *he* is *himself* our peace. And again: "He came and preached peace to you which were afar off, and to them that were nigh. For *through him* we both have access by one Spirit unto the Father." Read this aright and see that Jesus with his blood, which he shed on the cross, is present in his means of grace; so that whosoever accepts the gospel accepts him, and is reconciled to God; but whosoever closes his heart to the gospel rejects Christ himself, and remains under the wrath of God. As there is no salvation in any other, so there is no participation in him but by faith in his word.

By the word he has in fact created a new people of God, composed of Jews and gentiles. We also, with our fathers, were aliens from the commonwealth of Israel, and strangers from the covenants of promise, without hope, and without God. But the word came, and the Spirit therein made clear to us the cross; and now we also are made nigh by the blood of Christ. In the word of God we have our true certificate of citizenship in Israel. Christ is our only ground of salvation; and in him we are indissolubly joined together with the church of the Pentecost and of all time. Of his infinite mercy God has quickened us, raised us up, and lifted us to heaven in Christ Jesus. This is no idle dream; for we have the true gospel, the true Savior, the true life of love, and stand night and day before the throne of God. — O God, we bless thee for thy wisdom and mercy. Help us to believe the word, and to glorify thee. Amen.

The foolish builders, scribe and priest, Reject it with disdain; Yet on this rock the church shall rest, And envy rage in vain.
What though the gates of hell withstood; Yet must this building rise: 'Tis thine own work, almighty God, And wondrous in our eyes.

---

406. Wednesday after Twentieth Sunday after Trinity.

"The king's daughter is all glorious within; her clothing is of wrought gold."

Isaiah 61, 10. 11. I will greatly rejoice in the Lord, my soul shall be joyful in my God: for he hath clothed me with the garments of salvation, he hath covered me with the robe of righteousness, as a bridegroom decketh himself with ornaments, and as a bride adorneth herself with her jewels. For as the earth bringeth forth her bud, and as the garden causeth the things that are sown in it to spring forth; so the Lord God will cause righteousness and praise to spring forth before all the nations.

If you have seen a poor naked child receive a beautiful new dress, you also have witnessed her delight. *We*, also, were naked; and God gave us the most superb garment; shall we not rejoice? If the Spirit of God have enlightened you, your heart confesses that in yourself you are "wretched, and miserable, and poor, and blind, and naked." Now, the same Spirit of *truth* says, Gal. 3, 27: "As many of you as have been baptized into Christ have put on Christ." All carnally minded baptized persons have thrown away their glorious garment; but this must not prevent you from keeping that which God has given you. Have you not experienced the truth of that which the Holy Ghost says through the apostle? Have not we, who have been baptized into Christ, put on Christ? The Lord has said it; do you keep and ponder it in your heart, as it is God's will that you should do? *Faith* is the one thing needful; then certainly we poor, naked wretches ought to obey the Spirit of God, and *believe* that which the Son of God has given us. Do you not want your soul to *rejoice* in God? For what are you waiting? Even in your childhood, when you were baptized, the Lord put on you the garment of salvation, the perfect righteousness of Christ. So God declares; will you, then, deny it? The world feels no concern on account of its nakedness; but yours makes you unhappy. Truly, God has taken the matter in hand, even before you asked it of him; and has more than satisfied your want. The *Lord* says: "I have taken away thine iniquity, and put on thee beautiful garments." Shall you then say that it can not be true? No; say rather: I will accept as true that which *he* declares; I will believe without having seen, *because he has said it.* Sing then with truth: "I will greatly rejoice in the Lord, my soul shall be joyful in my God; for he hath clothed me with the garments of salvation, he hath covered me with the robe of righteousness." Brethren, in Christ we sinners are pure and beautiful in the sight of God; let us *believe* in him with the simple faith of children, and praise him with happy hearts! To do this grant us thy grace, thou God of mercy. Amen.

Most heartily I trust in thee, Thy mercy fails me never; Dear Lord, abide My helper tried, Thou Crucified, From evil keep me ever.
Now, henceforth, must I put my trust In thee, O dearest Savior; Thy comfort choice, Thy word and voice, My heart rejoice, Despite my ill behavior.

---

407. Thursday after Twentieth Sunday after Trinity.

Give us, O God, an ear to hear what the Spirit saith unto the churches.

Revelations 3, 14–22. And unto the angel of the church of the Laodiceans write; These things saith the Amen, the faithful and true witness, the beginning of the creation of God; I know thy works, that thou art neither cold nor hot: I would thou wert cold or hot. So then because thou art lukewarm, and neither cold nor hot, I will spue thee out of my mouth. Because thou sayest, I am rich, and increased with goods, and have need of nothing; and knowest not that thou art wretched, and miserable, and poor, and blind, and naked: I counsel thee to buy of me gold tried in the fire, that thou mayest be rich, and white raiment, that thou mayest be clothed, and that the shame of thy nakedness do not appear; and anoint thine eyes with eyesalve, that thou mayest see. As many as I love, I rebuke and chasten: be zealous therefore, and repent. Behold, I stand at the door, and knock: if any man hear my voice, and open the door, I will come in to him, and will sup with him, and he with me. To him that overcometh will I grant to sit with me in my throne, even as I also overcame, and am set down with my Father in his throne. He that hath an ear, let him hear what the Spirit saith unto the churches.

This is a most impressive sermon. Let us *all* lay it to heart! These are the words of *Jesus*, set down in order that *we* also may hear them. There are many who deceive themselves with a sort of Christianity in which there is no life. They neither have knowledge of their sin, nor do they seek the grace of God. They refuse to practice self-denial; and they live in sensuality, covetousness, hate, anger, pride, deceit, and other sins. They boast of Christ, though they mock and deride him in his saints and trample his blood under foot. "O you blind, deceived, and spurious Christian; certainly the word of God never taught you that you can be saved in this way; nor has it been preached by any of the prophets or apostles. On the contrary, the burden of their preaching is this: If you wish to receive forgiveness, you must repent, and renounce and hate your sins, and believe in Christ, your only Savior and Redeemer." (Joh. Arndt). — Others have begun to repent, but have then gone the way of Demas, spoken of in 2 Tim. 4, 10. They may perhaps keep up a certain appearance of piety, and have converse with the true Christians; and they "have a name that they live, — and are dead." — However, in the sight of God there is no greater abomination than that *lukewarmness* which he reproaches in the Laodiceans. He who is "the Amen, the faithful and true witness," — thus he here calls himself in order to wake us up; — *he knows your works*, and would rather have you to be cold than lukewarm. Give ear, then; awake, and know yourself! It is not the one that is wretched whom he will spue out of his mouth; — not the one who is sensible of his sin, and feels sorrow by reason of his misery; but the one that is satisfied with himself, and is rich and has need of nothing. When we no longer pray: "God be merciful to me a sinner;" when we no more feel the need of putting on Christ; when we have no desire to "behold the beauty of the Lord, and to enquire in his temple"; when we no longer have the wish to confess God, and to serve the brethren; — then we are lukewarm, and on the way to perdition. Deplorable self-complacency! For Jesus' sake, rouse yourself from your torpor! He chastises you by his word, and disciplines you by means of afflictions, because he loves you. He knocks at the door, because he wants to sup with you. Will you force him to reject you? Is it to become necessary for him to place another in the seat intended for you? You may yet "overcome," and then you shall "sit with him in his throne." Note this: You may overcome, and sit with Jesus in his throne, he says, "even as I also overcame, and am set with my Father in his throne." He still holds you in his heart; will you compel him to "spue you out"? to pronounce judgment and condemnation on you by his word? He yet loves you; yet there is time! Do return his love; go to your chamber, and pray with all your heart: Lord, wake me; and quicken me, and keep me. — Lord Jesus, if thou canst yet save me; if thou wilt yet have compassion on me, I humbly beseech thee to do it. "I would be, dear Jesus, where thou wouldst have me. I take thee, O Lord, into my heart with all thy grace and gifts." Faithful Savior, let us keep together; I can not live without thee, I must not lose thee. Chastise me, but do not cast me off; save, O save thine own, whom thou hast bought with thy life. Amen.

Just as I am, without one plea, But that thy blood was shed for me, And
that thou bid'st me come to thee, O Lamb of God, I come, I come.
Just as I am, and waiting not To rid myself of one dark blot, To thee,
whose blood can cleanse each spot, O Lamb of God, I come, I come.

408. Friday after Twentieth Sunday after Trinity.

*"I had fainted, unless I had thought to see the goodness of the Lord in
the land of the living."*

Hebrews 4, 9–16. There remaineth therefore a rest to the people of God.
For he that is entered into his rest, he also hath ceased from his own works,
as God did from his. Let us labor therefore to enter into that rest, lest any
man fall after the same example of unbelief. For the word of God is quick
and powerful, and sharper than any two edged sword, piercing even to the
dividing asunder of soul and spirit, and of the joints and marrow, and is a
discerner of the thoughts and intents of the heart. Neither is there any creature that is not manifest in his sight; but all things are naked and opened
unto the eyes of him with whom we have to do. Seeing then that we have
a great high priest, that is passed into the heavens, Jesus the Son of God,
let us hold fast our profession. For we have not an high priest which cannot
be touched with the feeling of our infirmities; but was in all points tempted
like as we are, yet without sin. Let us therefore come boldly unto the throne
of grace, that we may obtain mercy, and find grace to help in time of need.

Weary pilgrim among the people of God, a blessed sabbath rest
awaits you. The sabbath is the day of holy convocation, of divine
service, of liberty, and of the singing of praises to God. "There remaineth a rest to the people of God"; a condition of perfect repose,
with the full enjoyment of bliss in the fellowship of God and all the
saints. "Rejoice ye with Jerusalem; that ye may be satisfied with the
breasts of her consolation, and be delighted with the abundance of
her glory. Your heart shall rejoice, and your bones shall flourish like
an herb." (Isaiah 66, 10. 11. 14). If you, my reader, desire to enter
into that rest, you must walk with *fear*, and at the same time with
boldness. Neither the thoughtless nor the faint-hearted can gain admittance. Let the living word of God lay bare, melt, crush, and judge
your heart; but let it also heal and comfort you; so that you stand
confidently before his face, and boldly confess your faith before men.
The Son of God became our *high priest*; therefore we may be of good
cheer. He has not only atoned for our sins with his blood, which he
shed on the cross, and bore to heaven; but he was in all points
tempted like as we are, yet without sin. Thus of his own experience
he knows our struggles and our sorrows, our suffering and our labor,
and all our weaknesses; nay he knows better, and feels more acutely
than you do the condition of your sick and troubled heart, and the
sufferings with which sin and Satan afflict you. A *great* high priest
have we, Jesus the Son of God, great in power and great in mercy.
"Such an high priest became us, who is holy, harmless, undefiled,
separate from sinners, and made higher than the heavens." "Wherefore in all things it behooved him to be made like unto his brethren,

that he might be a merciful and faithful high priest in things pertaining to God, to make reconciliation for the sins of the people. For in that he himself hath suffered being tempted, he is able to succor them that are tempted." — We will, then, *labor* to enter that rest; *labor* hard to do it! *Here,* labor; *yonder,* rest! We will walk by the light of the word in the sight of God with holy earnestness, and come boldly before him sheltered under the wings of our merciful and faithful High Priest. — Accomplish this in us, O God, by thy Holy Spirit, for Jesus' sake. Amen.

Jesus, tender Savior, Hast thou died for me? Make me very thankful In my heart to thee.

Now I know thou livest, And dost plead for me; Make me very thankful In my prayers to thee.

Soon I hope in glory At thy side to stand; Make me fit to meet thee In that happy land.

---

409. Saturday after Twentieth Sunday after Trinity.

Psalm 36, 5–12. Thy mercy, O Lord, is in the heavens, and thy faithfulness reacheth unto the clouds. Thy righteousness is like the great mountains; thy judgments are a great deep: O Lord, thou preservest man and beast. How excellent is thy lovingkindness, O God! therefore the children of men put their trust under the shadow of thy wings. They shall be abundantly satisfied with the fatness of thy house; and thou shalt make them drink of the river of thy pleasures. For with thee is the fountain of life: in thy light shall we see light. O continue thy lovingkindness unto them that know thee; and thy righteousness to the upright in heart. Let not the foot of pride come against me, and let not the hand of the wicked remove me. There are the workers of iniquity fallen: they are cast down, and shall not be able to rise.

The *lovingkindness* of God is his undeserved goodness toward us; that we, in place of punishment and wrath, receive nothing but benefits. David praises it as something glorious in itself and precious to his heart. "How excellent is thy lovingkindness, O God!" *"Excellent,"* of great worth: the thought of the life and blood of God's Son is brought before us. *"Excellent," precious;* that is, a gem of value above all others. Such is the Lord's lovingkindness; there is nothing can be compared with it. It is of infinitely greater value than a thousand worlds full of the most precious things which could be created. That God loves us, and is good to us; — is there any price at which we would sell this truth? When David speaks of it as excellent ("jakar") it is as if he said: *"Thy rich and priceless* lovingkindness, O my God, is to me more precious than the pearls of greatest price, and is worth more to my heart than heaven and earth; it is *excellent* in itself and *excellent* to me!" I hope that you also, dear reader, know the lovingkindness of God, and prize it highly. How sadly blind and how terribly depraved are they who regard lightly the mercy of God! — I do not by any means say too much; truly they are "evil eyes" which do not see this sun, and do not heed its glory. When the Spirit of God enlightens us we understand that without it we were the most wretched of all creatures, abandoned to temporal and eternal misery, having no peace, given up to hate one another and to be trodden under foot by the devil; we understand that it is the mercy of God in Christ which gives us all good things, and we say with David: "Thy mercy, O God, is infinitely precious; it is better than life, and more excellent than heaven." Yet we feel that we do not grasp its full value. Of the bottomless ocean of the Divinity we can hold but a few drops; the love of God is a glorious sun, of which our poor eyes are able to see but a feeble reflection.

God, continue thy lovingkindness unto them that know thee; and thy righteousness to the upright in heart. Amen.

Every human tie may perish, Friend to friend unfaithful prove, Mothers cease their own to cherish, Heaven and earth at last remove: But no changes Can attend Jehovah's love.

In the furnace God may prove thee Thence to bring thee forth more bright, But can never cease to love thee; Thou art precious in his sight; God is with thee, God, thine everlasting light.

---

410. Twenty-first Sunday after Trinity. I.

Lord, let thy word punish us for our unbelief and strengthen our faith. Amen.

Gospel Lesson, John 4, 46–53. So Jesus came again into Cana of Galilee, where he made the water wine. And there was a certain nobleman, whose son was sick at Capernaum. When he heard that Jesus was come out of Judæa into Galilee, he went unto him, and besought him that he would come down, and heal his son: for he was at the point of death. Then said Jesus unto him, Except ye see signs and wonders, ye will not believe. The nobleman saith unto him, Sir, come down ere my child die. Jesus saith unto him, Go thy way; thy son liveth. And the man believeth the word that Jesus had spoken unto him, and he went his way. And as he was now going down, his servants met him, and told him, saying, Thy son liveth. Then inquired he of them the hour when he began to amend. And they said unto him, Yesterday at the seventh hour the fever left him. So the father knew that it was at the same hour, in the which Jesus said unto him, Thy son liveth: and himself believed, and his whole house.

The faith of all believers is not equally strong. There plainly is a wide difference between the man in our gospel lesson and the centurion who said to Jesus: "Speak the word only, and my servant shall be healed." The Lord has pleasure in them that believe in him with full trust and confidence; but neither does he disown those of weak faith, if they but be upright. He chastens and humbles all his own, and thus increases their faith; for this reason the son of this man was sick, and for this reason both you and I have our afflictions in the world. For this reason the Lord reproached the nobleman in our text, saying: "Except ye see signs and wonders, ye will not believe." For this reason also the word of God often gives us a different answer from that which we desire. — Although the woman of Canaan stands high above this nobleman in humility and faith, yet the Lord's manner of dealing with them is somewhat similar. She can bear it, and is therefore most thoroughly humbled, in order that her faith may gain a glorious victory; he is humbled to the limit of his strength to bear it, in order that his faith may increase. Both continue to pray; and the prayers of both are answered. Both have come to Jesus on behalf of their children; and both find more than they seek. — In the case of many the discipline by means of temporal affliction is in vain; but in the case of the upright it opens the door to the word of God. Look at the nobleman in our text. He had heard accounts concerning the Lord, but did not seek him. Afterward his son fell sick; then he remembered what he had heard, and went to Jesus. The Lord then reproached him in severe terms; and the nobleman humbles himself and sues for mercy. Thereupon the Lord brings the truth home to his soul; and now he is able to receive it. He believes without having seen, and then he is permitted to see also; — and he believes, and his whole house. Thus it is that the Lord deals with the upright; he humbles them, and creates faith; humbles them, and strengthens their faith. In like manner as he said to this man: "Thy son liveth," so he says to you: "Your soul lives, your sin is taken away, your death is destroyed; your prayer is answered, you and your house are saved. When your time comes, lay yourself down to sleep; you are in heaven, and your body shall be called forth to glory." The man went his way at the Lord's word, believing without seeing; go thou, and do likewise. He was not deceived; neither shall you be. None who trusts in the word of the Lord shall be disappointed. Go your way gladly; you shall find the Lord's words come true. — If your faith be weak, the Lord shall try you according to the measure of your ability to bear it, and chasten and strengthen your soul. Even though you may never become a mighty giant in faith, like Paul and Luther, yet you shall without any doubt obtain victory. The greater effort the devil makes to quench the spark of faith in you, the more brightly it shall burn. — Lord Jesus, I am full of frailties. Do not cast me off; but try, if there be truth in me; and strengthen my weak faith. Amen.

Lord, I believe; thy power I own, Thy word I would obey; I wander comfortless and lone When from thy truth I stray.

Lord, I believe; but gloomy fears Sometimes bedim my sight; I look to thee with prayers and tears, And cry for strength and light.

---

411. Twenty-first Sunday after Trinity. II.

Lord, put on me thy armor, and give me thy sword. Amen.

Epistle Lesson, Ephesians 6, 10–17. Finally, my brethren, be strong in the Lord, and in the power of his might. Put on the whole armor of God, that ye may be able to stand against the wiles of the devil. For we wrestle not against flesh and blood, but against principalities, against powers, against the rulers of the darkness of this world, against spiritual wickedness in high places. Wherefore take unto you the whole armor of God, that ye may be able to withstand in the evil day, and, having done all, to stand. Stand therefore, having your loins girt about with truth, and having on the breastplate of righteousness; and your feet shod with the preparation of the gospel of peace; above all, taking the shield of faith, wherewith ye shall be able to quench all the fiery darts of the wicked. And take the helmet of salvation, and the sword of the Spirit, which is the word of God.

In the fight against the devil our own strength is as nothing; but in the power of the Lord's might we are strong; so strong that "we are more than conquerors." The purpose of the apostle is to make us *earnest* by impressing us with the character and strength of the enemy. Let your mind dwell on the terms used to designate the enemy: "*Principalities, powers,* the *rulers* of the darkness of this *world, spiritual wickedness* in high places." The "*wiles*" of the *devil,* the strongest and most cunning of all created spirits, you must be able to withstand "in *the evil day*"; these terrible powers you, a poor broken reed, must overcome in the battles of life and in the agony of death, if you are to reach your crown. — The purpose of the apostle, however, also is to make our souls intrepid. I may be completely overawed on beholding the strength of the enemy; but then again, I am inspired with dauntless courage "in the Lord, and in the power of his might." I have been baptized into the *Lord;* by faith I am united to God the Almighty, who allowed himself to be attacked by all the power of wickedness, and has gained the victory. In him, and in the power of his might; mark you, in the *power* of the *Lord's might,* you shall surely tread the devil and his hosts under foot. It is a case of fighting for your life, while you are here; but the victory is assured, and its spoils shall last for ever. Put on the armor; work with one hand, but carry a sword in the other. "The whole armor of God." The apostle repeats it: "Put on the *whole armor of God,*" and "take unto you *the whole armor of God.*" First of all, you must be girt about with truth. This is the belt by which the garments are held in place; truth, *truth* in your innermost heart! Walk in the *light* before God and men, or you will stumble and be trampled under foot. In the next place, you must have on the righteousness of Christ; the breastplate which protects the heart and conscience against the dagger of every accuser. Furthermore, you must have your "feet shod with the preparation of the gospel of peace." That is to say, you must live all the time in the covenant of peace with God, in all your life gladly confess Christ, and suffer with him the ignominy of the cross. Do this, holding up the "shield of faith" against all the fiery darts of the wicked; that is, feeling assured of the presence of the invisible God, and of the truth of his promise; thus mortifying all the wicked thoughts and desires which are kindled in you by the tempter. The "helmet of salvation" is hope; that is, the soul's certain expectation of eternal glory, which gives you courage to hold up your head in all afflictions. Finally, you must use the "sword of the Spirit"; for you are not only to protect yourself, but to put your enemy to rout. Use the *sword of the Spirit,* the sword which is the Spirit; but the Spirit is the word of God. The Spirit of the Lord in the word shall, then, be your strength of soul and hand, wherewith you smite the devil, as did Christ in the wilderness. — That we shal in this way conquer in the strength of the Lord is as certain, as it is that we can by no possibility conquer in our own strength. Brethren, the crown of glory beckons; "put on the whole armor of God," and "be strong in the Lord, and in the power of his might!"

Almighty faithful God, be with us in the evil day, and protect us against the cunning and violent attacks of the devil. Lord God, make us strong in thee, and put on us thy whole armor; give us victory, and let us stand, having done all. Amen.

As true as God's own word is true, Nor earth nor hell, with all their crew, Against us shall prevail. A jest and byword are they grown; "God is with us;" we are his own; Our victory cannot fail.

---

412. Monday after Twenty-first Sunday after Trinity.

Lord, increase our faith. Amen.

Romans 4, 18–25. Who against hope believed in hope, that he might become the father of many nations, according to that which was spoken, So shall thy seed be. And being not weak in faith, he considered not his own body now dead, when he was about an hundred years old, neither yet the deadness of Sarah's womb: he staggereth not at the promise of God through unbelief; but was strong in faith, giving glory to God; and being fully persuaded that, what he had promised, he was able also to perform. And therefore it was imputed to him for righteousness. Now it was not written for his sake alone, that it was imputed to him: but for us also, to whom it shall be imputed, if we believe on him that raised up Jesus our Lord from the dead; who was delivered for our offences, and was raised again for our justification.

When we *believe* that which God has done for us in Christ, it is imputed to us for righteousness, as though we had done it ourselves. "If we believe," says the apostle. Therefore the statement that the *world* has been made righteous in Christ needs explanation. To be sure, the sins of *the whole world* were imputed to Christ, and *all* men are redeemed by his blood. Thus righteousness is granted and offered all men; but it becomes the possession of them only that believe. Your sin is imputed to Christ, whether you be a Jew or gentile, whether you be a believer or one of the wicked; but his merit is not received by you for righteousness, except you believe. *The believer is*, then, in truth *righteous before God*. The purpose of Paul here is to prove that *faith alone* justifies. Not circumcision, not birth, not works; but faith was imputed to Abraham for righteousness. It is, therefore, of the very highest importance that we *believe*; and it is this to which all scripture urges us.

Abraham and Sarah were old and decrepit, and could have no hope of issue. But God had spoken a promise; and to Abraham this was of greater force than were nature and reason. Giving glory to God, he became more strong and more sure in faith; and then he "saw the day of *Christ*." Abraham believed in Christ; therefore he was justified through his faith. *Christ*, not the virtue of his own faith, was his comfort and hope. Notice, that to Paul it is one and the same thing which is reckoned for righteousness to Abraham and to us, namely that which God has promised, that is Christ. — We have nothing but sin, and are decaying in death; and when we consider this, it is *against* all hope to expect eternal life. Yet, even as through the word Abraham was enabled to believe, so Christ is with us in the word; and thus we also are able to believe. Is it not true that Christ died and rose again for us? Is it not he who has given us the gospel, and baptism, and the Lord's supper? Is not he himself present in these means of grace as the Savior who died and rose again for us? And is not *the promise of God* more to be trusted than are your eyes; blind as they are in matters divine? Give glory to God, then; let him be true. "Against hope believe in hope"; and you shall be strengthened in your faith, and have the assurance beyond a doubt that he is able to do that which he has promised. How foolish is unbelief after all! Shall not God *be able* to perform what he has promised? Was *he* not able to give us his Son? Shall he not, then, be true to his promise, and through him make us righteous? Have compassion, merciful God, and create true faith in our hearts. Amen.

Dear dying Lamb, thy precious blood Shall never lose its power, Till all the ransomed church of God Be saved, to sin no more.

E'er since, by faith, I saw the stream Thy flowing wounds supply, Redeeming love has been my theme, And shall be till I die.

---

413. Tuesday after Twenty-first Sunday after Trinity.

Strengthen our faith, O God, and establish it firmly in thy word. Amen.

Matthew 16, 1–4. The Pharisees also with the Sadducees came, and tempting, desired him that he would shew them a sign from heaven. He answered and said unto them, When it is evening, ye say, It will be fair weather; for the sky is red. And in the morning, It will be foul weather to-day; for the sky is red and lowering. O ye hypocrites! ye can discern the face of the sky; but can ye not discern the signs of the times? A wicked and adulterous generation seeketh after a sign; and there shall no sign be given unto it, but the sign of the prophet Jonas. And he left them, and departed.

The Jews and their leaders certainly had seen all the signs necessary. With their own eyes they had seen Jesus heal the lame, the blind, the dumb, and the maimed; as is related in the chapter immediately preceding our text. However, unbelief is true to itself; they *would* not obey the truth, and therefore they could not believe. The Pharisees "desired that he would shew them a sign from heaven." Our modern infidelity says: "Those miracles are too old; give us fresh ones, and we will believe." Why, then, did not the Pharisees believe? They admitted of Jesus that "this man doeth many miracles" (John 11, 47); yet they did not believe. If the infidels of our day were permitted, like those of old, to see miracles before their very eyes, they would be as unbelieving as ever, and demand other signs. There was no want then, there is none now, of that which is necessary to faith. How could they explain the fact that all the scripture prophecies concerning the Messiah were fulfilled to the letter in Jesus? The explanation was easy to them: *"We will not* have this man to rule over us; hence he is a blasphemer; away with him!"* Nevertheless, they knew not that hereby was fulfilled the prophecy of Jonas. — There is no lack of signs at the *present* time. We have such evidences as the historical authenticity of the Bible, and hence the truth of all its miracles. Then there is the church of Christ itself, whose existence would be impossible, were not Christ risen from the dead. There is the Jewish people; and the apostacy of our times, by which infidelity fulfills the prophecies of the word of God, as did the Jews when they crucified Christ. And how does the world contrive to evade the power of the truth? By the same means as formerly: "That which we *wish* to be true is true. We are wise; we are many. Away with Jesus; crucify him!"

There was and there is a church of God notwithstanding; and there always *shall be* a church of God which *believes* the gospel and sees the signs. By means of these our faith is strengthened; and our heart lives in the scripture, which is fulfilled on us, as it was on the Lord himself. Blessed is he, whosoever shall not be offended in his cross! — Lord, thou dost still shew the world's wicked generation the sign of the prophet Jonas. Thou dost permit thy church, and thus thyself, to be cast out, and the waters to overwhelm thee; but dost rise again, and dost with thy preaching of repentance force the great and the small to do penance in sackcloth and ashes. Lord, teach us to understand the times, and to escape perdition in the day of thy judgments. Amen.

Among thy saints let me be found, Whene'er the archangel's trump shall sound, To see thy smiling face; Then loudest of the crowd I'll sing, While heaven's resounding mansions ring The riches of thy grace.

414. Wednesday after Twenty-first Sunday after Trinity.

Merciful Holy Spirit, enlighten us with thy gifts. Amen.

Hebrews 11, 1–6. Now faith is the substance of things hoped for, the evidence of things not seen. For by it the elders obtained a good report. Through faith we understand that the worlds were framed by the word of God, so that things which are seen were not made of things which do appear. By faith Abel offered unto God a more excellent sacrifice than Cain, by which he obtained witness that he was righteous, God testifying of his gifts: and by it he, being dead, yet speaketh. By faith Enoch was translated that he should not see death; and was not found, because God had translated him: for before his translation he had this testimony, that he pleased God. But without faith it is impossible to please him: for he that cometh to God must believe that he is, and that he is a rewarder of them that diligently seek him.

To the natural man the things of eternity are as incomprehensible as they are real. Their plane is higher than any which reason and the senses can reach. Here is God himself with eternal life in the means of grace committed to the keeping of his church; but in the eyes of unbelief there is nothing. The blind walk in the light; and yet to them there is no such thing as light. *Faith* alone discerns the things of heaven. Faith is, however, itself a miracle wrought by the Spirit of God; it can not spring forth out of the human understanding, nor can any man give it to another. *None but the Spirit of God can create it;* though he, to be sure does it through the instrumentality of the word and sacraments, administered by men. — As the things which faith discerns are of heaven, and as it is of heavenly origin, so faith itself is a thing of heavenly and divine nature. And as these heavenly things which are grasped by faith are true and real, nay the very essence of truth and reality, the living and everlasting; so faith also is not an imaginary something, but a real and living truth in the soul. It is not dependent on human wisdom, which is shifting and elusive; nor on human power and strength, which wither like the grass; nor on human virtue, which is nothing but imperfection; — no, faith has its origin in God's own word, and is immovably established on this rock, in the eternal truth, righteousness, and love of God; and like the life itself it is the irrefutable proof of its own truth. Faith is hid in the heart; but it manifests itself in the conduct of the Christians, and is the root of all divine science and of all truth and holiness on earth. Take faith out of the hearts, and you have taken away all the true theology and all true piety. Faith is not seeing and feeling, but the act of the heart in clinging with childlike confidence to the promise of God in the gospel. Use the word; ask the Spirit to illumine you; and walk uprightly before the Lord according to the measure of light given you. Then he shall strengthen your faith, and give you victory, as he did to them of old time. This shall never fail. — "Yet a little while, and he that shall come will come, and shall not tarry. Now the just shall live by faith; but if any man draw back, my soul shall have no pleasure in him. But we are not of them who draw back unto perdition; but of them that believe to the saving of the soul." — Grant us this mercy, O God, give us faith, and increase it from day to day. Amen.

O then, impute, impart To me thy righteousness, And let me taste how good thou art, How full of truth and grace: That thou canst here forgive Grant me to testify, And justified by faith to live, And in that faith to die.

---

415. Thursday after Twenty-first Sunday after Trinity

Lord Jesus, help us to believe; that we may see thy glory. Amen.

Mark 9, 17–27. And one of the multitude answered and said, Master, I have brought unto thee my son, which hath a dumb spirit: and wheresoever he taketh him, he teareth him; and he foameth, and gnasheth with his teeth, and pineth away; and I spake to thy disciples, that they should cast him out; and they could not. He answereth him, and saith, O faithless generation! how long shall I be with you? how long shall I suffer you? Bring him unto me. And they brought him unto him: and when he saw him, straightway the spirit tare him; and he fell on the ground, and wallowed foaming. And he asked his father, How long is it ago since this came unto him? And he said, Of a child: and ofttimes it hath cast him into the fire, and into the waters, to destroy him: but if thou canst do anything, have compassion on us, and help us. Jesus said unto him, If thou canst believe, all things are possible to him that believeth. And straightway the father of the child cried out, and said with tears, Lord, I believe; help thou mine unbelief. When Jesus saw that the people came running together, he rebuked the foul spirit, saying unto him, Thou dumb and deaf spirit, I charge thee, come out of him, and enter no more into him. And the spirit cried, and rent him sore, and came out of him: and he was as one dead; insomuch that many said, He is dead. But Jesus took him by the hand, and lifted him up; and he arose.

In this scripture lesson there are especially two thoughts which stand out in strong relief: 1) Jesus, and he only, is able to deliver from the sorest need. 2) He does not reject even the weakest faith. — We have a *strong* Savior, who is able to rebuke all devils, and deliver us from all spirits that vex us. There is no power of hell strong enough to resist him. This child in our text presents a striking picture of the lowest depths of human misery; and the heart of the father must have been torn into shreds by the cruel spirit. He would rather have seen his son a corpse than witness this horrible gnashing of teeth and these demoniacal features. Wretched parents, is there none can save you? No, none other; but Jesus *is able* to do all things. He charges the spirit to "come out of him, and enter no more into him"; and intimately as the spirit had entwined itself with every fiber of the child's soul and body, it is compelled to come out of him and spare his life. No man on earth has been so badly torn and maltreated by Satan, whether spiritually or bodily, that Jesus can not save him; and no misery is so great that Jesus can not change it into joy. If you be sore vexed by the devil, you still are so fortunate that Jesus is here and wishes to help you, — do but *believe!* As long as you refuse to call upon the Lord, and to believe that he is mighty to save, he can not manifest his power to you. Remember this, however: He *can* and *will* save you out of the *direst* need, if you will ask it of him with believing heart. Let your mind dwell on this thought; and he shall create prayer and faith in your troubled soul. There are thousands even now living who could tell you of his power to save. — If there be any who feels that his faith is altogether too weak, let him remember that for his special benefit the Spirit of God caused our Bible lesson to be written. Jesus must speak even of his apostles as a "faithless generation"; and they certainly were not likely to strengthen the man's faith. And the man himself; what does he say to Jesus? He says: "If thou canst do anything, have compassion on us, and help us." "If thou canst do anything"; — there is in the man very little faith. But he is honest, and sensible of his weakness; therefore he cries out, and says with tears: "Lord, I believe; help thou mine unbelief." To our merciful Lord Jesus this faith is sufficient; and he crowns it in glorious fashion. — As no power is so great that Jesus can not cope with it, even so there is no faith so weak that he will not accept it, if we do but seek him with uprightness. Where can be found the man who sought of him assistance against sin and the devil, and did not receive it?

Lord, we heartily thank thee for that thou dost not break the bruised reed, and dost not quench the smoking flax. O that we might be found to be upright, and that thou mightest sustain and strengthen our weak faith. This we humbly beseech of thee, merciful Lord Jesus. Amen.

If thou impart thyself to me, No other good I need: If thou, the Son, shalt make me free, I shall be free indeed.

From sin, the guilt, the power, the pain, Thou wilt redeem my soul: Lord, I believe, and not in vain; My faith shall make me whole.

416. Friday after Twenty-first Sunday after Trinity.

Lord, give us truth in the heart, and the full assurance of faith. Amen.

Hebrews 10, 19–25. Having therefore, brethren, boldness to enter into the holiest by the blood of Jesus, by a new and living way, which he hath consecrated for us, through the veil, that is to say, his flesh; and having an high priest over the house of God; let us draw near with a true heart, in full assurance of faith, having our hearts sprinkled from an evil conscience, and our bodies washed with pure water. Let us hold fast the profession of our faith without wavering; (for he is faithful that promised;) and let us consider one another, to provoke unto love and to good works: not forsaking the assembling of ourselves together, as the manner of some is; but exhorting one another: and so much the more as ye see the day approaching.

The veil barred the way to the holy of holies in the tabernacle; our flesh, that is our corrupted human nature, barred our way to heaven. But Christ was made flesh, yet without sin, and thus with his blood entered the presence of God for us; thereby "consecrating for us a new and living way." Himself by his death becomes our way to eternal life (John 14, 6). Having "put on Christ," and having been consecrated as priests (Exodus 29), and having had the soul sprinkled and cleansed with the blood of Jesus by the washing of the body with the pure, or holy, water of baptism, we have "boldness to enter into the holiest," and are able to speak to God without fear concerning everything which we have at heart. "By one offering Christ hath *perfected* for ever them that are sanctified." He has entirely taken away all our guilt, and overcome the sin in us; so that we have perfect righteousness, and the power of perfect holiness. And now "he ever liveth to make intercession for us." — Let us, then, come before God with a *"true heart"*; with a heart wholly *honest*; with one which does not *wish to keep and conceal anything*; but to reveal everything, and be cleansed *from all sin.* And "let us draw nigh *in full assurance of faith,"* not doubting that the blood of Jesus is counted payment *in full* of every debt, and assured that God is glad to see and hear us. This "boldness to enter into the holiest," this courage to speak freely in the presence of God, this "true heart" and this purity, and this "full assurance of faith" in a good conscience: —

how glorious and how precious are these things! *Thus*, then, let us walk in the new and living way! *Thus* let us confess our hope; *thus* let us be united in love! These three things our Bible lesson teaches us. Help us, O God, to do them, for Jesus' sake. Amen.

His Spirit in me dwelleth, And o'er my mind he reigns. All sorrow he dispelleth And soothes away all pains. He crowns his work with blessing, And helpeth me to cry "My Father" without ceasing, To him who dwells on high.

417. Saturday after Twenty-first Sunday after Trinity.

Psalm 57. To the chief Musician, Al-taschith, Michtam of David, when he fled from Saul in the cave. Be merciful unto me, O God, be merciful unto me: for my soul trusteth in thee: yea, in the shadows of thy wings will I make my refuge, until these calamities be overpast. I will cry unto God Most High; unto God that performeth all things for me. He shall send from heaven, and save me from the reproach of him that would swallow me up. Selah. God will send forth his mercy and his truth. My soul is among lions; and I lie even among them that are set on fire, even the sons of men, whose teeth are spears and arrows, and their tongue a sharp sword. Be thou exalted, O God, above the heavens; let thy glory be above all the earth. They have prepared a net for my steps; my soul is bowed down: they have digged a pit before me, into the midst whereof they are fallen themselves. Selah. My heart is fixed, O God, my heart is fixed; I will sing and give praise. Awake up, my glory; awake psaltery and harp; I myself will awake early. I will praise thee, O Lord, among the people; I will sing unto thee among the nations. For thy mercy is great unto the heavens, and thy truth unto the clouds. Be thou exalted, O God, above the heavens: let thy glory be above all the earth.

It was "in the cave" that David sang this "Michtam," this golden song. "My soul," he says, "is among lions; and I lie even among them that are set on fire, even the sons of men, whose teeth are spears and arrows, and their tongue a sharp sword. They have prepared a net for my steps; my soul is bowed down; they have digged a pit before me." In this dark cave he nevertheless tunes his harp, and is awake early, not to make complaint, but to offer praise. With his rejoicing he ushers in the morning; he sings praises to God before the rising of the sun. In the very jaws of his voracious enemies he lifts up his voice in song, that it may be heard among all nations; and the sound of it still fills the world. The secret of his exultation appears at the opening and the closing of the psalm: "Be merciful unto me, O God, be merciful unto me!" "For thy mercy is great unto the heavens, and thy truth unto the clouds." Here, again, two things are especially to be noted: 1) He puts his trust in *mercy*; and thus his own unworthiness does not stand in his way. No matter how great a sinner he may be, he can confidently expect the Lord to save him. 2) His hope is *in God alone*. God is the Most High; and his power is as much greater than that of all his enemies, as heaven is high above the earth. God has begun to help him; this much he has experienced repeatedly; and God does nothing by halves; he "performeth all things for me." As the mercy of God is great, so is his truth also. He does not permit deceit and wickedness to swallow up the innocent; but keeps his promise, and delivers all who in hope walk honestly before him.

The fact that David under these desperate circumstances was able to sing such a song of praise without a single note of complaint, shows clearly, that while afflictions *may* depress, and good fortune *may* lift up the soul, yet these things do *not constitute* our unhappiness and our joy. May we also learn this golden song, the secret of being able to praise and exalt God even in the dark cave! If you can not be merry, you shall at least receive grace to be stout-hearted, contented, and grateful. "Rejoice in the Lord alway," says Paul. This is God's will. May he to this end give us the grace of his Holy Spirit, for Jesus' sake. Amen.

Beset with snares on every hand, In life's uncertain path I stand: Savior divine! diffuse thy light, To guide my doubtful footsteps right. If thou, my Jesus, still be nigh, Cheerful I live, and joyful die: Secure, when mortal comforts flee, To find ten thousand worlds in thee.

---

418. Twenty-second Sunday after Trinity. I.

Have mercy upon me, O God, according to thy lovingkindness; according unto the multitude of thy tender mercies blot out my transgressions. Amen.

Gospel Lesson, Matthew 18, 23–35. Therefore is the kingdom of heaven likened unto a certain king, which would take account of his servants. And when he had begun to reckon, one was brought unto him, which owed him ten thousand talents: but forasmuch as he had not to pay, his lord commanded him to be sold, and his wife, and children, and all that he had, and payment to be made. The servant therefore fell down, and worshiped him, saying, Lord, have patience with me, and I will pay thee all. Then the lord of that servant was moved with compassion, and loosed him, and forgave him the debt. But the same servant went out, and found one of his fellowservants which owed him an hundred pence; and he laid hands on him, and took him by the throat, saying, Pay me that thou owest. And his fellowservant fell down at his feet, and besought him, saying, Have patience with me, and I will pay thee all. And he would not; but went and cast him into prison, till he should pay the debt. So when his fellowservants saw what was done, they were very sorry, and came and told unto their lord all that was done. Then his lord, after that he had called him, said unto him, O thou wicked servant, I forgave thee all that debt, because thou desiredst me: shouldest not thou also have had compassion on thy fellowservant, even as I had pity on thee? And his lord was wroth, and delivered him to the tormentors, till he should pay all that was due unto him. So likewise shall my heavenly Father do also unto you, if ye from your hearts forgive not every one his brother their trespasses.

God forgives every penitent sinner even his greatest debt; but they only who are willing to forgive others can receive and keep the grace of God.

By the *ten thousand* talents is meant our whole great debt to God by reason of our sins. When you have counted to 10 you return to the figure 1 and repeat the series of units; 10 is the symbol of completeness. Now ten thousand is 10 times 10 times 10 times 10; and a talent is equivalent to nearly 1,000 dollars. Ten thousand talents is therefore mightily significant of the enormity of our debt. This is one of the lessons taught by our Lord Jesus; but do we recognize its truth? When he adds that the servant "had not to pay," he shows us that we have absolutely nothing of value with which to put in an appearance before God. You owe ten thousand talents; but you have nothing whatever with which to make payment. This is the true state of the case. — Now, justice *demands* that payment be made. For yourself, you shall receive the punishment which you have deserved, and your "wife and children" likewise. The servant, however, humbles himself; and the Lord's mercy appears. If you acknowledge that God *in justice* should and could condemn you; nay that he *must* do it, if payment of your debt be not made; and if your heart sues for mercy; — then he is moved with compassion, and forgives you the whole debt. — The servant declares that he "will *pay* all." The doctrine is sometimes preached that he who is to receive mercy must have made himself entirely free from self-righteousness, nor have even a thought of himself paying any part of his debt. If this were true, it would be all but impossible for any sinner to enter the state of grace; but Jesus does not teach this disheartening doctrine. To be sure, the Spirit in the faithful "counts all things but dung, that they may win Christ"; but self-righteousness is still extant, and ever stands in the way of a perfectly fearless faith. For it is not our humility, but our self-righteousness which makes our *faith* weak. When the sinner refuses to admit his guilt, it is his self-righteousness which shuts him out from the grace of God; for then he does not plead for mercy. When, on the other hand, you admit the debt, and acknowledge that God's judgment is just, he forgives you everything, even though you still wish to make payment. Is not this distinctly taught in our gospel lesson? Even so David also declares, Psalm 32, 5: "I acknowledged my sin unto thee; and thou forgavest me the iniquity of my sin." In like manner John: "If we confess our sins, he is faithful and just to forgive us our sins" (1 John 1, 9). At the same time the Holy Ghost also teaches us, and ever more clearly, to know that forgiveness of sins is wholly *grace* on the part of God; so that we thus may leave behind us the Old Testament with its "patience" and "forbearance" of sin, and enter fully into the perfect "forgiveness" of the New Testament, a forgiveness which has its deep and living root in *the righteousness of Christ*. Give heed, now, to that which Christ here speaks to you: If you with upright heart confess your debt, all your sins are forgiven you; no matter how far you still may fall short of clearly discerning the true nature of justification.

See to it, now, that *you forgive your fellow servant!* If you do not, you again fall under the judgment of God's wrath. In the spirit of meekness you must help your neighbor onward to a knowledge of sin. *He* can not enjoy the consolation of forgiveness without making *confession*; but do not *you* be angry, nor wish for revenge on him. No matter who he is, or what he has done to you, it is your duty to forgive him with all your heart; so that you may be able to bless him, pray for him, feel the sorrow which love inspires for his unhappy condition, and the hope that he may repent; in order that he and you may be united in heaven. If your debtor pray to you to have patience with him, shall not you, whom so much has been forgiven, gladly forgive the little debt to yourself? What are an hundred pence as compared with ten thousand talents? — Truly, there must be a black pit of iniquity in us, since Jesus presents this servant to us as a glass in which we are to see ourselves reflected. And it must be a matter of supreme importance to forgive our debtors, since he has taught us to say it every time we pray the Lord's prayer. When one who has an unforgiving spirit prays the fifth petition of this prayer, he invites God's judgment upon himself; he refuses to forgive, and he prays God to deal with him in the same manner. The kingdom of Christ is the kingdom of forgiveness; in which mercy sits on the throne, and stretches out its scepter over all the people. The grace in the blood of Jesus, God's eternal love in Christ for us lost sinners, is the sun that gives light and heat to the whole city of Zion. He whose heart can not submit to this law, and who will not breathe this atmosphere, can not have his home in this kingdom.

Teach us, O God, to know our sin with heart-felt contrition; and forgive us all our trespasses, for Jesus' sake. Teach us also to believe thy mercy in Christ; and give us kind and gentle hearts, that we may gladly forgive one another as in thy sight. Yea, grant that in truth we may "from our hearts forgive every one his brother their trespasses." Amen.

Lord, we confess our numerous faults, How great our guilt has been: Foolish and vain were all our thoughts, And all our lives were sin.
'Tis not by works of righteousness Which our own hands have done; But we are saved by sovereign grace Abounding through his Son.

---

419. Twenty-second Sunday after Trinity. II.

The God of all grace make us perfect, stablish, strengthen, settle us. Amen.

Epistle Lesson, Philippians 1, 6–11. Being confident of this very thing, that he which hath begun a good work in you, will perform it until the day of Jesus Christ: even as it is meet for me to think this of you all, because I have you in my heart; inasmuch as both in my bonds, and in the defence and confirmation of the gospel, ye all are partakers of my grace. For God is my record, how greatly I long after you all in the bowels of Jesus Christ. And this I pray, that your love may abound yet more and more in knowledge and in all judgment; that ye may approve things that are excellent; that ye may be sincere and without offence till the day of Christ; being filled with the fruits of righteousness, which are by Jesus Christ, unto the glory and praise of God.

There is danger, dear Christian, — we will not hide it, — that you may fall; fall from grace, and away from God. You have not as yet reached the end of your journey; there may be many a dangerous piece of road yet before you. Bileam and Saul and Solomon and Demas, as well as the servant in the day's gospel lesson, are presented as examples for our warning, in order that none may feel secure and cease to watch and pray. On the other hand, there is a confidence and trust of the spirit in God, a firm feeling of assurance that he will keep us unto the end; and this assurance, or certainty, we will encourage in one another. That which Paul says on this subject here and elsewhere God wants us to hear and keep in our hearts. Paul declares that he is *"confident* of this very thing, *that he which hath begun* a good work in you *will perform it* until the day of Jesus Christ." Can you think that *God* would begin a thing, and only half finish it? Now, it is *God* who has begun the good work in you; and "he which stablisheth us with you in Christ, and hath anointed us, is *God*; who hath also sealed us, and given us the earnest of the Spirit in our hearts" (2 Cor. 1, 21. 22). We "are kept by the power of *God* through faith unto salvation ready to be revealed in the last time" (1 Peter 1, 5). *God* shall keep us in the fellowship with himself, and ever shed abroad his love in our hearts. This fountain is always full; its waters never cease to flow through the holy Christian church; and the Lord ever creates thirst after it in our souls. By this means we shall grow; and our love abound yet more and more, become ever more rich, full, strong, and prove itself in the practical affairs of life, "in knowledge and in all judgment," that we may shun every appearance of evil, "be sincere and without offence, and filled with the fruits of righteousness," *filled* with them so entirely that there may be room for nothing else. And these fruits "are *by Jesus Christ*"; not by you or me, but by "the Amen, the faithful and true witness," the eternal God. "It is for me," says the apostle, "to think this of you *all*"; not of some of you, but of you *all*. For I love you so well that "ye are in my heart to die and live with you"; but this is *Christ* in me, his love and mercy; and who shall be able to separate you from this love? — The plain purpose of the Holy Ghost in all this is to create in our soul full confidence in the power of the grace of God to sustain and keep us. He who acknowledges that himself can do nothing, but who trusts in God alone, and relies on the power of his grace, fully assured that he will perform the good work which he has begun; such an one is able to obey the admonition of the apostle in this same epistle: "Work out your own salvation with fear and trembling; for it is *God* which worketh in you both to *will* and to *do* of his good pleasure." *God* does not cease to work in you; *God* awakens in your soul the desire to pray and struggle; *God* gives you ever new strength unto holiness and every good work; *God* gives you continually the spirit of fear and of confidence. Therefore none may say: "I know not, if I can endure to the end." Rather let each declare: *"I am confident* of this very thing, that *he* which hath begun a good work in me *will perform* it until the day of Jesus Christ." Thus we "resist the devil stedfast in the faith"; and thus we fight. We do not sleep, but watch and *fight* in "the power of the Lord's might." — Lord, help us herein. Keep us, O God, that we fall not from thee; hold us fast to thee, thou strong God. Give us grace to say with thy apostle: "I know whom I have believed, and am persuaded that he is able to keep that which I have committed unto him against that day." Teach us more and more to know our own weakness, and to trust in thee, our God, alone. Give us the spirit of wisdom and revelation in the knowledge of thee. Work in us the fruits of righteousness; and let us be filled with them until the day of Christ, unto the eternal praise of thy name. Amen.

In vain would boasting reason find The path to happiness and God; Her weak directions leave the mind Bewildered in a doubtful road.

Jesus, thy words alone impart Eternal life; on these I live; Here sweeter comforts cheer my heart, Than all the powers of nature give.

420. All-Saints Day. I.

Speak, Lord; and give us grace to hear. Amen.

Gospel Lesson, Matthew 5, 1-12. And seeing the multitudes, he went up into a mountain: and when he was set, his disciples came unto him: and he opened his mouth, and taught them, saying, Blessed are the poor in spirit: for their's is the kingdom of heaven. Blessed are they that mourn: for they shall be comforted. Blessed are the meek: for they shall inherit the earth. Blessed are they which do hunger and thirst after righteousness: for they shall be filled. Blessed are the merciful: for they shall obtain mercy. Blessed are the pure in heart: for they shall see God. Blessed are the peacemakers: for they shall be called the children of God. Blessed are they which are persecuted for righteousness's sake: for their's is the kingdom of heaven. Blessed are ye, when men shall revile you, and persecute you, and shall say all manner of evil against you falsely, for my sake. Rejoice, and be exceeding glad: for great is your reward in heaven: for so persecuted they the prophets which were before you.

Here we are told *who are blessed*, and *what* it is to be blessed. "The poor in spirit"; these are the humble souls. They have nothing with which to stand before God, nothing of their own with which to make themselves blessed; they have neither *righteousness* nor *love*. "They that mourn"; these are the souls which have "that godly sorrow"; which grieve because they have sinned against God. "The meek" are they who for the sake of God suffer wrong without being provoked to anger. "They which do hunger and thirst after righteousness" are they who of their innermost heart, and with a longing which will not be stifled, desire to be able to stand before the righteous God. Hunger and thirst are the most imperative of the natural desires. So ardently do the saints desire righteousness; so heartily do they hate all wrong. "The merciful" are they who feel the distress of others as their own, and relieve it. "The pure in heart" brook no unchastity, anger, falsehood, nor any other wicked lust, in their hearts, but strive to be holy, as God is. "The peacemakers" are:

they who promote peace, gather the souls to the Lord, guide them in the way of peace, and unite them in one spirit. The peace-makers *gather*; the destroyers of peace scatter. Nevertheless, the saints must suffer persecution, slander, and all manner of evil in the world. — Yet they are *blessed*. They *are* blessed already, and they shall *be* blessed and saved *eternally*. They are "poor"; yet in Christ they possess all the treasures of the kingdom of heaven; righteousness and love, peace and joy. They "mourn"; yet they are happy, and shall have eternal comfort; "God shall wipe away all tears from their eyes." They are robbed and wronged in the world; but none can take their treasure from them. They shall inherit all things; for in Christ all things are theirs. Their hunger and thirst after righteousness shall be satisfied with the grace of Jesus; in him they are perfect before God, and shall at last be delivered from all sin, of whatever kind, in and about them. In the mean time they are entirely surounded by the mercy of God, in which they live and breathe night and day. They also understand more and more of the glory of God; and they shall *"see God" as he is*, which is the fulness of bliss. They are "the children of God," and are so called; they are like God, and wear the title of honor "sons and daughters" before all angels; and the kingdom of heaven with all its glory is theirs for evermore. — Rejoice, and be exceeding glad in all your afflictions; "great is your reward in heaven" for that which you now suffer; — a reward not by reason of any merit on your part, but by the grace of God. "For those who weep And those who sleep Beneath the portals narrow, The mansions rise Beyond the skies; We're going home tomorrow."

Lord Jesus, teach me thy way, and keep me from the path of the hypocrite. Let righteousness and truth lead me; for I believe in thee. Holy God, who art enthroned for ever; who dost dwell on high, and art nigh unto them that are of a broken heart and a contrite spirit! make me humble, and quicken my spirit and my heart. Let me be known of thee as one of thy saints on earth, that I may stand in the midst of the saved in heaven. Amen.

How happy is the man who hears Instruction's warning voice, And who celestial wisdom makes His early, only choice! For she has treasures greater far Than east or west unfold; And her rewards more precious are Than all their stores of gold.

---

421. All-Saints Day. II.

Lord, make our hope sure and living. Amen.

Scripture Lesson, Revelation 7, 1–12. And after these things I saw four angels standing on the four corners of the earth, holding the four winds of the earth, that the wind should not blow on the earth, nor on the sea, nor on any tree. And I saw another angel ascending from the east, having the seal of the living God: and he cried with a loud voice to the four angels, to whom it was given to hurt the earth and the sea, saying, Hurt not the earth, neither the sea, nor the trees, till we have sealed the servants of our God in their foreheads. And I heard the number of them which were sealed: and there were sealed an hundred and forty and four thousand of all the tribes of the children of Israel. Of the tribe of Juda were sealed twelve thousand. Of the tribe of Reuben were sealed twelve thousand. Of the tribe of Gad were sealed twelve thousand. Of the tribe of Aser were sealed twelve thousand. Of the tribe of Nepthalim were sealed twelve thousand. Of the tribe of Manasses were sealed twelve thousand. Of the tribe of Simeon were sealed twelve thousand. Of the tribe of Levi were sealed twelve thousand. Of the tribe of Issachar were sealed twelve thousand. Of the tribe of Zabulon were sealed twelve thousand. Of the tribe of Joseph were sealed twelve thousand. Of the tribe of Benjamin were sealed twelve thousand. After this I beheld, and, lo, a great multitude, which no man could number, of all nations, and kindreds, and people, and tongues, stood before the throne, and before the Lamb, clothed with white robes, and palms in their hands; and cried with a loud voice, saying, Salvation to our God which sitteth upon the throne, and unto the Lamb. And all the angels stood round about the throne, and about the elders and the four beasts, and fell before the throne on their faces, and worshiped God, saying, Amen: Blessing, and glory, and wisdom, and thanksgiving, and honor, and power, and might, be unto our God for ever and ever. Amen.

By these hundred and forty and four thousand is meant the entire church militant. That they are sealed in their foreheads signifies that God knows each one of them, makes them his peculiar care, and brings them out of all their tribulations. The righteous shall not be destroyed with the wicked; the angels of the Lord lead Lot out of Sodom, and the Christians out of Jerusalem before the destruction. The saints are the salt of the earth. As long as they dwell among the wicked, country and people will be preserved; but when the measure of sin is full, and the Lord takes his children away, destruction must follow. He who believes in Jesus has the seal of the living God in his forehead; the angels know this seal, and the devils are compelled to get out of its way. This is *one* of the things with which our text comforts the people of God in their afflictions. — The *other* is the sight of that great multitude which has already reached the home in heaven. It is a multitude gathered together out of all peoples of all generations, of all the twelve tribes, and all nations of gentiles who are become Israelites. And all are perfectly holy, cleansed from all sin in the blood of the Lamb; wholly righteous; without spot or blemish. All are victors, and carry the palms of eternal peace; they *were* in the midst of trials and struggles, but "came out of their great tribulation." With a loud voice all were singing praises to God and the Lamb. "They are before the throne of God, and serve him day and night in his temple; and he that sitteth on the throne shall dwell among them. They shall hunger no more, neither thirst any more; neither shall the sun light on them, nor any heat. For the Lamb which is in the midst of the throne shall feed them, and shall lead them unto living fountains of waters; and God shall wipe away all tears from their eyes." — How glorious a comfort is not this to the soul struggling against sin and poverty and care! Look; your home is over there! All these who stand before the throne and the Lamb, clothed with white robes, and palms in their hands, were even as you are; fought the same fight, and often thought, as you do, that they must be vanquished. Not many days ago they were weak and sinful, worn and weary, tempted and troubled; and now they are sinless and perfect, happy and blessed, exalted and glorious. Then they walked in gloom; now they dwell in the light. Then they were far away from the lover of their souls; now they are at home with him. Then they sighed and groaned; now they sing with gladness for evermore. You also are sealed unto this salvation; your place in heaven has been prepared for you from eternity, and is now awaiting you. If you believe in the Lord Jesus, and your righteousness be his blood, wherewith you wash yourself; then of a certainty you belong to the great white multitude, and shall receive grace of the Lord to assume your rank among the just men made perfect. — After the death of Melanchton there was found on his writing table a sheet of paper on which was written: "You shall enter the light; you shall see the Son of God; you shall learn those wonderful mysteries which in this life you have not been able to understand; such as the questions why we are created thus, how the two natures in Christ are united, and the like." And on the same sheet, to the left, was written: "You shall be wholly free from all sin, all labor, and all strife."

Lord Jesus, turn our eyes toward the glory of heaven; grant us grace to strive lawfully, and gain victory. Know us as being of thine own, and help us to confess thee fearlessly in the face of hate on the part of the devil and the world. Sanctify us wholly; and let us with truth be called the children of light, to the glory of thy name. Let our whole life bear witness that thy people are in truth a holy people. Amen.

O what array, O what the glorious host Comes sweeping swiftly down?
The chosen ones, on earth who wrought the most, The Church's brightest crown, Our Lord hath sent to meet me, — As in the far off years Their words oft came to greet me In yonder land of tears.

---

422. Monday after Twenty-second Sunday after Trinity.

Let me know thy holiness, O God, that I may see my sin, and fear thy judgment. Amen.

Job 15, 14–16. What is man, that he should be clean? and he which is born of a woman, that he should be righteous? Behold, he putteth no trust in his saints; yea, the heavens are not clean in his sight: How much more abominable and filthy is man, which drinketh iniquity like water?

We might say that according to this text man is as unholy as God is holy. However it would not be exactly correct; for nothing can properly be compared with the holiness of God. "The heavens are not clean in his sight." The glory of his countenance eclipses the purest sunlight. — Now, since God is so exceeding holy, what shall be our fate when we appear before him? How shall he which is born of a woman be righteous; a man abominable and filthy, which drinketh iniquity like water? And how can our Pelagians contrive to explain away this text? "Do learn to know the nature of Adam's offence and of original sin; that your depravity is greater than you can say or understand. Learn to know yourself; to know what you are become as a result of the fall; that from being the image of God you are become the image of Satan, with all his wickedness and malignity. For as the image of God means all the holiness of God, purity, end every virtue; and as man before the fall was wholly of heaven, spiritual, and pure as an angel; so man's inner nature is now become wholly of the earth, carnal, and brutish. In his anger and cruelty man has something of the nature of the lion; in malice and greed he is wolfish; in filth and gluttony he resembles the swine. If you will carefully examine yourself, you shall find in you a whole world of unclean beasts; and even in the one little member, the tongue, you shall find a nest of vipers and wicked spirits, 'a world of iniquity.'" (Joh. Arndt). This is the teaching of the Bible; almost literally what Paul writes in Romans 3, 10–18; it is truth unto salvation. How comes it, then, that only few men will listen to it, and that a still smaller number recognize the accuracy of this description of themselves? The trouble is that our conception of God is a faded picture. Come before the thrice holy and terrible God, in whose presence the seraphims cover their faces, saying, "Holy, holy, holy, is the Lord of hosts." Know *him* from whom you can not escape; who in his holy zeal spared not even his only Son, who had taken upon himself our sins, but gave him the full cup of wrath to drink, though he wept, and prayed that it be taken from him. Know our God, who is a consuming fire. Do this; and you shall cease to dream of your own piety, and you shall see your uncleanness and unrighteousness. Your disease is incurable; yet there is One says: "I am the Lord that healeth thee."

My God, I am shapen in iniquity, and in sin did my mother conceive me; and thus my heart is evil from my childhood. Have mercy on me, for Jesus' sake; forgive me, and heal me, that I may live and praise thee. Amen.

In vain we seek for peace with God By methods of our own: Jesus, there's nothing but thy blood Can bring us near the throne.
'Tis thy atoning sacrifice Hath answered all demands; And peace and pardon from the skies Are blessings from thy hands.

---

423. Tuesday after Twenty-second Sunday after Trinity.

O God, be merciful to us; increase our faith, and give us the true brotherly spirit. Amen.

Matthew 18, 15–22. Moreover, if thy brother shall trespass against thee, go and tell him his fault between thee and him alone: if he shall hear thee, thou hast gained thy brother. But if he will not hear thee, then take with thee one or two more, that in the mouth of two or three witnesses every word may be established. And if he shall neglect to hear them, tell it unto the church: but if he neglect to hear the church, let him be unto thee as an heathen man and a publican. Verily I say unto you, Whatsoever ye shall bind on earth, shall be bound in heaven, and whatsoever ye shall loose on earth, shall be loosed in heaven. Again I say unto you, That if two of you shall agree on earth as touching any thing that they shall ask, it shall be done for them of my Father which is in heaven. For where two or three are gathered together in my name, there am I in the midst of them. Then came Peter to him, and said, Lord, how oft shall my brother sin against me, and I forgive him? till seven times? Jesus saith unto him, I say not unto thee, Until seven times; but, Until seventy times seven.

This lesson shows with clearness that Christ *is in his disciples,* and that his church on earth is one with his church in heaven; exclusion from one is exclusion from the other. He who does not repent and receive mercy, and live in the fellowship of the Lord and his saints on earth, has no part in the bliss of heaven. — In the next place our text wonderfully strengthens our faith in the efficacy of *united prayer.* If the Spirit move two of us to go before our heavenly Father with the same petition, we never fail to receive that which we ask. Let Christian fathers and mothers bear this in mind, and pray together for their children; and the children for their parents. Likewise when two or more persons are of the same profession; or neighbors; or, in short, Christians having a common interest; when they have the same thing at heart; let them speak of it with one another, and agree as touching any thing that they shall ask, and lay before the Father this promise given by the Son.

Above all things, however, our text teaches us: Firstly, that we are to care for one another; and, secondly, that we must never tire of forgiving them that sin against us. When your brother sins against you, it is your duty to deliver him from the snare of the devil. It is not enough that you bear the wrong with meekness; you must do what in you lies to restore him to the right path. If you think of yourself only, and let the other go his own way, you say with Cain: "Am I my brother's keeper?" and you act in a spirit directly contrary to that of Jesus, who in love reproved even Judas and Pilate with a view to their good. Let it be your heart's desire to gain your brother; induce others to join you in praying for him. These two things belong together. — And you shall forgive your brother, *no matter how often* he may have sinned against you. As the heart of God is an *ever* living well which flows forgiveness for his children, even so shall your heart be toward the brethren. These words of Christ about forgiving "not seven times, but seventy times seven," how strikingly expressive of the truth that the kingdom of Christ is a kingdom of *sinners,* and rich in *mercy!* You need your brother's forgiveness as often as he needs yours; and how much more often do not both of you, then, need the forgiveness of God! Where, now, may we sinners come into possession of the necessary charity? We must beseech the Lord to increase our faith. Lead us, O Lord, into a thorough understanding of thy infinite mercy. Amen.

One there is above all others, Well deserves the name of friend. His is
love beyond a brother's, Costly, free, and knows no end. They who once his
kindness prove, Find it everlasting love.
O for grace our hearts to soften! Teach us, Lord, at length to love. We,
alas! forget too often What a friend we have above: But when home our
souls are brought, We will love thee as we ought.

---

424. Wednesday after Twenty-second Sunday after Trinity.

Psalm 7, 11–17. God judgeth the righteous, and God is angry with the
wicked every day. If he turn not, he will whet his sword, he hath bent his
bow, and made it ready. He hath also prepared for him the instruments of
death; he ordaineth his arrows against the persecutors. Behold, he travaileth
with iniquity, and hath conceived mischief, and brought forth falsehood. He
made a pit, and digged it, and is fallen into the ditch which he made. His
mischief shall return upon his own head, and his violent dealing shall come
down upon his own pate. I will praise the Lord according to his righteousness; and will sing praise to the name of the Lord most high.

Justice to all without respect of persons is the highest virtue of
a judge. Now, the highest perfection of justice is found in God
None can be compared with him in the strict justice with which he
rewards every man according to his works. This truth does not con-
tradict that other truth, which we learn everywhere, that the kingdom
of God is a kingdom of *grace*, in which forgiveness rules, and saves
sinners deserving of death. For he who truly knows his sin is covered by the merit of Christ, and is as righteous as is Christ himself.
It was the good pleasure, and therefore the righteous decree of God's
will, that Christ was to stand in the place of all, and that he who
believes and is baptized shall be one with him; thus making our sin
the sin of Christ, and the obedience of Christ our obedience. Now,
as the justice of God is absolute, the only begotten Son must needs
suffer in full the punishment which the world has deserved; there was
no abatement whatever. Neither shall even the smallest part of the
debt be forgiven, but payment *in full* be demanded of every one who
is not in Christ. The just punishment of all his sins shall be visited
on him. Often the retribution begins here, in order that the sinner
may be awakened to penitence; but if he continue in sin, a terrible
sentence of wrath shall be executed on him in the world to come.
The sword of God is whetted, his bow is bent; he has ordained his
arrows against the persecutors, and none can escape. No matter how
cunning the wicked may be, God shall find him, and visit just punishment upon him. Patience may spare him for a long time; but justice
is close at hand, and appears on the scene at last with its shining
shield and sharp sword. Do not doubt that a day is coming when
all things shall be revealed, and when everyone, without respect of
persons, shall receive according to that which he has done. The
justice of God is as exalted and sure, as are his omnipotence and love;
and equally with these it underlies everything which he has done
from everlasting.

Thou art he who trieth the heart and reins, righteous God. My defence is of God, which saveth the upright in heart. I will praise the Lord according to his righteousness; and will sing praise to the name of the Lord most high. Amen.

When the judge his seat attaineth, And each hidden deed arraigneth, Nothing unavenged remaineth.

What shall I, frail man, be pleading? Who for me be interceding, When the just are mercy needing?

King of majesty tremendous, Who dost free salvation send us, Fount of pity, then befriend us!

---

425. Thursday after Twenty-second Sunday after Trinity.

Give us, O Lord, thy spirit of wisdom and love.

James 3, 13–18. Who is a wise man and endued with knowledge among you? let him shew out of a good conversation his works with meekness of wisdom. But if ye have bitter envying and strife in your hearts, glory not; and lie not against the truth. This wisdom descendeth not from above, but is earthly, sensual, devilish. For where envying and strife is, there is confusion and every evil work. But the wisdom that is from above is first pure, then peaceable, gentle, and easy to be entreated, full of mercy and good fruits, without partiality, and without hypocrisy. And the fruit of righteousness is sown in peace of them that make peace.

Since the very essence of the devil is pride, we all are by nature vain, puffed up, wise in our own conceit, and self-willed; none has been born meek and lowly. Some are, however, even above others wise in their own eyes. When they are carried away by a spiritual revival, it is *possible*, to be sure, that the Spirit of God may humble them, and his discipline keep them humble; but they will, as a rule, sooner or later display their wisdom in such a way as to cause dissensions among the brethren. They imagine that they see more clearly than others the defects of society; they feel called upon to make "improvements" in the church; and their wisdom begets "envying and strife," a continual tossing to and fro, "confusion and every evil work." Such people are not "easy to be intreated"; they know it all. They pretend that in setting themselves apart and forming coteries of their own they are only following the example of our Lord Jesus; of Paul, and Luther, and other holy men. If they knew the living spirit of fellowship which characterized the Lord himself and his holy followers, and could feel the bitterness of *their* pain *in being cast out*, they would not charge them with having founded new sects. The separatists under consideration have so tender a conscience forsooth, that they can not endure the imperfections of society! Did they but in the love of Christ take upon their conscience the sins of their people, they would find something to do besides cultivating bitter roots which produce confusion. "Glory not, and lie not against the truth." This is not "the wisdom that is from above"; for the wisdom from above is "first pure," having no admixture of the devil's spirit of pride; "then peaceable," gathering and uniting them that are the

Lord's in the bond of peace. Furthermore, it is "gentle," kind and charitable toward all. It is "easy to be intreated"; ready to hear what others have to say, obedient to the truth, and willing to accept correction. It is "full of mercy and good fruits"; mark you, *full of mercy* and good fruits, "without partiality, and without hypocrisy," just, earnest, and upright. He that has this wisdom makes peace, and shall reap blessed fruit in this world and in the next. — Help us, O God, that none of us may hold himself aloof from thy grace. Let no bitter root grow up and yield confusion, defiling many. Give us the wisdom that is from above, and let us shew out of a good conversation our works with meekness of wisdom. Amen.

May he our actions deign to bless, And loose the bonds of wickedness, From sudden falls our feet defend, And guide us safely to the end.
May faith, deep-rooted in the soul, The flesh subdue, the mind control: May guile depart, and discord cease, And all within be joy and peace.

---

426. Friday after Twenty-second Sunday after Trinity.

Lord, let the word which thou wilt now speak to us strengthen our faith. Amen.

Isaiah 42, 1–4. Behold my servant, whom I uphold, mine elect, in whom my soul delighteth; I have put my spirit upon him; he shall bring forth judgment to the gentiles. He shall not cry, nor lift up, nor cause his voice to be heard in the street. A bruised reed shall he not break, and the smoking flax shall he not quench: he shall bring forth judgment unto truth. He shall not fail nor be discouraged, till he have set judgment in the earth: and the isles shall wait for his law.

The spirit in the kingdom of our Lord Jesus Christ is mighty and victorious mercy. Himself has taken upon his own shoulders our sins, and made our cause his own, and made himself answerable for us against all accusers; and thus we have to do with him only. And he deals with us like the merciful Savior that he is, and continues his efforts until he has healed us, and completed the work of saving us. He shall save all who accept the gospel invitation, of all peoples on the face of the earth, no matter how sorry the plight into which the devil may have brought them. Even if our faith be most deplorably weak, yet will he not reject us. "A bruised reed shall he not break, and the smoking flax shall he not quench." Thus we read in our text; and it is thus that we find him always. We all have many a time felt thus bruised and weak, and have disclosed our troubles to him, and received comfort and help. He is become the servant of the Lord, and was anointed to this very end, with meekness to help the afflicted. How carefully does he not take us in his hand; how indulgently does he not deal with us; how patiently does he not continue his efforts, even though the long course of treatment seem to effect no improvement in us! The bruised reed should become whole and vigorous. The faith in our heart should be strong and fearless; but alas, it is fragile and weak, and would fall to pieces at once, did not the hand of *him* who is meekness itself sustain us. The smoking flax

36

should be ablaze; it should shoot its flames as high as heaven in the pure atmosphere of grace; but it smokes and smokes, and is on the point of being quenched; yet he continues to add oil and keep the spark alive, that it might burn brightly at the last. He shall not cease his efforts, until the victory has been for ever won. — In thus saving us individually he preserves and perfects his kingdom. "He shall not fail nor be discouraged, till he have set judgment in the earth; and the isles shall wait for his law."

Ye servants of the Lord, do ye also bring forth judgment to the afflicted! Israel is one with their Lord; and to them, as to him, it is said: "I have called thee in righteousness, and will hold thine hand, and will keep thee, and will give thee for a covenant of the people, for a light of the gentiles; to open the blind eyes, to bring out the prisoners from the prison, and them that sit in darkness out of the prison house. I, the Lord, he that created the heavens, and stretched them out; he that spread forth the earth, and that which cometh out of it; he that giveth breath unto the people upon it, and spirit to them that walk therein. I the Lord thy God have spoken it." If it seem to you that your labor is in vain, remember that the Lord makes the earth to bring forth fruit, and will make darkness light before you.

Lord, we praise thee; we bless thy glorious name, and pray thee for grace to believe in thee, serve thee, and give thee honor for evermore. Amen.

Hail to the Lord's anointed, Great David's greater Son! Hail, in the time appointed, His reign on earth begun! He comes to break oppression, To set the captive free, To take away transgression, And rule in equity.

---

427. Saturday after Twenty-second Sunday after Trinity.

Psalm 86, 11-17. Teach me thy way, O Lord; I will walk in thy truth: unite my heart to fear thy name. I will praise thee, O Lord my God, with all my heart; and I will glorify thy name for evermore. For great is thy mercy toward me; and thou hast delivered my soul from the lowest hell. O God, the proud are risen against me, and the assemblies of violent men have sought after my soul, and have not set thee before them. But thou, O Lord, art a God full of compassion, and gracious; longsuffering, and plenteous in mercy and truth. O turn unto me, and have mercy upon me: give thy strength unto thy servant, and save the son of thine handmaid. Shew me a token for good; that they which hate me may see it, and be ashamed; because thou, Lord, hast holpen me, and comforted me.

The Lord had delivered the soul of David from death, by saving him from the hand of Saul, and from danger of his life at the time of Absalom's revolt. However, when we sing this verse, "Thy mercy is great toward me; and thou hast delivered my soul from the lowest hell"; we think of our salvation from spiritual death, and of the blessed gift of our new life in God. He who has thus learned the Lord's "way" has received a "heart *united* to fear his name": an upright heart which is wholly on the Lord's side, and struggles against all sin; — yet he prays that he may receive such a heart through an ever new revelation of the grace of God.

An *undivided* heart surrenders itself with *entire confidence* to the Lord. It regards only his word, and trusts only to his promise. It is as unmoved when sin and Satan rage against it, as when they hold their peace; it is of good cheer when threatened by distress and death, no less than when the outlook is most bright. It rests wholly in the mercy and truth of its almighty God. An *undivided* heart hates all sin with a perfect hate, and loves God with a perfect love. They whose heart is thus undivided have but one desire, which expresses itself in all that they think and say and do; one sun, which shines in the soul, and which they reflect; one life, whose beat is felt everywhere. There never is for one moment any corner of the heart in which the love of God does not live. Such a heart *"united* to fear his name" praises the Lord alway. It returns thanks not only for its joys, but for its sorrows as well; and nothing is able to silence it. "I will praise thee, O Lord my God; and I will glorify thy name for evermore." *To fear the Lord* with a whole heart is above all to praise and thank him. The divided heart complains; the undivided, praises.

If you have an upright heart, and walk in the light, you now feel, and will continue to feel while you live, how sadly deficient your heart is in singleness of purpose. You feel it to be divided, but it is "united"; you feel it to be sick, but it has been made whole. Everything in you *is* new; you believe in the Lord, love him, and praise him for all things. Yet you still suffer from the old things, and must accuse yourself of unbelief, of the lusts of the flesh, and of ingratitude. Pray with all the saints for a *perfect* heart; and in a blessed hour you shall receive it.

Bow down thine ear, O Lord, hear me; for I am poor and needy. Preserve my soul; for I am holy; O thou my God, save thy servant that trusteth in thee. Teach me thy way, O Lord, I will walk in thy truth; unite my heart to fear thy name. Amen.

Teach me, O teach me, Lord, thy way; That, to my life's remotest day, By thine unerring precepts led, My feet thy heavenly paths may tread. Informed by thee, with sacred awe My heart shall meditate thy law; And, with celestial wisdom filled, To thee its full obedience yield.

428. Twenty-third Sunday after Trinity. I.

Lord, give us the fear of God, and make us obedient. Amen.

Gospel Lesson, Matthew 22, 15–22. Then went the Pharisees, and took counsel how they might entangle him in his talk. And they sent out unto him their disciples, with the Herodians, saying, Master, we know that thou art true, and teachest the way of God in truth, neither carest thou for any man; for thou regardest not the person of men. Tell us therefore, What thinkest thou? Is it lawful to give tribute unto Cæsar, or not? But Jesus perceived their wickedness, and said, Why tempt ye me, ye hypocrites? Shew me the tribute money. And they brought unto him a penny. And he saith unto them, Whose is this image and superscription? They say unto him, Cæsar's. Then saith he unto them, Render therefore unto Cæsar the things which are Cæsar's, and unto God the things that are God's. When they had heard these words, they marvelled, and left him, and went their way.

Lucifer was dissatisfied, revolted, and became a devil. Korah, Dathan, and Abiram could not endure the supremacy of Moses and Aaron, but indulged in a tirade about the holiness of all the people, revolted, and went to perdition. In the days of David Israel had honor, riches, and good fortune; but they listened willingly to the voice of Absalom, became dissatisfied, revolted, and were torn up by internal dissensions. During the reign of Solomon they murmured against him; and after his death the ten tribes rebelled against their rightful ruler. He who is the rebel from the beginning, who hates obedience and subjection, seduced them, and created discontent in their hearts; so, when they refused willing obedience, they were forced to render the obedience of slaves. — At the time of Christ the Jewish people were subject to the Romans. When the multitude, on Palm Sunday, supposed that his purpose was to liberate them from Cæsar, they did homage to him; but because he is the king of true liberty, and demands self-denial, they cried out five days later, saying: "Crucify him; crucify him!" Shortly after this they revolted against the Romans, and were destroyed.

The lesson which *history* for our warning teaches us in a manner not to be mistaken is taught by the rest of the word of God also in distinct terms. Today we hear Jesus say: "Render unto Cæsar the things which are Cæsar's; and unto God the things that are God's." The Lord puts these two duties together. Rendering unto Cæsar the things that are his does not militate against, but is a consequence of rendering unto God the things that are God's. He only who gives God his own can give Cæsar that which is his. Bow in humility and the fear of God before the high and mighty Lord of heaven; give him the full confidence and love of your hearts; commit yourselves in faith and obedience into his hand; — and then render unto the government which he has placed over you reverence, obedience, and tribute. Obedience to the government as a result of obedience to God, this is the teaching of Christ. Willing submission to every ordinance of man, in that truly royal liberty which no power can put down, is one of the glories of the disciples of Jesus. Disobedience to the authorities, springing out of disobedience to God, is the spirit of Satan. Pride, and lust of power, and discontent; and, with it all, boasting about one's spirit of liberty, and the promise of ease; — these things are the curse of Absalom and of others who serve the flesh. That which Jesus teaches in our gospel lesson of today he declares also in his reply to Pilate: "Thou couldest have no power at all against me, except it *were given thee from above.*" The same truth he taught Paul also by revelation: "Let every soul be subject unto the higher powers!" Every man is in duty bound to obey the constituted authorities. "For there is no power but of God; the powers that be are ordained of God." The apostle could not have spoken with greater clearness. "There is no power but of God." If we believe the word of God, we know who it is has given us our government. "The powers that be are ordained of God. Whosoever therefore resisteth the power, resisteth the ordinance of God; and they that resist shall receive to themselves damnation. . . . For the power is the minister of God to thee for good. . . . Therefore we must needs be subject, not only for wrath but also for conscience sake." Thus wrote Paul; and we know that the government under which he lived was heathen, unrighteous, and cruel. To Titus and to all ministers of the word he wrote: "Put the faithful in mind to be subject to principalities and powers, to obey magistrates, to be ready to every good work." Now, to be "subject" to them means of our hearts to reverence and honor them as having authority over us in God's stead. And this is the teaching of all the apostles. Abstain from fleshly lusts, says Peter, and "submit yourselves to every ordinance of man for the Lord's sake; whether it be to the king, as supreme; or unto governors, as unto them that are sent by him for the punishment of evildoers, and for the praise of them that do well." This is directly contrary to the desire kindled by the devil in the carnal man; directly contrary to the spirit which now, in a higher degree than ever before, holds sway in the children of unbelief. When modern liberty dawned in France toward the close of the eighteenth century, the people deposed the government and Christ at the same time. The Christian doctrine that the powers that be are of God, and are to be honored and obeyed as the servant of God, and for God's sake, can by no possibility be reconciled with the assertion that there is no government but of the people, and that the people themselves are the supreme power. There is no reason why magistrates may not be chosen by the peole; but the Christian religion demands, that while they hold their office, they are to be esteemed and honored and obeyed as servants of *God*, placed in their positions by the Lord, and exersicing authority for him and under him.

False liberty, being slavery, has discontent as its companion; and being an untruth, it begets strife and calamity. Through the revolt of Korah and of Absalom the Jews destroyed themselves by the thousands; and in the destruction of Jerusalem they suffered as much from the internal dissensions as from the sword of the enemy. Disobedience means bitterness and self-destruction. On the other hand, subjection for the Lord's sake, being true liberty, gives joy and peace; being truth, it brings good fortune to the people. There is One has said: "Honor thy father and thy mother, *that it may be well with thee*, and thou mayest live long on the earth!" The expression "father and mother," however, includes all who have authority over us. The spirit of Christ is love; and love gathers, builds up, and strengthens. Even if the spirit of unbridled license had no evil result other than envy and bitterness in the minds of men, and conflicts between the classes into which society is divided, it would be more than bad enough; but contempt for the authorities brings upon us the judgment of God. — Be on your guard, then, Christian friends, and beware of the spirit of false liberty! This spirit is alluring; the beautiful word *liberty* is on its tongue always; it is wonderfully skilled in mixing together truth and falsehood; it clothes itself beautifully in the garment of light. I know a sure means of escape: "Bless the Lord alway, and forget not all his benefits" (Psalm 103). Then shall you become humble, and happy, and make peace, and impress on the young the wise man's words of gold, Proverbs 24, 21: "My son, fear thou the Lord and the king; and meddle not with them that are given to change."

Lord, teach us to know our unworthiness of thy many and great benefits. Give us humility and a submissive spirit; and preserve us from the evil spirit of self-will and bitterness. Give us true liberty in the heart, that we may gladly honor and obey those in authority over us, and cheerfully render to them the tribute imposed on us. Bless all whom thou hast placed in positions of authority over us. Give them wisdom, righteousness, and strength; and prosper their work, that the people may be benefited. We thank thee, O God, for this great mercy, that thou hast so long blessed us with the glorious benefits of liberty and peace. Drive away, we heartily beseech thee, the evil spirit of discord which threatens us; and grant that we may yet a long time lead a quiet and peaceable life in all godliness and honesty. Accept our thanks, and hear our prayer, for Jesus' sake. Amen.

God bless our native land! Firm may she ever stand, Though storm and night; When the wild tempests rave, Ruler of wind and wave, Do thou our country save By thy great might.

For her our prayer shall rise To God above the skies; On him we wait: Thou who art ever nigh, Guarding with watchful eye, To thee aloud we cry, God save the state!

---

429. Twenty-third Sunday after Trinity. II.

Lord, let us find the hidden treasure, sell all that we have, and buy it. Amen.

Epistle Lesson, Philippians 3, 17—21. Brethren, be followers together of me, and mark them which walk so as ye have us for an example. (For many walk, of whom I have told you often, and now tell you even weeping, that they are the enemies of the cross of Christ; whose end is destruction, whose God is their belly, and whose glory is in their shame, who mind earthly things.) For our conversation is in heaven; from whence also we look for the Savior, the Lord Jesus Christ; who shall change our vile body, that it may be fashioned like unto his glorious body, according to the working whereby he is able even to subdue all things unto himself.

These unhappy persons of whom the apostle can not speak without weeping, "the enemies of the cross of Christ, whose end is destruction," are none other than they who "mind earthly things." This statement is one of utmost gravity. Is it, then, so dangerous a matter to "mind earthly things"? Yes; so the word of the Lord says. If the earthly things be your treasure, your heart's best and dearest possession; your "God is your belly," you are an enemy of the cross oi Christ, and your way leads to destruction. Terrible thought! To be an enemy of the cross of the precious Savior! His blood, which brings salvation, you will have none of it; in your innermost heart there is aversion to a Savior who dies on the cross, and by this means reconciles us with God. And you are reluctant to bear affliction with him; you will not deny yourself, nor walk in his steps through poverty and suffering. Earthly riches, power, and honor are to you better than his love, and of greater value than the benefits of his death and resurrection. Let every one examine himself! We might possibly be these of whom the apostle speaks; for they are "many". The apostle says that they are many; and so says Jesus also: They are many who walk in the broad way to destruction.

As the people on the crowded streets of a great city divide into two currents setting in opposite directions, so do members of the whole human family. The children of the world hurry onward in their chase after the earthly things, and end in perdition; the people of God walk the way of the cross of Christ, and reach heaven.

Brethren, do not let the children of the world by their number and strength turn you back into the jaws of death. Let neither friendship nor enmity, neither threats nor promises, neither the craft of the Pharisees nor the shouts of the rabble crying "Hosanna," and then, "crucify him"; neither the spirit of license nor the spirit of sloth, lead you astray, and cause you to turn your eyes away from heaven. The path is narrow; but do you stay always in the company of the disciples, and walk in the steps of Jesus; follow him in obedience and self-denial, and you shall reach the blessed end of your journey. Our portion is not the fleeting good things of this world; "our conversation is in heaven." Upward, then; and homeward, in the company of all the saints! "He that findeth his life shall lose it; and he that loseth his life for my sake shall find it."

Lord Jesus, teach us to know the grace and the power of thy cross; give us the desire to follow in the steps of thy suffering; and grant that we may be faithful therein unto the end. Amen.

Teach me, O Lord, my days to number, And when this life I shall depart, Let me commend my soul to Jesus, And die with a repentant heart. O God, when tolls my parting knell, For Jesus' sake may all be well!

---

430. Monday after Twenty-third Sunday after Trinity.

Give us, O God, the true wisdom. Amen.

Proverbs 8, 10–17. Receive my instruction, and not silver; and knowledge rather than choice gold. For wisdom is better than rubies; and all the things that may be desired are not to be compared to it. I wisdom dwell with prudence, and find out knowledge of witty inventions. The fear of the Lord is to hate evil: pride, and arrogancy, and the evil way, and the froward mouth, do I hate. Counsel is mine, and sound wisdom: I am understanding; I have strength. By me kings reign, and princes decree justice. By me princes rule, and nobles, even all the judges of the earth. I love them that love me; and those that seek me early shall find me.

Should we not love wisdom, and follow it? Saint James says: "If any of you lack wisdom, let him ask of God, that giveth to all men liberally, and upbraideth not; and it shall be given him." A glorious promise! Yes; we will "seek wisdom as silver, and search for her as for hid treasures." "She is more precious than rubies; and all the things thou canst desire are not to be compared unto her. Length of days is in her right hand; and in her left hand riches and honor. Her ways are ways of pleasantness, and all her paths are peace. She is a tree of life to them that lay hold upon her; and happy is every one that retaineth her." — If you wish to honor God and benefit man; if you wish to walk honestly in the light of day; if you wish to be blessed, and to be a blessing to others; you must seek wisdom of the Lord. These four things you will find helpful: 1) Consider how sorely you stand in need of wisdom, if you are to do your whole duty as a father, a mother, a magistrate, an employer, a servant, or, in short, in any position in which God has placed you. Woe to them that walk blindly! Woe to the fool, who gropes in darkness, and does not know what he is doing! Bear in mind also that the natural man can not see the ways of the Lord. 2) *Pray* earnestly, persistently, and in faith; cling to the promise of God, and hold it up before him. "The Lord giveth wisdom; out of his mouth cometh knowledge and understanding." 3) Live according to your catechism; and obey the word of God in all things, as far as your knowledge goes. Take heed unto yourself, that you walk in the paths of the Lord's commandments. 4) Study the word with diligence, and keep it in your heart; ponder it, and do not forget it; make it a point, as far as possible, never to let a day pass on which you do not add a new passage to your store of Bible knowledge. — Observe these rules, neglecting none of them; so shall godliness and heavenly wisdom fill your soul. For you become "poor in spirit"; — and "are in Christ Jesus, who of God is made unto us wisdom, and righteousness, and sanctification, and redemption." (1 Cor. 1, 30).

Help us, O God, to incline our ears unto wisdom, and to apply our hearts to understanding; that we may understand the fear of God, and find the knowledge of God. Amen.

Almighty God, in humble prayer To thee our souls we lift: Do thou our waiting minds prepare For thy most needful gift.

We ask for wisdom: — Lord, impart The knowledge how to live; A wise and understanding heart To all before thee give.

The young remember thee in youth, Before the evil day! The old be guided by thy truth In wisdom's pleasant way!

431. Tuesday after Twenty-third Sunday after Trinity.

Lord, let thy word chasten us, and let it teach us obedience to thee. Amen.

Romans 13, 1–7. Let every soul be subject unto the higher powers. For there is no power but of God: the powers that be are ordained of God. Whosoever therefore resisteth the power, resisteth the ordinance of God: and they that resist shall receive to themselves damnation. For rulers are not a terror to good works, but to the evil. Wilt thou then not be afraid of the power? do that which is good, and thou shalt have praise of the same: for he is the minister of God to thee for good. But if thou do that which is evil, be afraid; for he beareth not the sword in vain: for he is the minister of God, a revenger to execute wrath upon him that doeth evil. Wherefore ye must needs be subject, not only for wrath, but also for conscience sake. For, for this cause pay ye tribute also: for they are God's ministers, attending continually upon this very thing. Render therefore to all their dues: tribute to whom tribute is due; custom to whom custom; fear to whom fear; honor to whom honor.

Paul writes this to the Christians in Rome, and teaches them that even such rulers as Tiberius and Nero are ordained of God. The first duty of government is *justice;* a good ruler punishes without partiality that which is evil, and wields the sword with strong arm for the defence of the oppressed, and for the execution of judgment on evildoers. And such a government is a great blessing; none of us fully understands how much gratitude we owe to God for good and just magistrates and other persons in authority. Unhappy is the people of whom it is said: "I will give children to be their princes, and women shall rule over them." All this does not, however, make void the truth that "the powers that be are ordained of God." If a people suffer under wicked rulers, it is the duty of Christians humbly to accept the correction which God administers; for every soul is to be "subject unto the higher powers," reverence them as God's ministers, whom the scripture for that reason also calls "gods," and be subject to them for God's sake. Our modern doctrine is that governments and magistrates are not the servants of God, but of the people, commissioned by the people to execute the will of the people. Let Christians beware lest they be deceived! Above the people is a higher Power, to whom rulers and subjects are answerable. Let our human authorities never forget that their power is of God; let them always remember this, in order that they may serve *God* with a good conscience, and let us never forget that those in authority over us are ordained of God. Let us bear this clearly in mind; so that we are subject for conscience sake!

Willingly we then render *tribute* and *custom* to whom they are due. All things of God and for God. We show all respect to those in authority over us; taking a course widely different from that followed by the ungodly men who "despise dominion, and speak evil of dignities." Subjection for God's sake and respectful behavior are the exact opposite of that servility which is the brother of impudence, both being the children of deceit. When authority commands we cheerfully obey; we bear wrong, but do not perpetrate it; — for we "obey God rather than men."

Lord, help us to be subject to every ordinance of man for thy sake. Give us the true spirit of liberty and of obedience. Amen.

Some trust in horses trained for war, And some of chariots make their boasts; Our surest expectations are From thee, the Lord of heavenly hosts. Now save us, Lord, from slavish fear; Now let our hope be firm and strong, Till thy salvation shall appear, And joy and triumph raise the song.

432. Wednesday after Twenty-third Sunday after Trinity.

Lord Jesus, let thy Spirit rule among us in all things. Amen.

Matthew 17, 24-27. And when they were come to Capernaum, they that received tribute money came to Peter, and said, Doth not your master pay tribute? He saith, Yes. And when he was come into the house, Jesus prevented him, saying, What thinkest thou, Simon? of whom do the kings of the earth take custom or tribute? of their own children, or of strangers? Peter saith unto him, Of strangers. Jesus saith unto him, Then are the children free. Notwithstanding, lest we should offend them, go thou to the sea, and cast an hook, and take up the fish that first cometh up; and when thou hast opened his mouth, thou shalt find a piece of money; that take, and give unto them, for me and thee.

As Jesus is the Son of God it was no more his duty to pay *tribute* to the temple, which belongs to his Father, than it is the duty of a royal prince on earth to pay tribute to the king. As Jesus by that which he here *says* bears witness of his divinity, so he proves his omnipotence and omniscience by his *deed*, in that he orders Peter to take the piece of money from the mouth of a fish. *He*, who is the only begotten Son of God, the Lord almighty, who had no need to pay tribute, *pays tribute* nevertheless. The love of Christ is the spirit of subjection and peace, which forms and strengthens social order; and this love he has given to his disciples. He not only is our perfect example, but he has made us his members; so that his spirit in us overcomes the flesh and the unruly spirit of the devil. Examine yourselves, you who wish to be more than Christians in name only; learn which is the spirit whom you follow; Christ's spirit of obedience, or the domineering spirit of the world; the love of Christ, which willingly bears the burdens of society, or the love of self, which is full of fault-finding and envy! Many boast of Christ and the liberty which is in him; but are so far away from the obedience of the lowly Savior and the free-born mind of the true Christians, that on the contrary they are the slaves of their own wilfulness, and are governed by a spirit of liberty which would bring about a condition of anarchy in the church, and destroy all social order.

If you would belong to my kingdom, says the Lord, you must deny yourself. If you would reign with me, you must put on my humility and obedience. If you would have the crown of glory over yonder, you must carry my cross here, and walk in my steps. —

Draw me, then, after thee, O Lord; and train me to follow in thy
steps. Give me grace to put on thy mind, and to follow thee faithfully. Let me be a good citizen of the state in which thou hast placed
me, and a living member of thy holy church on earth; and in heaven
a blessed member of the church triumphant, into which thou dost
gather all thy saints. Grant us this grace, most merciful God. Amen.

Give peace, Lord, in our time: Oh, let no foe draw nigh, Nor lawless deed
of crime Insult thy Majesty. O Lord, stretch forth thy mighty hand, And
guard and bless our fatherland.

---

433. Thursday after Twenty-third Sunday after Trinity.

Lord, let thy word chasten us and cause us to examine ourselves. Amen.

Titus 3, 1–7. Put them in mind to be subject to principalities and powers,
to obey magistrates, to be ready to every good work, to speak evil of no man,
to be no brawlers, but gentle, shewing all meekness unto all men. For we
ourselves also were sometimes foolish, disobedient, deceived, serving divers
lusts and pleasures, living in malice and envy, hateful, and hating one another.
But after that the kindness and love of God our Savior toward man appeared,
not by works of righteousness which we have done, but according to his
mercy he saved us, by washing of regeneration, and renewing of the Holy
Ghost; which he shed on us abundantly, through Jesus Christ our Savior;
that being justified by his grace, we should be made heirs according to the
hope of eternal life.

It is wonderful how often the apostles exhort the believers to
obey the civil authorities. This must, then, be a matter of vital
consequence, of the greatest importance for our salvation; and there
must be strong temptations for us men to be disobedient to those in .
authority over us. We should heed this well; for it has not been
written without good cause. If we allow free scope to our appetite
for power and our spirit of disobedience, we are not fit for *anything*
good, but fall into all the vices of heathenism. Note the words of
our text: Believers are to be "subject to principalities and powers,"
and "ready to every good work." These two things, subjection to
those in authority and readiness to every good work, belong together,
then; nay, they are one. Formerly, when we lived in heathenism,
our condition was a different one, says the apostle; for the heathen
spirit is foolish, disobedient, envious, and full of hate; directly contrary
to Christian subjection and obedience. Such we *were;* but now that
we have been regenerated and made partakers of God's mercy, we
have received a loving and meek spirit. Therefore we must now
prove ourselves wise, submissive, and obedient, to the glory of God.
In like manner Peter says: "Submit yourselves to every ordinance
of man for the Lord's sake; for so it is the will of God, that with
well doing ye may put to silence the ignorance of foolish men; as
free, but as the servants of God." Therefore, he that is submissive
and obedient to authority shows good sense, and has true liberty,
and does good; he understands the will of God, and obeys it. He,

on the other hand, who will not submit to authority is foolish and ignorant and wicked, knows not the meaning of liberty, and is a slave of the prince of darkness. — Christians, do not drift with the current; but prove that a new spirit dwells in you; prove that you are in truth the disciples of Jesus; prove the truth of the word of God, that submission to authority is a fruit of the new life created by the Spirit of God.

Lord, point out to us the royal path of humility, and give us strength to follow it. Teach us more and more to know that he whom the Son makes free is free indeed. Lord God, assist us against the evil spirit of wilfulness which threatens to take possession of the whole world. Have mercy, and save our people and our country, for Jesus' sake. Amen.

Lord God, we worship thee! For thou our land defendest; Thou pourest down thy grace, And strife and war thou endest.
Since golden peace, O Lord, Thou grantest us to see, Our land, with one accord, Lord God, give thanks to thee!

---

434. Friday after Twenty-third Sunday after Trinity.

Lord, give us the Spirit of grace and prayer, of humility and obedience. Amen.

1 Timothy 2, 1-7. I exhort therefore, that, first of all, supplications, prayers, intercessions, and giving of thanks, be made for all men; for kings, and for all that are in authority; that we may lead a quiet and peaceable life in all godliness and honesty. For this is good and acceptable in the sight of God our Savior; who will have all men to be saved, and to come unto the knowledge of the truth. For there is one God, and one mediator between God and men, the man Christ Jesus; who gave himself a ransom for all, to be testified in due time. Whereunto I am ordained a preacher, and an apostle, (I speak the truth in Christ, and lie not;) a teacher of the gentiles in faith and verity.

Paul here teaches us that, as our first and most important duty of all, we are to *pray for all men.* As one God embraces us all in his love, we are to love all, and pray for them with trust in God. Furthermore, as one mediator, the man Jesus Christ, the second Adam, whose kinsmen we all are, has gathered us in himself, and redeemed us all, we must feel ourselves a unit with all men, and thus pray for them. As Christ took upon himself the sin of all, so we are to take upon ourselves the cause of all; not to make atonement for them, as he did, but to make intercession for them. We shall make "supplication" that they may be saved. These our supplications we shall present as prayers; each for himself and for all together; and these prayers are intercessions, in which we lay before God the need of others, as if it were our own; even as did Abraham and Daniel, and above all our Lord Jesus. And in these prayers there is to be "giving of thanks"; in the first place, because all have been redeemed; and then, because we are permitted thus to take our troubles to the Lord in prayer; and finally, because faith does not doubt that our prayer will be answered. Such prayers and intercessions with giving of thanks are matters of the very highest concern.

Now, it is a striking circumstance that in the midst of his dissertation on the duty of making intercession for all men, that their *souls* may be saved, the apostle makes special mention of "kings and all that are in authority." "To be sure, the government of the state does not concern itself with the gospel, but with entirely different matters; and does not care for the souls, but for the bodies and bodily things;" and yet, the salvation of the souls is the ultimate purpose also of civic order in the world; and this is of great importance to the kingdom of God. For this reason Paul declares: We must pray for those in authority, that we may lead a quiet, godly, and honest life; for this is pleasing in the sight of God, who will have all men to be saved, and to come into the knowledge of the truth. He clearly establishes a relation of cause and effect between a peaceable civic government and a life in godliness, and again between these two things and the extension of God's kingdom. He who follows the disobedient spirit of the age goes directly against the ordinance of God; and thereby he also violates the love which he should have for the salvation of souls, and hinders the extension of the kingdom of God. Let all believers pray diligently for those who administer the affairs of the state; and let them bear the burdens with them in the sight of the Lord. It is a great blessing that God has joined us together in orderly society; and this would be true, even if we had a bad government. How much more, then, should we pray and give thanks for those in authority over us, when they are good and just!

We thank thee, Lord God, for thy wisdom and goodness toward us needy sinners. We thank thee for the government which thou hast given us; and we humbly ask thee to bless it, and preserve it, and strengthen it unto every good work. Give us grace, we pray thee, to lead a quiet and peaceable life in all godliness and honesty; a life acceptable in thy sight, and one which thou dost bless for the promotion of thy kingdom. Give us to this end thy Holy Spirit, for Jesus' sake. Amen.

Lord God, we worship thee! And pray thee, who hast blest us, That we may live in peace, And none henceforth molest us: O crown us with thy love; Fulfil our cry to thee: O Father, grant our prayer: Lord God, we worship thee!

---

435. Saturday after Twenty-third Sunday after Trinity.

Psalm 116, 10–19. I believed, therefore have I spoken: I was greatly afflicted. I said in my haste, All men are liars. What shall I render unto the Lord for all his benefits toward me? I will take the cup of salvation, and call upon the name of the Lord. I will pay my vows unto the Lord now in the presence of all his people. Precious in the sight of the Lord is the death of his saints. O Lord, truly I am thy servant; I am thy servant, and the son of thine handmaid: thou hast loosed my bonds. I will offer to thee the sacrifice of thanksgiving, and will call upon the name of the

Lord. I will pay my vows unto the Lord now in the presence of all his people, in the courts of the Lord's house, in the midst of thee, O Jerusalem. Praise ye the Lord.

We have a thousand things for which to thank the Lord; but forget to do it. In times of peace we fall into a sense of security; and in danger we are always prone to put our trust in human strength. Then it becomes necessary for the Lord to lead us into deep affliction, in order that we may *believe in him only, and bless his name.*

"I believed, therefore have I spoken," says the Psalmist. "The Lord led me into sore affliction; and thus I learned to trust in him. Of this my speech bare witness, in that I said: Every man is a liar, I and all others; none is to be trusted; but the Lord is my strength; he hath delivered my soul from death, mine eyes from tears, and my feet from falling." Note well his words, dear reader: "I believed, *therefore* have I spoken; I said in my haste, All men are liars." Here we are told that faith is born in agony, and that faith speaks; and we learn the remarkable truth that he who admits that "all men are liars" believes in God.

Now, when the Lord *chastens* me with affliction, *helps me to believe, and saves me,* what shall I render unto him in return for these benefits? "I will take the cup of salvation." I will accept his salvation, and let the Lord save me, as he desires; trust in him, and surrender myself to him. He has pleasure in mercy; I also will desire it. A good method of making payment, certainly. Furthermore, I will "call upon the name of the Lord." He is glad to have us call upon his name, and what more precious than to praise him? These are good terms which he has fixed for us. Finally, "I will pay my vows unto the Lord now in the presence of all his people." The "vows" of an Israelite usually consisted in thank-offerings; and in connection with them there always was a sacrificial feast with other godly men, who rejoiced with him over his deliverance. I will scatter about me the joy of salvation; feed the poor, bodily and spiritually; foregather with God's people; kindle their devotion, and be kindled by it. Truly, "I will pay my vows unto the Lord now in the presence of all his people, in the courts of the Lord's house, in the midst of thee, O Jerusalem. Praise ye the Lord!" Thus is ended the sorrow of the Lord's people.

Lord God, let me never more complain, and let me never put my trust in the power of man; but let me believe in thee, take the cup of salvation, call upon thy name, thank thee, and bless thee, and pay my vows unto thee. Truly, I am thy servant; I am thy servant, and the son of thine handmaid; thou hast loosed my bonds. Hallelujah!

Mighty God, while angels bless thee, May a mortal lisp thy name? Lord of men, as well as angels, Thou art every creature's theme.
Lord of every land and nation, Ancient of eternal days! Sounded through the wide creation Be thy just and lawful praise.

436. Twenty-fourth Sunday after Trinity. I.

Lord Jesus, awake us to believe in thee; and powerfully strengthen our faith. Amen.

Gospel Lesson, Matthew 9, 18–26. While he spake these things unto them, behold, there came a certain ruler, and worshiped him, saying, My daughter is even now dead: but come and lay thy hand upon her, and she shall live. And Jesus arose, and followed him, and so did his disciples. And, behold, a woman, which was diseased with an issue of blood twelve years, came behind him, and touched the hem of his garment: for she said within herself, If I may but touch his garment, I shall be whole. But Jesus turned him about; and when he saw her, he said, Daughter, be of good comfort; thy faith hath made thee whole. And the woman was made whole from that hour. And when Jesus came into the ruler's house, and saw the minstrels and the people making a noise, he said unto them, Give place; for the maid is not dead, but sleepeth. And they laughed him to scorn. But when the people were put forth, he went in, and took her by the hand, and the maid arose. And the fame hereof went abroad into all that land.

"The maid is not dead, but sleepeth." In these words the Lord declares his power to save from death. To our nature death is invincible, and to our eyes there is no deliverance from it. Every man whose thoughts are controlled by the laws of reason must surrender to death unconditionally, whether he be good or bad, wise or stupid. In every case he is helpless; he knows nothing, and has nothing, which can deliver him from death. To Jesus, however, death is a sleep; he is able with a word to awaken one who is dead, as one who sleeps. For he is Lord not only within the boundaries of created nature, but also *above* and *without*. He is able to do whatever he will, by supernatural as readily as by natural means. "Whatsoever the Lord pleased, that did he in heaven, and in earth, in the seas, and all deep places." Through faith only am I able to grasp this. My reason understands, to be sure, that God is infinitely great. When I consider that the sun is more than a million times as large as the earth, and yet is but as a grain of sand in the immensity of the universe which God has created; when I consider how he has marvelously formed me from the womb; I understand that God is great; but I also understand, — or possibly I do not, — that my thought can grasp but little or nothing of his greatness. Faith *alone* knows the glory of God, the power of God to create life from death.

In the gospels we always find our Lord Jesus in the midst of persons in affliction, who seek and receive help of him. Precious Savior, what a comfort this is for us; but do thou help me also to believe! This woman, "diseased with an issue of blood," the Spirit of God had made humble through her long affliction; and now he had also given her faith by means of the word. She was unclean and excluded from human society; but now she comes notwithstanding, because she believes that Jesus will make her whole. She well knows that no man could do it; but she believes that it is in the power of Jesus, and she is not disappointed. Let every one that is unclean, every sinner who is condemned by the law, and excluded from Israel, come to Jesus, and he shall save him. Jesus shall stop the issue of sin; its source shall be dried up; soul and body shall be cleansed and made whole. — The ruler of the synagogue in our text is another beautiful example of faith. When he had left home his daughter was at the point of death, and must, he thought, now be dead; yet he believes that Jesus is able to save her life. From his house comes the message that it is too late; but Jesus strengthens him, and he believes. Is his faith put to shame? Has *any* man who believed in the Lord been deceived? — "Yes," say you, "this is all very well, did I but have such a faith!" You are right. Remember, however, that he who will humble himself, and pray God to give him faith, shall surely receive it! It is a gift of God, and created by his Spirit; it is a light in the soul, of a nature entirely different from the light of reason; and the Spirit is here in the word, and wishes to enlighten you. Faith is sure of the unseen and incomprehensible; so that the heart chooses it, and surrenders to it. Faith trusts in the Lord's word, and builds on his promise without seeing. It knows that Jesus lives, and that he has given me his life; so that even though I die, yet I can not die. Because he died and rose again, and I am baptized into him, and partake of his body and blood; therefore my sin is no sin, — though in itself it is damnable, and gives me pain every day, — and my death is no death, no matter how much I may feel it to be death itself both in soul and body. The Lord holds me fast; and there is no power can separate me from him. — Has the faith of the saints, then, no infirmities, do you think? Alas, it has many such; but do you come here, and strengthen your weak faith by the sight of the omnipotence and grace of your Savior! The woman in our text was hardly without superstition; and though she is lovable in her fear and trembling, yet her faith wavered. Jairus was on the very point of sinking down into the gulf of dark unbelief; he had been lost, had not the Lord at the proper time spoken to him, saying: "Be not afraid, only believe!" Let neither your sin nor your distress, neither your unbelief nor your weakness, neither your hardness of heart nor your blindness, keep you away from our Lord Jesus; but rather let all these things impel you to come to him. No power of hell can prevent your coming. If you can do no more, cry out to him: "Lord, I believe, help thou mine unbelief!" Do this, and your help is come. — Lord, let thy Holy Spirit enlighten us with his gifts. Amen.

It is not death to die — To leave this weary road, And, 'midst the brotherhood on high, To be at home with God.

Jesus, thou prince of life, Thy chosen cannot die; Like thee, they conquer in the strife, To reign with thee on high.

---

437. Twenty-fourth Sunday after Trinity. II.

Give us, O God, the spirit of wisdom and revelation in the knowledge of thee. Amen.

Epistle Lesson, Colossians 1, 9–14. For this cause we also, since the day we heard it, do not cease to pray for you, and to desire that ye might be filled with the knowledge of his will, in all wisdom and spiritual understanding; that ye might walk worthy of the Lord unto all pleasing, being fruitful in every good work, and increasing in the knowledge of God; strengthened with all might, according to his glorious power, unto all patience and longsuffering with joyfulness; giving thanks unto the Father, which hath made us meet to be partakers of the inheritance of the saints in light: who hath delivered us from the power of darkness, and hath translated us into the kingdom of his dear Son; in whom we have redemption through his blood, even the forgiveness of sins.

You, faithful brethren, are delivered from the kingdom of darkness, from the power of the devil, and from the fellowship of his angels. The spirit of the power of the air, the spirit which is in the children of unbelief to darken their minds, and urge them on to all manner of wickedness, no longer dwells in you, nor has power in you. You have been translated into the kingdom of the Son of God; his blood has cleansed you; you have entered into heavenly places in Christ, and live in the society of the holy angels. For this you shall give thanks, and in it you shall rejoice. That which you now possess through faith, and enjoy in hope, you shall soon receive in glory; for the Father has made you meet to be partakers of the inheritance of the saints in light. This your fitness you shall prove by leading a godly life. You have made a beginning, and you should increase in godliness. The Spirit of God will give you all wisdom and understanding. He will give you an ever increasing knowledge of God, enabling you to see greater depths in the mystery of Christ; and he will give you more and more light and strength to walk in a way pleasing to the Lord. The more diligently you pray and use the word of God, the better shall you know the love of Christ, the stronger shall you be to serve him, and the more fruitful shall you be in every good work. When you are faithful herein, you receive all the time more light; the Spirit anoints your eyes, that you see the more clearly; and *fills* you with the knowledge of his will in all wisdom and spiritual understanding. Thus you are enabled to "walk worthy of the Lord;" think of it, "to walk worthy of the Lord unto all pleasing!" Not only are you yourselves beloved of the Father; but your *conduct* also shall be pleasing to the holy God; and not only pleasing, but *entirely* pleasing, you "being fruitful in every good work. You shall be *fruitful* in that which is good; and not only that, but "fruitful in every good work, strengthened with all might, according to his glorious power." Do hear and learn this, in order that you may not lose heart and strength for your sanctification: *His glorious power* strengthens you unto all patience and longsuffering; that you may easily persist, nor become weary

37

All who have tried it know how strong is the temptation to become negligent and to cease doing good, especially when the results are slow to appear. Patience is necessary, and longsuffering; persistence and unwearied courage, and a childlike mind toward God and all men. These you shall not lack, however; for the *Almighty*, who delivered you from hell and from all the power of the prince of death, shall strengthen you with all might, according to his glorious power, unto all patience and longsuffering with joyfulness. Blessed be his name! — Pray, then, for one another, and keep together under the standard of the cross! Ever more wise to know God, and to walk worthy of him; ever more holy and strong, more charitable and kind, more patient and happy! Give thanks to God, and bless him, and sing his praises always, until you stand before him, and see him face to face! — My God, I am, alas, as yet far, far away. But do thou, who didst give me an open ear, stretch out to me also thy strong hand and help me to lead a holy Christian life. Amen.

My God! permit me not to be A stranger to myself and thee: Amidst a thousand thoughts I rove, Forgetful of my highest love.
Call me away from flesh and sense; Thy sovereign word can draw me thence: I would obey the voice divine, And all inferior joys resign.

---

438. Monday after Twenty-fourth Sunday after Trinity.

Heavenly Father, draw us to thy Son, our Lord Jesus Christ. Amen.

John 6, 37-40. All that the Father giveth me shall come to me;. and him that cometh to me I will in no wise cast out. For I came down from heaven, not to do mine own will, but the will of him that sent me. And this is the Father's will which hath sent me, that of all which he hath given me I should lose nothing, but should raise it up again at the last day. And this is the will of him that sent me, that every one which seeth the Son, and believeth on him, may have everlasting life: and I will raise him up at the last day.

Every sinner who comes to Jesus, and abides with him in penitence and faith, is a gift from the Father to the Son. For "all that the Father giveth me shall come to me"; but "no man can come to me, except the Father which hath sent me draw him." Therefore no man is to brood on his election; if he wish to come to Jesus, this is because of the fact that the Father draws him; and it can not be that the Father would draw him without the earnest purpose of giving him to the Son. This declaration, "all that the Father giveth me shall come to me," is one exceedingly precious to sinners who seek mercy. And how many have not been comforted by that which follows: "Him that cometh to me I will in no wise cast out!" It has been the lifeline of thousands; it has drawn countless souls out of the waters of sin up into the city of God. It seemed to them that they must of necessity be cast out by reason of their many sins, their stubborn obstinacy, their hardness of heart, their faithlessness, their unbelief, and their love of self; in short; by reason of their thoroughly corrupt and wicked hearts; but he says: *Him that cometh* to me, no matter who or what he may be, I will *in no wise*, for no cause whatever, cast out; but will receive and save him. The invitation is so urgent that the poor heart could not resist it. Was any man, then, who comes to him cast out? Search the gospels from beginning tc end, and see if you can find a case in which a sinner sought Jesus, and was repulsed. Then make trial of it for yourself! Nor is it *possible* that the Lord could cast off any man who seeks him. The Father sent the Son into the world for the very purpose that he was to seek and save that which was lost; and can you then think it possible that the Son might cast off the miserable sinner whom the Father draws to him? No; the will of the Father is the will of the Son also, even to death on the cross for our sake. Our salvation is fixed and sure, thank God! And it is great and glorious likewise; for it is the will of the Father, that we may have everlasting life. We shall see the Son, and be raised up incorruptible in eternal glory. Death shall swallow us, certainly; but death is itself "swallowed up in victory," and thus it can do nothing but carry us into the kingdom of victory. — Dear heavenly Father, draw us to thy Son, and give us grace to believe the love with which thou dost love us; that we may overcome our unbelief, our sin, and our fear of death, and see light in the darkness. Lord, thou knowest how faint-hearted and unbelieving we are; have mercy on us, give us victory by thy word, give us a foretaste of the life everlasting, and give us perfect holiness on thy day of judgment. Amen.

Author of good! To thee we turn: Thine ever-wakeful eye Alone can all our wants discern, Thy hand alone supply. O let thy love within us dwell, Thy fear our footsteps guide! That love shall vainer love expel, That fear all fears beside.

439. Tuesday after Twenty-fourth Sunday after Trinity.

Lord Jesus, thou Son of the living God, let me hear thy voice. Amen.

John 5, 25–29. Verily, verily, I say unto you, The hour is coming, and now is, when the dead shall hear the voice of the Son of God; and they that hear shall live. For as the Father hath life in himself; so hath he given to the Son to have life in himself; and hath given him authority to execute judgment also, because he is the Son of Man. Marvel not at this: for the hour is coming, in the which all that are in the graves shall hear his voice, and shall come forth; they that have done good, unto the resurrection of life: and they that have done evil, unto the resurrection of damnation.

Death is a separtion of that which belongs together. When Adam fell from God, he died; and thus all men are now by nature dead in transgressions. This is the *spiritual* death which becomes *eternal* death, if a man be not born again before his time of grace is gone by. Of these "dead" the Lord says, that they "shall hear the voice of the Son of God, and live." He, he is the Living One for ever, who by becoming man brought life again into the human race; and his voice contains life, so that all who hear it are quickened. Now, this voice of the Son of God is nothing else than the gospel which is preached in his church. If you hear it, hear the heavenly truth which it contains, you come to life again through the life of the Son of God. He speaks it in such a way that the dead hear; and all who will hear rise from the dead, and live in God. But many stop their ears, and remain in death. Nevertheless, the time shall come when every man must hear. As we all are by nature spiritually dead, so we all are likewise subject to the death of the *body;* but the hour is coming, in the which all that are in the graves shall hear the voice of the Son of God, and shall come forth. The good shall come forth unto the resurrection of life, glorified, body and soul enjoying eternal life and happiness; while the wicked, who in this life did not hear his voice, shall come forth unto the resurrection of damnation, wretched in body and soul, condemned to suffer in everlasting fire. — Hear, then, ye children of men; hear now the voice of the Son of God, and live!

Merciful God, give us the open ear of the spirit, that we may obey thy call, and may become heirs of life. Lord Jesus, thou who didst become man for our sake, and by thy death and victory didst purchase ownership in the whole human race, so that thou hast the power to judge us all; grant, we beseech thee, that we may behold thee with joy when thou shalt come in the glory of thy heavenly Father. Quicken us now, that we may enter in with thee into the life eternal. Amen.

The Savior then comes unto our graves; His mighty command is given:
Then break from the deep the ocean waves, Each tomb and restraint is riven.
All earth hears the cry: Ye dead, come forth! In glory we go to meet him.
Then open the heavenly portals wide, The names of God's saints are given. God grant that we all in faith abide, And rise to the bliss of heaven! Our Father, may we in that great hour Find none of our dear ones missing!

---

440. Wednesday after Twenty-fourth Sunday after Trin.

Let thy word of life, O God, strengthen and quicken our hope of resurrection. Amen.

1 Corinthians 15, 35–44. But some man will say, How are the dead raised up? and with what body do they come? Thou fool! that which thou sowest is not quickened, except it die: and that which thou sowest, thou sowest not that body that shall be, but bare grain, it may chance of wheat, or of some other grain: but God giveth it a body as it hath pleased him, and to every seed his own body. All flesh is not the same flesh: but there is one kind of flesh of men, another flesh of beasts, another of fishes, and another of birds. There are also celestial bodies, and bodies terrestrial: but the glory of the celestial is one, and the glory of the terrestrial is another. There is one glory of the sun, and another glory of the moon, and another glory of the stars: for one star differeth from another star in glory. So also is the resurrection of the dead. It is sown in corruption; it is raised in incorruption: it is sown in dishonor; it is raised in glory: it is sown in weak-

ness; it is raised in power: it is sown a natural body; it is raised a spiritual body. There is a natural body, and there is a spiritual body.

The fact that our body decays should not frighten us; on the contrary, it shall give us the assurance that we are to be raised in glory. If the grain remained whole in the earth without dying, there would spring up from it no new grain; it *must* die in order to live, decay in order to be renewed. Thus it is with our body also. "Well," say you, "this may be true; but the grain puts forth new shoots while it still lives; our body, on the other hand, dies and is destroyed before the new begins to sprout." Are you, then, sure that our body has ceased to be, merely because we see it no more? In that which to your eyes seems to be empty space there are countless particles of matter. If we do not see even that which is of the earth, is it surprising that we do not see that which is of heaven? The matter of which your body is composed is renewed, perhaps several times in the course of your life, and yet you have the same body. There is in it a vital germ which can not die. The body may disappear from the eye of man, in the earth, in the sea, or in other bodies, no matter where; the Lord shall quicken it again, and give it a new and heavenly shape. We do not mean to say that your reason shall make you sure of this; "the resurrection of the body" is an article of faith. But suppose that you were ignorant of the nature of the seed which we sow; would you not call it foolishness to bury the grain in the earth? Or suppose that you knew nothing of the evolution of the butterfly; would you not regard the caterpillar in the cocoon as being for ever dead? What is to prevent the omnipotence of God from raising our body from the dead? As the new grain is one with the seed from which it sprung, so our new body shall be one with the body which we now have. "I know," declares Job 19, 25–27, "that my redeemer liveth, and that he shall stand at the latter day upon the earth; and though after my skin worms destroy this body, *yet in my flesh shall I see God; whom I shall see for myself,* and *mine eyes* shall behold, and not another." Nevertheless, as the new grain is a *new* and other body than that which was sown, so also the body of our resurrection. Now we have the image of the terrestrial, of Adam and of our Savior in his state of humiliation; then we shall bear the image of the celestial, that of our glorified Savior. Who can know the solemnity of death, feel its strength in his members, look into the dark and cold grave; and then read the Bible lesson before us without heartily thanking God for it? Our resurrected bodies shall be like unto the glory of the sun and the stars. How marvelous shall be the perfection, beauty and glory of all God's children! And this is a reason why we should now strive earnestly to sanctify both soul and body, and to make manifest to all the world that we have a *living hope.* Help us to do this, O God, for Jesus' sake. Amen.

'Tis sweet to rest in lively hope, That when my change shall come, Angels will hover round my bed, And waft my spirit home.
Soon too my slumbering dust shall hear The trumpet's quickening sound; And, by my Savior's power rebuilt, At his right hand be found.

441. Thursday after Twenty-fourth Sunday after Trinity.

Lord, make thy face to shine upon thy servant, and save me by thy mercy. Amen.

2 Corinthians 4, 7–18. But we have this treasure in earthen vessels, that the excellency of the power may be of God, and not of us. We are troubled on every side, yet not distressed; we are perplexed, but not in despair; persecuted, but not forsaken; cast down, but not destroyed; always bearing about in the body the dying of the Lord Jesus, that the life also of Jesus might be made manifest in our body. For we which live are alway delivered unto death for Jesus' sake, that the life also of Jesus might be made manifest in our mortal flesh. So then death worketh in us, but life in you. We having the same spirit of faith, according as it is written, I believed, and therefore have I spoken; we also believe, and therefore speak; knowing that he which raised up the Lord Jesus, shall raise up us also by Jesus, and shall present us with you. For all things are for your sakes, that the abundant grace might, through the thanksgiving of many, redound to the glory of God. For which cause we faint not; but though our outward man perish, yet the inward man is renewed day by day. For our light affliction, which is but for a moment, worketh for us a far more exceeding and eternal weight of glory; while we look not at the things which are seen, but at the things which are not seen: for the things that are seen are temporal; but the things which are not seen are eternal.

Did we look at the things which are seen, we were of all men most miserable; but we have another treasure: *Christ in us, and we in him; eternal glory and salvation.* For which cause we faint not. — When you suffer bodily pain, or the world oppresses you, or you are troubled with doubt and with gloomy thoughts; when you are cast down and feel nothing but death in mind and members, and yet believe, and pray, and confess Christ; then this is *his life in you,* and then God deals with you as with all his children, in order that his power may not be set at nought by your pride and self-confidence. Then Jesus is made manifest in you, and his name is glorified. You impart good things to other believers, and receive new treasures of them in return; and prayers and thanksgiving ascend constantly to God. Even this would be well worth the afflictions which we suffer; how much more, then, must it be true of *eternal glory!* What do all suffering and death amount to as compared with this glory? Note the grand words of the apostle: Our affliction is "but for a moment," while the glory is *"eternal"*; our affliction is "light" as compared with the "far more exceedingly weight of glory." Affliction is necessary; but therefore our dear God has disposed matters for us in such a good way that out of the *brief* and *light* affliction proceeds and is prepared for us an *eternal* and *exceeding great* glory. Now we die; but we shall come forth glorified in mind and soul and body, and live with God in the heavenly Jerusalem. "There shall be no more death, neither sorrow, nor crying, neither shall there be any more pain; for the former things are passed away." — Keep this steadily before your eyes, dear friend; live more than heretofore in hope; think more than heretofore on the last things; look every day more constantly forward to the consummation and the life eternal. — Give us this mercy, faithful God. Make us to rejoice in hope, be patient in tribulation, continue instant in prayer; and let us unto the end be among thy saints, who are renewed after Christ from day to day. Make us to see the things of heaven with ever greater clearness, that we may never tire of following him under the cross the little while we are yet to continue our earthly pilgrimage. O that this my poor earthen vessel might become ever more full of thy strength, Lord Jesus; in order that I might bless and glorify thee without ceasing, and stand at last among the number of the saved, to the eternal praise of thy name and thy blood. This we pray of our innermost heart. Amen.

And when thy awful voice commands This body to decay, And life, in its last lingering sands, Is ebbing fast away, Then, though it be in accents weak, And faint and tremblingly, O give me strength in death to speak, "My Savior died for me."

---

442. Friday after Twenty-fourth Sunday after Trinity.

God, let our heart be in heaven. Amen.

2 Corinthians 5, 1–10. For we know, that if our earthly house of this tabernacle were dissolved, we have a building of God, an house not made with hands, eternal in the heavens. For in this we groan, earnestly desiring to be clothed upon with our house which is from heaven: if so be that being clothed we shall not be found naked. For we that are in this tabernacle do groan, being burdened: not for that we would be unclothed, but clothed upon, that mortality might be swallowed up of life. Now he that hath wrought us for the selfsame thing is God, who also hath given unto us the earnest of the Spirit. Therefore we are always confident, knowing that, whilst we are at home in the body, we are absent from the Lord: (For we walk by faith, not by sight:) we are confident, I say, and willing rather to be absent from the body, and to be present with the Lord. Wherefore we labor, that, whether present or absent, we may be accepted of him. For we must all appear before the judgment seat of Christ; that every one may receive the things done in his body, according to that he hath done, whether it be good or bad.

We are willing that our earthly body should be dissolved. As the Old Testament tabernacle was not to remain standing, so shall this body also in which we are housed pass away. But we have an eternal habitation awaiting us, a heavenly city and a new and incorruptible body. For this we would gladly, were it this very day, exchange our present habitation. Nay, for this we sigh and yearn; yet not for that would we be unclothed, but rather wish that our body might be changed without passing through death, that mortality might be swallowed up of life. What unspeakable happiness it would be to come home to the Lord! Not for that we doubt that we shall be glorified. The Spirit of God, crying "Abba Father" in us, is the earnest of our inheritance. Neither are we disturbed by the fact that we do not see our heavenly home. We may at times be timid, because we *feel* only sin, and *see* only death; but by this means our heart is loosed from the world; and so when the Spirit teaches us that we now "walk in *faith*," that this is the order of salvation, the terms on which we are saved, the test of our obedience, — then hope becomes victorious. Yet we would so much like to escape our afflictions, to reach our home, to have passed safely over the dark gulf which lies between. "Happy the man who, all his troubles past, were safe at home in God's own heaven at last!" — And yet, whether at home or in a strange land, we live for the Lord; and our chief concern is that we may be accepted of him. For whether we shall die and rise again, or be changed in a moment, "we must all appear before the judgment seat of Christ; that every one may receive the things done in his body." *There is no conversion after death. Every one shall receive according to that which he has done in the body.* Saint Paul could not have made this statement, had it been possible for the soul to be converted when the body is in the grave. Soul and body are so intimately united that the soul can not be born again and sanctified apart from the body. Therefore it is of greater importance than tongue can tell that we here, in this life, become partakers of the grace of God, and live in newness of life.

Examine yourself, then, dear reader, and ask whether you feel the solemn import of death; whether you long after the heavenly habitation; whether you labor, that you may walk in a way to be accepted of God; whether you have the earnest of the Spirit that you shall inherit heaven; so that you dare die without fear, and go to meet your God!

Lord Jesus, give me thy Spirit; draw my heart to thee; and make me zealous to walk acceptably in thy sight. Let me not dream away my time of grace; but let me take thought that I may walk in the light before thee, and allow myself to be led by thy hand, dear Savior, and to be governed, chastened, comforted and guided by thy Spirit. Amen.

When all with awe shall stand around To hear their doom allotted, O may my worthless name be found In the Lamb's book unblotted! Grant me a firm, unshaken faith; For thou, my Savior, by thy death, Hast purchased my salvation.

---

443. Saturday after Twenty-fourth Sunday after Trinity.

Lord, today we again beseech thee, make us to rejoice in hope. Amen.

1 Corinthians 15, 20–27. But now is Christ risen from the dead, and become the first-fruits of them that slept. For since by man came death, by man came also the resurrection of the dead. For as in Adam all die, even so in Christ shall all be made alive. But every man in his own order; Christ the first-fruits; afterward they that are Christ's, at his coming. Then cometh the end, when he shall have delivered up the kingdom to God, even the Father; when he shall have put down all rule and all authority and power. For he must reign, till he hath put all enemies under his feet. The last enemy that shall be destroyed is death. For he hath put all things under

585

his feet. But when he saith, All things are put under him, it is manifest that he is excepted, which did put all things under him.

The Father has given the world to the Son; and the Son has undertaken to save it. By his death and resurrection he overcame our enemies; but he must deliver every individual who is to be saved from the power of the vanquished enemies; and this work he continues until the end of time. A patient has already been rescued from sickness and death when a physician who can be absolutely relied on to effect a cure has taken him under treatment, and administered the infallible remedy. So it is in the case of believers; sickness and death have been destroyed. But as the patient in the case supposed must for a time continue to feel the effects of the disease, which disappear gradually, so Christians continue to feel the ravages of sin and death, as long as they remain in this tenement of clay. Now, in what way is this brought about? The dominion of the devil over my *heart* is destroyed; but the power of death in my *body* increases and finally obtains complete victory, and delivers my body to the grave! Death consumes my strength, making me more weak from day to day. Now, why is this? Should I not become more healthy and strong? No, says the apostle; it is as it should be; for "the last enemy that shall be destroyed is death." This enemy must go on sapping the strength of your body, in order that you may be humbled by continuing to dwell in this ever more frail tenement; in order that your heart may die from the world; and in order that you may at last through death be wholly quit of "flesh and blood." What though death be strong in your body; it was strong in the body of Christ also; yet Christ rose again; and you shall rise again with him. — To every earnest Christian who knows the nature of death it is an "enemy"; and I am glad that the apostle calls it by this name. For though I am able to look it in the face without fear, nay rejoice in its coming, because it *must be my servant* to "ferry me over to the shores of eternal life"; yet I never can do otherwise than hate it and revolt against it in the innermost recesses of my being; for it comes from hell, is the devil's offspring, and is the enemy of everything which is of God. And it shall be utterly destroyed; Christ *has done* it, and *shall do* it; he "hath abolished death" (2 Tim. i, 10). When the new humanity of all the saints shall have been perfected; when the dead shall have been raised up, and heaven and earth shall have been transfigured; then shall the Son return to the Father his sceptre; then his work as a Savior is finished, and all things brought back to their original state of innocence; but to us the conditions shall be much more glorious than they would have been, had no Savior been necessary. Through the Son God is for evermore all in all. — Grant to us also this blessed experience, that we may see these things clearly in the light of heaven. Do this, merciful, faithful, and almighty God, for Jesus' sake. Amen.

O Jesus! shorten the delay, And hasten thy salvation, That we may see that glorious day Produce a new creation; Lord Jesus, come, our Judge and King! Come, change our mournful notes, to sing Thy praise for ever. Amen.

444. Twenty-fifth Sunday after Trinity. I.

Give us, O God, the enlightened eyes of understanding. Amen.

Gospel Lesson, Matthew 24, 15–28. When ye, therefore, shall see the abomination of desolation, spoken of by Daniel the prophet, stand in the holy place, (whoso readeth, let him understand:) then let them which be in Judæa flee into the mountains: let him which is on the housetop not come down to take any thing out of his house: neither let him which is in the field return back to take his clothes. And woe unto them that are with child, and to them that give suck in those days! But pray ye that your flight be not in the winter, neither on the sabbath day: for then shall be great tribulation, such as was not since the beginning of the world to this time, no, nor ever shall be. And except those days should be shortened, there should no flesh be saved: but for the elect's sake those days shall be shortened. Then if any man shall say unto you, Lo, here is Christ, or there; believe it not. For there shall arise false Christs, and false prophets, and shall shew great signs and wonders; insomuch that, if it were possible, they shall deceive the very elect. Behold, I have told you before. Wherefore if they shall say unto you, Behold, he is in the desert; go not forth: Behold, he is in the secret chambers; believe it not. For as the lightning cometh out of the east, and shineth even unto the west; so shall also the coming of the Son of Man be. For wheresoever the carcase is, there will the eagles be gathered together.

As the times were before the destruction of Jerusalem, exceptionally evil, so shall they be in the last days before the end of the world. Especially shall *doctrines of human invention* and *heretical sects* increase at a dreadful rate. In the first place, "false prophets shall shew great signs and wonders; insomuch that, if it were possible, they shall deceive the very elect." Even Saint John in his epistles speaks of false Christs, deceivers, and antichrists, who deny the Father and the Son; but what must the apostle have said, had he lived in our day? The Christian religion proves its power to conquer the world; the Lord's command to "go and make all nations my disciples" is being realized in all parts of the earth. And yet, how many thousands who have been baptized are there not who are become deceivers and infidels! How many are there not who have trampled under foot the apostolic doctrine of justification by faith; and how sadly have they not abused it, making it an excuse for lasciviousness! Who shall number the many who in our day have risen in revolt against the Lord and his Anointed; who deny the divinity of Christ, and revile the teaching of the church in regard to the Father and Son and Holy Ghost? And the people willingly allow themselves to be led astray. Our modern intellectual culture is born of the gospel, but turns against it to destroy it. The word of God is the light of the nations, the sun that illumines the peoples; yet men willingly surrender themselves to those who deny the gospel, and who thus lead them into black darkness. Wretched men to be thus blinded by the devil's own malevolence! Saint Jude also finds it needful to write to the faithful, and exhort them that they must earnestly contend for the faith which was once delivered unto the saints. By the spirit of prophecy he speaks in a wonderful way to us who live in these latter days. He warns against them that deny their only Lord God, and our Lord Jesus Christ; and who, being filthy dreamers, defile the flesh, despise dominion, and speak evil of dignities, and go in the way of Cain and Balaam and Core. (See the General Epistle of Jude.) Let us lay it to heart, and understand the signs of the times. — Secondly, to Jerusalem the terrible internal dissensions and schisms were certain destruction, as were the Roman legions thundering at the gates. In the Christian church it is becoming all the time more common to cry: "Lo, here is Christ, or there!" The apostles of infidelity, who place themselves outside of the communion of saints, and make war on the Christian faith, would not, be particularly dangerous did the faithful but present a united front. But the devil is acquainted with the rule, "*divide et impera*"; which means, divide, and rule; bring about dissensions among your adversaries, and the victory is yours! Christendom has never before been divided into so many sects as now. Somebody has a new idea on some doctrinal point; at once he organizes a church denomination of his own. Another has his private opinion in regard to church government, and starts a new sect. A third thinks that the discipline is too lax, and a fourth rather likes the style of preaching adopted by some separatistic exhorter; so they form new parties, dissolve the old bonds, sever the connection with their former brethren in the Lord. Many who shrink from fellowship with us on account of our imperfections do not shrink from sinning against the most earnest prayer of Jesus for the unity of his disciples; nor do they shrink from founding heretical sects, though the apostle, in Galatians 5, places this sin in the same class with adultery, murder, and drunkenness. Dear brethren in the Lord; let us be united, forbearing one another in love! The party spirit is not the spirit of the lowly and loving Savior; if we would belong to him, let us strive to be of the same mind with him! Go not forth after them that say: Behold, he is in the desert, but not in the church! Neither follow them that say: He is in the secret chambers, in the small church societies, not in the large ones! Remain true to that which you learned from the beginning; remain in the church which became your spiritual mother. Continue in humility and love; stay at your spiritual birthplace, and prepare yourself to meet the Lord, who shall come when he is least expected. Let this be your care, "in a holy life and the exercise of godliness to wait and long for the coming of the day of Christ." The words of the Lord concerning the destruction of Jerusalem have been fulfilled to the letter; that which he says concerning the end of the world shall likewise be fulfilled with equal certainty. Look and see, if the branch of the fig tree be not already tender. Are not our days becoming more and more like the days of Noe? And is not the church altogether too much like shattered and dismembered Jerusalem? Watch therefore; for ye know not what hour your Lord doth come!

Help us herein, O God, for Jesus' sake. Keep us united in thy love, and preserve us from the arts of seduction. Be merciful to thy

church, preserve thy believers, and make us one in thee, that the
cunning Satan may come to naught. Grant that we may always stand
with loins girt about with truth, with lamps trimmed and burning,
ready to go forth to meet our bridegroom. Amen.

"Wake, awake, for night is flying," The watchmen on the heights are
crying, "Awake, Jerusalem, arise!" Midnight hears the welcome voices, And
at the thrilling cry rejoices: "O where are ye, ye virgins wise? The Bridegroom comes, awake! Your lamps with gladness take! Hallelujah! With
bridal care yourselves prepare To meet the Bridegroom, who is near!"

445. Twenty-fifth Sunday after Trinity. II.

*Lord, let this thy word edify us, and make us steadfast in faith, rejoicing
in hope. Amen.*

Epistle Lesson, 1 Thessalonians 4, 13–18. But I would not have you to
be ignorant, brethren, concerning them which are asleep, that ye sorrow not,
even as others which have no hope. For if we believe that Jesus died and
rose again, even so them also which sleep in Jesus will God bring with him.
For this we say unto you by the word of the Lord, that we which are alive,
and remain unto the coming of the Lord, shall not prevent them which are
asleep. For the Lord himself shall descend from heaven with a shout, with
the voice of the archangel, and with the trump of God: and the dead in
Christ shall rise first: then we which are alive and remain, shall be caught
up together with them in the clouds, to meet the Lord in the air: and so
shall we ever be with the Lord. Wherefore comfort one another with
these words.

Just as surely as Jesus is risen from the dead, all his disciples
also which are asleep shall rise in glory. To Paul there is so intimate
a connection between the resurrection of *Christ* and *our* resurrection
that he declares, 1 Cor. 15, 13: "If there be no resurrection of the dead,
then is Christ not risen." It was for us that Christ died, and for us
that he rose again; his death is our death, and his resurrection is our
resurrection. The faithful are members of him; it can not be, then,
that he with a body quickened and glorified may sit on the throne of
heaven, while their bodies remain in the grave. Therefore when you
sorrowfully close in death the eyes of a friend who believes in Christ,
remember that this friend shall hear the voice of the Lord, and that
these eyes shall open again, and see the glory of Jesus. He is in the
hand and bosom of the Lord, like a sick child that is carried in its
mother's arms until it falls asleep to wake again healthy and happy.
— When our Lord Jesus on the last day shall descend from heaven
with the voice of the archangel, and the trump of God, all who are
in the graves shall hear his voice and come forth. We who are alive
at that time shall behold it. The graves shall be opened, and the
dead shall come forth, and the sea shall give up the dead which are
in it. As Christ at the moment when he was quickened found his
way from paradise to his body in the grave, so shall the souls of his
saints find their bodies, and bring them out of the grave. And in
the selfsame moment when the dead arise, we which are alive and

remain shall be changed, and that which is mortal in us be swallowed
up in life. Then shall be accomplished the final and absolute separation between the good and the wicked, which is described in Matthew
25; and all the saints shall then ever be with the Lord. — But your
soul must tear itself loose from the lusts of the world, and long only
after heaven! Prepare yourself, then, for that place, which you wish
to make your eternal habitation!

Lord Jesus, give us the grace of thy Holy Spirit, that we may
believe thy word, and await thy glorious coming. Let me in truth
be thine, my living Savior; let me be a member of thy body, and live
with thee in eternal glory. Come, Lord Jesus; come quickly! Amen.

Arise, the kingdom is at hand, The King is drawing nigh; Arise with
joy, thou faithful band, To meet the Lord most high!
Look up, ye souls weighed down with care, The Sovereign is not far;
Look up, faint hearts, from your despair, Behold the morning star!

446. Monday after Twenty-fifth Sunday after Trinity.

Let thy word, O God, create earnestness and faithfulness in our soul! Amen.

Matthew 24, 4–14. And Jesus answered and said unto them, Take heed
that no man deceive you. For many shall come in my name, saying, I am
Christ; and shall deceive many. And ye shall hear of wars, and rumors of
wars: see that ye be not troubled: for all these things must come to pass,
but the end is not yet. For nation shall rise against nation, and kingdom
against kingdom: and there shall be famines, and pestilences, and earth-
quakes, in divers places. All these are the beginning of sorrows. Then shall
they deliver you up to be afflicted, and shall kill you: and ye shall be hated
of all nations for my name's sake. And then shall many be offended, and
shall betray one another. And many false prophets shall rise, and shall deceive many. And because iniquity shall abound, the love of many shall wax
cold. But he that shall endure unto the end, the same shall be saved. And
this gospel of the kingdom shall be preached in all the world for a witness
unto all nations: and then shall the end come.

This is a truly appalling description of the time immediately preceding the end. Similarly Paul writes: "Know also, that in the last
days perilous times shall come! For men shall be lovers of their
own selves, covetous, boasters, proud, blasphemers, disobedient to
parents, unthankful, unholy, without natural affection, truce-breakers,
false accusers, incontinent, fierce, despisers of those that are good,
traitors, heady, highminded, lovers of pleasures more than lovers
of God; having a form of godliness, but denying the power thereof."
Verily, this is something which should make us all to pause and
examine ourselves! — Unhappy men are we, if we be of those here
described! O that we would earnestly consider this in the sight of
God! There are true believers among us; but they experience that
the spirit of unrighteousness is mighty in these latter days of the
world; they have difficulty in protecting themselves against the pride,
disobedience, want of charity, unbelief, love of pleasure, and all the

venom of Satan, which surround them. How sad a statement is
not this, which Jesus makes in regard to the Christians living in the
last days of the world: *"Then shall many be offended, and shall betray
one another, and shall hate one another.* And many false prophets shall
rise, and *shall deceive many.* And because iniquity shall abound, the
love of many *shall wax cold."* Let this be so solemn a warning to
us, that we may escape the awful danger. Even in the *very worst*
times it is *possible* for us to watch and win the victory. The Savior
says: "He that shall endure unto the end, the same shall be saved."
On another occasion he said to his disciples: "Ye shall be hated of
all men for my name's sake; *but he that endureth to the end shall be
saved."* To each one of us he shouts: "Be faithful; watch, and hold
fast; I will strengthen and keep you; surely I come quickly; endure
a little while; fear not that which you shall suffer; be faithful unto
death, and I will give you the crown of life!" He is faithful; hear
and obey him! Fear God; pray without ceasing; abstain from all
appearance of evil; and keep the covenant of brotherly love with the
children of God. Then shall the poison not kill you, nor the fire
consume you, nor the flood carry you away; but Satan with all his
cunning and power shall be put to shame.

Grant us this grace, our merciful and faithful God in Jesus Christ.
Amen.

Stand up, my soul, shake off thy fears, And gird the gospel armor on;
March to the gates of endless joy, Where Jesus, thy great Captain's gone.

Hell and thy sins resist thy course, But hell and sin are vanquished foes;
Thy Jesus nailed them to the cross, And sung the triumph when he rose.

---

447. Tuesday after Twenty-fifth Sunday after Trinity.

*Grant, O Lord, that we may be of thy saints, and may stand firm in
every trial. Amen.*

2 Thessalonians 2, 1-10. Now we beseech you, brethren, by the coming
of our Lord Jesus Christ, and by our gathering together unto him, that ye
be not soon shaken in mind, or be troubled, neither by spirit, nor by word,
nor by letter as from us, as that the day of Christ is at hand. Let no man
deceive you by any means; for that day shall not come, except there come
a falling away first, and that man of sin be revealed, the son of perdition;
Who opposeth and exalteth himself above all that is called God, or that is
worshiped; so that he, as God, sitteth in the temple of God, shewing himself that he is God. Remember ye not, that, when I was yet with you, I told
you these things? And now ye know what withholdeth that he might be
revealed in his time. For the mystery of iniquity doth already work: only
he who now letteth, will let, until he be taken out of the way. And then
shall that wicked be revealed, whom the Lord shall consume with the Spirit
of his mouth, and shall destroy with the brightness of his coming: even him
whose coming is after the working of Satan, with all power and signs and
lying wonders, and with all deceivableness of unrighteousness in them that
perish; because they received not the love of the truth, that they might be
saved.

We are to be always *prepared* for the second coming of the Lord; yet we must wait *patiently* for his own good time. As he has hid from us the hour of our death, so likewise the hour of his coming. Many things, however, are still to take place; but they are such as may be brought about so soon, that his coming may in a moment be at hand. "The gospel of the kingdom" was to "be preached in all the world"; but who shall say that this has not already been done? Even in the days of the apostles it was proclaimed at least in the far East and in the West; and in our times it has been preached to the people of the frozen North and to those in the islands of the South. The "falling away must come"; but it has begun ages ago. The powers of the deep are hard at work; the earth is being undermined on all sides, and the collapse may come at any time. Furthermore, according to Revelation 13, a beast shall rise up out of the sea; and another beast shall come up out of the earth, and cause the earth and them which dwell therein to worship the first beast. This is interpreted to mean, that there shall come forth out of the people a world-power; and it shall be quickened and strengthened by an idolatrous spirit and worship; for no rule can exist without some sort of religion. When these things have come to pass, says scripture; when this beast out of the sea of humanity has exercised its strength to "make war with the saints, and to overcome them"; when demoniacal powers perform wonders, and all the world follows the beast, and worships it, as though it were the truth itself; when there shall be sore trouble for the faithful, and the life of "the woman," the church of God, shall be as a life in the wilderness in the midst of the peoples; when, at last, this world-power formed of a partnership between earth and hell is in the hands of a single ruler, and we thus again have a world-power like that of old, fashioned especially after the Roman empire, as depicted in Revelation 17, making war on God's people; — then, and not till then, shall the Lord come and consume the antichrist.* Blessed is every one who has not received the mark of the beast! His name is written in the Lamb's book of life; and in his forehead the name of the Lamb that was slain, and the name of the Father, shall shine forth in eternal glory! — "Brethren, stand fast, and hold the traditions which ye have been taught, whether by word, or our epistle! Now our Lord Jesus Christ himself, and God, even our Father, which hath loved us, and given us everlasting consolation and good hope through grace, comfort your hearts, and stablish you in every good word and work!" To him be glory for ever and ever. Amen.

Awake, our souls, away our fears; Let every trembling thought be gone. Awake, and run the heavenly race, And put a cheerful courage on.
True, 'tis a strait and thorny road, And mortal spirits tire and faint; But they forget the mighty God, Who feeds the strength of every saint.

---

* But this "wicked one," this "antichrist," who causes the great "falling away" and makes war on God's church, *has*, according to the Confession of our Lutheran Church, *already come* in Papacy!

448. Wednesday after Twenty-fifth Sunday after Trin.

Preserve me, O God; for in thee do I put my trust. Thou art my Lord; I have no good beyond thee.

1 John 5, 18–21. We know that whosoever is born of God sinneth not; but he that is begotten of God keepeth himself, and that wicked one toucheth him not. And we know that we are of God, and the whole world lieth in wickedness. And we know that the Son of God is come, and hath given us an understanding, that we may know him that is true: and we are in him that is true, even in his Son Jesus Christ. This is the true God, and eternal life. Little children, keep yourselves from idols. Amen.

When Saint John here says that "whosoever is born of God sinneth not," and in the same Epistle, 2, 1, declares that "if any man sin, we have an advocate with the Father"; he clearly means that true believers do not live in sin; but walk in the truth, shun wickedness, and keep the commandments of God; yet without being sinless. "If we say that we have no sin, we deceive ourselves, and the truth is not in us" (1, 8). This is as certainly true as it is that if any do not purify himself, he is not a true child of God (3, 3). The whole world lies in wickedness, and thus all unregenerate hearts are ruled· by the devil. The children of God, on the other hand, have been set free; so that the devil can do no more than tempt them. They watch, and are on their guard, and the Holy Ghost is with them, and warns them, and chastens them; so that "the wicked one toucheth them not." As the children of the world are in the liar, so the children of God "are in him that is true." The words of the apostle are terrible in their solemn import, but at the same time they are full of comfort. "The whole world lieth in wickedness," *lieth in wickedness;* but we are in him that is true," *we are in the Lord.* "The god of this world hath blinded the minds of them which believe not;" but "the Son of God hath giveth us an understanding that we may know the true God, Jesus Christ." Here the apostle distinctly declares *that Jesus is the true God.* Scripture could not with greater clearness assert the divinity of Christ. The unbelievers deny Christ, the true God; and they say: "The devil is a myth; we are lords; we are in God; for the whole world is God." We know, however, that sin is not of God; and we know that every one who serves· sin is the slave of the devil; we know that Jesus has delivered us from the power of the devil; and we know that whosoever is of God and in God *sinneth not.* — "Little children, keep yourselves from idols!" Thus the apostle closes his letter. Be *assured* of your victory; but be vigilant always! Here a sifting out is taking place under dissensions and danger. Let the world keep its idols; idols of clay, and idols of gold, and intellectual idols! Do not receive the mark of the beast; but carry the cross, and follow Christ!

Faithful Savior, give us the assurance that the wicked one shall not touch us; and make us vigilant and faithful always and everywhere unto our dying hour. Thou knowest we were easily led astray by the alluring idols; but we put our trust in thee. Do not cast us off; and let our eyes never grow dim, but see thee with ever greater clearness. Amen.

Sure I must fight, if I would reign: Increase my courage, Lord; I'll bear the toil, endure the pain, Supported by thy word. Thy saints, in all this glorious war, Shall conquer, though they die; They see the triumph from afar, By faith they bring it nigh.

---

449. Thursday after Twenty-fifth Sunday after Trinity.

Lord, speak to our heart, that we may watch and walk in the light before thee. Amen.

2 Timothy 4, 1–8. I charge thee therefore before God, and the Lord Jesus Christ, who shall judge the quick and the dead at his appearing and his kingdom; preach the word; be instant in season, out of season; reprove, rebuke, exhort, with all longsuffering and doctrine. For the time will come when they will not endure sound doctrine; but after their own lusts shall they heap to themselves teachers, having itching ears; and they shall turn away their ears from the truth, and shall be turned unto fables. But watch thou in all things, endure afflictions, do the work of an evangelist, make full proof of thy ministry. For I am now ready to be offered, and the time of my departure is at hand. I have fought a good fight, I have finished my course, I have kept the faith: henceforth there is laid up for me a crown of righteousness, which the Lord, the righteous judge, shall give me at that day: and not to me only, but unto all them also that love his appearing.

The number of such as teach false doctrines is all the time increasing; and people always run after something new, something which tickles their itching ears. Therefore the Lord's true servants, and with them all humble and sincere Christians, must do their work all the more faithfully. They must walk constantly *in the sight of him* who soon shall come to judge the world; they must bear witness of him when it is convenient to them, and when it is not; they must not be exasperated on account of all the foolishness which they see, but with the meekness of Christ reprove, rebuke, and exhort the precious souls. They must keep watch over themselves, and keep an eye of love on the brethren; bear the cross without repining, and be faithful to the end in the Lord's work. Fidelity, ye brethren in the sacred calling, constant fidelity be your watchword; zeal for Christ, fresh courage, unswerving loyalty to the truth, and fearlessness in confessing it unto the end! *"Make full proof* of thy ministry," says Paul, and points you to his own example, but also to the crown that awaits you. There are especially three things which stir my heart in that which the apostle here says concerning his being ready to be offered, and his hope: 1) His example. He exhorts us to follow him, even as he followed Christ. "Let my example teach you that the Lord is faithful to give strength unto the end! To me it is a blessed thing to be offered; may it be the same to you when your time comes, as it soon will!" 2) The ranks are being thinned out. The old veterans are passing away to their reward in the church triumphant; while the difficuties are increasing, and we are now to take their place. Let us fill it with credit, stand united, lift high the banner of our confession of faith, and may we soon be gathered with them as victors! 3) The crown is worth fighting for; the day of triumph is coming, on which all the Lord's soldiers who remained loyal to him shall receive the crown of glory that fadeth not away. — Be strong, then, through grace; endure hardness, as a good soldier of Jesus Christ; strive lawfully, that you may be crowned! Lord, wake us, and strengthen us by thy Spirit; keep all who are thine faithful and fearless unto the end. Amen.

Awake, my soul! stretch every nerve, And press with vigor on: A heavenly race demands thy zeal, And an immortal crown.
A cloud of witnesses around Hold thee in full survey: Forget the steps already trod, And onward urge thy way.

450. Friday after Twenty-fifth Sunday after Trinity.

The Lord shall be thine everlasting light, and the days of thy mourning shall be ended.

Revelation 19, 1–9. And after these things I heard a great voice of much people in heaven, saying, Alleluia; Salvation, and glory and honor, and power, unto the Lord our God: for true and righteous are his judgments: for he hath judged the great whore, which did corrupt the earth with her fornication, and hath avenged the blood of his servants at her hand. And again they said, Alleluia. And her smoke rose up for ever and ever. And the four and twenty elders and the four beasts fell down and worshiped God that sat on the throne, saying, Amen; Alleluia. And a voice came out of the throne, saying, Praise our God, all ye his servants, and ye that fear him, both small and great. And I heard as it were the voice of a great multitude, and as the voice of many waters, and as the voice of mighty thunderings, saying, Alleluia; for the Lord God omnipotent reigneth. Let us be glad and rejoice, and give honor to him: for the marriage of the Lamb is come, and his wife hath made herself ready. And to her was granted that she should be arrayed in fine linen, clean and white: for the fine linen is the righteousness of saints. And he saith unto me, Write, Blessed are they which are called unto the marriage supper of the Lamb. And he saith unto me, These are the true sayings of God.

The great harlot "in purple and scarlet, and decked with gold, and precious stones and pearls, and having a golden cup in her hand full of abominations," this harlot "is that great city, which reigneth over the kings of the earth" (Rev. 17,4.18), the seat of antichrist, Babylon and Rome revived, a caricature of the heavenly Jerusalem. The days toward the latter end of the world are in scripture described as a time of dreadful trials to the children of God. The woman shall be "drunken with the blood of the martyrs of Jesus" (Rev. 17, 6); but all nations shall revel in the abundance of her riches" (18, 3). Their life shall be to eat, and drink, and plant, and build, and luxuriate in the pleasures of the flesh (Luke 17, 28. 30). "No man may

buy or sell, save he that has the mark, or the name of the beast"
(Rev. 13, 17); then the people of God shall have sore temptation.
These dire prophecies have been and are being fulfilled;* the
spirit of antichrist is even now at work; we also must make our
choice! To us also comes the warning word: "Come out of Babylon, that ye be not partakers of her sin, and that ye receive not of
her plagues!" Whom do you serve, and what is your God? Gold
and silver? or fine clothes, and luxuries, and delicacies? or influence
and power? Then you really live in the city of which it is said: "She
saith in her heart, I sit a queen, and am no widow, and shall see no
sorrow. Therefore shall her plagues come in one day, death, and
mourning, and famine; and she shall be utterly burned with fire;
for strong is the Lord God who judgeth her." (Rev. 18, 7. 8). Let
none of the faithful be infatuated with the pleasures of the world,
and abandon the cross. If Christ be your God, then lift up your
eyes. "He that sitteth upon the white horse is called *Faithful and
True,* and in righteousness he doth judge and make war. His eyes
are as a flame of fire, and on his head are many crowns. And he
hath on his vesture and on his thigh a name written, KING OF KINGS,
AND LORD OF LORDS." (19, 11. 12. 16). The marriage day approaches, and the bride is making herself ready! (Read our Bible
lesson over again). — Help me, thou who art called Faithful and
True; establish my steps in thy word, that neither pleasures nor sorrow may ever draw me away from thee. Give me grace to be arrayed in the fine linen, clean and white; cleanse me, and adorn me
with thy full righteousness. Amen.

Jesus, Sun of Righteousness, Brightest beam of love divine, With the
early morning rays Do thou on our darkness shine, And dispel with purest
light All our long and gloomy night.

---

451. Saturday after Twenty-fifth Sunday after Trinity.

Psalm 80, 1–7. Give ear, O Shepherd of Israel, thou that leadest Joseph
like a flock: thou that dwellest between the cherubims, shine forth. Before
Ephraim, and Benjamin, and Manasseh, stir up thy strength, and come and
save us. Turn us again, O God, and cause thy face to shine: and we shall
be saved. O Lord God of hosts, how long wilt thou be angry against the
prayer of thy people? Thou feedest them with the bread of tears; and givest
them tears to drink in great measure. Thou makest us a strife unto our
neighbors; and our enemies laugh among themselves. Turn us again, O
God of hosts, and cause thy face to shine; and we shall be saved.

In this psalm the people of Judah pray for the people of the kingdom of Israel, who had been led captives to Assyria. "When one
member suffers, all the members suffer with it." — As Jesus has
taught us to strengthen our faith by praying to God as "our Father,"

---

* According to the Confessions of our Lutheran Church these prophecies
refer primarily to the character and doings of Papacy, the Pope of Rome
being *the* Antichrist.

so the Spirit here calls the God of Israel by several glorious names of a kind to strengthen the faith of those who pray to him. The "Shepherd of Israel"; shall he not *care* for his own? He that "dwelleth between the cherubims"; shall he not *be able* to save? "The Lord," Jehovah; "God," Elohim, the glorious and heavenly majesty; "the God of hosts," Zebaoth, the ruler of the hosts of heaven and earth; — in him who has these names, and who is that which he is called, in *him* is the hope of Israel. Shall his wrath continue against his people, when the incense of their prayers ascends to him? The vine which he has planted with great care, shall he allow it to be destroyed by the heathen? No; he blesses it now, and *shall bless* it for evermore. The psalmist lets the church repeat three times the prayer: "Turn us again, O God of hosts, and cause thy face to shine; and we shall be saved." He thereby reminds us of that which is written in Numbers 6, 22–27: "And the Lord spake unto Moses, saying, Speak unto Aaron and unto his sons, saying, On this wise ye shall bless the children of Israel, saying unto them, THE LORD *bless thee, and keep thee*; THE LORD *make his face shine upon thee, and be gracious unto thee*; THE LORD *lift up his countenance upon thee, and give thee peace!* And they shall put my name upon the children of Israel; and I will bless them." This triple benediction, with its repetition of "the Lord," plainly points to the Trinity of God; something of which the Israel of old was no doubt dimly conscious. But our Articles of Faith interpret this benediction most beautifully. Therefore we are able to pray for God's Israel, his church on earth, with a more clear view and a more firm faith, than could the faithful of the Old Testament. Certain it is, the triune, almighty God is the Shepherd of the church, and leads us in the paths of salvation; no matter how long his anger may seem to burn, and prevent our prayers from reaching his ear. Yet a while "our enemies laugh among themselves," and ask, "where is your God?" But *his* righteous judgments go surely, though in secret, through the world; and it shall be said to Zion: "Fear thou not, and let not thine hands be slack. The Lord thy God in the midst of thee is mighty; he will save, he will rejoice over thee with joy; he will rest in his love, he will joy over thee with singing." — God, we bless thee, and pray thee to reveal thy glory. Protect that which thy right hand hath planted; keep us alive, that we may call upon thy name. Amen.

He will present our souls Unblemished and complete Before the glory of his face, With joys divinely great. Then all his faithful sons Shall meet around the throne, Shall bless the conduct of his grace, And make his wonders known.

452. Twenty-sixth Sunday after Trinity. I.

Lord, our soul is troubled; in thee only can it find rest.

Gospel Lesson, Matthew 11, 25–30. At that time Jesus answered and said, I thank thee, O Father, Lord of heaven and earth, because thou hast hid these things from the wise and prudent, and hast revealed them unto babes. Even so, Father: for so it seemed good in thy sight. All things are delivered unto me of my Father: and no man knoweth the Son, but the Father; neither knoweth any man the Father, save the Son, and he to whomsoever the Son will reveal him. Come unto me, all ye that labor and are heavy laden, and I will give you rest. Take my yoke upon you, and learn of me; for I am meek and lowly in heart: and ye shall find rest unto your souls. For my yoke is easy, and my burden is light.

The Son would rejoice exceedingly to reveal the mystery of grace to *all* men; but they *will not*; they *are determined* to walk in darkness. Their "wisdom and prudence," their pride and levity, make them blind to the light, and deaf to the word of the Lord. Give ear, then, ye who are needy, to the voice of the precious Savior, calling out to you, "Come unto me!" With these words he incircles us, and draws us to him. It is his earnest wish that we may come; and his invitation itself contains the strength which we need in order to accept it. When a king calls to him one of his subjects, the invitation *itself* is a passport which overcomes all difficulties, and clears the way to the royal presence; but here *he* calls to whom all things are subject, our King and Lord, Jesus Christ. None shall say: "I can not come." You can by the power of his grace, which invites you. Come, then; come to Jesus! "*Where* is he?" He is where his voice is, in the word and sacraments. O that you might see how near he is to you! But you shall not see it; for God has ordained that we are to believe; and he gives us grace thereto by his Spirit. How, then, shall I *come* to Jesus?" You must ask him for mercy, and commit yourself to him as your Savior. Believe that he is near you, and saves you; and give him thanks; then you *are* come, and you *have* rest. "But he invites only those who labor and are heavy laden. I do not know if I am one of them." My friend; put away your own wisdom, and learn this, that God gives all things of his *grace;* that he does not deal out in driblets, but pours out freely and abundantly with heavenly and lavish beneficence. Here he calls out to humanity in general; and he does not say: "Only such as labor and are heavy laden are permitted to come." No; he says: "Come, all ye that labor and are heavy laden;" or, in other words, all who desire to find rest. You certainly will not come, if you do not feel that you are heavy laden by reason of your sin; but if you then will come, it is his grace which calls you, and draws you; and the way is open. Now, dear reader, do you not feel that you are heavy laden and need rest? Do you not understand that you are blind, and that you need to be enlightened by the Spirit of God, in order that you may become wise unto salvation? If not, you at least stand at the parting of the ways, and have permission to enter *his* school, in which babes are instructed concerning the Father. Hear, all ye who understand that you can not by your own wisdom know God, nor by your own works find peace of soul and hope of life; hear the Savior's most loving invitation, and come to him, come to him! To all, with no exception, he calls out: "If *any* man thirst, let him come to me and drink!" "Let him that is athirst come; and *whosoever will*, let him take the water

of life freely!" Let none stay away! No matter who or what you
are, if you need salvation, come, for he calls you. You are lost; he
came for the very purpose of seeking and saving that which was
lost; *for that very purpose,* and none other. Blessed is he, whosoever
shall not be offended in him! He says: Take *my* yoke, *my* harness,
and with it carry *my* burden. I deliver you from the heavy yoke of
the law, from the bondage of works; for I have done all things for
you. Therefore when the law accuses you, all you have to do is to
refer the matter to me, and find rest in faith in my perfect righteousness. Then make my *love* your own, and serve one another. "Bear
ye one another's burdens, and so fulfil the law of Christ." When
we in love bear the infirmities of others, and help them in their bodily
and spiritual need, we carry the "burden" of Christ by means of his
"yoke". Love is the yoke; the troubles of the brethren are the burden.
We must *"learn"* of him: he *gives* us the grace without which we
can not take the yoke and lift the burden. He is a most patient
teacher, who does not reject us because we are slow to learn. Furthermore he gives us his patience and meekness, thus enabling us in
our turn to bear with others, and even to esteem them better than
ourselves; and thus neither our own unworthiness nor that of others
can prevent our finding rest in Christ.

Do not, precious soul, let it be in vain that Jesus calls you today
to come to him! Come, and learn to know his love; so that you
may surrender yourself to it, and may be delivered from the yoke of
the law; that you may be sensible of your unworthiness, that you may
be still before the Lord, and taste his peace. Then you *are* with him,
and yet you continually *come* to *him* anew; you *have* peace, and *receive* peace; *carry* his yoke, and *take* his yoke upon you; *are* his disciple, and *become* his disciple; until you are made perfect in love,
and enter on your rest in heaven.

Dear Savior, do thou interpret to me these thy precious words,
and draw me to thee. Thou knowest how many things there are
which would keep me away from thee, obscure my view of thee, and
make thy yoke seem heavy. Yet, precious Savior, thou knowest thy
servant; thou knowest how earnestly I pray thee for grace to believe
in thee, love thee, be like thee in lowliness and meekness, follow thee
in trouble and affliction, live in thy love, and exhaust all the strength
which thou givest me for the welfare of the brethren. Thou seest,
dear Lord, that in my heart I love thy yoke, and that I do not wish
to rid myself of thy burden. Draw me to thee, and after thee; so am
I truly blest. In thee alone has my soul found and will it hereafter
find rest. Praise be to thee, and to the Father and the Holy Ghost,
world without end. Amen.

When flesh shall fail, then strengthen thou The spirit from above; Make
us to feel thy service sweet, And light thy yoke of love.
So shall we faultless stand at last Before thy Father's throne; The blessedness for ever ours, The glory all thine own!

453. Twenty-sixth Sunday after Trinity. II.

Thy testimonies are very sure; holiness becometh thy house, O Lord, for ever.

Epistle Lesson, 1 Thessalonians 5, 12–23. And we beseech you, brethren, to know them which labor among you, and are over you in the Lord, and admonish you; and to esteem them very highly in love for their work's sake. And be at peace among yourselves. Now we exhort you, brethren, warn them that are unruly, comfort the feebleminded, support the weak, be patient toward all men. See that none render evil for evil unto any man; but ever follow that which is good, both among yourselves, and to all men. Rejoice evermore. Pray without ceasing. In every thing give thanks; for this is the will of God in Christ Jesus concerning you. Quench not the Spirit. Despise not prophesyings. Prove all things; hold fast that which is good. Abstain from all appearance of evil. And the very God of peace sanctify you wholly; and I pray God your whole spirit and soul and body be preserved blameless unto the coming of our Lord Jesus Christ.

Only they whom Christ has made free are able to lead the glorious life here described. We point to but a few of the many good things contained in this text, which is a veritable treasure house.

It is directly contrary to the spirit of the times to esteem "them which are over you in the Lord" *"for their work's sake."* It is rather the custom to worship *the men,* and despise their office. Let the disciples of the lowly Savior note this: "Esteem them very highly in love *for their work's sake."* — Then the following: "Warn them that are unruly, support the weak, be patient toward all men." We let the unruly do as they like, and the weak go down; we deal too indulgently with our own, and judge others too harshly. O that the words of the apostle might chasten us, and at the same time strengthen that which is good in us. Let none lose heart! — The apostle then goes on to say something most remarkable in connection with the preceding: *"Rejoice evermore!"* Can he mean this? Certainly he can and does. To the Philippians also he writes: "Rejoice in the Lord *alway!"* Joy, then, is to be the undercurrent under all the shifting sensations of our life; joy alway! "Rejoice in hope, be patient in tribulation, continue instant in prayer" (Rom. 12, 12). Here the apostle presents to us our duty, likewise in three successive steps: "Rejoice evermore! Pray without ceasing! In all things give thanks!" And he adds: "For this is the will of God in Christ Jesus concerning you." Then nothing must be allowed to prevent it; we can and shall do that which he says! Let every breath we draw and every beat of the heart be a song of praise in honor of God's love for us in Christ! To this end we must heed the instruction with which the apostle follows up his exhortation: "Quench not the Spirit! Despise not prophesyings! Prove all things; hold fast that which is good!" Let the gifts of the Spirit be cultivated; let no feeling of envy or contempt quench the holy fire, whether this burn in the wise or the simple. Let nothing prevent the proper use of the gifts. But on the other hand, neither is everything that glitters to be regarded as gold. "Hold fast that which is good; but abstain from all appearance of evil," even from the evil which appears in the shape of spiritual zeal. — "*Faithful* is *he* that calleth you, *who* also will do it." Practice obedience to him! He is "the very God of peace," the origin and source of peace; he shall take away everything which injures you; he shall destroy sin, which prevents your joy from being complete; and he shall sanctify you wholly, and preserve you blameless unto the coming of our Lord Jesus Christ. When the apostle is able to strengthen us in a hope such as this, he has the right to say: "Rejoice evermore; and in every thing give thanks!"

We bless thee, our God, who didst ordain us unto salvation in Jesus Christ, and didst in him call us to eternal glory. We thank thee also for the precious words spoken through thy apostle, and humbly ask of thee grace to believe and to obey the word. Amen.

Come, ye that love the Lord, And let your joys be known; Join in a song with sweet accord, While ye surround his throne. Let those refuse to sing Who never knew our God; But servants of the heavenly King May speak their joys abroad.

---

454. Monday after Twenty-sixth Sunday after Trinity.

Draw us to thee, Lord Jesus, and reveal to us thy glory. Amen.

John 5, 19-23. Then answered Jesus and said unto them, Verily, verily, I say unto you, The Son can do nothing of himself, but what he seeth the Father do: for what things soever he doeth, these also doeth the Son likewise. For the Father loveth the Son, and sheweth him all things that himself doeth: and he will shew him greater works than these, that ye may marvel. For as the Father raiseth up the dead, and quickeneth them; even so the Son quickeneth whom he will. For the Father judgeth no man, but hath committed all judgment unto the Son; that all men should honor the Son, even as they honor the Father. He that honoreth not the Son, honoreth not the Father which hath sent him.

Yesterday we heard Jesus say: "No man knoweth the Son, but the Father; neither knoweth any man the Father, save the Son, and he to whomsoever the Son will reveal him." As these words testify to his unity with the Father, so does also that which he says in the text before us, "Whatsoever things the Father doeth, these also doeth the Son *likewise*. For the Father loveth the Son, and sheweth him all things that himself doeth. The Son quickeneth whom he will, and unto him hath the Father committed all judgment. He that honoreth not the Son honoreth not the Father which hath sent him." If we are to know God, it must be in Christ; for *only in him* do we find God. When we come to the Son in the gospel, in which he is to be found, we come to the very God himself. Then we also become partakers of his divine power to quicken the dead; for he gives us a new life, which causes us to love him, and abstain from sin. In thus honoring him we honor the Father. Though we usually address our prayers to the Father, we may also pray to the Son; indeed our hearts may at times feel a special need of making their petitions to him. And if we know the Son, and can speak *to him* as to an intimate friend, we are the beloved of the Father, and shall fear no anger. The Son has *all* judgment. He who hangs on the cross for me, and with his blood makes atonement for all my sin, *he* and none other has the power to judge me. He must needs judge the impenitent for that they will not be saved; but to the needy who trust in him as their Savior he shall give everlasting life. For himself has said: "Verily, verily, I say unto you, he that *heareth* my word, and *believeth* on him that sent me, *hath everlasting life*, and shall not come unto condemnation; but is passed from death unto life."

In thee, Lord Jesus, have I found the Father; and in thee shall I for ever see him. Let me never fall into unbelief; but keep me with thee, and shew me thy glory. Lord Jesus, hold me fast, that I may abide with thee for evermore. Amen.

O draw me, Savior, after thee! So shall I run and never tire. With gracious words still comfort me; Be thou my hope, my sole desire. Free me from every weight: nor fear Nor sin can come, if thou art here.

---

455. Tuesday after Twenty-sixth Sunday after Trinity.

Let thy light shine for us, thou Spirit of God; and drive the darkness out of our soul. Amen.

1 Corinthians 1, 17–21. For Christ sent me not to baptize, but to preach the gospel: not with wisdom of words, lest the cross of Christ should be made of none effect. For the preaching of the cross is to them that perish foolishness; but unto us which are saved it is the power of God. For it is written, I will destroy the wisdom of the wise, and will bring to nothing the understanding of the prudent. Where is the wise? where is the scribe? where is the disputer of this world? hath not God made foolish the wisdom of this world? For after that in the wisdom of God, the world by wisdom knew not God, it pleased God by the foolishness of preaching to save them that believe.

Christ thanks the Father, "because he hath hid these things from the wise and prudent, and hath revealed them unto babes"; and to us he says: "Except ye be converted, and become as little children, ye shall not enter into the kingdom of heaven." Be, then, simple as a child; admit that with your natural wisdom you understand nothing of the truth unto salvation; and pray that God the Holy Ghost may kindle in you the light of *faith*. They have not entered into the heart of man, the things which God hath prepared for them that love him. These things are too foolish and too glorious to have been invented by man. If we ourselves were to have prepared a scheme of salvation, would we, do you think, have ordained that the Son of God should die for us, and we be justified freely by faith in him? No; this plan of saving sinners could have originated only with God; nor could we by any possibility have established this rule of life, that "he that believeth and is baptized shall be saved; but he that believeth not shall be damned." We never would have hit upon this plan; to us it would have seemed altogether too simple. — Nevertheless, because these things are of God, and are exalted above all wisdom, we must become foolish in order to learn them. Never think to be able with your reason to grasp the divine truth unto salvation; but *become a little child, and believe the gospel.* Look to him who hangs on the cross, and live; for it has pleased God by the foolishness of preaching *to save them that believe.* Bless the Lord for this in all eternity! Merciful God, give us grace to believe, by thy Holy Spirit, for Jesus' sake. Amen.

All our knowledge, sense, and sight Lie in deepest darkness shrouded, Till thy Spirit breaks our night With the beams of truth unclouded. Thou alone to God canst win us, Thou must work all good within us.
Glorious Lord, thyself impart! Light of light, from God proceeding, Open thou our ears and heart, Help us by thy Spirit's pleading; Hear the cry thy people raises, Hear, and bless our prayers and praises.

---

456. Wednesday after Twenty-sixth Sunday after Trin.

Lord, give us humble hearts which hunger after thy grace! Let thy Spirit by means of the word accomplish this in us. Amen.

Isaiah 57, 15–21. For thus saith the high and lofty One that inhabiteth eternity, whose name is Holy; I dwell in the high and holy place, with him also that is of a contrite and humble spirit, to revive the spirit of the humble, and to revive the heart of the contrite ones. For I will not contend for ever, neither will I be always wroth: for the spirit should fail before me, and the souls which I have made. For the iniquity of his covetousness was I wroth, and smote him: I hid me, and was wroth, and he went on frowardly in the way of his heart. I have seen his ways, and will heal him: I will lead him also, and restore comforts unto him and to his mourners. I create the fruit of the lips; Peace, peace to him that is far aff, and to him that is near, saith the Lord; and I will heal him. But the wicked are like the troubled sea, when it cannot rest, whose waters cast up mire and dirt. There is no peace, saith my God, to the wicked.

God is wroth with his proud and disobedient children. He smites them; but they increase their transgressions, and go on frowardly in the way of their heart. It may take a long time; and yet the prodigal son may come at last, and *humble* himself before his God. There is no peace to him who is separated from the Lord; the worm gnaws at his heart. Under the smooth surface is unrest; and ere you are aware of it, the troubled sea casts up mire and dirt. But when the wretched man humbles himself, the Lord comes in to him, and heals him. The Lord has established his throne *in the high and holy place,* with him also that is *of a contrite and humble spirit.* He is *the Holy One,* high above all sin, the perfection of purity; and yet he dwells in the *souls of miserable sinners.* If any would come very near to God, let him become less than the least in himself! "The Lord is nigh unto them that are of a contrite heart; and saveth such as be of a contrite spirit." O ye men, dust and ashes, unclean and wicked; humble yourselves, humble yourselves; know your misery, and give the Lord honor; then shall he gloriously exalt you. With love inconceivable he has fashioned the human heart in such a way that he may dwell in it, and it in him; but humility is the only door through which the high and lofty One enters our heart. — Lord, thou delightest not in the strength of a man; but thou takest pleasure in them that fear thee, in those that hope in thy mercy. Give me a humble heart and a simple and lowly spirit. Alas, my pride and my perverted mind! Lord, create humility and a living fear of God in my soul; so shall I in thee have much mercy and peace. Amen.

Lord, for ever at thy side Let my place and portion be! Strip me of the robe of pride, Clothe me with humility.

Meekly may our soul receive All thy Spirit hath revealed. Thou hast spoken; — I believe, Though the prophecy were sealed.

---

457. Thursday after Twenty-sixth Sunday after Trinity.

Psalm 138. A Psalm of David. I will praise thee with my whole heart; before the gods will I sing praise unto thee. I will worship toward thy holy temple, and praise thy name for thy lovingkindness and for thy truth: for thou hast magnified thy word above all thy name. In the day when I cried thou answeredst me, and strengthenedst me with strength in my soul. All the kings of the earth shall praise thee, O Lord, when they hear the words of thy mouth. Yea, they shall sing in the ways of the Lord; for great is the glory of the Lord. Though the Lord be high, yet hath he respect unto the lowly: but the proud he knoweth afar off. Though I walk in the midst of trouble, thou wilt revive me; thou shalt stretch forth thine hand against the wrath of mine enemies, and thy right hand shall save me. The Lord will perfect that which concerneth me: thy mercy, O Lord, endureth for ever: forsake not the works of thine own hands.

Wherefore will ye not all come and receive mercy at the hands of our God? Why will ye not all learn to sing praises unto his name? Have you any fear that *he* will not receive you? Is the sin of any man so great, or the heart of any man so wicked, that the Lord can not have mercy on him? By no means; but ye *will not!* Let us cry out with as loud a voice as possible into all the world, that God saves all lost sinners who will repent; so that not one need continue without peace under the yoke of sin, and then go to perdition. All the lies of Satan shall not shake the truth that Jesus receives sinners. — However, if you will not come and enjoy his lovingkindness, and take part in singing praises unto him, this must not prevent God's people from rejoicing and from praising the Lord. "Rejoice with all thy heart, O daughter of Jerusalem! The Lord hath taken away thy judgments, he hath cast out thine enemy; the king of Israel, even the Lord, is in the midst of thee; thou shalt not see evil any more." Blessed be thou, O God; I will praise thee with my whole heart; before the gods (all the mighty) will I sing praise unto thee. I will nevermore be able to give thee all the thanks which I owe. Me, a wretched worm of the dust, who am deserving of death, and whom thou shouldest have crushed under thy foot; — me thou hast made

thy child; my troubled soul thou hast given rest in thy loving bosom.
And thou hast promised me things yet more glorious; thou shalt
perform thy work in me, and I shall see thee as thou art in thy
heavenly beauty. Then I shall drink of the water of the river of life
clear as crystal, and walk in the light of thy countenance for ever
and ever. Blessed are they that do thy commandments, that they may
have right to the tree of life, and may enter in through the gates into
the city! — Once more, ye men; wherefore will ye not come to him?
You are miserable sinners and the certain prey of death; in your
hearts you admit it, no matter what you may say! — Our dear Lord,
we praise thee; we were like them that dream, when thou didst turn
again our captivity. Yet we still groan and weep: Lord, let our
captivity turn again as the streams in the south. Hear us for the
sake of thy mercy and thy truth. Amen.

When we pass through yonder river, When we reach the farther shore,
There's an end of war for ever; We shall see our foes no more: All our conflicts then shall cease; Followed by eternal peace.

---

458. Friday after Twenty-sixth Sunday after Trinity.

*Let thy mercies come also unto me, O Lord, even thy salvation, according
to thy word. Amen.*

John 6, 43–47. Jesus therefore answered and said unto them, Murmur
not among yourselves. No man can come to me, except the Father which
hath sent me draw him: and I will raise him up at the last day. It is written
in the prophets, And they shall be all taught of God. Every man therefore
that hath heard, and hath learned of the Father, cometh unto me. Not that
any man hath seen the Father, save he which is of God, he hath seen the
Father. Verily, verily, I say unto you, He that believeth on me hath everlasting life.

Our salvation is *wholly of God* from beginning to end. No man
awakens himself out of the sleep of sin; no man is truly penitent;
none comes to Christ for mercy; none believes the forgiveness of sins;
none is born again; except that God work all this in him. In like
manner the regenerated man's faithfulness unto the end is the work
of *God*. How comes it, then, that God does this for some men, and
not for all? Is it not true that he will have *all* men to be saved? —
We shall not here attempt to explain the mystery. The word of God
explains it, certainly; and yet it remains a mystery which only when
this life is done shall be fully revealed — to the glory of God's wisdom, love, and justice. — Yet if any be troubled and ask concerning
God's purpose with him, let him obey the Lord's call, and he shall
experience that the Father is drawing him, even *him* to the Savior.
Whenever serious thoughts of eternity stirred your heart, or you felt
a longing after God, it was the Father drawing you. When you
felt the emptiness of the world; when you were troubled, and yearned
after peace; when the word of God laid hold on you in your secret
heart; and the gospel commended itself to your conscience; when

despite your aversion to Jesus, there yet was something in you prompt-
ing you to give yourself to him; then all these things were the work
of the Father, who was drawing you to the Son. You might have
come to him, had you wished it; and if you remained away, you have
no excuse. On the other hand, dear reader, if you have learned
from the word of God to know yourself as a sinner deserving of
death; as one who knows nothing unto salvation save the blood of
Jesus Christ the Son of God; then the Father has drawn you, and
you are already come to the Son. It is *God* has taught you to know
your sin, and to ask mercy of Jesus. You already *believe* in him;
for you put your trust in him as your only Savior, and are persuaded
that he is the true God and eternal life. Give God the honor; he
has done great things with you. Soon you shall in the light of heaven
see clearly those ways in which his wisdom led you from the cradle
to the grave. He says: "I have loved thee with an everlasting love;
therefore with lovingkindness have I drawn thee." For this you
shall thank him with awe and worship for evermore.

Of our whole heart we confess that our salvation is wholly and
solely of thee, our God; and we pray thee to grant us this grace that
we may have our all in thee, thou eternal love. Amen.

Just as I am, poor, wretched, blind; Sight, riches, healing of the mind,
Yea, all I need, in thee to find, O Lamb of God, I come, I come.
Just as I am, thou wilt receive, Wilt welcome, pardon, cleanse, relieve;
Because thy promise I believe, O Lamb of God, I come, I come.

459. Saturday after Twenty-sixth Sunday after Trinity.

Psalm 31, 19–24. Oh how great is thy goodness, which thou hast laid
up for them that fear thee; which thou hast wrought for them that trust in
thee before the sons of men! Thou shalt hide them in the secret of thy
presence from the pride of man; thou shalt keep them secretly in a pavilion
from the strife of tongues. Blessed be the Lord; for he hath shewed me his
marvellous kindness in a strong city. For I said in my haste, I am cut off
from before thine eyes: nevertheless thou heardest the voice of my supplications, when I cried unto thee. O love the Lord, all ye his saints: for the
Lord preserveth the faithful, and plentifully rewardeth the proud doer. Be
of good courage, and he shall strengthen your heart, all ye that hope in the
Lord.

"Fear was on every side; while they took counsel together against
me, they devised to take away my life. But I trusted in thee, O Lord;
I said, Thou art my God" (v. 13. 14). The faithful are everywhere
surrounded by mortal enemies; but God is their strong fortress. They
are everywhere in mortal danger, and everywhere under safe protection. None can fully express the love felt for them by the mighty
Lord of heaven. Joh. Arndt says: "He who of his whole heart with
a living and sure hope gives himself to God possesses God *himself*
with all the treasures of his grace, with all his goodness and love.
God gives himself entire to him who gives himself to God. To him

who gives God his whole heart God gives his whole heart with all his goodness and his salvation." What a Tabor in the wilderness! "Thou shalt hide them in the secret of thy presence," says the Psalmist. The *secret* of his presence; that is, a sure hiding-place, unseen of human eyes! They live before the countenance of the Lord, and this is their protection. They flee to him; and "he maketh his face to shine upon them"; who shall dare touch them when they are under his eye? Thus Joseph is delivered from the wicked woman, Daniel from the lions, and his friends from the fire. But the deliverance is often *hid a long time*, even from the children of God themselves. Yet it always shews itself at the proper time; only our time is not his; for our *faith* is to be tried. David recounts his experience: "I said in my haste, I am cut off from before thine eyes; nevertheless thou heardest the voice of my supplication when I cried unto thee." Though I was unbelieving, thou didst hear me. The Lord knows our weakness, and saves us of his *"great* goodness." This he has hid from them that fear him, — hid it *from* them, and *for* them, — in order to reveal it before the eyes of all in due season. "O love the Lord, all ye his saints!" Rejoice in him with holy joy; and give yourselves to him with your whole heart. "Be of good courage;" hear this, ye timid ones, who fear his anger, and who see everything in dark colors; do hear and heed these words himself has spoken: "Be of good courage, and he shall strengthen your heart, all ye that hope in the Lord!"

My God, thou knowest thy servant. When I see thy face to shine I am of good courage; but when thou dost hide it from me my heart grows faint. Take not thy goodness away from thy poor child; but hide me always in the secret of thy presence, and keep me in thy pavillion, and strengthen my heart, and be unto me a strong city, for Jesus' sake. Amen.

Before the hills in order stood, Or earth received her frame, From everlasting thou art God, To endless years the same.

O God, our help in ages past, Our hope for years to come! Be thou our guard while life shall last, And our eternal home.

---

460. Twenty-seventh Sunday after Trinity. I.

Teach us, O Lord, that without the cross there can be no crown.

Gospel Lesson, Matthew 17, 1–9. And after six days Jesus taketh Peter, James, and John his brother, and bringeth them up into an high mountain apart, and was transfigured before them: and his face did shine as the sun, and his raiment was white as the light. And, behold, there appeared unto them Moses and Elias, talking with him. Then answered Peter, and said unto Jesus, Lord, it is good for us to be here: if thou wilt, let us make here three tabernacles; one for thee, and one for Moses, and one for Elias. While he yet spake, behold, a bright cloud overshadowed them: and, behold, a voice out of the cloud, which said, This is my beloved Son, in whom I am well pleased; hear ye him. And when the disciples heard it, they fell on their face, and were sore afraid. And Jesus came and touched them, and said,

Arise, and be not afraid. And when they had lifted up their eyes, they saw no man, save Jesus only. And as they came down from the mountain, Jesus charged them, saying, Tell the vision to no man, until the Son of Man be risen again from the dead.

The Savior is given an hour of rest as preparation for his great passion; and the disciples are permitted to see his glory before witnessing his struggle in Gethsemane. On the mountain his divinity shines out through the servant form which he had assumed, and reveals that he who suffers is in the bosom of the Father; in the garden it is hid by tears and the sweat of blood, and reveals itself only in his perfect obedience. All the disciples of Jesus follow him; but some follow him more closely than do the others, and hence are lifted up to greater heights, and thrust down to greater depths of joy and suffering. His life here below was labor and pain; but there were some bright hours in between. Last Sunday's gospel lesson, for instance, speaks of one such occasion of special joy; and he found rest daily in praying to the Father; and his soul rejoiced whenever hearts opened to receive the word of life. In like manner his Christians also must take up the cross, and experience many sorrows; but they likewise have their hours of happiness, giving them a foretaste of the life eternal. However, as not all are able to go farther into Gethsemane, so neither are all permitted to be with the Savior on Tabor. Some may at times be so distinctly conscious of the Lord's presence and of the powers of the world to come, that if it should continue, they would no more be in the world; they are so happy that they forget all suffering; they may speak with God by the hour, and it seems to them but a moment; in their soul is a rapture beyond utterance, a union of holy fear and the delight of love, which surpasses all understanding. But this experience is not common to all believers; and therefore you must not make it the test of your own state of grace and that of others. Neither shall you ask God to give you a greater measure of such happiness than so much as he sees that you are able to bear. Nevertheless, every Christian shall experience that the kingdom of God is righteousness, peace, and joy in the Holy Ghost; that the love of God is precious, and that his word is sweet. Every Christian is permitted to come to God in prayer, and learn that a day in the courts of the Lord is better than a thousand; and every Christian will have special seasons of joy more refreshing than the daily tenor of his life. For we at times need such a lifting up, in order that the mind may not faint under its burden, but be refreshed after the struggle, and be strengthened to undergo new trials; for which reason God has also granted us our ever recurring Sunday and our festival seasons. — Peter wished to build tabernacles on Tabor; as who would not? But the Lord did not bring you up into the mountain, dear friend, to let you now make your home there with him, but to enable you to go with him through the valley of Cedron without losing your faith. There is greater danger in joy than in sorrow. Yet we must taste the cup of joy, in order that our sufferings may be a benefit to us; for without an occasional sojourn on Tabor, without such seasons of joy, after the measure which each may be able to bear, we would succumb in the time of trouble. Follow Jesus more closely every hour; and your joys and sorrows will become more intense, and you will be transfigured after his likeness from glory to glory.

Lord, when shall I see thee in thy glory, and praise thee as I ought, thou light of all the heavens and fulness of all beauty? How long shall I walk in this wilderness, ere I reach the city of thy habitation, and see thee as thou art? Give me a clear spiritual eye to see thee; and give me now and then a foretaste of thy salvation; that I may not become weary, but may serve thee faithfully, and patiently bear whatever of suffering thou dost impose on me, and rejoice in the blessed hope of seeing thee face to face. Yet, O Lord, it is not mine to say what thou shalt do. Lead me, faithful God, according to thine own counsel; grant that I may never desire to rid myself of thy cross, but may ever more gladly carry it after thee; and receive me at last into thy glory. Amen.

Lord, guide me in thy secret way; With such a guide I shall not stray; Bring me into a heavenly frame, Unite my heart to fear thy name.
O King of nations, Lord of all, Before thee shall all nations fall; And every language shall confess Thy glorious everlastingness!

461. Twenty-seventh Sunday after Trinity. II.

Lord, let thy word stir us up, that we walk henceforth with living concern for our souls' salvation. Amen.

Epistle Lesson, 2 Peter 1, 12-18. Wherefore I will not be negligent to put you always in remembrance of these things, though ye know them, and be established in the present truth. Yea, I think it meet, as long as I am in this tabernacle, to stir you up, by putting you in remembrance; knowing that shortly I must put off this my tabernacle, even as our Lord Jesus Christ hath shewed me. Moreover, I will endeavor that ye may be able after my decease to have these things always in remembrance. For we have not followed cunningly devised fables, when we made known unto you the power and coming of our Lord Jesus Christ, but were eyewitnesses of his majesty. For he received from God the Father honor and glory, when there came such a voice to him from the excellent glory, This is my beloved Son, in whom I am well pleased. And this voice which came from heaven we heard, when we were with him in the holy mount.

Saint Peter continued unto the last to be as fervent as ever in spirit, and as zealous for the piety and the salvation of the brethren. The years did not impair his mind, nor weaken his zeal. Even now, with death near at hand, he is as full of fire as on the day of Pentecost, when the Spirit for the first time came upon him. This is as it should be. It is a sad thing when Christians with the lapse of time become lukewarm, and let the inner man grow old with the body; something which not rarely happens, especially in the case of such as have been suddenly converted, and have displayed extravagant zeal in the beginning of their Christian life. They become vain or lax; either of which conditions impairs their spiritual strength, and easily leads to their falling from grace. — As Paul in his life demonstrated whose devoted servant he was in faith, so Peter also and the other apostles. To this end the transfiguration on the mount had been of great importance; for it proves conclusively that the glory of God dwelt in Jesus while he was in the form of a servant; thus making it sure beyond a doubt that the man Jesus, who delivers himself up to death, is God's only begotten, beloved Son, in whom the Father is well pleased. It is this positive faith which makes Peter so energetic and robust even on the brink of the grave. He urges us to follow him herein; and in the chapter before us he mentions two things which shall surely help us to do this. 1) *Heed the light of God's word;* then shall the Spirit give you the assurance that Jesus has earned for you everlasting life, and has given you divine power to obtain victory over sin. 2) *Strive with all diligence to lead the life of faith in holiness;* whereto grace and strength are given you in the promises of God. So shall you "make your calling and election sure"; and "so an entrance shall be ministered unto you abundantly into the everlasting kingdom of our Lord and Savior Jesus Christ." The apostle has endeavored that we may be able after his decease to have these things always in remembrance. Shall not we, then, also make this endeavor?

Lord Jesus, help us to do this. Lead us with thee through thy death. Let everything which is displeasing to thee be crucified. Be with us through life, and take us to heaven when we die. We ask it in thine own name. Amen.

The hill of Zion yields A thousand sacred sweets, Before we reach the heavenly fields, Or walk the golden streets. Then let our songs abound, And every tear be dry; We're marching through Emmanuel's ground To fairer worlds on high.

---

462. Monday after Twenty-seventh Sunday after Trinity.

God, thou desirest truth in the inward parts; and in the hidden part thou shalt make me to know wisdom.

Matthew 5, 13–16. Ye are the salt of the earth: but if the salt have lost his savor, wherewith shall it be salted? it is thenceforth good for nothing, but to be cast out, and to be trodden under foot of men. Ye are the light of the world. A city that is set on an hill cannot be hid. Neither do men light a candle, and put it under a bushel, but on a candlestick; and it giveth light unto all that are in the house. Let your light so shine before men, that they may see your good works, and glorify your Father which is in heaven.

Lot was the salt in Sodom; Noah, in the last days before the deluge; and the faithful in Jerusalem, before the destruction of the city. As long as the righteous dwell among the ungodly the judgments of God are warded off; but when the saints disappear the eagles gather about the carcase. The proud men of the world do not know that the prayers of God's children are the props which sustain the country and nation. But if this be true, it behooves the faithful to strive the more earnestly after zeal and holiness. Let it again be said of us with full truth, as it was written of the early Christians: "They live among the others; but they distinguish themselves before them in a wonderful way by their conduct. They sojourn in their fatherland, but as strangers; they live in the flesh, but not according to the flesh; they dwell on earth, and live in heaven. They are misjudged, persecuted, condemned of all; yet they love all. They are poor, yet make many rich; they have nothing, and yet possess all things; they are cursed, and yet they bless. In a word, what the soul is to the body the Christians are to the world. The soul is in the body, but not of the body; the Christians are in the world, but not of the world. The flesh hates the soul, though this only prevents the flesh from giving itself up to its ruinous lusts; and the world hates the Christians, though these only resist its wicked and corrupt ways. . . . The soul is housed in the body, but it sustains the body; the Christians are housed in the world, but they sustain the world." (Epistle to Diognetus). — Away with all false pretence; with all hollow, ostentatious religion, which is a mere matter of form! Let the true life of the Spirit, the love born of God's love, burn and glow in our heart; that the light may shine round about, and the name of the Lord may be glorified! — Come, Lord Jesus, live in me; and let me always and everywhere live in thee. Let the celestial fire of thy love burn in my soul, and glow through my entire being; that my whole life may radiate thy love, and shew forth its praises. Amen.

My God, I love thee; not because I hope for heaven thereby; Nor yet because if I love not, I must for ever die.
Not with the hope of gaining aught; Not seeking a reward; But, as thyself hast loved me, O ever loving Lord!

---

463. Tuesday after Twenty-seventh Sunday after Trin.

Let the words of hope, O God, gladden and strengthen our hearts. Amen.

Revelation 7, 13-17. And one of the elders answered, saying unto me, What are these which are arrayed in white robes? and whence came they? And I said unto him, Sir, thou knowest. And he said to me, These are they which came out of great tribulation, and have washed their robes, and made them white in the blood of the Lamb. Therefore are they before the throne of God, and serve him day and night in his temple: and he that sitteth on the throne shall dwell among them. They shall hunger no more, neither thirst any more; neither shall the sun light on them, nor any heat. For the Lamb, which is in the midst of the throne, shall feed them, and shall lead them unto living fountains of waters: and God shall wipe away all tears from their eyes.

Tribulation first, and then glory! Peter wanted to remain on the mount. "Lord, it is good to be here; let us make here three tabernacles." No, Peter; it is too soon; you must yet a while suffer tribulation; the path to eternal glory leads by way of Cedron and Calvary.

The aged Jacob sighed: "I have waited for thy salvation, O Lord." Naomi lost both husband and sons; David was given tears to drink; and Jeremiah sang lamentations to move a stone. But behold them now before the throne of God, clothed with their white robes, and palms in their hands! There Moses is no longer troubled by the stubbornness of the people; there Job does not lose his riches, his children, his health, and his honor; there the eyes of Peter are not moist with tears; there Paul is rid of his thorn in the flesh; there Nehemiah is no longer a pitiful sight to see by reason of sadness on account of the city of God. Here on earth all believers have their afflictions, and are to be prepared to bear the cross after the Savior every day. But in the world to come they all are for ever delivered from all evil; for there sin has disappeared, and with it sorrow and suffering and death; "there is fulness of joy; at the right hand of God are pleasures for evermore." It could not be more beautifully expressed in human language, than it is in the words employed by the angel in our text: "The Lamb which is in the midst of the throne shall feed them, and shall lead them unto living fountains of waters; and God shall wipe away all tears from their eyes." The Lamb himself, the Lamb, who now has dominion over all things, and who now owns our heart; he shall care for us, and spread the tent over us. O how safe and how full of bliss shall be our habitation! And he shall lead us unto the living fountains of waters, where we shall drink without hindrance of the living streams of love; and the eternal God shall himself be our abundant comfort for all our tears on earth. Who, then, would not cheerfully suffer, and thank God for it? Fight the good fight for the crown; and the Lord shall give you a most glorious reward. Do not forget, however, that the blest in heaven are they *who have washed their robes, and made them white in the blood of the Lamb* Ponder this, and follow Jesus!

Lord, thou knowest how lukewarm I am, alas; and thou knowest how many obstacles bar my way. Stir me up, and strengthen me; and help me to renounce and cast from me everything which may endanger my salvation. Reveal to me even now so much of the glory to come, that I may rejoice in hope, be patient in tribulation, and continue instant in prayer Make me faithful, and guide me to the goal. Amen.

What are these in bright array, This innumerable throng, Round the altar night and day Hymning one triumphant song? "Worthy is the Lamb, once slain, Blessing, honor, glory, power, Wisdom, riches to obtain, New dominion every hour."
These through fiery trials trod; These from great affliction came; Now, before the throne of God, Sealed with his almighty name, Clad in raiment pure and white, Victor-palms in every hand, Through their great Redeemer's might, More than conquerors they stand.

464. Wednesday after Twenty-seventh Sunday after Trin.

O Lamb of God, bind our hearts inseparably to thee, and draw us into thy glory. Amen.

Revelation 14, 1–5. And I looked, and, lo, a Lamb stood on the mount Zion, and with him an hundred forty and four thousand, having his Father's name written in their foreheads. And I heard a voice from heaven, as the voice of many waters, and as the voice of a great thunder: and I heard the voice of harpers harping with their harps: and they sung as it were a new song before the throne, and before the four beasts, and the elders: and no man could learn that song but the hundred and forty and four thousand, which were redeemed from the earth. These are they which were not defiled with women; for they are virgins. These are they which follow the Lamb whithersoever he goeth. These were redeemed from among men, being the first-fruits unto God and to the Lamb. And in their mouth was found no guile: for they are without fault before the throne of God.

Here the song of praise from heaven, where the blest already enjoy eternal happiness, is heard by the church which still figths and suffers on earth. The saints have the Lamb's Father's name written in their foreheads; that is, they are his own, and they are like him. His Spirit and love, which saved them by the blood of the Lamb, are come upon them, and have imprinted themselves on them; so that now, when you see them, you read his name in their foreheads. — Their song of praise in heaven is so powerful that it sounds as the voice of many waters, or as the most terrific peals of thunder; and yet as beautiful as the sweetest strains of a harp; power and tenderness are in the most marvelous way united. They sing "a new song"; that is, a song of the things ever new which they see in God: and therefore a song which never grows old, and never wearisome. None on earth can learn it, save only those who know the power of redemption in the blood of the Lamb. "These are they which were not defiled with women." "For they are virgins"; not by abstinence from marriage, — else were Peter and several more of the apostles excluded, — but in purity of mind, in the soul's chaste love and faith toward our Lord Jesus during their life here below. A pure virgin means one who does not love the world, but serves God with single heart. "These are they which follow the Lamb whithersoever he goeth," are one with him, and always walk in his steps, imitating his obedience and patience. "These were redeemed from among men, being the first-fruits unto God and to the Lamb." Being precious and beautiful in his sight, they walk also as such, and are in mind and spirit fundamentally different from the world; "and in their mouth was found no guile; for they are without fault before the throne of God." They live in the truth. They do not reach sinless perfection here on earth; but they strive after it, nor cease their efforts before they reach it in the world to come. — Dear reader, you may, if you will, be numbered among the hundred and forty and four thousand; walk so as here is written! Help us thereto, thou Lamb of God, Lord of glory, by thy Holy Spirit. Give us the soul's chaste love of our heavenly bridegroom; open our ears to the tones proceeding from the church triumphant over yonder; and teach us to glorify the power of thy blood, that we may for ever sing the new song together with the angels before the throne. Amen.

Jerusalem, my happy home, Name ever dear to me! When shall my labors have an end In joy, and peace, and thee? When shall these eyes thy heaven-built walls And pearly gates behold? Thy bulwarks with salvation strong, And streets of shining gold? O when, thou city of my God, Shall I thy courts ascend, Where evermore the angels sing, Where sabbaths have no end.

---

465. Thursday after Twenty-seventh Sunday after Trin.

O Lord, that our faith might be living, and our longing after heaven be fervent! Amen.

Hebrews 11, 8–16. By faith Abraham, when he was called to go out into a place which he should after receive for an inheritance, obeyed; and he went out, not knowing whither he went. By faith he sojourned in the land of promise, as in a strange country, dwelling in tabernacles with Isaac and Jacob, the heirs with him of the same promise: for he looked for a city which hath foundations, whose builder and maker is God. Through faith also Sara herself received strength to conceive seed, and was delivered of a child when she was past age, because she judged him faithful who had promised. Therefore sprang there even of one, and him as good as dead, so many as the stars of the sky in multitude, and as the sand which is by the sea shore innumerable. These all died in faith, not having received the promises, but having seen them afar off, and were persuaded of them, and embraced them, and confessed that they were strangers and pilgrims on the earth. For they that say such things, declare plainly that they seek a country. And truly if they had been mindful of that country from whence they came out, they might have had opportunity to have returned: but now they desire a better country, that is, an heavenly: wherefore God is not ashamed to be called their God; for he hath prepared for them a city.

The faithful in the old covenant waited for the coming of Christ and for the salvation which had been promised them in him. They regarded the coming of the Savior, with atonement for sin and victory over the devil, as synonymous with the perfecting of his people and their occupation of their new home. Time has advanced, and we live in the midst of that for which they longed. Christ is come, the kingdom of heaven has been revealed, atonement for sin has been made, justification is an accomplished fact. We no longer dwell in the Canaan of the Jews, seeking God through the temple in the earthly city of Zion; we are come to "the heavenly Jerusalem, and to the innumerable company of angels, to the general assembly and church of the firstborn, . . . and to the spirits of just men made perfect, and to Jesus the mediator of the new covenant." But we are now in the midst of these things; the church is not as yet made perfect. We also walk in faith, and look for the rest eternal. Those already in heaven have no wish to return to the earth; and we also have bid the world farewell, and will not return to it. Their trust was in the word of God; and this is our reliance also. In regard to the country to which he was going Abraham knew nothing more than the Lord had told him; but at God's word he left home and kindred, not doubting that he would receive a good country. And was he disappointed, do you think? We have not seen our heavenly heritage; but we have God's own word for it. God, that can not lie, has promised us eternal life. He gives us grace to hold fast this promise; and none can rob us of our inheritance. — Together with the word of God, Israel had the country as earnest of the blessed rest in heaven. We have a greater pledge; namely, the church of Christ itself, with the holy means of grace and the Spirit therein, which bears witness in our hearts. We are already at the wedding; for we are "made to sit together in heavenly places in Christ Jesus." Shall any man, then, be able to make us doubtful of the reality of salvation, or of our portion therein? Let not the world flatter itself, that it can again make us blind! — "Blessed the man, O Lord, who for thy sake disengages himself from everything of the world, does violence to his nature, and with fervent zeal of the spirit crucifies the lusts of the flesh; so that the soul with clear conscience brings to thee its pure offering of prayer, and becomes fit to join the angelic chorus when all earthly things, of the body and of the mind, are shut out!" Grant us this mercy, heavenly Father, for Jesus' sake. Amen.

Then let my soul march boldly on, Press forward to the heavenly gate; There peace and joy eternal reign, And glittering robes for conquerors wait.
There shall I wear a starry crown, And triumph in almighty grace; While all the armies of the skies Join in my glorious Leader's praise,

466. Friday after Twenty-seventh Sunday after Trin.

The Lord liveth; and blessed be my rock, and exalted be the God of the rock of my salvation.

Hebrews 12, 1-11. Wherefore seeing we also are compassed about with so great a cloud of witnesses, let us lay aside every weight, and the sin which doth so easily beset us, and let us run with patience the race that is set before us, looking unto Jesus the author and finisher of our faith; who, for the joy that was set before him, endured the cross, despising the shame, and is set down at the right hand of the throne of God. For consider him that endured such contradiction of sinners against himself, lest ye be wearied and faint in your minds. Ye have not yet resisted unto blood, striving against sin. And ye have forgotten the exhortation which speaketh unto you as unto children, My son, despise not thou the chastening of the Lord, nor faint when thou art rebuked of him: for whom the Lord loveth he chasteneth, and scourgeth every son whom he receiveth. If ye endure chastening, God dealeth with you as with sons; for what son is he whom the father chasteneth not? But if ye be without chastisement, whereof all are partakers, then are ye bastards, and not sons. Furthermore, we have had fathers of our flesh, which corrected us, and we gave them reverence: shall we not much rather be in subjection unto the Father of spirits, and live? For they verily for a few days chastened us after their own pleasure; but he for our profit, that we might be partakers of his holiness. Now no chastening for the present seemeth to be joyous, but grievous: nevertheless, afterward it yieldeth the peaceable fruit of righteousness unto them which are exercised thereby.

We are yet in the field of battle; but above and about us is a cloud of blessed witnesses, who *have* fought and won, and who now by their example and presence are to give us strength to strive lawfully and to hold out until we stand in their ranks as victors. Let us, then, "lay aside every weight" which impairs our strength. "All things are lawful for me; but all things are not expedient." Cast from you whatsoever weighs you down and is a hindrance to you, or clogs your feet. "No man that warreth entangleth himself with the affairs of this life," says the apostle; "and if a man also strive for masteries, yet is he not crowned, except he strive lawfully." Those witnesses must give your faith good testimony. You are not as yet free from sin itself; purge yourself of it continually; for it continually seeks to ensnare you. Do not tolerate it in any way; or you may easily experience the truth of the saying: "Give Satan an inch, and he will take an ell."— The faithful Lord God shall graciously help you with his fatherly chastisement; but shall not rebuke you otherwise than as a father rebukes his children. When you are chastised and suffer as a Christian, you become like unto Christ. To be free from suffering and chastisement is to be outside of his kingdom; for all his people bear the cross. But you *must remain with him;* and you must above all things look to him in order to become strong in the fight. He saw before him at the end of his suffering our salvation as his joy and the prize of his victory; us there awaits at the end of our weary way an imperishable crown from his hand. Thus he became *the author* of faith, and is gone before us; thus he is its *finisher* also, and gives us strength. For his suffering is ours; and his victory, ours. It was in our stead, for our sin, he suffered, and it was our enemy whom he vanquished; and we are united with him as the members of his body. To look unto the cloud of witnesses about us makes us strong; but to look unto him, the author and finisher of our faith, Jesus, with the victory and salvation in his name, makes us invincible. What is all our suffering as compared with his; and what is all our tribulation as compared with the glory of "seeing him as he is"? Blessed be thy name, Lord Jesus! Let me truly experience the power of thy resurrection and the fellowship of thy suffering; and make me to keep my eyes fixed on thee always, even as thou, faithful Savior, dost keep me ever in thine eye and heart. Amen.

Lord, thou art my rock of strength, And my home is in thine arms. Thou wilt send me help at length, And I feel no wild alarms. Sin nor death can pierce the shield Thy defence has o'er me thrown: Up to thee myself I yield, And my sorrows are thine own.

467. Saturday after Twenty-seventh Sunday after Trin.

Lord, let thy faithfulness stir us up to penitence, and faith, and hope, and joy, and thanksgiving. Amen.

Hebrews 13, 8. Jesus Christ the same yesterday, and today, and for ever.

Truly, a sublime declaration! A good text with which to close the church year. Everything changes, but *he* is ever the same; all things become more gloomy and difficult, but in him there *is no shadow of change*. *His* power and love continue unchanged; his care for the church and for each individual believer is as great as it always has been. Our teachers pass away; but *he* remains. The apostles are dead; the fathers are dead; they who were the props of our youth are dead; our faithful and pious old leaders are dead; the pillars are shaken; the foundations are laid bare; but *he* lives, and is the same, and never deserts his church. As *he* loved you from eternity, *he* loves you today, and shall love you for ever and ever. *His* heart remains evermore unchanged, as it was when he burned with compassion, and became man, and gave himself to suffer the most agonizing death for us. John and Peter and Paul found *him* to be infinitely merciful and good toward sinners; and so *he* is toward us also. As you have yourself in faith experienced *his* mercy, when *he* translated you from death to life, cleansed you in his blood, gave you his peace, and comforted you with his love; as he has heretofore preserved you, supported you, borne with you, kept you, showered mercies upon you, and given you bread from heaven to eat; — so *he* shall continue to deal with you for evermore; he is the same yesterday, and today, and for ever. *His* arm is not shortened, nor *his* wisdom restricted. *He can* and *shall* preserve his church, and protect it against all its enemies; and *he* knows how to guide it through all difficulties. "Fear not," *he* says; "I am the first and the last; I am he that liveth, and was dead; and, behold, I am alive for evermore, Amen; and have the keys of hell and of death." The Lion of the tribe of Juda; the Lamb, which was slain, in the midst of the throne, has taken the book (i. e. the whole course of the world's development), and holds it in his hand, and opens its seven seals (Rev. 5). Shall *he* ever, do you think, be found wanting in power? or shall *he* fall short in wisdom? "Hast thou not known? hast thou not heard, that the everlasting God, the Lord, the Creator of the ends of he earth, fainteth not, neither is weary? there is no searching of his understanding." (Isaiah 40, 28). He is "Jehovah," who is and remains always the same. *He* it is, our Lord Jesus Christ, your Savior, your high priest, your prophet, and your king, who has guided you and saved you during the past year; and *he* shall guide you and save you through the year that is coming. You are growing older, and more needy, and more weary; you see more clearly how dark it is on earth; and you look back with sadness to the early days of your Christian life. Alas, it is gone by, that golden age, with the simplicity, the humility, the brotherly spirit, the bond of fellowship, which so beautifully knit the children of God together as one in the Lord; and evil times are come, with dissensions and schisms; and you are tempted to sit down and weep over your own distress and that of the church. Friend, dry your tears; *"Jesus Christ is the same yesterday, and to-day, and for ever."* Yet, why say that you must dry your tears? Rather will I say: Brother, let us weep. Let us weep tears of *penitence* on account of our sins during the past year, and tears of *joy* on account of the love and truth of our God! May the sorrow of repentance never die in our heart, nor the tears of joy be wiped away from our eyes; until we reach that place where there shall no more be any yesterday and tomorrow, but where it shall be said: "The day of eternity is here; and the marriage of the Lamb is come!"

Wilt thou come soon, Lord Jesus? "Surely I come quickly." Amen. Even so, come, Lord Jesus!

The grace of our Lord Jesus Christ be with you all! Amen.

O for a thousand tongues to sing My great Redeemer's praise! The glories of my God and King, The triumphs of his grace!

My gracious Master and my God, Assist me to proclaim, To spread through all the earth abroad The honors of thy name.

Look unto him, ye nations; own Your God, ye fallen race; Look, and be saved through faith alone, Be justified by grace.

Some short Morning and Evening Prayers,

for the use of such as do not use their own words when having family prayers.

Morning Prayer.

(The Catechism.)

I thank thee, my heavenly Father, through Jesus Christ thy beloved Son our Lord, that thou hast kept me this night from all harm and danger. I pray thee to care for me this day also, and to keep me from sin and all evil; that all my thoughts, words, and deeds, may please thee. I commit myself into thy hands with body and soul and all things. Let thy holy angels not depart from me, that the evil enemy may have no power over me. Amen.

The Lord's Prayer. The Benediction.

Another Morning Prayer.

I heartily thank thee, dear heavenly Father in Christ, for rest and sleep and thy protection this night, and for the day and the grace which thou again hast given us. When I awake I am with thee. Great and undeserved is thy goodness toward us. — Continue to surround us with thy angels, and keep us from all evil this day. Deliver all thy children from the craftiness and power of the devil; give us victory in all temptations, and patience in all tribulations; give us grace to do good every hour, to honor thee, and minister to one another with cheerful hearts. Let thy word today make progress on earth; bless it on the hearts everywhere, in homes and schools and churches, here and among the Jews and the heathen. Keep thy doctrine pure among us; and graciously preserve us from heresy and error. Bless our country and people, our president, and all in authority. Help us everywhere to walk before thee in the light, to be governed by thy good Spirit, and to bend our steps heavenward. Amen.

The Lord's Prayer   The Benediction.

Another Morning Prayer.

O God, thou fountain of life and peace; we thank thee for thy gracious protection and for the rest which we have enjoyed; for life and light and every good things. Keep us, we beseech thee, this day; compass us about with thy angels, bless our labor, and pronounce thy peace upon us. Let the Lord be magnified, which hath pleasure in the prosperity of his servant. And my tongue shall speak of thy righteousness and of thy praise all the day long. Our Father which art in heaven, etc. The Lord be with us! The Lord make his face to shine upon us, etc.

Another Morning Prayer.

Blessed be the Lord for evermore! Blessed be the Lord, whose mercies are new every morning! I laid me down and slept; I awaked; for the Lord sustained me. What shall I render unto the Lord for all his benefits toward me? I will take the cup of salvation, and call upon the name of the Lord. Keep thy servant, that I may be found blameless before thee. Let the words of my mouth, and the meditation of my heart, be acceptable in thy sight, O Lord, my strength and my redeemer. Our Father, etc. The Lord be with us! The Lord bless, etc.

Another Morning Prayer.

I will praise thee, O Lord my God, with all my heart; and I will glorify thy name for evermore. For thou art a God full of compassion, and gracious, longsuffering, and plenteous in mercy and truth. Today and for evermore will I give myself to thee with all my heart. Help me thereto by thy Holy Spirit. Teach me thy way; I will walk in thy truth; order my steps in thy word, and make thy face to shine upon thy servant. Let thy name be excellent in all the earth; let Satan be put to shame; let the peoples come to thee. Comfort the afflicted; preserve our country; be our sun and shield. Our Father, etc. The Lord be with us! The Lord bless us, etc.

Another Morning Prayer.

Lord my God, thou dost greet me with mercies every morning. How shall I thank thee as I ought? "Bless and santify my soul with heavenly blessing, that it may become thy holy habitation, a temple for thy eternal glory; and that there in this temple of God may be found nothing to offend thy divine and holy sight. — Look down upon me according to thy plenteous mercy and thy great compassion; and protect the soul of thy poor servant among the many dangers of this fleeting life. Attend me with thy mercy; and guide my feet in the path of peace to the bright and eternal home beyond the sky. Amen."* Our Father, etc. The Lord be with us! The Lord bless us, etc.

---

* Kempis.

Another Morning Prayer.

Heavenly Father, we heartily thank thee for each new day which thou dost give us, with peace and every blessing of soul and body. We humbly beseech thee, preserve our heart, our life, our home, our people. Deliver us from lying and ungodliness, unbelief, strife, injustice, and all the wickedness of the devil. Grant that today and always we may live together in the light before thee, with upright hearts willingly and gladly serve one another in love, and then be gathered together in eternal glory. Our Father, etc. The Lord be with us! The Lord bless us, etc.

Evening Prayer.
(The Catechism.)

I thank thee, almighty and merciful God and Father, through Jesus Christ thy dear Son, that thou hast graciously kept me this day. Forgive, I pray thee, all the sins with which I have today offended thee; and care for me, and keep me through the coming night. I commit myself into thy hands with body and soul and all things. Let thy holy angels not depart from me; that the evil enemy may have no power over me. Amen.

The Lord's Prayer. The Benediction.

Another Evening Prayer.

Praise be to thee, our God, who hast again helped us through the day, given us every blessing to enjoy, and delivered us from evil. Of our hearts we confess that we are not worthy of the least of all the mercies, and of all the truth, which thou dost shew unto us. Help us to thank thee always for all things; and let our offering of praise be acceptable to thee in Christ Jesus. Thou hast guarded us against sin; but we have failed to be vigilant, and have sinned; and we omitted much that is good. Help us to know our sin with heartfelt penitence, and to confess it with upright and humble soul; and forgive us all our debts for Jesus' sake, Give us all, O God, truly penitent and believing hearts. Do not let any of us retire to rest with thy wrath upon him; but turn us to thee, and be unto us a gracious God. Wake the souls everywhere, that sleep in sin; keep all thy believing children in the state of grace, and grant that we may increase in faith day by day. Extend thy kingdom into all the earth. Be with the ministers of thy word in demonstration of the Spirit and of power here and among the heathen. Bless those in authority and all our people. Preserve us this night from the malice of the devil, give us refreshing sleep and rest, and be thou our last thought, and our first. Help all who are in danger on land or sea, all who are sick and dying, and who are fighting against trials and temptations. Hide us and all ours in thy pavilion night and day, almighty and merciful God; and gather us at last to thee in heaven. This we humbly ask in Jesus' name. Amen.

The Lord's Prayer. The Benediction.

Another Evening Prayer.

God of glory and mercy; receive this evening also our poor offering of praise. Thou hast been our faithful support to this hour; infinitely great is thy mercy. Like as a father pitieth his children, so dost thou pity us. We pray thee to forgive us all our sins this day, and graciously to protect us this night. Let thy blessing rest upon our church and our country; give patience and comfort to all who are in distress. We commit ourselves and all ours to thy faithful care. Our Father, etc. The Lord be with us! The Lord bless us, etc.

Another Evening Prayer.

Bless the Lord, O my soul; and all that is within me, bless his holy name! Bless the Lord, O my soul, and forget not all his benefits; who forgiveth all thine iniquities; who healeth all thy diseases; who redeemeth thy life from destruction; who crowneth thee with lovingkindness and tender mercies! Let me sing praise unto the Lord, and rejoice in him; for he is my God and heavenly Father; and I am his child! Surely goodness and mercy shall follow me all the days of my life. To thee I commend myself and mine, thy whole church, our beloved country, and all who are needy and afflicted. Our Father, etc. The Lord be with us! The Lord bless us, etc.

Another Evening Prayer.

O Lord God of hosts, give us peace in our hearts, in our churches, in our country, in our homes; and in a blessed hour receive us into that happy home above, in which there shall be eternal joy and glory and peace. Have mercy on us; forgive us all our sins; defend us against the craftiness and power of the devil; be with us when we sleep, and when we awake. Blessed be thy glorious name for ever; and let the earth be full of thy glory. Amen. Our Father, etc. The Lord be with us! The Lord bless us, etc.

Another Evening Prayer.

O God our heavenly Father, forgive us all our sins of this day, for the sake of Jesus Christ. Let thy peace obtain victory in our hearts; and let no evil have dominion over us. Give thy angles charge to keep us this night and alway; us and all our dear ones, our home and our church, our country and all our people. Satisfy us with thy tender mercies in the evening and in the morning, and above all in our dying hour. We heartily thank thee for all thy goodness, and humbly commit ourselves into thy keeping. In Christ Jesus thou dost accept our thanks, and hear our prayer; and happy in thee we lay ourselves down to sleep. Our Father, etc. The Lord be with us! The Lord bless us, etc.

INDEX

to the Bible passages treated in this volume.

Page		
Genesis 2, 18. 21–24.. 95	Psalm 46 111	Psalm 143 96
4, 3–11 419	48............... 9	145, 14–21 394
17, 1–6 70	51, 1–9 429	Proverbs 8, 10–17....567
18, 17–19 80	51, 10–19 279	11, 23–25 413
24, 1–7 90	57................548	30, 5–9 398
Exodus 1, 22–2, 10..152	62, 1-8 296	Eccles. 11,9.10;12,1.2 86
4, 10–15 374	63, 1-7 527	Isaiah 1, 2–6.......426
15, 1–11 110	69, 21 209	1, 10–15 434
Leviticus 14, 2–8 104	72, 1–8 8	5, 1–7 423
Numbers 21, 5–9 324	73, 12–19 330	6, 1–7 319
1 Samuel 1, 20. 24–28. 83	73, 23–28 331	7, 10–15 201
1 Kings 17, 12–16....393	74, 1–9. 12.......125	9, 6. 7............ 41
18, 17–21 477	80, 1–7 595	12................ 64
Job 15, 14–16.......556	84, 1–7 499	13, 9–13 15
Psalm 2 115	86, 11–17 562	25, 6–9 105
6.................466	90................ 56	29, 10–14 427
7, 11–17 559	100...............256	29, 17–19 446
8.................532	102, 1–14 516	35................ 24
12................122	103, 1–5 470	40, 1–5 35
13................ 29	103, 8–14 357	40, 9–11 255
15................384	110...............291	40, 26–31 63
16................235	116, 1–9 494	42, 1–4 561
19, 7–12 140	116, 10–19 573	42, 5–10 28
22, 14. 15........209	118, 14–24 236	44, 1–5 299
23................250	119, 9–20 84	45, 4–8 71
24................ 6	119, 25–32 135	45, 22–25 74
25, 1–11 525	119, 41–50 378	49, 5. 6..........342
27, 7–14 117	119, 64–72 145	53, 1–5 144
31, 19–24 605	119, 97–105 505	53, 6–9 151
32, 1–5 439	119, 169–176 440	53, 10–12 134
34, 1–10 484	126...............263	53, 12 197
36, 5–12 538	130...............521	55, 1–5 347
37, 1–6 392	138............. 603	55, 6. 7..........265
37, 21–26 397	139. 13–18 473	55, 8–13 141
42, 1–5 500	142 450	57, 15–21 602

	Page
Isaiah 58, 5–8	387
58, 9–11	388
60, 1–6	69
61, 1–3	26
61, 10. 11	534
Jeremiah 31, 1–4	73
Lament. 3, 22–33	522
Ezekiel 3, 17–21	405
16, 9–14	461
34, 11–16	251
36, 25–27	326
Daniel 9, 15–19	37
Jonah 2, 1–9	155
Joel 2, 28–32	301
Micah 3, 5–12	408
5, 2–5	38
7, 18–20	523
Zechariah 3, 1–5	459
Malachi 3, 1–6	30
4, 1–6	21
Matthew 1, 20–23	39
2, 1–12	67
2, 19–23	65
3, 8–10	266
3, 13–17	146
4, 1–11	156
4, 12–17	106
5, 1–12	553
5, 13–16	609
5, 17–19	383
5, 20–26	379
5, 38–42	363
5, 43–48	364
6, 5–8	283
6, 19–23	478
6, 24–34	474
7, 12–14	402
7, 15–21	369
8, 1–13	97
8, 14–17	448
8, 23–27	108
9, 1–8	517
9, 9–13	355
9, 18–26	575
10, 37–42	131
11, 2–10	22
11, 25–30	596
12, 33–37	445
13, 24–30	118

	Page
Matthew 13, 36–43	120
13, 44–46	479
14, 24–33	113
15, 21–28	167
15, 29–31	444
16, 1–4	543
16, 13–19	373
16, 21–23	154
17, 1–9	606
17, 24–27	570
18, 15–22	557
18, 23–35	549
20, 1–16	127
20, 25–28	502
21, 1–9	3, 210
21, 10–16	213
21, 28–32	435
22, 1–14	528
22, 15–22	563
22, 34–46	506
23, 34–39	46
24, 4–14	589
24, 15–28	586
25, 1–13	16
25, 31–46	17
26, 1–16	215
26, 21–25	335
26, 39–46	162
26, 45–48	164
26, 49–54	166
26, 50–56	170
26, 59–68	174
27, 3–10	176
27, 23–25	186
27, 27–30	188
27, 31. 32	195
27, 33. 34	196
27, 39–44	204
27, 45–49	208
27, 57–66	223
28, 18–20	320
Mark 7, 6–13	504
7, 31–37	441
8, 1–9	389
9, 17–27	545
14, 26–31	160
14, 32–34	161
14, 66–72	172
15, 25	197

	Page
Mark 15, 28	196
16, 1–7	225
16, 14–20	286
Luke 1, 26–38	199
2, 1–14	42
2, 15–20	44
2, 21	58
2, 33–40	54
2, 42–52	77
4, 16–21	60
5, 1–11	369
6, 31–35	417
6, 36–42	358
7, 11–17	485
7, 36–50	356
8, 4–15	136
9, 57–62	343
10, 23–37	451
10, 38–42	139
11, 14–28	179
12, 16–21	332
12, 32–37	414
14, 1–11	495
14, 16–24	337
14, 25–33	340
15, 1–10	348
15, 11–16	351
15, 17–24	352
15, 25–32	353
16, 1-9	411
16, 10–13	418
16, 19–31	327
17, 7–10	130
17, 11–19	463
18, 9–14	430
19, 41–48	420
21, 25–36	12
23, 4–12	183
23, 17–24	185
23, 27–31	195
23, 34	197
23, 39–43	205
23, 46	220
24, 13–35	227
24, 36–48	230
24, 50-52	290
John 1, 1–13	49
1, 14-18	50
1, 19-28	32

	Page
John 1, 29–34	149
1, 35-42	372
1, 47–51	94
2, 1–11	87
3, 1–15	315
3, 16–21	306
3, 27–36	36
4, 6–14	100
4, 15–26	101
4, 30–34	85
4, 46–53	539
5, 2–9, 14	468
5, 19–23	600
5, 25–29	579
6, 1–15	189
6, 37–40	578
6, 43–47	604
7, 37–40	300
8, 1–11	361
8, 21–27	425
10, 1-10	309
10, 11–16	248
10, 23–30	253
11, 1–13	488
11, 20–27	490
11, 33–38	491
11, 39–45	492
12, 23–32	214
13, 1–15	217
14, 1-6	260
14, 7–13	262
14, 23–31	303
15, 1–6	323
15, 7–11	284
15, 17 21	295
15, 26-16, 4	293
16, 5–15	269
16, 16-22	257
16, 23–28	280
17, 1–5	264
17, 6-11	268
17, 11–19	272
17, 20–26	273
18, 1. 2	161
18, 4–9	165
18, 12-14. 19-24	171
18, 28–32	177
18, 33–38	182
19, 1	187

	Page
John 19, 4–7	192
19, 12–16	193
19, 18	196
19, 19–22	198
19, 23. 24	203
19, 25-27	207
19, 28. 29	209
19, 30	220
19, 31-37	222
20, 1–10	232
20, 11–18	233
20, 19–23	237
20, 24–31	240
21, 1–6	242
21, 7–14	244
21, 15 19	245
21, 20–23	247
Acts 1, 1–11	288
1, 13. 14	290
2, 1–11	304
2, 22–28	310
2, 29–36	312
2, 37–42	313
4, 8–12	428
6, 8–15; 7, 54–60	47
10, 34–41	229
10, 42 48	307
13, 38–41	344
13, 44–49	345
16, 25–34	457
26, 12-18	376
Romans 1, 16. 17	275
3, 19-22	66
3, 23-28	382
4, 1–8	403
4, 18 25	542
5, 1–5	493
5, 6–11	526
5, 12-16	438
5, 17–21	10
6, 3-11	381
6, 19 23	391
7, 1–6	454
8, 1–4	512
8, 5–11	481
8, 12–17	401
8, 18–23	360
8, 28–32	482
10, 4–10	75, 76

	Page
Romans 11, 33–36	317
12, 1–5	79
12, 6–16	89
12, 17–21	99
13, 1-7	569
13, 8–10	109
13, 11–14	4
14, 7–13	366
15, 4–9	13
1 Cor. 1, 4-8	508
1, 17–21	601
2, 9 13	447
3, 18–23	132
4, 1–5	23
5, 7. 8	226
5, 9–13	123
9, 19 22	133
9, 24-10, 5	128
10, 6–13	412
11, 23–29	218
12, 2–11	422
13, 1–7	365
15, 1–10	432
15, 20–27	584
15, 35-44	580
2 Cor. 3, 4-9	443
4, 7–18	582
5, 1–10	583
5, 14–21	150
6, 1–10	158
9, 8–11	396
12, 2–9	138
Galatians 2, 19–21	515
3, 5–11	456
3, 15–22	453
3, 23–29	59
4, 1–7	55
4, 21–31	191
5, 16–24	465
5, 25–6, 10	475
Ephesians 1, 3–7	510
1, 8-14	511
1, 17–23	7
2, 13–22	533
3, 5–12	377
3, 13–21	487
4, 1–6	497
4, 11–16	124
4, 22–28	519

626

	Page		Page		Page
Ephesians 5, 1–9	180	2 Timothy 4, 1–8	593	1 Peter 4, 7–11	294
5, 15–21	530	Titus 2, 11–14	51	5, 1–5	254
5, 22–33	91	3, 1–7	571	5, 6–11	349
6, 10–17	540	Hebrews 4, 9–16	537	2 Peter 1, 12–18	608
Philippians 1, 6–11	551	5, 5–10	278	1 John 1, 1–7	53
2, 1–4	501	10, 19–25	547	1, 8–2, 2	436
2, 5–11	211	11, 1–6	544	2, 4–11	513
3, 7–11	276	11, 8–12	103	3, 1–6	298
3, 17–21	566	11, 8–16	613	3, 13–18	339
4, 4–7	33	11, 23–27	114	4, 1–4	406
Colossians 1, 9–14	577	12, 1–11	614	4, 9–12	314
3, 1–6	241	13, 8	616	4, 16–21	329
3, 12–17	119	James 1, 2–12	92	5, 4–12	238
1 Thessalon. 4, 1–7	168	1, 17–21	271	5, 13–15	285
4, 13–18	588	1, 22–27	281	5, 18–21	592
5, 12–23	599	2, 10–17	385	Revelations 1, 4–7	11
2 Thessalon. 1, 3–12	19	3, 13–18	560	2, 8–11	336
2, 1–10	590	5, 19. 20	368	3, 1–6	121
3, 7–13	416	1 Peter 1, 3–6	322	3, 7–13	18
1 Timothy 1, 12–16	460	1, 14–19	471	3, 14–22	535
2, 1–7	572	1, 22–25	143	7, 1–12	554
6, 9–12	333	2, 1–6	62	7, 13–17	610
6, 13–21	409	2, 11–20	259	14, 1–5	612
2 Timothy 1, 6–12	27	2, 21–25	249	19, 1–9	594
2, 19–22	469	3, 8–14	370		
3, 14–17	82	3, 18–22	147		

www.ingramcontent.com/pod-product-compliance
Lightning Source LLC
Chambersburg PA
CBHW020350100426
42812CB00001B/13